U.S. Defense Spending: How Much is Enough?

U.S. DEFENSE SPENDING: How Much is Enough?

Edited by Carol C. Collins

Facts On File Publications
New York, New York ● Bicester, England

U.S. Defense Spending: How Much is Enough?

Published by Facts On File, Inc.
460 Park Avenue South, New York, N.Y. 10016
© Copyright 1983 by Facts On File, Inc.

Library of Congress Cataloging in Publication Data

Main entry under title:
U.S. defense spending.

Includes index.
    1. United States — Armed Forces — Appropriations and expenditures — Addresses, essays, lectures. 2. United States — Military policy — Addresses, essays, lectures. 3. United States — Defenses — Addresses, essays, lectures. I. Chambers, Carol. II. Title: United States defense spending.
UA23.U19   1983   355.6'22'0973   83-20603
ISBN 0-87196-816-9

International Standard Book Number: 0-87196-816-9
Library of Congress Catalog Card Number: 83-20603
9 8 7 6 5 4 3 2 1
PRINTED IN THE UNITED STATES OF AMERICA

Contents

Preface

Ronald Reagan's campaign platform in 1980, a year when American hostages were held captive in Iran and the Soviet Union invaded Afghanistan, included a pledge to undertake the "moral and physical rearmament" of the United States. The most striking characteristic of the Reagan budgets, unsurprisingly, has been the steady increase in the portion devoted to defense.

The question of whether we are spending too much or too little on defense cannot be answered within a single frame of reference. The nation might well be spending only a fraction of what the military establishment deems necessary to insure our national security, and still be spending far more than the economy will bear. Any discussion of what amount of spending constitutes "enough" must include at least these two variables.

Critics of the Reagan Administration's defense policy warn that the country cannot expect to maintain what approaches a "wartime" defense industry without experiencing serious consequences in the civilian sector. One frequently mentioned result is the large concentration of scientists and engineers—by some estimates over a third of the nation's total—involved in military research. Another is the reduced government funding available for such social programs as Medicare. According to this view, our military buildup is like a greedy fledgling, eating up all the nation's resources and starving the economy.

On the other hand, it is difficult to assign a dollar value to national security. The defense posture of the United States in recent years has been defined primarily by the vicissitudes of our relationship to the Soviet Union. This is not a book about foreign policy, and even less about arms control; nevertheless, it is necessary when measuring defense dollars to consider the demands placed on the military by our global perspective.

The final word on defense spending rests with Congress. The annual budget process is the unwieldy framework within which the sometimes competing claims of national security and the national economy are weighed and a level of defense expenditure is determined. The extremely wide range of opinion on what constitutes an appropriate level can be gleaned from the debate contained in the following pages. These editorials, drawn from major newspapers throughout the United States, reflect the strong feelings of American journalists about defense. They were chosen merely to present diverse points of view, without any attempt to favor one over another.

November, 1983   Carol C. Collins

Part I: The Soviet Threat

Discussions of American defense planning inevitably involve assessments of Soviet military capabilities and preparations. It is often pointed out that in the years following the Vietnam War, the United States cut back on its defense procurements while the Soviet Union plied ahead with both weapons development and manufacturing. As a result of those years, it is argued, the Soviets now have a larger supply of conventional arms and greater industrial capacity to produce weapons quickly in the event of war. There are also more Soviet troops immediately available for combat. Thus it is generally surmised that the Soviets would be at an advantage in a conventional war of short duration while the greater overall industrial and economic strength of the United States would cause the tide to turn in a longer conflict.

Difficult as it is to determine the precise strength of the Union of Soviet Socialist Republics in conventional weaponry—and analysts warn of the historical tendency always to overestimate an opponent's capabilities—it becomes many times more difficult to estimate comparative strengths and weaknesses in the nuclear arena. It is usually conceded that the U.S.S.R. has more vehicles to deliver missiles than does the U.S., but that the U.S. possesses a greater number of warheads (the portion of a missile containing the charge) and more sophisticated and accurate means of delivery. Experts on both sides of the question offer manifold arguments to support their view that the U.S. enjoys nuclear "superiority" over the Soviet Union, or vice versa, or that there exists a rough "parity" between the two superpowers. The question of which side would prevail in a nuclear conflict is freighted with so many uncertainties that the layman is most often lost along the way, understanding only that either nation has enough "megatonnage" in its nuclear arsenal to effectively destroy the other several times over.

Whether or not they are accurate, however, changing U.S. perceptions of Soviet military might are important because they are the cornerstone for the formation of a national defense policy. Since the mid-1960's, the U.S. has had to take into account the possibility of its own destruction, and this radical change in focus has completely altered the ramifications of our defense posture. With the accumulation of ever more powerful nuclear arsenals by both superpowers has come a twin realization: that conventional warfare carries with it a greater risk than ever before—of escalation into nuclear warfare—and that nuclear warfare itself could spell the destruction of both nations.

Soviet Military Preparations Said to Outstrip U.S. Efforts

A crisis atmosphere developed in 1981 as the Reagan Administration released declassified reports intended to bolster the contention that the U.S. was falling behind the Soviet Union in military production and capabilities, and to garner support for the President's proposed military programs. A Defense Intelligence Agency report released in September, 1981, stated that the Soviet Union surpassed the U.S. in almost every major category of arms production except major combat ships. The report emphasized that the Soviets had maintained high levels of arms production during the past five years, which was a period of U.S. cutback in defense spending. Defense experts pointed out, however, that the U.S. attempted to counterbalance the Soviet edge in weapons quantity with better, more technologically advanced weapons. A Pentagon report released in October, packaged in a glossy picture-filled booklet, also warned of the increasing threat to "Western strategic interests posed by the growth" of Soviet armed forces. Although containing no new information or systematic comparison with U.S. military capabilities, the report did disclose some previously classified data and photographs, including maps showing for the first time the estimated locations of Soviet missile launchers.

The pattern has continued in 1982 and 1983. In his address to the nation in November, 1982, in which he announced the decision to deploy 100 MX missiles in a "dense pack" basing system, President Reagan used electronic charts to depict a Soviet advantage in arsenals of ballistic missiles, nuclear warheads, missiles and bombers, as well as higher Soviet levels of projected defense spending. Most recently, in his March, 1983 televised address, President Reagan sought support for a proposed 10% increase in defense outlays. Using charts, graphs, and previously classified intelligence photographs, the President illustrated Soviet efforts to build what he called an "offensive military force" around the world. The Soviets, he said, were "spreading their military influence in ways that can directly challenge our vital interests and those of our allies." The photographs showed Soviet arms or facilities in Cuba, Nicaragua and Grenada. Sen. Daniel K. Inouye (D, Hawaii) delivered a Democratic rebuttal to the President's speech. Reagan had "failed to present an honest picture" of the comparative military strengths of the U.S. and Soviet Union because of his "urgency to defend" his defense budget, the Senator said. Inouye criticized Reagan for neglecting to mention the American "superiority" in submarine-based missiles, cruise missiles and total number of warheads. The purpose of the President's speech was to "instill fear in the hearts of the American people," he said, by giving the "impression that the United States is at the mercy of the Soviet Union."

THE INDIANAPOLIS STAR
Indianapolis, Ind., May 16, 1980

The price of letting United States conventional military preparedness slide may be higher than most Americans think.

Secret testimony by military experts before the House Appropriations Subcommittee on Defense points to a conclusion that the United States could not win a conventional war lasting more than 10 to 20 days with the Soviet Union.

That comes from Rep Jack Edwards of Alabama, ranking Republican on the subcommittee.

Edwards told Defense Secretary Harold Brown that the testimony convinced him "that the only way we could defeat the Soviets in a conventional war would be to resort to the use of nuclear weapons – not as an option, but as the sole means of waging successful warfare against the Soviet Union."

Elements of U.S. weakness, Edwards said in a letter to Brown, include a shortage of munitions and spare parts, lack of skilled personnel and poor readiness capability of aircraft.

"The Soviet Union," Edwards wrote, "has superior quantities of weapons and equipment, a superior production base, few manpower problems and a superior conventional force in being."

Facts provided by the Defense Department, he wrote, show "the armed forces lack depth. We lack all the necessary attrition assets to fight a conventional war, and a wartime logistical support base exists for perhaps 10 to 20 days of high intensity combat operations."

The details of the Edwards letter supports this grim accounting.

The bottom line is that in any confrontation or adversary relationship with the Soviet Union, the U.S. is operating from a position of weakness, a potent fact of which Soviet political overlords and warlords are undoubtedly aware.

Beyond doubt the roots of many noxious current events lie in the soil of U.S. military weakness: the obstinacy of the Marxist-dominated terrorists holding Americans hostage in Iran, the overrunning of Africa by Soviet "clients," the buildup of a Soviet military presence in Cuba, the attacking of Bahamian ships by Cuban-piloted MIG fighting planes, the Soviet invasion of Afghanistan, the Soviet intrusion in Kurdish rebel actions in Iran.

The Soviet behemoth and its proxies are on the move in many parts of the world. They are expanding because they know there is little to stop them.

The unwise neglect of U.S. conventional military capability has brought not only our own country but the world to a dangerous pass. The prudent action would be to change our course before it is too late.

The Miami Herald
Miami, Fla., May 12, 1980

UNSETTLING questions persist about how wisely President Carter and the Congress are acting to ensure that the nation can wage war effectively, if need be.

The key strategic issue is whether the balance of terror and power between the United States and the Soviet Union is shifting to give a meaningful edge to the Soviets.

The argument that has gained growing acceptance among the President, the Congress, and the public is that the rules of the game are in flux. The Soviet Union has come to match the United States in the murderous potential of nuclear armaments. It has widened its long-standing edge in conventional armaments and men under arms.

The Soviet Union continues to outspend the United States in developing new nuclear weapons. So there's fear that the U.S.S.R. could launch an attack that would destroy U.S. missiles before they got off the ground. And there is a concomitant fear that if nuclear standoff does maintain, it could be conventional warfare that counts after all.

Over the past two years, the President and Congress have indicated more and more that they agree with this opinion held by the U.S. defense establishment. The incredible, vexing irony is that they are moving so slowly to decide what to do about it.

All these months after President Carter decided to go ahead with development and deployment of the MX missile system, his Administration has yet to decide what the MX system will be like, much less work through its technical problems. And that is the missile system that the Administration is counting on to ensure that there is an effective U.S. nuclear deterrent in the latter part of this decade.

Granted, the MX system is controversial. There is genuine difference of opinion even among experts over whether it will work. The point, though, is that the controversy must be resolved, and soon, if the United States is not to be at military disadvantage later in this decade.

At the same time, it is more and more coming to be accepted that the United States is not adequately prepared for large-scale conventional warfare. Much U.S. military materiel is not operational, largely because maintenance budgets have been cut beyond all reason.

There is, again, genuine controversy over whether the United States needs increasingly sophisticated conventional weapons, or whether it would be adequate to maintain those that it already has. And many argue that far greater attention must be given to making those weapons reliable.

It almost defies belief that the President has intimated that the nation would take on defense of the Persian Gulf and perhaps Yugoslavia, yet Congress has not acted to ensure that the nation would have the manpower it needs. If the nation is to be prepared for conventional warfare, draft registration must be reinstated and the nation's reserves beefed up.

It is a sad but true comment on humankind that to assure peace, the nation must be ready for war. The sadder truth is that the United States is not ready. And until it is, peace will remain an illusion.

The Boston Herald American

Boston, Mass., June 11, 1980

This is no time for the United States to spike its guns.

To some this may sound like saber rattling. Actually, it is the sane and sensible conclusion of anyone who takes the trouble to look at a map of the world and see how much of it is dominated by the Soviet Union.

It is the conclusion of those who listen to our military and political leaders who agree, almost without exception, that the Soviet military machine has leaped and bounded far beyond the size and capacity of America's defense apparatus.

This nation's efforts to catch up have been sporadic, to say the least. Increases in defense spending planned under the Ford Administration have been cut by the Carter Administration. When Ford left office we had a five-year plan for developing and modernizing defensive weapons, the goal being at least to match the scope of Soviet military might.

When Carter entered the White House he gave every indication the Ford plan would be carried through. The Democratic Party platform on which Jimmy Carter ran in 1976 promised:

"Our strategic nuclear forces must provide a strong and credible deterrent ... our conventional forces must be strong enough to deter aggression."

What has President Carter been doing about that promise? Not enough to keep up with the Russians. He has cut back Ford's five-year plan by billions of dollars, partly by killing some projects and partly by delaying others. A recent estimate totals these Carter Administration cutbacks at $58 billion (B), an astronomical figure that is causing Americans to worry about the imbalance of weaponry between Washington and Moscow.

Inflation and unemployment will not be the only issues to trouble Carter in the forthcoming campaign. Defense has to be.

The News and Courier

Charleston, S.C., May 21, 1980

Intelligence estimates put the Soviet army strength at 170 divisions. The United States Army has 16. In any military emergency the capability of American ground forces will depend, then, on a rapid mobilization of Army Reserve and National Guard units that constitute another eight divisions — plus several hundred thousand individual combat replacements.

What is the readiness state of Reserve and Guard units? Are they fully manned and equipped? Are they adequately trained? Is the replacement pool sufficient to cover projected losses? The answer to each question is no.

The Army Reserve and National Guard are so deficient that the state adjutants general, meeting recently in Portland, Ore., issued the strongest protest National Guard commanders have registered.

For starters, they noted that the Guard and Reserve provide half the nation's combat forces and two-thirds of its support forces, but receive only five percent of the defense budget. The average Guard or Reserve unit has only two-thirds of the equipment required for active service, let alone combat. Guard and Reserve units are short 185,000 men. Specialists are particularly scarce. And the Army's replacement pool, the Individual Ready Reserve, continues to shrink as it has since termination of the draft in 1973.

As remedial actions, the National Guard commanders recommended:

—Equipment and training at least as good as that received by this country's potential advesaries.

—Some sort of selective service system.

—Enough ships and planes to move Guard and Reserve forces overseas quickly.

A final decision on the draft obviously must await resolution of the current national debate. There is, however, no reason to wait to provide adequate training and equipment as well as the air and sealift capabilities essential to a defense posture dependent on reserve troops.

Is anyone in the Carter administration listening?

Des Moines Tribune

Des Moines, Iowa, July 4, 1980

U.S. military spending is going up rapidly. Ronald Reagan says he would spend even more. The theory is that, without such spending increases, the Soviets eventually will conquer the West. The main proof offered for that theory is that they have spent more on arms than the United States has in recent years.

Once a genie like that gets out of the bottle in an American election season, it's unlikely to be put back. Politicians can make too much use of it. They like to run against the Russians.

Senator Edward Kennedy was pounding President Carter with the threat of a Soviet brigade in Cuba last fall. Then Carter clouted Kennedy with the Soviet invasion of Afghanistan. In a political alley like that, it was predictable that a tough old cold-war brawler like Ronald Reagan would emerge least bruised.

Maybe all of this has the folks in the Kremlin trembling and thinking twice, making every move on the basis of American responses to their military decisions. But that seems unlikely.

A central fact of superpower politics in the past decade is the increasingly friendly association of the United States and China. A slightly older but just as important fact is that the Soviet Union and China are almost in a state of cold war. Those are facts the Kremlin must consider in making its military budget and planning decisions. They are facts that probably shape the Soviet outlook as much as some kind of grand design of aggression.

Essentially, the Pentagon has to worry about the Soviet Union, but the Soviet leadership has to defend against both the United States and China. The Soviets have two major fronts to cover, the United States only one, a distant one. The Kremlin probably feels desperately insecure. The United States has no cause for similar panic.

Those billions that members of Congress and presidential candidates are throwing into the military budget are buying political points for them, but are unlikely to affect Soviet behavior.

St. Louis Globe-Democrat

St. Louis, Mo.,
September 24, 1980

Many Americans are astonished when they learn that the United States, supposedly the most productive nation in the world, has fallen far behind the Soviets in key conventional weapons such as battlefield tanks, armored personnel carriers, artillery, combat aircraft, surface ships and submarines.

Why should the Soviets have 50,000 modern battlefield tanks while the United States has only 12,675, most of which are vintage models from the 1960s?

Why should the Soviets have 55,000 modern armored fighting vehicles to 23,000 outdated U.S. armored vehicles, 7,800 combat aircraft to 5,200 U.S. combat planes, 273 major surface ships to 165 for the U.S, and 357 submarines to only 123 for this country?

The answer is that the Defense Department under President Jimmy Carter and Defense Secretary Harold Brown has opted for a strategy of (1) curbing defense spending; (2) relying on highly complex and costly weapons systems, and (3) delaying production until the systems are judged close to technologically perfect.

The case of the XM-1 Abrams heavy battlefield tank is a good example of how the Carter-Brown team has made United States conventional forces increasingly inferior to the Soviet forces. This tank has been under development for more than 20 years. It finally is nearing production on a limited basis — at a cost of $1.5 million a tank — and the Army may get 569 of them in 1981. But the Soviets in the meantime have produced four generations of battlefield tanks — each one better than its predecessor — and are turning out 2,600 of them yearly.

The cost of an F-14 for the Navy is $23 million. As a result the Navy gets only 467 of them instead of 521. The high price and complexity of U.S. aircraft also explains why the Soviets are turning out more than 1,000 combat aircraft in 1981 to only 378 for the United States.

The so-called "smart missiles" that Secretary Brown maintains will be among those that will save the U.S. from being overwhelmed by Soviet numerical superiority also have become so costly that some military men are beginning to question how far this trend can go. The Sidewinder missile that seeks out its target after being fired cost $3,000 when it was used in the Vietnam war. But the "improved" version being used today costs $160,000.

This new policy of producing far fewer and much more costly weapons is a reversal of successful military programs that prevailed before scientists such as Brown took over and started putting perfection in weapons' systems above practical battlefield considerations. Previously weapons were built so that they were "good enough" to perform their mission.

As pointed out in Forbes magazine, the United States during World War II concentrated on turning out large volumes of weapons that weren't the highest quality but they were good enough to do the assigned job. In 1944 the U.S. astounded the world by producing 104,000 airplanes. This country also produced 16,000 tanks a year and 104 ships in only two years.

"In World War II the M4 Sherman tank was possibly the least impressive tank in Europe. But waves of them overwhelmed Hitler's outnumbered, technological marvels," said Forbes.

Under Carter and Brown the trend away from this successful policy has accelerated and the United States finds itself becoming increasingly outgunned and outnumbered in crucially important battlefield weapons. The Soviets, who concentrate on getting weapons into production and then improving them in subsequent models, are pulling dangerously ahead. But nothing is being done to change this dangerous trend in U.S. weapons development.

The Detroit News

Detroit, Mich., July 7, 1980

President Carter is, above all else, the man who made defense a doomsday subject.

Under his not-so-tender care, the state of national preparedness for any kind of war has become as depressing as the failing economy.

His military-strategic mistakes defy explanation and are almost without number. His initial attitude toward the Soviets was all but childish, the product of dreams unbecoming a statesman. And if he can read a map, he has kept that talent hidden.

Four years ago, Mr. Carter campaigned for the presidency on a promise to slash defense spending. Now, as then, he naively ignores the frightening, ominous fact that the Soviet Union consistently spends 50 to 80 percent more than the United States on guns and troops — indeed, a huge $100 billion more in the past decade.

The invasion of Afghanistan ostensibly removed the scales from his eyes, but as far as the miserable Afghans are concerned, the fox had already dined on the chickens. And even now Mr. Carter seems to have learned little from his tragic and truly inexcusable miscalculations. He continues to insist that the henhouse door can be secured with a bent nail rather than a steel padlock. Just last month he rejected a congressional budget proposal because, in his view, it was too generous to the Pentagon.

At the outset of his presidency, Mr. Carter stunned wiser hands by unilaterally cutting America's armed might in the quaint belief that the Soviet Union would follow his example. His policy was as startling to Moscow (which took immediate advantage of this fortuitous lapse by deploying several new families of missiles) as it was to Washington.

The President canceled the B1 bomber, shut down the Minuteman III production line, halted development of the neutron battlefield warhead (needed in Europe to compensate for a three-to-one disadvantage in armor), delayed the Trident missile submarine, postponed development of the MX missile for three years, reduced the size of the Navy, and helped cripple the CIA to a perilous extent.

Such decisions signaled weakness, and retribution was swiftly delivered to the Carter White House. In Iran, the so-called student radicals invaded the American embassy and took 50 diplomatic employes hostage. Then, correctly assessing the deliberate impotency of the strange U.S. leader, the Soviet Union invaded Afghanistan, an act representing a major turning point in history. Not since World War II had Russian troops stormed across a nonsatellite boundary.

Mr. Carter struck back with a feather duster. The American hostages remain in Iran. The Soviet Union remains in Afghanistan.

There have been other events of importance that touch on the quality of the President's stewardship: A Soviet army brigade was discovered in Cuba, 90 miles from America's shores and overlooked for a year because Mr. Carter unilaterally cut off spy-plane flights over the island; MIG fighters capable of carrying nuclear weapons are in Cuba, too; the world computer system that is supposed to control American military operations is faulty; B52 bombers, old enough to qualify as antiques if they were cars, and even the newest F15 and F14 fighters, costing upwards of $25 million each, often can't get off the ground because there isn't enough money in the budget to maintain them; and the rescue raid into Iran (because of curiously poor planning) was a tragic failure.

Also: Pay has been so low in the military that some servicemen's families qualify for food stamps; because pay in the armed forces is inadequate, middle-management technical people are leaving in droves; and at a time when the Soviet Union has four million indi-

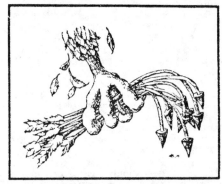

viduals under arms (plus another half-million border guards trained as combat troops) compared with America's 2,045,000, the Senate Armed Forces Committee proposed reducing the Army by two divisions for the want of men.

All-voluntary service isn't working. In response, Mr. Carter has restored draft registration, but balks at restoring the draft. His policies, even when properly directed, ineluctably fall short.

Ronald Reagan and the Republican Party must confront the continuing defense debacle with policies that will rebuild the nation's defenses and close the enormous lead in armed might opened up by the Soviets.

In addition, Mr. Reagan must restore the allies' confidence in American leadership, and press for a united posture against an adversary far more durable and powerful than Hitler.

Take heed, Republicans. A deeply worried America yearns for such a message.

Detroit Free Press
Detroit, Mich., August 25, 1980

THE QUESTION of American arms strength vs. the Soviet Union's came to the fore early in the presidential campaign, in part because veterans organizations were hearing from the candidates. They heard more of what they wanted to hear from Ronald Reagan than from Jimmy Carter.

Campaigns produce fundamental distortions in the discussion of defense. Mr. Reagan contends that U.S. strength has slipped dangerously under President Carter. He justifies his own call for massive new spending to attain absolute superiority over the Soviet Union by quoting a similar call by John F. Kennedy in 1960. What he does not note is that Mr. Kennedy's "missile gap" charge was subsequently discredited. It was an unfair charge: the rhetoric of a campaign.

President Carter, having campaigned four years ago with a promise to cut the military budget, now boasts correctly that he has substantially increased it, and that the real increases in spending have been greater than during the preceding Republican administrations. Mr. Carter also obviously has had an eye on the election in pressing anew for the MX missile system: an extraordinarily expensive and, in our view, unnecessary project.

Mr. Carter is being charged with weakening our defenses by dumping or delaying the B1 bomber, the costs of which have been estimated at $30-100 billion; a new nuclear aircraft carrier costing at least $2 billion; deployment of the neutron bomb in Europe; and some other proposed weaponry.

Carter had reason

In his principal decisions, we believe he was right. Even some strong advocates of the B1 now are conceding that, although they still want a manned bomber, this was not the right one to build. The vulnerability of giant aircraft carriers is more evident than ever, and the argument for an alternative — smaller naval vessels in greater number — seems valid. Europe itself, though it was unhappy with the way we shifted course, was rebelling against the neutron bomb when that proposal was dropped.

The fundamental question is whether the United States and its allies are behind, or falling behind, the Soviet Union and its satellites.

The Soviets have been through a period of rapid buildup in some armaments, with strong efforts to close the gap in the sophistication of weapons. It would be foolish to ignore that. And it would be foolish to believe we need no new efforts to parry the challenge: for instance, the cruise missile, modernization of the Navy, better maintenance of military equipment generally and incentives to make the all-volunteer army effective.

But Mr. Reagan seems much more willing than Mr. Carter to grant the Pentagon whatever it proposes in weaponry. And his call for absolute supremacy is an invitation to the Soviets to accelerate the arms race.

Are we weak?

Are we so weak? In 1979 the United States and its NATO allies spent $265 billion on military forces while the Soviet Union and its Warsaw Pact allies were spending an estimated $175 billion. We had 10,500 strategic nuclear weapons, to their 6,000; 9.5 million military personnel, to their 4.8 million; 445 major surface ships, to their 235. And these counts do not include one of the Soviets' most implacable enemies: China.

The quality of the NATO countries' weapons is better than that of the Soviets and their allies. There are types of weaponry in which the Soviets are more advanced, but Defense Secretary Harold Brown notes that our technology on balance "continues to surpass theirs by a considerable margin."

It is always possible to argue that the Soviet Union might cripple us with a nuclear first strike, but impossible to argue reasonably that we could not cripple it in return. The truth is that if madness prevailed in either country, or if there were a monstrous error of communication or judgment, the superpowers might move into a war that could destroy both countries. There is no certain way to prevent that without disarmament; in fact, if either side believed it could protect itself totally, the world might be more rather than less dangerous.

We should be hearing more in this campaign about arms limitation and less about what Mr. Carter has rightly called "an illusion of absolute nuclear superiority." What would the candidates do to bring progress in the arms talks? Can we soon ratify SALT II and move on to the next steps on strategic weapons? What can be done to limit conventional and tactical weaponry?

It is the answers to those questions that will tell us something about how safe we, and future generations, will be. A renewed arms race offers no security for anyone.

The Times-Picayune
The States-Item
New Orleans, La., November 17, 1980

We are fairly used to thinking of ourselves as vulnerable to the unthinkable — a first-strike attack by strategic missiles that come in from the upper atmosphere with some 15 minutes warning. But we retain the World War II continental-fortress idea of invulnerability to conventional air attack. That has been shattered by recent reports of Soviet bombers successfully testing our perimeter defenses and by the prospect that Soviet bomber development will soon make our present vulnerability a real danger.

Our national radar warning system dates for all practical purposes to the 1950s, when intercontinental ballistic missiles were still being developed and long-range bombers were the standard strategic strike force. ICBMs became the preferred weapon for both the United states and the Soviet Union, and the Soviets indeed dropped out of the bomber competition. (So did we, in effect, retaining our 1950s B-52s as our strategic air arm and concentrating on missiles and tactical fighters.)

Now, the air defense command says, our bomber defenses are geared "to guard against only a limited bomber attack." And that, aparently, not too well. Radars along different stretches of perimeter have different "floors" — heights below which planes cannot be detected — and some stretches have no radar converage at all. Further, the interceptor force to respond to contacts has dwindled to the point, says one defense special, where "we will be in trouble in the 1980s."

The Soviets in the '70s began building big bombers — the Backfire bomber that caused so much trouble in the SALT negotiations because the Soviets contended it was a theater weapon and we contended that, with midair refuelling capacity, it was an intercontinental bomber. It may seem passe in the era of ICBMs with multiple thermonuclear warheads to worry about a surprise bomber attack, but no one can foresee the opening gambits of a third world war, and it is a military adage that every war is begun with the weapons of the previous one.

If we must correct this suddenly important deficiency, it will cost a lot of money — new radar equipment, new interceptors, more manpower. And in this crazy game of strategic oneupmanship we may be locked in a struggle of money more than of armaments. We will have to divert a lot of the national budget to a new defense requirement — and one of the arguments for development of the U.S. cruise missile, which flies slow and low and has a tiny radar silhouette, was that it would force the Russians to divert billions to developing a radar shield against it.

The Reagan administration comes into office committed both to increased defense spending and to new negotiations with the Russians on realistic arms control. That gives each side the opportunity to try to get a handle on its problem with the other before the ante, in money and weapons, is irrevocably upped.

THE RICHMOND NEWS LEADER
Richmond, Va.,
November 21, 1980

Defending the nation became an issue in the 1980 presidential campaign; eventually it became a nail in Jimmy Carter's coffin. The Annapolis graduate was perceived — correctly — as the architect of a weaker, less respected America. Candidate Reagan promised change; he promised a stronger America. President Reagan will find help in bringing about that change in the person of Texas Republican John Tower — scheduled to become chairman of the Senate Armed Services Committee, if not Secretary of Defense.

Speaking informally at a press conference, Tower presented a wish list — no, a need list — that could be the Reagan administration's blueprint for improvement of America's defenses. Tower's wants:

● A new, manned, penetrating bomber that would be derived from the B-1 grounded by Carter.
● Continued development of the MX missile.
● A new submarine missile.
● More fighter planes.
● More ships, specifically a new carrier battle group — consisting of a carrier, carrier air wing, two cruisers, and support ships — as well as more amphibious vessels for the Marines.
● Deployment of the neutron bomb in Europe "to raise the threshold of risk for the Soviets," according to Tower.
● More pay for junior officers and senior non-commissioned officers, to end the flow of middle-management personnel out of the armed forces.

As for costs: Tower has said annual increases should range between 9 and 13 per cent after inflation, compared with the 6 per cent boosts envisioned by Carter. Truly, the dollar figures are boggling: This year's $157 billion defense budget would be upped by $3 billion to cover pay raises, fuel for naval operations in the Indian Ocean, and spare parts. By 1985, estimates call for a $294 annual military budget. Tower's "ball-park" figure for total defense spending from 1981 to 1985: $1.25 *trillion.*

Yes, Reagan's adversaries and the disarmament lobby will construe the proposed defense increases as mindless escalation of the arms race with the Soviet Union. Yet the Soviets are racing without us. Tower believes willingness to re-arm, and to be seen re-arming — to run the race and take the risks — will improve chances for negotiating a better strategic arms limitation treaty. He says the Soviets do not possess "enough industrial slack" — *i.e.,* physical capacity — to stay the course with a mobilized America dedicated to re-forging its arsenal. Hence Soviet enthusiasm for SALT II.

Tower's plans are plainly ambitious. They will cost money — *plenty* of money — as the Reagan years unfold. It will be money well spent. Defending the nation remains government's primary task, a task not addressed by a Carter administration seemingly bent on unilateral disarmament. Tower's list should draw support from Republicans, and from Democrats who have heeded the lessons of the Reagan landslide. Properly, broad support will be forthcoming. The nation will be the winner, and the world will be a safer place.

Minneapolis Tribune
Minneapolis, Minn., October 17, 1980

In contrast to the 1972 and 1976 presidential campaigns, this year's brings no serious proposals for reduced military spending. The leading candidates differ on many aspects of national security — indeed, they seem to relish blasting each other on defense issues — but the Democrat and the Republican and the independent are alike in advocating stronger defenses. They are also alike in failing to go beyond generalities in explaining their views.

Four years ago, Democratic challenger Jimmy Carter called for a cut of at least $5 billion in military spending; incumbent Carter now points to his administration's record of sustained real growth in the defense budget and promises more to come. This year, Republican challenger Ronald Reagan's main criticism of Carter's military policies is that the United States has spent too little. Independent John Anderson says the president has put too much into nuclear weaponry, too little into conventional forces.

But the issue cannot be framed solely in dollars. The first question to ask is whether the country's defenses are reasonably adequate now and likely to be in the future. With some reservations, we think the answer is yes. This is not to absolve the administration of serious mistakes, nor is it to dismiss entirely the other candidates' critiques of national security. But rational debate requires first a rational assessment of American military strengths and weaknesses — never an easy job, and always more difficult against a background of campaign hyperbole.

The most serious exaggeration is the charge by Reagan, amplified by many conservatives, of American military weakness. In their view, the United States should achieve "military superiority" over the Soviet Union; Reagan's frequently repeated phrase is "a margin of safety." The charge of weakness rests on such assertions as these: that Carter stopped or delayed the development of weapons like the B1 bomber, that he has dangerously restrained other military spending, that his advocacy of SALT II reveals a willingness to jeopardize American strategic strength and that he has a naive belief in Soviet willingness to cooperate.

The charge comes wrapped in awesome numbers. For example, the Soviet Union is said to have a 2-to-1 advantage over the United States in strategic bombers and missiles, and in major naval ships. But the numbers game is as deceptive now as always. No doubt there are worriers in Moscow who brood about America's 2-to-1 advantage in the number of strategic warheads and its larger advantage in aircraft carriers.

Still, numbers are essential ingredients of deterrence. But so are a lot of other things — targeting, accuracy, weapons vulnerability and diversity, skilled technicians, reliable command and control systems. To sum up, the Soviet nuclear armory could destroy American society; the American nuclear armory could destroy Soviet society. Soviet weapons are getting more sophisticated and destructive — as are American weapons, though the spurt of new ones will begin mainly in the mid-'80s. But no sane Soviet or American leader, now or in the foreseeable future, is likely to trigger the mutual destruction that nuclear war would entail.

Like most descriptions of nuclear strategy, the "essential equivalence" policy of the Carter adminis-

tration is a fuzzy term. But if the "superiority" demanded by the Reagan camp is a shade clearer, it is also a myth. After a generation of developing nuclear know-how and the weapons it made possible, the Soviet Union shows no inclination to accept a position of inferiority. Something close to strategic parity is likely to persist for a long time. It can be achieved through spending and development competition, or through mutual, negotiated restraints like SALT II.

Allegations of American military weakness extend to non-nuclear forces, and with more accuracy. The sorest point lately has been personnel: failure to reach enlistment goals and, worse, the drain of experienced military people into higher-paying civilian jobs. Although legislation to increase military pay and fringe benefits was enacted only weeks ago, it is already improving the personnel picture.

Unmentioned — at least by the Carter-Mondale campaign — is the president's responsibility for the armed services' personnel pinch. The pinch may be easing now, but many will remember Carter's disgraceful political performance last summer when he flew to a carrier returning from the Persian Gulf. Carter used that newsworthy event to announce his support for military pay increases, which he had opposed until then.

As with nuclear forces, Reagan wants superiority in conventional forces assured by more people and hardware — airplanes, tanks, ships. Here the Reagan-Carter contrast is particularly sharp.

According to William Van Cleave, a Defense Department official in the Nixon administration and now Reagan's chief defense adviser, the United States suffered a "decade-long process of (military) underspending," which was about to be reversed in the mid-1970s by the Ford administration. Carter prevented the turnaround, Van Cleave said, and the decline continued. But in the next breath he compared the situation today "with 1973, when the United States was a power to be respected and a powerful force . . . ." Thus a country suffering in 1973 from long underspending was somehow simultaneously powerful. Reagan's statements echo Van Cleave's words.

President Carter's statements in 1980 echo only faintly the words of candidate Carter in 1976. His broad goals are still commendable. Now, as then, he says the right things about defending freedom, pursuing justice, opposing tyranny. But the president's unpredictable shifts on specific defense policies dismay even those who have worked with him. Leslie Gelb, a leading State Department arms-control adviser from 1977 to 1979, well described a central problem of administration defense policy: "President Carter is a man given to overstatement, and given to marked inconsistency in his decisions."

Thus the dilemma. Anderson has virtually no chance of being elected. The two leading candidates offer a Hobson's choice: Erratic defense policies under Carter or predictable but dangerously misguided policies under Reagan. "History tells us that only the strong survive," said a former official belaboring the charge of weakness. The administration offered the right reply: "History tells us that the strong and wise survive." Unfortunately, Carter and Reagan display great zest for strength, but little evidence of wisdom.

Chicago Tribune

Chicago, Ill., October 14, 1980

As the debate over the state of America's defenses makes its way through appropriations battles and presidential campaigning, it is taking on the quality of one of those old comic book ads: 97-pound weakling goes to beach; beefy lout kicks sand in face; weakling takes muscle-building course; returns to beach with shapely maid on newly-muscled arm; lout kicks sand again; lout gets lights punched out.

In the defense debate, we have now had Afghanistan kicked in our face and we have signed up for the Charles Atlas course. The next panel, presumably, will have us returning to the beach with bulging Rapid Deployment Forces and clouting the ugly Russian in the jaw while NATO coos in admiration.

Nice comic book stuff, but it bears no more relation to reality than what happens on real beaches. The U.S. is not a 97-pound weakling; the U.S.S.R. is not Dick Butkus; and NATO is not a shapely, sighing maid.

It is certainly true that for several years the United States has been neglectful of its defense posture. We have grown a paunch. It has been prudent and proper for defense specialists and political candidates to jab contemptuous fingers at the paunch and demand a course of conditioning to tighten the flab and quicken the reaction.

But it is erroneous to allege that the U.S. is helplessly weak and that the Soviet Union is overwhelmingly strong. It is also dangerous, because our friends and our potential enemies are beginning to believe it. Our allies are alarmed that what Americans say about themselves might be true and that they must begin looking elsewhere for security guarantees. While that may have the beneficial effect of encouraging the allies to strengthen their own military positions [they have grown paunchy, too], it may also lead them to unnecessary and harmful accommodation of Soviet military and political ambitions.

It is especially dangerous if the Soviets begin to believe what we say about our weakness and their strength. They may be tempted to act on this myth of military disparity and plunge into some harebrained adventure that challenges essential interests of the supposedly impotent U.S. The resulting conflict would shatter that myth, but at what cost?

This may be one reason why Defense Secretary Harold Brown, many of whose subordinates have been decrying our "hollow army" and undermanned ships, went on record with a rebuttal of some of the weakness arguments. As he pointed out in a speech in El Paso, Tex., it never has been necessary in peacetime to keep every single fighting unit in combat-ready condition. Many units exist mainly as skeletal structures, ready to be fleshed out if the need arises. Ships and air squadrons can go into a standby status or undergo maintenance procedures that help to economize scarce resources without doing serious harm to the nation's military capability.

The Soviets do the same things for the same reasons. According to Secretary Brown, two-thirds of Soviet army divisions are in a condition that American reporting procedures would call "not combat-ready" — a higher proportion than in the U.S. Army, though the Soviets have more divisions.

It is also fallacious to base military disparity arguments on a simple count of guns, tanks, ships, and rockets. The Russians have more ships than the U.S. Navy, for example, but most of them are outmoded and vulnerable. The United States has chosen to mothball its obsolescence and depend on a leaner, newer, and more sophisticated Navy.

The secretary also pointed out an essential difference in the quality of the two opposing alliances, NATO and the Warsaw Pact. "The NATO allies are all voluntary members of the coalition," he said. "But the Soviet Union's Warsaw Pact allies are captives of their coalition. They would be fighting not to defend their freedom, but to further the conquests of their oppressor. No one can say what their reliability might be under such circumstances."

In fact, some military analysts explain the seemingly excessive Soviet military force in Eastern Europe by suggesting that the Kremlin anticipates using a large part of it against defecting allies.

None of which is a defense of the status quo in U.S. forces. There are weaknesses in the U.S. military posture, especially in manning levels, that are urgently in need of correction. Mr. Brown's analysis, although basically a sensible corrective to the general mood of doomsaying, was also a political defense of an administration trying desperately for re-election. There is much to be done to get rid of the flab. But having overstated the case for purposes of self-stimulation, let us now return to a better sense of the weaknesses—and the strengths—of a fundamentally powerful U.S. military force. It is an out-of-shape prizefighter, not a 97-pound weakling.

The Philadelphia Inquirer

Philadelphia, Pa., December 11, 1980

Make no mistake about it, one of the great debates of the next year is going to be about the U.S. defense establishment, and few of the voices which will carry any weight in the Congress, and fewer yet in the new national administration will be arguing that the present level of preparedness is adequate.

One does not need to be a Strangelovian zealot, pawing the ground in eagerness for a fast-sprint into a renewed arms race with the Soviet Union to find substantial merit in the arguments — or some of them — that the U.S. military has deteriorated to a point which is threatening to the national interest.

For the sake of the survival of humanity, as well as for the economic well-being of Americans and others around the world, it is vital to pursue negotiations on the limitations of weapons, especially nuclear ones. Although the record, including the debate about abandonment of the SALT II treaty, is far from satisfactory, President-elect Reagan has stopped short of rejecting the idea of serious limitations negotiations, and there is ground for hope that upon becoming president he will proceed on those lines.

Meanwhile, however, there is clear consensus in the Republican Party and in much of the Democratic as well that the U.S. defense structure is in a state of serious weakness and erosion. There are severe shortages of trained personnel in the all-volunteer defense force, and those who are trained are leaving far too quickly. Mobility of major force elements is restricted, in the kindest light, as has been dramatically demonstrated in the debates about the U.S. capability to respond to a total cut-off of crude petroleum from the Persian Gulf — a prospect which could bring the U.S. and most of the noncommunist industrialized world to a state of acute economic and political emergency.

There are other limitations, and other threats implicit in them, all further complicated by the fact that much of Western Europe is far from substantially equipped to cooperate in common defense of its interests and America's — and many of the principal NATO countries are showing increasing tendencies to draw back from what has been the sustaining and pre-eminent alliance against Soviet and communist-bloc adventures since soon after the end of World War II.

Beyond the anxieties about manning, training levels and mobilty of the U.S. Army, Navy, Air Force and Marine forces there are serious questions, involving commitments of enormous amounts of money, about basic military hardware: The bomber fleet, the fundamental major nuclear missile delivery systems, the naval war fleet.

As the Reagan transition teams go on with the job of putting together the policies and appointments which will constitute the new admnistration, it is clear that there is no unanimity about the question of defense. Powerful Republican voices on Capitol Hill disagree on substantial elements of manpower and hardware. Others who are expected to have high positions or influence within the administration are as discordant. It is President-elect Reagan who will have to draw the lines and to set the basic policy. It will be vital that he does so in an explicit, straightforward way.

The most valuable single point he could make when he is ready to speak out is that there is no more rationality in simply throwing money at defense problems than there is in indiscriminately pouring money into unproductive social programs.

"The worse thing that can happen," former Secretary of State Melvin R. Laird wrote recently in The Washington Post, "is for the nation to go on a defense spending binge that will create economic havoc at home and confusion abroad and that cannot be dealt with wisely by the Pentagon."

Mr. Laird hardly can be called a soft-liner. Nor can skepticism about the wisdom of setting gross percentages of increases in the defense budget be considered — responsibly — as negligent of the nation's true defense needs. Improvement is needed, clearly. But it must be done with austere, disciplined attention to cost and effectivness — and the ultimate practical purpose of each dollar that will be spent.

There is no more pressing question, in the short or long term, which Mr. Reagan will have to face than how to go about meeting that responsibility.

Roanoke Times & World·News

Roanoke, Va.,
September 13, 1981

The Defense Intelligence Agency has released a report telling, in essence, what everybody already knew: The Soviet Union in recent years has far outproduced the United States in most strategic and tactical weapons. In some cases the ratio is 3 to 1. In 1980 America turned out one-fourth as many tanks, a third as many armored vehicles, half the number of fighter planes, and half as many battlefield ballistic missiles as the U.S.S.R.

There's no question the United States needs to upgrade its battlefield weaponry and its ability to wage conventional war. Much of the so-called U.S. fighting force simply is not combat-ready.

But that's due more to shortcomings in personnel and training than to lack of adequate hardware. To the extent that the Defense Department focuses on numbers of weapons, it may distort the real needs. The United States would not want to maintain the size of standing army that required the quantities of guns, tanks and other weapons the Soviet Union does. It isn't needed; it would be contrary to our traditions.

Americans may well ask why the U.S.S.R. has so many weapons. One answer is in that country's vast size and its long, vulnerable borders; another answer is in its history of invasions by foreign hordes. No other large nation ever suffered as much in war as the Soviet Union, and it's still led by men who remember the terrible times of World War II. The Soviets arm because of profound anxieties and feelings of insecurity. Inwardly they are weak, and they know it. They seek security in numbers.

The United States needn't respond in kind, or be stampeded by the Reds' arms buildup. Gen. Maxwell D. Taylor, who served three presidents in high staff positions, agrees that we must redress the military balance. But he also sees a need for what he calls an essentiality review of the several programs the Defense Department proposes (e.g., whether the B-1 really is needed as a replacement for the B-52 bomber, or the MX in the place of existing ICBMs). The Pentagon shopping list is unrealistically long.

the Charleston Gazette

Charleston, W. Va., August 5, 1981

THE argument with which the Reagan administration justifies an unprecedented peacetime buildup of military strength is hardly a new one. Since 1945 we have heard with regularity the solemn assertion that the United States has fallen woefully behind the Soviet Union in military capability.

We have had the opportunity to test a few government figures who offered such a contention. Would they trade the American military capability for the Russian military capability? To this each replied that he hadn't exactly meant what he had just finished saying. What he meant was that it is necessary to remain a step ahead of potential enemies.

The Carnegie Endowment for International Peace is a non-partisan panel consisting of representatives from the military, academia, news media, science, law, and business. Among them are national security analysts — Lt. Gen. Andrew Goodpaster, former supreme allied commander in Europe; Lt. Gen. Robert E. Pursley, former commander of U. S. forces in Japan; Lt. Gen. Brent Scowcroft, national security adviser to President Ford; and Vice Adm. Patrick J. Hannifin, former staff director of the Joint Chiefs of Staff. According to findings recently released by the panel, America is not militarily enfeebled.

In defense-related technological areas — computers, radar, optics and the like — the panel found a clear American superiority in 14 separate areas of defense capability. It found America and Russia to be equal in six other fields. It found Russia to lead in none. As to deployed technological systems, the panel found America to lead in 14 areas, Russia in nine. The panel accepted CIA estimates showing that Russia spends more money on defense, but observed that the U.S. and NATO spending combined is greater than Warsaw Pact spending.

Costs, the panel warns, are hard to pin down and of little use in assessing relative strength. What is actually available is more important than the percentage of gross national product committed to defense, the panel agrees. Moreover, it points out that the practice of counting expenditures, personnel and weapons does not produce an accurate picture of military balance. Far more important than numbers is whether forces are adequate for the jobs assigned them.

The panel's findings suggest that the assessments of relative military strength as adduced by Pentagon lobbyists are unduly pessimistic. The United States is not yet a second-rate military power.

THE LOUISVILLE TIMES

Louisville, Ky., November 29, 1981

When the new secretary, Caspar Weinberger, took over the Department of Defense last week, he sent a formal message to the U.S. military establishment that he intended to "rearm America." That should warm the hearts of the ultra-conservatives and saber-rattlers, but it is a deception.

The United States can't rearm unless it first disarmed. And the fact is, although we are no longer able to conquer the world — as we could have done once — we are still better able to defend our borders and our people than any other nation in the world, including the Soviet Union.

This is not to say that the defense establishment is as good as it ought to be or will need to be. But it does mean that we must not be stampeded into a crushing round of defense over-spending. During this particularly vulnerable economic period in our nation's history, that could be the most debilitating course of all.

The doomsayers usually claim that simple numbers prove their contention that the United States is weaker than Aunt Tillie's bridge club. The problem is, their numbers are too simple.

They point with alarm, for instance, at the estimate of 1,400 Soviet intercontinental ballistic missiles, compared to our measly 1,054, or the 62 nuclear-armed Soviet subs which outnumber our mere 41. But our subs are better and less detectable than theirs. Even if a Soviet first strike wiped out our entire land-based ICBM force, which is highly improbable, our nuclear subs would likewise obliterate the Soviet Union. The third arm of our triad, the B-52 force, would provide an instant replay of hell.

In nuclear mathematics, 1,054 ICBMs plus 1,400 ICBMs equals absolute zero. With their present stock of atomic weapons, the United States and the Soviet Union would destroy themselves and the rest of the world in an all-out nuclear war. Who needs more?

The Pentagon groupies have other numbers, of course. A favorite is a comparison of the 4.8 million in the Soviet armed forces with our 2.3 million. But they rarely mention that 1 million of the Soviet troops are stationed permanently along the border with China, which has its own armed force of 4.5 million.

Our tactical air force is about equal to the Soviet Union's in numerical strength, but far superior in quality of men and equipment. We have comparably-sized navies; yet, two of the four Soviet fleets are in the Black and Baltic Seas, where they could be bottled up.

None of this is meant to imply that we should sit back and relax. Our defense spending has slipped from 8.7 per cent of our gross national product in 1969 to about 5 per cent. During the same period, the Soviet Union has poured between 12.2 and 13.6 per cent of its GNP into defense.

Our warhawks cite the dissimilarity of these numbers as evidence that our defense establishment is threadbare. The implication is that we should be spending on the Soviet scale.

That is about what it would take to fill all the military shopping lists being waved around. Although it is generally accepted that we ought to spend more money now on defense, we need not nor should not try to match the Soviet effort.

The general thrust of President Carter's final defense budget proposal, submitted just before he left office, was correct and should be adopted by the Reagan administration. Its priorities are on spare parts and maintenance of existing equipment, plus better pay and training for our existing force. Although that's not as flashy or expensive as some proposals, it would make the best use of what we already have.

But the Carter proposal also calls for a major investment in the MX missile system, which Mr. Reagan wisely has questioned. The MX could turn out to be the most expensive redundancy of all time. The money would be better spent for making Trident submarine missiles more accurate, or perhaps the accelerated development of cruise missiles and the Stealth bomber.

Similarly, a proposed huge new investment in NATO over the next five years, including the addition of five new U.S. divisions in Europe, might be avoided by insisting that our allies there finally get serious about paying for their own defense. The money we saved could better be spent in developing a truly effective Rapid Deployment Force, plus basing and supply facilities to protect our growing interests in the Persian Gulf area.

Mr. Weinberger insists that defense expenditures will be questioned as closely as all other programs. Unless he is serious, his proposed "rearming" could weaken America, not strengthen it.

The State

Columbia, S.C., February 8, 1981

FOR MONTHS now there has been an intermittent flow of worrisome news from Washington about this nation's military might in comparison with the Soviet Union's.

You've read some of those stories that question the success of an all-volunteer Army, Navy and Air Force. The reserves, which are counted as ready forces for mobilization, are in sad shape for manpower. Our supply of Navy ships has been substantially reduced, and Air Force pilots are flying bombers that are older than the crews.

Despite reassurances from President Carter about our military strength, there is a feeling in the country that there is a gap between our strength and that of the Russians. And the Russians continue to move ahead in nuclear and conventional armaments.

That feeling of unease about the United States' preparedness and ability to fight even a limited war abroad was a major factor in the election of President Ronald Reagan.

The figures now being tossed out to Congress by the Pentagon's leaders this week confirm, in our minds at least, that things are in worse shape than we'd thought.

The new secretary of defense, Caspar Weinberger, has the reputation of being frugal in spending the taxpayers' money. They call him "Cap the Knife"

in Washington because of his willingness to cut budgets. And when he took over the Defense Department, there was an air of expectancy that all that Pentagon fat we've heard about for many years was going to be pared away.

Thus, when he testified there would be some substantial increases over President Carter's defense budget requests, we got the feeling again that all certainly was not well in the military.

It was left to the chairman of the Joint Chiefs of Staff, Gen. David C. Jones, to recite the figures. President Carter asked for $6.3 billion in supplemental appropriations for this year, which would put the current Pentagon budget at $171.2 billion. General Jones says the military needs $8 billion more than President Carter requested. That would put the total at $178.2 billion.

Furthermore, General Jones says the Pentagon needs $196.5 billion for the fiscal year beginning in October, and probably an additional $30 billion late in that fiscal year.

Granted, some of these increases are due to various inflationary factors and to higher pay for employees of the armed services. But what we read into these figures is the size of the gap which has been allowed. The United States has lost its military superiority, or so it appears, and we may pay dearly for that in more ways than one.

Houston Chronicle

Houston, Texas, August 30, 1981

The Defense Department, in its plan to publish previously secret information detailing the Soviet defense industry and provide drawings and precise performance data on Soviet arms, has come up with an idea that should provide a much clearer picture of the Soviet military buildup than has been available heretofore.

The United States is having difficulty convincing European allies, and some Americans also, about the magnitude of the Soviet military machine. The statistics have been repeated often, and comparisons made with what the West is doing militarily, but none of this seems to have made much of an impression.

Few U.S. allies are increasing their defense spending by 3 percent as agreed to during the Carter administration, which means the Reagan

administration's goal of a 7 percent increase is a long way from realization. And Reagan's defense budget is drawing complaints at home and abroad.

The West Europeans appear to be worrying far more about the placement of U.S. weapons than in any threat from the Soviet Union.

The Soviets can pick up U.S. newspapers and magazines and get a fairly accurate picture of U.S. and West European military efforts, but information from the Soviet Union is scarce, sometimes giving a false impression of the Soviet effort.

It's about time the world got a better idea of why Reagan is putting so much emphasis on military spending and why the United States wants its allies to increase their defense budgets.

Rockford Register Star

Rockford, Ill., October 12, 1981

The annual migration of generals and admirals from the Pentagon to the halls of Congress was late this year, but with little else different from all the others which have gone on before.

It's late because this year the military didn't have to lobby Congress for huge budget increases. It got everything it ever dreamed of without asking. Now it's trying to keep it.

Never before in peacetime has the military top brass had so much to defend — or an administration so willing to listen to their blandishments.

Their battle plan for the annual invasion of Congress seldom varies, although it's being carried out with a little more flourish this fall. They start with dire warnings: The Russians (or somebody) are coming and we better watch out because we are hopelessly behind in military might and must give the Pentagon dollars by the billions to catch up. It's an annual tune designed to frighten the public and Congress into paying for a new bunch of military gadgets.

This year's military invasion of Congress is being led by Defense Secretary Caspar Weinberger (who once believed in balanced budgets). Its major weapon is a glossy, 99-page booklet, complete with multi-colored charts, photographs and drawings, all designed to picture a Soviet military capable of overwhelming the free world.

It may not be propaganda, as Moscow claims. But it certainly is public relations at its slickest. Why else translate the document into German, French, Spanish, Italian and Japanese? Why else the simultaneous telecast of Weinberger's press conference on it to Europe?

The Pentagon's glossy new booklet is not, of course, a pack of lies. For that matter, most of it already was common knowledge around world.

But it has its flaws. Facts are twisted or misused. Only part of the story is presented.

It hints at military weaknesses without offering any new information, meaningful comparisons or conclusions. It ignores areas where our military has commanding leads to focus on others where the Soviets have a meaningless numerical edge — meaningless because Russia is surrounded by enemies; America by allies.

It talks of massive numbers of Soviet combat ships without pointing out that most are small coastal vessels and many others are ancient with limited value. It lists massive numbers of Soviet bombers, while ignoring the fact that most are propeller-driven planes of no combat use.

It misuses comparisons of military strength and gross national product. It hints at technological shortcomings without producing any evidence that the long-established and almost total superiority of the United States has somehow changed.

It passes over military strength and expenditures by our allies.

It is exactly what it is designed to be: Not a factual military report but a public relations weapon designed to help the Pentagon get the biggest possible share of the national budget.

It's the military's annual cry of "Wolf!"

It is proper that the military should lead the fight to keep our nation strong and safe. There's not even anything wrong with them using public relations gimmicks to help. But let us not allow those gimmicks to create a national panic.

And let's not overlook the most important of all Weinberger's messages: The Kremlin has done massive harm to the Soviet economy by pouring so much of the nation's production into arms.

"They are totally untroubled by public opinion," Weinberger said of the Soviet leaders. "They can continue to injure their economy."

The same mistake can be made in the United States if we and our leaders are misled — are frightened into arming for unrealistic battles on improbable fronts.

THE MILWAUKEE JOURNAL
Milwaukee, Wisc., October 1, 1981

"There is nothing hypothetical about the Soviet military machine," writes Defense Secretary Weinberger in a glossy new Pentagon publication, "Soviet Military Power." He's right. And we agree with the secretary's dictum that the best defense for "free people of free nations" is to be well informed.

However, there is an important distinction between being well informed and having the wits scared out of you. The new booklet, unfortunately, accomplishes the latter at the expense of the former. And scared-witlessness is not a good base for decisions in a democratic society.

The deficiency of the Pentagon's publication, released elaborately in Washington Tuesday, is that "Soviet Military Power" is presented in a vacuum. The Russians have developed a formidable arsenal of advanced weaponry. But the vital point barely alluded to in the booklet is: compared to what?

The military capacity of the US is mostly presented by alarming indirection. As in: "Over the past 10 years, the Soviet Union is estimated to have taken the lead in development of directed energy weapons such as high-power lasers and possibly radio frequency." Such warnings are, indeed, alarming when supported by more objective sources. For instance, the respected Institute for Stragetic Studies in London last week reported that "the West has largely lost the technological edge which allowed NATO to believe that quality could substitute for numbers."

The reader of the Pentagon booklet, however, will find little by which to judge *relative* strengths of the US and Soviet Union — and we doubt that many Americans have readily at hand the Defense Department's annual "Military Postures" report, which does detail comparability. It is hard, then, to see how the lavish new publication fulfills the goal of helping to inform a free people.

There is a solid argument to be made for strengthening America's military forces. There is also value in counter-battery propaganda (the Russians are energetically howling about the Reagan administration's military emphasis even as they are furiously deploying their potent new missile, the SS-20, throughout Eastern Europe).

But there was, we fear, confusion at the Pentagon between these two modes of expression. As a result, the Weinberger monograph could have one of two principal results, neither helpful: burnishing the false image of an omnipotent tree-tall Russian, or encouraging the tendency to dismiss any warnings of Soviet military power as horsefeathers.

To inform a free people requires balance, proportion and comparison.

ARKANSAS DEMOCRAT
Little Rock, Ark., September 8, 1981

Just as Ronald Reagan warns the Russians not to engage in an arms race they can't win, word comes from a defense intelligence study that the Russian economy is sinking under the weight of rising defense spending. Is that what Mr. Reagan is talking about?

Some people don't like his saying the things he does to Russia. He has told them (as Khrushchev once told us) that their system is outmoded and doomed to fail. Now, he's telling them that they can't beat us in an arms race. But he didn't start that. Soviet Premier Leonid Brezhnev did. When Mr. Reagan announced the defense buildup, Brezhnev said that trying to surpass Russia was "unacceptable."

Of course, it should have been unacceptable to us that the Russians should have had the 10 clear years of outspending us that has enabled them to catch and surpass us in arms. Those were the palmy years of domestic social spending, which Mr. Reagan is now ending – so that we can do what we've got to do about defense.

As to who will surpass whom, the defense intelligence report declares that Russian defense spending has stagnated Soviet living standards and slowed economic growth almost to a standstill.

In Russia, of course, government allocates all national expenditures, which isn't the case here – where even Mr. Reagan's $1.6 trillion in projected defense spending represents only a 7 per cent real increase and a much smaller percentage of national output than is the case with Russia. Our worry is about the inflationary effects – not the depressive effects – of such spending. When he answers Russia's boast that we can't win with a boast of our own, Mr. Reagan would seem to be speaking from the catbird seat.

THE INDIANAPOLIS NEWS
Indianapolis, Ind., September 14, 1981

Americans who remember the 1960 presidential campaign may recall that John Kennedy bore down hard on the defense vulnerabilities of the country, somewhat in the same way that Ronald Reagan did.

Kennedy's buzzword was "missile gap." He said the Soviet Union was far ahead of the U.S. in strategic weapons and that it would be his policy to "bridge the missile gap" as rapidly as possible.

After he became President, Kennedy learned he had been misinformed. There was no missile gap.

Joseph C. Harsh, the respected authority on international affairs who writes for The Christian Science Monitor, believes it may be a parallel scene — that U.S. armament, taken in the aggregate, may not be as inferior to the Soviets as Americans have been led to believe.

Harsh partly documents his view by citing an annual study done by the International Institute of Strategic Studies. The report confirms that from 1983 to 1986 the Soviets may have more power in their Intercontinental Ballistic Missiles (ICBMs) than the U.S. in the same weapons. But the U.S., says the study, has long range bombers which carry strategic weapons. The Soviets have no bombers of similar capacity. Moreover, the U.S. maintains 20 strategic submarines on station, armed with 3,200 nuclear warheads, as opposed to 7 to 10 such submarines for the Soviets.

The study also doubts the ability of the Soviets to destroy the 1,064 U.S. ICBM silos. To accomplish this feat would demand 2,000 perfectly aimed and coordinated warheads — a technological impossibility. Even if the Soviets could pull it off, they would need to make allowance for U.S. military assaults with an arsenal of weapons before their second wave could be launched.

The conclusion is that the competence of the U.S. capability for deterrence has been underestimated. Thus, the arguments continue. The News has previously provided the best available statistics showing the Soviets are far ahead in overall firepower, with the admonition that domestic efforts must be doubled in order to assure essential deterrence against possible aggression.

On the other hand, the "authorities" were wrong in 1960. Could they be mistaken now?

Harsh raises the possibility because of President Reagan's preoccupation with moving quickly toward a balanced budget. The collision course between such budget-cutting and increasing the defense budget is inevitable. And this is the main cause of the impasse in Washington.

The logical resolution of that impasse is to give up or postpone the creation of the controversial MX missile or the B-1 bomber, or both. The MX missile has created a storm of controversy over satisfactory siting. No one wants to give it a home for obvious reasons. In previous discussions it has been theoretically positioned on railroad cars, in movable silos, on submarines and in airplanes. The President is still weighing the evidence. Also, the argument rages on, as it has for 15 years, about the B-1 bomber. The President is pondering that one, too.

Meantime, it is relevant to note that if the Soviets were moved to make a surprise attack, they could wait four years before these superweapons would be in place.

If the President, says Joseph C. Harsh, should take this recent study seriously, he could save $100 billion by abandoning the MX missile and another $50 billion by grounding the plans for the B-1 bomber. To save $150 billion would put the budget in clover, would reassure investors, would probably bring down interest rates and cause an upsurge in employment. It is a tempting picture, but it is clouded by a host of pressure groups, senators and representatives who have their own set of priorities based on their special sets of facts.

Two questions hang like the sword of Damocles: Does the nation possess sufficient military power today and tomorrow to deter the Soviets? Are the MX missile and the B1 bomber expendable?

The average American desperately wants to know the answers to these questions. He deserves to know, if anyone does, and the President, if he has been misled as John Kennedy was, should back up and start over. What is needed now is not more debate and oratory, but some honest answers based upon facts.

THE WALL STREET JOURNAL

New York, N.Y., October 2, 1981

Secretary Weinberger's slick new 99-page guide to Soviet military power is but the latest effort by the Reagan administration to prove to an unbelieving world what should be obvious: The Soviet Union is a dangerous and expansionary power.

We find it disquieting that such efforts are necessary. And it is even more disquieting that they have not made much evident impact on public opinion in the U.S. and Europe. The parallel between this ho-hum response and the prevailing disbelieving attitude in the U.S. and England when Hitler was arming for World War II is by no means perfect, but neither is it imperfect.

The administration itself has to some degree contributed to this mood by bowing so quickly to arms-talk pressures, thus setting itself up for the old Russian ploy of first conducting a massive arms buildup outside existing limitations and then trying to negotiate restrictions on the other side's attempts to catch up. But the administration has made at least four significant efforts to awaken the U.S. and Europe to the new dangers.

The first, the State Department's white paper on El Salvador, drew immediate fire from the left, including the social democrats of Europe who, through naivete or worse, have helped sponsor the Communist drive to conquer Central America. The effectiveness of the counterattack was reflected in a Senate vote a few days ago to slap so-called human rights restrictions on the administration's aid to the Salvadoran government in its bloody war with Communist-led guerrillas.

The next administration effort was to link terrorist groups around the world to Soviet-sponsored training camps. This too provoked a counterattack. The thought that those cold-blooded assassins assaulting democratic institutions might be something other than freedom fighters was brushed off by many as conspiracy mongering.

Then, of course, there were the recent "yellow rain" disclosures, particularly significant because they make clear that the Soviet Union has not lived up to its commitments on the control of chemical and bacteriological warfare. The implications of this for future arms-control talks are obvious. And indeed, reports of Soviet use of such horror weapons are not new; we editorialized about them in this space in February, 1980. Yet the administration had been so shell-shocked by the reaction to its previous complaints about Soviet conduct that it presented this one with great caution.

Finally, there was this week's Pentagon briefing book on Soviet power. There was not much new in it, either. The basic numbers on tanks, planes and missiles have been monitored not just by the Pentagon but by other analysts, such as Britain's International Institute for Strategic Studies, for years. They are formidable: 50,000 Soviet tanks, 9,000 winged aircraft and 5,200 helicopters; 22,000 artillery pieces; 1,700 warships; 7,000 nuclear warheads on intercontinental missiles; 3.7 million troops, not including KGB forces and construction troops.

How was this greeted? Various critics said it failed to make comparisons in quality and quantity with U.S. and NATO forces; it doesn't take account of the problem of alcoholism in the Soviet Union; it was a Pentagon ploy to defend the defense budget against cuts, etc.

Now, of course, it is the custom and practice in the U.S. to ask questions and we would not want to see that change. But there may be something here that goes beyond normal debate.

The nagging fear is of what the more respected analysts of the Soviet military buildup have always predicted would happen: that the Western democracies would begin at some point to doubt their ability to stand up to the various forms of intimidation that the Soviets have learned to apply—that instead of being outraged they would become more conciliatory.

If this is happening, it is ironic that it should be happening when the Soviet Union has genuine internal problems. Predictably, those problems, reflected in low morale and productivity, are used by some in the West to argue that the Soviet threat is diminishing. That argument, however, does not take account of the special circumstances of Soviet political life, where the ruling party depends for its existence on the same instruments it uses to threaten the outside world: military might, KGB terrorism, political manipulation of the population. And history suggests that heavily armed, expansionist nations become more, not less, dangerous during periods of domestic economic adversity.

The Reagan administration has been trying to build public support in the U.S. and Europe for a more vigorous U.S. role in defending against Soviet intimidation and infiltration of the world's democracies. It obviously will have to persevere more convincingly. But anyone who thinks these are mere scare tactics is indulging in a dangerous form of escapism.

The Birmingham News

Birmingham, Ala., October 3, 1981

Americans would be extremely foolish to be taken in by attempts to discredit Defense Secretary Weinberger's report on Soviet military power. While the report helps to explain why the United States must move quickly to improve its military capability, it is not a quickie effort meant only to support President Reagan's announcement regarding the MX Missile and the B-1 bomber.

The 99-page book containing the new assessments obviously was not compiled overnight. The information it contains about Soviet military power is consistent with earlier published independent intelligence from abroad.

The dangers that exist for the United States from Soviet military blackmail of its NATO partners are already painfully evident in irrational anti-U.S. violence and demonstrations against new defensive nuclear weapons in the capitals of Europe, despite 250 SS-20 missiles the Soviets have targeted on European cities.

Clearly its military machine far exceeds Soviet needs for defensive purposes. The sacrifices the costs of the armaments have exacted from the civilian population in terms of creature needs speak more eloquently than words of Soviet intent to create a military machine capable of offensive warfare on two fronts.

Only in technology and expertise does the Atlantic Alliance come close to matching Soviet military strength. And each year the gap widens. If the United States is to negotiate arms agreements with the Kremlin, it will have to negotiat from a base of credible military capability. Otherwise such talks will be used only to widen the gap between Western and Soviet military capability.

At this point, it seems Western leaders, along with the United States, are losing the propaganda war with the Soviet Union as well. Financed by the Kremlin, so-called pacificist and leftist groups are claiming that in the event of a confrontation between the Soviets and the United States, Europe would become the battleground and ultimately a nuclear-polluted wasteland. Leaders of these groups are, in effect, saying it is "better to be Red than dead."

Because the United States has the capability through its satellites to track Soviet military advances, it is a U.S. obligation to warn potential victims of Soviet aggression. Warnings, however, are worthless, if Europeans choose to bury their heads in the sand and ignore reality as they did while Hitler built his war machine.

"THE RUSSIANS ARE LEADING! THE RUSSIANS ARE LEADING!"

The Atlanta Journal
THE ATLANTA CONSTITUTION
Atlanta, Ga., November 27, 1982

The president of the United States wasn't leveling with you when, in his recent speech booming the MX missile, he said that "in virtually every measure of military power, the Soviet Union enjoys a decided advantage."

Those charts he used to scare the daylights out of you told only half the story.

The Soviets do indeed have 1,200 atomic warheads mounted on intermediate-range missiles in Europe against zero for the United States, as he asserted.

But their range is too limited to span the ocean, and be used against us. And NATO already has planned a deployment of U.S. Pershing missiles in late 1983 to counter the Soviet deployment.

When it comes to total warheads carried by land-based and submarine-based missiles, the two superpowers are roughly in balance, with about 7,500 apiece; and that is by far the more significant figure, representing the number of individual atomic explosives each country could heave at the other in the event of all-out nuclear war.

The president also kept mum about the number of bombs carried by the U.S. fleet of long-range bombers, which is superior.

And our advantage will rise shortly with the arrival of 3,000 new missiles now on order, and the deployment next month of 16 B-52 bombers — each carrying 12 nuclear-tipped cruise missiles that can be launched far outside Soviet air defenses and fly more than 1,500 miles to targets deep inside the country.

Such deliberate misrepresentation might help the president to ram another huge military-spending bill through Congress — were it not so transparent, so easily refuted and, ultimately, damaging to his personal credibility.

But one worries more about the cumulative effect of his alarums on the Soviets. Let us hope that President Reagan, who misses no opportunity to repeat his demonstrably false propaganda that the Soviets have the edge, never convinces the Soviets of that.

FORT WORTH STAR-TELEGRAM
Fort Worth, Texas, June 25, 1982

In a world grown increasingly cynical, might more than ever today is being equated with right.

That is one of the principal reasons so many of the world's so-called nonaligned nations have tended to list so much in their nonalignment toward the Soviet Union. There is a widespread belief, fostered to a considerable extent by American advocates of increased defense spending, that the United States lags behind the Soviet Union in military muscle.

In terms of sheer numbers of soldiers, missiles and other pieces of hardware, that is true. But from the standpoint of technological sophistication of arms and effectiveness in combat, that now appears to be a questionable assessment.

The spectacular success of the Israelis, using mainly American-manufactured aircraft and tanks against Syrian forces equipped with Soviet-made hardware, suggests that the United States still enjoys a decided technological advantage over

the Soviets in conventional arms that compensates for the Soviets' superiority in numbers.

That demonstration of the quality of American arms will not be lost upon those governments that based their relations with the two superpowers upon assessments of which is militarily stronger. It should go a long way toward dispelling the myth that the United States has become a defanged tiger.

It is unfortunate that such renewed respect for American military power should have to arise Phoenix-like out of the ashes of the deplorable events that have occurred in Lebanon in recent weeks. Perhaps it is unseemly to speak of such a side effect of the conflict in view of the dimensions of the tragedy that has unfolded and the perilous political repercussions that it could engender.

But the fact of the superior performance of American-made arms in the fighting in Lebanon cannot be ignored by the Third World countries, by the Pentagon or by the Soviet Union.

The Des Moines Register
Des Moines, Iowa, April 5, 1982

President Reagan's assertion that the Soviet Union has "a definite margin of superiority" in nuclear weapons over the United States has led the experts to resume counting missiles, launchers, warheads — what Winston Churchill at the beginning of the atomic age called the odious apparatus of modern war.

You can cook the numbers any way you want to. The important

thing is to count the right elements and to forget about comparisons that don't matter.

Notwithstanding administration efforts to play down Reagan's remarks, no authoritative official has ever before asserted Soviet superiority in nuclear arms, not even in the current administration. Reagan's use of the word "superiority" was at least careless.

Previous administrations, Republican and Democratic, have used terms like "rough parity" and "essential equivalence" to describe the U.S.- Soviet balance. Former National Security

Adviser Zbigniew Brzezinski used a new term the other day: "ambiguous equivalence." That probably says it as well as anything.

You could devise a nuclear-weapons numbers game that showed the Soviets at an advantage. For example, they have 1,398 intercontinental ballistic missiles and the United States has 1,052. But if you count the number of warheads on those missiles, the advantage goes to the United States, with about 9,000 as against the Soviets' 7,000.

One thing that can't be counted or easily measured is quality. There, the United States seems to have an important edge, according to most observers.

But beyond a certain point, it no longer has any meaning to claim that you're No. 1, or that you're superior. The numbers game becomes pointless once you have enough military strength to do the job you want to do.

Both the United States and the Soviet Union have the ability to blow each other to ashes. So who is No. 1. It doesn't mean anything. The matter was stated with clarity the other day by Paul Warnke, the former director of the U.S. Arms Control and Disarmament Agency:

"It doesn't make a damn bit of difference. The fact that they might have a 2-megaton warhead compared to our modest ones of something like 400,000 tons of TNT only makes one difference: How big is the hole going to be where the high school used to be?"

The Hartford Courant
Hartford, Conn., December 12, 1982

For most Americans, the argument on defense boils down to a single question: Are the Russians ahead?

One answer comes from President Reagan: "Today, in virtually every measure of military power, the Soviet Union enjoys a decided advantage," he said on Nov. 22.

If the Russians are conclusively ahead, the nation will provide for the Pentagon to catch up. That aspect of America's psyche — the spirit of competitiveness — will not tolerate a second-best place in defense.

But the evidence does not point to a United States fallen behind. At worst, there is a sharing of first-place position with the Soviets. The sharing is called nuclear parity, which strategists say is the requisite for arms control.

Let those in a better position to know tell the story:

• "Would you rather have at your disposal the U.S. nuclear arsenal or the Soviet nuclear arsenal?" asked Chairman Charles H. Percy at a hearing of the Senate Foreign Relations Committee last April 29. Defense Secretary Caspar W. Weinberger replied, ". . . I would not for a moment exchange anything, because we have an immense edge in technology."

• "I would not trade," said Gen. John Vessey, chairman of the Joint Chiefs of Staff, in response to a similar question a month earlier at a hearing of the Senate Armed Services Committee.

• "The Soviets do not have anything like strategic superiority in the sense of a militarily or politically usable advantage in strategic nuclear forces," said former Defense Secretary Harold Brown on April 30.

• "The United States is the dominant military and economic power not only in that (Pacific) theater but also in every other theater of the world," said Adm. Robert Long, commander-in-chief of U.S. forces in the Pacific, on March 16.

• "The U.S. Navy's sea-based tactical aircraft and carriers represent the single most important advantage over the Soviet navy, and are far superior in both numbers and quality," said Navy Secretary John F. Lehman on March 24, 1981.

• "We are in the strongest position that we've ever been when it comes to tactical aircraft," said Air Force Brig. Gen. Del Jacobs last June 6, when asked how NATO and Soviet forces compare.

• "I, myself, believe they've gotten weaker. . . They are in a weaker position today than they were 14 or 15 years ago," said former Defense Secretary Robert S. McNamara on April 8, when asked about reports that the Soviets have tipped the geopolitical balance in their favor.

• "Just one of our relatively invulnerable Poseidon submarines — less than 2 percent of our total nuclear force of submarines, aircraft and land-based missiles — carries enough warheads to destroy every large and medium-sized city in the Soviet Union," said President Jimmy Carter on Nov. 23, 1979.

These testimonials dispute, if not disprove, President Reagan's claim that the Soviets enjoy "decided advantage."

The pervasive skepticism toward leapfrogging investments in defense is well-founded. Americans are far more sober-minded today about presidential claims than they were in the days when every word on defense and foreign policy uttered from the Oval Office was considered to be certifiably true.

Mr. Reagan wants to spend $1.9 trillion on the military over the next six years. That amounts to $36 million every hour, day and night. The exotic hardware planned for our future includes MX, Trident II, cruise and Pershing II missiles, and B-1B and Stealth bombers.

These are crucial to peace and eventual disarmament, contends the president. To which the American people are saying, Show Me.

The News and Courier
CHARLESTON EVENING POST
Charleston, S.C., June 5, 1983

Twenty years ago with liberal, Democratic John F. Kennedy at the nation's helm, 9 percent of the gross national product was spent on defense. Today, that figure is down to 6.7 percent of the GNP while Soviet defense expenditures, in constant dollars or percentages, have grown constantly.

Yet there are those in leadership positions in Congress and elsewhere that airily claim another $15 billion or $20 billion can be cut from defense without weakening the U.S. posture or any ill consequences. They say that but don't bet on it.

A history lesson is appropriate. On the eve of World War II, Austria was weak, Czechoslovakia was weak, Poland was weak, Latvia was weak, Estonia was weak, Lithuania was weak, Belgium was weak, the Netherlands was weak, Norway was weak, France was weak, the Philippines were weak and Indochina was weak. With relative ease, all were conquered or occupied by a stronger power.

On the other hand, Hitler THOUGHT the Soviet Union was weak so the Germans attacked. Hitler was wrong. Japan's Tojo THOUGHT the United States was weak so the Japanese attacked Pearl Harbor. Tojo was wrong. It doesn't have to be actual weaknesses that make certain nations prey to others — merely the perception of weakness.

This country, when compared militarily to the only nation that would be an aggressor, the Soviet Union, is much weaker today than it was 20 years ago. If the trend continues, then the point will be reached when we will be unable to respond to a power confrontation with the Russians, and, with the excuse of sparing lives, the United States will surrender. The brightest torch of freedom in the world will be snuffed out.

The price of defense is high. So is the price of freedom. They're synonimous.

Chicago Tribune

Chicago, Ill., March 15, 1983

When an orderly community is confronted with an outside danger it reacts typically in one of two ways, depending on the kind and the quality of its leadership. One reaction is for the leaders to calmly evaluate the danger, inform the community of its precise nature and organize a prudent defense against it. The other reaction is for the leaders to overestimate the peril, run shouting through the streets and get the citizenry into a paroxysm of confusion and panic.

The first reaction is the one most likely to save the community. The second can be more dangerous than the danger itself.

The Reagan administration is coming close to following the second course, the path of panic, in its reaction to the Soviet military threat. Instead of careful evaluation the President and his advisers are indulging in overblown rhetoric. They call American armed forces inferior to the Soviet Union's large but cumbersome military machine. They begin to look rattled, unsure of themselves, of their armed forces and of their people; they begin to look frightened and even frightening.

For all its vigor and truculence, the President's fire-and-brimstone speech to the National Association of Evangelicals last week is the kind of shouting that disturbs many Americans. It is not that what he said was false, but that it was exaggerated and was delivered in language poised near the edge of frenzy. It might have been suitable to carry on that way to an audience of evangelicals accustomed to Bible-thumping fury, but the President's words reach throughout the land to those for whom such rhetoric is disturbing. Screaming "fire!" in a crowded theater may be a bad idea even if the theater is actually on fire.

It is much the same with Defense Secretary Caspar Weinberger's new book on the size and growth of Soviet military forces, released with much doomsaying about how the Soviets are getting ready to fight a protracted nuclear war and conquer the world.

Of course it is prudent and necessary for the United States and its allies to mount a sensible defense against Soviet military power. But it is imprudent and unnecessary to discuss the matter as if it were an imminent fight to the nuclear finish against Satan incarnate. The Russians are not devils—they are merely Russians, no more and no less, people of average height and moderate intelligence and a fairly well-honed sense of self-preservation.

Americans sense that reality, and that is why the administration's shrill reaction to a manageable threat is hurting its own cause. It is more the administration than the Freeze Movement leaders that is responsible for the likely passage of a freeze resolution in the House of Representatives. The Freeze Movement obtains its essential force from a widespread concern among the people that the government's leaders are on the verge of doing something foolish. And the only place they get that impression is from the leaders themselves.

At heart, President Reagan's proposals for strengthening U.S. military power are sound. There are the post-Vietnam years of neglect to be made up for, obvious weak spots to be corrected. If Americans are told of the nation's defense weaknesses in a calm, clear and honest manner, they will support corrective measures. If they are persuaded that the administration is pursuing arms control in good faith, they will be less likely to look upon defense spending as excessive. But if they are harangued and threatened they will balk.

BUFFALO EVENING NEWS

Buffalo, N.Y., May 20, 1983

An increase in defense spending is clearly necessary, and Congress is currently debating just how large the increase should be. But the Reagan administration, in pressing its defense requests, has sometimes been on shaky ground.

Sen. Carl Levin, D-Mich., says the effect of some of the statements by President Reagan and defense officials has been "to exaggerate needlessly" the Soviet threat. To keep the defense debate in perspective, Sen. Levin offered data from the Defense Department and other sources.

Sen. Levin particularly objected to Mr. Reagan's statement last November that "today in virtually every measure of military power, the Soviet Union enjoys a decided advantage." In this connection, Mr. Levin noted the contrast between the hard-nosed views of many of our civilian leaders and the assessments of our capabilities by high military leaders. Gen. John Vessey, chairman of the Joint Chiefs of Staff, when asked by Sen. Levin if he would swap our forces for Soviet forces, said he would like some of the things the Soviets have but that, overall, his answer would be: "Not on your life."

Similarly, Deputy Secretary of Defense W. Paul Thayer said a few weeks ago that "United States forces are outnumbered 2 to 1 in military personnel and by even greater ratios in most categories of military hardware." And yet in 1980 — even before the current effort to expand the nation's defenses — Gen. David C. Jones, a former chairman of the Joint Chiefs, said: "There is too much pessimism about our current capability ... I would not swap our present military capability with that of the Soviet Union, nor would I want to trade the broader problems each country faces."

The Soviet Union is, indeed, ahead in some categories, and that is worrisome, but just to "show there is another side," Sen. Levin cited data showing that the United States is ahead in strategic nuclear warheads and bombs, 9,543 to 8,072; in carrier-based attack aircraft, 720 to 65; and in heavy and medium bombers, 328 to 245.

What is needed in the defense debate is less heat and more light. Defense spending should be increased, but at a pace that will ensure that the money is spent wisely and effectively.

THE TENNESSEAN

Nashville, Tenn., March 13, 1983

IT is as predictable as the seasons that when the Pentagon is having difficulties with its budget in the Congress, it issues another "report" on how great are the strides of the Soviet Union toward military superiority.

So, Defense Secretary Caspar Weinberger has issued a new report which he says documents a "relentless" Soviet drive toward such superiority in all fields, including space warfare.

The 107-page document devoted attention to what the Soviet is doing in space, noting that "the development of a large manned space station by 1990" is one of the goals of the new heavy-lift launcher system now in development.

It suggested that, before the end of the century, the Soviet will send aloft space stations that could weigh more than 100 tons and be able to support a large crew for extended periods. It said the Russians could be able to launch their first prototype of a space-based laser anti-satellite system in the late 1980s or very early 1990s.

The report contains no real surprises, or nothing that has not been speculated on before. It does provide details on a wide variety of Soviet weapons. It is interesting, in view of the fact that several days ago government specialists on the Soviet Union reported that its military spending from 1976 to 1981 rose at a slower rate than they had estimated — about 2% a year instead of more than 3%.

It does not take much analyzing to figure out why the report has been turned out. It is an obvious attempt to muster support for the administration's embattled defense spending plans at a time when even Republican loyalists are demanding that military spending be trimmed.

And it may be partly to offset the testimony of Defense Department program analyst Franklin Spinney, who has told committees that the price of the administration's massive defense buildup has been understated.

Mr. Spinney said the Pentagon has systematically underestimated future defense costs for at least three decades. He said it is ordering a range of weapons now, based on projections of multi-year development costs that are unrealistic. The planners seem to think unit costs will go down over a period of time. Instead, unit costs have consistently gone up, doubling, tripling and even quadrupling in the cost per unit.

Furthermore, the Pentagon's shopping list continues to include exotic, "gold-plated" weapons systems whose efficiency in battle is extremely doubtful. The Soviet Union, however, tends to stick to basics and practicality in sea, land and air weapons.

While the Congress is sharpening its budget ax, it should scrutinize again some of those exotic U.S. systems and put its emphasis on those things that are really needed for combat readiness of this country.

THE DAILY HERALD

Biloxi, Miss., March 7, 1983

President Reagan has resisted staunchly efforts to trim back on the rate of increase in U.S. defense spending but, increasingly, questions are raised as to justification.

The nation's governors, for one, have urged reductions to reduce budget deficits and to accommodate more funds for domestic programs in a year of skin-tight state budgets.

The president has proposed a 10 percent annual increase in defense spending amounting to a total outlay of 29 cents of each budget dollar. But the governors, in a rare display of bipartisan unity, asked the increase be held between 3 and 5 percent. Mr. Reagan chose to rebuff their intrusion into matters of defense which are the prime federal responsibility under the Constitution. However, the political message is certain to be seriously studied by the administration in light of expectations that Reagan will seek reelection.

Then along came *The New York Times* with a story stating that Central Intelligence Agency specialists now believe the CIA has been over-estimating the growth rate of Soviet military spending over the past six years.

The Soviets' defense spending, allowing for such factors as inflation and industrial inefficiency, may be growing at a rate no higher than 2 percent annually, according to the CIA. If so, this is substantially lower than the 5 percent figure Reagan has frequently used in justifying U.S. expenditures.

However, there's a balance factor which should not be overlooked.

The Defense Intelligence Agency, disputing the latest CIA interpretations, asserts the Soviets, in dollar amounts, spent 44 percent more than the U.S. for defense in 1981, to the tune of $222 billion to $154 billion.

Further, the DIA said, the Soviets spent $45 billion for research and development which, as a line item, did not come under the category of defense.

It is comforting to be told that the U.S. still leads the Soviet Union by 15-1 in basic technologies with military applications, as the Pentagon recently revealed. But it is evident the Soviets are striving mightily to close the gap.

Which brings back the question, how much defense spending is justified?

By the very nature of our constitutional government, the responsibility for answering that rests squarely on the shoulders of the commander-in-chief who sits in the White House Oval Office.

As his predecessor, President Carter, was accused of underspending and permitting a dangerous weakening of defenses, Mr. Reagan now is chided for proposed expenditures deemed proportionately too high.

So long as a president remains convinced the nation's security requires the defense outlays he has requested, he may be challenged by dissenters but should not be unduly shackled by hasty legislation born of political discontent.

Detroit Free Press

Detroit, Mich., May 12, 1983

THANK SEN. Carl Levin, D-Mich., for reintroducing a real world context to the debate over American defense spending. His new booklet, "The Other Side of the Story," is intended as a counter-argument to the administration's contention that the United States underwent a decade of neglect in the 1970s and is now behind in virtually every military area against the Soviet Union.

But in addition to his own charts and numbers, which demonstrate that although the United States is behind in some weapons systems it is ahead in others, Sen. Levin discusses the less quantifiable factors that determine the outcome of battles. The Soviet Union, he reminds us, must fear "unreliable allies; lower quality military personnel and tactical leadership; a huge frontier with a hostile China; noisy, therefore more vulnerable submarines; serious geographical constraints on naval access to the open oceans; far less capable pilots; airlift deficiencies," and so on. Even the most sophisticated hardware does not automatically equal effective power, he says. "If we have to go to the Persian Gulf to carry out a commitment to defend our interests with military power," the senator points out, "the MX missile won't do us much good."

Sen. Levin's rebuttal has already been dubbed "Chart Wars" and that is too bad. The hazard of the military spending debate is that it will disintegrate into a numbers war, a simple quibbling over whose figures are accurate. The far more important questions, in fact, the only truly relevant ones, involve the purpose and effectiveness of our defense system: In what instances will American foreign policy goals be best met by military intervention, by diplomacy, by economic sanctions or assistance?

Charts don't win wars. On paper, analyses of the European powers in 1914 would convincingly have predicted that no nation could sustain a conflict longer than a few months. Force comparisons of Germany and the Soviet Union in 1939 would have demonstrated, wrongly, that the latter must lose, not only because Soviet weapons were inferior, but because Stalin's purges had decimated the Soviet senior officer corps. If possession of hardware were enough, both France and the United States should have won in Indochina. Clearly other factors were at play.

If the Soviet Union must cope with unreliable allies, the United States must deal with our own allies' electoral and economic cycles, their differing perceptions of the world and their interests. However superior are America's Pershing II missiles, they will be of limited value if Western Europeans refuse to deploy them.

If the Soviet Union is handicapped by the quality of its military personnel, similarly the United States as a military power is limited by the quality of education and training of its own armed forces. The Army defended itself against charges of declining literacy among recruits several years ago by saying that the recruits were only a reflection of the society that produced them. The Army was right. Americans who cannot read an instruction manual will have trouble repairing sophisticated machinery in the heat of battle. Americans who have no grasp of their own history and political culture, or that of other nations, will not understand what they are defending.

National security entails far more than weapons. The best weapons systems for the job might not be the ones that most profit defense contractors. And any attempt to fit this nation's budget priorities with its actual security needs is welcome.

THE INDIANAPOLIS STAR

Indianapolis, Ind., May 24, 1983

Critics airily say that the United States can cut $15 billion or $20 billion from its defense budget with no ill consequences. They may feel certain. They cannot be certain.

When John F. Kennedy was president the nation spent 9 percent of its gross national product on defense. Today it spends only 6.7 percent of GNP on defense. Meanwhile, the Soviet Union is allocating more and more of its GNP to military spending.

Wishful thinking enters as much into the debate over defense spending as it does into anything. It is pleasant to think that the United States could spend two-thirds or half the amount that the Soviet Union spends on its armed forces — without risking bad consequences.

But is relative military weakness of no consequence? On the eve of World War II, Austria was weak, Czechoslovakia was weak, Poland was weak, the Baltic states of Lithuania, Latvia and Estonia were weak, Belgium was weak, Norway was weak, the Netherlands was weak and France was weak.

All were occupied or conquered by stronger powers.

Hitler thought the Soviet Union was weak. The Nazis attacked the Soviet Union. Hitler was wrong.

Japan's warlords thought that the United States was weak. They attacked Pearl Harbor. They were wrong.

In the real world, not only the weakness of nations makes them prey to aggressors but the perception of weakness makes them prey to aggressors.

The United States, vis-a-vis its only probable adversary, the USSR, is much weaker today than it was 20 years ago. If it continues to weaken, the time will come when confrontations with Soviet power or the power of Soviet proxies anywhere will lead to surrender by the United States. That in turn would spell the end of freedom in this country.

The price of strength is high. But it is worth paying, since it is also the price of freedom.

Part II: U.S. Policy— Global Strategy

National nuclear policies and strategic doctrines are of necessity somewhat divorced from reality, since there has never been a nuclear war. The United States, like the Soviet Union, can adopt a stance only through a kind of second-guessing of the other's probable actions in a hypothetical conflict. If, for instance, one nation believes it possible to "win" a nuclear war, then that nation would presumably be more likely to launch a first strike, or to allow a conflict with "tactical" nuclear weapons to escalate into a strategic exchange between the two nations. To take it a step further, if one nation assumes that the *other* nation believes such an exchange to be winnable, then its leaders might feel impelled to guard against a first strike by deploying nuclear forces in such a way as to make the attack suicidal for the nation that initiated it. The reasoning is akin to a chess game in which no pawns have yet been moved but each opponent has tried to plan his entire game based on an assessment of the other's abilities and probable counter-moves. Part of the strategy is never to reveal too much of your own thinking; hence, the U.S. has never stated whether it would or would not launch its missiles immediately upon receiving radar warnings of a Soviet attack, the so-called "launch-on-warning" option.

A growing willingness on the part of the U.S. to entertain the possibility of a "limited" nuclear war appears to be indicated by new civil defense programs and by Pentagon documents detailing plans for an extended nuclear conflict. The thinking behind this kind of preparation goes beyond the so-called "mutual assured destruction" doctrine of previous years, which assumed that the U.S. could deter a Soviet attack through the threat of massive nuclear reprisal against Soviet industries and cities. Instead, the trend is to believe that the U.S. would not actually retaliate in this way, since it might invite destruction of its own cities; according to this theory, the U.S. must also be able to "prevail" in a protracted exchange of missiles with the Soviet Union. The result is a massive arms buildup calculated to permit destruction not just of Soviet cities and industries but of all the Soviet Union's intercontinental nuclear forces, with the assumption that this enhanced destructive capability will then provide a sufficient threat to act as a deterrent. Whether or not this kind of policy is effective in the long run, the immediate result is that hundreds of billions of dollars are spent for its implementation. There are many newspaper editorialists who feel the U.S. is woefully unequipped to meet the threat of nuclear conflict. Many others feel there is an inherent paradox in accumulating more nuclear weapons when the use of such a large arsenal is conceivable only in the very situation its existence is meant to prevent: a full-scale nuclear war.

Nuclear Warfare Strategy Changed; Soviet Military Sites Targeted

Presidential Directive 59, released by the White House Aug. 5, 1980, detailed a new strategy adopted by the Carter Administration in the event of a nuclear war with the Soviet Union. The new policy gave priority to attacking military targets in the U.S.S.R., lessening a previous emphasis on massive retaliation against Soviet cities and industrial complexes. The directive reflected changes in the thinking of senior Administration officials, who as late as January 1979 held that the United States' massive nuclear arsenal, with its potential to destroy every large and medium-sized city in the Soviet Union, sufficed to deter any threat of nuclear war. The officials, including Defense Secretary Harold Brown and National Security Adviser Zbigniew Brzezinski, maintained that the Soviets no longer believed in the concept of "mutually assured destruction," and were currently developing the "counterforce" capability to fight a prolonged but limited nuclear war. They concluded that the Soviets would be less inclined to launch "pinpoint nuclear attacks" in a first strike if the U.S. could deny them eventual victory by destroying vital Soviet military capability.

The Philadelphia Inquirer

Philadelphia, Pa., August 19, 1980

Enormously serious and complex questions about U.S. nuclear strategy must be thoroughly analyzed in public discussion, and satisfactorily answered, before any steps are taken to implement a new directive issued by President Carter which projects the possibility of a "limited" nuclear war with the Soviet Union.

Defense Secretary Harold Brown acknowledged existence of the directive last week, and discussed its substance, after details already had been widely published. Secretary of State Edmund S. Muskie was understandably angry about not being consulted or informed. Zbigniew Brzezinski, the President's hawkish national security adviser, apparently was a major architect of the directive, which has been under consideration for several years and incorporates concepts that were discussed during the Ford and Nixon administrations.

Thus the idea isn't new but the directive is. In essence, it directs the Defense Department to add an important new option in its nuclear strategy. While Soviet cities and industrial complexes would continue to be major targets of the U.S. nuclear force, more emphasis would be placed on pinpointing military targets. Long-range U.S. missiles would be zeroed in on Soviet military bases, including missile launching sites, and on troop concentrations and underground shelters for military and government leaders.

A great peril of a limited nuclear strategy is that it seeks to make nuclear war more credible and therefore more likely. Critics argue that the strategy would seem to be fatally flawed in its basic assumption that a limited nuclear war could be fought between two superpowers without escalation to all-out mutual destruction.

Heretofore, a U.S.-Soviet nuclear exchange has been thought of in terms of mass annihilation of cities and tens of millions of people. In a matter of hours, if not minutes, both countries would be wastelands of nuclear horror. Most if not all survivors of initial blasts would suffer lingering deaths from radiation. No sane person would ever start such a war; hence the strategy of mutual deterrence. The objective of the nuclear balance of terror is to prevent a nuclear war that nobody could win.

In theory a nuclear war limited to military targets could go on for weeks or months, maybe even years, because there would be no mass destruction of cities and civilian populations. It would be like a conventional war, with nuclear weapons. Improved accuracy of nuclear warhead delivery systems is said to make the targeting of relatively small military installations thousands of miles away technologically feasible.

Proponents of the "limited" war option argue, with some logic, that striking military targets would be less horrible than wiping out cities and populations, and that having the option might possibly avert all-out nuclear war. What, however, would be the chances of preventing what started out as a limited nuclear war from becoming all-out nuclear war? Would adding a "thinkable" option to the nuclear arsenal make nuclear war more thinkable and therefore more likely? Would emphasis on military targets increase the temptation to launch a first strike?

President Carter and his election opponents, Ronald Reagan and John Anderson, need to give their views on these agonizing questions with unrestrained candor. The voters must know where they stand, and the nation must not drift into a change in nuclear strategy without understanding fully the arguments for and against and the possible consequences.

The Oregonian

Portland, Ore., September 6, 1980

President Carter's recent overhaul of U.S. nuclear strategy, while necessary, was a chilling reminder that a so-called "limited nuclear war" today may be a real possibility.

Carter's directive, which called for aiming missiles not only at Soviet cities but also at military targets, was a necessary and foregone conclusion. The Soviets did not share our view that no country can "win" a nuclear war, and it was necessary to play by Moscow's rules.

Firing missiles at Soviet cities was so horrible to contemplate and would risk such devastating attacks on our own cities that an American president, faced with a limited attack on the United States, might capitulate rather than wield a sword of Damocles that would annihilate both countries. The new policy of targeting military installations is a more credible threat, and hence a more effective deterrent.

Unfortunately, the price of making a war less terrible is that it becomes more likely. There is a real possibility that nuclear weapons will be used in combat within the next two decades, but the scenario is different from what most Americans expect.

A nuclear war between the United States and the Soviet Union is a very remote possibility, although it is not inconceivable that a superpower losing a conventional war — particularly in some hotspot of the Third World — would resort to nuclear weapons.

The gravest danger of nuclear confrontation is in the so-called pygmy and pariah nations, where leaders find that a few nuclear missiles may compensate for weakness in conventional arms.

Many countries with historic enmities, such as India and Pakistan, Iraq and Israel, already have shown interest in acquiring nuclear capabilities. Brazil, Argentina, South Korea and South Africa — all countries plagued by feelings of insecurity — are also said to be looking for the bomb.

They may well find it. A junior at Princeton University developed a workable plan for an atomic bomb by studying only public documents. Highly enriched uranium or plutonium is increasingly available because of the proliferation of civil nuclear reactors.

The Carter administration is right to discourage the spread of new reactors that use highly enriched fuels. The world also must pressure France and Germany not to sell nuclear fuels or enrichment technology to the likes of Iraq and Argentina.

Nuclear proliferation is not strictly a national or regional concern. The enduring poison of radiation threatens all people who inhabit the planet. Everyone's interest is in ensuring that nuclear war, even limited nuclear war, is not added to the mistakes of history.

JUST A LITTLE BIT PREGNANT

THE INDIANAPOLIS NEWS
Indianapolis, Ind., August 20, 1980

Most of the criticism of President Carter's recently announced shift in nuclear strategy misses the mark.

The revised nuclear strategy gives priority to attacking military targets and the underground shelters of Soviet political leaders rather than destroying cities and industrial complexes. It has drawn fire, mostly from the political left, for allegedly making nuclear war more thinkable and therefore more probable.

The purpose of the new strategy, however, is to deter the Soviet Union from making a nuclear first strike, and the reasoning behind it is basically sound. What is important to Soviet leaders is not so much their population centers (they may be expendable in the Kremlin's military calculations) as the security of the instruments of their military-political power. The new strategy aims directly at the power of the Soviet state, at what the Kremlin in its reverse order of values cherishes the most.

The real problem with President Carter's strategy shift, so far little discussed, is not its theory but the question of its credibility. The United States does not now have, and may not have for several years, the military capability to give it any effect.

Brig. Gen. Al Knight, U.S. Army-ret., calls the new strategy "the right thing at the wrong time." It is the wrong time, he says, because the "U.S. does not have the operational strategic weapons systems needed to execute such a policy" and will not have them until the late 1980s.

The new doctrine, Gen. Knight notes, cannot be applied to existing weapons programs, but depends upon the MX missile system which will not become operational until close to the end of the decade. Meantime, he says, the doctrine will be operating in a "vacuum." The U.S., he concludes, "faces impending strategic vulnerability now to the mid-1980s." It is a time when the Soviets, as well as concerned allies, will question America's nuclear credibility.

Why was the new doctrine announced at this time, apparently so prematurely? The recently adopted Republican platform calls for a "clear capacity to destroy military targets," and President Carter's prompt endorsement of a similar position blurs the distinction between the two parties on the issue. The President has reduced his political vulnerability even while, ironically, increasing the nation's.

But now that the doctrine has been announced, it may be possible to minimize the dangers of the interim period by speeding up the new weapons programs. Gen. Knight puts it this way: "To have any credibility, the new doctrine must be applied *now*. This will require an acceleration of strategic programs, and the initiation of new ones to fulfill the declaratory objectives of the new doctrine."

In the interests of a credible national defense posture, will President Carter commit himself to that also?

Sentinel Star
Orlando, Fla., August 18, 1980

IT IS really a matter of semantics, but when the words used are "nuclear devastation," and "mutually assured destruction," the semantics take on a special significance.

During the last 10 years the entire American nuclear defense strategy has been under scrutiny by successive presidential administrations. Within the last month, reports have surfaced to the effect that the traditional American theory of nuclear warfare has been radically altered.

No longer is the nuclear might of the United States tied to what had been called the Mutual Assured Destruction (MAD) strategy. This plan called for the targeting of American nuclear warheads against major Soviet population and industrial centers. The theory behind this strategy held that the Soviets would never launch a nuclear at-

tack against the United States knowing that to do so would cause incineration of Moscow, Leningrad and other Soviet cities.

Several factors, such as increased numbers of increasingly accurate warheads, caused successive presidents beginning with Richard Nixon to revise the MAD strategy. And within the last three years, former Secretary of State Henry Kissinger became its most outspoken critic.

The factors involved in prompting the shift in our basic strategy are relatively simple to identify. Primarily they involve increased throw weight and accuracy of Soviet missiles and hardening of Soviet industrial and military sites as well as massive Soviet emphasis on civil defense.

These factors led to American defense planners facing the possibility that their Soviet counterparts could conceive a nuclear war as "winnable" whereas before it had been theoretically unthinkable because of the inherent losses.

Thus, if Soviet leaders believe they could survive with sufficient resources an American nuclear attack, the concept of mutually assured destruction is voided.

That would leave an American president faced with the threat of pre-emptive Soviet attack against our nuclear weapons with one of two options: either surrender or respond to a limited Soviet strike by pulling out all the stops and attacking Soviet cities.

So in place of the MAD theory, the United States is adapting a policy calling for "graduated response."

The reason all this policy reform is so much semantical gymnastics is that no one, least of all the planners involved on both sides of the Iron Curtain, feel that what starts as a limited nuclear war will remain limited very long. And escalation of a limited nuclear war would lead inevitably back to that mutually assured destruction of everything standing.

The irony of the situation is that for the American nuclear arsenal to remain an effective deterrent to Soviet nuclear extortion, the words governing its use must be changed to reflect reality. And that reality is the possibility that an American president, relying on a policy limiting him to either doing nothing or doing everything — with no options in between — might bow to Soviet ultimatums instead of responding in kind.

Thus, rewriting the words outlining presidential options becomes a major aspect of the defense of the Western world.

TULSA WORLD

Tulsa, Okla., August 18, 1980

THE FLAP over President Carter's failure to consult Secretary of State Edmund Muskie on a basic change in U. S. strategic nuclear strategy has obscured the fact that an unreal and unworkable policy has been junked.

That was one based on the doctrine of mutual assured destruction (MAD). It theorized that neither Russia nor the U. S. would start a nuclear war because the resulting holocaust would destroy the major Cities of both countries.

No one, the theory held, could possibly start a war that would almost certainly leave millions of casualties.

Thus the U. S. nuclear force was aimed at Cities rather than industrial and military installations.

The President's new order changes that. U. S. nuclear power will henceforth be focused on military installations.

The basic problem with the MAD doctrine was that the Russians never agreed to it. Their approach was to train nuclear missiles on U. S. military targets. Thus if attacked, the U. S. President would have to decide to incinerate millions of Russian civilians with whatever missiles survived a Russian first strike.

After that, the Russian installations would be largely intact and capable of continuing to rain missiles on the U. S.

That such a doctrine could survive two decades or so is the mystery. It was based on an unrealistic view of the world. It would be nice if the Russians had agreed to the idea, but all the evidence is that they didn't.

The Presidential decision is therefore a good one, despite the anguished cries of those in the State Department who want to continue to argue about arms limitations and treaties at the same time the Soviets construct a system capable of knocking out U. S. missiles in a first strike.

The Providence Journal

Providence, R.I., August 22, 1980

Discussion of U.S. plans for waging nuclear war, normally confined to inner Pentagon offices and a few academic institutes, has a way of bubbling into public view during periods of disquiet. Now the Carter administration has gone public to describe what it calls a "refinement" of U.S. war plans, stressing an ability to conduct limited nuclear attacks against selected enemy military targets. What kind of a change in U.S. strategy (if any) is really under way, and why?

As Defense Secretary Harold Brown outlined it in a speech at the Naval War College on Wednesday, the administration has reviewed its strategic plans (particularly its list of targets in the Soviet Union) with an eye toward giving U.S. leaders more "flexibility" in responding to crises. A U.S. ability to retaliate selectively against key Soviet military targets could help keep a nuclear conflict limited, Dr. Brown said. Soviet awareness of this ability, he added, will dampen any Kremlin temptation to wage a surprise attack.

This was a speech of unusual significance, and several observations are in order. The first, a fact that Secretary Brown freely acknowledged, is that the Carter administration has hardly undertaken a "new" nuclear targeting strategy. Since the dawn of the superpowers' nuclear rivalry, U.S. military planners have been continually evaluating a broad mixture of targets, military and civilian. Of the 25,000 or so possible Soviet targets already mapped, large cities account for only a few hundred. Thus, President Carter's celebrated and still-secret "Presidential Directive 59," setting forth the doctrine, appears to be more of an updating and a revision of strategy than any drastic departure.

The growing U.S. emphasis on selected military targets (as distinct from an all-out bashing of major cities) springs from at least two sources: the technological, as smaller warheads and more accurate guidance systems have permitted more precise targeting; and the need to counter a growing Soviet ability to threaten U.S. missiles. By drumming home the idea that the Soviets could not prevail in a nuclear exchange, the administration figures, as Dr. Brown said, "to strength our deterrent and thus increase stability."

In choosing to publicize plans normally kept under wraps, the Carter administration appears to have several aims: to give another post-Afghanistan warning to Moscow not to stir up further trouble; and to reassure our allies that the United States remains militarily able to counter any type of serious threat. It would be surprising, too, if domestic political considerations had not played a part in the administration's decision to talk strategy publicly.

Overall, though, its central goal is sound. Confronting a huge Soviet military buildup, the United States has no choice but to strengthen its own deterrent forces, modernize its command and control systems and develop flexible nuclear strategies to cope with whatever sort of unspeakable showdown might someday confront us. To this extent, the administration is keeping on the right track.

It is not pleasant to contemplate these issues, but neither is it possible for the public to hope that by ignoring them they will go away. Ronald Reagan's challenge to President Carter on this country's nuclear capability and readiness to defend itself has at least helped to force the public to face and think through that which it would rather not think about, and that is all to the good.

THE SACRAMENTO BEE

Sacramento, Calif., August 18, 1980

Although the details haven't yet been supplied, the Carter administration has acknowledged the adoption of a new nuclear war strategy that would target Soviet missiles, military installations and political leadership as well as Russian cities and industry. Given the emergence of long-range Russian missiles that can wipe out America's land-based Minuteman force, the new U.S. strategy may be an inevitable consequence. Until more is known, however, no sure judgment is possible.

It's unfortunate that this fundamental change in nuclear policy has come out in fragmentary fashion, making it open to conjecture that it was leaked by administration officials in response to the Republican platform calling for nuclear superiority instead of parity with the Russians. It's even more unfortunate that the administration failed to involve Secretary of State Muskie in the deliberations preceding the plan's adoption, thereby reinforcing the impression that critical elements of American defense and foreign policy aren't properly coordinated at top levels. Indeed, the question has arisen in some quarters as to whether hard-liners in the Pentagon and the National Security Council have stolen a march on the new secretary of state, who was promised a full voice in matters bearing upon foreign affairs.

The strategic change is not exactly new. The idea that the United States should be able to match the Soviets' first-strike capability is implicit in the development of the MX missile, whose prime targets would be Russian missiles and other military installations. It also is implicit in such proposed weapons as a new manned bomber, the large Trident II submarine-launched missile and the ever more accurate family of cruise missiles.

The new strategy conceives for the first time of the possibility of "limited," and perhaps prolonged, nuclear warfare with the Soviets, something that may also, by making such warfare "thinkable," increase its likelihood. Until now, American strategy has rested upon the belief that both sides would be deterred from atomic warfare because its inevitable consequence would be the mutual assured destruction ("MAD") of each others' cities and populations. The new strategy envisions something less than that; but it entails the obvious risk that what might start as limited nuclear warfare would escalate rapidly to wholesale incineration.

Given the awesome implications of the revised nuclear policy, both for America and all other nations, the administration will have to provide the fullest explanation of the thinking behind it and the justification of the potential risks it will entail, particularly with respect to the future of nuclear arms control. The Muskie episode should impel the White House to reorder the way it goes about such key policy-making to assure that such deliberations will fully involve the State Department and the Arms Control and Disarmament Agency, which were largely excluded from this decision.

The implementation of the strategy presumably will require congressional approval of the new arms it contemplates. We trust that in the course of that process all of the possible consequences of this new decision will be fully explored, and that the American people will have the advantage of a national debate on a matter so important to their survival.

ST. LOUIS POST-DISPATCH
St. Louis, Mo., August 11, 1980

Under the cover of the hullabaloo of the Democratic convention, the Carter administration has quietly and without public debate adopted a radical new nuclear strategy certain to be perceived in Moscow as threatening and provocative — as it is — and certain to require the diversion of untold billions of American tax dollars from useful social investment. According to *The New York Times*, Mr. Carter has signed a presidential directive that gives priority to attacking military targets in the U.S.S.R., rather than cities, and incredibly envisages the possibility of fighting a prolonged nuclear war, as if there were any such thing.

In effect, it is a first-strike strategy in disguise. *The Times* says that prime targets are to be Soviet military forces, for which read Soviet land-based missiles, which may sound somewhat innocuous at first hearing. Isn't it morally more acceptable to attack the uniformed enemy rather than innocent civilians? Perhaps so. But won't that drive the Russians into adopting a similar

posture? And if both sides subsequently achieve a first strike capability against each other's forces, won't that enormously increase the pressure on each side to strike first in any emergency in order to eliminate or reduce the size of the opponent's retaliatory strike? That's what critics of first-strike say of this Strangelovian business, and it is hard to disagree.

Critics contend also that the new strategy will require much larger and more advanced weapons systems than now exist. The new $30-to-$100 billion MX mobile missile would be only a down payment (which may be reason enough to forgo the MX). Additional billions will have to be spent on submarine-launched missiles to support the first-strike threat. And costly new reconnaissance and communications equipment will be required to assure necessary precision. But if the net result of this vast expenditure of treasure is to create a world even more dangerous and unstable than it is now, as seems likely, then what is the benefit of the new strategy?

SAN JOSE NEWS
San Jose, Cal., August 7, 1980

QUIETLY, and without the public debate the subject deserves, the Carter administration has made a fundamental change in this nation's nuclear weapons strategy.

The revised policy gives priority to striking military targets and political command centers, rather than targeting entire cities and industrial concentrations. The logic behind this, according to one administration official quoted anonymously, is to have "more choices than Armageddon or surrender."

According to early reports, first published in this and other newspapers Wednesday, the possibility of fighting a prolonged nuclear war, lasting weeks and perhaps even months, is envisaged in the revised strategy.

That is absolutely chilling.

There's no way we or other journalists, working with the scant and fragmentary amount of information which has been made public, can draw definitive conclusions on the key question: Will this new policy make nuclear war more likely?

But it certainly sounds as if it could.

When the Mercury News laid out our basic positions on national and international issues last May, we stated our basic approach to this subject. We repeat it now:

The United States should maintain a credible nuclear deterrent — without losing sight of the fact that our very existence depends on nuclear weapons literally serving to deter war, not to wage it.

Approval of new weapons systems should always be within that context.

It sounds as though Washington is now talking about using nuclear weapons to wage war. And the supposition that this would be a "limited" war is hardly comforting.

New weapons systems certainly are involved. Both the MX and the cruise

missile systems are central to the revised policy.

It should be pointed out that the policy really isn't all that new; the notion that we could fight and win a limited nuclear war with the Soviet Union has been around since the 1960s. But from then until now, it failed to prevail over the alternative approach attributed to former Defense Secretary Robert S. McNamara, who contended that Washington and Moscow could deter a nuclear war by amassing arsenals capable of destroying each other's cities.

The McNamara view first came under attack during the Nixon administration. As early as 1973, former Defense Secretary James Schlesinger was calling for a national debate on his contention that the United States should be able to deliver "selective" nuclear strikes against the Soviet Union.

The Carter administration has approached the question without national debate, and indeed with scarcely any publicity at all. Only now do we learn that, a few weeks ago, the president signed a directive drastically changing this nation's approach to the single most crucial issue any president faces.

Was the decision — or its timing — a political response to the election platform approved last month in Detroit, where the Republican party went on record favoring a "clear capacity to destroy military targets"? There's no proof of that, but one can't help but ask the question.

Certainly the Democrats, like the more hawkish Republicans, are going to insist that no one wants a war, and that the whole point of the new strategy is to possess a stronger deterrent against war

But election year rhetoric aside, is all this in fact making a nuclear war more likely? We don't know. But to have to consider the possibility at all is profoundly troubling.

The Times-Picayune
THE STATES-ITEM
New Orleans, La., August 10, 1980

Lost in the maelstrom of presidential politics was President Carter's recent decision to alter the nation's basic nuclear weapons strategy. The new policy is aimed at giving the United States the capacity to make pinpoint nuclear strikes against military targets in the Soviet Union.

This new approach is based on the growing idea, once unthinkable, that a limited nuclear war between the United States and the Soviet Union is possible. Evidence suggests that the Soviets are already moving in that direction, and the United States must be able to respond in kind.

Since the dawn of the nuclear age, U.S. strategy has been based on the concept of massive retaliation against Soviet cities and industrial targets. The strategy was solidified under former Defense Secretary Robert S. McNamara in the 1960s under the tag "Mutual Assured Destruction," or MAD.

When he became president in 1977, Jimmy Carter appeared to embrace the McNamara concept. Three factors are cited for his decision to go with the new strategy, known as Presidential Directive 59: (1) Recent developments suggest to U.S. defense officials that the Soviets might no longer subscribe to the concept of mutual deterrence and are moving toward a "limited" nuclear war capability; (2) advances in U.S. weapons technology, such as the Air Force's MX mobile rocket and air-launched cruise missiles, provide the necessary pinpoint strike capability; and (3) political pressures in the wake of Mr. Carter's decisions to cancel production of the B-1 bomber and the neutron bomb left him vulnerable to charges from Ronald Reagan that he is "soft" on defense. The recently adopted Republican Party platform calls for a limited strike capability.

The question remains, of course, whether the United States and the Soviet Union could keep a nuclear exchange limited. Some have argued that just the potential for a limited exchange increases the possibility of a nuclear war between the superpowers. Yet the advance in nuclear weapons technology and the Soviet push in that direction seem to have made a change in U.S. nuclear strategy inevitable. The shift to a limited capability does not, of course, cancel the potential for massive retaliation and the deterrent value it holds.

Los Angeles Times

Los Angeles, Cal., August 15, 1980

The Carter Administration's "new" nuclear strategy, deliberately leaked by the Administration last week, is not really all that new. The puzzling question is why the Administration chose this particular time to trumpet an evolutionary step in what has been U.S. policy since at least 1974—and to do it in a way that invited confusion and misunderstanding both at home and abroad.

Presidential Directive 59, as the revised strategic policy is formally known, was approved by President Carter in late July, and was to have been disclosed by Defense Secretary Brown in a speech later this month. For reasons that remain obscure, its essentials were leaked last week—reportedly by national-security adviser Zbigniew Brzezinski.

PD 59 provides that in the event of a less-than-all-out Soviet nuclear attack—one that hit U.S. missile silos, for example, but spared American cities—the U.S. response will emphasize counterblows against military targets rather than destruction of Soviet cities and industrial complexes.

Actually, according to knowledgeable sources, there has never been a time when substantial numbers of this country's nuclear warheads were not targeted on Soviet military complexes. Judging by Russian military literature, the same is true of Soviet targeting.

What has changed over the years is the strategic balance, and the perception among defense experts as to what kind of attack most likely would occur.

In the early postwar years, when the United States enjoyed an overwhelming superiority in nuclear striking power, the priority of military targets in event of war was taken for granted. It wasn't thought necessary to base the American deterrent on the threat of killing millions of Russian civilians.

But in the 1960s, as the Russians began to narrow the American lead, a new policy was announced by Defense Secretary McNamara—the so-called doctrine of "mutual assured destruction," or MAD, as it is called by its critics.

Under this theory, the Soviets were put on notice that any nuclear attack—whether on U.S. population centers or military targets—would trigger a massive American nuclear counterattack on Russian cities.

The doctrine assumed that the Soviets would respond in the same way to an American first strike. With each side holding the other's civilian population as hostage, neither could attack without risking the annihilation of its civilization. Or so it was thought.

As Soviet nuclear striking power continued to grow, however, U.S. military and political leaders had to face some uncomfortable questions.

Was any President of the United States really prepared to commit national suicide in response to a limited Soviet attack on Western Europe or on American missile silos—an attack that initially, at least, spared U.S. cities? Could we really expect either friend or foe to believe that we would?

As long ago as 1969, Henry A. Kissinger concluded that the answer was no. He urged President Nixon to make the U.S. deterrent more credible by disavowing the fiction that his only choices, in event of a real or threatened Soviet attack, were surrender or national suicide.

The ultimate result was a so-called counterforce doctrine, enunciated by Defense Secretary Schlesinger, which suggested that the appropriate response to a Soviet attack on U.S. missile silos, for example, would be a counterblow against Soviet missiles or military-related industry.

The destruction of Soviet population centers would still be the ultimate deterrent, but would not necessarily be the American response of first resort.

The plain purpose of the shift in targeting emphasis, restated in one form or another by all of Schlesinger's successors at the Pentagon, was to make war less likely by making the American deterrent more credible to the Kremlin.

However, critics have contended that the policy, by downgrading the threat of instant Armageddon, might make nuclear war more thinkable and therefore more likely. (Many of the same critics are seemingly unconcerned by evidence that the Soviets are dedicated to a counterforce strategy of their own, and have been all along.)

President Carter seemed to share the skeptics' view of the flexible-response strategy early in his term. But he nonetheless has approved new weapons—the MX mobile missile and the air-launched cruise missile—that are necessary to maintain flexible response as a viable doctrine.

Aside from the pointed inclusion of the Soviet political leadership as priority targets and the speedier installation of survivable command and control systems, it is hard to see what will be done now that wasn't going to be done anyway.

If that is the case, why did the Administration feel compelled to dramatize what seems in fact to be a modest, evolutionary shift in policy—and, in the process, to give Moscow an opportunity to huff and puff and make this country's European allies more nervous than they already are?

Maybe Carter wanted to remove the ambiguity as to his own perception of national strategy. Maybe he wanted to whet the Soviet appetite for resumption of arms-control negotiations as soon as the November elections are over. Maybe the Pentagon thought PD 59 would help fend off critics of the MX missile program.

However, Brzezinski's reported role in leaking the revised policy—and Secretary of State Muskie's professed pique at not being fully consulted—suggests that bureaucratic infighting might have been a factor.

Inevitably, the suspicion also arises that Carter, now facing an election challenge by a hawkish-sounding Ronald Reagan, felt the need to embellish his own credentials as a strong-defense man.

That suspicion may or may not be fair, but the Administration itself created the problem by the timing of PD 59 and the maladroit manner in which it was made public. □

DAYTON DAILY NEW

Dayton, Ohio, August 9, 1980

You have to begin with the premise that any strategy for nuclear war is madness.

The more aggravating problem is that *any* theory to avoid nuclear war, through deterrence by force or through unilateral disarmament, also can be seen by some as mad.

In that light, the Carter Administration's new strategy for avoiding or fighting nuclear war (the strategies for both are the same, you know) is as logical as the strategy it would replace. The debates over it will not end in the forseeable future.

The U.S nuclear strategy has been to keep enough power to wipe out the Soviet population if the Russians should strike us first. That would seem fearful enough.

But some America's military analysts fear that the Soviets don't buy that mutual deterrence argument. Indeed, there is some evidence they think it is possible to fight a nuclear war and win it, as opposed to Americans who think the whole shooting match would be so devastating that nobody would dare start it.

So the Carter Administration proposes to sharpen its forces to hit specific Soviet military targets with such accuracy and force that the Soviet leadership woould be blown clean out of its bomb shelters right away.

The theory is that this and related capabilities would allow the United States to fight a limited nuclear war over a long period. In other words, Americans want the same capability Russians are developing. Logical enough.

So the intent is to avoid an all-out nuclear war yet deter aggression. The catch — all these theories have and will always have catches — is that the Russians might feel this could give the United States a first strike capability, so might be *more* willing to pull the trigger first when tensions get high. So does force deter violence or incite new dimensions of it? Does preparation for a "limited" war reduce the scale of destruction or make the first volley more likely? There are no answers; there are only opinions among parties faced with massive life-and-death questions.

Either side is likely to gain something of a first-strike ability simply because the arms race has led to such sophisticated killing machines. The new strategic plan will require even more of the powerful, accurate weapons and surveillance systems.

What ought to be clear, if those in America and Russia could recognize it together, is that there is no security in any of this. The next step ought to be ratification of the SALT II treaty — even though this would not change U.S. strategy or forbid it the weapons systems our war planners want.

Nuclear strength, at best, only buys time for humankind to come to the overriding realization of its oneness rather than its delusion of separateness. In the long run, no lesser theory will save us.

Rocky Mountain News

Denver, Colo., August 14, 1980

THE failure to inform Secretary of State Edmund Muskie of its switch in nuclear arms strategy is another example of the administration's confused approach to foreign policy.

In general, the new U.S. policy gives priority to attacking military and political targets in the Soviet Union rather than targeting nuclear warheads on cities and industrial complexes. It is designed to give the United States a nuclear response short of all-out nuclear war.

Whether that policy is any better than the old one for avoiding a world nuclear holocaust is debatable. But that is not the issue involved in the dustup between Muskie and the Pentagon and the White House.

Muskie learned of the new policy by reading it in the newspapers last week. He made his displeasure known to reporters accompanying him on a trip the other day.

The White House seems to be trying to gloss over leaving Muskie out by saying that nuclear arms strategy is more a matter for the Defense Department than for the State Department.

That is poppycock. Our nuclear stance is a basic element of foreign policy. To leave the secretary of state out of discussions of a major change in nuclear policy is simply incredible.

Secretary of Defense Harold Brown said further that officials of the State Department were in on discussions before Muskie was appointed. That excuse doesn't wash either; Muskie has been in office three months, certainly long enough for someone to have told him that a major nuclear arms policy change was in the works.

There are indications, too, that the policy change came as a surprise to U.S. allies. To allay concern in allied capitals, Secretary Brown sent messages to defense ministers of the North Atlantic Treaty Organization reassuring them that the United States has "no desire" to fight a nuclear war.

The episode is hardly one to inspire confidence in the administration either here or abroad.

The Houston Post

Houston, Texas, August 15, 1980

President Carter's approval of a shift in U.S. nuclear arms strategy is a logical extension of improvements in the superpowers' strategic weaponry. The modification, which will make the Soviet Union's military-industrial complex and top officialdom potential targets of our missile arsenal, is not, in a sense, really new. Selective targeting has long been an option in our nuclear battle plans. But only with the development of the MX and cruise missiles, highly accurate warheads and sophisticated communications and reconnaissance equipment has the policy become practical.

The Soviet Union does not accept the doctrine of mutual assured destruction of U.S. and Russian population centers that we adopted in the 1960s as a deterrent to nuclear war. But, like us, they have lacked the ability to deliver their nuclear warheads with the precision that selective targeting requires. In the meantime, our intelligence agencies report, the Soviets have developed an extensive civil defense program, with emphasis on protecting the government leadership and key military and industrial installations, while trying to ensure the survival of as much of the population as possible.

The civil defense buildup has been accompanied by a concerted effort to improve the accuracy of Soviet nuclear weapons. U.S. defense officials now say the Russians have made such rapid progress toward this goal that our land-based intercontinental ballistic missiles will be vulnerable to a first strike by Soviet ICBMs by the mid-1980s.

The new strategy, approved by the president in a directive last week, has been under discussion for the past six years. This "countervailing strategy" was first broached publicly by James Schlesinger when he was secretary of defense in the Nixon administration. Critics accused its proponents of "thinking the unthinkable" — a limited nuclear war. The same complaints are already being voiced about the president's recent decision, which is certain to provoke a new debate on nuclear policy. Yet those who oppose the latest modification in that policy seem to ignore abundant evidence that the Soviet leadership believes a nuclear war is winnable.

This does not necessarily mean that Brezhnev and company would risk a nuclear exchange on a whim. But if certain conditions prevailed, they might think the unthinkable, particularly if they believed we had only one arrow in our strategic bow and might be reluctant to use it. We need the new alternate strategy, just as we still need the "balance-of-terror" doctrine, to let the Kremlin leaders know that we are prepared to meet them at any level of nuclear conflict they might contemplate.

AKRON BEACON JOURNAL

Akron, Ohio, August 13, 1980

UP TO NOW, no one has worried much about what would happen after a nuclear war between the United States and the Soviet Union.

We've been conditioned to think of such an event as the beginning of the end. We've been told there aren't likely to be any survivors. And the devastation would very likely be so complete that anyone who did survive would probably wish he hadn't.

However, there's a different message in recent reports coming out of Washington, a message that might encourage some Americans to resume work on their bomb shelters.

The Carter administration, it is said, has a new strategy for fighting a nuclear war with the Soviets. Rather than firing missiles at Soviet cities and industrial complexes, and killing millions of people, the administration reportedly now prefers to aim our nuclear weapons at military targets, including troop concentrations and missile bases.

This would give the United States the capability of fighting a prolonged but limited nuclear war, presumably one in which the end of civilization would not be inevitable.

The policy reportedly was approved by the President earlier this month after nearly four years of debate. It has not yet been officially confirmed by the White House.

Nevertheless, the reports contain some disturbing implications.

For one thing, there is the obvious conflict between the new strategy and the principles involved in the stalled SALT II agreement.

To execute the strategy could pull the United States into a new arms race and greatly endanger the chances of winning an acceptable agreement with the Soviets to limit spending on nuclear weapons.

Another problem is that the new strategy invites an acceptance of the idea of waging a nuclear war. It does so by suggesting that a nuclear war can be limited and that it doesn't have to end in the destruction of mankind — or at least whole nations.

But who would want to bet his shirt on that possibility, let alone the future of the planet? Is it really reasonable to believe that the course of a nuclear war can be controlled once the first missiles are launched? The answer should be obvious.

Defense Secretary Harold Brown has described the new strategy as a means of deterring Soviet action that could lead to a nuclear war. It is not, he added, an indication that the United States wants to fight a nuclear war. Let's hope so.

Beyond philosophical concerns, though, there are two that are much more practical. One is the apparent decision by the Carter administration to embrace the new strategy without first trying to secure the approval of the State Department and Secretary of State Edmund Muskie.

The other is apparent failure to notify American allies of the new strategy before reports leaked to the press. That's not unlike the manner in which the allies learned of the President's plans for arming Western Europe with neutron bombs.

Secretary Muskie told reporters he was unaware of the new nuclear game plan until he read about it in news reports. Administration officials acknowledged that talks which gave birth to the final strategy did not include either the State Department or the Arms Control and Disarmament Agency, although they said senior State Department officials had taken part in earlier discussions. Secretary Muskie was finally briefed Tuesday.

Why President Carter would reach a decision of such magnitude and importance without involving Secretary Muskie is puzzling, very puzzling. It suggests that, whether for political or practical reasons, the President is relying more heavily on advice from the Defense Department and the National Security Council than his State Department as he continues his quest for a second term.

A clear, detailed explanation of the new strategy and its objectives ought to be forthcoming from the Carter administration.

There remains far more hope for mankind in mutual efforts with the Soviets to limit nuclear weapons than in spending billions and billions more to prepare for a prolonged but limited nuclear war.

Reagan Administration Decides To Assemble Neutron Warheads

Defense Secretary Caspar Weinberger announced Aug. 10, 1981 that the Reagan Administration had decided to assemble neutron warheads, reversing the Carter Administration policy of producing individual components of neutron weapons but not assembling them. The announcement revived the controversy over the neutron bomb, which produced a far smaller blast but more intense radiation than conventional atomic weapons. It could thus be used against enemy tanks without causing massive damage to the surrounding population centers. It was intended to defend Western Europe against Soviet tanks, which outnumbered North Atlantic Treaty Organization tanks by about four to one. Weinberger said the assembled neutron warheads would be kept in the United States and would not be deployed in Western Europe except in case of war, and then only with NATO approval. Weinberger said in defense of the decision that Western European opposition to the deployment of neutron warheads was "largely a tribute to the effectiveness of the Soviet propaganda campaign against this weapon." He also referred to the Reagan Administration's eagerness to alter the "record of vacillation" established by Carter's handling of the problem. Although he did not mention the Persian Gulf area, other officials indicated that the weapons were considered to be potentially effective in the event of a Soviet attack in that region. Reagan had the authority to order production of the neutron bombs as a result of the congressional authorization for the Department of Energy for fiscal 1981, which included funds for the production and stockpiling of neutron weapons.

THE PLAIN DEALER
Cleveland, Ohio, August 13, 1981

We think President Reagan was right to make his momentous decision on the neutron bomb. It does not deploy the bomb, it merely puts it in the armory. If the Soviets are so aroused by it, it may turn out to be a powerful bargaining chip.

As for the Europeans, one should not make light of their great apprehension of just what the Soviets are capable of. On the other hand, the grim reality in Europe today is not the neutron bomb, which is not there, but the great armed might of the Soviet Union, which is. There are signs that the Soviets are chipping away at the will of the West to resist. In such a climate, the neutron bomb may be a means of rebuilding Europe's backbone. Or it may turn it into jelly.

Everyone remembers former President Jimmy Carter's coaxing of West German Chancellor Helmut Schmidt to help sell the neutron bomb to the NATO allies, followed by Carter's pulling the rug from under Schmidt by deciding not to develop the weapon. The Pentagon's vision is that these weapons will be used to counter the Soviet Union's massive superiority in tanks and other armored weapons, especially in Europe.

It is also not surprising that the reaction in Western Europe should range from cool to hostile, given the widespread fear and respect of the Soviets, the suspicion of America's sincerity in its role as defender of Europe, the memory of Carter's perfidy, and the rebirth of the anti-nuclear movement.

What is more significant is that in France, which recently elected a socialist government, there was acknowledgement of the reality that the Soviets have amassed awesome forces and weaponry on NATO's eastern flank and that Soviet actions and doubletalk on disarmament had made the American decision inevitable — or at least understandable.

To be sure, there are legitimate questions about the timing of President Reagan's announcement. Congress is on vacation. A new round of disarmament talks with the Soviets is due in the fall. Down the road, a point that is reported to have worried Secretary of State Alexander M. Haig Jr., the Western allies have to be persuaded to accept medium-range missiles there in 1983. Revival of the neutron bomb controversy might jeopardize this move, Haig argued.

There is genuine fear, of course, that the neutron bomb will prove too attractive, if that is the word. Because it can achieve its primary goal of checking armored attack with minimum damage to surrounding property, it might be brought into use quite soon in any engagement, critics say, inviting the other side to use even more terrible nuclear weapons.

Yet its advocates see the neutron bomb as perhaps the most rational weapon of its type and can make a convincing case for getting it ready, especially when the likely adversary has the means to steamroller over Western Europe or into the Persian Gulf.

The Morning News
Wilmington, Del., August 13, 1981

Twenty years ago today the East Germans started to put up the Berlin Wall. That violated the four-power agreement concerning free access to West Berlin. But the United States, France and Great Britain stood by motionless while their former ally, the Soviet Union, aided and abetted the East Germans in their wall building.

What would have happened in 1961 if the Western allies had stepped in and torn down the wall? Would there have been war and, if so, what kind of war — nuclear or conventional? Would the East Germans and Russians have halted the wall construction only to wait for another opportunity to break the pact? Or would decisive Western action in 1961 have brought about an era of coexistence stretching to today?

We shall never know. There is no "redoing" of history. There is only speculation. The same kind of what-if questions can be asked about Western reaction to Russian intervention in Czechoslovakia just 13 years ago this month. We can speculate about other Russian-American confrontations and wonder whether we would be better off, safer and in less need of rearming had any one of the confrontations been handled differently.

What then about the Reagan administration's policies of stern threats (as in the case of El Salvador and alleged Cuban-Russian involvement there) and the rush to strengthen the American military, including the just-announced production of the neutron weapon? Are these actions that will keep us safe or propel us into war?

The arguments put forth by Secretary of Defense Caspar Weinberger in support of neutron weapon production explain well the new administration's approach to threatening international situations. The ready availability of the neutron weapon, the secretary has been saying, will act as a deterrent against a Soviet invasion of Western Europe and protect against unfriendly takeovers in the Persian Gulf.

The neutron weapon, we are told, while extremely effective on the battlefield in destroying tanks and those in them, does not cause the kind of widespread destruction and contamination we have all come to fear from nuclear warfare. This is not to say that the neutron weapon is gentle or harmless, only that it is less likely to hurt civilian populations or result in long-lasting contamination.

This month is not only the anniversary of the Berlin Wall and the ending of the Czechoslovakian spring but also of the atomic bombing of Hiroshima and Nagasaki. Accounts of the death, destruction and frightful illnesses inflicted on hundreds of thousands of innocent civilians with those two attacks *could* make the design of the neutron weapon appear benign, if there were ever anything benign about warfare.

Will production of the neutron weapon be a deterrent to attack? Might it provoke attack? Those questions can be asked about any aspect of the arms buildup but the unhappy truth is that only unfolding events will provide the answer.

Edmonton Journal

Edmonton, Alta., August 11, 1981

President Ronald Reagan, by approving the production of the neutron bomb, has chosen the arms race over arms limitation.

The neutron bomb (actually an eight-inch artillery shell or a Lance missile warhead) carries an explosive force of 1,000 tons of dynamite (one kiloton). By comparison, the bombs that destroyed Hiroshima and Nagasaki were rated at 20 kilotons and the largest bombs now are rated above 50 million tons (50 megatons).

But the neutron bomb emits very high levels of neutrons and gamma rays. It kills soldiers, mostly by radiation, while minimizing destruction to adjacent property and population. (Critics say its radiation damage, beyond the target area, has been underestimated.)

The most likely area of use is West Germany where the neutron bomb could be used against Soviet tanks and armored personnel carriers.

There is abundant cause for worry over the massing of Soviet armored divisions close behind the Iron Curtain. The armored vehicles are offensive weapons and threaten the security of adjacent Western nations.

But security — European and global — would be better served by a reduction rather than an escalation of the arms race. SALT II, while not directly limiting Soviet tank forces, would have achieved bilateral reductions in the strategic armaments which threaten the entire world. That agreement was signed by then-President Carter. But Ronald Reagan campaigned against it and SALT II was never ratified by the American Senate.

The American abandonment of SALT II was defended on the grounds that the deal was stacked too heavily in favor of the Soviets. The other view was that America simply was not interested in stopping the arms race; that Uncle Sam would rather fight than switch from a big stick to the pursuit of peace.

President Reagan, by proceeding with the neutron bomb that Carter had stalled, confirms that America, far from being part of the solution to international tensions, will continue as part of the problem.

Even within the "logic" of the arms race, tactical nuclear weapons, including the neutron bomb, may be a mistake. While such weaponry fills a gap for the military, that gap — between limited conventional weapons and unlimited nuclear weapons — was seen to give some hope that nuclear war could be avoided. Because either side could annihilate the other several times over (the argument ran), neither side would be so insane as to drop "the bomb".

But with the gap blurred between conventional and nuclear weapons, one can more realistically project a gradual escalation from use of conventional weapons, to tactical nuclear weaponry, to full-scale nuclear weapons — and to mutual annihilation.

Critics of the neutron bomb also argue that conventional defences against tanks could be equally effective, for the neutron bomb, while irradiating most tank troops, might not immediately immobilize them; they could fight on for several days before dying.

The "logic" of Mutual Assured Destruction (MAD) now is falling to the "logic" of surgical kill. To the military mind, it looks better on the battlefield. To the peaceful mind, it only rationalizes an arms race that must be halted.

Richmond Times-Dispatch

Richmond, Va., August 13, 1981

President Reagan's decision to authorize production of the neutron bomb corrects a serious mistake that the Carter administration made. This weapon belongs in the United States' arsenal, and the vacillating Jimmy Carter erred when he reversed himself and canceled plans to develop it.

Opponents of the bomb, some of whom surely have been influenced by Soviet propaganda, are attempting to persuade the world that it is a horrifying new breed of weaponry, more terrible than the nuclear bomb. This is not so. A nuclear device itself, the neutron bomb is in fact less destructive than the nuclear bomb; and its development might actually reduce the chances of a nuclear holocaust.

This weapon emits radiation as deadly as that which comes from nuclear bombs already in existence, but it produces far less heat and explosive force. It would therefore cause far less physical damage. This would enhance its value as a tactical weapon for use in such densely settled areas as Europe, and experts consider it an especially effective defense against a Russian tank assault on our NATO allies.

Critics of the bomb argue that the fact that it would be less destructive than ordinary nuclear weapons increases the likelihood that it would be used and, therefore, increases the chances of a nuclear conflict between Western democracies and the Soviet Union. Russia intensifies these fears by denouncing the neutron bomb as an immoral weapon and its development as a dangerously provocative act that would trigger a new arms race. To placate the Russians, some timorous Europeans and Americans would delay development of the bomb indefinitely.

But this is an unrealistic, and potentially suicidal, view. It is no secret that the Soviet Union already is engaged in a massive program to increase its military power. It is no secret, either, that the most effective deterrent to a Soviet assault against Western Europe is the fear of American intervention in behalf of its allies. If it had to deal with the European countries' defense forces only, the Soviet Union probably could waltz its way to the English channel — and even to England. To fail to strengthen Western Europe's defense system while the Soviet Union is growing stronger would be to increase the possibility of Soviet aggression. By enhancing American military strength, development of the neutron bomb would increase the deterrent effect of the United States' military commitment to Europe. Thus, as Defense Secretary Caspar W. Weinberger has said, President Reagan's decision to produce the weapon should decrease, rather than increase, the possibilities of a conflict — nuclear or otherwise — between the United States and the Soviet Union.

It is important to stress that the weapons would be stockpiled on American territory. They would not, at the moment, be deployed in any Western European country. But they could be sent there or even to the Mideast quickly if the need for them arose.

Some critics of the president's decision say that it was poorly timed, that it will inflame neutralist passions in Europe and undermine American efforts to promote the deployment of medium-range missiles in NATO countries two years from now. So far, however, Europe's reaction to the president's move has been less volatile than these critics had predicted. But the reaction of our European allies should not be a decisive factor anyway. In the final analysis, the United States must prepare prudently for its own defense no matter how unconcerned its allies might prove to be about the Russian threat. Adding the neutron bomb to American defense structure will be a prudent act.

OKLAHOMA CITY TIMES

Oklahoma City, Okla., August 11, 1981

HIGHLY emotional reaction to President Reagan's decision to proceed with production of the neutron warhead was to be expected, but it shouldn't be allowed to hide the facts that support the action.

Critics in this country and abroad seek to associate fear of the "enhanced radiation weapon," as it is known in technical jargon, with the general hysteria over nuclear warfare. It was just such reaction that prompted former President Jimmy Carter to shelve production of the neutron bomb in 1978.

Under Reagan's order, the Lance missile and eight-inch artillery shells will be furnished with the nuclear material tritium to make complete enhanced-radiation weapons. They are to be stockpiled only in the United States and would be deployed in Europe only after full consultation with U.S. allies.

The weapons are designed to produce far more radiation and far less blast and heat than other tactical nuclear weapons. Of course, describing them, simplistically, as weapons that "kill people without severe damage to the surroundings" invites their condemnation as inhumane and barbaric.

But, in truth, the neutron bomb is designed for tactical use on the battlefield, where the target would be enemy soldiers. Few sane people want war but, if it comes, soldiers are going to be killed, and it probably makes little difference to them if death comes by radiation or by machine gun bullets.

Western European leaders are understandably reluctant to welcome Reagan's decision, recalling how Carter pulled the rug out from under West German Chancellor Wilmut Schmidt, who had stuck out his neck in 1978 in agreeing to have the neutron weapon placed in his country. Yet they should realize that neutron weapons would spare European cities the kind of destruction inflicted on them in the past two world wars.

In ordering production of neutron weapons, Reagan is further redeeming his campaign pledge to rebuild U.S. defenses and restore the nation's military credibility.

FORT WORTH STAR-TELEGRAM

Fort Worth, Texas, August 13, 1981

The Soviet propaganda machine has surpassed itself in reacting to reports of President Reagan's decision to proceed with the manufacturing and assembling of neutron weapons.

Russian propandists have called it "cannibalistic."

The earlier characterization of the neutron bomb as a "capitalist" weapon is perhaps understandable, if viewed from a Marxist-Leninist perspective. The neutron bomb often is characterized simplistically as a weapon that kills people and spares buildings.

But cannibalistic? We can only suppose that what is meant is that people who would employ such a weapon would be capable of eating other people.

What makes the neutron bomb decision cannibalistic to the Soviets is the fact that they do not yet have it. What they do have is a superabundance of tanks that would be very vulnerable to neutron weaponry. But it is a safe bet that the Russians have been working on the neutron bomb themselves.

It is a gross distortion to describe the neutron bomb as more of a people killer than other bombs.

Indeed, it may be less "inhuman" than other nuclear weapons because it is designed to kill soldiers in tanks on battlefieds without killing civilians in cities many miles away.

President Reagan's decision to assemble the neutron weapons is merely a logical followup to former President Jimmy Carter's decision to make them. It is a decision that should add credibility to our posture as the guardian of the free world, regardless of how some of our allies react to it. That decision should have been made by the previous administration.

Among other things, the neutron bomb will serve to counter the Russians' chemical and biological weapons capability. The Soviets have built up a huge stockpile of such "cannibalistic" weapons.

The Dallas Morning News

Dallas, Texas, August 11, 1981

"**N**EUTRON bomb decision draws Soviet outcry," reads the headline. Why, to be sure; and so did the Marshall Plan draw Soviet outcries, and the Berlin airlift and every other post-World War II American initiative designed to strengthen the forces of freedom over against the forces of slavery.

The Soviets are not stupid. They understand all too well the uses of neutron weapons, which are missiles and howitzer shells equipped with warheads that produce high radioactivity without a lot of accompanying physical damage.

Against a Soviet *blitzkrieg* through Western Europe, such weapons would be critical. They might neutralize the massive Soviet edge in tanks.

American forces in Western Europe might today be equipped with neutron weapons were it not for the Carter administration's having taken fright from the anti-neutron propaganda campaign unleashed by the Soviets four years ago. To deployment of neutron weapons Carter wouldn't say yes and he wouldn't say no. He decided to produce but not assemble the various components.

Now the Reagan administration says, assemble them, though "deployment outside U.S. territory," the State Department comments, "is not involved."

Ultimately it will be involved. And here the plot thickens. Can we persuade NATO to approve the weapons for use on European soil when already the alliance is embroiled over the question

of our deploying new medium-range missiles two years hence?

Secretary of State Haig reportedly opposed putting the neutron weapons together at this time, fearing negative European reaction. Defense Secretary Weinberger said — and evidently the President agreed — we can't let Europe tell us what weapons to build. Wherein Weinberger and Reagan, we think, have it just about right.

Left-wing opposition in Europe to beefing up American military capabilities is not impressive to Americans who remember why the beefing up is necessary. It is for the purpose of better protecting Europe.

What Europe must decide in due course is whether it wants to be protected by the American "nuclear umbrella," because that umbrella is tremendously expensive. It is the United States that bears the burden of the alliance, contributing to national defense 5.2 percent of GNP, against 3.3 percent in West Germany, 3.9 percent in France, 2.4 percent in Italy and so on. Only Britain comes close to matching our effort.

If Europe does not wish to be defended, doubtless other uses can be found for our money. One doesn't want NATO tugged into the Soviet orbit. But already strategic thinkers like Lawrence W. Beilenson argue we could better spend our money on long-range missiles than ground troops in Europe. Such as Beilenson are bound to get a more attentive hearing, the louder Moscow's clients or sympathizers in Europe yell about weapons that "kill people instead of property."

The Evening Telegram

St. John's, Nfld., August 11, 1981

One of the necessary attributes of a successful actor is a good sense of timing, especially when it comes to the point of delivering the telling "punch" lines. President Ronald Reagan, into the White House via Hollywood, California, showed decidedly bad timing during the weekend when he announced that the United States would proceed with the manufacture of the neutron bomb.

It is bad enough that the U.S. has decided to proceed with the assembly of this dreadful weapon, the components for which have been ready and stockpiled for years, after the Carter administration rejected the plan. But he made the announcement on the very day that the population of Japan, and millions more people around the world, were commemorating the holocaust that almost annihilated the cities of Hiroshima and Nagasaki, August 6 and 9, 1945.

The understatement of the year came from a West German spokesman who said the decision was "exclusively an affair of the U.S. government;" as though the neutrom bomb, the socalled Doomsday weapon, had nothing at all to do with the potential destruction of most of the human race. The neutron bomb is the "most obscene" if that's possible of all these modern weapons. It is designed deliberately just to kill people and leave property, in the widest sense of that term, intact. Hence the Soviet Union has sarcastically termed it the "capitalist" bomb, and announced they too have the capability to make it and will do so.

The West German statement is strange because that country, in the European theatre, is much like Canada in North America, a buffer between the U.S.A. and the USSR. Nuclear weapons are alteady already deployed on German soil and more will be in place in a few years as a result of a NATO

decision. These will certainly include the neutron bomb when and as soon as it's built.

The move is another, perhaps fatal step, in the lunatic escalation of nuclear weapons. An article on this page quotes military experts as estimating that the two superpowers between them have some 35-40,000 weapons stockpiled or in launching sites. Any one of these is many more times more powerful than the bombs that killed Japanese civilians in numbers that exceeded the entire population of Newfoundland at that time, 36 years ago. Not only that, but the explosions left a legacy of disease, deformity, incredible suffering and heartbreak, of which the end is not yet in sight.

Other experts say that besides this "overkill", the U.S. already has a distinct technical edge on the Soviet Union, and if all nuclear tests were stopped now, that advantage would remain. There are two potential treaties that have been on the carpet for several years — the 1974 Threshold Test Ban Treaty, which limits weapons to 150 kilotons, and the 1976 Peaceful Nuclear Explosives Treaty which also permits explosions of 150 kilotons each, but also allows an aggregate of 1,500 kilotons "for group explosions". It sounds almost cosy.

It also sounds idiotic, almost maniacal, and shows more plainly than anything else that mankind, despite his "large brain" that distinguishes him from the other animals, is a great deal more stupid than these socalled "dumb" creatures. This is even more frightening, when you read and hear about patently brilliant people, scientists, engineers, generals, even some politicians, discussing it as though it were a fireworks display, the matter of a "limited nuclear exchange", that at the very least would eliminate one-tenth of the earth's population in one fell swoop and leave a large part of the planet in desolation.

The Charlotte Observer

Charlotte, N.C., August 14, 1981

"It is difficult to conduct a reasonable argument about nuclear warfare, for war begins where reason ends."
— Observer editorial, Aug. 3, 1977

It's unlikely that President Reagan's decision to assemble the neutron bomb moves the world significantly closer to nuclear war, as some of his critics fear; but neither does it "correct a wholly wrong and enormously damaging decision by his predecessor," as the Wall Street Journal contended this week.

Development of the neutron bomb began in the Kennedy administration, and no president since has removed it from the list of potential U.S. weapons. Jimmy Carter agonized — commendably, we think — before deciding to stop short of assembly, while announcing that the option of deploying the weapons remained open.

Mr. Reagan's decision only affirms more emphatically a belief in the weapon's deterrent value; and, it probably makes somewhat swifter deployment possible.

A 'Reasonable' Argument

The neutron bomb, in the form of short-range missile and artillery shells, produces less blast than other nuclear weapons, but releases deadly radiation over an area approximately a mile in diameter. It is far more effective in killing troops than non-nuclear battlefield weapons, but does much less physical destruction than other nuclear weapons.

It's possible to make a reasonable case for its deployment, as Secretary of Defense Caspar Weinberger did in a Viewpoint page column in Thursday's Observer. Available U.S. and allied conventional forces are considered inadequate to confront a massive Soviet invasion in Europe. The neutron bomb would provide an option between a conventional war in defense of Europe, which presumably we would lose, or using far more destructive nuclear battlefield weapons, or launching a nuclear attack against the Soviet Union.

But despite the buildup of Soviet border forces, there's reason to question the seriousness of the threat of an invasion, given the Soviet Union's problems with Poland and China and its vulnerability to nuclear attack from all sides.

Neutron bombs in western Europe may be a more *credible* deterrent — to a Soviet invasion — than our ability to blow Moscow off the face of the earth, since it would provide a more limited response; but is it as *powerful* a deterrent? Would the Soviets be more tempted to launch an invasion if the most they would risk — based on our own strategy — would be retaliation with neutron bombs?

If we accept what has been a widely held assumption since Soviet nuclear development first created the "balance of terror" — that the awesome destructiveness of nuclear weapons was the most powerful deterrent to their use — we must conclude that having more limited, more precisely targetted nuclear weapons erodes that deterrent. And making the prospect of a direct U.S.-Soviet military confrontation less terrifying surely doesn't make it less likely.

A Frightening Scenario

While scientists can calculate the immediate effect of a neutron bomb, no one knows for sure what the lingering consequences of extensive use of such weapons would be.

Although the Soviets strategically have little need for neutron bombs, they are believed to have large stockpiles of deadly nerve gas, and a neutron bomb defense against an invasion might remove whatever inhibitions they have against the use of gas, in retaliation.

Thus the scenario moves further and further beyond reason, into the realm of frightening absurdity. And what is the next step? How extensively can we set off highly radioactive nuclear explosions near the Soviet border and still feel secure within our own borders?

Pentagon planners have the duty to play out computerized war games and make educated guesses about what might happen under various circumstances. But experience, not guesswork, suggests that the world has been able to keep the nuclear genie bottled up precisely because the consequences of letting it loose have been unthinkable.

The president has the duty, in an unpredictable world, to keep as many defense options as possible open to the United States. But it is far from certain that Mr. Reagan's decision, and the policy direction it represents, for all its apparent reasonableness, makes this a more secure world.

Reducing The Threat Of War

Four years ago, when Mr. Carter was wrestling with the neutron bomb decision, we concluded in an editorial that "the argument over the neutron bomb is yet another sign of the foolishness of thinking that advanced weaponry equals national security. If the threat of war is to be reduced, it will be by worldwide arms reduction, not by increasing the sophistication of weapons."

That was an accurate assessment then, and it is still true today.

THE SACRAMENTO BEE

Sacramento, Calif., August 13, 1981

President Reagan's decision to begin constructing neutron bombs was a mistake. Apparently taken without warning, much less consulting, either our European allies or Congress, the decision is an impolitic snub that is not justified by any military emergency. Indeed, by ignoring the new weapon's potent symbolism in Europe, Reagan could lose more politically than he would gain tactically by deploying it.

If the point of Reagan's European strategy is, as his aides have said, to prevent the "Finlandization" of Western Europe — to prevent these countries from making political concessions to the Soviet Union out of fear of the Soviet military threat — then the American counterthreat should not be even more frightening to our NATO allies. And given European fears about the neutron bomb, its production is likely to create, if anything, an even greater motivation among the Western allies to avoid confrontation and make concessions.

European fears are centered on the fact that the existence of a new, "less damaging" tactical nuclear weapon would make it that much easier to take the step from non-nuclear to nuclear warfare. This is, of course, the primary deterrent value the neutron bomb is supposed to have: The Russians are also intended to believe that the United States would be willing to respond to a tank offensive with neutron bombs, even though it might not be willing to risk the use of existing tactical nuclear weapons. But to precisely the extent that the deterrent threat is credible, so is the risk of actually using a nuclear weapon. And by making this critical threshold easier to cross, the United States would be embarked on a strategy that has more to do with fighting a nuclear war than deterring one.

The distinction is crucial in Europe, and it should be here — especially when there is so little to be gained by blurring it. It might be worth considerable risk to have on hand a tactical weapon that would correct the imbalance in European tank strength between NATO and the Soviet alliance, but that has to be balanced against the danger of increasing the possibility of a nuclear conflict. Such a decision cannot be prudently made in isolation from our European allies, whose land we would seek to protect. It can only make it more difficult for European leaders — even if they are otherwise willing — to create domestic support to increase their own participation in NATO and other mutual defense arrangements.

The Reagan administration already has access to stockpiled parts for a neutron bomb. It is unlikely to gain much — either in battlefield strength, in diplomatic progress in Europe or in diplomatic leverage with the Russians — by putting these parts together.

St. Louis Globe-Democrat
St. Louis, Mo., August 11, 1981

The so-called neutron bomb (the warhead actually is carried on an eight-inch howitzer or a Lance missile) was developed principally to protect Western Europe from the massed armored forces of the Soviets and their Warsaw Pact allies.

North Atlantic Treaty Organization forces have 11 armored divisions to oppose 31 Warsaw Pact armored divisions.

The "enhanced radiation" weapon is the one European military commanders called for as the best means of stopping an all-out tank attack on their outgunned, outnumbered forces. It is a tactical weapon that retains virtually all of the radiation of a nuclear weapon but eliminates most of the heat and blast effects. Radioactivity from a neutron weapon can kill the crew of a tank that is within a one-mile radius of the burst. Thus it could be used against a massed Warsaw Pact armored attack without devastating the homes, the industry and the people whom the defenders were trying to protect.

It would have been deployed in Western Europe in 1978 if President Jimmy Carter had not suddenly reversed his field in April of that year after many months of trying to convince NATO leaders that it was in their interest to deploy the neutron bomb.

The neutron bomb is back in the news once more as President Ronald Reagan has taken the logical step of ordering the assembling of its components that have already been produced.

Reagan knows that as long as NATO forces are so badly outnumbered by Warsaw Pact armor they are going to need a weapon to counter this very heavy Communist advantage. Furthermore, the United States has more than 250,000 troops in forward positions in Western Europe, along with their dependents. These U.S. forces deserve the best protection they can get from the huge concentration of Communist armor. The neutron bomb could be the weapon that prevents U.S. forces in Europe from being overrun in the event of a full-scale war.

The claim that the neutron weapon would lower the threshold of nuclear war and thus increase the likelihood of a nuclear exchange is not valid. Both sides already have deployed hundreds of conventional tactical nuclear weapons that could be used in the event of full-scale fighting.

The Soviets, who are complaining so bitterly about President Reagan's order, have deployed more than 250 medium-range SS-20 missiles against Western Europe. Each of these missiles has three warheads with a range of 2,500 miles. Just one of these warheads, if detonated, would inflict five times the radiation of the largest U.S. tactical neutron weapon. The nations of Western Europe, as far as is known, don't have a single medium-range nuclear weapon to offset the intimidating Soviet SS-20 advantage.

Patently, the Soviets have twisted the situation to their advantage again. They have gullible Westerners worrying about the possible deployment of tactical enhanced radition weapons while the Russians escape major criticism even though they have deployed medium-range nuclear weapons targeted on all the major cities of Western Europe that have many times the radiation potential of the neutron missile.

The lessons of the past show that the Soviets will never negotiate away the awesome conventional and nuclear superiority they now have over Western Europe. Western European countries have only one viable alternative — to match the Soviets in every respect or face the possibility of being Finlandized by intense Soviet psychological warfare exploiting their military superiority. Deployment of the neutron weapon would be a major constructive step.

Des Moines Tribune
Des Moines, Iowa, August 14, 1981

Former National Security Adviser Zbigniew Brzezinski this week challenged Defense Secretary Caspar Weinberger's claim that the neutron bomb could be moved to Europe for use in "only a few hours." Europeans seem reluctant to have it stored there.

Brzezinski provided — unintentionally — another reason to oppose President Reagan's decision to start manufacturing and stockpiling the new bombs. He said the neutron bomb — which expends most of its energy in radiation rather than blast and thus kills people while doing less damage to structures — would be used primarily to blunt an attack by Warsaw Pact forces.

It cannot fully achieve that role, Brzezinski said, unless it is stored in Europe. It won't do to keep the bombs stateside, he added, because there is "no way to get them to Europe in a few hours. It would take several days, probably."

Several days — or even several hours — might be enough time for an attacker to eat up a lot of territory. Thus Reagan may come under pressure to give local commanders in Europe authority to order the use of the neutron weapons in the event of a surprise attack.

A Pentagon spokesman said Wednesday that, under current policy, only the president can order the use of any nuclear weapon. That should always be the case. These arms are too terrible to be used by any authority other than the president's — and they should never be used unless there is no other way to protect America's most fundamental interests.

Since the neutron bomb has at least the potential to force a revision in that policy, it should be left where President Carter left it: on the drawing board.

The Toronto Star
Toronto, Ont., August 17, 1981

To no one's surprise, President Ronald Reagan's decision to go ahead with the on-again-off-again neutron weapon has produced an emotional outcry. The reaction is easy to understand, for no human being today can take lightly the appearance of what seems to be yet another new nuclear weapon.

Unfortunately, however, the issue has become greatly beclouded by myth, emotion and propaganda that it is not easy to make a clear judgment. Contrary to widely-held belief, for instance, the neutron weapon is not an offensive device. Its range is limited to that of the missile that could carry it — the Lance, which flies about 75 miles. It is not a weapon of general devastation, but one designed for a local and specific mission. Its task is to halt Russian tanks, if and when they invade the West.

It is not a new weapon. Both the Russians and the Americans have been at work on it for nearly 30 years. In November, 1978, Leonid Brezhnev told visiting U.S. senators that the Soviets had tested the neutron weapon "many years ago" but had not put it into production. Obviously, Moscow's tactical needs are different from those of the Western alliance.

The neutron bomb does differ from other A-weapons. It inflicts less damage from blast and intense heat, but it has enhanced radiation — intended to penetrate Soviet armor. By design, the lifetime of this radiation has been reduced literally to hours, to enable the allied forces — and civilians — to enter the battle area.

The bomb, therefore, is a local, tactical weapon designed for a specific mission. Indeed, the Russians conceded this much in excluding it from the now-shelved SALT (Strategic Arms Limitation Treaty).

In its mission, it would replace some of the "dirty" nuclear warheads that would be employed now, and the damage done to civilians would, therefore, be less. And, contrary to some of its critics, it is not likely to lead to global annihilation. It is merely a minor part of the nuclear deterrent which has so far helped keep the two giants from the final, all-devastating combat. To assume that the introduction of a tactical weapon is somehow going to impel the leaders in Washington and Moscow to risk mutual destruction is naive.

But Reagan's decision raises other questions: Why now? And why announce it in this manner? This, in Western Europe, is a season of political unease, with the neutralist spirit alive and swelling, especially in Scandinavia, the Netherlands and West Germany. The only exception, interestingly enough, is Socialist-led France.

All these countries have been pressing Washington to begin disarmament talks with Moscow. To throw the neutron bomb into the cauldron at this point is a major political blunder. At the least, it creates problems even for regimes as pro-American as that of Bonn. At worst, it gives the Soviet propagandists yet one more opportunity to drive a wedge between the United States and its European allies.

Some years ago, an official of the French Atomic Agency assessed the new weapon neatly: "The neutron bomb means for tanks what the introduction of the machine-gun once meant for the infantry."

We are now, tragically for all of us, in an era when the nature of military hardware has been escalated from the musket and the machine-gun to that of miniaturized nuclear shells and missiles. But, given the changed military yardsticks, the neutron weapon is still one of limited mission and limited range — a low-grader among the hundreds of varieties in the arsenals of nuclear powers.

Why Moscow should so vehemently oppose it is easy to understand: The neutron weapon seems to check the overwhelming advantage the Soviets have in tank power. If they can thwart the production of this weapon through protests of their own or through demonstrations in the streets of Western Europe, so much the better.

But if they succeed, a heavy part of the blame will fall on Washington's own inability to understand that what might be sound military action can easily turn out to be a dreadful political boner.

SAN JOSE NEWS

San Jose, Calif., August 12, 1981

A single B-29 bomber flew over Hiroshima, Japan, on Aug. 6, 1945, at 8:15 in the morning, local time ... An atomic bomb carried from Tinian Island in the Marianas was dropped ...

The combined heat and blast pulverized everything in the explosion's immediate vicinity, generated spontaneous fires some distance away, produced winds that fanned the flames in Hiroshima's crater-like configuration so powerfully that they burned almost 4.4 square miles completely out, and killed between 70,000 and 80,000 people (flash burns killed 20-30 percent, radiation 15-20 percent), besides injuring more than 70,000 others.

A second bomb, dropped on Nagasaki, on Aug. 9, killed between 35,000 and 40,000 people, injured a like number, and devastated 1.8 square miles.

— Encyclopaedia Britannica

THE coincidence of dates is uncanny. On Aug. 6, 1981, 36 years to the day after Hiroshima, the administration of President Ronald Reagan decided to notify United States allies that neutron bombs are now being produced by this nation. And on Aug. 9, the anniversary of Nagasaki, newspapers broke that news to the American people.

In fact, the neutron bomb went into production weeks ago, Defense Secretary Caspar Weinberger said Monday. That revelation and others came out of an extraordinary series of seven separate television interviews Weinberger conducted in an effort to sell acceptance of the administration's decision to assemble and stockpile the bomb.

The administration's almost frantic efforts to sell the notion that the neutron bomb is necessary should be a tip-off — a warning that something very dangerous, even deadly, is going on here.

It's not just that the very concept of the neutron bomb — a weapon designed to kill people but minimize property damage — seems inhumane. There is a terrible irony in the very idea of a bomb that would kill humans and other living things slowly and painfully with enhanced radiation while leaving buildings and other structures undamaged by its blast effect. But that's not the principal problem.

It's not just that the administration's rationalization that the bomb is needed to counter the Soviet Union's 45,000 tanks in central Europe may be specious. Indeed it may be; in the current issue of Scientific American magazine, Paul Walker, a member of the Union of Concerned Scientists, argues that the danger of a "blitzkrieg" by Russian armored divisions may be overrated. He may be right, and the neutron bomb may also be less than cost-effective, as Walker maintained in a telephone interview with UPI Monday. But that's not the principal problem either.

It's not just that Weinberger seemed self-contradictory when he argued that it wasn't necessary to consult our NATO allies in advance, because assembling the bomb was an internal U.S. matter — and then went on to say that it could be deployed in Europe in "only a few hours."

It's not just that Weinberger was disingenuous in implying that Congress, and not the Reagan administration, really made the decision to assemble the bomb. The fact is, the fiscal 1981 defense authorization bill directed the president to produce and stockpile all of the *separate components* of the neutron bomb, but not to assemble them as usable.

It is the Reagan administration, not Congress, which has decided to do what the Carter administration proposed and then vacillated away from — i.e., to assemble the bomb as a usable weapon.

Weinberger tried hard to blur that distinction, by stressing that Carter's inept fumbling "gave the impression of a weak, irresolute America." He's right about that. It did. The Reagan team's projection of a bellicose America isn't necessarily any better, but even that is not the chief reason that Americans should be alarmed.

The real cause for concern is that once again the world has moved closer to nuclear war — and once again it is the West, not the Soviet Union, which has taken another step toward total annihilation of life on Earth.

It was we who began, and it has been at nearly every crucial juncture we who have escalated this seemingly inexorable rush toward doomsday. We were first to develop and test the atom bomb. We were the first to use it, at Hiroshima and Nagasaki. We took the lead in raising the level of destructiveness by developing the hydrogen bomb. We introduced the multiple warhead. And now — although both France and the Soviet Union have developed and tested the neutron bomb — once again it is the United States which has become the first nation actually to produce and stockpile this weapon too.

The awful implication of the neutron bomb is not that it merely adds another layer to a worldwide nuclear arsenal that already exceeds the potential for more than a million Hiroshimas. That would be bad enough, but this latest step is pregnant with an even more bizarre and terrible notion — the concept that the United States should be prepared to fight — and could expect to win — a *limited* nuclear war.

The madness of such reasoning did not originate with the Reagan White House. The concept of limited nuclear war has been kicking around Washington ever since the Nixon administration, and the Carter administration brought it out in the open with Carter's own on-again, off-again flirting with the neutron bomb, and with his now infamous Presidential Directive 59, which explicitly abandoned the one absolute commitment that has kept us all alive until now. And that is the knowledge that our very existence depends on nuclear weapons literally serving to deter war, not to wage it — and that approval of new weapons systems must only occur within that context.

Of course a limited nuclear war would be preferable to blowing up the world — if it were possible to have one without the other. But the fallacy is the assumption that once any nuclear weapon is used, it will be possible to limit the escalation of destruction. Former Defense Secretary Robert McNamara put his finger on the flaw in such reasoning years ago.

You can conduct a limited nuclear strike, McNamara said, and you can be perfectly clear in your own mind that that's all you expect in response. But you have absolutely no guarantee that that's all you'll get.

And that's the problem with the current vogue of talking about "precision nuclear strikes" — the very kind of thing for which a neutron bomb would be used. The underlying assumption is that we could cross the crucial threshold between conventional and nuclear war, with both the White House and the Kremlin carefully calculating, even as the missiles homed in on their own troops and bases and silos, precisely what the limits would be on the next strike, and the next counter-strike, and the one after that, and the one after *that* — with cool heads constantly in control, so much in control that no one on either side would make a fatal miscalculation.

To believe that requires a faith in our own leaders — *and in the Russians'* — that transcends all logic.

Weinberger would have us believe that all opposition to the neutron bomb grows out of a "well-orchestrated propaganda campaign based in Moscow." Certainly there is such a campaign. But one hardly needs to parrot the communist line to question the production of the neutron bomb. One needs only to be sane.

Years ago, just after Hiroshima, Lewis Mumford, the eclectic social historian, planner and prophet, wrote words that come to mind now:

"We in America are living among madmen. Madmen govern our affairs in the name of order and security ... And the fatal symptom of their madness is this: they have been carrying through a series of acts which will lead eventually to the destruction of mankind, under the solemn conviction that they are normal responsible people, living sane lives, and working for reasonable ends ...

"These madmen have a comet by the tail, but they think to prove their sanity by treating it as if it were a child's skyrocket. They play with it; they experiment with it; they dream of swifter and brighter comets ...

"Why do we let the madmen go on with their game without raising our voices? Why do we keep our glassy calm in the face of this danger? There is a reason: we are madmen too. We view the madness of our leaders as if it expressed a traditional wisdom and a common sense.

"We view them placidly, as a doped policeman might view with a blank, tolerant leer the robbery of a bank or the barehanded killing of a child ... Our failure to act is the measure of our madness. We look at the madmen and pass by.

"Truly, those are infernal machines that our elected and appointed madmen are setting. When the machines go off, the cities will explode, one after another, like a string of firecrackers, burning and blasting every vestige of life to a crisp.

"We know that the madmen are still making these machines, and we do not even ask them for what reason, still less do we bring their work to a halt ...

"We are thinking only of the next hour, the next day, the next week, and that is further proof that we are mad; for if we go on in this fashion, tomorrow will be more heavy with death than a mortuary."

St. Louis ⚞ Review

St. Louis, Mo., August 14, 1981

The timing was too bad to be accidental. While the rest of the world was observing the anniversary of the use of atomic weapons over Hiroshima and Nagasaki, the United States announced that it would begin production of a new weapon, the neutron bomb.

Obviously, the Reagan administration considers it important not only that the United States possess great military power, but also that it be perceived as ready and willing to use that power.

We cannot quarrel with that premise. Vacillation by a world power is as dangerous as a bully-boy attitude daring a response. The possession of great power carries awesome responsibilities for the prudent use of that power so that conflict by miscalculation never occurs.

We also can see that much of the opposition to the neutron bomb is propagandistic and emotional. It really doesn't matter much if the nuclear weapon that ultimately lights the skies is one of "enhanced radiation" (which sounds like a new Christmas tree ornament) or not. Our enemies delight in describing the bomb as a particularly capitalistic weapon, designed to kill only people while leaving important things like buildings and railroads unscathed. We know that there is another side to the coin and that the neutron bomb is a more sophisticated weapon than its predecessors. It can be more accurately targeted and its radiation although more intense is more controlled in extent and duration.

Nor are we impressed with the moral fervor of the condemnation of the weapon in foreign lands. The Soviet especially has embarked upon a massive increase in atomic power. Soviet strategic needs are less well served than those of the West by neutron type weapons and their criticism of the neutron bomb is hypocritical unless it also contains a real determination to slow their own nuclear buildup.

But in spite of these realities, we are appalled by this decision of the administration to escalate an already out-of-control nuclear arms race. The only reasonable justification for the introduction of any new nuclear weapon is to increase national security, but in the reality of the situation, the decision can only threaten security even more. Does anyone really think that the Soviet will allow this escalation to go unmatched? Have they done so with any other weapon we have unveiled? They will respond, either with new weapons of their own or by increasing the numbers of their own existing warheads. Is this security?

Where is our national sense of urgency to end this mad race into the jaws of death? In the case of the neutron bomb could we not at least have used it as a threat, proposing that unless meaningful arms limitations were achieved by mid-1982 that then we would begin its production? We were not reluctant in 1945 to drop a second atomic bomb on an already broken Japan as a sign of our determination to end the war. We are not reluctant now to begin construction of a new weapon to show the world that we possess overwhelming military power. Where is the urgency to take similarly resolute steps toward disarmament to show the world that we are as serious about peace and disarmament as we are about war and destruction?

The San Diego Union

San Diego, Calif., August 13, 1981

There can be no doubt about the compelling military logic of President Reagan's decision to order production of neutron warheads for the Army's tactical nuclear weapons.

Allied tanks defending NATO's central front are outnumbered 4-1 by those of the Soviet-led Warsaw pact. Neutron warheads for the U.S. Army's Lance battlefield missiles and 8-inch howitzers would help considerably to lessen the odds.

The intense, armor-piercing radiation released by the neutron warhead together with its comparatively slight blast and fireball make it an ideal equalizer should massed Soviet tank forces ever strike across heavily populated West Germany.

This explains Moscow's hyperbolic reaction at the merest mention of neutron weapons. The Soviets have invested staggering sums during the last decade and a half to achieve military superiority over NATO. They aren't pleased at the prospect of seeing that superiority diminished, especially by such relatively inexpensive technological innovations as the neutron warhead.

Three years ago, Leonid Brezhnev and company orchestrated a world-wide propaganda campaign designed to pressure then-President Carter into foregoing production and deployment of neutron weapons. To Mr. Carter's eternal discredit, he rewarded this shabby exercise in disinformation by canceling plans to produce neutron warheads and stockpile them in Western Europe.

Mr. Carter noted then that the decision could be reversed if the Soviets failed to demonstrate reciprocal restraint in their own arms building and foreign policy.

Since then, the Soviets have invaded Afghanistan, threatened Poland, fomented additional mischief in the Middle East, helped arrange the shipment of arms to Marxist guerrillas in Central America, and expanded an unprecedented military buildup that poses the greatest threat to global peace and security since World War II.

Clearly, Mr. Reagan's decision to add enhanced radiation weapons to the American arsenal was abundantly justified.

It is less clear, perhaps, that this was the best time to announce what should have been a comforting decision for Western Europe's NATO countries.

The European appeasement lobby awakened by the original debate over neutron weapons, and by NATO's 1979 decision to deploy a new generation of American Pershing and cruise missiles beginning in 1983, has grown ever more vociferous.

So intense is the pressure from the left that even such staunch NATO supporters as West German Chancellor Helmut Schmidt now find it imprudent to publicly welcome Mr. Reagan's decision to proceed with neutron warhead production. NATO governments are even less inclined to invite renewed protests by agreeing, as West Germany did in early 1978, to permit neutron weapons on their soil.

Secretary of State Alexander Haig, a vigorous proponent of neutron weapons during his tenure as commander of NATO's ground forces, nevertheless reportedly urged Mr. Reagan to delay his decision so as not to exacerbate the alliance's political strains.

The President chose instead to act on the advice of Defense Secretary Caspar Weinberger, and his own judgment that NATO's political problems have to be faced squarely sooner or later.

Still, Mr. Reagan tempered his decision by noting pointedly that the neutron warheads would remain on U.S. soil, which should dampen protests from the European left.

Meanwhile, the Soviets will know that NATO's newest and most lethal anti-tank weapon is in production and could be flown to U.S. troops in Europe within hours in a threatened crisis.

That kind of knowledge diminishes the threat of a Soviet attack, and makes it less likely that any of NATO's weapons will ever have to be used.

The Washington Post

Washington, D.C., August 11, 1981

THE PRESIDENT has gotten himself into a whole new predicament by his decision on the neutron bomb. He has entered a volatile emotional thicket that has been the scene of Atlantic alliance turmoil for 20 years. Mr. Reagan has also handed Europe's burgeoning left, not to speak of the Soviet Union, a powerful propaganda club to use against the United States, and he has taken a step to overload the European nuclear circuit and diminish chances that the new Pershing II and ground-based cruise missiles will be deployed in Europe.

The neutron bomb is no ordinary nuclear weapon. It is a tactical battlefield weapon designed especially for use in Europe in the event of a Soviet invasion. Many Europeans are upset, as well they might be, to think in those terms. It upsets them further to consider the special physical characteristics of the neutron bomb—it is heavy on radiation as against blast and heat—that make its use feasible on European territory. It is not simply that these characteristics lend themselves to propaganda: Nikita Khrushchev's line of 1961—that a neutron bomb meant "to kill people but preserve all riches" and that it embodies "the bestial ethics of the most aggressive exponents of imperialism"—is still being peddled. It is precisely because the neutron bomb seems so feasible that many Europeans have long feared that it would be used.

The strategic argument for the neutron bomb is summarized on the opposite page today by the secretary of defense. The essential case is that this weapon, being relatively small and controllable, would give NATO a credible nuclear deterrent that, even if employed, would not likely produce a general war. The con side holds that neutron bombs, being practical, would lower the barrier against nuclear usage and lead on to a full exchange.

The special and familiar emotional past of the neutron bomb ensures, however, that the issue will not be resolved on strategic grounds. Even before Mr. Reagan decided to move from building to assembling the parts of this weapon, a strong anti-nuclear current was running in Europe and a strong current of distrust of the Reagan hard line as well. Already, the critical alliance effort to deploy new missiles to counter the Soviet buildup of SS20s was an uphill struggle. Prudence dictated that Mr. Reagan reserve a move on the neutron bomb until he had climbed that hill. Instead, he chose to make it steeper. He may be moving NATO toward a fateful crisis.

The Dispatch

Columbus, Ohio, August 12, 1981

PRESIDENT REAGAN'S decision to begin production of the neutron bomb marks a substantial change in nuclear warfare strategy. The implications are enormous.

The bomb embodies a macabre concept: An invading army can be destroyed but the buildings in the invaded territory can be left relatively undamaged and suitable for future use. The bomb carries twice the radiation but less than 10 percent of the explosive power of a conventional nuclear weapon. It ends life in roughly a three-quarter mile radius of the impact point, but the radiation dissipates within minutes and the territory can be quickly occupied by friendly forces.

The bomb is designed to be effective against Soviet tank forces in Europe which outnumber NATO tanks four to one. The bomb's "discriminating" features are designed to appeal to the West Europeans who inhabit the probable battleground for the next East-West war. Civilians can be evacuated when the war starts and will have homes to return to after the war is waged.

And therein lies the bomb's real significance. The neutron bomb advances the idea that a limited nuclear war can be fought and won, and that the world will be fit for life once the war ends. This idea has long contended with a contrary notion that nuclear weapons should be made so big, pack such destructive power and cause such horrible damage that they will never be used. This is the basis of the deterrence policies both sides have embraced for decades.

The neutron bomb may signal the start of an era in which nuclear warfare is sanctioned, terrible human suffering — albeit limited in numbers — is acceptable and the desire for battlefield victory exceeds other considerations.

Reagan's decision to produce, stockpile but not deploy the bomb is a measured step, one that addresses the neutron bomb issue with the same caution that President Carter displayed when he decided to manufacture the bomb's components but not assemble them. The difference is that the bomb will now be ready for use and can be included in warfare strategy.

Reagan's move seems calculated to pressure the Soviet Union to begin substantive negotiations on nuclear arms limitations and reductions. The president has long maintained that the United States must demonstrate to its enemies that it has the will to be secure and the might to negotiate from a position of strength.

In moving ahead on the neutron bomb, Reagan is demonstrating his will, increasing U.S. might, but raising considerably the stakes in the nuclear arms race. It is a gamble the president feels he has to take. We hope it pays off.

ARKANSAS DEMOCRAT

Little Rock, Ark., August 20, 1981

The Russians are calling Ronald Reagan's decision to build and assemble the neutron bomb barbarous — and demanding that the Geneva convention outlaw the thing. Our European allies, on whose soil the bombs would be implanted, are merely grumbling. They know well enough that the neutron bomb is their only deliverance from the giant Russian conventional forces poised just across their borders.

In artillery and missile form, the bomb would deter the Russians from marching and rolling into Western Europe. Despite their tremendous nuclear superiority, that's how the Russians will come if they come at all. In time, American Pershing and cruise missiles will be installed on NATO soil as a face-off to the giant Russian SS-20s — but nuclear war isn't the scenario for Europe. A missile fired from either side there would point to Armageddon; whereas a Russian ground attack wouldn't — or so the Russians figure — necessarily result in our countering with the only thing that would stop it, short of neutron bombs: nuclear missiles. For missiles would bring Armageddon, too. The bottom line is that the Russians count on us not choosing nuclear war just to save Europeans from ground attack.

But the neutron bomb spoils the Russian scenario. It can neutralize superior conventional forces. Its intense radiation would wipe out marching men and tank-crews alike while only lightly damaging surroundings. In effect, the neutron bomb would be a conventional response to a conventional attack.

The Russians (echoed by many pacifists everywhere) have denounced the bomb from the first as a new species of horror because it "kills only people." The answer to that absurdity is that death from non-destructive radiation is no different from death by nuclear explosions — and that the only "people" dying from the radiation would be Russian aggressors, super force blackmailers trading on the terror of nuclear war to conquer by conventional means. The neutron bomb – the great neutralizer of superiority in tanks and men – is the civilized world's response to only conventional blackmail. It is a weapon for peace.

THE BLADE

Toledo, Ohio, August 17, 1981

SOVIET reaction to President Reagan's order to produce and stockpile neutron warheads can be classified as knee-jerk predictable. One would expect no less that a Tass denunciation of the weapon as "the most inhumane type of mass annihilation."

Tass conveniently neglected, of course, to mention that the Kremlin itself has tested a neutron weapon of its own, as reported by the French defense minister.

Actually, the President is not plowing new ground. Former President Carter, after backing and filling over the issue in the latter part of his term, finally decided to produce components for neutron warheads but not assemble them. The Reagan order goes only a step further to put them together and store them as another deterrent to Soviet military action.

From that standpoint the action makes sense. Reaction in most western European capitals was calm, with acceptance of the step as an American prerogative as long as the warheads are not placed immediately in their territories. The exceptions were mainly the Scandinavian countries where peace movements sometimes take on a somewhat rosy hue. The Swedish foreign minister, for example, called the Reagan decision "a further dangerous and alarming escalation of the arms race between the superpowers," adding that "if one really wants peace, one can't exclusively plan for war."

The fact is that the Soviet Union maintains a huge edge in numbers of tanks in central Europe. These would be the main targets of neutron warheads, designed to kill tank crews by intense radiation but with reduced explosive effect. While all weapons of mass destruction are inhumane, this one is somewhat less so than, say, a "dirty" nuclear blast that would spread death and destruction over a much wider area.

The Soviet Union also enjoys a big lead in numbers of troops and tactical nuclear missiles in the European theater. The Administration's decision is logically designed to help overcome the present imbalance between Warsaw Pact and NATO forces. In the meantime, arms-control talks could still begin if Kremlin leaders are disposed to seriously discuss that subject. But to paraphrase the Swedish foreign minister, if one wants peace, one cannot forget about planning for war, either.

Chicago Tribune

Chicago, Ill., August 12, 1981

A great fog of confusion and sophistry filled the air two years ago when President Carter bumbled the decision on deploying "enhanced radiation warheads," better known as neutron bombs, in Europe. Now that President Reagan has begun to rectify that error by ordering the assembly and stockpiling of neutron weapons in the United States, the same fog is rolling back in. It should be cleared away, and those who are confused will find these points helpful.

● The neutron bomb is an anti-tank weapon, not a diabolical gadget designed to wipe out German burghers and their families while preserving their homes and factories for use by the victorious neutron-bombers. It produces a large amount of short-lived radiation without a great deal of blast and heat, which is an ideal way to attack massed tank and troop formations without wide-spread destruction or contamination of nearby towns and villages.

● The neutron bomb is an effective means of preventing a Soviet attack on Western Europe but is virtually useless to an attacking Soviet or Warsaw Pact force. The Soviets have built an enormous tank force in Eastern Europe, 19,500 of them compared with only 7,000 on the NATO side. Such a force is far more than would be needed for the defense of Eastern Europe, so must be considered a potential invasion threat. The best way to forestall such an invasion would be to deploy anti-tank weaponry that would render the tanks useless without devastating the West European battlefield. Since NATO's 7,000 tanks are obviously too few to invade Eastern Europe, and since no such invasion is even remotely contemplated by the Western allies, the Soviets would have little reason to deploy neutron weapons.

● Deployment of neutron weapons in Western Europe would not make it more likely that a conventional war would turn nuclear, as many critics assert. An overwhelming Soviet armored assault against the West would almost certainly result in the use of tactical weapons of the older, dirtier, more destructive, but less effective design if no neutron bombs were available. The availability of the highly-effective neutron bombs, on the other hand, would make such an attack much less likely in the first place.

Thus the enhanced-radiation weaponry is not Dr. Strangelove madness but a sensible response to a very real threat. Still, the howls from the West Europeans will be loud, almost as loud as the howls from the Kremlin.

The response to the Soviet howls is simple: If the Russians were not building an invasion-sized armored force in Eastern Europe, we in the West would feel no need to deploy dangerous weapons to defend against it. Get rid of the tanks, comrades, and we'll get rid of the anti-tank weapons.

The response to the West Europeans is equally simple: If you don't like the way the United States is defending you, do it yourselves. Britain is turning its navy into razor blades, West Germany is cutting its real defense expenditures, the Dutch army is unionized, and the French petulantly refuse to take part in the military side of the NATO alliance. All seem willing to let the United States bear the main burden of their defense, so they have little right to complain about how we go about it.

The fact is that the President's decision on the neutron weapons is less revolutionary than the furor surrounding it would indicate. President Carter, after a great deal of foolish indecision, ordered that the components of neutron weapons be manufactured. Mr. Reagan took one step further by ordering the components be assembled into usable artillery shells and Lance missile warheads and stockpiled on U.S. territory. They will not be moved into Western Europe without the agreement of the host countries involved — and if the Warsaw Pact tanks start lining up on the borders, the West Europeans might be glad that the neutron weapons are available.

By making this decision in a forthright manner, President Reagan is serving notice on the Soviets that the United States is willing and able to meet the armored threat from the East. There is none of the on-again off-again confusion of the Carter administration to tempt the Soviets to behave even more threateningly. The Soviets can fume all they want, and they can even produce their own neutron weapons even though they would be of little use to them. But in the end they will have to realize that this President will not shirk his duty to defend the West.

The Wichita Eagle-Beacon

Wichita, Kans., August 11, 1981

And so we raise the ante in the nuclear arms race. There is no doubt the administration's decision to proceed with the production of neutron weapons does that; the only question now being whether it also will deter the Soviets from attacking this country or its allies — its intended purpose — and in the process spur them into getting serious about nuclear arms reductions.

Certainly both sides should get serious about that, and in that connection, it's encouraging to learn President Reagan already has had several contacts with Soviet President Brezhnev about the possibility of resurrecting the arms reduction talks. Reintroducing the neutron bomb into the arms-talks equation complicates the prospects for achieving a suitable accord in ways no one really can predict.

It's hard to believe, though, that if the United States does indeed go into neutron weapons production, the Soviet Union won't be long in following. It only makes sense, before the United States takes that step, for Soviet and American negotiators to get together and at least agree on the two countries' common points of understanding.

The biggest difficulty the administration might have with its neutron weapons proposal is in selling the idea to the United States' Western European allies. West Germany and France, in particular, whose soil is soaked with the blood of thousands of their own citizens, as well as of Allied soldiers, have known the horrors of war. They understandably aren't anxious to invite another because of nuclear stockpiles within their boundaries. Nor does simply storing the neutron weaponry in the United States until it's needed "over there" resolve that problem, or alleviate those concerns.

Even the contemplation of using nuclear arms of any sort in a confrontation between superpowers should give every citizen — American and Soviet — cause for introspection and, yes, prayer, for the safety of the nations — all nations. Much caution, deliberateness and diplomacy are called for, as the administration starts down this new road.

The Burlington Free Press

Burlington, Vt., August 14, 1981

The Defense Department's announcement this week that the nation is producing neutron bombs was disconcerting for its apparent acceptance of the idea that a limited nuclear war is possible.

The decision is an indication of a persistent delusion in the military mind that the use of tactical nuclear weapons will not trigger a massive exchange of long-range bombs by the United States and the Soviet Union. Some Pentagon leaders apparently have yet to grasp the idea that no one will survive a nuclear holocaust.

The rationale behind the production of neutron bombs is disturbing. Because the bomb produces more radiation and less blast and heat, it tends to be more effective against people and causes a minimum amount of damage to buildings and other structures.

Should Russian armor spring out of the East in a drive toward Western Europe, the neutron bomb could destroy the horde and create less havoc than a conventional nuclear weapon, according to defense officials. But it appears that strategic thinking comes to a shuddering halt, after contemplating the success of that hypothetical mission. Military leaders seem willing to rule out the possibility that the Soviet hierarchy would be so rankled by the destruction of its ground forces that it would order a full-scale nuclear assault on the United States. In the ensuing exchange, millions of American and Soviet citizens would be killed and wounded and the survivors would be doomed within days of the attack.

Soviet leaders already are dismayed by the news of the production of the neutron bomb and no doubt are responding by stepping up construction of their own weapons, if they have them, or putting in motion plans to develop neutron weaponry. Once again, the arms race will be escalated.

The production of the neutron bomb is but another signal that the United States and the Soviet Union are on a collision course that can only end in nuclear disaster if the two nations refuse to sit down and work out sensible agreements on putting an end to the madness of the arms race.

Minneapolis Star and Tribune

Minneapolis, Minn., August 13, 1981

So badly did the Carter administration bungle the enhanced radiation warhead, or neutron bomb, that a worse performance seemed impossible. But the Reagan administration's handling of the same issue not only is more inept, but could prove more harmful to the United States. If top officials seriously debated the wisdom of adding this new kind of nuclear weapon to the arms inventory, no signs appeared in the casual announcement last week that production had begun. And if Defense Secretary Weinberger was aware of the decision's adverse impact on NATO allies, he chose to dismiss it.

In light of the earlier experience, you would expect the Reagan administration to do better. President Carter announced in 1977 that the United States would produce and deploy the neutron bomb, but only with the concurrence of American allies. The key was Chancellor Helmut Schmidt; West Germany forms NATO's front line and would become the primary base for neutron bombs. Despite criticism from his own party, Schmidt supported the American policy — which Carter reversed the next year by indefinitely deferring final production. That incident contributed strongly to European misgivings about Carter.

Unlike the Carter plan, the current one does not envision deployment in Europe; technically, therefore, U.S. production of neutron bombs requires no other countries' consent. But the weapons are intended primarily as deterrents to the Warsaw Pact; intended for ultimate use, if not immediate basing, in Western Europe. Their heat and blast effects would be less severe than those of standard nuclear weapons designed for battlefield use, and their lethal radiation greater. Thus neutron bombs have the advantage of potential use against tank and troop concentrations with less destruction of built-up surroundings. The disadvantage is that neutron bombs may be seen as a partial substitute for conventional forces and could increase the likelihood of an early resort to nuclear weapons in a European crisis.

Because Europe is so intimately involved, the pros and cons — political as well as strategic — deserve debate within and among NATO governments. The 1977 decision satisfied only half that requirement: The Nuclear Planning Group, a NATO subdivision made up of defense ministry representatives, recommended neutron bomb deployment on military grounds. But without corresponding consultation on political consequences, national leaders were unprepared for the firestorm of public criticism that had much to do with Carter's reversal.

Western leaders applied lessons from that unhappy experience to subsequent deliberations on the larger, more-complex question of the Soviet-West European nuclear balance. They paired their December 1979 decision to modernize intermediate-range U.S. missiles in Europe with an initiative for arms-control negotiations on the same issues. The two decisions were preceded by long discussions among two working groups. Though the issues are far from settled, they did not explode unexpectedly on the European political scene.

The Reagan administration seems determined to unlearn from experience. Then-Gen. Alexander Haig shepherded the missile discussions through NATO as its military commander; as secretary of state, he would be the logical official to lead comparable consultations on the neutron bomb. Instead, Defense Secretary Weinberger has led the charge with such arrogance as this: "There is no particular reason to consult anyone any more than there would have been to consult on the production of the 155-millimeter conventional artillery bomb." The administration did notify allies that neutron bomb production had resumed, but only when the news was about to appear in the press. And Weinberger, dismissing critics as fools or worse, attributes European opposition to the success of Soviet propaganda.

Of course the Soviets oppose the neutron bomb, just as they do every other Western defense measure, and of course some in the West echo the Soviet line. But others challenge the strategic wisdom of the neutron bomb, just as diverse critics like Ronald Reagan and Leonid Brezhnev challenge the Carter plan for MX missile deployment. There may be a case for building the neutron bomb. But the administration all but destroys it by deriding dissent, ignoring allies and asserting, as Weinberger did this week, that peace is best assured by more arms.

The Pittsburgh Press

Pittsburgh, Pa., August 12, 1981

President Reagan will need to employ all of his determination and diplomatic skill to stick to his decision to build neutron weapons — battlefield devices that cause more radiation and less blast and heat than regular nuclear warheads.

The Soviet Union, through a vast campaign of propaganda and intimidation, forced President Carter to back down on producing the weapon in 1978, and it already has started to play the same tattoo on Mr. Reagan.

As before, the Russians will be aided in their campaign by self-styled "peace" groups both in the United States and in Europe — some of which are sincerely pacifist while others are followers of the communist line.

★ ★ ★

The Kremlin's dislike for the neutron warhead is understandable — from its point of view.

For this weapon was designed specifically to strike at armored units in Central Europe, where the Soviet-led Warsaw Pact has a 3-to-1 tank advantage over the United States and the NATO allies.

Apart from Moscow's self-interest, there is a respectable argument against the neutron warhead.

Its opponents say that because it can be focused on killing soldiers while limiting civilian deaths and property destruction, the neutron bomb is more likely to be used than a regular atomic weapon — thus increasing the chance of triggering a major nuclear war.

However, the Warsaw Pact's lead in manpower and conventional arms is so great that an all-out attack on Western Europe would have to be answered with nuclear weapons — if Western Europe were to have any chance of repulsing the onslaught.

In such event, it obviously would be better to use weapons that could cripple Soviet tank formations without destroying nearby cities with the blast and fallout that would result from the use of current nuclear bombs.

★ ★ ★

A great deal is at stake in the neutron-warhead issue.

With its propaganda drive and threats, Russia is seeking a veto over the weapons NATO could use in its defense. Yet NATO cannot let any potential enemy control such decisions without gravely weakening itself.

Indeed, if the Soviet Union succeeds in manipulating America's allies into rejecting the neutron weapon, and later the medium-range cruise missile, the unraveling of NATO will have begun.

And that, in all probability, would lead to the withdrawal of U.S. troops from Europe — and Soviet political domination of the entire continent.

The Boston Globe

Boston, Mass., August 11, 1981

There are, in today's world, two ways to think about any particular weapon: It will be used or it won't be used. If, in today's world, a weapon like the neutron bomb were really used, it is highly likely that the whole world would be at war with massive exchanges of many kinds of warheads. Death and destruction would be massive. In this case, the addition of any particular system (the neutron bomb) to the arsenal is essentially superfluous.

The alternative is that the bomb is not going to be used. In that case, it is not necessary and does not have to be built, at least in the context of the world as it is today. The United States does, after all, have any enormous array of tactical and strategic nuclear weapons on hand. It has developed most of them with a minimum of objection from either domestic or foreign critics. It will probably continue to do so. The Soviet Union has an essentially similar arsenal and continues to develop its own weapons.

Some people cherish the notion that somehow it may be possible to fight a "limited" nuclear war in which the neutron bomb would have a role to play. Its purported ability to deliver lethal doses of neutron radiation to clusters of enemy troops with a minimum of physical damage to structures seems attractive from a tactical point of view. In the history of modern warfare, however, escalation has been the norm, not restraint.

The real danger in the neutron bomb is that those making policy will begin to formulate it on the premise that there could really be a "limited" war with the Soviet Union in Europe or elsewhere. Given such an assumption, they might approach disputes with greater willingness to force some particular conflict to the ultimatum stage.

The Reagan Administration's decision to push ahead with the assembly and domestic storage of the neutron bomb, possibly foreshadowing its stationing in Europe, does nothing to enhance either America's safety or that of its allies. The argument that such weaponry would help contain such a war, preventing it from becoming Armageddon, is simply not credible. The neutron bomb adds nothing to the deterrent value of this country's enormous strategic arsenal, which guarantees the total destruction of the Soviet Union should war actually break out.

All that the bomb and the Administration's announcement of it have managed to do is arouse its domestic critics and the Soviet Union to no particular purpose. There will probably be ample opportunities for muscle-flexing in the future over real rather than artificial issues. It makes little sense to stir the pot just for the sake of stirring.

Buffalo Evening News

Buffalo, N.Y., August 12, 1981

Any nuclear weapon is horrible, but the neutron bomb is less horrible than most, since it has far less blast and heat than other nuclear weapons. It is designed for use against troops rather than cities, and it has little lingering radiation or widespread fallout. In Europe, it could help offset NATO's 3-1 disadvantage in tank forces in relation to Soviet forces.

President Reagan's decision to produce and stockpile the weapon has inevitably stirred controversy. The way the weapon is often described — "it kills people but leaves buildings intact" — makes the neutron bomb sound like a devilish new device that places material possessions above humanity. Actually, the neutron warhead is a small, battlefield weapon, designed to be deployed in artillery shells or the Lance battlefield missile.

Because the neutron bomb is less deadly than the intermediate-range nuclear missiles that NATO has decided to start deploying in 1983, foes of the weapon maintain, with some logic, that it could lower the "threshold" of nuclear war and make that dread event more likely. On the other hand, the fact that the neutron weapon could be used without mass destruction also makes it a more credible weapon, and thus one with potentially greater deterrent value. Every nuclear weapon would fail in its purpose — deterrence — the moment it was fired.

The timing of Mr. Reagan's decision was opposed by Secretary of State Alexander Haig because Western Europe is at present engaged in a controversy over the stationing of intermediate-range cruise and Pershing-2 missiles to meet the threat of Soviet nuclear missiles already in place. The neutron warhead is likely to create an additional dispute.

The warheads, however, will merely be stockpiled in the United States and will not be deployed without the consent of allied nations. Mr. Reagan might also have been influenced in his decision by the failure of our allies to live up to their commitments to increase defense spending. Even without any plans for deployment, the stockpile of neutron bombs would have some deterrent effect on Moscow.

THE COMMERCIAL APPEAL

Memphis, Tenn., August 11, 1981

THERE WASN'T all that much new about President Reagan's decision to start producing the neutron warhead.

All his decision really meant was that the military now can put together the pieces that President Carter already had ordered produced and stored.

That means, of course, that if those bombs should be needed somewhere in the world they will be more readily available than they would have been if the pieces first had to be assembled. But it doesn't necessarily mean a dramatic change in U.S. policy about the possibility of using such weapons.

Whether having such weapons is good or bad may be a matter of long and perhaps even bitter debate in the United States, but it is likely to be a useless debate. Once a nation has the ability to produce a weapon it is going to produce it, even though it knows that doing so may well induce other nations to match it or even to raise the ante by finding an even better weapon for the same purpose.

President Carter, of course, wanted to stockpile the neutron bombs around Europe since that region is the one where they most likely would be needed. The bombs are considered first-rate defensive weapons against tanks. One of the Soviets' great advantages in Europe at present lies in its abundance of tanks.

Having the neutron weapons stockpiled in Europe would have made them quickly available against the Soviet tanks should the Kremlin ever have decided to move against western Europe. Having them stockpiled in the United States obviously will mean the response to any move the Russians make would be less immediate, but President Reagan thinks the fact that the neutron weapons now will be ready to go in itself will deter any rash Soviet military actions.

The Kremlin, of course, is aware of the potential of the neutron weapon against its tanks and is nettled by that realization. So it is not surprising its propagandists immediately have said the American move will require the Russians to build their own version of an "enhanced radiation" weapon.

IF THAT IS ALL that comes of this, the result will not be all that bad.

The real question is what happens if either nation ever feels compelled to put such weaponry to actual use.

If the United States employs the neutron bombs against Soviet tanks, will the Kremlin be satisfied with simply retaliating with its equivalent neutron bombs? Or will the Soviet officials decide that since the United States has resorted to nuclear warfare — albeit on a limited or "theater" scale — the next move should be something higher?

And if the decision is to escalate, what form will that escalation take? Will it be a token intercontinental missile with its multiple warheads in hopes that such a demonstration will be sufficient to force withdrawal of the allied forces in Europe? Or will it be what now is known as a preventive strike that is really defensive but which would involve an attempt to wipe out all the land-based nuclear forces of the United States?

No doubt such theorizing will be dismissed as impractical by those who control the buttons that will make the ultimate decisions as to whether we all live or die and whether there will be any world left for anyone to fight over. And, of course, it is a foolish exercise if for no other reason than that so few of us have any control over it.

Arkansas Gazette.
Little Rock, Ark., August 11, 1981

Thirty-six years ago this month, the United States brought World War II to an abrupt close by dropping atomic bombs upon the Japanese cities of Hiroshima and Nagasaki. They were crude and relatively small devices, dropped from bombers, but even so, 97,000 died at Hiroshima and 77,000 perished at Nagasaki. In the ensuing years, the United States and others, especially the Soviet Union, have made startling technological advances in nuclear weaponry, but they seem to have lost sight of where this sophistication is carrying the planet Earth.

This point comes home dramatically in the relatively modest step that President Reagan, in painful irony, took last week on the anniversary of the Hiroshima blast: The United States will assemble and stockpile enhanced radiation weapons, known popularly as neutron bombs.

Components for neutron warheads have been manufactured and stockpiled since former President Jimmy Carter decided in 1978 that this was as far as the United States should move. President Reagan's decision means that these parts will now be assembled and kept in the United States. Apparently less than 400 warheads will be needed, at least initially. They are to be mounted on the Lance battlefield missile and eight-inch howitzer shells. They are designed for use against Soviet tanks in Europe because they rely on radiation for their principal killing power. The neutron bomb is to be the United States' answer to the 3-to-1 advantage over NATO that the Soviets have in tanks, for the blast will penetrate the armor and kill the tank crews while leaving the equipment and buildings virtually undamaged.

There is a certain practicality in the intention of design, but to contend, as has Presidential Counselor Edwin Meese III, that availability of the neutron warhead should deter Soviet aggression and encourage arms control is at best illogical and at worst absurd. Instead, easy availability will tell the Soviet Union to produce its own enhanced radiation weapon or to use instead some other kind of tactical nuclear weapon. There is no good reason to expect that the Russians would have the same regard for preserving those picturesque villages in, say, West Germany or France, that the United States has.

To argue that the cause of arms control and peace are served by the circumstance that the United States' neutron warheads will not be deployed on European soil, in deference to many of our allies, really begs the question. After all, among other things, this is the jet age. Any neutron warheads stockpiled in the United States are only a few hours away from firing mechanisms that are deployed in Western Europe.

Many Europeans who oppose the neutron warhead contend that the weapon invites escalation from the tank battlefield to the whole of the continent. The fear is that Western Europe would serve as the battleground for the United States and the Soviet Union, which would remain relatively intact. Their objections are well-taken, but the history of nuclear weapon development, and the theory of nuclear warfare, argue much more persuasively that the spark of a single neutron warhead, even a device as small as one kiloton devastating an area in a radius of 550 yards, would likely lead to a full-scale strategic exchange, leaving a planet incapable of sustaining meaningful life.

Those who say that both sides would exercise discipline in limiting their use of nuclear weapons of any magnitude simply ignore the record of nuclear one-upmanship written out for the last 36 years. Neither side has exercised discipline in the development of ever more exotic nuclear weapons, each in response to the other.

The second Strategic Arms Limitation Treaty negotiated by three American administrations and signed by former President Carter, but never ratified by the Senate, would have broken this pattern at the strategic level and could have brought mutual reductions in a subsequent agreement. Once the new pattern had been set, the nuclear powers could easily have applied the same principles to tactical and medium-range nuclear weaponry.

Despite the administration's view that production of the neutron warhead will encourage arms control, it plainly will have the opposite effect. An abiding hope now must be that the Reagan administration will soon come to its senses and vow, through SALT, to reduce the threat of mutual destruction by mutual reductions in all kinds of nuclear armament.

The Houston Post
Houston, Texas, August 14, 1981

President Reagan's decision to assemble and stockpile neutron bombs in this country has reopened a sensitive issue. But opponents of the weapons, which are not bombs but warheads for missiles and artillery shells, are relying more on emotion than logic in arguing against them. The characteristics of the neutron warhead — its ability to kill by huge doses of highly concentrated radiaton while causing limited damage to property — are cited as the main reason for not using it. From its inception, the idea of a weapon designed to kill people while minimizing damage to real estate has been regarded as horrendous. Yet is it any more immoral than a weapon that inflicts equal amounts of destruction on both life and property?

Proponents of the neutron warhead see it as an alternative to conventional nuclear weapons that spread radioactivity as well as fire and blast damage over a much larger area. In a densely populated region like Europe, they argue, the neutron weapon would be less destructive than conventional nuclear arms. Anti-nuclear groups in Western Europe contend, however, that neutron warheads would increase the threat of nuclear war by making the use of such weapons more acceptable.

The administration says it does not now plan to deploy neutron weapons outside this country and that it would consult closely with our allies before such a step were taken. Reagan's decision to assemble and stockpile neutron weapons is defended as a logical follow-up to President Carter's decision to make components of the warhead but not to assemble them. Unfortunately, Carter's indecision on the neutron bomb issue has complicated present administration policy on the weapon.

When the question of deploying the warhead in Europe was first broached in 1977, many Western European leaders were opposed to it. But West German Chancellor Helmut Schmidt was persuaded to support deployment. Once Schmidt was out on a limb over the issue, the Carter administration sawed it off by deciding not to produce or deploy the weapon. That understandably soured Schmidt on the neutron bomb and hurt U.S.-West German relations.

The most vociferous opponent of the bomb, however, has been the Soviet Union — and with good reason from the Kremlin's perspective. The weapon could be a powerful deterrent to an attack on Western Europe by numerically superior Warsaw Pact forces — an equalizer in effect. The neutron warhead was designed to stop a Soviet tank attack. The high levels of radiation emitted would penetrate tank armor and kill the occupants. It also has been suggested that the neutron bomb could make a useful bargaining chip in talks on nuclear arms control in Europe that are expected to begin around the first of the year.

The primary purpose of the controversial new weapon, however, is defense. We are not going to use it to attack the Soviet Union or its Warsaw Pact allies. If the weapon is ever used, it will be to stave off defeat by an enemy that has engaged in a military buildup far beyond its legitimate defense needs, an enemy that has more than 200 medium-range nuclear missiles aimed at Western Europe.

THE CHRISTIAN SCIENCE MONITOR
Boston, Mass., August 10, 1981

The new furor over America's neutron bomb dramatizes the necessity of improving conventional means of deterring aggression so that this weapon is never used. The production of the "enhanced radiation warhead," to use its more descriptive name, should at least be part of a clearly defined overall defense doctrine. Even such an advocate of the weapon as Reagan transition adviser William Van Cleave has said that it is worthless without such a doctrine.

Perhaps the United States has developed a doctrine to a greater extent than is evident. But neither the White House nor the State Department explained the neutron bomb's role in a larger scheme of things as the reports of President Reagan's decision to produce it came out over the weekend.

Rather there appeared to be disagreement within the administration on the decision to go ahead at this time. The reported situation behind the scenes echoed the unusual public moment in February when Defense Secretary Weinberger gave his personal opinion in favor of going ahead — and Secretary of State Haig was sufficiently concerned to cable NATO members that this did not represent official US policy.

Europeans have been understandably wary about the neutron weapon not only because of President Carter's on-and-off position but because of growing popular disapproval of the planned deployment of new theater nuclear weapons on European soil. The enhanced radiation warhead would add the exploitable image of a battlefield nuclear weapon that could be exploded as close to the ground as 500 feet with insignificant blast damage to property but with neutron radiation fatal up to half a mile. Europeans are concerned, too, about the radiation sickness predicted for civilians around the edges of the battlefield.

Critics note that the killing or incapacitation of troops would ordinarily not be swift, so that they could fight effectively for a half hour or more before succumbing perhaps weeks later. Besides this disadvantage as a weapon, there is the question of whether the warhead's low-yield characteristics make it more likely to be used than other nuclear arms and thus a more credible deterrent. If the idea is to make the use of nuclear arms more thinkable, this is a kind of credibility the world can do without.

Moscow reportedly has not done much with low-yield battlefield weapons and still sticks to the concept of massive reaction should the West start using nuclear arms of any degree. Indeed, according to an Arms Control and Disarmament Agency report submitted by the last administration, the deployment of neutron warheads in Europe might increase Soviet propensities to use regular nuclear weapons in a war. The report said that fitting the warheads on missiles and artillery shells, as the present administration has now decided to do, would have "only slight impact" on "the course of ongoing arms control negotiations, efforts to stem nu-

clear proliferation, deterrence and stability in Europe, or the destructiveness of war should it occur."

In the light of all this, why would the US want to start stockpiling such weapons? For one thing, they would then become available for deployment to serve the intended purpose of stopping any attack by Soviet tanks in Central Europe, where Soviet armor is reported to have a three-to-one superiority over the allied forces. Among immediate reasons cited is Mr. Reagan's agreement with Mr. Weinberger that the Europeans should not be allowed a kind of veto over US arms decisions, nor should such decisions be left hostage to allied backing for the new theater nuclear weapons. The US has already agreed to theater arms control talks in connection with those weapons. This administration evidently wants to get back to the more independent US nuclear decisionmaking familiar before Mr. Carter agonized back and forth on European attitudes toward the neutron bomb.

To be sure, the allies should not have a veto over the US. On the other hand, to consult with them and recognize their apprehensions is not to grant such a veto. The US wisely says it has no intention of reaching a decision on deploying the warheads without full consultation.

It is hypocritical in the extreme for Moscow to try to make propaganda hay out of calling on the US to forgo this escalation in the arms race. The Soviets have been pushing that race to the point of missiles threatening Europe and other moves that mean both the Europeans and the Americans must look to their defenses. The case for the necessity of the enhanced radiation warhead in this equation has not yet been proven. It behooves America and its allies to bolster their other defenses while the controversy clears.

ST. LOUIS POST-DISPATCH
St. Louis, Mo., August 26, 1981

In the wake of President Reagan's announcement that neutron weapons have been put in production, Chancellor Helmut Schmidt has braved a bitter political storm by publicly arguing that he will not unilaterally ban the weapon's deployment in West Germany. The chancellor has restated the 1978 West German cabinet decision that outlined Bonn's three conditions for deploying the weapons in Germany: neutron weapons must be deployed in other NATO nations as well as West Germany; the European deployment of the weapons must be a joint NATO decision; and NATO and Warsaw Pact nuclear arms control negotiations must have failed.

By stressing that a European neutron weapon deployment would only be made "after very careful considerations," Chancellor Schmidt is attempting to defuse this highly emotional issue and to buy political time for President Reagan.

Secretary of State Alexander Haig has pledged that the U.S. will begin European nuclear arms control talks with the Soviets before the end of the year. However, many West Europeans, including some high ranking West German politicians, are already questioning American sincerity. These critics argue that the U.S. is not interested in arms control talks and is only concerned with deploying a whole new generation of U.S. tactical nuclear weapons in Europe — of which, the neutron ordnance and the 572 Pershing II missiles and ground-launched cruise missiles are a major part.

Chancellor Schmidt fears that many West European are starting to believe that the Soviets are more willing to control nuclear weapons than are the Americans. If that becomes the majority opinion, U.S.-West European relations will be in for a very rough period. It is for President Reagan to prove this thinking wrong.

THE SUN
Baltimore, Md., August 14, 1981

The neutron bomb is an awesome weapon. Just like any bomb, its purpose is to kill people, but it kills them in a different and extremely effective way — by releasing massive doses of radiation. In the process it does not blow everything to smithereens: It leaves intact cities and buildings and bridges, and weapons of war such as tanks. It just kills people.

This the bomb President Reagan wants to build and stockpile. Is he out of his mind? Not at all. As horrible as it would be if it were used, the neutron bomb will give the United States and the nations of the NATO alliance something they desperately need — a truly effective deterrent against the Kremlin starting a war. In fact, the bomb may be the best way to keep the world from destroying itself.

Poised on the border of Western Europe are the Soviet and Warsaw Pact armies, supposedly the strongest military force the world has ever seen. If these armies invade Western Europe, the experts seem to agree, they would be victorious in a matter of weeks or even days, such is the power of their infantry divisions and their armor. NATO forces would be almost powerless to stop the onslaught. Powerless, that is, with one exception: The West could resort — as it has said it will in such an event — to massive nuclear retaliation.

As Secretary of Defense Caspar Weinberger points out in his article on the Letters/Opinion page, the neutron bomb as an alternative is much saner than the suicidal defense policies the United States and other NATO forces now embrace.

And that threat of massive nuclear retaliation is no guarantee the Soviets and their allies will not

start a war. They might start a conventional war, which they know they could win, in the belief that the United States and NATO would not launch its big atomic missiles for fear of being wiped out themselves. And a crisis situation, such as Poland, could further tempt a Soviet gamble.

In sum, too much of a risk for the world to bear. The neutron bomb puts the Warsaw Pact on notice that the West is now able to neutralize the advantage the East has in troops and armor without resorting to total nuclear war. It removes any doubt the Kremlin may have as to the resolve of NATO in the event that Western Europe comes under attack.

President Reagan's decision to stockpile neutron weapons is a message Moscow understands. Indeed, the Soviet Union's outrage would be nonexistent if the president's action were not one that puts an end to the superior advantage — and an end to the danger inherent in such an advantage — of the Warsaw Pact.

The Kremlin's suggestion that it, too, will have to develop neutron weapons for defensive reasons is ludicrous — the West, after all, hasn't the troops and the armor to threaten the East. So, if the Soviets produce neutron weapons, such production will do nothing to alter the balance of power.

There is one sure way to end production of neutron weapons, and we bet the Soviet Union is well aware of it. If the Kremlin is truly serious about disarmament, it need only negotiate in good faith to reduce its stockpile of conventional weapons. Then, and only then, should the United States rethink its position on stockpiling neutron bombs.

The Register

Santa Ana, Calif., August 23, 1981

Few people can fail to be concerned about nuclear weapons that serve as instruments of mass destruction. Even if such weapons are used for defensive purposes, they are likely to kill thousands, perhaps millions, of innocent bystanders. It would probably be a happier world if such weapons were abolished from the face of the earth. But a glance at reality indicates that such an abolition is unlikely. Even if people were willing to accept the enhanced supra-national power that would be necessary to enforce a ban on nuclear weapons (and we're not the only people who would question the creation of such a power) as a trade-off for a nuclear weapon-free world, the likelihood is that not even a powerful and repressive world government would be able to enforce an effective ban on nuclear weapons.

Given that reality, perhaps the best that friends of liberty and justice can hope for is the possibility that future weapons choices will be available with reduced mass-murder consequences. In the face of the fact that nuclear weapons exist, perhaps we should strive for weapons that are defensive in nature, selective in application, and able to inflict maximum damage on invaders and aggressors while minimizing the effects on our own population and on local civilians and noncombatants.

In light of that background, it is difficult to understand the uproar over the tentative decision to deploy enhanced radiation warheads (popularly nicknamed "neutron bombs") in Europe.

Ideally, of course, the United States should not be paying for 42 percent of Europe's defense and mass destruction weapons should be eliminated. We'll continue to hold that ideal out as an ultimate goal, and do what we can to move toward it. But a decision on neutron weapons must be considered in the context of current reality in Europe.

Part of that reality is that the Warsaw Pact nations have beefed up and modernized their forces in the past decade or so, while NATO forces have remained at a fairly static level. The Warsaw Pact troops have newer tanks, antitank weapons, artillery and armored vehicles than do the NATO troops. An honest debate is possible about whether this Warsaw Pact build-up is the prelude to an invasion or blackmail of Western Europe, especially in light of the communist bloc's problems in Poland, a key element of Warsaw Pact military planning. But the prudent thing for NATO is to have a credible defense against such a possible invasion even if an actual invasion is unlikely.

At present the NATO deterrent against an invasion from the East includes tactical nuclear weapons in the form of artillery shells and the short-range Lance missile. These weapons range in size from 10 to 50 kilotons. They embody the most objectionable aspects of nuclear weapons. Their use would probably leave a 1-1/4 mile radius of devastation that would be a radioactive crater for decades, as well as producing radioactive fallout for miles around.

The neutron weapons are designed to produce intense blast and radiation within a small area (140-yard radius); out to 900 yards they would produce a deadly spray of neutrons; up to a mile away the neutrons would cause some radiation sickness and death; effects beyond a mile would be minimal; fallout is virtually nothing.

The superiority of such a weapon for *defensive* purposes is easy to understand. They could be focused with a reasonable amount of precision on invading tanks and troops while sparing most of the surrounding population and their homes and factories. Bear in mind that if these weapons are used at all, they would be used in Western Europe.

Without neutron weapons, Western Europe would face two choices if the Warsaw Pact mounted an invasion. It could use the tactical nuclear weapons now in place (destroying huge areas and killing millions of civilians) or succumb after a half-hearted resistance.

The most serious argument against neutron weapons is that they could be destabilizing because they might be used. The suggestion is that the use of low-destruction nuclear weapons like the neutron warheads would release some kind of psychological trigger, making it more likely that escalation to a full-scale nuclear war could occur.

One should not ignore that psychological aspect. But this argument is seriously misleading. The strategic advantage of neutron weapons is that they are a more credible deterrent than 10 to 50 kiloton tactical nukes. One could understand a certain reluctance on the part of West Germans to obliterate their homeland in the face of an invasion threat. If one-kiloton neutron weapons were available, however, they would help to constitute a believable defense posture.

Neutron weapons may make defense against invasion of Western Europe more credible. They would greatly reduce the harm to bystanders and their property, compared to present systems.

Again, we're not fans of any weapons system, nor do we take lightly the threat of killing anybody. But in light of the current situation and the possible threat, we have trouble understanding the intensity of the objection to neutron weapons in some quarters.

The Oregonian

Portland, Ore., August 11, 1981

President Reagan's approval of production of the neutron bomb is a mixed blessing, politically and militarily.

The Aug. 8 announcement is a clear sign that the Reagan administration holds firm in its resolve to shore up U.S. military capacity and in the national commitment to the defense of others. Nevertheless, the president will be forced to deal with troublesome issues related to the neutron decision.

First, the neutron bomb, more properly known as an enhanced radiation/reduced blast weapon, has been surrounded by such negative public perceptions that Reagan will have to make clear its precise application in the West's defensive scheme. In fact, the administration has announced it will build the shells with neutron tips and not deploy them in Europe at this time.

Opponents have called the weapon cruel and inhumane because it is designed to destroy human beings with limited effect on property. The weapon's supporters have said that as long as nuclear weapons are part of the West's arsenal, the neutron bomb would be one of the best ones because its limited target area allows it to be used on attacking troops while sparing civilians and communities on the edge of a battlefield. Deployment of the neutron bomb is unlikely to garner any more support until its strategic purpose is better defined.

Second is the question about the ultimate use of the weapons. A later decision to deploy them, most likely in Western Europe, will cause tremendously bitter debate in the affected countries, and that debate will make few friends for the United States, even though the weapon is supposed to be used for defensive purposes.

Third, the weapon's effectiveness is still very much in question. Although it is designed to incapacitate military personnel such as tank drivers, it does not take effect instantly. Thus, even after escalation to nuclear warfare, attackers might be able to accomplish their maneuvers before suffering disabling effects.

Fourth, the administration may be politically motivated to propose this tough military program to point to if a decision is made in the future to scrap another program such as the MX missile. However, if the hope is to use the neutron bomb as a bargaining chip in future negotiations with the Soviets, something to cast aside in return for a Russian promise to do so with another program, the administration may have to think again. The Soviets already have said that they would consider developing the weapon if the United States does, making mutual cancellations of its production an exercise in futility if it can be stopped now.

Finally, the issue points up the administration's dangerous disinclination to rely more heavily on the buildup of conventional deterrent forces. These, The Oregonian believes, are central to any non-suicidal defense scheme. The best that can be said of Reagan's go-ahead for neutron bomb production is that it may encourage our European allies to increase their conventional arms capacity rather than face last-resort deployment of the ironically misnamed "clean bomb."

Post-Tribune
Guarding Your Interests Daily

Gary, Ind., August 12, 1981

The Kremlin is openly irate and several of our European allies — plus, of course, the dove wing at home — are more than a little irritated by President Reagan's decision to go ahead with production and stockpiling of neutron atomic warheads.

If it provoked the sort of anger which might make Moscow, through fear, more willing to talk nuclear arms control in terms Washington would consider more reasonable, then that might be to the good. If it spurred only angry rhetoric from Pravda and Tass, then that could be shrugged off by us and understood by our friends. But if — and this is highly possible — it steps up the nuclear arms race one more notch it could be both costly and dangerous.

Further, were these weapons of greater total destructiveness as was the case with the hydrogen bomb and the MIRV (multiple targetable) systems, the complaints of our European allies might be easier hushed on grounds we had to make the superpower decisions because we were the only member of the Western Alliance capable of carrying them out.

Since the neutron weapons, however, are designed for battlefield rather than intercontinental use, it means their most conceivable use would be to try to stop an armored thrust from the Warsaw Pact area into West Europe. That being the case, the neutron warheads — to be fired from howitzers or on relatively short-range missiles — would have to be launched in Europe to be effective.

The Pentagon has sought to calm West European fears — which only West Germany's Helmut Schmidt among government leaders had the nerve to buck both when President Jimmy Carter first pondered neutron development and again now — by announcing there are no plans "at this time" to consider deployment outside the United States.

It's rather obvious, though, that it would make tactical sense only to stockpile such an arsenal where it could be quickly air-shipped abroad should use of the warheads be thought needed.

The loudest original protest in this country was aimed at the awkwardly expressed — though partially accurate — claim that such weapons were "cleaner" than others in the nuclear arsenal and could kill people by radiation, even through the walls of armored tanks, with less accompanying demolition of surrounding structures. The real point there is that the neutron weapon's destructiveness can be somewhat more confined making it more conceivable as a battlefield weapon than one of total area destructiveness.

Therein, though, could lie its principal danger. If destructiveness can be more confined there might be more temptation to use such a weapon — as, for example, to stop an invasion by the obviously stronger Soviet tank forces into West Europe. Once, however, any type of nuclear weapon is used, the other side might almost certainly take that as an excuse to loose the other atomic weapons in an exchange sure to destroy civilization as we know it.

Running such a risk is, of course, not the Reagan administration's aim. It is sincere in the argument that only by stepping up American strength in every military field can we hope to restrain Soviet expansion or the eventual possibility of a Soviet first nuclear strike.

Still, in a world where at least two major powers hold the capability of mutual devastation, provocation may be the most immediate danger.

On those grounds we would have preferred keeping wraps on the neutron warhead. That no longer seems possible since the weekend's announcement.

We fall back, therefore, on the hope that the next Washington nuclear move might be toward a resumption of talks and away from further provocative escalation — justifiable or not.

The State

Columbia, S.C., August 13, 1981

NO ONE in his right mind likes to think about nuclear warfare, either tactical or strategic. But the existence of nuclear weapons of various sizes and kinds is a fact of modern life that all the hand-wringing and wishful thinking cannot change.

President Reagan has given the go-ahead for the production of yet another kind of nuke, a tactical weapon called the neutron bomb. This baby causes chill bumps to rise on many individuals because it kills people while causing minimum damage to property.

A decision to build a weapon described in that manner might seem to some to display a callous disregard for human life. It's immoral, one might say.

But is it? The neutron bomb was designed with one principal purpose in mind: to deter or blunt a massive armored attack in Central Europe without doing as much damage to the structures and people on the edges of the battlefield as the use of regular nuclear weapons would do and that even all-out conventional war can do. The neutron bomb's high radiation would penetrate tanks and kill crews. But it produces less heat and blast damage than regular nukes and churns up much less radioactive debris than would be sucked up into the atmosphere. One aim is to reduce civilian casualties.

Indecisiveness about building the neutron weapon contributed heavily to Jimmy Carter's reputation as a weak President. Mr. Carter decided to build the weapon and persuaded the reluctant government of West Germany, the likely first point of a Soviet land attack in Central Europe, to accept it on its soil. The Russians launched a massive propaganda campaign against the new bomb. Many Europeans, including West Germans, became alarmed, and Mr. Carter stopped production.

The reversal of that decision by Mr. Reagan is just one of the many ways he has shown that he intends to be known as a bold and resolute President.

The Soviets, predictably, have again broken out the grossest hyperboles their propagandists can think up. They called the neutron bomb "the most inhuman type of weapon of mass annihilation," ignoring the much greater destructive power of regular nukes. They said that "the same cannibalistic instincts prevail now in the White House" that caused President Truman to order the first use of atomic weapons at the end of World War II. The decision to build the bomb, the Soviets said, confirms that the "prattlings" of the United States about its interest in arms control are a "rude deception designed to camouflage the Reagan administration's course for preparing a nuclear war."

Mr. Reagan obviously hit the Soviets' sore point. The USSR has a sizable advantage over the NATO forces in tanks, manpower and some other conventional weapons. Defense Secretary Caspar Weinberger, leading the verbal counterattack for the United States, said the sharp Russian reaction was expected because the new bomb would "neutralize their advantage" in conventional forces. "If you have this weapon, you can prevent Day One (of a Soviet invasion) from occurring."

We believe Mr. Weinberger is reading the Russians rightly. We cannot forecast what the USSR's response will be beyond the propaganda onslaught. If the Administration hasn't miscalculated — and we don't think it has — the deterrent value of this bomb could increase Soviet caution, lead to realistic arms control talks down the line, and enhance the likelihood that peace can be maintained.

The Birmingham News

Birmingham, Ala., August 11, 1981

President Reagan's decision to assemble the so-called neutron bomb and stockpile it in the United States was a necessary one. The battlefield device will not be deployed in other countries in the immediate future and may never be, short of a shooting war with the Soviet Union.

As expected, the decision has been greeted with alarm by anti-nuclear activists in most of Western Europe. The Soviet Union has also added its voice to those who object to its manufacture, and that is not unreasonable considering that Soviet soldiers would be the bombs' targets in event of war.

It is regrettable that so much misunderstanding about the device still exists. The U.S. media must take some responsibility for not shedding real light on the subject and accepting the rhetoric of left-wing European groups and Soviet propagandists.

The decision to develop the bomb was made in the beginning not at the urging of the U.S. military but because influential members of the West German government insisted on it. However, after facing criticism at home, those officials later retreated when former President Carter refused to back them up and waffled on the decision to manufacture the device.

The bomb has been labeled by Europe's leftist media and the Kremlin as a weapon designed to destroy people instead of buildings. Such was not and is not the intent of the designers. The bomb was designed with a low explosive yield so as to restrict its effect to the battlefield and not kill helpless civilian populations a few miles distant.

The bomb does have a relatively high radiation yield and would kill enemy troops, but that is what it is designed to do so that an invasion from Eastern Europe could be met without destroying West European civilization in the process.

If bombs could be labeled humane or inhumane, the neutron bomb is certainly more humane than some others that take a terrible toll in civilian lives as they did during World War II.

With the present imbalance between Soviet forces and armaments in Eastern Europe and NATO, the neutron device will be another deterrent, not a panacea for defending Europe. And eventually, if the Kremlin is unsuccessful in using threats of war to blackmail and neutralize European governments, the countries which now object to the bomb's manufacture very well could seek to have it stockpiled on their own soil in the not-too distant future.

THE LOUISVILLE TIMES

Louisville, Ky., August 12, 1981

The neutron bomb, which kills people while leaving structures and machinery intact, would, according to Pentagon theorists, deter Soviet tank armies from plunging into Western Europe.

But this ingeniously selective nuclear weapon is also politically explosive. The very mention of it by a highly placed American official, as Secretary of State Alexander Haig tried in vain to remind his colleagues in the administration last week, causes alarm and consternation in much of Western Europe. Indeed, the neutron bomb can do as much to deter cooperation among NATO allies as it does to keep the Soviet tanks at bay.

Whatever its military significance, therefore, the President's weekend announcement that the United States will produce the bomb was, from a foreign policy standpoint, singularly inept. The likely result will be to place further strain on a shaky alliance and to reinforce those forces in Europe that are pushing for unilateral disarmament.

While Mr. Haig can match the most hawkish Reaganaut when it comes to anti-Soviet bombast, he is also sensitive to the political problems facing Chancellor Helmut Schmidt of West Germany and the trend toward neutralism in Holland, Scandinavia and even Britain. And he understands that the neutron bomb will weaken rather than reinforce Western defenses if it undercuts pro-NATO leaders. Unfortunately,

he lost the Oval Office debate to saber-rattling Defense Secretary Caspar Weinberger.

While American hawks like to condemn what they consider "better-red-than-dead" defeatism, Europeans do have ample cause to worry about the growth of nuclear arsenals on both sides of the Elbe. They foresee a nuclear disaster that might begin with the firing of a small neutron weapon at Soviet tank units and escalate into an exchange of tactical nuclear weapons. Europe, according to this scenario, could end up as a "nuclear sponge," while the two superpowers remain unscathed.

The neutron bomb unquestionably has military virtues that might at some point make its deployment desirable. Because it releases intense, but short-lived, radiation that could kill enemy soldiers without excessive danger to civilian populations or their cities, it seems well-suited for use in densely populated Central Europe.

As critics point out, however, these same characteristics could also have the insidious effect of sanitizing nuclear war, of making it seem less awful. No matter how you cut it, moreover, building the neutron weapon is an escalation, a raising of the nuclear stakes. The other side will now feel obliged to build one, too.

The Europeans' much saner approach is to make "improvements" in the NATO missile arsenal contingent on another stab at arms control talks with Russia. Because Europe is also leery about the deployment of new medium-range and cruise missiles to counter those installed by the Russians, Secretary Haig agreed last spring to approach Moscow about reductions on both sides before the weapons are in place.

However, the administration has repudiated the SALT treaty and shows little enthusiasm for arms control talks. Now it has decided, without consulting European leaders, to spend a billion or so of the trillion dollars that will flow into Pentagon coffers in the next several years on a weapon that can be counted on to stir up strong passions in NATO capitals.

The argument that the decision is strictly an American one requiring no discussions with other governments will carry little weight with our allies. While it's true that neutron weapons will be made and stored in this country, they are clearly designed for European battlefields.

Mr. Reagan's damn-the-torpedoes approach will please those who hunger for a showdown with the Soviet Union. Given the current state of European politics, however, the President would have better served the long-term goal of Western unity if he had listened to Mr. Haig's plea to proceed cautiously and at a more propitious time.

THE MILWAUKEE JOURNAL

Milwaukee, Wisc., August 12, 1981

The Reagan administration's decision to assemble and stockpile the neutron bomb is worrisome. It is a weapon intended to check invasions by conventional forces — tanks and infantry. But because it is nuclear, its use would immediately put the US and the attacker (presumably Russia) on the ladder of nuclear escalation. There probably would be little chance then of turning back from full-scale nuclear war.

Admittedly, Defense Secretary Caspar Weinberger makes several plausible points in favor of the neutron bomb (actually a warhead whose delivery would be by shell or missile). He argues that the weapon can (1) deter the Russians from invading with their superior tank forces and manpower and (2) give this country a bargaining chip in eventual negotiations with Moscow on arms reduction.

It also can be argued that the neutron warhead is no more ugly than any other weapon. All instruments of war are monstrous, from the hand grenade to the hydrogen bomb. However, there *is* an important distinction between conventional and strategic nuclear weaponry; the latter can destroy human civilization. We fear that the neutron weapon blurs the distinction and that Weinberger is encouraging the dangerous fallacy of "limited" nuclear combat.

As for the sanctimonious howling by the Russians about "this barbarous weapon," we are unimpressed. Naturally they don't like it, because its purpose is to repeal their advantage in conventional warfare. However, Moscow's threat to meet the

challenge with a program of its own has to be taken even more seriously. Not that a neutron bomb in Soviet hands would be so alarming. Its supposed usefulness is as a defensive weapon against massed assault, which is not the way the US would fight a war against the USSR. But if the Kremlin has some other weapon program in mind as a countermove and is not just blustering, the US could find that it has not improved its bargaining position after all.

There also has to be concern for allied reaction, even though the weapon is to be stockpiled in the US, not deployed abroad. Many Europeans are neutralist-minded these days, particularly in the smaller countries, so a new emotional issue has been handed to agitators against a strong NATO — particularly against deploying medium-range nuclear missiles on European territory to offset the threat of Soviet SS-20 missiles aimed at Western Europe.

All things considered, we wonder why the Reagan administration didn't just sit tight. Components for the neutron bomb were already on hand, thanks to the Carter administration's decision to make them but not assemble them. It has not been explained how much time is being saved in the extra step of assembling the warheads, except in Weinberger's statement that they could be on their way to a hot spot where they are needed (not necessarily European) in a matter of hours.

Maybe the shortened time is important, although it would seem that the move could be delayed until war clouds actually gather. For now, we're just afraid that readying the weapon will be unnecessarily provocative.

Seven-Year Civil Defense Program Authorized by Reagan

President Ronald Reagan March 29, 1982 issued an order for a $4.2 billion program to prepare a civil defense plan in case of nuclear attack. According to a spokesman for the Federal Emergency Management Agency, the program was intended to double the number of people who could be expected to survive a nuclear attack. (Current estimates put the survival rate at 40% of the American population.) Reagan's civil defense plan relied on an advance warning of at least one week before a nuclear attack, based on the assumption that a surprise attack was less likely than "a general exchange that would come out of a period of heightened international tension" with the Soviet Union. It called for evacuating residents from 380 "high-risk areas" such as missile fields, strategic bomber bases and nuclear submarine ports. The evacuated residents would be moved to "host areas" chosen by the states. Special shelters would be provided for "key industrial workers" in the "high-risk areas" and for "key defense and population relocation support industries." A Defense Department official termed the seven-year program a "modest" effort that represented "little more than insurance—insurance that in circumstances short of a central strategic exchange, some lives might be saved that would otherwise be lost."

BUFFALO EVENING NEWS

Buffalo, N.Y., April 5, 1982

At a time when President Reagan is supposed to be seeking ways to cut back on federal spending, he has announced plans for a seven-year, $4.2 billion civil defense program that can only be described as unsettling — literally and figuratively. It involves the relocation of up to two-thirds of the American population, including the evacuation of every major city in the country.

The program is based on the assumption that nuclear war might not come as a bolt out of the blue but as the climax to weeks of rising tension. This would, it is imagined, enable everyone to get out of high-risk areas.

There are several major flaws in this whole idea, starting with the intriguing question: What would the Russians be doing, assuming they were planning a nuclear strike, during the week or so it would take to clear out our cities? Indeed, the very act of evacuation could be expected to dangerously heighten tensions that were already existing.

Beyond these catastrophic issues, there are such practical matters as the feeding and housing of two-thirds of the population away from home and trying to operate a country made up mostly of such "refugees."

Sen. Alan Cranston, D-Calif., has described the evacuation plan as a "total waste of money and an economic tragedy." Adm. Noel A.M. Gayler, former commander of American forces in the Pacific, similarly called it a waste and said it could not save lives. One argument for the plan is that the Russians already have a substantial civil defense program, but Adm. Gayler asserted that the Soviet program "is a turkey, as they are beginning to realize."

It is hard to believe that this evacuation idea is a serious proposal, and yet, far out as it is, it is less strange than some other ideas that have been reported as emanating from the Pentagon.

Thomas K. Jones, deputy under secretary of defense, reportedly expressed this hopeful view of nuclear war in an interview: "Everybody's going to make it if there are enough shovels to go around." He explained: "Dig a hole, cover it with a couple of doors and then throw three feet of dirt on top. It's the dirt that does it."

Later, Mr. Jones said some of his remarks in the interview had been taken out of context and misinterpreted. He said he did not recall saying, as had been reported, that the United States could recover completely from a nuclear war in two to four years. The Los Angeles Times, which has a tape recording of the eight-hour interview, stands by its report.

This kind of casual talk about nuclear war has stirred fears in some quarters that the Pentagon considers it as some kind of military option, rather than a cataclysmic disaster for the human race.

President Reagan has tried to counteract this impression, saying in his recent news conference that, in a nuclear war, "I don't think there could be any winners."

Nevertheless, the image of his administration is not enhanced by some of its more extreme spokesmen — nor by the current plan to spend vast sums developing a program for evacuating most of the American people on the wholly implausible premise that the nation would have at least a week's advance notice of an imminent Soviet nuclear attack.

The Star-Ledger

Newark, N.J., April 3, 1982

Many of us have short memories and tend to forget the major public policy debates of the past. And that is why these debates so frequently repeat themselves.

In the early 1960s, President John Kennedy proposed that the nation make an enormous investment in fallout shelters that would be used in the event of a nuclear attack. The President said this could save lives. Much of the nation disagreed.

Opponents of the plan argued that a nuclear attack would be so devastating that the fallout shelters would be of minimal assistance. The plan wasn't abandoned but it was put on the back burner and we have heard little of civil defense since then.

Suddenly, the controversy has re-emerged. The Reagan Administration is asking Congress to appropriate $4.2 billion for a new seven-year plan to beef up civil defense. The Administration claims this will "provide for survival of a substantial portion of the population in the event of nuclear attack."

There are a couple of new elements and arguments since the debate of two decades ago. The earlier program concentrated more heavily on private fallout shelters in individual homes while this stresses moving people from the city to the countryside. And proponents of civil defense argue that because the Soviet Union has built a huge system, this country should emulate it.

* * *

But in most respects, the same arguments, pro and con, are being repeated from two decades ago. The arguments against spending huge amounts on civil defense are just as convincing and the arguments in favor of it just as unconvincing as they were then.

On one level, the construction of an elaborate civil defense system would raise false hopes that we could come through a nuclear attack in reasonably good shape. Most of the scientific evidence seems to indicate that a nuclear attack remains a totally devastating possibility.

The secondary arguments for a nuclear system are plagued with false assumptions. It seems most unlikely that there could be orderly evacuation at a time of widespread panic. And even if there could, irradiated crops, water supplies and wildlife and the absence of hospitals and sewer systems would make survival impossible. Nor is the fact that the Soviets built an elaborate system that may be fatally flawed a good precedent for our doing the same.

Moreover, the cost argument weighs heavily against it. It makes no sense at all, at a time of fiscal crisis, when budgets are pared to the bone and many deserving domestic programs must be heavily pared, to spend $4.2 billion on a system whose benefits are, even under the most favorable assumptions, likely to prove illusory. The best way to deal with this program is to relegate it back to the history books from which it emerged far too soon.

THE LOUISVILLE TIMES

Louisville, Ky., April 1, 1982

Apparently unable to find any more empty military defense crannies in which to stuff greenbacks, the Reagan administration has turned to that proven abyss, civil defense. The President's proposed budget includes $252 million, about double the amount being spent this year for civil defense to "provide for survival of a substantial portion of the U. S. population in the event of nuclear attack."

Even though the plan calls for six more years of appropriations, that amount is peanuts, of course, in the magnanimous world of Reagan defense spending. Yet, it is less of a bargain if one considers that the plan it would put into effect is worthless.

In brief, it calls for orderly evacuation of millions of Americans from large- and medium-sized cities into small towns in case of nuclear attack. That assumes at least several days' warning from the Soviet Union before it fires off any missiles. It also assumes that no one would panic, that our transportation network could handle the largest mass evacuation ever seen in the world and that our small towns would welcome and care for this horde from the cities.

As Thomas K. Jones, deputy under-secretary of defense for strategic theater nuclear forces, told a *Los Angeles Times* reporter in January, it could even be easier than that. Our secret weapons for survival are shovels and doors, according to Mr. Jones. Each American has only to dig a trench, lay a couple of doors atop it and cover them with three feet of dirt. After Armageddon is over, we all climb out of our trenches, and everything is back to normal in two to four years.

A Senate Foreign Affairs subcommittee wanted Mr. Jones to elaborate in person on these intriguing ideas, but he dodged them until yesterday, when he appeared under threat of a contempt citation. Mr. Jones now says he was misquoted or misunderstood, although the reporter claims he has tapes to back up his story. Nevertheless, a statement the Defense Department tried to send the subcommittee in place of the elusive Mr. Jones a few weeks ago offered a much grimmer rationale for the civil defense proposal.

It conceded that it is impossible "to obtain levels of protection from the effects of all-out nuclear war that would reduce significantly the unspeakable horror of such an event." The proposed civil defense program, it suggested, is "a minimal effort ... that might diminish the loss of lives ...."

That's still way too optimistic. Perhaps even estimates that up to one-fourth of the human race would somehow survive are also wildly optimistic. Certainly populations of target areas such as the United States and Soviet Union wouldn't do nearly that well.

In part, at least, this latest boondoggle may result from our keep-up-with-Ivan outlook in Washington these days. The Soviet Union has poured billions into a similar screwball scheme which retired Adm. Noel A. M. Gayler, former commander of U. S. forces in the Pacific, typifies as "a turkey."

It is also dangerous, because it is liable to breed a false sense of security. All-out nuclear war would obliterate the world. The only way to survive one is not to have one, and disarmament is the only way to make sure of that. Our government's energies must be devoted to ridding the world of nuclear weapons, not convincing the world that it can survive them.

The Detroit News

Detroit, Mich., April 7, 1982

Civil defense evacuation plans come and go. Remember in the early 1960s when everyone was building a bomb shelter for protection against a Soviet attack? Now the Reagan administration has its plan, only this one would cost taxpayers $4.2 billion in the next seven years — not counting inflation. That's right, $4.2 billion!

The idea is for the 145 million people in cities of more than 50,000 population — such as Orlando — to be evacuated to rural areas for hiding. Unlike the earlier plans, though, the government would not ask for civilian help until a nuclear attack was imminent. Instead, during peacetime, the government would train 20,000 instructors in shelter management who would then teach millions of others in a crisis.

There is one catch. For the plan to work, the United States would have to be alerted to the attack at least several days ahead of time, preferably a week.

That kind of puts a damper on the whole thing. If for some reason the Soviets aren't polite enough to let us in on their planned attack, or if our intelligence agents slip up just this once, the plan wouldn't work.

Might it even be possible that, given this much notice, the Soviets might just switch their targets from the cities to the rural evacuation areas? Nevertheless, the supposedly budget-cutting administration seems intent on pushing this plan through Congress, asking for nearly $252 million this year.

The worst part of this whole thing, however, is that it tries to make us think that a nuclear war might be palatable — something that can be fought and, indeed, won.

Talk about disasters. This plan is one we can do without.

'TO FIGHT THE UNWINNABLE FIGHT, TO SURVIVE THE UNSURVIVABLE WAR ...'

ALBUQUERQUE JOURNAL

Albuquerque, N.M., April 9, 1982

A Pony Express mentality seems to be directing the Reagan administration's plans to protect millions of Americans from the horrible consequences of a nuclear attack. Let's hope the attitude is shorter lived than was the 19th century mail service.

But how else can anyone explain the strange expectation that the Soviet Union would give us eight days warning before it launches its missiles? That's the time it took the Pony Express to get a letter across the country by horseback.

The administration plans to spend $4.5 billion in the next seven years to plan for evacuation of 319 "high risk" cities and 61 defense installations. Albuquerque would be one of the choice targets.

There are obvious advantages to an eight-day warning. We could all stock up on supplies at the local grocery and department stores. We could pack the family car with survival gear, pets and the family jewels. We could even say goodbye to our friends and lock up the old homestead. The latter seems somewhat foolish since we'd have to presume nothing would be left to return to if we somehow survive an attack and its horrible aftermath.

You can't help wondering, however, what the United States and the Soviet Union would be doing those eight days while Americans docilely prepared to move 50 to 60 miles to host areas away from their cities. And what would the Soviets be doing when its satellites showed us streaming out of our cities? The least they'd do is re-target their missiles to the host areas.

The insanity of the scenario is breathtaking. Between them, the United States and Soviet Union have 50,000 nuclear warheads. President Reagan wants 17,000 new nuclear weapons in the next decade. When we build more, the Soviets will build more. Nuclear weapons, after all, have become predominantly weapons of political intimidation. The Soviets seek advantage while the United States seeks relief from anxiety.

The survivors of a nuclear attack could not be fed or cared for, even if they were miles away from ground zero.

There's a strange perversity in the evacuation plan. If Americans are worried about possibly having to dodge nuclear warheads, they're not as likely to worry about unemployment, financing a new home or car or paying last year's taxes.

Rather than planning mass evacuations based upon faulty assumptions, attention and the $4.5 billion could be better focused on preventing doomsday.

Chicago Defender

Chicago, Ill., March 30, 1982

President Reagan has come up with a policy for people to follow in the event of a nuclear attack. It's a beaut. Just go to the telephone and ring up a few numbers and get some nuclear-emergency advice. Ostensibly you will be told where to relocate (if you can get through the rubble). In case of a serious international crisis — as if it isn't serious enough now — you can learn what to do before leaving home in an evacuation, what to take along, what to leave behind, and so forth.

Phone books are now being distributed in a few towns in Maine, the first to contain nuclear-emergency advice. This great news has been announced by a David M. Sparks, regional director for the Federal Emergency Management Agency in Boston.

A better idea is for millions of citizens to go into the streets, as they have done in Europe, and demand an end to official insanity in all countries.

The Dispatch

Columbus, Ohio, April 6, 1982

THE REAGAN administration might better address the realities of the Soviet nuclear threat — and probably save money — by withdrawing its plan for a $4.2 billion civil defense buildup and placing its support behind the development of an emergency medical deployment force capable of responding quickly in the aftermath of a limited nuclear attack.

The administration's current proposal, aimed at helping the country survive an all-out nuclear attack, is being pushed by the Federal Emergency Management Agency which oversees civil defense. The plan calls for a 7-year buildup in preparedness. A key component of the plan is "crisis relocation" — the movement of large portions of the population out of potential target areas and into "safe" zones.

The plan rests on four questionable assumptions: (1) the "safe" zones would be able to receive and sustain large numbers of refugees; (2) sufficient warning of an impending attack would be received in time to undertake a mass relocation; (3) the relocation would be orderly, and (4) there would be areas in the nation that would be spared the consequences of an all-out nuclear attack.

The "safe" zones are so designated because they are lightly developed and of little strategic value to the U.S. defense effort. It is precisely this lack of development, however, that would make it difficult for these zones to accommodate large influxes of people — or to sustain the additional life once the refugees arrived. Inadequate water, food, medical and sanitary facilities would very likely doom any survivors.

There is little chance that sufficient warning would be received to allow for a mass population relocation. A surprise attack is just that, and it is foolhardy to think the Russians would indicate their intentions to launch an attack. But even if there were a warning, there is nothing to prevent the Soviets from aiming a few of their extra bombs on the "safe" zones to which the refugees are fleeing.

If a relocation were ordered, officials would be hard-pressed to prevent panic and insure an orderly flow of people and vehicles to the destination zones. Even minor accidents or vehicle breakdowns could snarl exodus arteries, causing delays and prompting riot.

And while it is impossible to predict the actual consequences of an all-out nuclear attack, evidence is growing that the combination of the initial radiation, firestorms, blast waves and fallout would end animal and plant life across the continent. Those who did survive would likely soon succumb to disease and starvation.

In short, the only way to survive an all-out nuclear attack is to prevent one.

A more prudent civil preparedness undertaking would be the development of an emergency medical deployment force that could respond to the needs of victims of a limited attack.

It is conceivable that the United States and the Soviet Union would exchange single strikes before calling a halt to hostilities and mediating differences. In that instance, survivors in the attack zone would require immediate and substantial outside assistance. And unlike the case of an all-out attack, there would exist outside resources to call upon following a limited exchange.

The emergency medical deployment force would have medicine, food and personnel readily available and would have vehicles capable of transporting aid to the attack zone and victims from the zone to hospitals across the country where they could receive additional treatment.

The emergency medical deployment force would coordinate and utilize existing resources and well serve the nation's needs in a time of tragedy. It should be considered as an alternative to the mass relocation proposal.

The Philadelphia Inquirer
Philadelphia, Pa., April 3, 1982

The Reagan administration has been thinking about the unthinkable. Now it proposes to do something about the unthinkable. It has announced a $4.2 billion, seven-year civil defense plan designed to "provide for survival of a substantial portion of the population in the event of nuclear attack."

Can the administration seriously believe that if there *were* a nuclear attack "a substantial portion of the population" would survive? Does it seriously believe Soviet leaders believe a substantial portion of their population would survive?

One objective of the proposal is to "assist in maintaining perceptions" that the "strategic balance" is favorable to the United States. In other words, the administration assumes that if the men in the Kremlin see how serious the United States is about defending its population from a nuclear attack they will recognize the folly of mixing it up with this country and stay their finger from the button.

That suggests something wrong with the administration's perceptions. What has maintained the strategic balance over the years has been the perception of leaders on both sides that there is no defense from nuclear attack. The basic folly of the administration's plan is that it makes the unthinkable thinkable. It does not make the unthinkable sensible.

There are other flaws. One is that the planners are going on the working assumption that the President would have at least a week's advance notice to get the American people moving out of "high-risk areas" to "host areas."

What do the planners think the Soviet leaders would do when they saw, through their satellite communications (and on American television), the mass movement of Philadelphians to Coatesville, New Yorkers to the wilds of Connecticut, Washingtonians to Roanoke and so on? Would the Soviet leaders, planning a sneak attack to wipe out this country, be gentlemen enough to wait until millions of Americans had removed themselves to (presumed) safety?

Where are those "host areas"? Taking "new federalism" to a new extreme, the administration proposes to leave designating "host areas" up to the states.

And how will millions of Americans get to wherever they're supposed to go? The administration has been slashing funds for transportation programs of all kinds — mass transit, Amtrak, Conrail. Railroads are capable of moving large numbers of people, but the administration considers it unthinkable that Washington should assume any responsibility to help them buy rolling stock or repair their tracks.

The administration ought to think about spending that $4.2 billion and more to provide for the survival of America's moribund transportation network. Call it civil defense. Call it national security. Call it anything, but it makes more sense than a plan that will not deceive the Soviets but could create illusions of security among Americans.

Detroit Free Press
Detroit, Mich., April 24, 1982

THERE IS NOTHING particularly new about the idea of evacuating the population of vulnerable areas if nuclear attack is threatened. President Reagan's emphasis on an evacuation program, however, is the most serious effort in that direction yet. It arouses some concern that the nation's leaders are more inclined than they have been in the past to believe nuclear war is thinkable.

There certainly should be sober consideration of what should be done in the event of nuclear attack. But there is also serious question about the practicality of any plan that requires moving 4.3 million residents of Michigan from the state's urban counties to areas less likely to come under attack. Michigan's tentative plan, for instance, would send 164,094 frightened residents of Detroit and the Grosse Pointes heading north to Grand Traverse County, a wide-open space south of Traverse City that would hardly be prepared to receive them.

Such an evacuation would require at least a week's advance notice, a luxury that would not be likely. Even if there were that much notice, the results would still be utter chaos: traffic jams from Lake Erie to Lake Michigan, fighting, looting, thousands crowding into areas unable to feed and shelter them.

President Eisenhower initiated the interstate highway system as a useful device for dispersing urban populations in event of war and his administration experimented with a three-day evacuation of the president and 15,000 federal employes in 1954. In 1978 President Carter endorsed a similar "crisis relocation" program, and asked an unenthusiastic Congress to provide more than the $100 million allocated to civil defense that year.

This time around, President Reagan is asking for $4.2 billion over seven years to finance the evacuation program. Committed to more arms and a bigger bang as it is, the Reagan administration may be attempting to minimize the risks of arms escalation with a civil defense system that seems to give promise of life and nationhood after the bombs fall.

But very few responsible people believe that a nuclear war could be contained, and that the world as we know it would continue to exist afterward. However ingenious, civil defense systems are no substitute for real arms control.

Governments, Barbara Tuchman pointed out in a recent talk at the University of California at Los Angeles, are unlikely to agree to arms limitation. Ego, lack of agreement on how to proceed, and even the thought of losing the next election work against it. But, finally said Ms. Tuchman, the utter finality of a nuclear war is so obvious that fright may succeed in bringing a settlement that is not attainable by reason.

Real arms control could be achieved by populations truly alarmed at the consequences of an unrestricted nuclear arms race. A civil defense plan that lulls us into thinking that nuclear war is survivable — and therefore possible — will do far more to damage our national security and to obliterate our future than to protect it.

The Seattle Times
Seattle, Wash., April 22, 1982

RANDY Revelle, King County executive, is dead right about at least one issue: The federal "plan" to evacuate the Puget Sound area in case of an imminent nuclear attack is ridiculous.

Revelle last week told King County department heads not to spend more time working on the evacuation plan, because the effects of a nuclear war would be so devastating that the plan wouldn't do much good.

The Federal Emergency Management Agency developed the "crisis relocation" scheme last fall. In a 72-hour period, citizens supposedly would pack up their cars as if for a camping trip and in an orderly, neighborhood-by-neighborhood exit, drive to "host areas" in other counties east of the Cascades, to the north or south.

For one thing, it is ludicrous to think that any evacuation would remain orderly and would not turn into a chaotic, panicky rush that would jam the bridges and main highways out of town. Traffic accidents, cars out of gas, and other snafus would quickly make the plan moot.

And what would evacuees do if they did reach their destination? Clearly, Yakima County could not absorb an extra 401,000 residents, as the plan envisions. The food, shelter, medical and sanitation problems would be staggering — even before the area was hit by radiation fallout that would make it uninhabitable anyway.

Some civil-defense experts have suggested that people could dig holes under their cars, or dig holes and cover them with doors with a few feet of dirt piled on top. But where will all the shovels come from — not to mention the doors?

And can you imagine living in a hole for a few weeks without much food or water, waiting for the fallout danger to decrease? Once the radiation sickness, epidemics, and looting got going full blast, so to speak, it wouldn't exactly be our idea of an ideal summer vacation.

William Mayer, regional director of FEMA, defends the plan. He told The Times' Sally Macdonald: "It wouldn't be life as usual for the evacuees. It would be hell. But we could get them out."

We have doubts about Mayer's last statement, although we wholeheartedly agree with the first two. It would be hell. The living would envy the dead.

But there's another reason why spending more time and money on an elaborate evacuation plan is absurd. It might make nuclear war more thinkable because such a conflict supposedly would be more survivable. We'd much prefer that nuclear war remain just as unthinkable as possible, thanks.

THE MILWAUKEE JOURNAL
Milwaukee, Wisc., April 15, 1982

"Crisis relocation planning" is a premiere phrase at the Federal Emergency Management Agency these days. Sounds sort of comforting, doesn't it?

But what the label conveys is a delusion embedded in an absurdity. "Crisis relocation planning" is the centerpiece of US civil defense policy, and what it essentially means is: If tensions between the nuclear superpowers verged on war, folks in the cities would take to the hills.

That's flip, but is there anyone two degrees this side of comatose who can regard this Daffy Duck notion with anything but grotesque giggles?

The administration wants to spend $4.2 billion in the next seven years to institute an evacuation system for the 380 areas in this country deemed "high risk" nuclear targets. Under the plan as now formulated, for example, 965,000 Milwaukee area residents would be evacuated to 16 other counties.

The theory is that dispersal of millions of Americans to outlying regions would give them a greater chance of surviving an exchange of nuclear warheads — hundreds, if not thousands, of warheads in an all-out conflagration. However, even with several days of warning, this wall-to-wall dispersion would have to be accomplished in an atmosphere of frantic apprehension. And, remember, in a normal urban environment mere raindrops can tangle a rush hour.

In short, the plan presumes fantastic managerial capacity to regulate transportation and traffic, to provide emergency shelter, food and medical care, to enforce law and order and — well, you get the point. (The civil defense proposal seems to ignore the frightening possibility that a nationwide relocation in a time of severe international stress might itself contribute another destabilizing element in a crisis.)

But let's grant, for argument, that a massive evacuation might get millions of Americans beyond the range of the worst *immediate* effects of multi-megaton nuclear blasts. What about the post-attack period? What about a water supply? Food? Medical care for widespread radiation poisoning? "Survival" could be, at best, a mockery.

So why go through this deluding drill? The civil defense scurrying is, we submit, little more than a reflex governmental action animated by a deficient impulse.

Worse, debating a concept as bizarre as "crisis relocation" detracts from concentration on what can and must be done to diminish the possibility of nuclear war. That means effective arms control and reduction, intensively and intelligently pursued.

"I believe that the only real defense against nuclear annihilation is to get the nuclear bomb under control by prompt and vigorous international negotiation," Rep. Henry Reuss (D-Wis.) said the other day. Just so.

There is, fortunately, a good deal of skepticism within Congress over the administration's plan. Indeed, there are those in the administration who roll their eyes at the ill-conceived strategy.

"We have always been able to send people to their death," writes Jonathan Schell in "The Fate of the Earth," a new book on nuclear war, "but only now has it become possible to prevent all births and so doom all future human beings to uncreation."

Against that prospect, which is neither fanciful nor hysterical, "crisis relocation planning" becomes a monstrous joke.

St. Louis Globe-Democrat
St. Louis, Mo., April 15, 1982

Opponents of Civil Defense have succeeded to a large degree in confusing the issue so that many Americans believe spending money for this purpose is a total waste. Nothing could be further from the truth.

Civil Defense, if properly carried out, could serve as a major deterrent to a possible Soviet missile attack. In the event of a Soviet ICBM attack, it could save tens of millions of lives if there is time to carry out plans for evacuating non-essential workers and their families from cities during the period of a nuclear confrontation with the Soviet Union.

The Russians have developed a comprehensive, nationwide Civil Defense program which calls for removal of all but essential workers and government officials from cities if there is the possibility of a nuclear war. This gives the U.S.S.R. a major advantage over the United States in the event of a confrontation between this country and the Soviet Union.

If the Soviets have time to implement their Civil Defense plans and remove most of their population from urban areas, an American president would be at a big disadvantage. He would know that the Soviets might believe they could launch a nuclear first strike with their huge SS-18 ICBMs on the United States which would devastate most of our intercontinental ballistic missile silos and B-52 bases. The Soviets then would be in a position to send an ultimatum to the U.S. to surrender or face attacks on our cities from the remaining Soviet super missiles — the SS-17, SS-19s, SS-11s and SS-13s.

Patrick J. Breheny, regional director of the Federal Emergency Management Agency, makes the excellent point that about 90 percent of the funds spent on Civil Defense can be put to good use in the event of major disasters such as a chemical spill, a nuclear plant emergency, a tornado, earthquake and many other emergencies requiring the moving of large numbers of people and providing rescue operations on short notice. If Civil Defense is blocked, so are these vital rescue operations in the event of a disaster.

President Reagan is the first president to recognize the need for revitalizing this country's defense against a nuclear or bomber attack. He has drawn up plans for a seven-year program to improve U.S. Civil Defense and has requested $252,340,000 for fiscal 1983 to start the program, almost double the current budget of $133,300,000 million.

Opponents of Civil Defense claim that creating a strong network would mean the U.S. believes a nuclear war could be fought and won. Therefore, they conclude, none should be provided. This again is totally wrong. Providing an adequate Civil Defense doesn't mean the U.S. believes a nuclear war is winnable.

It only means that the government and defense planners are taking prudent steps to protect the lives of Americans in the event the Soviet Union or some other nation should launch a missile attack against the United States. In addition to a strong Civil Defense, the U.S. also should deploy an anti-missile network to provide further deterrence to a possible Soviet missile attack.

THE DENVER POST
Denver, Colo., April 21, 1982

THIRTY years ago, when yellow-and-black Civil Defense stickers began showing up on public buildings, ostensibly to direct people to the nearest bomb shelters, one local physicist used to tell his children that the initials "CD" stood for "cruel delusion."

What the scientists have known for decades has finally become a major concern of the general population — there is no real survival from a nuclear war. A few might survive the initial blast, fewer still the lingering radiation. But the human organization we call civilization — institutionalized food gathering and distribution, medical care, education, transportation, security, even religion — would not survive.

This week, organizers all over the nation are calling attention to the chilling irrationality of nuclear war with a series of programs called Ground Zero Week. Local activities began Sunday with a rally at the State Capitol. In graphic and sometimes grisly terms, speakers have been describing the effects on buildings and people at growing distances from the impact crater — ground zero — of a nuclear blast. The message is pretty one-sided: there is not much hope.

Attendance hasn't been massive. Not many people are eager to wallow in the gloomy prognostications. But these aren't vacant-eyed radicals from the fringes of society calling attention to the threat. These are respected public officials and professionals, many with expert knowledge on the physics and politics of the nuclear horror.

There seems to be a new willingness not to ignore the possibility of a nuclear miscalculation. For so long, because nuclear war was simply unthinkable, people assumed no one was thinking about it. Now, however, with the national administration again discussing the chances of "survivability," there is a surge of reaction.

It's reflected in national polls, to which politicians pay great attention. An NBC News-Associated Press survey in the last week of March, for example, showed 74 percent of the public in favor of a freeze in the production of nuclear weapons in both the United States and the Soviet Union. A smaller number — about 50 percent — favors U.S. disarmament if the Soviet Union agrees to disarm as well. But three-quarters of the poll's respondents recognize the folly of continuing to build nuclear bombs when both sides already have more than they need, as Winston Churchill said, to "bounce the rubble" several times over.

Public opinion is the ultimate political force. Public displays of opinion help reinforce the politicians' sense of what the voters want. This week's Ground Zero programs, while they may not be fun to attend, thus are important contributions to the grass-roots agitation to finally remove the "unthinkable" from the list of national policy options.

THE ARIZONA REPUBLIC

Phoenix, Ariz., April 17, 1982

AS the movement to freeze nuclear arms grows, the national debate over U.S. civil defense is heating up.

At first glance, it would seem that if there are fewer nuclear weapons in the arsenals of the superpowers, then the need for more civil defense is lessened.

However, that is conventional wisdom, not the logic of Washington.

President Reagan proposes a $4.2 billion program for civil defense over seven years.

The House Armed Services Committee voted the president most of what he wants for the fiscal 1983 budget, but Senate Armed Services slashed the request by nearly half.

There is increasing uneasiness in Congress and across the country over administration emphasis on "limited nuclear war."

The Pentagon has been quick to note these concerns and is now stressing stronger civil defense as a deterrent.

The core of the plan is to prepare the evacuation of 380 cities and other "high risk" areas in the nation in the event a nuclear attack appears likely.

The evacuation of major cities is an incredible logistics problem that is not only impractical but would invite chaos.

No nuclear power would offer a week or two weeks' warning of attack and, even if U.S. intelligence learned of such a strike, where would the fleeing millions go to protect themselves?

Officials of five cities — from Sacramento, Calif. to Cambridge, Mass. — have rebuffed federal evacuation plans.

There is a limited civil role in defense.

It involves more extensive communications, medical plans and associated emergency supplies, as well as public education.

The assumption that millions of Americans could or want to survive a nuclear war has never been established.

Even if it were, many survivors accept that such a life might well be far worse than the pain of death.

THE LINCOLN STAR

Lincoln, Neb., June 2, 1982

Are plans for mass evacuation of urban areas and medical treatment in the event of nuclear war prudent responses to the ultimate threat or simply invitations to disaster?

That question is at the center of a growing national debate over new civil defense measures. In Nebraska, plans are slowly being drawn to evacuate and relocate populations in the state's four "highest risk" areas. And physicians have been asked to join in planning on how to respond to major disasters, including nuclear war.

Advocates of such disaster planning say that with sufficient warning up to 80 percent of the American population can be saved. At the very least, evacuation and treatment plans have value as life-saving gestures and are better than nothing, they argue.

But critics say that the new civil defense planning actually increases the danger of nuclear war. "It (nationwide evacuation planning) brings in the whole notion that nuclear war is winnable and thinkable," Bryan Coyne, coordinator for the Nebraska Nuclear Weapons Freeze campaign said in a Star story Tuesday. "I don't consider nuclear war winnable or survivable."

But some people obviously think otherwise, beginning at the top. Although the rhetoric has been toned down somewhat, President Reagan, Vice President Bush, Secretary of State Haig and others have talked for some time about limited nuclear war and the probability that the U.S. can survive a nuclear war and prevail in the aftermath. A significant element in the nuclear power industry is similarly inclined.

We recall a recent conversation with a pro-nuclear power engineer who challenged the notion that a massive nuclear military exchange would destroy life on this planet as we know it.

He said, in so many words, that the average civilian outside the blast zone could survive a nuclear attack much the same as he or she would survive a tornado: in the basement, with bottled water and plenty of food on hand and a radio tuned in to get survival instructions. The householder would, of course, need to make sure basement windows and doors were tightly sealed so that radioactive particles did not filter in, he said. And he warned that when survivers venture outdoors they ought not to run their hands over the filmy substance which would be covering cars and other objects.

Gee — if it's that simple, let's go to war, what the heck.

But it's not that simple.

Civil defense planners talking up evacuation and physicians who pretend seriously to plan for taking care of survivors of a nuclear exchange do not differentiate between theory and practice and they ignore human nature. Not the least of the problems confronting a successful evacuation is adequate warning. Are we so sure we can tell what the Soviets are up to? Then there is the need for a total absence of panic, iron discipline and a friendly, hospitable host population to welcome all us city-dwellers calmly leaving the high-risk areas. Not to mention feeding, watering, bedding us down and cleaning up after us for an extended period of time. And will there be enough surviving physicians, blood, hospital beds, trauma units, splints, bandages, ambulances, nurses, cleared emergency routes, etc., etc. if the bombs drop?

These planners better sober up. Trying to convince the American public that it can survive a nuclear holocaust and be top dog in a world worth living in is immoral. It endangers all of us.

THE LOUISVILLE TIMES

Louisville, Ky., May 7, 1982

The Reagan administration is disturbed because its civil-defense plan to evacuate millions of Americans to the countryside in case of nuclear attack is under fire from outside critics who call it ridiculously impractical. The plan, to cost an estimated $4.2 billion over seven years, needs public credibility and congressional support to survive.

So, this is the worst possible time for its own support troops to be shooting the administration in the foot. But that, according to a recent Knight-Ridder News Service story, is precisely what is happening:

✔ The U. S. Postal Service has prepared an Emergency Change of Address form that evacuees are supposed to mail on their way out of town, and a Notification of Safe Arrival to be posted when they get to South Succotash Falls. When asked what the point of it all is if the big-city post office is vaporized by an SS-20, a Postal Service spokesman replied that "It's easy to pick apart the little details. There's nothing certain about life, anyway."

✔ Pamphlets from the Federal Emergency Management Agency include handy reminders to lock the doors and take your credit cards on your way to Armageddon, and to brush fallout particles from your clothing afterwards.

✔ Finally, Internal Revenue Service guidelines note that tax collections will resume not later than 30 days after "the immediate post-attack period."

It's not surprising. After all, it's coming from the same clear thinkers who have put all of our economic marbles on Reaganomics and bet all of our hopes for world survival on tough talk and thousands of additional nuclear weapons.

Haig Rejects "No First Use" Atomic Arms Policy

Secretary of State Alexander M. Haig Jr. April 6, 1982 rejected the possibility that the United States would adopt a "no first use" policy, saying that the U.S. nuclear arsenal would be ineffective as a deterrent if the West were to declare it would never be the first to use nuclear weapons in a war. Haig's remarks were reportedly planned to preempt the publication of an article scheduled for publication in the spring issue of Foreign Affairs magazine. The forthcoming article, authored by four former senior government officials, argued that the U.S. strategy of "flexible response" required reexamination in the light of the buildup of nuclear arsenals during that period. That strategy, adopted by the North Atlantic Treaty Organization in 1967, barred an unprovoked nuclear strike by NATO members but did not rule out the possibility of retaliating with tactical nuclear weapons if the Soviet Union were to launch a massive conventional attack. In their article, the four former officials argued that any such use of nuclear arms carried with it a "high and inescapable risk of escalation" into a general nuclear war, and recommended instead that the West strengthen its conventional forces. Haig attacked the proposal as shortsighted: "Those in the West who advocate the adoption of a 'no first use' policy seldom go on to propose that the U.S. introduce the draft, triple the size of its armed forces and put its economy on wartime footing," he said, maintaining that these steps would be necessary "to counter-balance the Soviet conventional advantages and geopolitical position in Europe."

The Philadelphia Inquirer

Philadelphia, Pa., April 11, 1982

Secretary of State Alexander M. Haig Jr., and thus the Reagan administration, took so seriously the arguments put forward in an article published last week in the arcane journal Foreign Affairs that he delivered a major foreign-policy address rebutting it, timed for maximum impact in Europe as well as the United States, *before* the article's publication.

Whether Mr. Haig's elaborate speech qualified as a pre-emptive first strike or a retaliatory second strike might better be left to the judgment of history. Since both combatants were firing off words and ideas, not megatonnage, the battle will go on — which is very doubtful if the superpowers begin firing off any nuclear weapons.

It has become increasingly obvious, even to many in the highest hawk-roosts, that a major-powers nuclear exchange would mean nothing less — there cannot be more — than obliteration of the human race.

The Foreign Affairs article was written jointly by McGeorge Bundy, George F. Kennan, Robert S. McNamara and Gerard Smith — all men of vast experience in superpower politics, and hardly to be seen as fluttering doves. The most important contention of the piece was that the United States should abandon the option, held as a more-or-less sacred element of the doctrine of nuclear deterrence, of "first use." That is to say, the writers urged that the U.S. government declare that even if the Soviet Union, with or without its Warsaw Pact allies, invaded Western Europe with conventional military forces, the United States would not counterattack with nuclear weapons.

Mr. Haig's ringing and scholarly defense of the first-use option was that to give it up and to maintain mutual security with America's European allies would force the United States to "reintroduce the draft, triple the size of its armed forces and put its economy on a wartime footing." The threat of nuclear retaliation to conventional attack, in other words, is a matter of efficiency and economics.

There is logical merit in both sides of the argument — *as the argument is being addressed.* The trouble is that it is the wrong argument.

The right argument, which is gaining increasing recognition throughout the world, is how civilization, for all the real conflicts of interests between the superpowers and among others, can collectively prevent its suicide.

To extend the debates about theories of credibility of deterrence, an honorable global obsession since Hiroshima, is to continue to accept that the use of nuclear weapons to settle grievances or to prevent political losses is a reasonable prospect. Or an acceptable thing. Or even a possible thing.

If there were further need to validate that, it is well served by the fact that every conclusion and course of action that derives from the assumption of acceptability of nuclear war ends up pressing for increases in the world's nuclear arsenals. Pieties about the virtue and wisdom of arms limitation and reduction become lip service.

There is an alternative. It will be difficult, requiring great courage and fierce moral resolve. It is for the American government — and by persuasion and politics others, including the Soviet Union — to establish as its highest principle and most urgent necessity the fact that nuclear war is simply unacceptable. It is for the leaders of this country and this planet to insist — as is the common interest of each of them and their countries and their posterities — that every other element of international political debate be tested against that simple principle and imperative.

Until that is done, the human race will continue to walk a perilous path. It can lead nowhere but to the precipice of its own total destruction.

The Oregonian

Portland, Ore., April 12, 1982

A proposal by four former U.S. presidential advisers — all accused of being hawks during their tours of duty — that the United States renounce its option to strike first with nuclear weapons in case of attack should not be dismissed out of hand.

The nuclear threat to strike first has been used since the Truman era as a means of offsetting Soviet numerical superiority in conventional weapons. Any plans to abandon such a strategy were recently renounced by Secretary of State Alexander M. Haig Jr., who argued such a policy would mean a resumption of the draft and greater defense expenditures.

The authors of the proposal, published in Foreign Affairs, are McGeorge Bundy, security adviser to Presidents Kennedy and Johnson; Robert S. McNamara, secretary of defense in the same administrations; George F. Kennan, former ambassador to the Soviet Union and a leading expert and presidential adviser on the Kremlin; and Gerald Smith, chief Nixon delegate to the SALT negotiations and ambassador-at-large under Carter.

They all support a buildup of conventional weapons and believe in a strong nuclear deterrence. But all four fear Western civilization will be destroyed once the first nuclear bomb is used. They fear even a limited use of nuclear weapons, as has been proposed, risks catastrophe far greater than the nation could possibly suffer even if it lost a conventional-weapon war.

What has changed the thinking of these men, most of whom supported first-strike policies in the past, is the gigantic proliferation in recent years of nuclear weapons. When McNamara and Bundy were being pilloried as hawks in the Vietnam War era, there were only some 6,000 nuclear weapons. Now, McNamara pointed out, there are 50,000. And more are scheduled to be built, escalating the level of terror.

These are rational, realistic men who have come to the conclusion that the world cannot long survive the nuclear buildup; that something has to be done to turn it all around. A pledge by both the United States and the Soviet Union that neither would be the first to use atomic weapons would be a major step toward disarmament. The Soviets have long proposed renouncing first-use strategy because they knew the United States held nuclear superiority, a superiority these ex-officials and others believe the nation still holds.

The group is not opposing a conventional arms increase, but is arguing that it need not be as extensive or as costly as Haig believes. What can be learned from further study is how costly and how much sacrifice would be required to build up conventional weapons, a job already under way on a large scale.

There is a question that neither group has addressed. That is how believable the U.S. promise is to use nuclear weapons first if attacked. We cannot be certain, when the chips are down, that any administration would sacrifice Washington, New York or even Portland, Ore., for West Berlin. Charles de Gaulle didn't believe it, and he ordered the French to build their own nuclear arsenal, which they have done.

The Salt Lake Tribune

Salt Lake City, Utah, April 12, 1982

A plea by four former high level government officials that the United States and its European allies prepare to renounce the first use of nuclear weapons is yet another manifestation of rising nuclear holocaust fear.

The former officials are Robert S. McNamara, defense secretary in the Kennedy and Johnson administration; McGeorge Bundy, former national security adviser to Presidents Kennedy and Johnson; George F. Kennan, former U.S. ambassador to the Soviet Union, and Gerald C. Smith, former director of the Arms Control and Disarmament Agency and leader of the Nixon administration arms negotiation team. Some of them either helped shape the existing possible first use policy or tacitly supported it during their government service.

That these men now reject a strategy of more than three decades, a strategy that seems to have worked, is a telling example of lost faith and convincing reflection of nuclear policy enlightenment now dawning in the United States and Europe.

The four, it should be noted, do not suggest immediate renunciation and they insist that a no-first-use pledge be accompanied by sufficient buildup of NATO conventional forces to prevent a Soviet invasion of Western Europe.

For 33 years the West has relied on the threat to resort to nuclear arms as a counter to superior Soviet forces in the region. In view of today's advanced nuclear devastation potential, however, reliance on a strategy which accepts use of nuclear weapons to stop a conventional assault invites the onset of the ultimate nuclear horror.

Though their proposition is eminently reasonable in theory, the former officials' plan rests on the dubious premise that the United States and its European allies are prepared to pay the additional costs of raising a conventional force strong enough to discourage Soviet invasion.

Secretary of State Alexander Haig, who rejects shifting to a no-first-strike policy, contends that such a change would require that the United States reintroduce the draft, triple the size of its armed forces and put its economy on a wartime footing. Mr. Haig is convinced that this country and its NATO allies are not willing to pay the price of lifting the nuclear threat shield. Sad to say, he is correct.

Mr. McNamara et al apparently harbor similar doubts. In their Foreign Affairs magazine article, they declare that "It seems clear that the nations of the Alliance together can provide whatever (conventional) forces are needed and within realistic budgetary constraints. But it is a quite different question whether they can summon the necessary political will."

This inability to drum up the "necessary political will" to provide a sufficient conventional deterrent is a longstanding failing which, as noted, has also been the underpinning, indeed the only grudgingly acceptable rationale, for refusing to forswear first use of nuclear weapons in case of Soviet conventional attack.

Although the terror of nuclear war was recognized even before the first bombs were exploded in 1945, the terrible probabilities of wide-ranging nuclear destruction have been squarely assessed and faced only recently by an increasingly aroused public demanding an end to "nuclear madness."

The old strategies, no matter how well they have served, are now suspect if they ultimately rely on or are likely to lead to nuclear conflict. Mr. Haig and the rest of the Reagan administration are wed to the traditional logic. Mr. McNamara and party, the advocates of an across-the-board nuclear weapons freeze, and even those who would accept unilateral nuclear disarmament are seeking a better way.

Renunciation of first use of nuclear weapons in Europe would significantly advance that glorious quest only if the sponsors' precondition of greatly strengthened NATO conventional forces is met. That stern challenge looms as the crucial test for nuclear banishment advocates here and abroad.

Arkansas Gazette.

Little Rock, Ark., April 9, 1982

There is a growing body of thought within high but unofficial councils concerned with strategic policy that any use of nuclear weapons, no matter how small, must be avoided if full-scale nuclear war, indeed, even the end of human life, is to be avoided as well. The essential idea — a sound one — is that once a nuclear weapon is used by either side, the escalator to nuclear holocaust has been set inexorably into motion.

This fundamental assumption, in any event, seems to underlie the call by four senior officials from past administrations for President Reagan to seriously consider renouncing the option of "first use" of tactical nuclear weapons should the Soviet Union launch a massive conventional attack upon Western Europe.

The four have outlined their call in *Foreign Policy* magazine, and they delivered an advance copy of it to Secretary of State Alexander Haig. The four are distinguished figures: Robert S. McNamara, former secretary of Defense and World Bank president; McGeorge Bundy, President John F. Kennedy's national security adviser and former Ford Foundation president; Gerald Smith, President Richard M. Nixon's arms limitation negotiator; and George Kennan, former ambassador to the Soviet Union and Yugoslavia.

They draw a distinction between "first use" of a nuclear weapon and a "first strike." The latter designation, in policy discussions generally, refers to an unprovoked and sudden (perhaps surprise) nuclear attack on the other side. The United States long has promised that it will not launch a "first strike."

The United States, however, has never ruled out "first use" of tactical nuclear weapons if it should become necessary to blunt a massive assault by the Russians against outmanned North Atlantic Treaty Organization forces in Western Europe. This position has reflected a policy that was adopted in the early days of NATO and formally reiterated in 1967 as "flexible response."

The four former officials are saying essentially that many changes, including technological changes, have taken place in the interim and this may be the opportune time to reconsider the option of "first use."

Given its rigidity, the administration's immediate response has been disappointing but not surprising. Within hours of receiving his visitors, Secretary Haig went across town to Georgetown University to publicly reject the proposal, saying it would be "tantamount to making Europe safe for conventional aggression."

Clearly enough, as the four have pointed out, the alternative would be to strengthen the existing conventional forces, through the efforts not only of the United States but also of the NATO allies. Without saying so, they imply that the Europeans must assume a greater role in their own defenses than they have in the past.

The administration in recent weeks has assumed a stern defensive posture on nuclear arms policy questions that does not bode well for halting and reversing the arms race and its likely result: nuclear war. President Reagan and Secretary Haig have rejected calls in Congress and in the grassroots for a mutual freeze on nuclear weapons. And now Mr. Haig rejects a responsible proposal for renouncing "first use" of nuclear weapons. It is a harsh, negative and hauntingly dangerous administration position.

THE MILWAUKEE JOURNAL
Milwaukee, Wisc., April 8, 1982

Washington is a city where drama often obscures substance. However, the heavyweight debate between Secretary of State Haig and the George Kennan foursome over whether America should flatly renounce the "first use" of nuclear weapons was an unusually constructive chapter in political discourse.

The winner, in our view, was the case for repudiating first-use advanced by the impressive quartet: George Kennan, former US ambassador to Russia and the nation's senior scholar of the Soviet Union; Robert McNamara, defense secretary under Presidents Kennedy and Johnson; McGeorge Bundy, national security adviser in those administrations; and Gerard Smith, chief US negotiator for SALT-I.

"A posture of effective conventional balance and survivable second-strike nuclear strength is vastly better for our own peoples and governments, in a deep sense more civilized, than one that forces the serious contemplation of 'limited' nuclear scenarios that are at once terrifying and implausible," the four men say in a jointly written article in the April issue of Foreign Affairs.

The essay is lucid, persuasive and prudent. It was released at a press conference Wednesday, after Haig, getting wind of the article and press conference, hurriedly scheduled a Tuesday speech in which he rejected the argument before it was publicly made (a pre-emptive strike, so to speak).

Haig argued that "flexible response" — the doctrine that NATO forces could respond to Soviet attack with, say, theater nuclear weapons to inhibit further aggression — does not involve the assumption that any nuclear conflict could be "controlled." He contended that flexible response provides "the deterrent effect of a possible nuclear response, without making such a step automatic."

That doctrine, embraced by Reagan, has been around for a decade. But its premises are increasingly untenable, and appalling, we think.

Kennan and his associates correctly rejected the notion that any nuclear exchange could be restricted — and thus the flexible response as a deterrent is invalid and, in fact, threatening in itself. It also is politically destabilizing both between thè superpowers and within the Atlantic Alliance.

A necessary complement to renunciation of first-use would be stronger conventional military forces to help sustain Western deterrence. That could be the catch, of course. It might well be necessary for the US to resort to some form of draft.

A strengthened NATO conventional force is feasible and financially practical, the Foreign Affairs article argued, "but it is a quite different question whether they (the members of the Atlantic Alliance) can summon the necessary political will." It is vital that the will be summoned if the threat of catastrophic nuclear war is to diminish.

Renouncing first-use by the US and NATO — with the Russians invited to make a similar pledge — would be no panacea. However, it would do more to restrain nuclear holocaust than would a continuing accumulation of atomic weaponry ever less susceptible to control.

The issue is complex. But informed discussion at the level of the Haig-Kennan exchange can stimulate the reasonable formulation of policy on which the fate of the planet may well depend.

TULSA WORLD
Tulsa, Okla., April 9, 1982

PRESIDENT Reagan is being urged to renounce first use of nuclear weapons in a conventional war in Europe, a development that would all but guarantee Soviet domination of Europe in a short time.

This advice comes from former Defense Secretary Robert McNamara, former national security adviser McGeorge Bundy, former strategic arms negotiator Gerard Smith and George Kenan, former U. S. Ambassador to the Soviet Union.

It is advice that the Democrat and Republican presidents under which they served never took — and with good reason.

Despite the current hysteria, the threat of nuclear warfare against the Soviets if they ever dare to attack western Europe is what has maintained peace in Europe for 37 years.

The four former officials admit that the U. S. and NATO countries would have to be prepared for a massive buildup in conventional weapons should first use of nuclear weapons be renounced in advance.

That, of course, would mean resumption of the draft and even greater spending on the military that President Reagan is seeking. Finally, it would result in a confrontation of armed forces far stronger than in Europe at the end of World War II.

Further, the temptation to "adventure" on the part of the Soviets would be much greater than it is now. They would certainly become more beligerent, particularly during the lengthy buildup of western forces to follow the "renuniciation" by Reagan.

Give the former officials credit for wanting to find a way to reduce the chances of nuclear war. But this suggestion not only won't do that, it will assure the Sovietization of western Europe by removing the only restraint that has prevented it for nearly four decades.

The Pittsburgh Press
Pittsburgh, Pa., April 12, 1982

Four former national-security officials have urged the United States and its allies to pledge not to be the first to use nuclear weapons in Europe. But Secretary of State Alexander Haig has rejected their proposal out of hand.

Too bad. Mr. Haig spoke too quickly — in fact, one day before the proposal was even published.

The idea has both merits and drawbacks. It is vastly complicated, and it deserves more than instant dismissal.

★ ★ ★

The officials, basically hawks turned doves, are Robert McNamara, former defense secretary; McGeorge Bundy, adviser to Presidents Kennedy and Lyndon Johnson; George Kennan, former ambassador to Moscow; and Gerard Smith, President Nixon's disarmament negotiator.

They want the NATO alliance to give up its strategy of "flexible response" — which means use of either conventional or nuclear weapons to counter a Soviet attack in Europe.

They say this policy only adds to the risk of nuclear war.

In its place they would have NATO strengthen its conventional forces sufficiently to deter Russia from risking aggression.

In reply, Mr. Haig said a "no first use" policy with regard to nuclear weapons would make Europe "safe for conventional aggression" — because of Russia's superior ground forces.

That, he added, would force the United States to "reintroduce the draft, triple the size of its armed forces, and put its economy on a wartime footing."

This is rhetorical overkill, and it does not reflect a reasoned analysis of the question.

Mr. Haig would do better to sound out our NATO allies and find out if they have the political will to put up more ground troops to lessen the chance of Soviet aggression.

★ ★ ★

After all, first use of nuclear weapons in event of war in Europe would not guarantee victory. It might, in fact, ensure the initiator's own devastation.

Consider, for instance, this scenario:

The Soviets massively invade West Germany. The allies cannot stop them and resort to battlefield nuclear weapons to warn the Kremlin against continuing. Russia promptly replies with larger, more radioactive weapons, destroying armies, military depots, ports, rail centers and communication lines.

At this point Russia essentially would be the winner.

America's options would be to accept that fact or to fire its strategic missiles — triggering the incineration of this country, the Soviet Union and the Europe that was to be "saved."

If indeed there is significant risk of such an Armageddon, we and our NATO allies should seek out a better strategy. And if the debate can be turned in that direction, the four former officials will have performed a valuable service.

Pentagon Plan to Prevail in Prolonged Nuclear War Reported

A new strategic U.S. plan for winning a prolonged nuclear war against the Soviet Union had been prepared and was awaiting President Reagan's approval, it was reported Aug. 15, 1982. The Pentagon document, which envisioned a nuclear exchange lasting as long as six months, was prepared in response to a directive written by Reagan in the fall of 1981. That directive, ordering the Pentagon to come up with a plan for prevailing over the Soviet Union in a prolonged nuclear exchange, was part of a top-secret national security document designed to supersede Directive 59, a nuclear strategy document approved during the last six months of the Carter Administration. Defense Secretary Weinberger, in defending the Administration's strategy, pointed to evidence that the Soviet Union had increased its capacity to fight a prolonged nuclear war, and said the U.S. had to make similar preparations. He mentioned the increased accuracy of Soviet missiles, the ability to reload silos and launchers, the hardening of command centers to shield against attack, increased civil defense preparations and heavy spending for ballistic missile defenses.

In a related development, a U.S. Postal Service plan to continue mail delivery following a nuclear holocaust was unveiled at a congressional subcommittee hearing Aug. 12. The 400-page civil defense plan called for relocation of the Postal Service headquarters after the destruction of Washington, D.C., the protection of its employees and the distribution of emergency change-of-address forms to the surviving population.

The Salt Lake Tribune
Salt Lake City, Utah, August 12, 1982

Now that the unthinkable — nuclear war — has surfaced to public consciousness, people here and abroad are letting their governments know in strong terms what they think about it. The earlier U.S. protests about nuclear power plants have spread to include demonstrations against nuclear weapons — blockades of a Trident submarine in Puget Sound, a Strategic Air Command base and a nuclear research firm.

It may not be fair to fully blame President Reagan's inordinate fear of Russia and his resultant nuclear sabre-rattling for the growing rash of anti-nuclear activities, but it's certainly a major factor.

The present widespread fear of nuclear war is a phenomenon largely coincident with this administration.

In the Carter-Ford-Nixon eras, there were some protests, mostly limited to nuclear power and nuclear proliferation, but nothing on the current scale. Until the past year, the idea of nuclear war was an abstraction, an event too horrible to contemplate, something no sane national leader would initiate, unthinkable.

Then Reagan acknowledged the possibility of a "limited" nuclear conflict and the whole thing hit the fan. It became "possible" and the resulting tide of fear sparked mass protests in the western world, arrests of activists and public pressure that brought a nuclear freeze resolution to within two votes of passage in the House. (House Democrats plan to reintroduce the measure and hopefully it will pass this time.)

Civil defense plans for mass evacuations and bomb shelters, at a cost of $4.5 billion, have been resurrected — the whole panoply of futile protection measures formerly abandoned as irrational.

Since it's impossible to stuff the nuclear genie back in the bottle, the only option is to handle it with all the wisdom, safeguards and diplomatic prudence possible. And not terrorize the public with careless rhetoric.

President Reagan, having raised the specter of potential nuclear devastation, could bury it with a few well-chosen words, followed by concrete actions. He could support the nuclear freeze, modify U.S. demands in disarmament talks to a reasonable degree of fairness and possible acceptance by Russia or any other initiative to convince the world he is sincerely committed to reducing the nuclear threat.

But that's asking the leopard to change his spots.

Reagan reassured European leaders at the Versailles summit that he is not as tough as portrayed, then reverted to his old stance upon his return home. He said in a public speech, "There has been a historic change in Washington. We are on the defensive no longer."

He could be on the defensive in November. He has a lot of voters frightened.

The Morning News
Wilmington, Del., August 12, 1982

THE VERY SIGHT OF the black on white news report was revolting, shocking. Secretary of Defense Caspar Weinberger was not only confirming that planning has been done for possibly fighting a long nuclear war, but was defending the rationale behind such planning.

It's necessary to prepare for a protracted exchange, said the secretary, to help minimize chances of a "hair-trigger" incident. (Incident?) It is a plan based on a perception that it is desirable to avoid firing all our nuclear weapons immediately in response to a Soviet attack, to have the goal of "prevailing" in the drawn-out exchange and ending it on favorable terms with some nuclear arms intact.

Nobody has ever conducted a long nuclear war. Nobody knows how it would work. Would bomb bursts creep across the adversaries' maps? Would Wilmington and Vitebesk receive missiles on Monday, Kalinin and Georgetown Tuesday, Baltimore and Leningrad Wednesday? Would Voroshilovgrad and Dover be next and Kharkov and Philadelphia on Friday? Would Odessa on the Black Sea and Odessa on the Appoquinimink be taken out on Saturday, or would the parties rest from their unholy labors on the Sabbath or on Sunday?

Does it mean devastation management by objective, violation of this many thousands of military and that many thousands of civilian bodies according to a strict timetable?

Then you read the account again and you realize that this is the Pentagon talking.

You have to remember what it is like in the Pentagon, in all of those cubicles, big and small, along the endless corridors that are spokes to that huge, five-sided wheel — planners of this headquarters shunned the idea of a *round* wheel, which might be a clue to us.

These are hard-working people, professionals, the people we pay to think the unthinkable. When they talk of the defense mission, it isn't the same as when we do.

"War fighting" to these folks, has a very low priority in the defense mission, far below *deterrence of aggression*, for instance, or *war planning*. Deterrence and planning, however, are meaningless without ability and will to actually fight — and regrettably kill, and that ability and will must be stressed in public.

It all could mean we really don't know, can never know what Mr. Weinberger or any defense secretary really means. What does he mean when he concedes that nuclear war is not "winnable" but adds, "We certainly are not planning to be defeated"? Is prolonged nuclear war even possible? "I just don't have any idea," said the secretary. "I don't know that anybody has any idea." But does that compute with his declaration: "You show me a secretary of defense who's planning not to prevail and I'll show you a secretary of defense who ought to be impeached."

It is all too remote, all too abstract.

But it is damnably expensive, damnably frightening.

ARGUS-LEADER

Sioux Falls, S.D., August 22, 1982

During a year wnen Americans and other nationals the world over have demonstrated their feelings against nuclear war and for a nuclear freeze, it's upsetting to realize that the Pentagon continues to plan for one.

It would be more upsetting if there were no American plans.

The latest Washington ruckus over defense planning concerns changes the Reagan administration is supposed to have made in a secret document that was drawn up last year to supersede former President Jimmy Carter's directive.

Carter's Presidential Directive 59 drew criticism because the plan presumed mankind could fight and survive nuclear war as it did conventional wars of the past. Now, according to a report by the Los Angeles Times, President Reagan's planning entails setting a goal to win a protracted or extended nuclear war. That period might be one of several months.

Air Force Gen. David Jones, a native of Aberdeen, S.D., and chairman of the Joint Chiefs of Staff under both Carter and Reagan, said before he retired in June that preparations for fighting a limited or protracted nuclear war would be throwing money into a bottomless pit.

Said Jones, "I don't see much of a chance of nuclear war being limited or protracted...I see great difficulty in keeping any kind of nuclear exchange between the Soviet Union and the U.S. from escalating."

The general is right. The public is also right in wanting to avoid a nuclear war. There would be nothing left if the world were that unfortunate.

Nevertheless, the Department of Defense should be ready with contingency plans for the worst. Plans involving nuclear war are only an extension of other secret planning for combat in many areas of the world. Very few, if any, of them will ever be used.

If there were no plans, DOD would be derelict in its duty — and so would the country's president, whether Reagan or any of his predecessors.

Most nations — particularly the major ones — have war plans for possible use against usually friendly nations. Russia and the United States, because they are superpowers, of necessity have plans for Doomsday.

We take the optimistic view that the two superpowers eventually will find a way to reduce their nuclear stockpiles and maintain present deterrence with a lesser capability. That's the best hope for peace and avoiding a nuclear accident that might involve major countries in a conflict.

Surely, it is the duty of the public and politicians to question the basic concept of nuclear war and to criticize planning for such a calamity. There's another side to that.

If the Japanese had realized how furiously the United States would react to their sneak attack on Pearl Harbor, they might not have sent their carrier task force against Hawaii.

The lesson of Dec. 7, 1941, aside from demonstrating the need for preparedness, was that even if losses had been much worse, this country's response would have been just as determined. That rationale applies as well to any future attack — conventional or nuclear.

Both the Soviet Union and the United States, we'd like to think, are smart enough to find a way to avert the ultimate calamity.

No Russian president or prime minister will tell the Kremlin to stop planning for nuclear war, including how to protect its people if the Americans attack. No American president should tell the world that if someone drops nukes on Pearl Harbor this country will lie down and quit. That would be an invitation to blackmail.

Arkansas Gazette.

Little Rock, Ark., August 25, 1982

Evidence continues to accumulate that the Reagan administration does indeed believe that a nuclear war would be winnable if the United States only had enough weapons and used them in just the right way.

President Reagan's vow to "rearm America" remains a cornerstone of his administration, as White House chief of staff James A. Baker III made clear enough in a recent appearance on CBS's "Face the Nation." Mr. Reagan continues to resist any suggestion of cuts in the whopping Defense budget. Earlier this month, Energy Secretary James B. Edwards, presiding at an underground nuclear test in Nevada, remarked that "if we're going to get into war, I want to come out No. 1, not No. 2," adding: "That's the Reagan administration goal — peace through strength."

And now comes the news from the *Los Angeles Times* that a plan for winning a prolonged nuclear war has been prepared in response to a presidential directive and has been delivered to President Reagan. The plan, says the *Times*, provides guidelines on how the United States could win a war lasting up to six months by protecting its command, control and communication systems.

It is hard to imagine a nuclear war lasting six days, much less six months. Such a lengthy conflict would require repeal of human nature, for it assumes that neither side would use more than a few megatons, carefully measured over a period of months. It doesn't take many megatons to reduce either the United States or the Soviet Union to rubble. Any rational analysis of these and other factors leads to the conclusion that fighting and winning any kind of nuclear war in any rational sense is impossible.

ADMINISTRATION PLANS FOR SIX-MONTH NUCLEAR WAR.

— NEWS ITEM

The Wichita
Eagle-Beacon
Wichita, Kans., August 23, 1982

There are a lot of words that apply to the government's plans for delivering mail and collecting taxes in the wake of a nuclear war: naive, macabre, ominous. But perhaps the most fitting one is: dumb.

It simply is dumb to be focusing on such mundane matters in a scenario keyed to national — if not world — disaster. Who's going to worry about whether the mail is late if the country has been decimated by nuclear war? It does little good to have such concerns now; surely no one would propose more timely standards after a blast of A-bomb attrition. And what government that had just participated in a nuclear holocaust would have the gall to try to collect income — or any other kind of — taxes from the survivors?

The depressing truth is becoming more evident; that even the most ambitious civil defense plan in the world (which the latest U.S. "head for the hills" proposal would not be) could be only of marginal use in the event of an all-out atomic war. It's misleading for leaders to imply anything otherwise.

But, true to form, that hasn't stopped the government from pursuing a policy of overkill in dealing with the perceived problems of getting along in a post-holocaust world. Last December, it published a manual of no less than 16 chapters, outlining the battle plan for getting the mail through after the war — and probably the world — is through. That not only is dumb, but it tends to perpetuate the dangerous, growing myth among government decision-makers that nuclear war may be winnable. Dependable mail service and conscientious tax-paying will be among the least of humankind's worries if anyone ever tries that theory out.

Minneapolis Star and Tribune
Minneapolis, Minn., August 17, 1982

The acronyms in the headline are not original. Former Defense Secretary Robert McNamara devised the deterrence principle known as MAD, or mutual assured destruction. Despite the growth in numbers of nuclear weapons, paralleled by growth in their accuracy, that 1960s idea has undergirded a generation of sound strategic thinking. For either superpower to unleash a nuclear attack would be madness, given the devastation that retaliation would bring.

The second acronym gains significance week by week. It came from the fertile and far-sighted mind of Spurgeon Keeny, a scholar at the National Academy of Sciences, who last fall wrote about strategic planning in the Reagan administration. According to Keeny, strategists were figuring how to spread a lot of nuclear weapons across a lot of targets and still have enough to fight a long nuclear war. In a Foreign Affairs magazine article Keeny warned of the risk inherent in that idea, which he called Nuclear Utilization Target Selection — NUTS. Developments in recent months suggest that NUTS has taken root. The Defense Department last week completed a plan, ordered in 1981 by President Reagan, for the United States to fight and win a protracted nuclear war with the Soviet Union. Earlier this year an internal Defense Department document contained similar language. And the administration has been pushing a $4.2-billion plan for evacuating cities in case of nuclear threat.

Advocates of expanded civil defense cite as one reason the Soviets' similar program. Rep. Jim Leach, an Iowa Republican, responds appropriately: "To match a dumb strategy with a dumb strategy is itself dumb." So, too, with NUTS. The United States has about 30,000 nuclear warheads, one third of them designated "strategic." The rest are smaller — many of them the size that destroyed Hiroshima and Nagasaki. No matter how many cities the Soviets or Americans evacuated, no matter how many people burrowed underground, a fraction of existing nuclear weapons could destroy their societies. Assumptions that nuclear war could remain controlled, limited, prolonged and, in any imaginable sense of the word, winnable are dangerous wishful thinking.

Officials in the Carter administration said in 1980 that a greater emphasis on U.S. capacities for low-level nuclear war-fighting could strengthen deterrence. But Harold Brown, then defense secretary, warned that even the most limited use of nuclear weapons would "very likely" bring about general nuclear war. Gen. David Jones, recently retired chairman of the Joint Chiefs of Staff, has said the same thing. The best endorsement of MAD is the absence of nuclear war. The Reagan administration's case for NUTS is as flimsy as it is frightening.

The Pittsburgh Press
*Pittsburgh, Pa.,
August 18, 1982*

Most Americans don't know whether to feel reassured or dispirited about the U.S. Postal Service's plan for continuing mail delivery after a nuclear war.

Officials told a skeptical subcommittee of the U.S. House of Representatives the other day that an elaborate postal chain of command has been established and that steps would be taken to protect postal workers.

It's nice to know that neither snow, nor rain, nor heat, nor gloom of night, nor atomic bombs can stay the couriers from their appointed rounds.

What's disheartening is that postal officials think the possibility of a nuclear war is serious enough to devise their plan. Even more depressing is the thought that there may not be many people around to either write or receive mail.

Postal authorities might better occupy their time in figuring out how to get the mail delivered on time and keep postal rates down before planning for any holocaust.

The Kansas City Times
Kansas City, Mo., August 17, 1982

That was a real rib-tickler up on Capitol Hill Thursday, the way members of the House Post Office Subcommittee poked fun at the Postal Service for its otherworldly audacity in thinking it could deliver the mail after a nuclear war. Such a setup cheap shot that, shucks, it was guaranteed page one and a spot on the evening news, no matter what. Making fools out of bureaucrats is a great spectator sport. The theater of the absurd playing to a full house.

You've got to give Congress credit, though. Those guys do know how to alert the press — surely you didn't think all that coverage was by accident — and make mincemeat out of myopic turf-minded government officials who charge ahead like the Postal Service and the Internal Revenue Service have been doing, trying to divine how to meet the basics of government in a primitive society. That's what post-nuclear war America will be, all right — primitive. Barbaric. Even, brutal, we'd bet. Not much time to write letters and earn enough to pay taxes to Washington. Oops, our mistake. Well, whatever would be the capital.

Since the radioactive ruins of the world's longest-playing democracy would be smoldering testimony to the failure of political leaders to prevent the war through negotiations and disarmament, citizens can take heart in knowing that the post office and the tax-collecting branches will be hard at work, doing their bit to rebuild America.

The absurd aspect of this exercise is the agencies that will be lucky to function in a post-nuke world are looking ahead, while those that can do something to lessen the prospects of incineration seem more determined than ever to test their pet theory that, indeed, there can be an America after a nuclear war.

Reagan Urges Antimissile System; Soviets Ask Space Weapons Ban

"I am taking an important first step," President Reagan announced in a nationally televised address March 23, 1983. "I am directing a comprehensive and intensive effort to define a long-term research and development program to begin to achieve our ultimate goal of eliminating the threat posed by strategic nuclear missiles." What Reagan proposed was that American scientists "turn their great talents" to developing an antiballistic missile system capable of destroying Soviet missiles before they could reach their targets. The President described the development of an ABM system—which presumably would employ lasers, microwave devices, particle beams and projectile beams, and be based at least partly in space—as "a formidable task, one that may not be accomplished before the end of the century." Deployment of an ABM system would represent a fundamental revision in U.S. nuclear strategy; for the last 35 years, the U.S. has relied on the threat of massive nuclear retaliation against the Soviet Union to deter an attack and maintain a so-called "balance of terror" between the two powers. That policy had effectively prevented a nuclear war for three decades, Reagan conceded, but said that the Joint Chiefs of Staff and other advisers had convinced him of the "necessity" of developing an antimissile system that could prevent a Soviet attack from ever occurring. This new policy, President Reagan said, "could pave the way for arms control measures to eliminate the weapons themselves."

The Soviet Union reiterated its long-standing appeal for a ban on space weapons a month later. Yuri V. Andropov, Soviet Communist Party general secretary, called for an international agreement banning weapons in outer space. "Recent developments," Andropov charged, "have demonstrated that the use of space-based military technology is being assigned an ever greater role in United States strategic plans, including those announced by the top United States leadership." The Soviet leaders' words echoed the fears of many Americans that outer space, once the province of peaceful scientific enterprise, was rapidly becoming another potential theater for nuclear conflict.

Newsday
Long Island, N.Y., April 21, 1981

"May the shoreless cosmic ocean be pure and free of weapons of any kind. We stand for joint efforts to reach a great and humanitarian aim—to preclude the militarization of outer space."

Leonid Brezhnev said that last week after the space shuttle Columbia's roundabout trip from Florida to California. Was it just rhetorical boilerplate, or a signal that Moscow would like to talk seriously about limiting weapons in outer space?

We don't pretend to know, but it could be worth the Reagan administration's while to find out.

For domestic consumption, the Soviet media have treated the space shuttle primarily as a platform for testing killer satellites and laser weapons. It's not clear just what the shuttle is expected to do for the Pentagon, but Columbia can put a 65,000-pound payload into orbit—more than five times as much as the Russians can send up. The Kremlin can't be very happy about that.

On the other hand, the Soviet Union has tested a number of killer satellites with apparent success, and the Pentagon isn't very happy about *that;* it could be very bad news for this country's surveillance, navigation and communication satellites. So both sides might benefit if they could avoid an arms race in orbit.

Presumably it would be difficult to verify compliance with an agreement to limit space weaponry; in practice it might be impossible. But if there's a chance to avoid pouring defense billions into the shoreless cosmic ocean, it should be fully explored.

The Hartford Courant
Hartford, Conn., June 12, 1981

"In military history, land conflicts progressed to use of the sea and then of the air as requisite technology became available. We are now at another frontier for the application of military power — space."

That quote, from a recent issue of the Naval War College Review, neatly summarizes the evolving relationship between technology and warfare. As the "requisite technology" developed, conflicts followed that made use of it.

Technology is now being developed that will make it possible to extend the human battlefield to space. Indeed, Connecticut's own United Technologies Corp. might even help make that prospect a reality.

It is working on plans for a mirror that would concentrate and aim a laser beam to destroy missiles.

In spite of the unexplained failure of an Air Force test using a laser beam to bring down a supersonic air-to-air missile recently, the development of laser weapons for space is a virtual certainty.

Both the United States and the Soviet Union possess the technological know-how to make it feasible to put a directed-energy weapon, such as a high-energy laser, into space. Such a weapon might be able to kill a long-range bomber or a ballistic missile in flight.

A successful laser weapon would be able to destroy even the fastest-moving target instantly, since laser light can travel a mile in the same time it takes a plane moving at twice the speed of sound to travel an eighth of an inch.

The era of orbiting battle stations, and possible Star Wars, could be here in a decade or two.

To assure that that happens, the Pentagon and some members of Congress are playing up the threat of a Soviet dominance of space with the advanced weaponry it has been working on.

The Soviets, no doubt, are plowing ahead with their laser weapons development because of the threat of U.S. dominance of space, a spectre they may see as more real since the successful flight of the Columbia space shuttle in April.

The dismal spectacle of an arms race in space confirms the adage that the more things change, the more things stay the same. And it gives added dimension to the description of space as the final frontier.

The Providence Journal

Providence, R.I., August 31, 1981

Is a new form of warfare about to splash onto the computer terminals of the generals and admirals charged with defense of this country — and all other countries? U.S. forces already are experimenting with this new field, one of electron shields, lasers, computer manipulation of the earth's magnetic field. The aim, of course, to destroy the ships and planes and missiles of an enemy.

If this sounds like Star Wars, it isn't far removed. This is no movie fantasy, though. The United States has an Electronic Security Command, and it has 12,000 electronic warfare specialists around the world, playing out scenarios of battle in this new medium.

The electronic battlefield grows out of the enormous amount of communications equipment that modern military forces use, not only to send messages between all commands, but also to trigger missiles and even aircraft. Electronic commands speed up the process of ordering weapons into battle, but they are vulnerable to interception or even counter-commands from enemy intelligence units that have succeeded in penetrating electronic security.

Thus, the new Star Wars units could theoretically "blind" command and control stations, leaving generals out of touch with their troops and weapons. But retaliation might do the same to an aggressor's forces.

The commander of the new U.S. unit maintains the Russians are far ahead of this country in developing such capability. Moreover, he laments the advantage the Russians have in training far more scientists and engineers — as much as six to one, he contends.

Maybe it is time for this country to review the incentives it provides for scientific training, just as it did after the Russians launched the first space vehicle, Sputnik. The war of the future will not be fought with weapons of the past, and Americans had better stay in the forefront of research if they expect to stave off the aggressors of the 21st Century.

THE DAILY OKLAHOMAN

Oklahoma City, Okla., October 20, 1981

BRINGING all military space operations under the control of a single command center, as proposed by the Air Force, has led to apparently uninformed speculation about a plan to abolish or abandon the National Aeronautics and Space Administration (NASA).

There is no such plan, and the speculation is totally unfounded.

The suggested Consolidated Space Operations Center at Colorado Springs deals only with U.S. Air Force space operations. There will continue to be separately funded civilian space missions by NASA.

One principal reason for the new control center is security. It's not hard to see why. All of America's space operations have been open and above board, although a number of military satellites have been launched — mostly from Vanderberg Air Force Base in California — with a minimum of publicity.

The very openness of the U.S. space program has been in marked contrast to most Soviet space activities. But as more and more space vehicles are launched on military missions, it becomes obvious that our propensity for telling all should be limited to civilian operations in space.

The space shuttle will be positioning orbiting civilian laboratories which will experiment with the manufacture of exotic alloys and difficult pharmaceuticals in space. Launching communications satellites into geosynchronous orbit will continue,

as will scientific observation satellites.

But the security factor argues strongly for a separate military space fleet. Among those pushing the idea is Sen. Harrison Schmitt, R-N.M., a former astronaut, who says "there is a clear necessity for a public shuttle fleet and a defense fleet — one operated by NASA or a NASA spin-off and one operated for defense."

As chairman of the Commerce Committee's subcommittee on science, technology and space, Schmitt has endorsed proposals for a U.S. Space Command as the space operational agency for all of our military services. His proposals go beyond the Air Force plan for combining all of its space activities under one control center.

But this concept may run into a complication because of the fact that the North American Air Defense (NORAD) is a joint U.S.-Canadian command established by treaty. Any merger of NORAD with an expanded U.S. military space command would presumably involve a new treaty with Canada extending the scope of NORAD. But this does not appear to represent any insurmountable diplomatic obstacle.

Combining all military space operations under a single command is a classic example of an idea whose time has come. What the command will comprise may not be what is now proposed in every detail, but the concept is an essential part of the future of North American defense strategy.

The Houston Post

Houston, Texas, June 28, 1982

The Air Force's recent decision to create a Space Command emphasizes the growing importance of space as a theater of military operations. The U.S. space shuttle, on its fourth and final test flight, is carrying a top secret Pentagon payload. Nearly half of the shuttle flights through 1984 will be solely for military purposes.

The Soviet Union, in the meantime, has orbited a new space station, Salyut 7, as a companion to its Salyut 6, which has been in orbit four years. It has been manned much of the time by Soviet cosmonauts. The Soviets have developed a killer satellite and are pressing research on other devices with military space application, including a laser weapon. U.S. government sources reported earlier this month that the Russians launched a shuttle-like craft and recovered it from the Indian Ocean after one and a quarter orbits; Moscow later denied that it was a shuttle vehicle test.

The United States is moving forward with renewed momentum on its own military space projects. The Air Force's new Space Command, when it is activated Sept. 1, will give this country its first central authority from which to direct military operations in space. These will include defense-related uses of the shuttle. Strained U.S.-Soviet relations have acted as a catalyst to the military space race. Shortly before creation of the Space Command was announced, former Secretary of State Alexander Haig disclosed that the Russians had carried out a series of complex tests with anti-satellite weapons. We plan to test a satellite killer of our own soon, a two-stage rocket fired from an F-15 jet fighter.

Washington and Moscow have been inclined to view their military competition in space from a somewhat narrow "them-and-us" perspective. But space is no more the sole province of the superpowers for military purposes than it is for civilian purposes. Just as electronically guided "smart" weapons, such as the French Exocet missile, have been acquired by several nations, so might weapons designed for space use. This should give impetus to the negotiation of an international treaty banning all weapons from space, just as nuclear weapons are now banned.

It is unlikely that an agreement could be reached ruling out all military use of space, nor would it necessarily be desirable. Space is the ultimate high ground, an invaluable vantage point from which to observe Earth. Both we and the Soviets depend on satellite reconnaissance to keep track of military activities not only in each other's respective territory but worldwide. Still, a verifiable treaty eliminating weapons from space could save costly preparations for extraterrestrial conflict and remove the threat of attack by arms in orbit.

Richmond Times-Dispatch
Richmond, Va., August 11, 1982

If you haven't heard of High Frontier, you probably soon will. It is a strategic concept, envisioning armed satellites and a complementary ground-based anti-missile system, that would, according to a Heritage Foundation report, "(1) slam shut the window of U.S. military vulnerability; (2) fast-thaw the nuclear freeze movement; (3) preserve America's narrowing technological lead in space; and (4) greatly limit the damage from a Soviet first-strike attack." And its cost ($50 billion over five years), relative to such budgetary black holes as the MX missile system, is palatable.

The idea, put forth by a space-/defense team headed by former Defense Intelligence Agency chief Daniel Graham, is that the United States would sow outer space with a double layer of conventional satellites capable of detecting and destroying more than nine out of 10 Soviet ICBMs before they reached American territory. Surviving missiles, reads the High Frontier scenario, would be "cleaned up" by normal U.S. ABMs. If, somehow, a few reached their target, their destructive impact would be blunted by a vigorous civil defense program. Then it would be our turn.

Among the touted virtues of High Frontier is that, being a near-perfect defense — imagine, analogously, deploying a battalion of Dick Butkuses in front of a goal line — it would end the arms race. The United States would have no need to build new offensive systems; those that the U.S.S.R. built would be irrelevant, since anything they threw up could be swatted down. Thus High Frontier would remove the shadow of nuclear worlddeath that has darkened mankind's soul for decades. Pretty heavy spaghetti. But, considerations of technical credibility to one side, might we sound two warnings?

It is one of the curiosities of the nuclear world that the most provocative arms systems are those that bolster defense. This is because great defensive superiority would allow one side to launch a first strike with virtual impunity. Hence, implementing High Frontier — which would place the Soviets in a position of strategic-geopolitical inferiority for the foreseeable future — could trigger the Armageddon that it is intended to preclude.

Moreover, what technology does, higher technology can undo. Who is to say that Soviet scientists, sooner or later, could not invent some device that would befuddle our satellite detectors and permit their missiles to rain on American cities? High Frontier — which, like calls for a nuclear freeze, is viscerally appealing — could induce a state of false security, leaving us with gaping security gaps in both offensive and defensive weaponry.

This does not mean that the concept should be abandoned. Quite the contrary, especially since the Kremlin is known to be working on its own killer-satellite system: By the mid-1980s, say defense experts, it may have in orbit laser-armed machines that could sweep the welkin of Allied spacecraft. But it does suggest that more than a $50 billion price tag stands in the way of High Frontier's rhapsodic promises.

St. Louis Globe-Democrat
St. Louis, Mo., June 28, 1982

Now that the Air Force has created a Space Command for dealing with U.S. military operations in space, the time has come to give serious consideration to deploying a non-nuclear space defense system against enemy missiles or an accidentally-fired ICBM.

Two things concerning space have been apparent for a long time:

— It is inevitable that the United States, the Soviet Union and other technologically-advanced nations will expand their military operations into space.

— The nation which first deploys an effective space defense system against enemy missiles will gain the kind of superiority the United States once had when it had a monopoly on nuclear weapons.

Lt. Gen. Daniel O. Graham, AUS, Ret., who headed a research team which developed a plan for a non-nuclear space ballistic missile defense system, says the U.S. could use existing hardware to deploy an effective defense against Soviet missiles in a matter of years if the decision was made to go ahead with the system and give it top priority.

Critics of Graham's proposed space defense plan claim it would "escalate the arms race." But, in fact, an effective space defense would nullify the Soviets' enormous offensive missile threat and greatly reduce the chances of an atomic war.

Instead of being a weapons system designed to kill tens of millions of people, the mission of a space defense would be to save more than 100 million Americans from possible annihilation from a Soviet missile attack and also to intercept any missile that might be accidentally fired at this country.

The Virginian-Pilot
Norfolk, Va., June 26, 1982

The Soviet Union has been uneasy all along about the American space shuttle. A machine that is rocketed into space, performs as a space ship (in an environment where the laws of aerodynamics do not apply) and returns to Earth as an airplane represents an awesome technological achievement with military implications. Moreover, Defense Department involvement in space activity has been considerable all along, but with the space shuttle *Columbia* preparing to undertake its first explicitly defense-related mission on Sunday, the Kremlin's propaganda organ is in a frenzy.

Snapped Pravda: "American brass hats make no secret that they regard outer space as a potential theater of operations. The Pentagon also is planning to put laser weapons, spy satellites and anti-satellite systems into near-Earth orbit [and] to spread the arms race to outer space."

The Russians fear, not unreasonably, that the U.S. could become the first nation in space with exotic weapons and surveillance systems that could place it at a fatal disadvantage. They would not be similarly troubled, of course, if they and not we were in the lead. They were exultant when Sputnik beeped the message that the Soviet Union had beaten the U.S. into space — an event that energized both the American space program and American education.

Although a Russian cosmonaut has not yet walked upon the moon, the Soviet manned space program still goes forward. Two cosmonauts and a French pilot were sent aloft Thursday to join two Soviets already aboard the orbiting Salyut 7 space station. It would be disingenuous to suggest that the Soviet space effort is propelled solely by scientific and industrial motives; to say that the military component of the Soviet space program is substantial is to understate the reality.

It would be well, of course, if space remained uncontaminated by the war virus. The United States and the Soviet Union agreed in the Sixties to neither test nuclear weapons in space nor "place in orbit around the Earth any objects carrying nuclear weapons or any other weapons of mass destruction, install such weapons on celestial bodies, or station such weapons in outer space in any other manner."

Pravda apparently is not accusing the United States of violating these commitments — only of planning to place military hardware in orbit that could enhance U.S. satellite spying on the Soviet Union and "kill" Russian spy satellites. Well, that's a subject for sober discussion also. The Pentagon fears, not unreasonably, that the Soviet military is seeking the capability that Pravda accuses the United States of seeking.

At this point, there being no agreement to bar spy satellites and killer satellites from space, the question may be one of who will "git thar fustest with the mostest." But putting space off limits to the arms race and martial competition generally is a worthy goal that the superpowers may yet take up.

For now, the first order of business is to dismantle some of the doomsday weapons of which the superpowers possess a redundancy — a topic being addressed by the talks on intermediate-range ballistic missiles in Europe and the START talks on intercontinental ballistic missiles and aircraft scheduled to begin on June 29. In the overall, disturbing arms picture, *Columbia's* modest defense-related mission is a detail.

DESERET NEWS
Salt Lake City, Utah, January 22, 1983

Most Americans seem to think of the U.S. space program as an adventure in exploring the unknown, not as a struggle for military supremacy or national survival.

But an ominous document released this week by the Department of Defense threatens to change all that. In a 136-page budget plan for 1984-1988 defense spending, military leaders have ordered preparations to "wage war effectively from outer space."

Even more disturbing, the Defense Department indicated that by moving quickly, the U.S. could head off any future treaty banning weapons in space, and at the same time, add a new dimension to the nation's military capability.

"We must ensure that treaties and agreements do not foreclose opportunities to develop these capabilities . . .," the document said.

The 1967 Space Treaty already bans nuclear weapons in space or on celestial bodies. But the pact may not mean much. Military planners apparently have other options in mind that would exploit non-nuclear technology now becoming available.

Among these are systems to fire some kind of force from space vehicles. Just what that "force" would be was not spelled out, but the military is known to be working on such science-fiction ideas as laser and particle beams.

The document said that space-based weapons could provide almost instantaneous access to any point on the globe. It said the Department of Defense will "vigorously" pursue the technology to make this possible.

While the guidance document is deliberately vague about the nature of most of the futuristic weapons systems, it was clear about the first priority — the development of an anti-satellite weapon to be operational by 1987.

Also envisioned are military uses for the space shuttle, an approach that has already begun with several early shuttle flights.

The Department of Defense has responsibility, of course, of making sure the U.S. keeps up with the latest technology and is able to counter any new threat from the Soviets, but all the same, the planning to be able to "wage war from space" is a chilling move.

Even more disturbing is the military thinking that would have the nation rush to new weaponry before any treaty might interfere. Somehow, at the moment, this makes the search for peace seem even more difficult than it already is.

THE DAILY HERALD
Biloxi, Miss., April 12, 1983

Three weeks ago, when President Ronald Reagan called for long-term development of military technology to render nuclear missiles "impotent and obsolete," he was greeted with more scoffs than applause.

His idea isn't as much science fiction as the scoffers would have people believe. It is, rather, the initial step toward solving the present arms race between the U.S.S.R. and the U.S.

Disarmament talks between the two countries continue and continue without achieving either a halt in new weapons production and deployment or a reduction in the number of nuclear weapons already in place. Little encouragement is being produced by the talks.

The negotiating stalemate and the perception many people have that a nuclear war is now being considered as possible because some believe it is survivable has generated a worldwide peace movement that itself contains an inherent danger. Those who want peace at any price themselves remove the necessity for an aggressor nation to use arms — nuclear or conventional — to achieve conquest.

Deterrence, as Defense Secretary Caspar W. Weinberger said this week, "would be strengthened because we would remove an aggressor's capability to attack us rather than merely threaten retaliation after an attack has taken place."

The concept of Mutual Assured Destruction, holding that the other side could sufficiently withstand a nuclear attack to launch a counterattack, has prevented World War III but now seems to be weakening. Americans would be more secure knowing the nation's military could intercept and destroy ballistic missiles before they reached our country.

Such an antiballistic missile defense system doesn't yet exist, but experts say it is possible to devise one, using laser beams and charged particle beams.

The research and development may indeed constitute a major challenge, but the size of the challenge can be kept in perspective by considering America's response when the late John F. Kennedy issued the challenge to put a man on the moon in less than a decade. When he spoke, moonwalking was the stuff of science fiction, not reality. In less than ten years, it became history.

For each side to continue to build more missiles, bigger missiles, more sophisticated missiles and ditto for launching platforms may be an unbreakable cycle, as some contend. Building an effective anti-missile defense system is more sensible. And it would be more encouraging to see these efforts directed toward defense rather than toward weapons whose only use is offensive.

FORT WORTH STAR-TELEGRAM
Fort Worth, Texas, March 30, 1983

If proof were needed that the sort of "defensive" umbrella of anti-missile capability advocated last week by President Reagan is more than mere *Star Wars* sci-fi stuff, it came in the almost violent reaction from Soviet leader Yuri Andropov.

In the fear-war of nuclear blackmail, he whose missile is, being gored cries the loudest.

Reagan may have done the nation, and the world, a distinct service by bringing up the subject in a televised speech on national defense.

He brought it out of the closet, and subsequently it has turned out that both the Soviets and we ourselves have been quietly pursuing such missile-killing technology all along. Lasers, particle beams, non-nuclear anti-satellite systems — they are all well beyond the thinking stage, even beyond the drawing board in some cases, on both sides of the Iron Curtain.

These mind-boggling anti-weapon weapons may smack of Buck Rogers, but they appear to be the next generation of international armament, and thus the next generation of international arms diplomacy.

It is not only well for the United States to pursue this field of military technology — at more than the current $1 billion a year pace — it is essential.

At worst, lasers and particle beams and defensive missile killers will become the next lap to be run in the arms race. At best, they hold out the promise of nullifying the current, and mutual, threat of nuclear holocaust.

Either way, progress in this field is inevitable, and it behooves the United States not to be laggardly.

If there were doubts about this, Andropov's angry shouting should end those doubts. He calls U.S. anti-missile plans "insane" and a "bid to disarm the Soviet Union."

Which is exactly what Soviet scientists are bidding to achieve, vis a vis American nuclear deterrents, with their own research and development.

The greater danger may be that Soviet shouting, and U.S. responses such as Defense Secretary Caspar Weinberger's brushing off of Andropov's statement as "standard Soviet disinformation" will cloud the issue.

There is an opportunity here, in terms of turning the arms race to truly defensive weapons, for defusing the threat and reaching a greater stability between the two great nuclear powers, and it shouldn't be lost in rhetoric such as Andropov's.

Weinberger is right that freedom from fear of nuclear attack would be an enormous step for mankind. The next big job, while development continues in this technology, is to sell the Soviets on the idea.

the Charleston Gazette

Charleston, W. Va., April 9, 1983

PRESIDENT Reagan's call for "Star Wars" defense devices to stop ICBMs in flight without killing people has triggered worldwide reaction.

Comments from scientists, world leaders and political analysts ranged from it's wishful thinking, technologically impossible, a ploy to justify ever-greater defense spending, a decoy to make the Herculean job of negotiating disarmament seem less urgent, a shift from the nuclear age into the death-ray age, to a skillfully used ploy that has trumped the peace movement.

Physicist Uwe Henke of the Fusion Energy Foundation says a "foolproof" system could be built in 10 years. Physicist Edward Teller of H-bomb fame said Reagan's decision may "convert the Cold War into real peace." Other physicists say the concept is a pipe dream. Jerome Wiesner, former president of Massachusetts Institute of Technology and nuclear adviser to President Kennedy, says that, were Flash Gordon gizmos to halt 95 percent of 10,000 Soviet warheads, the 5 percent remainder would destroy America. Wiesner also says that space-station lasers can't repel cruise missiles that hug Earth's surface.

Soviet reaction has been predictably paranoid: the Kremlin fears that, if America is shielded from missile attack, the Pentagon will be free to launch a first strike.

Soviet fears, along with nuclear jitters around the globe, might be eased if America promised to share missile-stopping technology with the world. William F. Buckley Jr., friend of the president, recommended in a column that the U.S. share its discoveries with the world. Subsequently Reagan acknowledged this possibility.

Research is aiming toward Buck Rogers weaponry: x-ray lasers, free-electron lasers, proton beams, neutral particle beams — all predicted to have power to destroy ICBMs in flight; all still conjectural. Meanwhile, a few militarists say present-day, air-to-air rockets mounted on orbiting space stations, the "High Frontier" concept, could stop missiles without killing people.

If any revolutionary approach proves workable — even 95 percent workable — the U.S. could give it to the U.N. as international guardian against ICBM strikes from any direction. With more and more nations acquiring nuclear capability, danger never can be completely eliminated. But wouldn't U.N. sentry duty against missiles be a small step to protect the human race from incineration?

U.N. peacekeeping forces have contained several world crises. What worse crisis is imaginable than a world about to throw missiles hither and yon? What bigger peacekeeping mission is imaginable than to prevent this castrophe?

Pittsburgh Post-Gazette

Pittsburgh, Pa., April 7, 1983

Congressmen and columnists have been ridiculing Mr. Reagan for his so-called "Star Wars" push for a futuristic anti-missile defense. Yet as ill-timed and hastily conceived as the president's March 23 announcement was, his proposal may well be more than a pipe dream.

In the next two years, the Army will flight-test an experimental anti-ballistic weapon capable of destroying incoming Soviet nuclear warheads by non-nuclear means. The missile would not require high explosives because of the destructive capability inherent in its interception speed — 15,000 feet a second.

A Defense Department spokesman said experiments are being done to improve the potential weapon's accuracy and that it could be ready for deployment in three to five years.

There are problems with the system. Nuclear missiles could — depending on their design — detonate in the atmosphere when hit by such a defensive weapon. By itself, therefore, it could not eliminate the devastation that probably would result from a large-scale nuclear attack.

But another system being studied might meet that requirement. Dr. Uwe Parpart, a physicist at the Fusion Energy Foundation in New York, says the United States could have within 10 to 12 years a space-based system of laser weapons capable of "foolproof" protection against missile attack.

He also claims that a ground-based laser system that could defend key targets such as command centers and military bases could be deployed in about seven years if Congress were willing to invest about $10 billion from its annual defense budget of more than $200 billion.

Making such systems foolproof may seem like something from a science-fiction movie, but so did walking on the moon 10 years before Neil Armstrong took his giant step. Thus, while Mr. Reagan can only blame himself for the criticism heaped on him by scientists, defense experts and his own staff, his bad timing should not subject a serious proposal to ridicule.

The Times-Picayune
The States-Item

New Orleans, La., March 30, 1983

The furor that has followed President Reagan's remarks about developing absolute defenses against globe-spanning missiles is an even greater indication of the temper of these times than the fact that he decided to inject it into an address designed to gain support for his reasonable plea for a bigger defense budget.

He may have thought the idea would be a comforting thought for the long haul beyond these difficult days when armed defense costs so much money and seems to give so little confidence. But in suggesting that such a defense might be found and was worth putting money into finding, Mr. Reagan laid himself open to attack both as a dangerous would-be destabilizer of a balance of nuclear terror whose trim is a matter of bitter controversy and as a pious scientific dreamer who simply doesn't know his subject.

Mr. Reagan was not specific in what he meant, and neither official clarifiers nor critics have done much better. Everyone seems to be imagining futuristic laser and particle-beam weapons and pointing out that not even scientists are agreed on whether such things will work or would be practicable. And in a world that outlawed anti-missile defense systems on the principle that no country would launch a nuclear attack if it could not defend itself from one, the idea of a country's developing an impenetrable defense is enough to cause global goosebumps.

With all due respect to technology, we find it hard to imagine a feasible system of defense that would protect the United States from any kind of offensive weapon, from ICBMs coming down from space to cruise missiles slipping in a few hundred feet above the ground. Science fiction writers can conjure up all-purpose "force fields," but we wonder how far the idea would get through the Pentagon's R&D.

But it is no secret that both the United States and the Soviet Union have been researching lasers and the particle-beam principle and that space has been put to cautious military purposes. The Soviets already have a satellite that can destroy other satellites, and the United States is developing a satellite-killer system. Such research and development are necessary both to keep abreast of advancing technology and to prevent others from advancing beyond us in offensive weaponry.

The actual effect of Mr. Reagan's program will probably be to put more money into the field, a field in which defense is already a basic element. It will doubtless not produce an anti-doomsday machine, nor will it wreak havoc with the arms balance. The best defense against the cost of accelerating such programs to both nuclear superpowers and the threat of one side's achieving or seeming on the point of achieving invulnerability is still to negotiate control and reduction of the present weapons that are creating so much very real fear.

THE TENNESSEAN

Nashville, Tenn., March 25, 1983

IN his television speech, President Reagan pressed his case for a continued military buildup and support for his military budget, but the surprise of his talk was his call for a national effort to create an impregnable defense against nuclear attack.

The President called his proposal a "vision of the future that offers hope," in what appears to be a step toward the beginning of a sweeping, long-range change in national strategic doctrine. He said he has ordered an intensive research program aimed at an "ultimate goal of eliminating the threat posed by strategic nuclear missiles."

It is a vision of the future that is more chilling than hopeful. It obviously would mean the ultimate militarization of outer space. It would spur the Soviet Union to meet that challenge as soon as possible. Nobody at this point can say if the plan is technologically feasible, militarily desirable, or even in the range of what the nation could afford. In fact, nobody knows what the cost would be.

At best it seems to hold the false promise of eventual security from nuclear attack. But as history has proved, weapons of offense inevitably find cracks in the best weapons of defense. In a world where technology constantly moves forward, it is folly to talk of any guaranteed defense.

The superpowers have had two assumptions in their separate policies of deterrence in a nuclear age. One is that there is not presently any effective defense against nuclear attack, and the other is that if one came from either side, retaliation would be swift and sure. That is, in effect, a balance of terror as both sides have built up larger and larger nuclear arsenals.

If either side could create a credible and effective defense, that balance would be shattered, but with what results nobody can predict.

Although he offered no details, presumably the President's proposal apparently would include research into laser beams to destroy missiles as they rise and the use of anti-missile missiles both inside and outside the atmosphere over the U.S..

While research on such things is permitted under a 1972 treaty, that treaty limits anti-missile defenses in both the U.S. and the Soviet Union. Presumably, at some point of development, the treaty would have to be abrogated.

While moving toward a hoped-for defense against missile attack, Mr. Reagan said "we must remain constant in preserving the nuclear deterrent and maintaining a solid capability of flexible response" in event of a Soviet move against this country.

The curious thing about the speech, although it dwelled on defensive plans, was that the thrust was aggressive and warlike. It seemed almost an after thought that the President stressed he was "totally committed" to seeking nuclear arms reductions in negotiations with the Soviet Union. If that commitment is so strong, why should he talk of futuristic plans and more missiles in the meantime.

The best defense against nuclear holocaust would be in both sides seriously negotiating to cut down on their nuclear arsenals rather than accumulating more and more weapons. Mr. Reagan makes it sound as if the U.S. stands naked before the Soviet threat, which it most certainly does not. The game of numbers of nuclear missiles is misleading. If 10 such missiles on both sides would render unthinkable destruction on both, what does it matter if there are a thousand more? How many times can a country be destroyed?

Mr. Reagan may have intended all this as a "hard sell" for his military budget in the Senate, since shortly before he spoke, the House had rejected his military budget and halved the spending goal. But in doing so, he raised new concerns and apprehensions — as well as a brand new controversy over defense spending.

THE INDIANAPOLIS STAR

Indianapolis, Ind., March 25, 1983

First it was retired Army Lt. Gen. Daniel Graham and the High Frontier, then more recently nuclear scientist Edward Teller with Operation Savior. Though the names differ, the concepts are the same: a totally defensive strategy against nuclear weapons.

Both plans have sparked intense interest among ordinary citizens as well as knowledgeable scientists and technicians. The concept has also generated a burgeoning hope that fear of a nuclear Armageddon can be buried once and for all with other artifacts of primitive civilizations.

The non nuclear space age preventive strategy has now moved from the nation's living rooms and town halls into the world's consciousness, thanks to President Reagan's address Wednesday night.

The president proposed a formidable program to exploit technology in order to find the means of intercepting and disabling nuclear missiles after they have been launched but before they can reach the ground and wreak wholesale death and destruction.

The president's program is visionary, yes, but also feasible. The devices that would be tested — lasers, microwaves, particle and projectile beams — are still in the early stages of development. But scientists for some time have felt that beam defenses — employed by satellite and ground bases — could revolutionize nuclear strategy.

Gen. Graham speculated it would take 12 years to phase in the three-stage High Frontier plan, which has been discussed previously in this column. The president suggests decades of costly research and development, with superweapon success realized possibly before the end of the century.

"But is it not worth every investment necessary to free the world from the threat of nuclear war?" he asked. The answer is a clear and unequivocal, if not universal, yes.

The Soviets doubtless will declare the defensive doctrine another variant of the first-strike, pacifists will see it as a diversion to cover up an interim massing of nuclear capability and allies may fear it will dampen arms reduction talks and possibly trigger a first strike by the Soviets.

Those reactions should not deter the president from dedicating himself and the nation to pursuing what is by design and essence the best hope for defusing global fears.

Because decades will be required to fully deploy the defensive strategy, the United States remains perilously vulnerable to attack, a stark fact demonstrated by graphic comparisons of Soviet and U.S. weapons production and by top secret photos of Soviet military hardware and installations in Central America and the Caribbean.

The president served notice that our present nuclear deterrent posture must be maintained and strengthened until the space age defense system is in place.

Yet less than an hour before the president spoke, the House of Representatives adopted a Democrat-drafted budget that contains a mere 4 percent increase in military spending. That contrasts with the 10 percent increase Mr. Reagan contends is essential to reducing the gross disparity between U.S. and Soviet defense capability.

The president asked for public reaction to negate the House action and realize the higher military spending needed to stiffen our present deterrence posture. Both he and the nation's security need that reaction

RAPID CITY JOURNAL—
Rapid City, S.D., March 27, 1983

Depending on who is voicing the opinion, President Reagan's call for a national effort to develop means to defend against a missile attack was either a visionary view of the future or dangerous talk that could lead to new dimensions in the arms race.

A proponent of the switch in emphasis from offense to defense is Dr. Edward Teller, the physicist who created the hydrogen bomb. He contends that if the U.S. invests enough in anti-ballistic defensive measures, the arms race could be directed from offensive to defensive weapons and the threat of nuclear holocaust would be lessened.

Teller points out that because the machinegun and trenches of World War I made mass offensive attacks impossible, defensive strategy prevailed in the post-war period. However, in 1940 the German army skirted the Maginot Line, considered to be the ultimate in defense. Thereafter, offensive weaponry began to dominate, culminating with nuclear weapons.

In the U.S. and Soviet arms buildup, both sides have concentrated on developing offensive nuclear weapons. The theory of Mutual Assured Destruction (MAD) evolved as a formula which might prevent each country from attacking the other.

Teller feels if the technology of defense can be developed to the point that it cannot be defeated except by a much greater effort on the part of the offense, then war will not be winnable for the side that started it. The only course left would be for both sides to turn to a defensive strategy.

However, plans to deploy a new generation of weapons in space is seen by some scientists as posing a greater threat than the security they seem to offer on the surface.

Basis of that view is that the development of offensive weapons is much cheaper than defensive weapons and that for every defensive innovation, there is a much cheaper way for offensive weapons to circumvent it. If that is true, there's the possibility political leaders might decide they could launch an attack and defeat attempted retaliation with defensive weapons. That would pull the nuclear "trip wire" tighter because both sides would have to seriously consider launching the first strike.

Whether there will be a switch in emphasis from offensive to defensive weapons will depend on technological developments. Recent advancements in radar, long wave infrared sensing, and computer technologies have encouraged researchers to suggest a number of very accurate anti-ballistic missiles could be developed.

Whatever course this country follows, the search for defensive technologies will take years or even decades. But until other ways are found to lessen the nuclear threat, pursuing that search would be a prudent course.

The Des Moines Register
Des Moines, Iowa, March 25, 1983

Lift that peacekeeper mantle from President Reagan's newest initiative "to free the world from the threat of nuclear war" and there lies a very dangerous proposal.

In 1972, the United States and the Soviet Union reached perhaps their most important arms-control agreement when they signed the Anti-Ballistic Missile Treaty, limiting the deployment of defensive missile systems. It was difficult, given the technological momentum of defensive-weapons research, but the overwhelming sentiment on both sides was that an ABM system (1) could not work and (2) would encourage a first-strike mentality.

Now Reagan wants to revive the illusion that a good defense can end the arms race. In answer to it-can't-work thinking, he offers the hope of new technology. Yet he offers it to a world in which one weapon can destroy a city and hundreds of thousands of people, a world in which only the perfect defense will suffice. What laser can provide that?

As for the destabilizing effect of defensive weapons, Reagan said only that he recognizes "certain problems and ambiguities." These include, presumably, the fact that either superpower, operating under the illusion that it could limit retaliatory damage to acceptable levels, would be greatly encouraged to make a first strike.

How must this look to the Russians? If the United States were to achieve — or think it had achieved — the ability to shoot down retaliatory Soviet missiles, wouldn't the men in the Kremlin have to consider that America might be planning a devastating first strike? Certainly the Pentagon would make that assumption about the Soviets if it were discovered that they had an ABM system.

It is such fears that brought about the ABM treaty, a significant achievement that Reagan now proposes to violate in intent if not in word. With his speech, he has invited the Soviets to embark on yet another surge forward in the arms race, this one still more costly and more dangerous than the last.

THE BLADE
Toledo, Ohio., March 31, 1983

PRESIDENT Reagan's call for a strong American effort to develop highly sophisticated anti-missile weapons is not as wild-eyed an idea as some of his critics are making it out to be. In typical Reagan fashion the President has advanced a thought-provoking proposal which merits serious consideration.

It is, to be sure, a radical departure from the MAD concept (mutual assured destruction) under which both superpowers face the certainty of a nuclear response to any first-strike action one might consider. Under that deterrence idea, defensive weapons against nuclear missiles have had no meaningful role.

That does not mean that plans should not be considered now for possible development some time in the future. Under the President's proposal, defensive systems might eventually become a significant part of the national defense picture.

It is true that deployment of anti-ballistic missile systems is outlawed by the SALT I treaty of 1972 with the Soviet Union, except for one permissible installation on each side. But that does not prevent research and development of such systems which, in fact, has been going on in the scientific communities of both countries for quite some time.

Scientists in the United States are divided on the practicality of the Reagan plan, with some referring to it as a pipe dream of "death rays" designed to knock out Soviet missiles before they can reach their targets. Others, however, see it as well within the realm of possibility. The Pentagon already has contracts out for the design of space-based laser systems, for example, some of which are well advanced.

Anyone who thinks these kinds of weapons are beyond the bounds of believability might recall that many scientists — while accepting the theory — were uncertain that the atomic bomb would work, either, at the time it was being developed. And Americans listened with incredulity when President John Kennedy pledged the United States in 1961 to put a man on the moon and return him safely within a decade. But the technical and scientific genius of this country was brought to bear on the problems involved with unprecedented intensity, culminating in the moon walk of Ohioan Neil Armstrong and his companion, Edwin Aldrin, in 1969.

It is known that Soviet scientists are proceeding with their own advanced research on anti-missile devices. That alone suggests that the United States cannot afford to ignore that facet of defense. On the other hand, it does not mean that both powers cannot proceed with efforts to achieve reductions in offensive nuclear missiles, such as have been going on in Geneva.

If there is one thing that arms races of the past have demonstrated, it is that today's breakthrough is tomorrow's passe system. President Reagan is not talking about pie-in-the-sky "Star Wars" weaponry in encouraging this kind of advanced research. He is outlining attainable scientific achievements which might one day be essential to this nation's defense.

...AND WE'VE ASSEMBLED A CRACK TEAM OF EXPERTS TO ADVISE US ON THE PROJECT...

SPACE-AGE DEFENSE

©1983 SAN DIEGO UNION

The Detroit News

Detroit, Mich., June 6, 1983

The skeptics who scoff at President Reagan's proposal to build space-age defensive systems would do well to read the "High Frontiers" thesis of Lt. Gen. Daniel Graham.

Gen. Graham, former deputy director of the CIA and a military adviser to Mr. Reagan during the campaign, developed the thesis for the Heritage Foundation last year. It is a benchmark work that is reflected in President Reagan's March 23 call for a switch to a defensive posture that could, by the turn of the century, render intercontinental ballistic missiles (ICBMs) impotent.

The general begins with the assertion that today's strategic doctrine is not defensive. The two superpowers possess sufficient missiles to destroy each other's society, and there is no defense against them except for the anti-ballistic missiles (ABMs) in place around Moscow.

The peace has been kept for 38 years by a "balance of terror" that holds civilian populations hostage. In theory, no nation could attack another without risking a retaliatory holocaust. This is the doctrine of Mutually Assured Destruction (MAD).

The old strategy has been invalidated by the Soviet Union because (says the presidential strategic arms commission) that country "probably possesses" enough weapons with sufficient accuracy to destroy America's 1,047 ICBM silos "using only a portion of their own ICBM forces." The United States can't do such damage to the Soviet Union using *all* of its weapons. This is what is meant by the "window of vulnerability."

Gen. Graham is against "MAD-ness." He says the United States and its allies can't hope to match the growing mass of Soviet weaponry, strategic and conventional, and would be foolish to play a quantitative game that the Soviet Union could win.

Instead, the United States should do an "end run" around Soviet global strategy, engaging Moscow on technological high ground where Moscow is weakest. This leads away from proliferation of nuclear weapons (it might even make the MX missiles unnecessary) to the acquisition of

earth-orbit, non-nuclear defensive weapons designed to *destroy* nuclear warheads before they do harm.

"High Frontiers" postulates three main layers of defense, all of which employ known technologies:

● A "point" defense system, batteries of launchers at ICBM sites that would throw out swarms of unguided rockets — small, steel-case projectiles with enough mass and velocity to smash a warhead just before it reaches detonation range. These could be in use within two or three years.

● Space-borne "trucks" that orbit the earth, each with sensing, control and guidance devices, and numbers of non-nuke projectiles that knock out missiles just after launch. These could be operational in the 1990s.

● Laser, particle-beam energy, or microwave weapons to destroy missiles in space. These technologies, now under intensive research here and in the Soviet Union, could be ready in a decade.

Back in 1962, the skeptics thought John F. Kennedy was daft when he committed the United States to put a man on the moon within the decade. But the goal was achieved seven years later. From that day, anything in space became possible.

Since then, we have witnessed faultless space shuttle flights, and most people are now indifferent to the everyday miracles of satellites that bring us TV programs, distant telephone calls, insights into our geography, more accurate weather forecasts, more accurate navigation for ships and planes, and even such spin-off products like better ovenware.

But what of the legal arguments?

Liberals decry space defense, arguing that the atmosphere should be sanitized of weaponry and, further, that the ABM treaty and resolutions of the United Nations prohibit militarization.

This is naive. Space is already militarized. Both sides use passive systems to "sky spy" the other side and the disarmament treaties forbid interference with such "eyes."

In addition, the Soviet Union has never shown much interest in far space. The USSR launches 75 satellites a year, four or

five times more than the United States, all in low earth orbit. Seventy percent have purely military roles, 15 percent combine military and civil uses, and only 15 percent purely civil purposes.

The Soviet Union is the only nation that has successfully killed one satellite with another, a crude experiment that has no known peaceful applications.

On the second point, the ABM treaty is ambiguous and Gen. Graham's weapons are outside its definitions. In any event, the treaty sets up a forum for discussion of new issues and can be canceled by either side on six months' notice.

Space is the last arena where the Soviet Union wants a High Noon meeting with the United States. Why? Because the United States has the lead in miniaturization of components and can do infinitely more with one pound of freight. Further, the United States has the space shuttle delivery and maintenance capability the Soviet Union lacks.

Gen. Graham meets two other critical arguments head on. It would be foolish to demand a perfect, impermeable — and very costly — space defense system. A simpler system that can destroy, say, 20 percent of the first-strike missiles would cast doubt on the success of a pre-emptive strike, and that doubt could well prevent the attack. America's retaliatory power would be restored without building another ICBM. And spaceborne non-nuclear weapons would be incapable of killing a single Russian because they are *defensive,* not *offensive.*

Gen. Graham's blueprint for "assured survival" is a doctrine of hope, the opposite of the despair and resignation implicit in an "assured destruction" policy.

President Reagan also believes it is better to build weapons that eat nuclear warheads than to build more warheads. But he also knows that one system can't be trashed until a better system is operational.

Gen. Graham's central message is this: It is wiser to don a bullet-proof vest than expose a bare chest to Moscow's military might.

The San Diego Union

San Diego, Calif., July 31, 1983

When Ronald Reagan announced his support for an actual defense against nuclear attack this spring, the idea was dismissed out of hand as a Star Wars concept, light years from reality. Yet a few days ago, the Air Force used a laser weapon to shoot down five consecutive sidewinder missiles moving at 2,000 miles an hour. E.T., call your office.

Unfortunately, the Pentagon seems apathetic — even negative — about proposals to build a defensive shield not in the next century, but now.

Defense expert John Gardner, head of a Pentagon study on defense technology, testified in April that there are "no technological barriers" to building a non-laser fleet of satellites capable of knocking out about 98 percent of any Soviet missile attack, and doing it by 1987. Yet when Gardner solicited help from industry contractors in July, he specifically asked them *not* to "emphasize early deployment." He said the United States is looking for plans that will take until the "post-2000 era" to begin.

Mr. Gardner's argument, and the argument of many critics of strategic defense, is that most of the quick-to-deploy systems would knock out "only" 95 to 99 percent of a Soviet attack. In other words, they would save 50 to 150 million lives, but that's not good enough for nuclear war.

That may or may not be valid strategy. Nuclear physicist Edward Teller argues, convincingly, that a fast, cheap, but crude defense system is precisely what's needed. Early defenses would immediately close the vulnerability of U.S. missiles (at less than the MX will cost). And they would solve some of the technological kinks that any defense system will face — like how to defend our defensive satellites against attack themselves.

Then, when more exotic technology comes along, we'll be ready.

Valid or not, all these strategic points are, well, strategic — not technological.

Reagan science adviser George Keyworth has been overseeing that report — due on the President's desk by October — from the White House. We suggest Mr. Keyworth draft a swift memorandum reminding Mr. Gardner that his job is to conduct research, not manipulate grand strategy.

What a shame it will be if that memo is never sent — and a proposal to end the madness of Mutual Assured Destruction strategies gets buried in the "out" file of a Pentagon bureaucrat.

The Des Moines Register

Des Moines, Iowa, June 20, 1983

President Reagan's Star Wars talk has been an abundant source of comedy material for gag-writers, but the sad fact is that the day isn't far off.

From Livermore, Calif., comes a report on a $55 million accelerator built to develop a gun — about the size of a conventional navy gun or missile launcher and probably lighter — that will shoot 50 billion electrons a second at a missile or a plane, destroying its interior with heat.

The problem is that the electron beam would come out like a bolt of lightning, and scientists are trying to figure out how to straighten and aim it.

"Electron bullets are lethal objects, that much is not in question," said Richard Briggs, head of the weapons project at the Lawrence Livermore Laboratory. "But we don't know how to hold the electrons in a beam, and we are not sure how far the beam can be cast."

It would be nice to think that someone was spending $55 million on finding a way to abolish the idea that an electron gun or any other weapon is necessary. But that's too much to hope for: like thinking that science could solve the mystery of socks' disappearing in the laundry.

Houston Chronicle

Houston, Texas, July 29, 1983

An "integrated laser subsystem" aboard an Air Force cargo plane "successfully defeated" five Sidewinder missiles fired at it from a fighter-bomber. That's about all the Air Force is reporting, saying details are classified.

Laser is an acronym for "light amplification through stimulated emission of radiation." President Reagan has ordered research into the possibility of using high-energy laser beams to knock out strategic missiles as they travel through space toward their target.

The president's program was called *Star Wars* gimmickry by some. Not so. Not when there is already the capability of intercepting air-to-air missiles traveling 2,000 mph.

The terse Air Force announcement may have the same significance in the future of warfare as that day in 1942 under the Chicago University football stadium when an atomic reaction was first sustained.

The Star-Ledger

Newark, N.J., August 13, 1983

Down in the Pentagon they're all excited about the latest achievement in high-flying technology. For the first time ever, an airborne laser has disabled air-to-air missiles.

The experimental laser weapon, carried aboard a modified Boeing 707 jetliner, crippled five Sidewinder missiles. The Sidewinders had been shot from an A7 Corsair fighter-bomber in what could be classified as a high-tech shootout.

What has the Pentagon brass dancing on air is that the new success carries the nation one tiny step closer to President Reagan's "Buck Rogers" defense strategy, as articulated in a May speech.

The latest laser experiments have been going full blast for several months now, and while the initial results are encouraging, the nation is still has a long way to go to duplicate the advanced defense techniques envisioned in the Buck Rogers comic strips, circa the 1930s.

No planning for the defense of the country should exclude a reasonable, bilateral, mutually verifiable nuclear arms reduction agreement with the Soviet Union.

Such an agreement, however, depends as much on the leaders in the Kremlin as it does on the occupants of the White House, and to date there has been little indication to suggest that the Soviet Union is serious about negotiating an arms retrenchment pact.

Part II: U.S. Policy—
Arms Spending Decisions

Decisions about major weapons systems are the concrete evidence of a nation's defense policy. It is at least partly for this reason that "big-ticket" items such as the MX missile system or the B-1 bomber program excite a great deal of controversy.

The MX program grew out of the belief that the land-based missiles of the United States, the Minutemen and Titans, were vulnerable to a Soviet surprise nuclear attack. The MX missiles were designed to meet that threat by rendering the Soviet land-based missiles equally vulnerable—and, in addition, to reduce U.S. vulnerability by being themselves difficult to target. Since the mobile "racetrack" basing was first proposed by President Carter, of course, the MX has become a missile without a home, as each new basing system has been rejected by a skeptical Congress.

The development of the B-1 bomber and the naval building program reflect similar strategic considerations. The land-based missiles are considered the least "survivable," or most vulnerable, delivery system in the nuclear arsenal. Least vulnerable are the submarines carrying ballistic missiles, and somewhere in between are the traditional bombers carrying nuclear bombs. The most recent additions to the strategic nuclear arsenal are the cruise missiles, which can be launched from planes, from the ground, or from ships or submarines. (Cruise missiles are highly accurate missiles capable of flying close to the ground to evade radar detection.) President Carter cancelled the B-1 program in 1977, on the grounds that air-launched cruise missiles carried by modified B-52's would be more effective than another larger manned bomber. The Reagan Administration, operating under a different theory of nuclear deterrence, has decided to press ahead with the B-1, claiming that the B-52's will soon be unserviceable, and in addition to pursue development of the Stealth "advanced technology" bomber.

A portion of the defense budget that receives less publicity is the substantial part devoted to the maintenance of U.S. armed forces around the globe. By some estimates, about 75% of the proposed 1984 defense budget will be funnelled into supporting active units of the Army, Air Force, Navy and Marines in Europe, Asia and other overseas bases, as well as maintaining the Rapid Deployment Force. (By contrast, the combined cost of the MX and B-1 programs would come to about 5% of the total budget.) This less visible spending is also the result of national policy; in recent years, the U.S. has grown increasingly interventionist in defending its perceived interests abroad. If it is to maintain this level of activity overseas, the U.S. must have larger forces. The means of recruiting these forces, and the separate question of the level of wages to be paid them, are also a part of the larger defense spending picture.

Reagan Administration Attempts to Resume Nerve Gas Production

The production of chemical weapons has been banned in the United States since 1969, when President Nixon renounced their use and ordered the destruction of U.S. germ warfare stocks. Then and now the discussion of "nerve gas" and other chemical weapons has centered upon moral issues involved in their use rather than upon their strategic value. The Reagan Administration, however, in seeking to revive the development of so-called "binary" weapons, has argued that they are necessary because the Soviet Union is stockpiling similar chemical weapons and has refused to negotiate a treaty with the U.S. prohibiting their use. (The term "binary" derived from the use of two relatively harmless chemicals contained in separate compartments in bombs or artillery shells. When the bombs or shells exploded, the chemicals combined to form a deadly nerve gas. These weapons were considered safer for U.S. troops to use and store than "unitary" chemical arms.) The first spending bill passed under the Reagan Administration, the supplemental appropriations bill for fiscal 1981, included a $20 million appropriation to equip an existing Army plant in Pine Bluff, Ark. for making binary munitions. The U.S. and its Western allies had become concerned in 1980 over reports that the U.S.S.R. was using chemical weapons in Afghanistan, and the North Atlantic Treaty Organization had repeatedly urged member nations to upgrade their defenses against chemical weapons. President Reagan continued to press for funds to produce binary weapons in his 1983 defense authorization request, but was handed a defeat when the $54 million earmarked for actual production of the weapons was eliminated by House-Senate conferees. (The Senate had narrowly passed the funds, but they were dropped by the House, which passed a ban on binary weapons production.) High-level Administration officials, including Secretary of Defense Caspar Weinberger and Secretary of State George Shultz, lobbied Congress to include binary weapons in the fiscal 1984 authorization. The House again voted against the funds, in June, while the Senate passed them by a vote of 50 to 49, with Vice President George Bush casting the deciding ballot. The bill fashioned by conferees in August included the $130 million for production of binary bombs and artillery shells; chemical arms opponents in the House have vowed to fight the provision when the bill reaches the House for final passage.

WORCESTER TELEGRAM
Worcester, Mass., September 29, 1980

Almost without warning, the issue of whether the United States should embark once again on a program to develop offensive nerve gas weapons surfaced in the U.S. Senate.

The plan, a modest $4 million beginning for a nerve gas production facility in Arkansas, gained quick preliminary approval.

For more than a generation now, the superpowers have had a silent agreement that bombs, planes, guns and explosives would be enough. None has wished to be identified with the horrible, choking, grovelling death associated with nerve gas.

In fact, the United States and the Soviet Union have been negotiating a treaty to limit use of chemical weapons.

There is a worry that the Russians are ahead in the production of nerve gas and in the production of machinery to decontaminate aircraft and personnel who might come in contact with chemical weaponry.

There is a suggestion that we then must outproduce the competition in order to deter the use of such weapons.

There is a problem in the fact that we may well be way behind in the production of protective gear for our troops and in decontamination equipment and procedures.

Some in Congress argue well that we should make our investment in the area of protecting personnel and equipment from the possibility of attack with nerve gas. Bombs and rockets can do a more effective job of deterring attack in the first place and of responding to any attack than can chemical weapons.

Building a nerve gas production facility in Arkansas does not answer questions about how we would deliver such weaponry to the battlefield, how we would protect our troops from a chemical attack. It does raise questions of safety for people in this country.

Congress should look to the greater problems that have surfaced recently with our military machine. Equipment must be upgraded, the personnel problems solved and the issue of making the all-volunteer military an effective fighting and defensive force addressed.

Chemical warfare stands well below other critical items on a list of military problems that need solving.

The Honolulu Advertiser
Honolulu, Ha., September 28, 1980

During World War I, 30 percent of all American casualties were caused by poison gas. That experience led most nations to curb the use of chemical agents during war.

But it was not until 1969 that an American president took action to stop all work on biological arms and begin to reduce our chemical weapons stockpile.

NOW, HOWEVER, the House and Senate have done an about-face and passed separate bills which would fund construction of a new factory to produce chemical weapons — particularly "binary" nerve gas shells. These are artillery rounds and bombs which contain separate relatively safe chemicals that are mixed before the weapon explodes to produce a deadly poison gas.

A conference committee must now decide the fate of the construction authorization. It should hold up the $3 million both chambers set aside for the project, and allow the administration to complete a review of the consequences of rejoining a chemical weapons race.

The fact is that even now we are at a disadvantage with the Soviets. They have continued an active chemical arms production and research effort during our moratorium and, according to the Los Angeles Times, the Soviet army may have 20 to 30 times as many chemical-warfare units as does the United States.

That alone might be cited as a compelling reason to begin our own production now, but there also are reasons for caution.

FIRST, WHERE would nerve gas stockpiles be placed? It seems unlikely our NATO allies would be enthusiastic about having their countries used as chemical arms storage sites. And, especially after the Titan missile mishap in Arkansas, many American communities would not be pleased with such a prospect.

Second, what are the related costs of such a decision? For instance, there will be a need for more trained soldiers. This comes at a time when skilled manpower appears hard to come by in the armed services, and when competition for defense dollars is keen.

Third, will production of chemical weapons mean the United States has given up on its efforts to institute a treaty banning such lethal arms? Or will American policy be to achieve nerve gas parity with the Soviets, only to then try and exact a freeze or reduction in chemical stockplies?

There are many fiscal and social costs as well as military factors involved in these decisions, and they should be weighed carefully before we commit ourselves to establishing a facility to again produce nerve gas.

The Providence Journal

Providence, R.I., June 8, 1981

The Senate vote was a squeaker.

On May 21, by a tally of 50 to 48, the U.S. Senate approved President Reagan's bid for $20 million to equip an Arkansas plant for production of binary nerve gas weapons. The decision was somewhat of a piece with others supporting the Reagan military build-up; but the closeness of the vote reflected a deep controversy running to the nature of such weapons.

Advocates of producing these weapons make several forceful points. For one thing, they note, the Soviet Union has been racing ahead of the United States in testing and producing its own sizable stocks of chemical weapons for possible combat use. Thus, they say, we should catch up so not to be caught, in some future conflict, at a serious disadvantage.

Moreover, it is argued (with some reason) that the new type of chemical weapon is safer than the type still in U.S. stockpiles. The binary system consists of two gases kept separate (and each, by itself harmless) until they are mixed when their artillery shell container is fired.

Both these arguments, however, hinge on a debatable premise: that such devices employed in war would give American forces a needed combat edge that they could not better obtain from other weapons in their arsenal.

Nerve gas is deadly and unpredictable in its effects, subject to tricks of the weather and posing threats to friendly troops and civilian populations as well as to enemy forces. The idea of its use assumes an unlikely, slow-moving conflict involving massed ground troops, as was the case in World War I when poison gases were last used on a large scale. The United States since 1925 has steadfastly supported the Geneva Protocal banning the use of poisonous gases in combat; and in 1969 U.S. production of chemical weapons was halted by President Nixon.

To abandon this half-century of restraint seems both unnecessary and risky. Clearly, given evidence of the Soviets' own chemical-warfare buildup, the United States should work on defensive measures (improved gas masks, protective clothing) and combat tactics to cope with such agents. But a new array of chemical munitions would vastly complicate any future combat situation, bringing little advantage in relation to the added risks. As Oregon's Sen. Mark Hatfield said, in unsuccessfully urging defeat of the measure: "This is insane. This is launching us into a system that could bring disaster to this earth." Senators Pell and Chafee, it is worth noting, also voted against this measure. They should keep up the fight.

THE TENNESSEAN

Nashville, Tenn., June 12, 1981

IN a close vote recently the U.S. Senate agreed to the Reagan administration's plans to spend $20 million for new binary chemical weapons. It was a vote that should have failed.

Defense Secretary Caspar Weinberger lobbied for the funds, arguing that deferral would be "tantamount to unilateral disarmament," which is arrant nonsense.

The vote signals the reversal of U.S. policy on chemical and biological weapons over more than a half century. President Franklin D. Roosevelt asserted in 1943 that the "use of such weapons has been outlawed by the general opinion of civilized mankind," and vowed the nation would never use such weapons unless they were first used by its enemies.

That policy was reaffirmed in 1969 by the then President Richard Nixon, and in 1975, President Gerald Ford ratified the convention prohibiting the use of biological weapons.

It is curious why the Reagan administration would reverse such long-standing policy. Its argument is that the Soviet Union is ahead of the U.S., which is probably right. But the best deterrent is not one of trying to stockpile more chemical weapons than the Soviet has, but to step up defensive capability against such weapons in the form of better gas masks, protective clothing and combat training.

The administration is doing that by seeking more funds for chemical warfare defenses. It would have been better off to concentrate on that rather than asking for a down-payment on a proposed $3 billion chemical warfare program the nation does not need. The U.S. and NATO already have enough chemical warfare weapons stockpiled to respond to any such use by the Soviet Union. In this case would it not be better to use negotiation rather than proliferation?

SAN JOSE NEWS

San Jose, Calif., May 29, 1981

EVEN while creating other ways to kill and maim each other's soldiers and civilians, the world's nations have avoided any widespread use of chemical weapons ever since World War I — on grounds that chemical warfare is particularly hideous.

But now that ban is beginning to break down. The Reagan administration and Congress are jumping into a chemical weapons race with the Russians that could rival nuclear arms stockpiling in the sheer monstrosity of its potential for human destruction.

Abandoning a 12-year ban on U.S. production of nerve gas and other chemical warfare agents, the administration has committed itself to a new generation of "binary" chemical weapons. The name derives from the fact that the active agents are stored as separate components that don't combine and are not lethal until the shell containing them is fired. This supposedly makes binary weapons safer to store than the aging stocks of chemical warfare agents the Army already has on hand.

The House already has appropriated money for binary nerve gas production at the Army's chemical warfare facility at Pine Bluff, Ark. And last week the Senate approved $20 million for howitzers to launch canisters containing binary weapons.

The argument for all of this, not surprisingly, is that we must keep up with the Russians, who presumably have been building new offensive chemical weapons. For us not to do likewise, according to Defense Secretary Caspar Weinberger, would be "tantamount to unilateral disarmament."

That reasoning has been cited for all sorts of other military buildups, but surely there are limits to the logic that if the Russians find a fiendish new weapon, we not only have to have the same thing, but we need more of it than they do.

The recent U.S. administrations that banned production of offensive chemical weapons did not discontinue work on defenses against such weapons, which is only prudent. This administration, however, has adopted the philosophy that the best defense against chemical warfare is the offensive ability to wage that same kind of war. There is a point, however, at which the logic of escalation becomes dangerously irrational. Suppose it were discovered that the Russians had gained a demonstrable military edge of some sort by testing an especially gruesome variety of nerve gas on their own citizens in concentration camps where civilians were used as guinea pigs. Would we feel compelled to do likewise?

If that kind of ethical question does not halt the rush toward chemical stockpiling, a practical consideration should. Implicit in the Senate debate last week was the understanding that the new binary canisters and the howitzers for shooting them are needed in the event of a Soviet invasion of Western Europe. Yet all of our NATO allies have officially disavowed use of chemical weapons, and don't even want nerve gas stored on their soil. So what is the Army going to do — line up those howitzers along our eastern seaboard and fire the binary canisters all the way across the Atlantic?

THE CHRISTIAN SCIENCE MONITOR

Boston, Mass., May 26, 1981

The news dictates comment on another military matter, and we beg the reader's indulgence for a page that must seem like our own defense buildup. The Senate has responded to an unusually intense administration lobbying effort and gone along with House approval of $20 million for the production of nerve-gas weapons. Now President Reagan ought to seize the opportunity to work no less vigorously for Soviet and world agreement to outlaw these and other means of chemical warfare. A first step would be to end his suspension of the Geneva talks in which Moscow and Washington have for years been seeking chemical disarmament along the lines of the 1972 international convention against biological warfare.

There is no moral excuse for any nation to use such horrifying weapons, ones to which unprotected civilians are more vulnerable than the increasingly well-protected military. And the difficulties of effective military use add to the reasons for resisting a new arms race in the chemical realm. At the least the United States should not plunge ahead — in a program for which $20 million would provide only the first "module" — without the full public airing that has never taken place.

Two arguments have been advanced *for* plunging ahead. One is a supposed — but undocumented — Soviet buildup of chemical weapons, and their possible use in Afghani-

stan. Another is the supposed — but disputed — "safety" in handling of the binary nerve-gas weapons the administration wants.

One technical problem is that the binary weapons have not been fully tested, as existing chemical weapons have been. Indeed, the particular artillery shell designated for the first production module would be an uncertain version of a well-tested nerve-gas artillery shell already in good supply and with a recognized record of full safety.

Complicating the matter further is the reluctance of the US's NATO allies to accept more stores of chemical weapons on European soil. They know the projections of millions of civilian casualties, contrasted with relatively few military casualties, if such weapons were used in a 10-day war. (The binary shell itself is known to have a leakage problem that could result in trailing its cargo over the people of the side firing it.)

The experience of World War I shows that

despite the agony, the use of chemical weapons was never militarily decisive except in a first surprise use on unprotected victims. Now Moscow's buildup of protection against chemical warfare is known, even though its production is not; and the US also is making strides in protecting personnel.

Experience likewise shows, as in the case of biological warfare, that when the sides see that a weapon is really not to their benefit they can be persuaded to limit its production and use. Chemical weapons could be seen in this light, if thoughtless action does not bring an arms race neither side wants. Last year in the Geneva talks a step of progress was achieved toward agreement on how the outstanding question of verification could be approached. Mr. Reagan's combination of suspending the talks and asking for the $20 million makes it incumbent on him to reassure friend and adversary alike that his country continues to abhor such weaponry.

ST. LOUIS POST-DISPATCH

St. Louis, Mo., June 6, 1981

The vote by the Senate to provide $20 million for retooling a nerve gas plant in Pine Bluff, Ark., represents a new and ominous turn in U.S. defense planning. The plant is to produce a type of chemical munition called binary artillery shells. These shells contain two separate chemical mixtures, which are combined in flight and form a lethal nerve gas. The total cost for the program is estimated at $2.5 billion.

Proponents of the program argue that binary shells will be safer to handle and will counter new Soviet chemical weapons. The first argument may be true, but it is unproven. The second argument is based more upon the emotional desire for "keeping up with Ivan" than it is upon sound military planning. The U.S. already has a large chemical weapons arsenal — estimated at between 28,000 and 38,000 tons. The size of Soviet stockpile is unknown but is believed to be several times larger than that of the U.S.

It is unlikely, however, that the gas weapons already on hand will ever be used. Apart from the moral considerations against their use, the restraint on chemical warfare lies in the fact that they are militarily counterproductive. The effects of gas are hard to control; they literally change with the wind. Gas poisons the battlefield for both friend and foe, making even the most basic actions, such as eating or changing clothes, impossible. Even with chemical warfare suits and gas masks, soldiers are only able to fight for a few hours. The history of gas in combat shows that it does not provide the attacker with a war-winning weapon.

With an already large chemical arsenal, the Reagan administration's plans to reopen nerve gas production would be a waste of money. If the money is to be spent on chemical warfare, it should go into developing better gas masks and protective suits for American soldiers.

The Oregonian

Portland, Ore., May 26, 1981

Sen. Mark O. Hatfield has called the plan adopted by Congress to spend nearly $20 million to equip a facility to manufacture nerve gas "insane." It is all of that, of course, and more.

Last year, when the same appropriation was before the Senate and Hatfield blocked it by threatening a filibuster, Secretary of Defense Harold Brown was secretly arguing that forcing the issue risked inflaming public opinion in Europe and thereby jeopardizing efforts to install new missile defenses in NATO countries.

What the appropriation does is to provide money for construction of a facility to manufacture binary nerve gas at Pine Bluff, Ark. This is a material that does not become lethal until its two chemical components contained in artillery shells are mixed and released as a deadly gas on impact.

Soviet forces have long had important chemical-gas warfare capabilities, and NATO commanders have been responding by equiping their forces with protective clothing and masks to meet the threat. Whether a stockpile of U.S. binary gas will prove a deterrent is anybody's guess, since, unlike strategic weapons, the gas would be used in tactical situations where it

would not always provide a margin of victory and might prove an inferior response.

Whatever dubious military values are claimed for binary nerve gases, civilian populations of Europe and other parts of the world would become the victims as the chemicals would be sucked into the atmosphere and transported over great distances, damaging all forms of life.

The $20 million appropriation (it was $19 million last year) is only the foot in the door, as it does not buy any gas production. Under a 1975 law, Congress is required to certify that national security requires production. But if the votes exist for appropriations, they may be there for certification.

At a time when painful cuts are being made in the budget, affecting the lives of most Americans, Hatfield is correct in saying, "This is insane, to ask the American people to buy a weapons system in 20 minutes that would change the whole face of the earth." That Congress is rubber-stamping this appropriation is a disgrace. It is a waste of tax money, and it hurts the nation's world image without compensatory security gains.

The Washington Post

Washington, D.C., May 27, 1981

CONGRESS has appropriated $20 million for a plant to make new chemical weapons. The relatively small amount of money clouds the significance of the decision, which breaks a decade-long moratorium on the production of these weapons.

True, this is not a decision actually to make the weapons. But it is the key first step. Once the plant is built, it is unlikely that it will not be used. It would cost several billion dollars to construct a modern chemical arsenal. Before Congress and the administration start down that road, a number of questions need to be debated.

Unlike traditional chemical weapons, the new type —called "binaries"—are inert until after they are fired. They remove any danger to people who manufacture, transport or use them; the new technology thus makes chemical weapons more attractive to military commanders—and presumably also to terrorists.

But despite their improved safety, chemical weapons are still of questionable military utility at best. Strategists argue that the United States must be able to retaliate in kind to a chemical attack. But why? On a practical level, troops wearing protective gear are largely unaf-

fected by chemicals, so that many other types of weapons would provide a much stronger response.

Because most of the casualties from chemical warfare would be civilians, nearly all Western European countries oppose—or legally forbid—the production or storage of chemical weapons on their soil. A U.S. chemical arsenal could therefore disrupt rather than strengthen NATO forces. At the very least, a prior agreement needs to be reached with our NATO allies before money is spent on weapons that might never be allowed on European soil.

U.S. production of binary chemical weapons could damage or destroy one of the most hopeful arms control opportunities still available. A treaty outlawing chemical warfare has been under negotiation for several years. And while it is a more difficult undertaking than banning biological warfare, the agreement already reached in that closely related area suggests that a satisfactory treaty on chemical warfare can be achieved.

It is a truism that not all defense spending contributes to the nation's security. The decision to begin making a new generation of chemical weapons is an example. It should be reconsidered.

ALBUQUERQUE JOURNAL

Albuquerque, N.M., May 28, 1981

Nerve gas kills civilians. At least soldiers have a chance; they are trained to fight in nerve gas environments and are often protected by special clothing and masks. If the United States goes ahead with its nerve gas program, as seems possible at this point, the world-wide implications are not positive.

In 1969 President Nixon announced the United States would unilaterally reduce its chemical warfare stocks and stop producing more. The law requires a president to state publicly his stance on getting the country back into the nerve gas business.

Ronald Reagan has apparently made that statement by pushing a proposal which has passed the Senate to provide $20 million to equip an Army installation at Pine Bluff, Ark., for production. A supplemental spending measure passed by the House includes the $20 million.

The money would pay for a substance known as DF, one of two "binary" agents. The two agents are harmless by themselves but lethal when mixed. The other agent, DC, is available commercially.

The Army has nerve gas in stock. Some of it is in leaking canisters at the Rocky Mountain Arsenal near Denver. But officials say much of it is intact and can kill just as many people as it could when first produced.

So why make more? Because it is thought, though not confirmed, that the Soviets are stockpiling chemical warfare agents. It has also been reported the Soviets have tried out the gases on tribesmen in Laos and on civilians in Afghanistan. Again, these charges are not confirmed.

The issue, then, is whether the United States will honor the long-traditional agreement among nations to stay out of the nerve gas business, or keep up with the Soviet military machine by producing more than it already has.

This matter deserves — demands — a lot more public debate than it has yet engendered. Of course there are military realities, and the new administration is clearly ready to face them. Yet, there are humane considerations that must be given equal weight.

By building up their own supplies, the Soviets have the leverage of threat of a horrible weapon. It would be even greater leverage if this country did not have the same weapon. Whatever one's idealism, that is a strategic reality. The Soviets would not likely talk about a nerve gas ban when they have an arsenal and we do not. But if the Soviets tried to gas some people, what would stop a nuclear retaliation?

At the same time, arsenals in Arkansas and Colorado would not seem to have much deterrent effect. And most U.S. allies not only abhor the idea of nerve gas use, they refuse to allow it to be stored in their countries.

Which brings us to the real victims of nerve gas warfare: civilians. Many soldiers for the Soviets and NATO are prepared for nerve gas warfare. The Soviets have hermetically sealed tanks. But civilians have nothing to protect them from this heinous and deadly type of warfare.

The superpowers already have enough nuclear capability to kill most of the world's civilians. They have in stock enough chemical agents to do the same. The strategic equivalence thinking that is behind this push for more nerve gas is not a compelling reason to make more.

Wisconsin State Journal

Madison, Wisc., June 12, 1981

The U.S. Senate has voted, 50-48, to take the next step toward producing a new type of lethal nerve gas.

The Reagan administration argued strongly, and wrongly, for a $20-million supplement to the defense budget to equip an Arkansas factory for making a new type of artillery shell containing the nerve gas.

Administration spokesmen said the weapon would contain two chemicals which become lethal, only when mixed as the shell is fired. Thus, it would be "safer" for U.S. troops, who Pentagon spokesmen say could be threatened by leakage old-type chemical gases now in storage.

Besides, it was argued, it will take more congressional action before the new nerve gas can be manufactured. (On the other hand, it will take one less step if the House concurs and the factory is equipped.)

Finally, Sen. John W. Warner, R-Va., said the nerve gas is needed to put the U.S. in position to "threaten retaliation" against possible use of nerve gas by the Soviet Union.

It has been suggested that a European war is the most likely place for use of nerve gas, but there is major opposition in Europe to storing such weapons there.

Chemical-warfare weapons have been developed and stored by the military for decades, just in case. Defenders say war isn't pretty; if the foe is prepared to use nerve gas and other gases, so must we.

But do Americans want to be able to "threaten retaliation" against possible use of nerve gas by the Soviet Union? We have gases now. Do we need more? Will our allies agree to store and use the new nerve gas?

What does this do to the intent and integrity of the nearly 100 nations, including the United States, that have signed a treaty prohibiting them from being the first to use nerve gas in war?

Not enough good answers have been provided to justify another step toward the manufacture of this *new, improved* nerve gas. The House should reject the proposal.

Roanoke Times & World-News

Roanoke, Va., May 29, 1981

Recreating the aftermath of the first full-scale gas attack in World War I, Dr. Robert Jones wrote in the British journal *New Scientist* in 1977 that the abandoned Allied trenches were "tenanted only by the dead garrisons, whose blackened faces, contorted figures, and lips fringed with blood and foam from their bursting lungs, showed the agonies in which they had died."

The image is horrible. Any method of killing people could be called inhumane, and some ways surely are worse than with chemical weapons. But there is a mystique about poison gases that, since 1918, has deterred their widespread use in war — a feeling that some weapons are simply too terrible to employ.

So far, this feeling also has prevailed since World War II about atomic bombs. The conviction that, once unleashed, nuclear warfare would lead to uncontrollable horrors has kept them in check: The balance of terror, some call it.

That feeling has not restrained the superpowers from stockpiling nuclear weapons. Similarly, the Soviet Union is generally conceded to have built up a fearsome ability to wage war with gas. There were reports early in 1980 that the Soviets had used it against insurgents in Afghanistan. That was never substantiated, but there's no doubt the Russians use gas in their own battle training, and some of their soldiers are said to have died from it.

Civilized minds rebel at the idea (there were strong protests in the Senate last week), but maintaining the balance of terror also may require increased U.S. investment in chemical warfare. The United States has fallen behind the U.S.S.R. in this capability. Treaties like the 1925 Geneva accord are admirable expressions of international intent, but the ability to retaliate in kind remains probably the strongest deterrent against first use of gas in war.

With this as with weaponry in general, the superpowers must guard against trying to outdo each other in firepower. The more weapons there are, the more chance they'll be used; and the greater investment in them, the poorer the whole world is for it.

The Charlotte Observer
Charlotte, N.C., February 11, 1982

Although the decision by the Reagan Administration to seek resumption of nerve gas production wasn't unexpected, it is, by the very nature of the subject, shocking and appalling. It reverses a 13-year-old policy affirmed by one of Mr. Reagan's Republican predecessors, Richard Nixon.

Whatever his faults, Mr. Nixon was not an irresponsible peacenik, unconcerned about matters of national defense. He was, however, sympathetic to an international effort dating at least to the end of World War I to assure that chemical weaponry will never again be used.

There are powerful reasons for that objective. The first is in the effect of the weapons themselves. Nerve gases cause paralysis of the respiratory system and death by suffocation. More importantly, their deadliest effects are on civilian populations. Enemy soldiers are likely to have gas masks and protective suits to shield them from chemicals.

Civilians Will Die

The chief strategic value of such weapons is too force the enemy to operate in an encumbered state, burdened with protective equipment that reduces mobility and perhaps adds to psychological stress. Civilians, meanwhile, lacking protective equipment, will be out of luck. They will die — and their deaths will be excruciating.

Those factors fuel a growing moral outrage at the heart of congressional opposition to nerve gas production. But senators such as Republican Mark Hatfield and Democrat Gary Hart are also armed with pragmatic arguments.

Mr. Hatfield, whose views on the subject spring from his serious, born-again Christianity, maintains that our existing stockpile of deadly chemicals is ample and far from obsolete.

NATO Allies Opposed

He also notes that our NATO allies are generally opposed to chemical weapons and aren't anxious to use them even in response to, say, a Soviet nerve gas offensive in Europe. They would not be inclined to kill off their own very dense civilian populations for the sake of encumbering invading Soviet troops.

If, despite that, U.S. leaders decided it was necessary to use such chemicals, Sen. Hart contends that stockpiles now in Europe "are more than sufficient to deter Soviet first use."

He says he is concerned, however, that we do not have enough modern equipment to fully protect our own soldiers from the threat of nerve gas. Such protection is a crucial deterrent to the use of chemical weapons.

If we lack gas masks and protective suits in sufficient quality or numbers, then they should be developed, and appropriations for that purpose are imminently justifiable.

Sens. Hart and Hatfield also contend that the administration's nerve gas decision is apt to send shock waves through our NATO allies — jeopardizing the tenuous solidarity on which our European defense objectives currently depend.

For reasons such as these, there is a very strong chance that Congress will block appropriations for the president's chemical warfare request.

Moral Issues

But amid all the pragmatism of congressional debates, the sweeping moral issues raised by the administration's decision — and, indeed, by some of its other defense strategies — ought not to be put aside.

Almost no one opposes this administration's general effort to strengthen U.S. defense capability. What's disturbing is a change in rhetoric and the thinking that apparently underlies it. The move to deploy more tactical nuclear weapons and the decision to add to our capacity for chemical warfare suggest ominously that there is no longer the sense among our leaders that the use of such weapons is essentially unthinkable.

No one is suggesting that Mr. Reagan *wants* to engage in chemical warfare. But what's uncomfortably clear, in comparing his policies to those of his predecessors, is this:

A president who wants to create such weapons is more likely to use them than a president who doesn't.

Arkansas Gazette.
Little Rock, Ark., February 13, 1982

Just as many in Washington, particularly in Congress, had feared, President Reagan has decided to reopen the chemical weapons race with the Soviet Union. In a letter to House Speaker Tip O'Neill this week, Mr. Reagan formally notified Congress that he was resuming production at the Pine Bluff Arsenal of nerve gas shells, scrapping a moratorium on nerve gas weapon production that has been in effect since 1969.

The decision is expected to encounter fierce opposition in Congress, especially in the Senate, where Senator Gary Hart of Colorado and Senator David Pryor of Arkansas already have taken a lead in opposition. The Senate, it should be recalled, came within two votes last year, when Mr. Reagan was at the peak of his legislative prowess, of blocking the administration request for $20 million to prepare for resumption of production at the arsenal should the President decide that new weapons are needed.

Any legislative battle is likely to come as part of the debate over the proposed 1983 budget that Mr. Reagan also sent to Congress this week, but far more is at stake than the relatively modest expenditure — $30 million — for production of binary nerve gas weapons. There is less to argue about, as a matter of fact, elsewhere in the total $705 million chemical weapons item in the budget. More than 70 per cent of the total is to be spent on defensive measures such as protective clothing. Indeed, if the United States is vulnerable to Soviet use of chemical weapons, it is because not enough defensive measures have been taken even for battlefield troops.

The United States already has ample supplies of nerve gas — enough to kill every human on earth. By resuming production of such weapons, the United States would only be substituting a more advanced version, but also would very probably trigger a new race with the Russians in exotic chemical weapons. The administration, in arguing for resumed production in advanced forms, follows much the same logic that it has on strategic and tactical nuclear weapons, such as the MX missile and the B-1 bomber: the more the better and hang the cost.

As anticipated by the Pentagon, the binary nerve gas weapons would be produced in two separate parts, for a 155-millimeter artillery projectile and an aerial chemical bomb called the "Bigeye." Each part of the weapon would contain a chemical that was generally non-toxic. The two parts, with separate chemicals, would be assembled immediately before firing and the two chemicals, in liquid form, would mix into a deadly nerve gas on the way to the target. The advantages of binary weapons is that they are safer to store than are existing nerve gas weapons, although the evidence is far from convincing that the existing weapons pose a danger if stored, maintained and handled properly.

Even so, there is another dimension to Mr. Reagan's decision to push ahead and Congress will be made well aware of it in the coming months. Like the neutron warhead, nerve gas is intended primarily for tactical battlefield use to deter any Soviet advances against NATO forces in Western Europe. Many in Europe do not want either the neutron bomb or nerve gas stored, ready for use, in their backyards. The Pentagon, in a backgound statement, seems to be at least a little sensitive to these feelings, by stressing that "no decisions or recommendations have been made regarding deployment of chemical weapons." It pledged, as well, that the allies would be fully consulted before any additional decision is made on stockpiling nerve gas outside United States borders.

The Reagan administration, in any event, has not made much of a case for resumption of nerve gas production. It will have its full opportunity as Congress considers whether to provide the money in the 1983 budget. There may be a case for additional protective measures, for troops as well as civilians, but resumption of weapons production after 13 years would surely decrease the chances for lasting peace and true national security.

THE ANN ARBOR NEWS
Ann Arbor, Mich., February 11, 1982

JUST when you thought life was dangerous enough, the peril factor gets raised another notch.

Despite the fact that chemical warfare is banned by the Geneva Conventions and that production of chemical weapons in this country has been halted since 1969, President Reagan wants to resume their manufacture.

"Considering the current world situation," Reagan said, "particularly the absence of a verifiable ban on production and stockpiling chemical weapons, the United States must also deter chemical warfare by denying a significant military advantage to any possible initiator."

Reagan is talking about the Russians, of course. They're alleged to have the best capability in the world in chemical warfare.

(It has also been documented that the Russians used some lethal airborne substance in Afghanistan to wipe out resistance there).

A top Pentagon weapons expert recently told a congressional hearing that the Soviet Union's store of chemical warfare munitions is believed to be from four to 10 times larger than the U.S. stockpile.

So Reagan is responding to another perceived area of Soviet dominance. Five years of negotiations on a possible ban on chemical warfare have gotten nowhere.

THE KEY QUESTION is whether chemical arms is a productive area of competition. What is to be gained by adding another dimension to the arms race?

Given the risks involved in storage and the extreme danger of working with this stuff in the first place, why is the U.S. committed to playing catch-up before it has exhausted the negotiating process?

And why, with so much detail given to massive overkill in weaponry, are we in effect launching a new chemical weapons arms race?

Rep. Patricia Shroeder, D-Colo., probably put her finger on it best when she said of Reagan's request, "This makes no sense at all unless you are really going to use it on a civilian population."

War is hideous enough. Nuclear attack and aftermath are almost too horrible to think about. Chemical warfare is barbarism.

We aren't deterring the Russians one bit by resuming production. We don't even know what their capacity is; we just have the educated guesswork of the same defense establishment people who earlier brought us the missile gap (non-existent) and the nuclear submarine deficiency and now the chemical arms "disadvantage."

THE APPROPRIATE relosponse is NO. No to President Reagan, no to resumption of chemical arms production, no to the busybodies in the Pentagon and yes to renewed negotiating vigor with the Russians to live by what's left of humanitarianism and the Geneva Conventions.

THE LOUISVILLE TIMES
Louisville, Ky., February 15, 1982

A Pentagon official offered a chilling commentary on the progress of modern war recently when he noted that poison gas, a weapon that repelled the civilized world 50 years ago, is now considered comparatively attractive.

After chemical weapons were used by both sides in World War I, most countries signed the Geneva Protocol of 1925, which bans poisonous gases and liquids from armed conflict. (The United States didn't agree until 1975). Spraying the enemy has since been considered a breach of battlefield etiquette, although substantial evidence indicates the Soviets have resorted to it in Afghanistan and Southeast Asia.

As the Reagan administration prepared recently to resume the production of deadly nerve gas, however, a Defense Department spokesman put forth the reassuring argument that chemical killers might be an agreeable alternative to nuclear ones. After all, said he, gas is cheaper and won't do much damage away from the battlefield.

This is apparently an extension of the soothing argument that neutron bombs are acceptable because, while sizzling people, they do little harm to buildings.

Actually, the difficulty of controlling the movement of gas once it is unleashed and the resulting threat to civilians in a densely populated area like Europe is only one of several reasons why Mr. Reagan should change his mind about our need for this gruesome weapon.

The administration's argument for chemicals is the usual: The Soviets are ahead of us both in their ability to use and defend themselves against poison attacks. Therefore, we must match them by stockpiling nerve gas in new, admittedly safer "binary" containers.

The large amount of gas we still have in storage, however, will make the Soviets think twice before moving a conflict on to the chemical escalator. If our nuclear deterrent remains credible,enemies will have a powerful incentive to refrain from chemical attacks.

In view of the mounting evidence that Moscow has revived chemical warfare in remote corners of the world, the U.S. can seize the moral high ground and strengthen its alliances in both Europe and the Third World by staying out of the nerve gas race.

The millions of dollars earmarked for nerve gas should be spent on developing techniques to defend both troops and civilians against chemical attack. The world should then have little trouble directing its outrage at the country responsible for bringing back a form of warfare that is universally condemned.

DESERET NEWS
Salt Lake City, Utah, February 11, 1982

Should the United States get back into the business of producing weapons of chemical warfare?

After a 13-year moratorium, President Reagan is proposing to do just that. But if the Pentagon isn't more candid than it has been so far about the move, its fate could be determined more on the basis of budget constraints than on the basis of Soviet provocations.

This week Mr. Reagan sent Congress a military budget that includes $705 million for chemical warfare. Of that amount, $30 million would be earmarked for eventual production of two binary nerve gas weapons, a 155mm artillery shell and a Bigeye bomb.

Binary weapons have two chemical components that are not lethal when packaged separately but become highly toxic when combined while a projectile is carrying them in flight. Such weapons would be less dangerous to store than present chemical agents. All of the present agents were produced before 1969, when President Nixon halted their output. Much of these old chemical agents, the Pentagon says, are stored in shells that fit only weapons that have been phased out or will soon be abandoned.

Add to this the many recent reports about Russia's use of chemical weapons in Afghanistan, Laos, and Cambodia and the White House's concern about this part of America's defense posture becomes understandable.

But beyond that point, the Pentagon's efforts to justify ending the U.S. moratorium look ingenuous. The idea behind the proposed new U.S. program, the Pentagon insists, is to induce the Soviets to agree to "a complete and verifiable ban on the development, production, and stockpiling of chemical weapons." If such a treaty is concluded, this argument goes, the U.S. can call off its production of new chemical warfare agents. Until then, the implied threat of U.S. retaliation supposedly would deter the Soviets from using their chemical weapons.

But since the Soviets have violated three different treaties in their current use of such weapons, why would a new treaty be more effective?

Since Moscow hasn't agreed to on-site inspections when Russia was behind in the arms race, why should the Soviets change when they have a 35-to-1 advantage over the U.S. in chemical warfare units, a 14-to-1 edge in chemical stockpiles, and a 14-to-1 margin in production facilities?

In fact, don't such lopsided margins suggest the U.S. would have to do plenty of catching up before our new chemical weapons would have a deterrent effect?

For that matter, why should Soviet aggression be deterred by new U.S. chemical weapons when it has not been deterred by other new American weapons, such as the recent decision to go ahead with production of the neutron bomb?

Finally, why should Russia be worried when the European members of NATO have made it clear they do not want the new U.S. chemical weapons stored on their soil?

Until better answers are provided than have been forthcoming so far, the new chemical weapons program will look less like a deterrent than like an opportunity to save $30 million in a budget that can use plenty of trimming.

The Washington Times

Washington, D.C., August 8, 1983

Vice President Bush cast the tie-breaking vote in the Senate to end the U.S. moratorium on making chemical weapons, in force since 1969. It was a solid day's work by the Veep.

But there's a piece to go before production of modern "binary" nerve gas weaponry can be cranked up. The House has voted to sustain the ban, and opponents say they will fight the production approval that is contained in a conference-committee report on the 1984 defense authorization bill.

Chemical warfare is understandably repellent, the horrible connotation lending itself to deep opposition. But that is not the point. There is compelling evidence (compelling to those not predisposed to disbelief) that the Soviets have lavishly used chemical weapons in Afghanistan, for example, and have supplied toxins for use by their proxies in Southeast Asia — the "yellow rain" — notwithstanding treaty prohibitions.

More to present point, the use of toxic weapons is integral to Soviet tactical doctrine, and the Kremlin doesn't have a moratorium on the stuff, so far as we are aware. In an attack on NATO forces, the Soviets would unleash clouds of nerve gas and similar toxins; Warsaw Pact forces are thoroughly drilled in how to do it. That is the reasonable expectation, given the status of Western chemical-war deterrence.

U.S. supplies are old, degrading, and tricky to use. Soviet planners need hardly tremble at retaliation from those stocks. The West is well aware of how potent a chemical war-fighting capacity the Soviets possess — which means that NATO troops would immediately have to take protective measures in any emergency, and protective measures against such weapons are cumbersome and drastically reduce military efficiency.

Therefore, does not the argument to provide NATO forces with comparably modern chemical weapons, and thus a deterrent, become persuasive? It should.

Agreement by the conference committee to permit the Pentagon to begin in 1985 assembling the binary nerve gas shells (in which two components are separated until fired and toxically activated) stunned opponents in the House. A provision similar to the Senate's failed there by 14 votes, and a later vote to delete 1984 money for a binary artillery shell carried by 95 votes. Fine.

The opponents, led by Foreign Affairs Chairman Clement Zablocki of Wisconsin, are pledging to fight the nerve-gas approval when the conference report comes up on the House floor shortly. But we imagine longer vision will prevail, now that the Senate has taken a sensible stand, even if narrowly.

Of course chemical weapons are nasty (though so is a .30-caliber bullet), but failure to take action to prevent use of such gasses by establishing a clear deterrent is even nastier. Who knows, the Kremlin might even get a millimeter more serious about reaching agreement on banning all chemical weapons if it is convinced the U.S. intends to end this woeful weakness in its arsenal.

AKRON BEACON JOURNAL

Akron, Ohio, July 20, 1983

THE SENATE seems bent on proving that deterrence has no moral limits. The Senate, supported by the Reagan administration, voted last week to put America back in the nerve-gas business for the first time since 1969.

Only two positive things can be said of such a vote: First, it is not the final word; the House voted down a similar measure a month ago so the fight is still on. Second, the vote was a squeaker — 50-49 with Vice President George Bush deciding the issue — so there is little political momentum to overturn the House defeat.

But it is disheartening to see so many in the Senate who would spend $130 million to produce weapons so horrible they are outlawed as uncivilized even for war.

Only the Soviet Union has major stockpiles of chemical weapons. So the thin excuse used in asking renewed production is: The other side has them, and so must we, as a deterrent and a "bargaining chip."

Neither argument holds up. The United States already has chemical weapons to use as a bargaining chip. And chemical weapons are not strictly weapons of war because soldiers on a battlefield can be protected from them. Civilian populations are the main target.

This is one arms race that cannot be justified by economics, military strategy or, certainly, civilized conduct. The Congress should act quickly, in conference committee, to overturn the Senate's unwise vote.

The Hartford Courant

Hartford, Conn., July 17, 1983

Vice President George Bush's deciding vote in the Senate Wednesday for a new generation of nerve gas bombs and shells makes him a contender for the title of the most dangerous man of our time.

Mr. Bush — in his capacity as president of the Senate — broke a tie to tip the vote, 50 to 49, toward realizing the nightmare vision of a chemical war that would doom thousands of innocent people to a horrible, excruciating death.

Of course, that possibility doesn't seem to faze Mr. Bush. He is the person, after all, who once professed as a presidential candidate that an all-out nuclear war with the Soviet Union was something that the United States could both survive and win.

But the vice president wasn't directly responsible for the futile and stupendously expensive nuclear arms race in which the two superpowers are engaged. His vote last week, however, gave him a direct role in starting what Sen. David H. Pryor of Arkansas said "could mark the beginning of a new kind of arms race."

There has been no open race for dominance in chemical weaponry since 1969, when President Richard M. Nixon called a unilateral halt to the production of U.S. chemical bombs and shells.

But half the Senate, responding to twisted and tired Pentagon arguments that such weapons are now needed as a "bargaining chip" to get the Soviet Union to seriously negotiate arms limitations, opted to get the nation back on the race track. To their credit, both Connecticut senators opposed the weapons.

The House voted last month to scuttle the program, but now the issue goes to a House-Senate conference committee, where its chances of survival are considered better than even.

The Senate vote came when Sen. Pryor proposed deleting authorization for $130 million for setting up production facilities for a new nerve-gas bomb in Pine Bluff, Ark., and for producing new 155mm nerve gas shells.

Despite the "improved" design of the proposed new weapons, they add nothing to the nation's capacity for fighting a chemical war. They only make such a war more likely.

The United States already has more than 3 million nerve gas projectiles, as well as land mines, aerial spray tanks and bombs. If any of these weapons were used in heavily populated Western Europe against a Soviet invasion, the most likely victims would not be the armies that are prepared for them, but the civilians without protection and escape.

Allegations that the Soviets have introduced the use of chemical weapons in Laos, Cambodia and Afghanistan should strengthen the resolve of this administration to negotiate a treaty to prohibit their development and production, and to eventually destroy them.

Building more of the weapons ourselves would only provide the Soviets with a pretext for expanding their production and use. Further, the production of a new generation of chemical weapons would stimulate research on both sides for even more lethal chemical and biological agents to throw against each other.

Nothing now can undo the disgrace of Mr. Bush and the 49 senators who voted to reopen this ugly competition. But if enough Americans express enough outrage, it can still be stopped.

SYRACUSE
HERALD-JOURNAL
Syracuse, N.Y., July 25, 1983

Shame on George Bush.

A vice president hadn't been called on to break a tie in the U.S. Senate since 1977. When Bush did it last week, he cast the decisive vote in favor of moving ahead with the production of nerve gas.

As President Reagan's understudy, Bush has a responsibility to uphold administration policy. But what a shame it had to be on something as morally offensive as nerve gas.

▽   ▽

The administration used the same old line: We need to produce new nerve gas to deter the Russians. When will we stop using that fallow argument in place of ethical leadership?

How about, just once, deterring Russians by shaming them into the moral mainstream instead of following them into the gutter?

The Soviets believe the end justifies the means. We should show the world it can do better than that.

▽   ▽

Richard Nixon imposed a moratorium on the production of new, lethal gas 14 years ago. Times have changed; we know the Soviets have continued to develop nerve gas and there is evidence in Afghanistan and Laos that they, or their puppets, have used it on humans.

But why must we respond to a nerve gas threat with our own lethal chemicals?

In addition to being ethically unacceptable, nerve gas is of dubious military value. Western nations have other means of deterring the Soviet Union than killing civilians painfully with gases that attack the nervous system.

Besides, production of nerve gas bombs and shells endangers us.

▽   ▽

Proponents tout the safety of the proposed new line of chemical warfare weapons. However, last year, the Pentagon postponed its request for funds when it found the nerve gas bomb can explode while still in an aircraft headed for a target. So much for safety.

Fortunately, the battle is not over. Thanks to Bush, the Senate approved development funds. But, earlier, the House of Representatives rejected the expenditure by a wide margin. House members need to stand firm in that rejection.

ARGUS-LEADER
Sioux Falls, S.D., July 15, 1983

One message the U.S. Senate didn't have to send to Moscow this week was the 50-49 vote approving $130 million for production of new nerve gas weapons for the first time since 1969.

The one vote majority, obtained only by Vice President George Bush casting the deciding vote to avoid a tie, doesn't say anything to the Russians. That's despite the contention of supporters of the nerve gas program that only if the United States modernizes its own chemical weapons will the Soviet Union negotiate seriously to reduce its own stockpile.

On June 23 the House voted 256-161 to kill the nerve gas program. The disagreement between the House and Senate will have to be resolved in a conference committee. That group can do the nation a favor two ways: either by deleting the nerve gas appropriation from the defense bill or by failing to reach agreement, thus stymieing new production of chemical weapons.

Two senators from opposite sides of the aisle had the right analysis of nerve gas weapons. Sen. Mark Hatfield, R-Ore., said there is no case for this weapons system and described it as grotesque and barbaric. Sen. Edward Kennedy, D-Mass., said, "Those who would lose their lives are civilians. We are talking about killing millions of people."

Sen. David Pryor, D-Ark., was the chief sponsor of the amendment to strip the money for nerve gas weapons production from the defense bill, despite the fact that the weapons would be constructed at Pine Bluff in the senator's home state. He said existing stores of older U.S. chemical weapons provide an adequate deterrent against the Russians.

South Dakota's senators split their vote: Sen. James Abdnor voted for the nerve gas program, Sen. Larry Pressler voted against it. If Abdnor has a chance to vote again, he should change his mind.

None of the combatants in World War II used poison gas, which both sides employed in World War I. This country used Agent Orange and other defoliants in Vietnam to strip the countryside so the North Vietnamese and the Viet Cong couldn't grow crops. That blighted the food chain and was a mistake that should never be repeated. There have been charges, so far unproved, that the Soviet Union and its allies have used illegal chemical weapons in Laos, Cambodia and Afghanistan.

In 1969, President Richard Nixon ordered a unilateral halt to the production of U.S. chemical weapons. Since then there have been unsuccessful efforts to negotiate an international ban with the Soviet Union.

The United States should persevere in its goal to prohibit chemical weapons. They simply aren't needed. Both superpowers have sufficient deterrence in nuclear and conventional weapons to discourage any kind of warfare.

There is ample justification, for instance, for spending $5.2 billion on the B-1 bomber for research and purchase of the first 10 planes. They are badly needed to replace aging B-52s which present hazards for their Air Force crews. On another issue, we'd like to think that an arms agreement with the Soviet Union eventually will make it unnecessary to proceed with the MX missile.

There are many strong messages for the Kremlin in the $200 billion defense authorization bill for fiscal 1984 that the Senate has under consideration. The bill demonstrates resolve — but it doesn't need money for nerve gas weapons to make a point to the Soviet Union.

Rockford Register Star
Rockford, Ill., July 22, 1983

Pentagon proliferation of nuclear missiles in the name of "nuclear control" is frightening enough. But Senate action to unleash a new wave of nerve gas weaponry in the name of peace is obscene.

Nerve gases, correctly indentified as "grotesque and barbaric," have no conceivable defense value. They are a threat not to armies, but to civilian populations — a truly barbaric threat.

That is why every American administration since 1969 has disowned such weapons and why many of them have sought ways to dispose of existing supplies.

Not this administration. The United States Senate has voted its approval of new nerve gas weapons. The vote was close, 50-49. And the plan faces serious challenge in the House, which already has rejected the plan once.

But the Senate vote is more meaningful than a one-vote margin might indicate because Vice President George Bush cast the tie-breaking 50th vote. That puts the entire administration clearly on record behind this obscene plan.

Is there any excuse for producing new nerve gas weaponry? Only the same old claim that somehow production of new weapons is the only way to disarm. That claim is as grotesque as the weapons being planned.

The Seattle Times

Seattle, Wash., July 15, 1983

CONGRESS last year fought a bruising battle over nerve-gas weapons, similar to the round that ended in the Senate this week with a tie-breaking vote by Vice President Bush.

As happened last year, appropriations to resume production of the weapons were approved in the Senate but rejected in the House. A conference committee went along with the House. We hope history repeats.

As before, both parties split deeply on the issue. Seventeen Republican senators, including Slade Gorton, voted against nerve gas and against the administration. Fourteen Democrats, including Henry M. Jackson, voted for the administration request for $130 million to produce nerve-gas artillery shells and production equipment for the Bigeye nerve-gas bomb.

Earlier, the House had voted 216-202 to scuttle the program. We hope the conference committee that will resolve the issue goes along with slender majority sentiment. Among other things, we are impressed with Sen. David H. Pryor's argument that existing stores of the deadly gas provide an adequate deterrent against the Russians.

Pryor's argument gains weight from the fact that the home state of the Arkansas Democrat is where the nerve gas would be produced. It requires strong conviction to vote against home-state jobs.

Rejecting a resumption of nerve-gas production would be a strong signal to a skeptical world of America's interest in the control of deadly weapons of mass destruction. It would strengthen the confidence of U.S. allies in this country's willingness to move forward in nuclear-arms negotiations with the Soviet Union.

It is true that the Russians not only are continuing to produce chemical weapons but have used them in Afghanistan and, by proxy through Vietnam, in Southeast Asia.

Because of that, we do favor the appropriation of funds for continued research on antidotes and other defensive measures in the chemical-weapons field.

The Des Moines Register

Des Moines, Iowa, July 15, 1983

The Reagan administration hasn't yet met a weapon it doesn't like. If the MX missile, the B-1 bomber, laser beams in space and Pershing missiles in Europe aren't enough for you, then consider the latest favorite in the Reagan arsenal — nerve gas, the weapon too horrible for Richard Nixon.

The House of Representatives in June voted to kill the new $130 million chemical-weapons program proposed by President Reagan, which would build a new family of nerve-gas artillery shells and a nerve-gas bomb. The nerve-gas program came up Wednesday in the Senate, with the outcome in doubt. When all senators present had voted, the tally was 49-49, which would have killed the plan.

But Vice President George Bush rode to the rescue of the weapons, casting the tie-breaking vote in a rare exercise of his authority as president of the Senate, which permits him to vote in case of a tie. Now House and Senate negotiators will have to wrangle over whether to put the nation back into the chemical-weapons business.

This country has not produced nerve-gas weapons since 1969, when President Nixon halted production to try to negotiate a treaty with the Soviet Union to ban them. No treaty has resulted, so now Reagan and his allies contend — in a familiar refrain — that the only way to reach a ban on chemical weapons is to begin producing them.

The United States has a stockpile of older, cruder chemical weapons, but their caretakers at the Pentagon warn that the old bombs are getting leaky, so new ones are needed.

Nerve gas is a horrible, indiscriminate weapon that would kill masses of civilians if unleashed in battle. As a bargaining chip, it is morally bankrupt. As a weapon for possible use, it is, as Republican Senator Mark Hatfield of Oregon labeled it, "grotesque and barbaric."

A decision to begin building nerve-gas weapons, after a 14-year lapse, would represent another escalation of the obscene arms race. We cannot believe that the United States is unable to defend itself without these symbols of barbarity.

At some point, it is necessary to put a stop to this fascination with weapons of indiscriminate death. That point has been reached with nerve gas.

•

Once again, Iowa's two conservative Republican senators split on a critical vote. Charles Grassley voted against the nerve-gas program; Roger Jepsen voted for it. If Jepsen had voted no, the vice president could not have rescued nerve gas from defeat. The White House owes Jepsen another one.

The Wichita
Eagle-Beacon
Wichita, Kans., July 15, 1983

The Senate's 50-49 vote for renewed production of binary nerve gas, which this nation has not made since 1969, is a dangerous step that could have the potential of launching the world on the ultimate chemical "bad trip." Sen. Mark Hatfield, R-Ore., surely reflects the feelings of millions of thinking Americans in characterizing that kind of weaponry as "grotesque and barbaric." It is not to the credit of Vice President George Bush that he cast the tie-break vote that put the otherwise-divided Senate on record as favoring the armed forces' stockpiling of a type of weapon most of the world thought it had renounced after gas warfare first was used in World War I.

Proponents say the nerve gas program is needed as a bargaining chip in this nation's arms negotiations with the Soviet Union. Only if we modernize and expand our own chemical weapons arsenal, they argue, will the U.S.S.R., which has been accused of waging chemical warfare in Afghanistan and elsewhere, be willing to discuss mutual chemical weaponry reduction.

Like nuclear weapons, which we have been urged to build more of to provide another bargaining chip, nerve gas has the capability of destroying human life far beyond the perimeters of battle zones. In fact, the greatest number of casualties resulting from its use in war might well be civilians. This is because the Soviet army, at least, is known to have equipment to protect soldiers against a nerve gas attack.

Even in peacetime, renewed production could pose dangers to Americans. A few years ago, some obsolete chemical materiel stored in Colorado began leaking toxic fumes and had to be removed to a remote area in Utah. It's significant that one opponent of renewed production of binary artillery shells — containing chemicals that would become lethal only when mixed by detonation — is Sen. David Pryor, D-Ark., in whose state they would be assembled. He says existing stores of such weapons provide an adequate deterrent against Soviet chemical aggression.

Now it is up to the House, which voted 256-161 last month to kill the nerve gas program, to hold the line.

Reno Gazette-Journal
Reno, Nev., July 15, 1983

With Vice President George Bush breaking a tie vote, the U.S. Senate Wednesday approved $130 million to produce nerve gas weapons.

And to what end?

According to the Reagan administration, to force the Russians to negotiate.

That seems to be the answer, and the excuse, for every type of weapon proposed by this administration. If the United States must spend billions upon billions, if it must produce every terrible weapon known to man to the nth degree, then it must be to make the Russians negotiate.

Under this philosophy, carried to its extreme, the United States might just as well bomb the blazes out of Russia right now. That would really make the Russians sit up and negotiate. After the Russians bomb the blazes out of the United States, of course.

Somewhere in this dangerous one-upmanship, there must be a midpoint between building every weapon possible and failing to preserve the security of the United States. Somewhere there must be a policy which says certain weapons should not be built.

Surely that is the case with nerve gas. Gas weapons were considered so inhumane that the nations of the world banned them after World War I. On the same grounds, the United States has not produced one in 14 years. The justification for that moratorium remains as firm today as it was then.

Of course, the Russians seem to be using chemical warfare in Afghanistan, and Vietnam seems to be using it in Southeast Asia. As far as is known, the Russians and Vietnam are the first countries to use chemical weapons since World War I.

But that is not sufficient reason for the United States to produce these weapons. A nation with moral standards need not sink to the level of its enemy in every instance to protect itself. In fact, it must not.

Skeptics will point out that the United States already produces H-bombs, the most terrible of modern weapons. That is true. But that is not sufficient reason to produce yet another cruel weapon.

Nor do battlefield tactics demand the production of chemical bombs. Europe and this country can be defended without them.

Fortunately, the House has voted to kill the nerve gas program. When the matter goes to a conference committee, the House should hold firm for common sense and humanity.

Detroit Free Press
Detroit, Mich., July 16, 1983

MICHIGAN CAN take some solace in the fact that Sens. Carl Levin and Donald Riegle were among the minority that voted against the resumption of nerve gas production. The nation can take some hope in the fact that the Senate's approval of new nerve gas weapons is not the final word on them. Since the House earlier voted down a return to the production of nerve gas, the final decision still belongs to a conference committee.

That decision should be a flat no.

The United States now owns 37,000 tons of nerve gas, enough to kill every man, woman and child on earth 50 times over. Two important points need to be made about that. One is that chemical and biological weapons are inherently non-discriminatory; that is the basis for treating them as a class apart from others. Airborne and waterborne poisons stray easily from their targets. Women, children and non-combatant men are as vulnerable as soldiers. The experience of World War I was that soldiers who directed nerve gas at the enemy too often found the uncontainable terror wafting back at themselves.

The second point is that the United States already possesses a redundant offensive capability. To the extent that possession of such weapons constitutes a deterrent against Soviet chemical warfare, the United States should feel secure.

The proponents of new chemical weapons point out a number of real problems with our current stockpile. But these will not be solved by producing new weapons. The present nerve gas arsenal is often described as aging. That does not mean the gas itself is no longer effective. It means the containers are beginning to deteriorate, posing a safety problem in storage.

The senators who voted for new nerve gas weapons were voting for binary weapons — so-called because they come in two containers that can be stored and transported separately and assembled for use on the battlefield. Binary weapons would certainly be safer than nerve gas in rusting canisters. But greater safety could also be attained by better storage of the existing supply, and that would not run the risk and expense of escalating the arms race, or the environmental risks in disposing of the old weapons. In any case, the safety factors should be addressed, if only because the nerve gas is most likely going to remain right here with us. Our European allies have resisted the deployment of nerve-gas weapons on their soil.

Advocates of nerve gas production point out that when President Nixon stopped the manufacture of chemical weapons in 1969, the Soviet Union proceeded apace and resisted negotiated controls. Resumed American production, they say, would provide a deterrent and a bargaining chip in arms control talks.

Possibly. But it's far more probable that the greatest American vulnerability to Soviet chemical warfare lies not in our existing offensive arsenal, which is more than ample, but in our virtual lack of defenses. Where the United States, and all NATO allies except perhaps Great Britain, seriously lag behind the Soviet Union is in the adequacy of their protective gear and training for chemical warfare. Congressmen who have shown little interest in funding such things as defense against chemical warfare, or in providing more than a 30-day wartime supply of ammunition to NATO, have no business funding a new generation of nerve gas weapons.

Reagan Seeks Enlarged Naval Fleet

Nearly one-sixth of the defense funds Reagan added to Carter's fiscal 1982 budget request were to be spent building new ships and refurbishing old ones in order to expand the Naval fleet. The Navy sought to increase its fleet from 12 carrier task forces (an aircraft carrier plus its escort ships) to 15, or from about 450 ships to 600. Most controversial were the plans to reactivate a mothballed aircraft carrier, the *Oriskany,* and two old battleships, the *Iowa* and the *New Jersey.* The $139 million to begin work on the *Oriskany* was cut out of the budget, but funds for the two battleships were passed: $328 million for the *New Jersey* and $91 million for the *Iowa*. Both ships had been commissioned during World War II, and were to be refitted to carry long-range cruise missiles. Proponents argued that the old warships could be renovated for far less than it would take to build new ones, and could be used to fill in until new carriers were completed.

The Washington Star
and Daily News
Washington, D.C., March 6, 1981

The striking news about the Reagan defense budget, beyond the fact that it is to be far bigger than Mr. Carter's, is the emphasis on naval shipbuilding: an emphasis that is, in our judgment, overdue.

Whatever the Carter administration's successes or failures in upholding our end of the "correlation of forces," it permitted a significant *relative* decline in U.S. naval power. In 1977, the Ford administration bequeathed to Mr. Carter a program aimed at a 600-ship fleet by the year 2000 — this at a time when the Soviet Union, never historically a great naval power, was investing rubles hand over fist in a blue-water navy whose size and professionalism our own experts found both impressive and threatening.

Nonetheless, the Ford projections were trimmed by about 50 per cent, at the risk of results vividly foreshadowed after the collapse of the shah of Iran's vaunted protectorate over the Persian Gulf. It became necessary to strip a carrier task force from the Pacific to establish a U.S. presence in the Gulf, for without it there could be no credible "projection" of U.S. military power there at all.

In the spring, summer and early fall of 1978 — before the shah's flight, in fact — Mr. Carter's curtailed shipbuilding budget precipitated much debate in Congress, focused on his initial resistance to a new nuclear carrier. It was said, with considerable truth it now seems, that the navy was being withdrawn from harm's way to the patrolling of the major trans-Atlantic sea lanes. The secretary of defense claimed, in response, that "the U.S. Navy will continue . . . to have the capability to operate in areas of relatively high threat, such as the Northern and Southern flanks of NATO." He did not admit that this "capability" would require U.S. naval strength in the Pacific to be stripped to exiguous levels — as in fact it was after the Iranian crisis and the Soviet challenge in the Indian Ocean brought home the folly of naval cutbacks.

It is the usual story of penny wise, pound foolish. Had the Carter administration accepted and followed Mr. Ford's naval plans, the augmented capability for which the new Navy secretary John Lehman is bidding would be moving along, at less cost. Even in May 1978 when the Carter cutbacks first came under strenuous debate in Congress, two truths about naval strategy seemed indisputable: First that it would be a calamity, strategically and psychologically, for the U.S. to concede Soviet naval supremacy where U.S. naval presence has traditionally been strong and influential. And secondly, that while military economizing has its place, it is folly to derive a naval strategy from budgetary considerations — as the Carter administration seemed to be doing. It is one thing to impose budgetary discipline in the light of an established naval strategy, another to fix a budget figure and then derive a naval strategy from it.

The Carter administration, though warned, violated both principles, even as the eventual cost of correcting a shipbuilding cutback was growing at double-digit inflationary figures. And this is to speak not only of ships but of personnel capable of taking them to sea — who were, and were known to be, leaving the Navy in droves because compensation levels were inadequate.

Looking back on it, the debate over the naval estimates in mid-1978 marked a critical turning point in the maintenance of U.S. military strength. And economizing wasn't the only negative force. Much of the opposition to a continuation of the U.S. naval tradition from within the Carter administration seemed to derive from the fear that a far-flung naval presence is not a stabilizing force but a liability and a threat. Events have revealed the light-headedness of that view. There was and is no obvious response to that essentially isolationist argument — except the one that counts: Isolationism has failed at every outing as a war-avoidance policy in this century.

We do not suggest here that Secretary Lehman's rebuilding plans should not be scrutinized carefully, and in no respect more than the plan to recondition old carriers and battleships, turning the latter, as we understand it, into cruise-missile launching platforms. What is not debatable for us is that the U.S., a continental nation bordering two great oceans, importing some 50 per cent of its oil and sharing far-flung defense responsibilities, should remain a naval power second to none. Whatever fiscal sacrifices are necessary to meet that goal will have to be made.

The Courier-Journal
Louisville, Ky., January 13, 1981

THAT NEW SOVIET attack submarine that caught the U.S. intelligence community by surprise seems sure to revive arguments about the utility and survivability of American aircraft carriers. The big new Russian sub, code-named "Oscar," apparently is designed to launch long-range, anti-ship cruise missiles. The likely targets of these missiles, in a major war, would be U.S. flattops.

Navy officials say a fleet of such missile-firing subs would make our carriers 10 times as vulnerable as they are now. Carrier admirals and their supporters in the Navy and on Capitol Hill doubtless will use Oscar to bolster their case for speeding up deployment of new fleet air defense systems. Those who believe carriers are obsolete will, of course, draw a quite different conclusion: that there's no way to defend a big target traveling 30 miles per hour from scores of missiles traveling hundreds of miles an hour, so it's foolish to build more carriers.

The carrier critics may be right — up to a point. Cruise missiles, whether launched by Oscar or by Soviet long-range bombers, probably will make U.S. carriers "sitting ducks." At the least, the cruise-missile threat could force U.S. carrier task forces to devote so much attention to defending themselves that they would have little time, and few combat aircraft, left for other missions.

But it's a bit early to write the obituary on aircraft carriers. Whatever their limitations in an all-out war with the Soviet Union, they still have potentially enormous value in lesser conflicts, especially in regions far from U.S. or allied air bases. The Persian Gulf is an obvious example. Planes from American carriers operating in the Indian Ocean and Arabian Sea would be needed if a country in that area — Iran, for instance — tried to shut off oil shipments by closing the Strait of Hormuz.

Carriers are also a handy means of "showing the flag." That term has become synonymous, in some minds, with American bullying of small countries. But in a nasty world where governments, as well as free-lance terrorists, seize hostages, gunboat diplomacy still seems to have its place.

None of this, however, answers two big questions in Washington: how many carriers does the Navy need, and must every new one be a nuclear-powered behemoth? At the moment, the Navy has 13, including two that date back to the Korean war and soon will be retired. A new $2 billion nuclear-powered carrier is under construction, and still another has been authorized by Congress, over President Carter's objections.

This seems like enough. It may be more than enough, since carrier construction is consuming dollars badly needed for other, less sophisticated ships. Critics of the Navy's emphasis on carriers point out that a big ship, however capable, can only be in one place at one time. By building a small number of very expensive ships, especially carriers, the Navy has come to the point where it is hard pressed to cover the world's oceans. And that makes it all the more difficult to keep track of all those Soviet submarines, including Oscar.

Roanoke Times & World·News
Roanoke, Va., February 28, 1981

Concern about declining U.S. military strength is often based on the Soviet Union's willingness to spend a greater portion of their gross national product on defense. That argument is flawed, however, by the fact that the United States is much the wealthier of the two powers. The United States should be able to expend a lesser percentage of its wealth on defense than the Soviets and still keep pace.

More important than the degree of effort is the result. And on that, the commander of the U.S. Navy's Atlantic fleet delivered a disturbing message in Roanoke recently. Adm. Harry D. Train II, in town for a visit to the local reserve center, said the Russian navy has, over the past decade, developed in both size and sophistication to the point that America no longer enjoys clear pre-eminence on the seas.

The 500 active ships in the U.S. Navy today, Train said, represent less than 10 percent the number during the height of World War II, and only a third the number as recently as the Cuban missile crisis of 1963.

From other sources come other, equally worrisome numbers. According to the International Institute for Strategic Studies, the U.S.S.R. leads the United States in major surface warships (289 to 173) and in submarines (257 to 81),

not to mention Soviet margins in such non-naval categories as tanks, more than 2-1, and tactical warplanes.

If the China card is played, the numbers don't look so bad — much of the Soviet military effort goes toward protecting a long border with an unfriendly nation, a problem the United States doesn't face. Moreover, total military spending of Washington and its NATO allies is greater than the total of Moscow and its Warsaw Pact allies.

But if the situation is not so grim as sometimes pictured, neither is it cause for great cheer. Despite its hostility to the U.S.S.R., China cannot yet be regarded as a proven friend of the West, whose own alliance is showing signs of strain. The Soviet drive for a strong navy cannot be explained by the need to protect a long land border. Since the Soviets don't require a powerful navy to protect their economic interests and access to resources, the admiral said in Roanoke, their goal must be to provide muscle for their military and political aims.

Train also said he is heartened by President Reagan's commitment to more military spending. The perception from which that commitment is derived — that the United States, despite its greater wealth, is falling behind the Russians in military capability — is no illusion.

The Dispatch
Columbus, Ohio, March 5, 1981

MAJOR CHANGES in U.S. naval strategy have been placed in force by the Reagan administration to counter Soviet threats and they call for hot pursuit.

Abandoned is the Carter administration strategy of pulling back from the northern and southern flanks of North Atlantic Treaty Organization territory. Criticized was the Carter strategy of drawing ships from the Mediterranean and Pacific to provide protection for the Indian Ocean-Arabian Sea-Persian Gulf hot spot.

The new strategy, according to Navy Secretary John Lehman, will be to counter the Soviet threat to America's vital interests. That means Navy squadrons on patrol in the Iceland-Britain gap, defense of the Western Alliance's flanks and even keeping the Russians away from northern Norway.

It will take a lot more tools than the Navy now has — about 600 active warships compared to the present 456. And the key increase will be the ability to launch about 15 aircraft carrier battle groups.

Congress will be asked for a $660 million downpayment on a new nuclear-powered carrier. Too, another $1 billion will be needed to refit the USS Oriskany, a mothballed carrier, and the old battleships Iowa and New Jersey. The latter project will take about three years.

That length of time, along with the seven years needed to build a brand new carrier, is a matter that bothers John J. Spittler of Columbus, president of the Navy League of the United States.

Spittler contends that "our eagle of peace—American industry" has had its wings clipped. He says that while the U.S. military-industrial complex was able to answer the challenge at the outset of World War II, it no longer can turn the trick. It has atrophied.

He says that when President Reagan calls for a 600-ship Navy, the nation must not only be ready, it must be able. That will require a Congress that gives industry more than a purchase order — it also must convey complete confidence and support.

America's new hard line on national defense will exact some new hard decisions.

THE INDIANAPOLIS STAR
Indianapolis, Ind., April 27, 1981

Until 1975, the Soviet Navy had mainly a defensive posture, but since then it has been a long-distance force designed to dominate any maritime area that is the focus of Soviet ambition.

That includes the Caribbean, Latin America, the Indian Ocean, Africa and the coastal regions and vital sealanes of Asia, as well as the "front yard" of the North Atlantic and "back yard" of the North Pacific.

To further the Soviet naval strategic capability, the Soviet naval wizard, Adm. Sergei G. Gorshkov, designed an ultra-modern surface fleet to operate beyond the passages where the North Sea, Baltic, Black Sea and Pacific fleets can be choked off.

The punching power of the new fleet is augmented by nuclear submarines and naval air forces using the versatile Backfire bomber, which with air refueling is capable of intercontinental ranges.

Soviet yards are producing nuclear and conventional craft in numbers that astonish Western naval experts. By the mid-1980s the fleets are expected to include nuclear carriers.

The first Soviet nuclear cruiser, the Kirov, with its fanastic combat design and equipment including sophisticated missiles, anti-submarine weapons, helicopters and long-range conventional guns, strongly impresses Western experts.

The long-distance naval forces will give Soviet expansionists an alternative to nuclear attack and long-drawn-out ground warfare.

They also put the United States in a dangerous position of numerical and technological naval inferiority which could spark Soviet adventurism and the risk of war between the great powers.

What should be the U.S. response to this challenge?

Obviously, U.S. naval forces need strengthening, new technology, more ships, better missiles, meshing of naval capabilities with those of the air and ground forces, power to interdict arms shipments and defense of the oil lanes.

President Reagan's proposed increase in ship production shows he is aware of the need for a stronger navy.

Vital to strength is a pay scale high enough to retain skilled officers and enlisted men who man the ships and operate the equipment. Congress must address this factor realistically. An informed public will offer essential support.

The Soviet naval challenge is one of the most critical threats in U.S. history. It must be dealt with intelligently and bravely.

THE BLADE

Toledo, Ohio, May 21, 1981

ON the face of it, the idea seems absurd. The navy wants to recommission two World War II-era battleships, and the proposal has attracted a good deal of discussion. It is difficult to say whether or not the navy needs two recommissioned battleships. But when the question is put another way, whether new ships should be built or the two battlewagons and another vintage aircraft carrier should be put back into service, the issue takes on another dimension.

The navy, if it gets what it has proposed, would use the battleships New Jersey and Iowa as floating platforms for long-range cruise missiles equipped to strike ships or land targets with either nuclear or conventional warheads. The battleships might be sitting ducks, of course, but probably no more so than the large expensive aircraft carriers. At least three additional carriers are on the navy's shopping list in its effort to expand the fleet from 12 fighting groups to 15.

In addition to the two battleships, the seaworthiness of which has been rather extensively debated, the navy has suggested recommissioning the old aircraft carrier Oriskany. All told, these three older ships might be put back into service for not much more than the cost of one new carrier, and they would essentially be used for the same purpose — to serve as floating missile launching platforms.

The battleships in particular have heavy armor of a type built to withstand the attack of missiles bearing conventional warheads. And they are relatively "low-mileage" ships. Moreover, they can be put back into service much quicker than any carriers or other new ships could be built.

If there is any flaw in the pro-battleship arguments, it is that the navy's estimates of what it would cost to put them back into service are somewhat vague. Of course, Congress will have to weigh the alternatives. But in light of the navy's ambitious expansion plans, some of which Congress seems inclined to go along with anyway, the proposal to refit the three vintage ships may turn out to be the more feasible and less costly alternative.

Los Angeles Times

Los Angeles, Calif., March 18, 1981

There is a strong case for building a larger and more powerful Navy, as President Reagan is planning to do. So far, however, the Administration has not adequately answered the questions raised by skeptics.

In geopolitical terms, the United States is an island nation that, in contrast to the Soviet Union, is heavily dependent on foreign sources of oil and other important raw materials. To the degree that hostile or potentially hostile forces gain the ability to threaten the sea lanes, the national security of the United States and its major allies is imperiled.

U.S. naval strength relative to that of the Soviet Union has slipped in recent years. Adm. Thomas B. Hayward, chief of naval operations, warned Congress a few weeks ago that, with the new emphasis on safeguarding Middle Eastern oilfields, the Navy is simply stretched too thin to meet all its commitments.

It is against this background that Reagan has proposed to expand the Navy by a third to 600 ships, built around 15 combat battle groups instead of the existing 12.

Even with a substantially expanded defense budget, there won't be enough money to do all the things that the military services believe are necessary. It is important to spend available funds in ways that will buy the most effective forces for the money.

Applying that standard to the Navy, question No. 1 is where the Pentagon expects to get the 100,000 to 150,000 men and women that would be required at a time when it is seriously short of trained manpower. Until the Administration has a credible answer to this question, talk of a 600-ship Navy is a bit unreal.

Assuming that this issue is resolved, the spending program for the Navy—as for the other services—raises certain questions that should be explored by appropriate committees of Congress.

The Navy, for example, wants to spend several hundred million dollars to bring two battleships out of mothballs. Provided the manning problem can be dealt with, the idea makes sense from the standpoint of getting more firepower at sea quickly and at much lower cost than it would take to build new ships. It isn't clear, though, whether supplementing the big warships' shore-bombardment guns with 300-odd long-range cruise missiles is the most practical and cost-effective option available.

A question of more fundamental importance is the Navy's continued emphasis—even into the next century, it seems—on large aircraft carriers that, by virtue of their high cost, squeeze older ships out of the budget.

Even within the Navy, many officers worry that the big carriers are becoming increasingly vulnerable to Soviet surface-to-surface missiles. They argue that the Navy should begin hedging its bets by building a larger number of smaller surface ships, including small carriers capable of launching vertical or short-takeoff fighter planes.

This viewpoint, which got short shrift in the new Navy budget, deserves a more serious hearing from the new Administration.

The Boston Herald American

Boston, Mass., March 13, 1981

"War once declared, must be waged offensively, aggressively. The enemy must not be fended off, but smitten down." — Alfred Thayer Mahan.

The Reagan administration's new naval doctrine, announced by Navy Secretary John Lehman, is nothing less than a reaffirmation of the wise dictum laid down nearly a century ago by America's foremost seapower theoretician.

The notion that a good offense is the best defense is particularly applicable to a U.S. naval strategy capable of yielding victory over the Soviet Union at sea.

One of the U.S. Navy's overriding responsibilities in any general East-West war would be the protection of thousands of miles of vulnerable sea lanes on five oceans. Should these sea lanes, most especially those in the Atlantic Pacific and Indian Oceans, be cut by Soviet submarines, aircraft, or surface ships, vital American allies and the United States itself would be isolated.

Japan and Western Europe would be left to face Soviet forces on their own, and the United States would be denied the oil and strategic minerals essential to its economy and to defense production.

The Carter administration, attempting presumably to justify its draconian cuts in Navy shipbuilding programs, seemed prepared to adopt a passive strategy under which the Navy would be compelled to simply await Soviet attacks on the sea lanes.

But that defensive strategy conceded the Soviets the crucial initiative at sea and, worse yet, denied the U.S. Navy a fighting chance to exploit the Soviet navy's most serious strategic handicap.

In contrast to the U.S. Navy, which enjoys easy access to open seas from numerous warm water ports, Soviet warships are based in the restrictive and often ice-clogged waters of the Arctic Ocean, Baltic and Black Seas, and the Sea of Japan.

Submarines and surface ships leaving any of the four largest Soviet naval bases must pass through narrow choke points vulnerable to attack. And what better way would there be to preclude threats to allied sea lanes than by bottling up the Soviet fleets in their ports?

But, of course, a U.S. Navy capable of blocking the passage of Soviet fleets to deep water must have more and better ships — the kind that can fight and survive in close proximity to the Soviet land mass.

The 450-ship fleet Carter bequeathed the Reagan administration is at least 150 ships short of the total needed to fulfill projected wartime demands, including sustained attacks on Soviet choke points.

Thus, Secretary Lehman and the Reagan administration have proposed to double the Navy's shipbuilding program. Even then, it may be eight years before the Navy has enough ships appropriately armed to carry out an offensive strategy that offers the best hope of protecting allied passage on the world's oceans.

Clearly, then, there is no time to lose in getting on with the job of rebuilding the Navy and, in the process, making it strong enough to preserve the peace or, failing that, to prevail over a larger Soviet fleet in any war at sea.

St. Louis Globe-Democrat

St. Louis, Mo., June 2, 1981

The moment of truth, a bitter pill to swallow, has arrived for the U.S. Navy.

No longer are there any ifs or buts about the situation — now the American Navy no longer is No. 1. Instead, it finds itself trailing behind the Soviet Union.

As the Russian navy was gaining fast and closing the once vast gap between the two sea forces, room remained for hedging. Those days of equivocating are gone, for the time being at least.

No less of an authority than Secretary of the Navy John Lehman Jr. has conceded that "we have lost our maritime superiority." Last August, the Navy's top admirals met in Washington to review the situation and acknowledged that the slim margin of U.S. superiority that had been reported only a year earlier no longer existed.

In recent testimony on Capitol Hill, Rear Adm. Sumner Shapiro, chief of naval intelligence, reported that "we no longer can depend on superior American technology to offset Soviet numbers." He pointed out that Russian technological advances "in some cases are superior to our own."

The gains scored by the Reds in fewer than two decades are staggering. Today the Soviet naval fleet counts 647 major ships composed of 372 submarines and 275 surface warships. The U.S. has 454 major battle vessels, including 119 submarines and 335 surface ships.

That gives the Russians a frightening 3-to-1 superiority in submarines and a total of 193 more vessels than the U.S. Navy has at its disposal. With such odds facing the U.S., it is not surprising that in some quarters the Soviet sea buildup that began in earnest in the early 1960s has been compared to the growth of the German navy prior to World War I that led to the decline of the British Empire.

What a contrast the current situation is to the days of former Rep. Carl Vinson, Georgia Democrat who died Monday.

Vinson battled in the forefront for a first-class Navy while serving in Congress for a half-century before retiring in 1965. He played a key role in launching a two-ocean Navy prior to World War II and was one of the main driving forces behind the Navy's phenomenal growth during the war.

In the trying times that exist today, it is comforting to see the emphasis the Reagan administration is placing on a strong national security to help preserve world peace. Now the Navy appears to be in good hands again. One could hardly find a better qualified person to rebuild the Navy than the enthusiastic and optimistic Lehman, who has the vision to see the day when sea leadership will be recovered anew by the U.S.

Now the U.S. has an overextended 2½-ocean Navy trying valiantly to police three massive areas. The fleet is short some 20,000 petty officers but it is shaking out of the doldrums. Re-enlistment of first-termers is up 6 percentage points and climbed 14 percent among second-termers over two years ago. For 1½ years now the Navy has attained its recruiting goals and more than three-quarters of the new volunteers have college diplomas.

The Reagan administration has a goal of 600 active ships, 46 more than exist today. The number of battle groups would be increased from the present 12 to 15. In an effort to speed up the production pace, two of the new groups may be built around reconditioned World War II battleships rather than aircraft carriers.

With the U.S. heavily dependent on imported oil and strategic materials, a Navy equal to the task is essential to protect American merchant vessels and to keep vital trade lanes open.

Flags are flying at half mast mourning for Vinson. He died at age 97, no doubt thankful for being able to live long enough to see the U.S. Navy again accorded the proper attention and support it deserves and needs to help keep this nation free.

The Wichita
Eagle-Beacon

Wichita, Kans., May 10, 1981

Plans to pull two World War II battleships out of mothballs, equip them with sophisticated electronic gear and cruise missiles, and recommission them make a certain amount of sense. The great, gray leviathans Iowa and New Jersey are said to be in remarkably good condition, represent a considerable military investment laid idle, and the Navy is in need of updating to stay competitive with the Soviet Union's growing fleet of warships.

Navy Secretary John Lehman obviously is impressed with the ships' capabilities, calling them "as fast as any on the oceans today," and noting they were built to withstand the incredible impact of 18-inch artillery. "That's a far more formidable threat than any conventional warhead the Soviets can throw against us," he observes.

That, however, doesn't erase memories of battleships going down at Pearl Harbor. Nor does it address the fact that, outfitted with cruise missiles likely to be carrying nuclear warheads, the Iowa and the New Jersey almost certainly would be targeted for atomic strikes themselves, rather than conventional attack in a major conflict.

Ships this size would be nearly impossible to hide from today's advanced surveillance systems and missiles, making a direct hit on one of them much more likely. In the event both were lost to such an attack, a lot more than the $1 billion retrofitting expense would be gone.

So, too, probably would be about 3,000 Navy personnel and a sizable portion of the cruise missile arsenal.

The proposed cost of putting the two huge battleships back to sea is about equal to building three much smaller, new frigates. Given that, leaving existing, apparently serviceable ships tied up at dockside may seem a comparative waste of equipment and defense dollars.

Actually, it underscores the fact the needed modernization of the U.S. Navy isn't likely to lend itself either to cheap or easy solutions. Successful modernization isn't likely to begin by investing heavily in trying to make 40-year-old warships perform tomorrow's missions.

Houston Chronicle

Houston, Texas, May 21, 1981

John F. Lehman Jr. has all the appearance of being the right man in the right place at the right time.

Lehman presides over a U.S. Navy whose forces have been allowed to dwindle — by half — while its commitments have been increased, and while the Soviets have steadily forged a large and sophisticated fleet able to project its interests and power throughout the oceans.

Lehman intends to do something about that in his role as secretary of the Navy and cutting edge of the Reagan administration's policy to rebuild and reassert American naval power. And he has been going about his task with a vigor that matches the seriousness of the problem.

That vigor, as well as his optimism, outspokenness and tough attitude toward the Russians, has apparently been a little surprising. It is a common theme of remarks about the secretary, who has received more attention than is usual for the relatively anonymous service secretaries in these days of centralized Defense Department command.

Surprising it may be, but this seems to be just what the Navy needs. When the Navy has reached the point where it "is unable fully to meet its peacetime commitments," then the Navy is standing in need of a forceful, visible and constant public advocate. The quote is from the chief of naval operations, Adm. Thomas B. Hayward, and the assessment is not really disputed.

Building the Navy to more than 600 ships from its present 450, regaining its margin of superiority over the Soviet fleet, and establishing a superior fighting capability are not easy or cheap tasks — and certainly no task for the fainthearted. Secretary Lehman seems to be anything but fainthearted, which could be some of the best news the Navy has had in a long time.

THE SACRAMENTO BEE
Sacramento, Calif., June 4, 1981

The Reagan administration's plan to enlarge the Navy to 600 ships by 1989 includes building three additional nuclear aircraft carrier task forces. According to Sen. William Proxmire, a member of a defense appropriations subcommittee, each of the huge nuclear vessels and its supporting ships and personnel would cost an estimated $30 billion to build and run. Given the history of cost overruns for such projects, the actual cost would no doubt be far greater.

Thus, for 10 years the nation would be committed to a Navy for which, in Defense Secretary Caspar Weinberger's words, huge nuclear carriers "would be the backbone," at a cost running to $90 billion or more.

Proxmire and Sen. Gary Hart of the Senate Armed Services Committee have become outspoken critics of this kind of Navy. The nuclear carrier task force, Proxmire contends, would be "a large floating target for advanced Soviet missiles." Hart argues that diverting so much money to carriers would deprive the Navy of other important needs, including swifter, more maneuverable missile cruisers.

Navy Secretary John Lehman insists that the big carriers could withstand repeated hits by modern Soviet missiles because of their mass and structural strength. He argues that their defense systems, watertight compartments and superior damage control would enable the carriers to carry out their missions even if hit by missiles.

Arguments between experts on the effectiveness of such supercarriers will continue, as they have for the past several years. A lay person might wonder, however, if this isn't another time warp reminiscent of the 1930s argument over huge battleships. Critics said they would be sitting ducks for air attacks from carriers. World War II proved them right. It seems more than possible that big nuclear carriers will likewise be vulnerable to the increasing sophistication of deadly cruise missiles and other modern weapons difficult to defend against.

Beyond those arguments, however, the administration's approach lacks a coherent specification of the mission the carrier task forces would be expected to fulfill, and how they would fit into broader U.S. defense and foreign policy objectives. The nuclear carrier issue also reflects a basic flaw in the administration's entire approach to defense: Vast expenditures are sought for military equipment and programs as if more and bigger is better, when that seems less and less the prospect for modern warfare.

The administration is having second thoughts about the Carter administration's terribly costly, environmentally destructive basing plan for the MX missile. That same pause is certainly warranted before staking billions on a carrier "backbone" that may be obsolescent before it's built, and whose mission 10 years hence remains unclear.

THE DAILY OKLAHOMAN
Oklahoma City, Okla., July 20, 1981

Over the years, few journals have earned a reputation that matches the credibility of "Jane's Fighting Ships," the London-based annual survey of the world's navies.

Thus when Jane's documents an ominous buildup of Russia's offensive naval capability, coinciding with continued decline of comparable U.S. and allied strength, the warning should be taken seriously.

In its 84th edition, Jane's concurs in a common description of U.S. naval forces as "a one-and-a-half ocean navy striving to carry out a three-ocean job."

The present era is called "an emergency for the U.S. Navy" highlighted by Soviet completion of 40 naval vessels during the last two years while our navy got 18 and the British only one. Announced cutbacks in the British surface fleet will further strain NATO defenses.

Meanwhile, the Soviet Union is proceeding at an unprecedented pace to expand and modernize its navy, including a new nuclear carrier and other missile-firing surface vessels as well as a new generation of the world's largest and deepest diving nuclear submarines.

President Reagan has pledged to reverse the decline of American naval strength that sunk to such a low ebb under the Carter administration. But as Jane's noted, allied navies are plagued by bureaucratic delays in planning and construction. Expediting the administration's plan to increase our fleet from 400 to 600 ships merits an immediate and high defense priority.

The Hartford Courant
Hartford, Conn., May 2, 1981

After World War II, the United States was indisputably the most powerful maritime power on Earth, while the Soviet Union had only a weak defensive naval force.

That situation did not change materially until the early 1960s, in particular after the Cuban missile crisis. The Soviet Union then embarked on a massive naval buildup under Adm. Sergei G. Gorshkov. Today, the Soviet fleet closely rivals that of the U.S. Navy.

But even the most vehement advocate of more U.S. defense spending must admit that today, despite the best efforts of the Soviet Union, the United States still has the most powerful navy in the world.

It is now flexing its muscles quite impressively in the Indian Ocean, where its strong presence is being used to counter Soviet advances in Africa and Asia, and to discourage a possible Soviet invasion of Mideast oil fields.

American superiority on the seas is almost certainly going to continue for some time into the future because of the substantial budget increases slated for the Navy under the Reagan administration.

In fact, Navy Secretary John F. Lehman Jr. puffed at a recent strategy conference in Newport, R.I., that the national security deserves nothing less than absolute maritime superiority. There can be no acceptance of "parity" between U.S. and Soviet naval forces, he said.

He insisted that a shipbuilding program that would create a 600-ship Navy by the end of the decade must be embarked upon; any talk about a strategy involving a 400-ship Navy is, in Mr. Lehman's view, "defeatist."

If people like Mr. Lehman continue to preside over the rest of this decade, we wonder whether they will be content with 600 ships in 1990. Why not 700? Or 800? Or 1,000? The Soviets, spurred by our own naval buildup, will undoubtedly follow suit in an effort to catch up with or even surpass the size and quality of the U.S. Navy.

And, if this government still brooks no talk about "parity," more ships with more weapons with greater sophistication would be required to maintain superiority. In the familiar holy name of National Security, then, we might be embarking on still another arms race, this one seaborne.

And the race could be futile. Although the American submarine fleet is without question a crucial part of the nation's defense capability, highly vulnerable surface ships, like aircraft carriers and refitted battleships, would be of little use in a global nuclear war. In that kind of war, the sea battle would be largely irrelevant.

A major naval buildup might encourage the United States to conduct simultaneous limited wars around the globe, a dangerous and anachronistic notion for the 1980s.

For now, the United States seems stubbornly uninterested in a break in the competition. It opposes, for example, a special United Nations conference to discuss creation of a "zone of peace" in the Indian Ocean. The Soviets, of course, have taken full propaganda advantage by making known their willingness to participate in such a conference and to engage in force reduction talks.

To at least some Third World countries, notably India, that makes the Soviets look like the ones desirous of peace — however undeservedly — while the United States looks like a gunboat diplomat.

In the short term, the United States could help ease growing tensions in the Indian Ocean by agreeing to talk about the "zone of peace" concept. In the longer term, this administration should re-examine its insistence on absolute naval superiority when the clear implication is a future naval arms race and increasing world instability.

CHARLESTON EVENING POST

Charleston, S.C., July 27, 1981

Pentagon sources indicate the Navy may reduce its presence in the Indian Ocean/Arabian Sea — an area where two carrier battlegroups have cruised since late 1979. The seizure of the U.S. Embassy and hostages in Tehran, and the Soviet invasion of Afghanistan prompted the decision to set up the force. The sources stressed there is no intention of ending the Navy's presence, only reducing it to ease the strain on crewmembers kept at sea for months on end.

Last year the aircraft carrier Nimitz returned from a nine-month deployment to the area, having spent during one period 144 continuous days at sea. Even if liberty can be scheduled for the crew, the ports — Karachi, Pakistan; Mombasa, Kenya; Muscat, Oman and the Seychelle Islands to name a few — don't offer much to a sailor on the town. Many are Moslem and honor the rigid restrictions of that faith. And the temperatures in the area range from hot to hotter.

When the planned expansion of the Navy to 15 carrier battlegroups becomes a reality, then two groups can easily be scheduled on a three-month rotating basis as our national interests dictate. At the same time, the commitments of the Navy to the Western Pacific, the Mediterranean and North Atlantic can also be honored.

But the reality of today is that the Navy's assets, both ships and men, have been stretched to the limits of endurance trying to meet its obligations. It's about time a few of the obligations were eased.

The Virginian-Pilot

Norfolk, Va., June 16, 1981

The Reagan administration is pledged to rebuild the U.S. Navy, inferior in numbers to the Soviet Navy. Retired Admiral Stansfield Turner, who headed the Central Intelligence Agency during the Carter presidency, thinks well of Navy proposals to prepare four *Iowa*-class battleships for active service as cruise-missile platforms. But he suggests the Navy shouldn't stop there—that it should proceed to distribute cruise missiles to the fleet.

He has a point. If the name of the game is to increase firepower as well as the number of weapons platforms, it surely makes sense to apply new technologies broadly. This is particularly so when technologies could boost the Navy's firepower greatly at relatively modest cost. Admiral Turner would have the Navy make extensive use of vertical short takeoff and landing (VSTOL) aircraft and remotely piloted drones, as well as cruise missiles. These missiles and aircraft, which Admiral Turner argues the Navy has been slow to embrace, would do much to erase Soviet warships' edge in firepower.

The U.S. Navy still retains an imposing lead in anti-submarine-warfare capability. And the Soviet Navy—for all its otherwise impressive achievements—has yet to fully enter the aircraft-carrier age. But land-based Soviet naval aviation equipped with cruise missiles constitutes a formidable threat that demands formidable replies.

Numbers are not the whole story when talking about the superpowers' naval forces. The Soviet Navy is disadvantaged geographically, being split into four fleets that must pass through constantly monitored choke points to reach the great oceans. Nonetheless, more warships with more punch are a must.

Admiral Turner's remedy would mean more bang for the buck. And it would expedite strengthening of the Navy. "We should insist," he says, "that the relatively small accompanying investment in cruise-missile technologies be made and that the Navy install a cruise-missile capability against fixed and moving targets on as many ships, aircraft, and submarines as possible. We must not end up with only a few showcase battleships with little fighting potential."

Navies don't come cheap. But any administration that prizes cost-effectiveness as well as military superiority should ponder the Turner prescription.

The Times-Picayune
The States-Item

New Orleans, La., July 27, 1981

U.S. naval power has been sorely neglected in recent years, while the Soviet Union has been seeking dominance of the world's oceans. Fortunately, the Reagan administration appears to be committed to reversing the dangerous trend.

The offensive capacity of the Navy is to be expanded with the phased introduction of 150 surface ships armed with modern missiles. The ships will supplement the power of the Navy's aircraft carrier groups, says Adm. Thomas B. Hayward, chief of naval operations.

The need to modernize and increase U.S. naval forces has been dramatized by the growing Soviet naval challenge in several regions. Recently, "Jane's Fighting Ships," the authoritative British journal that keeps track of the world's navies, warned that the United States has "a one-and-a-half ocean navy striving to carry out a three-ocean job." The annual survey of world warships said Western navies are plagued by low budgets, bureaucracy and political indecision "at a time when there are grave dangers inherent in the naval situation."

In the last two years, the Soviet Union completed 40 naval vessels while the U.S. fleet received 18 and the British navy one, the survey reported. In addition, Britain's Royal Navy recently announced plans to reduce the number of surface ships it has committed to the North Atlantic Treaty Organization, leaving the United States to take up the slack.

The buildup of Soviet naval presence in the eastern Mediterranean, the Indian Ocean and the Western Pacific is stretching U.S. carrier forces thin. Top U.S. naval and NATO officials view the situation in the eastern Mediterranean as particularly challenging because of the strategic importance of NATO-member Turkey, which shares borders with the Soviet Union, to the stability of the region. A strong U.S. naval presence is deemed vital to counter growing Soviet naval strength in the eastern Mediterranean. The withdrawal of a U.S. carrier battle group from the Mediterranean to the Indian Ocean has increased concern over U.S. naval capacity in the Mediterranean.

In the Western Pacific, the Seventh Fleet is outnumbered by the Soviets, according to Adm. Hayward, and the "quality of the Russian Pacific fleet has improved."

Considerable debate is going on among U.S. naval officials, members of the Reagan administration and Congress over the best means of strengthening naval capacity. Much of the debate focuses on the type of additional carriers needed. Adm. Hayward and other top Navy officials see a need for at least two more nuclear-powered carriers, while the sentiment in Congress is for smaller, conventional carriers.

The ultimate decision is a matter for the experts. But on the question of the need to vastly upgrade U.S. naval forces, there is little room for debate in view of the clear Soviet ambition to control the seas.

San Francisco Chronicle

San Francisco, Calif., July 7, 1981

FOR YEARS NOW, the U.S. Navy and protagonists of a strong American sea arm have been ringing the warning bell about the extraordinary buildup of Russia's oceangoing muscle. Back in 1979, the authoritative manual that is Jane's Fighting Ships said the U.S. and other non-Communist countries had allowed their naval strength to decline to a point where they would be vulnerable to Soviet military blackmail

And earlier this year, the chief of naval operations, Admiral Thomas B. Hayward, gloomily testified before Congress that the Navy had lost its margin of superiority.

BUT THE POLITICAL climate here at home has changed. And the Navy is proposing a vast program to add ships and aircraft intended to meet President Reagan's goal of attaining clear naval superiority over the Soviet Union before the end of the decade. The Navy wants 143 ships and 1890 aircraft built, and four battleships and two carriers taken out of mothballs. That is approximately 75 percent more seapower than had been planned by the Carter administration.

The bill will be no small item — some 120 billion over five years. Despite such expense, this nevertheless seems to us to be a bold and necessary move considering the great importance of a naval presence should some tinder spot, like the Persian Gulf, flare again. It is a project that deserves to be launched, but one that also warrants the most careful kind of scrutiny as it proceeds down the ways.

Take, for instance, the decision to double the number of nuclear-powered submarines from seven to 14. This will enable the Navy to reach its goal of 100 attack submarines — weapons that are considered by many strategists to be the most effective in the American arsenal

SUCH A DECISION — to emphasize the silent potency of the submarine for maximum deterrent effect — would appear to be sound military planning. But do we really need to trundle out those old battleships with all their vulnerability to attack from the air and beneath the sea? Some of the new technology is suspect, too. As some military critics have noted, a high-powered aircraft, with electronic equipment that is supposedly the apogee of the art, but breaks down with regularity, is nothing more than a costly albatross.

There is no doubt that a strong navy is important to U.S. security, and can be a vital factor in maintaining world peace. Nevertheless, if money is to be spent, on such a large scale, during a period of national belt-tightening, on the stronger navy that we need, it must be expended intelligently on the most effective weaponry

THE TENNESSEAN

Nashville, Tenn., July 20, 1981

THE Navy has proposed a plan of massive shipbuilding and aircraft procurement to meet President Reagan's goal of clear naval superiority over the Soviet Union before the end of the decade. But that plan needs very close scrutiny at the White House.

The Navy proposes building 143 ships, as opposed to the 80 planned by the Carter administration, plus bringing four battleships and two small aircraft carriers out of mothballs. The plan also includes two nuclear-powered aircraft carriers and 14 attack submarines.

The two 95,000-ton aircraft carriers, each costing $3.3 billion, would be the proposed centers of new battle groups.

If one can assume that any future conflict between nations would remain in the realm of a conventional war, the large new carriers and reconditioned battleships might be worth the cost, even though in the era of cruise missiles they still would make large and tempting targets.

The likelihood of any future war with a major enemy remaining conventional for very long is distressingly small and escalation to nuclear exchanges most probable. In that case, the big ships would be immediately targeted by nuclear missiles of the cruise type or others.

A strengthened Navy is something that has fairly wide support since there has been an erosion of its strength in terms of numbers and the fleet is aging.

But if the nation wants sea power, it would seem that the money for the big new carriers might be spread out into a number of smaller ships, capable of carrying their own nuclear weapons.

These and attack submarines would at least make enemy targeting more difficult since there would be more to shoot at, while some of them, at least, would be able to unleash their own deadly weapons in any retaliatory strike. Perhaps the admirals need to think more seriously about tomorrow's kind of war in their planning today.

BATTLESHIP NEW JERSEY RECOMMISSIONED. — NEWS ITEM

TULSA WORLD
Tulsa, Okla., December 2, 1981

THE U.S. Senate was torn Monday between nostalgic romanticism and present-day reality in the debate over resurrection of two mothballed battleships. Romanticism won.

The Senate voted to spend $91 million to begin reactivation of the USS Iowa and $237 million to continue restoration of the USS New Jersey. How else can you explain the decision except in terms of yearning for the past, when battleships were the backbone of the navy and heart-stirring symbols of American might?

But this is not 1904 or 1917 — or even 1943. In light of the country's 1981 defense needs — more modern weapons and better-paid personnel — the decision borders on the incredible.

Most naval scholars agree that battleships, as primary instruments of seapower, were outdated before Pearl Harbor.

The Japanese put this country's entire battleship fleet in the Pacific out of action in a single carrier-launched air raid on Dec. 7, 1941. In the end, it made little difference. Carriers had become the decisive weapon.

The Japanese enjoyed a 10-0 advantage of battleships at the beginning of the Pacific war. Every one of these was knocked out of action by 1945, thanks to American air power. The big floating gun platform is much more vulnerable today than in 1945 because of surface-to-surface and air-to-surface missiles, weapons available to every third-rate military power in the world.

The Senate's vote is a tribute to what British naval historian Richard Hough called the "greatness and grandeur" of the dreadnought. But that was a long time ago.

The Senate's action is a costly indulgence in nostalgia at the expense of taxpayers.

THE ATLANTA CONSTITUTION
Atlanta, Ga., December 15, 1981

Pentagon officials have decided the United States should seek superiority over the Soviet Union on the seas. Considering how much valuable material and energy products move across the world's oceans to this country and our allies, that approach makes sense.

The United States used to have a clear superiority on the oceans. Since World War II, however, the strength of the Soviet armada has been growing by leaps and bounds. Today's Soviet fleet is sophisticated and has been built over a number of years, and represents a large investment. The Soviet navy now has a momentum that will be difficult to overcome. Each year new ships, aircraft and research vessels are put to sea.

Thus, a major part of U.S. military planning actually has been done for us in the Kremlin. The United States has no choice but to meet the threat.

Consider this:

American dependence on overseas oil and non-fuel minerals has increased to the point where almost half of the oil we consume is imported. All of the 46 minerals in the U.S. strategic minerals inventory are imported.

The value of U.S. overseas trade keeps growing. The dollar value of U.S. exports quadrupled between 1946 and 1972, and has quadrupled again since then.

In more than 200 international incidents cataloged since World War II, the Navy has been called upon to respond to more than 75 percent of them.

As it relates to warfare, U.S. policy has been to fight the enemy as far away from home as possible. Having forward-positioned forces is one way of keeping the fighting away from our own territorial borders.

Naval fighting takes two basic forms: blockade and battle. Blockade is the preferred one, and historically has proven highly effective. But a blockade is possible only with superior forces.

And if for this reason alone, maritime superiority for the United States makes sense in peacetime and in the event of war.

DESERET NEWS
Salt Lake City, Utah, December 7, 1981

Few parts of its defense plans have generated more scorn and derision for the Reagan administration than its plans to take a couple of old warships out of mothballs and return them to duty.

These plans have come to symbolize what its critics insist is the new administration's preference for throwing U.S. military weight around rather than helping needy people.

What's more, the critics say, the plan is unrealistic in view of the age of these ships, which go back to world War II.

Actually, re-fitted old ships can under the right circumstances render valuable service, as they did in World War II, the Korean Conflict, and the Vietnam War.

Though the administration wants to increase defense spending and new ships and missiles are on order, they won't be ready for another four to eight years. As a result, U.S. forces could be caught short of vital equipment at a time when Soviet military capability is especially strong.

Nowhere is the problem more acute than in the U.S. Navy, where a single Nimitz-class nuclear-powered aircraft carrier can take up to eight years to build.

To help fill the gap, the administration is proposing to renovate two World War II-era battleships, the New Jersey and the Iowa. Though both chambers of Congress have allocated money for the New Jersey, the House of Rreparesntatives so far has refused any funds for the Iowa. The House action is a mistake.

While many of the old armaments would be retained, these ships would be fitted with modern missiles able to strike targets 200 to 300 miles away. And they could be modernized more quickly than new ships can be built.

Right now the Navy needs fast, powerful, missile-launching ships in the Indian Ocean in case of a crisis in the Middle East. Some or all of these three old ships could be used there.

In safeguarding national security, special circumstances can require special responses or weapons. That goes for cold wars as well as hot ones.

The Union Leader
Manchester, N.H., August 3, 1981

Old battleships never die ... they just wait patiently in mothballs.

The last time Uncle Sam needed one of these big fighting ships was in 1969, when the U.S. Navy called upon the New Jersey — more affectionately known as the "Big J" — for 328 days of bombardment support duty off South Vietnam.

After serving in three wars, the "Big J" went into mothballs and, for a long time, it appeared that the era of the battleship had come to an end.

Now comes word that the New Jersey is being returned to service. Not only that, but two more of the big ships, renowned in sea battles of years past for the firepower of their 16-inch guns, may be recommissioned in the future.

Obviously, it will take a lot of facelifting to get these battleships back in fighting shape. Fact is, the 888-foot New Jersey will undergo a $330 million renovation project to turn it into a modern missile-firing dreadnought.

That, of course, is a lot of money.

but, as Secretary of the Navy John H. Lehman Jr. points out, two battleships can be renovated for the cost of building one new frigate and the restoration takes less time than building a new ship.

The "Big J" may be getting older, but she hasn't lost her punch. Even though it has been 38 years since the ship was first commissioned, the New Jersey, with a top speed of 33 knots, still will rank among the fastest of the conventionally powered ships in the U.S. Navy.

At a time when America is shoring up its defenses, it's good to see a tried and true veteran of the seas being recalled to active duty.

And her return no doubt will be greeted with great enthusiasm by the proud officers and enlisted men who fought and won many big battles — thanks to her powerful weaponry — during three wars.

Welcome back, "Big J."

Navy Warships' Future Questioned After Falklands War

The war between Great Britain and Argentina over the Falkland Islands in 1982 intensified debate in the United States over naval strategy. The sinking of an Argentine cruiser and the destruction of a British destroyer in early May, with the loss of hundreds of lives, were particularly instrumental in prolonging congressional debate about the advisability of building large warships. The loss that made the deepest impression on U.S. military analysts was the sinking of the British destroyer *Sheffield* by two French-built low-flying Exocet missiles, fired from an Argentinian jet. The two missiles, estimated to cost $200,000 each, quickly brought down the 4,100-ton *Sheffield,* whose cost was put at $50 million. The *Sheffield* was a modern destroyer, commissioned in 1975. The Falklands battle came at a time when the Defense Department was requesting funds for a massive ship-construction program for the Navy, which was to include two giant, *Nimitz*-class nuclear-powered aircraft carriers. In a letter circulated in the Senate May 5, Sen. Gary Hart (D, Colo.) observed that "surface ships have proven more vulnerable than many expected . . . Billion-dollar cruisers . . . are not a very good trade for two torpedoes." Hart's conclusions were disputed by Secretary of the Navy John Lehman, who noted that only large aircraft carriers could provide the kind of defense needed to protect fleets against attacking airplanes. "The British don't have any air cover," he said in explaining the British losses at sea, which included another destroyer and two frigates, plus a container ship carrying supplies. The Argentine plane that fired on the *Sheffield* "could not have gotten anywhere near our ships," he asserted.

The Hartford Courant

Hartford, Conn., May 9, 1982

The war for the Falkland Islands should give those advocates of a 600-ship American Navy plenty to think about.

This is the first war essentially being fought with high-technology missiles, and it has become disturbingly clear just how vulnerable surface vessels have become.

That ancient ark of American origin, the Argentine cruiser General Belgrano, was helpless against the two Mark 24 torpedoes, guided by wires and acoustic homing devices, fired by the British nuclear-powered submarine Conqueror. It was the first sinking of the war. The second sinking, of an unidentified Argentine patrol boat by a British helicopter, was caused by missiles equipped with radar homing devices with a range of 15 miles.

The British, in turn, lost their 4,100-ton British destroyer HMS Sheffield when it was hit by French-made missiles fired from a distance of 20 miles by an Argentine fighter-bomber.

Clearly, many surface vessels are just sitting ducks in the age of remote-control war.

And yet, the Reagan administration is pushing a $168 billion, five-year program that involves, among other things, the construction of two new 90,000-ton aircraft carriers.

The proposed carriers would cost about $4 billion apiece, but how long would they last in a war against missiles? "About two days," said Adm. Hyman G. Rickover, father of the nuclear Navy, in his farewell testimony before Congress earlier this year. In fact, one well-placed $100,000 missile could nullify the entire multi-billion-dollar investment.

Another administration proposal — the restoration of some mothballed battleships — seems even more ludicrous in the light of what's happened in the Falklands. They were widely considered too vulnerable to be of much use in battle even before World War II, and no amount of retrofitting is likely to change that assessment now.

Certainly a substantial investment is needed to keep America's edge on the seas. But instead of putting out great lumbering targets for sophisticated missiles — already in the hands of mini-powers like Argentina — the emphasis should be on less vincible ships.

The money for the giant aircraft carriers could be diverted to produce twice as many smaller, more maneuverable carriers, or to build a different variety of vessels altogether.

The best investment would be in the production of large numbers of small, conventional submarines to supplement the Trident fleet. And all naval vessels, from frigates to carriers, should be equipped with the best available anti-aircraft and anti-missile weapons.

The administration wants to create a deterrent to war by rebuilding the Navy. But the potential adversaries of the United States are also watching how easily surface ships are being dispatched in the Falklands. They are less likely to be deterred by a U.S. Navy that concentrates on launching still more sea-going dinosaurs.

DAYTON DAILY NEWS

Dayton, Ohio, May 13, 1982

The missile that sunk the *HMS Sheffield* sends a potent warning to the United States: Don't rebuild the Navy to fight the last war.

President Reagan and Congress are preparing to spend $168 billion to rebuild the U.S. fleet. Given the steady and monstrous buildup of Soviet naval forces — 1,179 vessels compared to the 600 the United States is aiming for — modernization is necessary. But the United States also is building in some risks, as with the two new large aircraft carriers being proposed.

Basically, the debate is whether to build two large, $3.4 billion aircraft carriers or more smaller ones. The sinking of the *HMS Sheffield* is cited by both sides to support their own cases.

The crushing of the $50 British million ship by a $200,000 missile emphasized that naval warfare is now more clearly in the realm of missiles. Unless surface ships are loaded with their own missiles or anti-missile systems, they may be sitting ducks even against militarily weak nations.

Proponents of large aircraft carriers argue that the big flattop is needed to hold all the modern jets to control the sea surface, and that one big carrier would need fewer sophisticated escort ships than several smaller carriers would. For that reason, Congress is likely to approve money for another large nuclear carrier to be launched in the 1990s.

Since the U.S. fleet already has several large carriers, it ought to more seriously consider smaller new ones. The Soviet Navy has developed primarily as an anti-carrier force. U.S. submarine commanders know that American carriers are highly vulnerable. The Navy is risking a lot by putting so many eggs in so few baskets.

The carrier is no longer a reliable strategic weapon anyway. The old notion of moving the carriers close to the Soviet Union is now suicidal. Soviet attack-subs, Backfire bombers and long-range missiles are too potent a threat. Aside from nuclear submarines, the United States has to rely on missiles, not carrier-launched jets, to hit Soviet bases.

Carriers are still needed to project U.S. air power closer to some distant trouble-spots just as surface ships, though more vulnerable these days, are needed to transport personnel and equipment.

But it makes more sense to build more smaller ships that can be dispersed and to continue placing more stress on new missile technologies.

CHICAGO Sun-Times
Chicago, Ill., May 8, 1982

The Falkland Islands naval engagements are the biggest since World War II. So it is fitting that the Senate pay close attention to what's been happening there as it begins debate on the administration's $168 billion ship and aircraft procurement program.

A cruiser, a destroyer and a patrol boat have been sunk by comparatively inexpensive, electronically guided, "smart" projectiles—both torpedoes and airborne missiles. And the question is whether big, high-cost warships—especially 95,000-ton Nimitz-class aircraft carriers—have been rendered obsolete by sophisticated missile technology.

Navy Secretary John F. Lehman Jr., who has two such big-deck carriers in the budget, thinks not. He argues persuasively that if the British had the defensive weapons and aircraft of one such carrier in the South Atlantic, the Argentine missile that sank the destroyer Sheffield could never have reached target, and if the target was a Nimitz, it would have survived a hit.

Maybe so. But when a Nimitz-class carrier costs $3.4 billion to build, and its auxiliary ships cost $10 billion more, a second opinion is in order.

One comes from Sen. Gary Hart (D-Colo.) and others of his military reform caucus, legislators who have made themselves experts in military strategy and procurement.

Hart, no dove, wants our Navy built up. But he argues for light flattops—not as light as the 20,000- and 29,000-ton British vessels that can launch only jump jets, but 40,000-ton carriers that accommodate the same fighters that a big-deck ship does.

These would have tactical virtues. They would be dispersable for greater safety and divisible from their battle groups for multiple missions. But their glowing virtue in a time of red-ink budgets is that *four* of them can be built for the price of *one* Nimitz-class carrier. Hart is for building four of them and shelving the two Nimitzes. So are we.

With "smart" missiles proliferating, even in Third World military forces, $3.4 billion is a lot of chips riding on one keel.

San Francisco Chronicle
San Francisco, Calif., May 10, 1982

THE SINKING OF HMS Sheffield, a modern, $41-million-dollar destroyer, by a $250,000 French missile which mated rocketry with electronic guidance systems certainly shocked more than the British Admiralty. The admirals had obviously misjudged the threat of modern weaponry not all that different from weapons in their own arsenals.

And this has already prompted some thought in the Pentagon, which has had the ability to employ naval vessels in in-shore bombardment and support roles, without too much thought of air cover, in the last two wars fought by the U. S. Navy: Korea and Vietnam.

The fact of the matter is, however, that such air-to-surface missiles as the French sold to the Argentinians have been available to nations all over the world for some time now and it makes no difference whether they sup at a Soviet or at a Western hand. Surface vessels, always vulnerable, are now more vulnerable than ever before because of highly-efficient, incredibly-swift and long-ranged missiles and, of course, torpedoes of the sort which destroyed the Argentine cruiser.

IT IS IMPROBABLE, the U. S. Navy tells us, that an American destroyer like the Sheffield would have been operating in an area of hazard without air protection. That air cover is able to provide electronic and radar protection to ensure that no hostile aircraft can come within 450 miles of a carrier battle group.

Nonetheless, the Sheffield example is sobering. Striking range against ships by a foe detected only by radar has been increased substantially. And, undoubtedly, some rethinking is necessary. The incident came as this country is deciding upon construction of new nuclear carriers and a time when a study of carrier vulnerability has been classified although this was not originally intended.

The Dallas Morning News
Dallas, Texas, May 8, 1982

WORLD War II proved that no matter how big and powerful the naval vessel — whether Germany's Bismarck or Britain's Prince of Wales and Repulse — the right weapons, used rightly, can sink it.

The point is worth reflecting on as congressional debate quickens over the Reagan administration's $96 billion ship-building program. The point is not, as some have alleged, that surface ships are too vulnerable to pour much money into. The point is that, vulnerable or not, no one in the past 40 years (or the past 4,000) has come up with a replacement for ships.

The Falklands fighting has brought the lesson up to date. That surface vessels can be sunk or destroyed by "smart" weapons has become tragically plain. But so is it plain that ships do vital and unique things — like project national power into places where it could not otherwise penetrate.

How else could the British make plain to Argentina their determination to recover the Falklands, save through dispatching the fleet? The Falklands are hard enough for Argentina to reach by air — far less for Britain, which lacks land bases on the South American continent.

The evolving congressional debate over surface ships centers so far on the nuclear-powered Nimitz-class carriers that the administration wants to build. Sen. Gary Hart of Colorado thinks such ships, priced at $3.7 billion each, are dinosaurs. He would build smaller vessels, so as to disperse our power more widely. Sen. Sam Nunn of Georgia wants more reliance on land-based than on sea-based power.

Here are two interesting criticisms — neither of which obviates the need for the carriers. Sen. Hart doesn't reckon with the fact that the Soviet Union has enough anti-ship missiles to sink the whole U. S. Navy. Building a lot of carriers doesn't solve the problem. Building powerful carriers that can defend themselves, even while taking structural damage, won't necessarily — but might — solve the problem.

As for land bases, where, first of all, is the certainty that they can survive political changes? Look what happened to U.S. bases in Iran.

How, in the second place, do you deal with relatively inaccessible areas like the South Atlantic? Just where would we put a land base?

Nor should the value of ships as symbols be forgotten — a value recognized throughout history. To know that the Americans can get somewhere is one thing; actually to see the Americans passing by on patrol is quite another thing.

No, there's no substitute for a powerful, wide-ranging Navy: The sort we don't have anymore, thanks to post-Vietnam cutbacks that reduced our fleet to the smallest level since Pearl Harbor. If the administration gets its way, we'll have a 600-ship fleet by the end of the century. It won't be cheap, but then national security rarely is these days.

THE BLADE
Toledo, Ohio, May 15, 1982

THE naval warfare in the South Atlantic in which two major surface ships, one British and one Argentine, have been scuttled by sophisticated weaponry raises some pertinent issues for American defense planners.

The lessons are not entirely clear, partly because the details of both attacks have not been fully disclosed and partly because the forces involved are not precisely the same as those that might be deployed by a U.S. naval task force in battle. Nevertheless, it is impossible to ignore one salient point — that surface naval vessels are vulnerable to a single missile or torpedo. This throws into serious doubt the value of building large ships, such as massive nuclear aircraft carriers, which might turn out to be sitting ducks. At present the navy is seeking money to add two big carriers to its current total of 13 and to take four battleships out of mothballs, ostensibly to serve as seagoing missile-launching platforms.

Navy Secretary John Lehman, Jr., holds that the British-Argentine conflict proves the validity of his thesis that big carriers would not be as vulnerable because of their effective air power which would serve as a shield. This is undoubtedly true up to a point, but there are two major questions left unanswered: Could even a strong air defense protect against all potential missiles that might be thrown against large ships? And second, could a carrier's planes still carry out attack missions that would be entrusted to them while at the same time adequately protecting the mother ship against incoming missiles?

There are arguments to be made for the big-ship approach, but the United States should not rush headlong into construction of such vessels simply because the navy secretary thinks that is the thing to do. This question involves not only naval units but the overall military stance of the nation, including land and air forces. Our defense posture should be assessed in that light, keeping in mind the warning by retired Adm. Elmo Zumwalt that the navy may be creating "a seaborne Maginot Line."

There is, despite the hidebound mentality of some navy brass, an argument to be made for a navy of smaller, more numerous, and more mobile vessels — including a versatile submarine force — in order to cope with any situation that may occur anywhere in the world. Few things are more unpredictable than the circumstances of a future military conflict.

It is especially important at a time when the nation is on the verge of a record arms buildup involving large increases in spending, that defense planners, civilian and military, weigh the options carefully and avoid putting all our military eggs in only a few big baskets.

Houston Chronicle
Houston, Texas, May 6, 1982

Among the volumes of "lessons" being drawn from the Falkland Islands dispute by politicians, military men, historians, journalists and others, none is more compelling for this country than the need for a strong Navy.

As the Senate considers the Reagan administration's proposed defense budget, which includes plans for the largest naval expansion ever in peacetime, it is well to consider the lessons about naval strength now being acted out by the British and the Argentines in the South Atlantic.

A time-honored military axiom spun from basic physics has it that force will rush in to fill a vacuum. The nation which lets its naval power dwindle does so at the peril of encouraging aggressors. For Britain the entire Falklands crisis, and in particular the loss of the destroyer Sheffield in a sea battle, are bloody testament to that.

As recently as 1977 Argentina backed down from invasions of the Falklands, impressed by British maritime strength. When Argentinians seized the moment in early April, they were acting in large part because British naval forces were substantially weakened from what they had been in 1977. So many ships and planes had been moth-balled that the Argentinians felt they could move on the Falklands with little fear of effective British retaliation.

There may yet be enough bite left in the British lion to prove the Argentinians wrong, but that would not disprove the theory; it would only call into question the Argentinians' timing. If they had waited six months longer the lone British Vulcan which bombed the airstrip at Port Stanley would have been mothballed. Later still, and one of the two British carriers involved in the operation would have been in Australian hands. Much longer, and who knows, the British may have been reduced to buying passage for all their troops on Caribbean cruise ships.

Britain no longer has an empire, but in recent weeks the British have relearned the importance of naval strength. The United States never had an empire, but it has far-flung strategic interests requiring naval strength.

Navy Secretary John F. Lehman Jr. has asked the Congress to provide the funds necessary for the United States to reacquire "clear maritime superiority" across the globe. In view of the sequence of events leading to the Falklands dispute, we can settle for nothing less.

Lincoln Journal
Lincoln, Neb., May 6, 1982

Do you think it too much to expect that as the White House and its military people pore over combat reports from the South Atlantic, there may yet be second thoughts about spending $1.7 billion to recondition four World War II battleships?

Alas, probably so.

Still, the torpedoing of Argentina's only cruiser, the 13,645-ton General Belgrano, by a British submarine, and the sinking of a $50 million modern British destroyer by a missile fired from an airplane some 20 miles away ought to give someone in Washington pause.

Why was it necessary for the British to strike at the Argentine cruiser anyway? Its 15 six-inch guns had a maximum range of only 13 nautical miles and the ship — born in 1938 as the U.S.S. Phoenix and a survivor of Pearl Harbor — was positioned well beyond the 200-mile radius of exclusion which Britain has proclaimed around the Falkland/Malvinas Islands.

One need not be a veteran of anything other than the Nebraska Navy to guess the immediate "significant threat" which the 44-year naval vessel posed to the British task force was bound up mainly in the missiles it carried in its weapons inventory.

Heat-seeking, acoustically-homing or radar-guided missiles fired at moderate distances are the principal threat to enemy aircraft. Comparable missiles fired at greater distances can strike at ships themselves. The death of the British destroyer Sheffield proved that once again.

Even ruling out a nuclear war, should the United States become involved in a major conflict, the opposition is likely to be far better armed than is Argentina.

Navy Secretary John Lehman this week denied a *Philadelphia Daily News* report about the technical inadequacies of the four battleships scheduled for revival.

At the same time, however, Lehman did confirm that a sophisticated, computerized anti-missile defense system will not be installed on the recommissioned giants. The newspaper originally was told the system would be unable to survive the recoil and shock of the battleships' gun blasts.

Swell. Battleships that are so physically immense they personify national strength and power in harbors around the world will end up with less anti-missile protection than other capital ships — and when missiles, not bombs, are the primary modern surface weapons threatening such ships.

To be sure, Lehman has an answer for that.

He says the battleships would never be without a screen of protective air support to knock down cruise missile planes miles away.

Which also means none of the four battleships could venture out of port without the companionship of a big-deck aircraft carrier — further bunching the Navy's biggest and most expensive ships.

Couldn't that $1.7 billion the Reagan administration wants to spend on juicing old-style battleships buy the U.S. Navy ship platforms which make more sense in the last years of the 20th century and better fit the Navy's essential mission of protecting world shipping sea lanes?

The Courier-Journal

Louisville, Ky., June 2, 1982

A NAVAL armada such as the one Britain has deployed around the Falklands is a grand and awesome sight. But precision-guided cruise missiles aren't easily awestruck — nor, apparently, are Argentine pilots. And that goes far to explain why four proud British warships now lie at the bottom of the South Atlantic.

The British naval losses, which also include a sunken cargo ship and several damaged frigates and destroyers, haven't been serious enough to endanger the armada's basic mission: recapture of the Falkland Islands. But it comes as a shock to learn that a third-rate military power such as Argentina can inflict so much punishment on one of the world's most modern navies.

For Americans, who boast the biggest and best collection of fighting ships, the Falklands war raises some obvious and troubling questions. If a relatively inexpensive, French-made Exocet missile can knock out a British destroyer from 30 miles away, couldn't similar Soviet weapons do the same to our ships? And if British anti-aircraft missiles and carrier-based jets can't fully protect their fleet from determined Argentine air attack, would one of our carrier battle groups fare any better against the Soviet Union's more numerous and more effective long-range naval bombers?

Navy Secretary John Lehman, himself a reserve naval pilot, brushes such questions aside. The real lesson of the South Atlantic, he says, is that only big aircraft carriers, such as America's nuclear-powered *Nimitz*, and high-performance aircraft, such as F-14 fighters and E-2C radar planes, can ensure survival in the dangerous new world of sea-skimming anti-ship missiles.

No doubt the British would be delighted to have the *Nimitz*, with its 90 or so planes, off the Falklands — instead of the small-deck *Hermes* and *Invincible*, which together carry only 30 to 40 Harriers and a few dozen helicopters. A couple of squadrons of F-14s probably would make quick work of attacking Argentine jets before they got close to their targets.

Giant carriers and supersonic combat jets *are* useful — especially for intimidating or, if necessary, fighting Third World upstarts. But if that were the only mission of the U.S. Navy, this nation would have more than enough sea-going firepower in our current fleet of 12 carriers — much less the 15 that Mr. Lehman wants.

But of course our navy is designed to do more than execute gunboat diplomacy. Its ultimate mission is to defeat the Soviet navy and keep the sea lanes open in time of war.

The Soviet Union is no Argentina. In a full-scale war — one that crossed the nuclear threshhold — our aircraft carriers and their escorts would be prime targets of Soviet nuclear missiles. Similarly, Soviet fleets would come under U.S. nuclear attack. Neither navy — except for submarines — would last long in such a conflict.

But even a war between U.S. and Soviet forces in which only conventional weapons were used might quickly result in enormous naval losses. Even before the Falklands war, some military analysts were warning that the U.S. Navy had badly underestimated the vulnerability of our aircraft carrier battle groups, including the giant carriers themselves, to cruise missiles and long-range torpedoes.

Most of America's top naval brass firmly believe in the aircraft carrier and are extremely sensitive to suggestions that their pride and joy is a sitting duck. That's doubtless why the Navy has classified as "secret" an unpublished article about last year's Ocean Venture exercise by the Atlantic Fleet. The article, by an officer who was chief analyst of Ocean Venture, reportedly concluded that simulated submarine attacks on carriers participating in the exercise were far more effective than the Navy admits.

Nevertheless, the Reagan administration plans to build two more nuclear-powered carriers, at a cost of $3.4 billion each, and Congress has approved the down payment in fiscal 1983. Critics argue, persuasively, that this money — or a fraction of it — could be more wisely spent on more anti-ship cruise missiles and attack submarines, and on converting B-52s into long-range naval patrol bombers.

This isn't to suggest that the Navy should scrap its carriers. The war for the Falklands has proved that carriers are valuable, even necessary, for certain kinds of fighting. But it is foolhardy to think that American carriers could survive for long within easy range of land-based Soviet aircraft and their missiles, much less carry the battle to the Soviet homeland, as some admirals envision.

Our naval strategy, tactics and budgetary priorities need serious rethinking. Stamping "secret" on the work of critics is a poor way to start.

Chicago Tribune

Chicago, Ill., October 10, 1982

Could America win its next war if it is compelled to fight one? It didn't win the last one, in Vietnam; it was fought to a standstill in the one before that, in Korea; and a number of military thinkers believe it could do no better in the future. They believe that the United States is prepared to fight the wrong kinds of wars in the wrong kinds of places with the wrong kinds of weapons. There is a growing sense of uneasiness in the U.S. military, a suspicion that all the billions being spent on defense may be buying a blunder on the scale of the Maginot Line that failed to slow the Germans in World War II.

There have been fundamental changes in the world since the last great U.S. military victory (the end of the colonial era, the communications boom) and in war (guerrillas, terrorism, high technology). Yet the basic structure of the U.S. military and the basic kinds of weapons it uses have not greatly changed since World War II. The three services—Army, Navy and Air Force—are organized in the same large and often unwieldy units that were needed to fight the mass battles of that war. The central weapon of the Army remains the heavy tank; of the Navy the large aircraft carrier; of the Air Force the manned high-performance bomber and fighter.

Should changes be made, and if so, what should they be?

Most military thinkers say that no great changes are needed, that except for a little tinkering here and there the present structure is just fine. The Army is building its huge M-1 tank, the Navy is campaigning for more giant carriers and the Air Force is building the B-1 bomber. The commitment to NATO, and to the stationing of more than 300,000 troops in Europe, remains firm, as does the commitment to Korea and Japan.

But others are calling for a complete re-evaluation. Their view is cogently expressed in the current issue of Foreign Affairs. Written by retired Adm. Stansfield Turner, a former director of the CIA, and Capt. George Thibault, chairman of the Department of Military Strategy at the National War College, the article questions a basic U.S. assumption—that the deployment of forces behind prepared defenses in Europe and Korea and the existence of about a dozen large-carrier task forces meets this country's global military needs.

They call instead for a doctrine they call "preparing for the unexpected." They contend that U.S. forces are more likely to be needed in unexpected places on short notice than in the carefully prepared theaters of Europe and Asia. They ridicule the idea that U.S. naval forces could hope to approach, blockade and destroy Soviet ships in port, which is one justification for large-carrier task forces.

What is needed, they write, is a doctrine of flexibility that will permit manageable units of U.S. forces to move quickly into crisis areas and to destroy the Soviet navy on the high seas, where it is most likely to be encountered. This, they say, is a "maritime strategy" that depends on controlling the sea and using it to project power around the world. That means a basic change in types of ships and weapons and in the organization of the forces.

Their main target is the large aircraft carrier. Adm. Turner has long advocated the construction of many small carriers instead of a few large ones on the ground that the big carriers are easy and tempting targets. An enemy could cripple our Navy by destroying only a few of them, and so will devote considerable money and effort to the task. By spreading the target value among a larger number of ships the enemy's problem becomes more difficult and the Navy's survivability is enhanced. The Navy resists the Turner thesis on the ground that the small-carrier doctrine requires low-performance short take-off aircraft armed with high-performance missiles, and that no such aircraft presently exist.

The Turner reply: Make them. One reason they don't exist is that there are no carriers that need them. He points out that any large carrier conceived today will not be operational for nearly 10 years and will have to serve for 30 years after that, or until around the year 2020. In the meantime, technological advances in missiles will make the small-carrier concept steadily more compelling. The sooner we start, he contends, the sooner we will have the kind of Navy that is needed.

The rest of U.S. forces should similarly be spread into smaller and more flexible units that can work independently or be pulled together in larger aggregates for larger tasks, such as 2,000-man Marine units equipped for "rapier thrusts" into problem areas. Armored units, the writers argue, should be far more mobile—which might be achieved by making armor and artillery lighter, faster and smaller. Also needed are more and better transport ships and planes to move U.S. forces quickly and in the numbers that might be needed.

One of the great dangers of an inadequate conventional strategy is that it makes nuclear war more likely. As long as conventional forces are able to serve the country's needs there will be no temptation to consider the nuclear option. But if the U.S. is caught unprepared for some challenge to basic national interests—a Soviet move against Middle East oilfields, perhaps—it would be a dangerously different matter.

The Turner-Thibault vision is, of course, a minority opinion. Adm. Turner occasionally tends to crankiness on the small-carrier subject (and the Navy establishment occasionally tends to apoplexy in denouncing it). Yet clearly there is something wrong with a global strategy that depends so heavily on a great many soldiers sitting, idle, in European barracks and a very few giant aircraft carriers sitting duck-like on the sea.

Congress and the military establishment should commence a serious debate on the question of whether America could win its next war—because if the answer is yes, there is much less chance that we will have to fight one.

The Birmingham News

Birmingham, Ala., December 30, 1982

President Reagan has personally recommissioned the USS New Jersey as what proponents describe as the first of a new class of warship — a vessel carrying the traditional firepower of a battleship but also equipped with sophisticated electronics and missiles.

Rear Adm. Walter T. Piotti Jr., director of the Navy's surface warfare division, said the $326 million renovation gives the New Jersey "a war-fighting competence relevant to the 1980s and beyond." Earlier this month, the admiral told the House Armed Services seapower subcommittee that the modernization was "one of the most successful and cost-effective Navy programs of modern times."

Other naval experts are less than enthusiastic about the program, however. They point out that the same amount of ordnance could be mounted on a far less costly platform than a battleship — which, in itself, will present a tempting target to any enemy. The economies of renovation are as well offset by the hefty operating costs of a ship carrying a complement of some 1,600 men.

As for the New Jersey itself, the recommissioning marks another stage in what has been an intriguing history. The ship was first launched Dec. 7, 1942, a year after the Japanese attack on the Pacific Fleet in Pearl Harbor. It has since been taken in and out of service three times, with its most recent service coming off the coast of Vietnam, where its massive, 16-inch guns were used to bombard land targets.

The modernization of the 58,000-ton, 887-foot vessel, which can cruise at 35.5 knots, included installation of eight armored launchers for Tomahawk Cruise missiles, advanced cruiser-style communications equipment, as well as reactivation of the 16-inch turrets and 5-inch gun mounts.

Perhaps, however, the greatest benefit of the program — which, if the Navy has its way, will be followed in two years by the recommissioning of the USS Iowa, with the USS Missouri and USS Wisconsin to follow — lies in the flag-showing capacity of the great ships. The battleship remains an enormously impressive sight, as visitors to the USS Alabama in Mobile can testify, and the appearance of such a sight in various harbors around the world could carry a significant message.

How well a battleship might function in a modern war is another question entirely, however, and it of course must be our most fervent prayer than the thesis will never be tested.

THE DAILY OKLAHOMAN

Oklahoma City, Okla., December 20, 1982

NEWS that the first of four U.S. battleships has been restored and will shortly join the active fleet is being highly touted by a top-ranking admiral as "one of the most successful and cost-effective Navy programs of modern times."

Rear Adm. Walter Piotti Jr. says the $400 million refitting and re-equipping of the U.S.S. New Jersey has been "a singularly successful initiative," and the World War II-era battlewagon has passed all sea trials with flying colors. It's been fitted with modern defensive missiles, electronic gear and helicopter landing facilities.

The New Jersey's three sister ships — the Missouri, Iowa and Wisconsin — are programmed to be de-mothballed later, if the Pentagon admirals have their way.

The old battleships admittedly are a magnificent sight, and certainly were formidable firepower platforms in their day. But you don't have to be a military expert to question the wisdom of returning four of them to active fleet duty at a projected total cost of nearly $2 billion.

Still fresh in memory are those two modern British destroyers lost to French exocet missiles in the Falklands War with Argentina. Ships that cost millions were taken out with missiles that cost a few paltry thousands. It's reasonable to suggest that if destroyers were that vulnerable, how much more vulnerable is a huge battleship to modern weaponry?

The Navy must assume its share of cost-cutting to help reduce staggering budget deficits, and leaving those three 40-year-old battleships in mothballs would seem to be a good place to start.

The Virginian-Pilot
Norfolk, Va., December 31, 1982

The two *Nimitz*-class nuclear attack-aircraft carriers that the U.S. Navy ordered from Newport News Shipbuilding this week are scheduled to be completed near the end of the Eighties — at roughly the same time that the Soviet Navy is expected to field its first big-carrier battle group. The 60,000-ton Soviet carrier currently under construction probably will be nuclear powered. So not only in the United States, but also in the Soviet Union, naval planners have concluded that a low number of big carriers is superior to a larger number of smaller carriers.

The naval war fought by Great Britain and Argentina over the Falkland Islands reaffirmed the conviction in the minds of many, including then-Chief of Naval Operations Thomas B. Hayward, that the United States is building the right kind of navy. A consensus formed that the British Navy would have made quicker work of the opposition and sustained fewer losses had it sailed into battle with large-deck aircraft carriers transporting high-performance, fixed-wing aircraft and radar surveillance aircraft. This combination would have given the British the capability of destroying enemy warplanes before they got close enough to harm the naval task force sent to reclaim the Falklands from the Argentine invaders.

The U.S. Navy hopes to have 15 big-carrier battle groups operating by 1990, compared to the 14 now in existence. The 96,000-ton CVAN-72 and CVAN-73 that will rise on the ways at Newport News Shipbuilding are central to attainment of that goal. As they are phased into the fleet, older carriers will be retired.

Of more immediate concern to Southeastern Virginia is the prospect that the construction contracts for two more carriers will stabilize the Newport News shipyard's work force at more than 25,000 throughout this decade.

While many other areas of the nation are suffering through economic depression, Virginia's economy is afflicted by mild recession because of the steadying federal presence in the northern and southeastern sections of the state. The two *Nimitz*-class carrier contracts are a multibillion-dollar boost to regional prosperity. An inevitable boost, once the go-ahead came down from Washington. Among American shipyards, only Newport News Shipbuilding spawns supercarriers.

THE COMMERCIAL APPEAL
Memphis, Tenn., December 29, 1982

"WE MUST be able in time of emergency to venture in harm's way, controlling air, surface and sub-surface areas to assure access to all the oceans of the world," President Reagan said as he recommissioned the World War II battleship USS New Jersey.

The Navy is touting this 40-year-old vessel as "the most modern warship in the world" and says the $326-million renovation was "one of the most successful and cost-effective Navy programs of modern times."

If the Navy gets its way, the USS Iowa will be recommissioned, too, in two years, and the USS Missouri and the USS Wisconsin will follow if Congress provides the money.

BUT DOUBTS about the cost and about the usefulness of these ships as we approach the 21st Century continues, even among defense experts.

The President's high praise for the New Jersey came a week to the day after Britain's secretary of state for defense, John Nott, reported to the House of Commons on the state of United Kingdom defenses.

Nott spoke from Britain's recent experience.

"A lesson of the Falklands — which some dispute, but how I do not understand — is that surface ships are highly vulnerable to modern missiles," Nott said.

"As the Eighties progress, the weight of the potential strike from these systems will be such that point defense systems, however multiplied, will be hard pressed to cope.

"It will be increasingly difficult to prevent some submarine-launched missiles in particular and indeed some air-launched missiles getting through. And, as we have seen recently, one missile can cause immense damage to the modern surface ship, however we strive to improve their survivability.

"The Argentines had two modern submarines and five, just five, air-launched missiles.

At the present time the Soviets have some 2,000 submarine and air-launched missiles including the most up-to-date stand-off systems; the weight of missile strike against surface platforms would be immense.

"We must therefore continue the gradual shift away from the surface fleet into maritime air and submarines. We must go for smaller, less expensive and less vulnerable surface platforms.

"We must continue the process . . . of changing the emphasis of the fleet to meet the missile threat — which we have only barely glimpsed in the Falklands."

That certainly doesn't not sound like a prescription for recommissioned battlewagons.

CONGRESS would do well to heed Secretary Nott's warnings before it approves new projects which seem intended to prepare this nation to meet future wars with the weapons of the last great war.

Battleships, regardless of how much they are updated with electronic and missile gear, could prove to be the Maginot line of the future.

ST. LOUIS POST-DISPATCH
St. Louis, Mo., December 30, 1982

At the recommissioning of the battleship New Jersey, President Reagan said, "The price of peace is always high." The president is correct — an adequate defense is never cheap — but bringing back the Iowa class battlewagons is an exercise in military nostalgia too expensive at any price.

The irony is that much of what the battleship apologists say about the New Jersey and her three sister ships is generally true: With a top speed of 33 knots, they are still among the fastest warships in world; their main armament of nine 16-inch guns is unparalleled in terms of firepower and range; and their foot-thick armor belt and foot-and-half-thick turret armor, make these vessels the least vulnerable ships on the highseas. Designed and built over 40 years ago, the 58,000-ton Iowa class battleship is a truly remarkable warship.

However, this is a naval era of 40-knot nuclear-powered attack submarines, supersonic bombers, 25-mile-range ship homing torpedos and 300-mile-range nuclear-armed cruise missiles. In certain highly specialized roles, like amphibious gunfire support, the battleships might be useful. But similar arguments could be made favoring the return of dragoons (horse-mounted infantry) and the mule corps for anti-guerrilla operations in mountain areas.

Norman Polmar, a repected naval expert and former editor of "Janes' Fighting Ships," summed up the issue very weil: "There are other, cheaper ways to get gunpower on a ship. We're talking about 1,800 men to tote around nine guns or 40 missiles. It is not cost-effective."

Recommissioning the battleships is military romanticism. This is not naval power but the illusion of naval power. America needs to build a fleet for the 21st century, but President Reagan is wasting our money on a Hollywood navy.

Radar-Evading Bomber Developed; Carter Scored for Disclosure

News that the United States had developed a bomber that could evade detection by radar was publicized by the Defense Department in late August, 1980. The so-called "stealthy aircraft" had been tested secretly since 1978, according to the Pentagon. It was built in a shape that minimized reflection of radar beams and in addition was coated with a special material that diffused radar waves. Republican presidential candidate Ronald Reagan Sept. 4 denounced the Carter Administration for "a cynical misuse of power and a clear abuse of the public trust" by disclosing the work on the aircraft. Reagan charged that the White House had deliberately leaked news of the plan to improve President Carter's "dismal defense record." He said the disclosure was a "grievous blow" to national defense, since it gave the Soviet Union a "10-year start" on developing a similar plane.

In hearings Sept. 4 before a subcommittee of the House Armed Services Committee, Defense Secretary Harold Brown said disclosure of the "stealthy aircraft" was necessary because the press had learned of its existence. A Pentagon spokesman told the subcommittee that one military journal had known of the aircraft in 1978 but had not published the information until August 1980.

The Dallas Morning News
Dallas, Texas, August 29, 1980

WHAT YOU do, when your defenses are down, is whistle in the dark. President Carter has tried to whistle up some support lately by announcing a major technological advance that supposedly would enable bombers, reconnaissance planes, missiles and fighters to cross Soviet borders because they would be "invisible" to the most sophisticated Soviet radar detection devices.

The new techniques, revealed by Defense Secretary Harold Brown in a hastily called news conference, are called "stealth technology."

The stealth technology is an exciting prospect. But as U.S. Sen. John Tower, who has long experience in the Senate Armed Services Committee, pointed out, the super-secret technology won't be available until the 1990s. In the meantime, there are serious gaps in the United States defense, a condition aggravated by the Carter administration's flip-flops and foot-dragging on military expenditures.

As numerous defense experts observed, the President's revelations about the stealth research not only may have jeopardized security precautions, but most likely were politically motivated. The announcement seemed blatantly calculated to help Carter boost his sagging defense posture before the November elections.

What the country needs, instead of grandstanding and empty promises, is a comprehensive revitalization of our total defense effort. Evidence continues to crop up showing that the country's defense readiness is in a dangerous state of neglect and disarray. Our B52 bombers are older than some of the men flying them. And qualified servicemen are in such short supply, ships have had to borrow personnel to go to sea.

Another telling example: The main computer network that would signal a nuclear attack on the United States has serious flaws that are not being addressed. The system miscued twice in June and erroneously signaled a Soviet nuclear attack on the United States. The errors put the nation's defense forces on full alert for three minutes.

Defense specialists have been warning since 1973 that the computer network is faulty. The system ties together the nation's nuclear arsenal through a worldwide chain of 35 computers at 27 key military installations. The government's own watchdog agency, the General Accounting Office, concluded the network "is not sufficiently responsive, reliable or secure, as demonstrated by its performance record."

The GAO report said response to some questions required hours when they should have taken only minutes or seconds. The GAO report also said the system had a failure rate of 62 percent in one test of its use.

This means our country is relying on an early warning system that could fail 62 percent of the time. That's not something calculated to make you sleep any sounder tonight. Even with Jimmy Carter whistling political lullabies outside the window.

Arkansas Democrat
Little Rock, Ark., August 28, 1980

So the United States has been working for three years on an "invisible" bomber – one that Russian radar wouldn't be able to spot until it was over its target. The defense calls this "stealth" plane a major technological advance, and it can't be anything less – even if the plane doesn't yet exist and the announcement is politically timed to offset the finding that the Russians have our big missiles covered.

But though "stealth" is seven or eight or more years away from operational status, the good news, according to Secretary of Defense Harold Brown, is that the stealth principle can meanwhile be applied in part to existing missiles – even to tanks. That gives the Russians something to think about even if it does put them on notice to get going with a similar program of their own.

Not that it involves true invisibility. It's simply that the mode of construction plus a special coating will make the planes (and other weapons) invisible to radar, except very close up. It appears to be largely a matter of minimizing bulk and eliminating the broad-side surfaces that create radar images. But for strategic purposes, that's invisibility as near as not to matter.

The thought that the stealth principle will make vulnerable their entire defense establishment – missiles, planes and even civil defense installations – is bound to give the Russians the kind of nightmares that Russian missile superiority is now giving us.

Ironically, it's reported that our own early warning system against Russian attack has some shortcomings of its own. But the problem can't be anything like what the stealth program will hand Russia.

St. Louis Globe-Democrat
St. Louis, Mo., August 26, 1980

The new breakthrough in technology that will enable American bombers, cruise missiles and fighter-bombers to avoid detection of enemy radar detection units is undeniably a remarkable achievement and could give the United States some much-needed breathing room in which to rebuild its depleted defenses.

The technology, called "Stealth," will prevent Soviet radar from spotting a U.S. bomber until it is too late to knock them down, according to Defense Secretary Harold Brown.

Brown understandably would not release any details of the new development but military and scientific sources say the concept involves a variety of techniques, including the use of radar-absorbing materials and revolutionary changes in aircraft design that would cause radar beams to be deflected from U.S. aircraft into the air rather than rebounding back to the Soviet detection equipment.

There also have been reports that the concept includes reducing the infrared "signature" given off by engine heat, which would defeat the ability of sensors to detect aircraft or vehicles in deepest darkness.

As heartening as the breakthrough is, it hardly calls for Secretary Brown's claim that this discovery "alters the military balance significantly."

For the fact is that this country doesn't have any "Stealth" bombers on hand and defense experts estimate that it could take eight to 10 years to get a "Stealth" plane into service.

Furthermore, due to the administration's halting development of the supersonic B-1 bomber in 1977, apparently with Brown's approval but against the recommendations of the Joint Chiefs of Staff, the U.S. has been left with its ancient, outdated, subsonic B-52 bomber fleet in which many of the pilots are younger than the planes. By now this fleet is down to about 325 planes from its original strength of 625 due to attrition, losses in the Vietnam war and the mothballing of more than 100 of the old planes.

The B-52s are so slow in relation to today's standards that they could be spotted visually on a daylight raid. If the B-1 program hadn't been stopped the nation by now would have a good-sized fleet of these modern, supersonic planes with a much slimmer silhouette that, even without the new technology, would be able to penetrate Soviet air defenses, according to military authorities.

Now that the new technology is available there is even greater reason for moving ahead with production of the B-1 as rapidly as possible. The added speed, coupled with the radar-defeating capability, would make it a strong deterrent against a possible Soviet air or missile attack. For even if the Russians should gain the capability to knock out the greater part of our land-based missiles, they would be deterred by knowing that they had no sure defense against the United States' B-1 bomber fleet.

Unless the White House improves its security measures, however, there is some question as to how long this country will be able to keep the secret of "Stealth." Columnists Rowland Evans and Robert Novak report that many details of the new discovery leaked out from a meeting that Sen. John Stennis and two staff members held with top Pentagon officials who unveiled the technology.

"Many of its most intimate details were precisely explained on the evening television news and in newspapers the following day," Evans and Novak said.

That, unfortunately, has been the story of too many of our breakthroughs. The Soviets, via their den of spies at the United Nations, their Embassy and Consulate, get our secrets almost as fast as our military.

The Knickerbocker News

Albany, N.Y., September 16, 1980

The United States has been working on top-secret technology that, when perfected, would make our aircraft virtually invisible to Soviet detection equipment. Until a few weeks ago, the "Stealth" project was tip-top secret, one of the most closely guarded in Washington, a town that thrives on rumors, leaks and loosely kept secrets.

Someone from the Pentagon leaked generalities about the project to various news media, and made very sure the word would get out. After the original leak, Defense Secretary Harold Brown called a press conference and not only confirmed the Stealth project existed, but told the world more than anyone could possibly have expected to learn about such a hush-hush matter. White House staffers have since admitted the project was noised about in order to counter some of the criticism President Jimmy Carter is taking because of his military budget reductions.

We find it difficult to believe Mr. Carter's White House would spill its metaphorical guts and endanger national security in order to score a few political points, but that appears to be what happened. Just when the president needed a little boost in the popularity britches, just when Ronald Reagan's charges that our national defense posture is slumping began stinging hardest, a magical leak springs forth from a Pentagon that had been silent on Stealth for many years, through several presidential terms of office.

If, as the White House defended itself, the Russians have known about Stealth for years, why haven't the American people? Would the Russians have had to extract Stealth details bit by bit, spending time, money and spies if Secretary Brown hadn't passed it on free via national television?

There has been a lot of knee-jerk reaction recently against the press and the rest of the news media, which disclosed the Stealth information it had been fed. The cry has been loud and sharp, in some cases — "Jail 'em!" Punish the messenger for telling the tale, in other words.

This is the height of the ridiculous. Where do these leaks come from? In virtually all instances, from inside the government. And, most times leaks are put out by government itself to serve its own purposes — as trial balloons, for political gain, to stir up sentiment for or against an issue.

That is what happened in this situation, a leak of top secret Pentagon information to grab the president a few political brownie points with the electorate. Talking about slapping penalities on the media may make a few politicians look like avenging angels to their constituents, but it's hardly an intelligent solution to the problem.

How far will Mr. Carter go to get re-elected? We are afraid to find out, if the Stealth incident is any indication.

Des Moines Tribune

Des Moines, Iowa, October 16, 1980

Two months ago, Defense Secretary Harold Brown told a press conference about a new technology that he said will allow the United States to build aircraft "that cannot be successfully intercepted with existing air-defense systems." The technology, called "Stealth," will make future U.S. warplanes almost invisible to enemy radar, officials claimed.

Brown's press conference produced heavy and sustained flak. Republicans charged that the administration disclosed details about Stealth to make itself look good on military issues. It was alleged that the disclosures gave the Russians a 10-year warning of U.S. plans.

The whole truth about Stealth, however, appears to be as difficult to locate as the warplanes the technology is supposed to conceal.

A Washington Post survey of several non-government specialists in military technology produced a consensus that high Defense Department officials probably have exaggerated their claims for Stealth. The technology, they agree, is promising, but several physical laws seem to limit the concealment that it is possible to give.

It is difficult to evaluate the claims and allegations, political and military, because so much of the subject involves secret data. The secrecy can become ludicrous. Scientist Edward Teller claims there is a way to overcome the Stealth technology, but — citing security considerations — he hasn't said what that way is. Thus, a secret weapon apparently imperils a secret technology.

It would help if Stealth's defenders and critics would provide factual evidence. No doubt some of Stealth's secrecy is needed. But neither is there doubt that much of the Stealth secrecy — like secrecy generally — is unnecessary.

There is a tendency for both sides to overstate their case. The Stealth disclosures probably won't help the Russians as much as the Republicans think. And the reliability of technology — both military and civilian — is easy to overstate, too. Technology is entrancing, and secrecy has an allure of its own. But a proper understanding of Stealth requires that some of this top secrecy and high technology be replaced with some down-to-earth facts.

The Evening Gazette

Worcester, Mass., September 17, 1980

When Secretary of Defense Harold Brown spilled the beans on our "Stealth" bomber a week or so back, there was whatfor to pay. The Republicans jumped all over Brown for endangering the national security, Brown countered before a congressional committee that he hadn't said anything that would help the Soviets one bit, Henry Kissinger said that he and former President Gerald Ford had considered the Stealth bomber a matter of the highest priority secrecy and The Washington Post fretted that it had been used as a conduit for the leak.

Now U.S. Rep. Bob Carr (D-Mich.) has weighed in with a novel argument: Breaking the news about Stealth was far better than keeping it secret because "If Stealth were kept secret, it would have no effect on Soviet decision-making and would fail." It would fail, that is, because it would not deter the Soviets from military action.

"Stealth," says Carr, "is a fundamental military breakthrough, comparable to the invention of radar. The world doesn't need to know how it works, but the world does need to know we have it. It began to have a major beneficial effect on the psychological strategic balance the moment Brown put it into the headlines."

Well, maybe so. It's hard to measure the "psychological strategic balance" of world power. Some might think it might depend partly on our keeping the Soviets guessing about what we have up our sleeve.

Brown's announcement about Stealth probably did not astound the Kremlin quite as much as some claim. After all, Aerospace Daily, on July 23, 1976, had a long lead article about famed aircraft designer Kelly Johnson and the "stealth" aircraft he was designing for Lockheed.

"The goal is to reduce aircraft visibility through new technology," the article said . . . the Air Force and DARPA (Defense Advanced Research Projects Agency) have been searching for ways to reduce aircraft signatures through combinations of aerodynamic configurations, absorptive materials, paint schemes and electronic countermeasures." That should have given Moscow a few clues about what we were up to.

But we do find it interesting that Brown chose to unveil the existence of this new marvel right in the midst of a presidential election campaign in which Ronald Reagan was charging the Carter administration with being asleep at the defense switch.

The Stealth bomber may not change the world power balance, as Brown claimed, but it may help the Democratic power balance in the coming election.

FORT WORTH STAR-TELEGRAM

Fort Worth, Texas, August 27, 1980

The "stealth plane" may be hazardous to the enemy's military health.

But not if the enemy knows about it.

And that is why U. S. Sen. John Tower got hot under the collar about the Carter administration confirming the existence of technology to build the stealth plane — one that is invisible to radar.

Sen. Tower said the administration is playing fast and loose with American security. He said Jimmy Carter is using word about the airplane to make political hay. He said the president is using the airplane to enhance his image. He also said the president's men have been leaking information about the airplane on Capitol Hill to try to kill any chance for a bomber that could be deployed quickly.

The administration countered by saying it was all right to confirm existence of the technology capable of making warplanes virtually invisible to radar because word about the capability had already leaked.

It is too bad that word did leak out about the new technology. And we have no way of knowing whether the administration did indeed have the information leaked so it could shoot down any plan to build another bomber. But it does have a nasty smell to it.

But, be that as it may, there was no reason to confirm that the new technology exists. We should at least have tried to keep the enemy guessing. Why present the enemy with the information on a silver platter?

As Sen. Tower said, everyone privy to the details of this technology was clearly aware — or should have been — of the need to keep this promising technology secret for as long as possible so as not to alert the Soviet Union to the need to develop countermeasures.

To leak such information, he said, goes beyond the bounds of propriety, even in an election year.

But politics or no, there was no reason to confirm the technology. Surely the enemy knows too much about our military capability as it is.

Let's keep our military secrets secret.

Let us not, through our own actions, turn out to be our own worst enemy.

Sentinel Star

Orlando, Fla., August 27, 1980

IT IS difficult not to be suspicious of a recent Carter administration announcement that the United States has perfected technology rendering certain nuclear weapons delivery systems immune to Soviet defenses.

This is not to say that, if true, the announcement is not welcome. Defense Secretary Harold Brown, in an unprecedented statement last week, said the new technology called "stealth" would effectively nullify the Soviet investment of $100 billion in air defense systems.

He also said that possible application of the technology to other weapons systems like tanks and ships would greatly enhance their survivability in a conflict. He added that the Soviets had no known countermeasures or similar technology in development.

So why the suspicion?

It is, after all, the height of the political season and President Carter knows full well that one of the most prominent of his many political Achilles' heels is his defense record. He killed the manned bomber program, severely cut back shipbuilding, held back on cruise missile deployment and reversed himself on development and deployment of the enhanced radiation warhead. All of these decisions were unilateral — and futile — attempts to get the Soviet Union to decrease its defense spending by setting a pacific example.

Ronald Reagan is hammering on those decisions. And what better response from a man recognized as pre-eminent in political sensitivities than to announce that all the while his administration has been working on a stunning breakthrough that would revolutionize strategic concepts?.

Further cause for suspicion is the wording of Mr. Brown's response to questions about funding. For while he said the administration decided that now was the time to announce the existence of the technological triumph, he added that the administration had not decided and would not decide "until next year" whether to recommend "actual production" of a stealth bomber.

Defense advocates recognize too well the familiar Carter administration ploy of announcing with great fanfare newfound commitments to defense programs which are then never funded or very quietly shelved months later.

If stealth technology becomes applied reality because of Mr. Carter's political motivations, then it will be a case of reaching a beneficial goal for dubious reasons. But if all the fanfare amounts to so much eyewash that will be discarded after a successful election, then Mr. Carter is playing personal politics with questions of national survival.

WORCESTER TELEGRAM.

Worcester, Mass., August 26, 1980

It's not easy to keep up with defense developments, especially as selectively disclosed in the hot blasts of a presidential campaign.

Last week, Defense Secretary Harold Brown that: 1, the Soviet Union probably had the capacity to wipe out our land-based Minuteman missiles with a sneak strike by their own rockets and, 2, we have developed some way of protecting our aircraft from Soviet radar detection.

"This so-called 'stealth technology," Brown told reporters, "enables the United States to build manned and unmanned aircraft that cannot be successfully intercepted with existing air-defense systems. We have demonstrated to our satisfaction that the technology works."

Brown also said that the discovery "alters the military balance," which may well be true if the facts are as he reported.

Questions arise. For example, if we can build bombers that can't be detected, do we need the MX missile system that Brown has been so insistent on having? Also, how long is it likely to be before the Soviets learn the secret of the "stealth technology"?

With Ronald Reagan charging that the Carter administration has let our military defenses slide to the point where we are No. 2 to the Soviets, it is natural to expect counterassertions by the administration. Already, Brown has taken a more active political role than any previous secretary of defense.

But where does the truth lie? Have we really had a breakthrough that alters the military balance, or have our defenses gone slack?

The American people are going to hear a lot on this subject, not all of it enlightening, in the next two months.

The News and Courier

Charleston, S.C., September 4, 1980

President Carter seeks to amaze credulous voters by taking the wraps prematurely from something called "Stealth" and treating it as a "breakthrough" in defense weaponry — a good reason, the administration implies, for voting Carter in November. As a political tactic, this is sneakier than most. Who would believe that the president of the United States, commander-in-chief of the armed forces which will deploy "Stealth" — if it gets to that point — would be trotting out military secrets to be used as electioneering material! And it isn't a secret, mind you, to which the Carter administration holds any proprietary rights, as if it had developed what amounts to a high-class paint job for fighters and bombers at its own expense and initiative.

As far back as World War II, scientists and designers were following a line of investigation which the president has now told the Russians is about to yield results. German submarines were covered with a rubbery material intended to soften outlines and blur the image returned to Allied radar scopes. "Stealth" despite its intriguing name hasn't exactly sneaked up on us. It is quite possible, of course, that Americans with their superior technology have carried it to the point where it has real promise of being what Mr. Carter says it is, a scheme which will permit aircraft to get through the radar beams.

That's good, maybe, but don't let Mr. Carter steal credit he isn't entitled to. This is no "breakthrough." It isn't going to give American planes any permanent advantage. What the Americans can do in this line, the Russians can do, and will do it sooner, now that they know we do it.

To say that the Russians would have done it anyway doesn't excuse the sophistry of the Carter approach. Mr. Carter is playing on the gullibility of people who want to believe in some kind of quick fix. He is claiming credit for an achievement — if that's the right word — which belongs to other people in other administrations as much as to him and his administration.

Surely the Russians will rejoice in the news of "Stealth" and the progress it is making. Americans should shake their heads and ask: Who wants to follow a commander-in-chief who gives away military secrets in order to get votes?

Los Angeles Times

Los Angeles, Calif., August 28, 1980

The Administration's disclosure that an "invisible" aircraft has been developed looks crassly political; it tends to erase President Carter's vulnerability to Ronald Reagan's charge that the 1977 cancellation of the B-1 bomber project was a dangerous mistake.

But if the new technology is as good as Defense Secretary Harold Brown says it is, it does represent a potentially remarkable new contribution to U.S. national security.

References to an "invisible" bomber actually are misleading. The new technology has not yet been applied to a bomber, new or otherwise. When it is, the aircraft will be perfectly visible to the naked eye, but will be able to escape radar detection until it is too late for defending forces to shoot it down. Or so the Pentagon says.

The so-called Stealth bomber technology involves both an unorthodox shape, designed to reflect the fewest radar beams, and special coatings to absorb or diffuse radar signals.

Brown says flatly that bombers, cruise missiles or fighter aircraft utilizing the technology "cannot be successfully intercepted with existing Soviet air defense systems."

It should be noted, however, that despite the effusive claims made for the Stealth radar-foiling technology, which has been tested on experimental flights over Nevada, the Administration is not committing itself to build a new bomber incorporating it.

That decision presumably will be made by March 15, the deadline set by Congress for an Administration decision on whether to proceed with an updated B-1, a stretched version of the smaller FB-111 or an entirely new manned bomber.

Some skeptics claim that the Soviets will be able to cope with Stealth bombers or cruise missiles by merely stepping up the power of their radar systems. Defense officials insist that it won't be that easy, that the Russians will be forced to spend many billions of dollars beefing up an air-defense system that is already said to represent a $100 billion investment.

In any event, it would take at least until the late 1980s to build a bomber fleet incorporating the Stealth technology. It obviously becomes relevant to ask whether the Russians can upgrade their radar systems faster than the United States can put a new Stealth bomber into service.

Even if the answer proves to be yes or maybe, the Stealth technology is a valuable development, portions of which can apparently be applied to existing bomber, fighter or cruise-missile designs rather quickly.

This can be extremely important not only in the context of making the U.S. strategic deterrent more credible but also in such areas as the Persian Gulf, where American fighter-bombers may someday face the task of penetrating Soviet-built radar systems in order to defend U.S. and allied interests.

Buffalo Evening News

Buffalo, N.Y., September 13, 1980

One wonders when the election campaign is going to get down to dealing with something important. Last week, the Democrats and Republicans got into a flap over the new "invisible" plane that is being developed, and both sides seemed to be playing politics with the issue.

In late August, the Carter administration announced that the Pentagon is developing a plane, named "Stealth," than can evade detection by enemy radar. Defense Secretary Harold Brown called the plane "a major technological advance of great military significance."

Ronald Reagan promptly charged that the administration "has breached one of this nation's most closely held military secrets in a transparent effort to divert attention from the administration's dismal defense record." He called the disclosure "a grievous blow" to the U.S. that had given Russia a 10-year head start in developing countermeasures. "The KGB is no doubt gleefully celebrating," he said.

The charges do not seem to hold much water. The plane was first mentioned in a trade journal in 1975, and since then there has been regular mention of its development. What was not known to the public (and apparently still is not) were the details of the top-secret project. In announcing the project, Mr. Brown spoke of it only in general terms.

Mr. Reagan did have a point, however, in accusing the administration of making the announcement for political purposes at a time when its defense policies are under heavy attack. Mr. Brown said lamely that attempts to keep the plane's existence secret would have been likely to stir competitive reporting and create more dangerous news leaks. He said he was creating a "firebreak" by acknowledging all that had been disclosed so far and then clamping down on any new leaks.

Rep. Samuel Stratton, D-N.Y., chairman of an investigating subcommittee, rightly scoffed at this explanation, declaring that if the first line of defense against leaks didn't work, there was little reason to have confidence in the second.

We indeed hope that there are more precautions than such "firebreaks" to maintain the secrecy of this important project. Politics aside, a plane that can be made invisible to radar would obviously have great military value. The Soviet Union no doubt is already working on ways to improve its radar system to make the Stealth plane less elusive. Nevertheless, this breakthrough at least raises the possibility of creating a new generation of long-range bombers as part of the nation's strategic nuclear force.

Stealth Debate Continues; Pros, Cons of 3 Bombers Weighed

President Carter's final budget, submitted in January 1981, included funds for researching the "Stealth" aircraft project. As the year wore on, however, the debate over the new technology intensified. Much of the debate centered on the condition of the existing force of B-52 bombers: The Reagan Administration felt a new bomber would be needed by 1987, while the Carter Administration had said it would not be necessary until the early 1990's. If the aging B-52's remained in working condition until the delivery of the new Stealth bombers, then an equally controversial plane, the B-1 bomber, could be dropped from the drawing board—and had, in fact, been eliminated in 1977 by Carter. But if the B-52s did not last, or delivery of the Stealth planes was delayed, the argument went, then the U.S. would be left for some years without any effective long-range bombers unless the B-1s were built. Critics of the B-1 program said that the expensive bomber would soon prove obsolete, with the Soviets able by the end of the decade to track the plane and shoot it down. Critics of the Stealth program called the proposed bomber a "paper plane" that couldn't be realized until at least the mid-1990's. President Reagan, in his strategic weapons program announced in October, opted for a joint program of both B-1 building and Stealth development, but at a high cost; by Air Force estimates made in June, the cost for 100 B-1s would be $18 billion, and that for 100 Stealth bombers would be $22 billion.

Detroit Free Press

Detroit, Mich., February 24, 1981

BY THE 1990s, the United States can have a fleet of Stealth bombers, designed without flat surfaces so they will be "invisible" to present-day and presumably future Soviet radar. No decision is at hand for Stealth production. But the bomber seems likely to be built if the new technology is as good as advertised and there is no big breakthrough on strategic arms limitation.

A major debate is beginning on what to do between now and the advent of Stealth bombers. The outcome will determine whether the country spends a moderate amount of money or an enormous amount, even as it is beginning to pay heavily for the Stealth fleet.

The options are to rely during the 1980s upon our existing fleet of B52s, enhanced with long-range cruise missiles; to modify the existing FB111, a smaller bomber now in service; or to build a new version of the B1, canceled by former President Carter four years ago before it reached production stage.

The Reagan administration apparently has determined to ask for $2.5 billion in the next budget for either the B1 or the modified FB111, with a temporary delay on a decision about which one. The country would be committing itself to a huge spending program in either case. The Pentagon estimates the bill for a fleet of 150 modified FB111s at $7 billion and for a fleet of 100 B1s at $18 billion. Given past experience with such figures, we probably can assume costs of several times that much.

President Reagan has dramatized the meaning of a trillion dollars by saying it means a stack of thousand-dollar bills 47 miles high. We suspect the bill for an initial fleet of B1s would be something like a stack of thousand-dollar bills four miles high. No one knows yet what the Stealth fleet would cost, but probably it would be much more than that.

Why is there a need for either the B1 or the modified FB111? Advocates of both say there will be a time during the mid-1980s and afterward when the country will be more vulnerable to Soviet attack unless it

has one of these new weapons ready to strike. But Air Force planners acknowledge that the modified FB111 could be ready only in very small numbers by 1985 and the B1 only in small numbers by 1986. So the administration is talking about huge expenditures for a weapon that would be a primary part of U.S. defenses for only several years, until Stealth bombers are in service.

We do not believe the need for either the B1 or the FB111 has been demonstrated, nor do we like the political aspects of the decision-making process that is unfolding. Advocates of these new bombers use the same logic that is called upon by advocates of the MX missile system: that U.S. land-based missiles are more vulnerable to Soviet attack now than ever before. But that argument overlooks the enormous capacity of U.S. sea-based and airborne missiles, which are capable of destroying much of the Soviet Union and are a powerful deterrent to any attack on land-based missiles.

The Air Force's high command wants the B1. Two officers who are leading experts on the choice, however, prefer the less expensive FB111: Gen. Richard Ellis, commander of the Strategic Air Command, and Gen. Alton Slay, who has just retired as commander of the unit responsible for developing new aircraft.

Gen. Slay nevertheless is ready to assent to B1 production, he says, because he believes the political climate in Congress is more favorable to it. Is that the right basis for such a decision, rather than demonstrated military need? We do not think so.

At a time when the administration is asking for retrenchment in almost every kind of non-military spending, it seems to want to impress the Soviets by throwing big sums into weapons systems that may or may not be needed. Congress should take a more tough-minded position than that. American strength lies not just in military power but also in the health of the economy. Megabucks spending for unnecessary weapons is not a good way to strengthen basic industry, control inflation and otherwise make the economy strong.

THE RICHMOND NEWS LEADER
*Richmond, Va.,
February 26, 1981*

President Reagan has begun re-forging the American arsenal. He expects to ask Congress next year for about $2.5 billion to begin building a fleet of long-range manned bombers that could hit the Soviet Union or any other enemy — hard. About these bombers, much remains to be decided. Yet the Reagan administration shows determination to succeed with this project, and Congress seems willing as well. Heartening news.

Plans call for two new kinds of bombers to be built, in a two-phase program. After a study, the U.S. is scheduled this summer to decide either on a modified version of the B-1 killed in 1977 by President Carter, or on an enlarged FB-111. These planes would replace the B-52s now in use — many of which are older than the men who fly them. They are to be operational in the mid-years of this decade. Air Force officials consider the B-1 the better plane; the FB-111 would be cheaper and more quickly developed. A more advanced bomber, incorporating much of the Stealth technology that caused such a fuss when it was revealed during the 1980 campaign, should be flying in the 1990s.

After grounding the B-1, the Carter administration decided to place the nation's defensive bets on the land-based MX missile system, an overly complicated enterprise that would move nuclear missiles between silos on a track in the Utah and Nevada desert — presumably confusing the Soviets. Yet: The MX also will take the better part of a decade to complete; it will be hugely expensive, subject to sabotage, do much environmental damage, and cause political problems — while the Soviets could continue targeting on the site. Missiles placed in submarines — large and small — and manned bombers seem a more sure way of meeting defense obligations.

A new fleet of manned bombers. It will be costly, with the final figure running into uncalculated billions. Yet it will be money well spent, because defending the nation remains any administration's prime priority — a priority sadly neglected during the past four years of Jimmy Carter's Democratic, unilaterally-pacifistic stewardship. President Reagan was elected, in part, to re-forge the nation's arsenal; President Reagan's resurrection of the moribund manned bomber development program shows his determination to redeem his campaign vows. Good.

11/12/81, THE PHILADELPHIA INQUIRER
THE WASHINGTON POST WRITERS GROUP
AUTH

Coming Soon

'JUST WHAT YOU'VE ALWAYS WANTED...'

THE B-1 BOMBER

A MERE $39 MILLION (EACH)

· US AIR FORCE

LIQUOR

'WE CAN SCRIMP A LITTLE MORE AT HOME, AND CHARGE IT!'

THE CHRISTIAN SCIENCE MONITOR

Boston, Mass., March 11, 1981

Hour after hour, day after day, the sturdy B-52 bombers of the US Strategic Air Command (SAC) thunder down their far-flung runways and roar into the skies — as they have done now for over two decades. The bombers form the backbone of the air wing of the US strategic deterrent, along with land-based ICBMs and sea-launched missiles. Now, the new Reagan administration argues that the warhorse B-52s are increasingly vulnerable to Soviet air defenses and that the US must immediately begin development of a new force of advanced (nuclear-bomb-carrying) long-range bombers that will be capable of penetrating Soviet air defenses right into the 21st century.

For the American public, the question of whether or not to develop a new manned bomber will involve costly — and crucial — military and political tradeoffs. The administration's initial request for $2.5 billion in the fiscal year 1982 budget would be only the tip of the budget wing in an enormous weapons program that could eventually reach well in excess of $18 billion by the mid-1980s. These are monies that will be lost to budget-starved civilian programs, as well as to such needed Pentagon initiatives as upgrading manpower and recruitment benefits.

Nor must it be forgotten that the military traditionally wants all that it can get in the way of weaponry, whether the need be actual or illusive, and no matter how difficult it is to absorb the new hardware. The Spinney Report, for example, now being widely discussed in military circles (put out by a civilian analyst for the Defense Department) comes to the startling conclusion that the more the US spends on overly sophisticated weapons systems (aircraft in particular), the less able it is to wage effective warfare.

The reason for this is that such systems are subject to numerous technical "glitches" and thus are often out of service, tend to be more dependent on replacement parts, and require larger numbers of skilled operational manpower than can usually be recruited into a volunteer military establishment.

On the other hand, in the eyes of senior Pentagon officials, not to build a new bomber could endanger the nation's security in the next decade or so.

What alternatives do beleaguered American taxpayers face, as they attempt to wade their way through the crosscurrents of claims and counterclaims that will mark an intense congressional haggling over the bomber question? There are essentially five:

● Develop the B-1 bomber cancelled by President Carter in 1977 but kept alive over the years by federal research funding. Research and development costs of the B-1, which has a supersonic "dash" capability, have already come to almost $6 billion. Four prototypes of the B-1 have been built.

● Develop a less-costly "cut-down" subsonic derivative of the B-1 incorporating the technology of that original prototype.

● Adapt the existing medium-range FB-111 to fill a penetration bomber role.

● Develop the top-secret Stealth aircraft technology (designed to escape radar and other detection methods) as quickly as possible, with the hope of having Stealth bombers in operation by the late 1980s or early 1990s. The cost of a full-scale program is not known, given the secrecy surrounding the technology. Nor is it certain that such aircraft could be operational by 1990, or sooner.

● Continue the Carter administration approach of modifying existing B-52 bombers to serve as a "standoff force" that would fly astride the borders of the Soviet Union (or other potential adversaries) equipped with air-launched cruise missiles (ALCMs). In other words, while many B-52s would still be assigned a "penetration-bomber" role, the primary emphasis would be on using the B-52s as "carriers" of cruise missiles, which would then themselves adopt the "penetration" role.

While top Pentagon officials do not like to overly trumpet the fact — given the growing political support for a new bomber — they are in fact highly impressed with the continuing performance of the B-52 (which has been substantially modernized in recent years with a new wing, new avionics, and so on), and concede that it could serve adequately through the remainder of this century.

Although the above are the theoretical options facing US taxpayers and Congress, it must not be overlooked that in great part the alternatives are already being narrowed by political and economic considerations. While the administration has indicated it will not reach a decision on which bomber to go with until later this year, probably in June, the Pentagon has already suggested that it favors a B-1 subsonic variant or an adaptation of the FB-111. The B-1, for its part, is now incorporating an array of advanced technologies.

Stretching the FB-111, a course that has been favored by top officers of SAC, would easily be the least costly of these two alternatives in immediate dollar terms. The plane, as noted, already exists and could serve as the backup to the B-52 until the Stealth bomber comes into production in the 1990s. Estimates for refurbishing the aircraft run from $6 billion to $7 billion, compared to more than double that for the cheapest B-1 variant. The ultimate cost, including operating and tanker expenses, would likely be much more however, bringing total outlays close to the dollar projections for the B-1.

Perhaps the most compelling argument against the FB-111 is that given the huge outlays involved it might be economically sounder to commit funds directly either for the B-1 or the Stealth. The FB-111, after all, is an "older" technology, a "child of the 1960s." The plane would also carry a smaller nuclear "payload" than the B-1.

One factor that lawmakers will want to weigh carefully is whether the US has the "time" to await development of the more technologically advanced Stealth bomber. The answer seems in part to depend on the stability of the other two legs of the US nuclear triad in the mid '80s. If a decision on the MX mobile missile is delayed, would the ICBM leg of the nuclear triad be "endangered"? Also, the Trident submarine program has been experiencing major problems, ranging from delays to structural difficulties.

If the ICBM or the submarine arms of the triad are in any way vulnerable or weakened, that would seem to provide justification for the US moving ahead as quickly as possible on either developing the FB-111 option, or going ahead with the B-1. At least one arm of the triad would remain unquestionably secure through this decade.

A potent bomber force would be a reasonable alternative to a vastly more costly (and highly questionable) land-based MX system. Moreover, it must be stressed that the nuclear-equipped bomber, unlike the land or sea-launched missile, provides maximum tactical flexibility. Besides carrying a wide assortment of weapons, the aircraft can be recalled from its target or redirected to a new target as a military situation develops.

The task for the United States, given budget restraints, will lie in ensuring that its important manned bomber force has the precise mix of aircraft.

The Detroit News
Detroit, Mich., July 30, 1981

The "stealth" bomber is a secret project. The scant information available on it was disclosed by President Carter and his defense secretary, Harold Brown, during last fall's presidential campaign.

The two were under steady attack for making a hash out of national defense. Late in the campaign, Mr. Carter and Mr. Brown tried to justify their earlier cancellation of the B-1 bomber with the announcement that a new and remarkable stealth bomber was in the wings and would make the B-1 obsolete.

Mr. Carter and Mr. Brown claimed a "technological breakthrough." But if Verne Orr, the present Air Force secretary, is right, the Carter-Brown announcement was premature, to say the least.

Mr. Orr says he has examined the state of stealth research and it is "just a paper airplane." There are drawings, he said, and a couple of contractors are trying to sell the project by making highly questionable, if not exaggerated, claims.

The stealth technology is so new, and so tricky, that such an airplane is 10 or 12 years away from squadron service, Mr. Orr says. Development costs for stealth will be "tremendous," and, Mr. Orr adds, "I don't think there's any mood to pull all the stops."

The shape and surface materials of the proposed bomber would absorb radar rays, to make its detection difficult, if not impossible. But, some aeronautical engineers say, planes shaped to fool radar have an alarming tendency to crash because they are aerodynamically unsound.

This fall, Defense Secretary Caspar Weinberger has to make up his mind about the manned bomber — whether to order a modified B-1, wait for the development of stealth, or adopt a smaller and less flexible FB-111. No matter what happens, stealth will eventually be developed because it offers the promise of a world technological lead.

But aging B-52 strategic bombers, many older than the pilots that fly them, must be replaced soon. The B-1 is a remarkable machine and it is ready. The FB-111 is less acceptable because it is small and less flexible.

The U.S. strategic position was seriously weakened by the Carter administration. Mr. Reagan has to move rapidly to repair the damage, and the B-1 offers promise for doing just that.

You can't plan a defense strategy around a "paper airplane."

The Oregonian
Portland, Ore., March 22, 1981

The B-1 bomber is creeping up on the U.S. budget. Rockwell International Corp. is building a $20 million plant at El Segundo, Calif., feeling confident the project canceled by President Carter in 1977 will be back in the air by the end of summer.

The manned bomber, whether a B-1, a fanciful "Stealth" model or a proposed stretched out F-111, is vulnerable to new technology that will assure its detection virtually when it is launched. It will be blasted in a flurry of hundreds of guided, smart missiles hurled at it along an entire flight path tracked by satellites.

Aircraft like the B-1, now called the B-1 variant, will cost at least $132 million each in 1981 dollars and a lot more by the time the first squadron of 15 becomes operational by the end of this decade. If the Stealth bomber is built, it would not become operational by the early 1990s. In either case, detection, tracking and interdiction technology will be further advanced, while there is real doubt among military critics that systems to protect these machines can keep pace, considering how vulnerable the bombers would be if flown in combat today. Remember, bombers this expensive are expected to see service for upwards of 40 years, making it vital that we pick a technology capable of growth and not tied to outmoded concepts.

Aside from the lobbying pressures from industries and labor unions that would profit from a big bomber program, there is the fact that the Air Force traditionally has been proud it can put a man over the target, no matter what the risks or the costs. But in hanging on to this nostalgic notion, the Air Force is putting its heart where its head ought to be and the Pentagon is putting our money on the wrong weapons.

The Courier-Journal
Louisville, Ky., February 25, 1981

AMERICANS who voted for Ronald Reagan because he promised to restore U.S. military strength by building a new manned bomber (among other things) may get more than they bargained for. It now seems the Air Force will get not one but two bombers.

The Reagan defense team is committed, as was the Carter administration, to developing a totally new bomber based on "stealth" technology that can make a plane almost invisible to radar. But a stealth bomber wouldn't be available until 1990. Meanwhile, the Air Force is worried that its 300-plus B-52s, the newest of which is 20 years old, will become increasingly vulnerable to mechanical breakdown and to improvements in Soviet air defenses.

So Defense Secretary Weinberger plans to seek congressional approval for an interim bomber that would replace a portion of the aging B-52 fleet and that would be available more quickly than the stealth aircraft. Top candidates are the B-1 bomber that Jimmy Carter cancelled in 1977 and the FB-111, a tactical fighter-bomber already in service.

Either approach would be costly. Reviving the B-1 project and building 100 bombers would cost $12 to $18 billion, depending on whether the Air Force bought the original, already tested version of the B-1 or an improved version incorporating some stealth technology.

Under the competing plan, 150 existing FB-111s would be lengthened to accommodate more fuel, more powerful engines and new electronic equipment to foil enemy radar. The "stretched" FB-111s would cost about $7 billion.

Each approach has its champions within the Air Force. B-1 advocates say their plane would be much more capable and would last longer than the FB-111. Those who favor the stretched FB-111 do so not out of love for the plane but because it would be cheaper and could be brought into service sooner. They worry that if the Pentagon spends the extra billions for the B-1, Congress may be reluctant to approve money for other Air Force projects, such as the stealth bomber and the mobile MX missile.

There is, of course, another alternative, but you won't hear it mentioned by the Air Force. Why not build *neither* plane? The Pentagon could use some of the money it would save to press development of the stealth bomber and to accelerate deployment of air-launched cruise missiles. The great advantage of cruise missiles, of course, is that they can be launched more than a thousand miles from their target. So bombers that carry them don't have to penetrate those formidable Soviet air defenses.

Even aging B-52s are adequate for the job. In fact the Air Force plans to use some of them as cruise missile carriers even if it gets the B-1 or the FB-111.

The argument for an interim bomber assumes that cruise missiles, with their relatively small nuclear warheads, aren't enough. The Air Force insists that planes capable of penetrating Soviet air defenses and dropping big multi-megaton bombs also are needed.

But if the day ever comes that U.S. bombers are sent into the Soviet Union, their path almost surely will have been cleared by cruise missiles and ballistic missile warheads aimed at Soviet air bases and radar installations. Even big, lumbering B-52s should have little trouble reaching their targets under those conditions — assuming they don't break down on the way from old age.

Age *is* a problem. The B-52 force won't last forever. But a new stealth bomber is a more promising replacement than either the B-1 or the FB-111. Admittedly, the stealth bomber wouldn't be coming off the assembly line until 1990. But the improved B-1 that some Air Force generals want wouldn't go into production until 1985, and even the first stretched FB-111s wouldn't be available until early 1984.

That means the interim bomber would cost the nation $7 to $18 billion so that some B-52s could be retired five or six years earlier than if the Air Force waited for the stealth plane. That doesn't look like much of a bargain.

Nevertheless, Congress, in a defense authorization bill last year, went on record as favoring development of a new manned bomber and demanding that the Pentagon come up with a bomber plan by March 15 of this year. So sentiment on Capitol Hill for an interim bomber is strong. It remains to be seen whether that sentiment is strong enough to overcome evidence that strongly suggests the Air Force should make do with its B-52s until a stealth bomber is available.

Pittsburgh Post-Gazette

Pittsburgh, Pa., November 5, 1981

Everyone agrees that the supersonic B-1 bomber has been designed to strike targets inside the Soviet Union. So it must be particularly unsettling to Air Force top brass that the Pentagon's own recent booklet entitled "Soviet Military Power" casts considerable doubt on the B-1's ability — or that of any other aircraft for that matter — to penetrate Soviet airspace.

"The diverse capabilities of Soviet air defense systems will be enhanced by improved command and control procedures to avoid destroying friendly aircraft while rendering the airspace over ground forces virtually impenetrable to enemy aircraft," the Pentagon study notes.

Soviet air defenses deploy more than 5,000 early-warning radar and an interceptor force of nearly 2,500 aircraft. As the orthodox U.S. view of Soviet air defense recognizes, moreover, the electronic mesh raised to protect Soviet airspace will be tightened with further research and improvements in the Soviet's own system of AWACS.

That discrepancy between Pentagon estimates of the capability of a preferred weapon and the apparent invulnerability of its target has troubled critics of the B-1 for some time. The proposal for sending an incredibly expensive weapon and its crew on a suicidal and pointless mission seems like misguided strategy. Anyone failing to see the contradictions in the B-1 plan can at least take the word of the Central Intelligence Agency. While Mr. Weinberger pleaded with the Senate last week for B-1 funding, Sen. Ted Stevens of Alaska revealed that CIA defense specialists in a secret briefing had backed the dependable B-52 bomber force as being just as capable as the B-1 of handling foreseeable missions through this decade.

Just as the Pentagon's assessment of Soviet military strength failed to place that threat in the context of NATO's own strategic capabilities, the administration's request for revival of the B-1 fails to evaluate the military context in which the weapon would be used. If an austerity-minded Congress undertakes such scrutiny on its own, it will make sure that the B-1 doesn't get off the ground.

Chicago Tribune

Chicago, Ill., August 2, 1981

No doubt about it, the B-1 is a terrific airplane. It literally flies itself. It is equipped with a computer that pilots the $200 million marvel 200 feet above ground at nearly the speed of sound without slamming into cliffs or apartment buildings. The pilot is but a passenger, a somewhat redundant monitor who watches the lights and dials and screens and confirms that the computer is doing his job for him. Terrific.

It is so terrific that it is almost as good a weapon as a cruise missile, except that it costs about 100 times as much as a cruise missile. Which is the main reason we don't need the B-1. We didn't really need it when the splendid engineers at Rockwell dreamed it up, and we need it even less now when we must save every spare dollar to build up a credible defense force.

The mission of the B-1 has been changed so many times that it is more goulash than airplane. It started out as one thing — a supersonic manned penetrating strategic bomber — and wound up as something quite different. As presently conceived, it is intended primarily to carry cruise missiles to the fringes of the Soviet Union and release them for their flights to target. It no longer really needs its treetop flight capability or its supersonic speed. It does not really need all the computer capability, the swing wings, or the powerful engines. It doesn't really need its prodigious 6,000-mile range.

Worse, it is already becoming obsolete even though only a handful of prototypes have been built and flown so far. Advances in Soviet radar and anti-aircraft defense capabilities are rendering it useless as a penetrating bomber, and cruise missile technology makes it pointless to have manned strategic bombers at all.

Nevertheless, the Reagan administration is seriously considering revival of this steel-and-titanium dodo bird in a production program that would put around 100 of them in the air at a cost of at least $20 billion by the end of the decade. A series of alternative proposals now on the desk of Defense Secretary Caspar Weinberger suggest three possible ways to go on finding a successor to the aging fleet of B-52s that now constitute the strategic bomber fleet.

The first is the B-1, which was shelved by President Carter in 1977. The aircraft would be reconfigured primarily as a cruise missile carrier for strategic purposes, and secondarily as a long-range bomber for conventional missions.

The second is a crash program to develop and deploy that intriguing mystery plane, the "Stealth" bomber, which would incorporate advances in construction to make it extremely difficult to detect on enemy radar.

The third is both: continued development and production of the B-1 and concurrent development of Stealth technology on a non-crash basis.

The chief attraction of the first alternative, going ahead with the B-1, is certainty. Even though the B-1 is not the airplane that the United States needs to replace the B-52, there is at least the knowledge that it works and can be produced according to a reasonably predictable schedule. The Stealth bomber, on the other hand, depends on technology that so far is pretty much confined to paper and to theory. Even with a costly crash program it could turn out to be less impressive than the theories promised, or it could turn out that the Soviets could overcome its "invisibility" by relatively easy advances in radar technology.

The third alternative — doing both — would offer the advantages of both programs and would avoid the danger of putting all the country's bomber eggs in one basket. Doing both would also cost about twice as much.

But there is another alternative, a fourth way to retain the bomber leg of the strategic triad without throwing away billions of dollars on an aircraft that will soon be obsolete.

That fourth approach is to convert part of the B-52 fleet to serve out their final years of usefulness as cruise missile carriers (which is already planned anyway) and to design a system for cruise deployment on a more modest aircraft as a supplement to or replacement for the B-52s. Meanwhile, the Stealth bomber can be developed as the eventual replacement for the B-52.

That solution would retain the bomber leg of the strategic triad, which in effect would become the cruise missile because manned penetrating bombers of the conventional B-1 design are obsolete. At the same time, it would carry forward development of a genuinely new generation of bomber, the Stealth. If the Stealth technology proves inadequate, or if Soviet defensive measures outstrip its capability, at least the enormous costs of production can be avoided.

It would be nice if we could have it all: the self-flying B-1 superbomber, the workhorse cruise missiles, and the no-see-um Stealth. But we can't afford it all, so something has to go. That something should be the B-1, which no doubt is the loveliest flying machine that ever quickened a Pentagon pulse — but which couldn't even deliver a first-class letter to the Kremlin.

Lincoln Journal

Lincoln, Neb., October 6, 1981

The B-1 bomber, says Missouri's senior senator, Thomas F. Eagleton, in phrasing that would engage and enliven Harry Truman's soul, "is a turkey."

Agreed.

Not that the sleek, four-engine swept-wing subsonic bomber isn't a marvel of the most advanced technology. It truly is. After all, taxpayers should have something to show for a B-1 program research and development cost in excess of $2 billion.

But the technical qualities and characteristics of the plane which Jimmy Carter tried to ground permanently in 1977 are not the issue.

The root question is whether the United States, in defending against the possibility of deadly war with the Soviet Union, absolutely must have an intercontinental manned bomber capable of penetrating that enemy's borders.

If one reflects on that specific proposition and all its ramifications, the answer favorably weighs in for such an aircraft under only one condition; that is, in mortal combat between the United States and the Soviet Union, neither side will resort to use of atomic and nuclear weapons.

We both will pledge to kill each other exclusively under World War II engagement rules, or as they existed up to a cloudless day over the Japanese city of Hiroshima. So-called conventional war, that is.

Under such a condition, of course, it is then madness and mind-boggling profligacy to think as well about yet another generation of still more sophisticated and potent nuclear weapons, whether land (MX) or sea-based (Trident II).

Nuclear-style war with the Soviets, or the permanent threat of catastrophic nuclear destruction, is, however, at the heart of our global military strategy. We can have a conventional war with Libya, or Mexico, or South Africa, and use medium-range attack bombers. But not the Soviet Union.

Therefore, what need have we for an intercontinental B-1, and one which even the White House concedes will have border penetrating advantages for only a relatively brief time period? What is required here, again trying to defend against a war with the Soviets, are more platforms for airborne cruise missiles.

Properly building on the Carter administration's equipment initiative, the Reagan administration's strategic renewal program calls for deloyment of more than 3,000 airborne cruise missiles. The first squadron of cruise-missile equipped airplanes — B-52Gs — is to be operational next year.

The administration's position, as quoted in the *New York Times,* is that "if we did not build the B-1 now, we would have to start development of another aircraft ... to replace the B-52s as cruise missile carriers."

Precisely.

Get at it then.

The hardware for such airborne platforms ought to come a good deal cheaper, too, than the $15 to $20 billion cost estimated for construction of 100 B-1s.

The News and Courier
Charleston, S. C., November 14, 1981

The Defense Department appropriations bill for this fiscal year is still in the formative stages in Congressional committees and promises to be one of the biggest bones of contention to face the Reagan administration. Already pegged in the $200 billion range by both the House and Senate subcommittees, the bill will be energetically attacked by liberals when it reaches the floor. They see huge outlays for weapons systems diverting funding from pet social programs. The administration would do well to identify, isolate and reexamine those specific defense programs that will draw the most flak.

One sure candidate for reappraisal is the B-1 bomber, a weapons system whose cost estimates vary so widely and escalate so rapidly it has already been labeled "the flying Edsel." Earlier this year, the prime contractor, Rockwell International, said the B-1 costs would run $11.9 billion. By July, the Air Force upped the figure to $19.7 billion. The following three months witnessed further upward reappraisals until late last month Defense Secretary Caspar Weinberger indicated a project cost of $27.9 billion. Last week, the Congressional Budget Office predicted the final price tag will run close to $40 billion. In addition to the spiraling cost, there are serious reservations expressed by Republicans, conservatives and strong defense advocates as to the need for the system in the first place.

The B-1 project is already more than 10 years old. It has been advertised by its proponents as the long-awaited and much needed replacement for the aging B-52s, currently America's only manned strategic delivery system. As the project gathered and lost advocates over the years, never receiving full approval, research in the field of manned bombers continued. Now, Air Force designers have roughed out an even better bomber, one that would be impervious to enemy radar — the Stealth. Estimates are that Stealth will be operational by the mid-1990s.

While not wishing to start a debate about the need, in the first place, for manned bombers in the age of missiles, an excellent case can be made to cancel permanently the B-1 program and concentrate the energy and funding on speeding up the Stealth project. Such a move by the administration could be the *quid* for a *quo* that is higher on Defense's priority list.

The Dallas Morning News
Dallas, Texas, November 4, 1981

LAUNCHED from a White House rostrum just a month ago, the B1 bomber already is encountering heavy flak as it tries to penetrate the fog of Congress.

The President proposes building 100 B1s to replace aging B52s, thus undoing Jimmy Carter's 1977 decision to kill the B1 program aborning. The B1s would come into service in 1987. Then, in the early 1990s, along would come the "stealth" bomber, the so-called "invisible" aircraft. Thus the third leg of the strategic triad — ground-, air- and sea-launched missiles — would be rendered as sturdy as the others, if not in fact sturdier.

But money is starting to overshadow the B1 debate, as it overshadows nearly everything in Washington these days. Costs for the B1 program are rising — from $19.7 billion last spring to $20.5 billion, owing to plans for improved equipment. Defense Secretary Weinberger himself acknowledges that inflation will drive costs still higher.

Senators on both sides of the aisle accordingly have declared or hinted that the nation cannot afford both the B1 and the "stealth" bomber. Senate Republican whip Ted Stevens quotes approvingly a CIA study showing that B52s, fitted with cruise missiles, could effectively do the B1's work. A major struggle could be in the making. And what a dreary prospect that is.

The B1 bomber program should have been cranked up four years ago. Here we are with a second chance to strengthen, in the near as opposed to the distant future, our capability to deter nuclear war. And some lawmakers waffle.

Well, it won't do. The "stealth" concept is a splendid one, and clearly we must embrace it. But what happens while we wait for "stealth" planes to come on line in the early '90s? The B52, excellent plane as it is, dates back to 1962. The B1 is designed to fly lower; its contours present less of a target for Soviet missiles; it can get off the ground more quickly in case of Soviet attack.

The Air Force protests that the CIA report cited by Sen. Allen is outdated — that the B1, as presently designed, is even less visible to radar than previously.

The B1 is expensive? Yes, to be sure; but here is an arresting statistic: In 1976 we could have built 244 B1s for $20 billion, which as we say is the understated cost of 100 today. The longer we put off needed programs, the more expensive they get.

Alas, putting off such programs has become a habit with Americans in the past 15 years. As the Pentagon's share of the budget has shrunk steadily, so has this country's ability to warn off or repel its enemies. However formidable-seeming, $20 billion is one-thirty-fifth of a $700 billion budget. It is little enough, one would think, to help get America's defenses up to snuff after a decade of neglect and decline.

Why not build the B1 and "stealth" *both*, when the choice is your money or your life?

Houston Chronicle
Houston, Texas, November 12, 1981

Second thoughts about the defense budget are now being heard in Congress.

The critics of a strong national defense were stilled by the results of the presidential and congressional elections a year ago. The voters left no doubt that they did not want a second-place military. The higher military budget submitted by President Reagan met little opposition. But now, with cuts in welfare and social programs going into effect, those opposed to more defense spending are finding their voices again.

The critics say that there are costly overruns in major defense items. They say that new weapon systems are too expensive. They claim that today's recruits can't operate the modern weapons. They say the Pentagon is neglecting maintenance to build costly weapons. Once again, the cry of "butter, not guns" is being heard.

The B-1 bomber is a case in point. The nation has depended upon aging B-52s so long the planes are older than some of the pilots. President Carter in 1977 canceled the B-1, weakening that leg of our strategic triad of bombers, ships and missiles.

President Reagan decided the B-1 is necessary to fill the defense gap until a more advanced "Stealth" bomber even less detectable by radar can be developed. There was little reaction from anti-military groups at first, but now they are speaking out against the B-1. A Democratic senator is protesting the cost, which has, of course, risen since a Democratic president mistakenly canceled the program. Others say the B-1 is a "bomber without a mission" and that it would be best to wait until a more advanced plane is ready in the 1990s. If this group holds true to form, they probably will then oppose the "Stealth" plane also as unnecessary and too costly.

While Congress fiddles around, the Soviet Union is turning out a steady stream of Backfire bombers and deploying one new missile after another. The longer this country delays in rebuilding its defenses, the greater the cost will be and the greater will be the threat to peace.

Stealth Gains Ground as Criticism of B-1, B-52 Grows

As estimates of the cost of the B-1 bomber rose in 1982 and 1983, the debate over the role it would play as part of the U.S. air-based nuclear defense was rekindled. Reports that the Stealth bomber would be operable by 1990 or 1991 caused opponents of the B-1 to declare that the four- or five-year period of its usefulness, between the demise of the B-52s and the advent of the Stealth bombers, did not justify its expense. (An independent Pentagon study released in June, 1982 estimated that the cost of 100 B-1 bombers would come to $26.7 billion.) In any case, they said, the B-1 was too large a plane and too easily detectable by radar to be strategically useful beyond the end of the decade. Proponents of the B-1 program countered that the B-52s were already beginning to reach the end of their usefulness, pointing to several accidents involving the veteran planes in late 1982 and early 1983. Arguments on both sides were complicated by the possibility that either the B-1 or B-52, though potentially unsuited for penetrating Soviet air defenses, could be used in the future to carry and launch cruise missiles.

BUFFALO EVENING NEWS
Buffalo, N.Y., March 21, 1982

The new Stealth bomber, which is designed to evade enemy surveillance efforts, will be ready for operations as a long-range nuclear deterrent force in 1991. The date, a long-kept secret, slipped out in testimony by a Pentagon official before a congressional hearing.

Opponents of the new B-1 bomber have been very much interested in arriving at a firm date for the Stealth aircraft, since the only justification for the B-1 is as a stopgap to replace the obsolescent B-52 bombers until the Stealth bombers are ready. Present plans call for the B-1 to go into service in 1987. This means that the entire B-1 program, estimated to cost $40 billion, would last only four years, until the superior Stealth bombers take over.

This seems an incredible outlay to fill a small "window of vulnerability" — which may or may not exist. The old warhorse B-52, which has been a reliable part of the nation's strategic arsenal, is viewed as incapable of penetrating Soviet defenses for the entire decade.

However, the cruise missile provides a means of lengthening the valuable life of the B-52. Armed with cruise missiles, the B-52 could remain a credible nuclear deterrent beyond the reach of Soviet air defenses. It could, in fact, be more effective than the proposed B-1, which some experts doubt could penetrate Soviet defenses much better than the B-52.

The manned bomber remains an important part of the "triad" of strategic defenses — a concept that includes land, sea and airborne nuclear forces and thus avoids putting all our defense eggs in one basket.

But for the airborne force, we should be concentrating on the Stealth bomber, rather than wasting $40 billion on a plane that will last for only four years.

Opponents of the B-1 now fear that the Pentagon's commitment to the B-1 may induce it to go slow on development of the Stealth. Some Pentagon officials are saying that the B-1 could penetrate Soviet defenses until the mid-1990s, thus reducing the urgency of the Stealth program.

In the current defense budget, $2 billion was allotted to preliminary B-1 development. At the time of passage, perceptive military experts in Congress declared that there were other military goals that should be given priority before the B-1.

Sen. Sam Nunn, D-Ga., who favors a strong defense, said he didn't think there would be enough money to go around. He declared: "I believe either the B-1, the MX or the Stealth program will have to be canceled or significantly delayed, or I believe that our conventional force posture and our readiness will be severely eroded."

Congress approved a start on the B-1 program last year amid an atmosphere of approval of greater defense spending in general. While President Reagan is right in his determiniation to rebuild the nation's defenses, Congress should not uncritically approve every defense request, especially if the money could be better used elsewhere.

The date for the completion of the Stealth bomber, inadvertently revealed by the Pentagon, should prompt the lawmakers to re-examine the entire B-1 program.

Lincoln Journal
Lincoln, Neb., March 26, 1982

Americans were first informed the United States was working on some kind of red-hot new-fangled "invisible" bomber called Stealth during the 1980 presidential campaign.

Jimmy Carter's people, with political gain being the objective, deliberately leaked reports about the hush-hush radar-deceiving research project.

Presumably that was to signal voters Annapolis graduate Carter certainly was not asleep at the military switch, as Republicans were charging. It was also to flesh out Carter's earlier rationale for canceling the B-1 bomber program.

Things didn't quite work out for Carter. But development of the very expensive Stealth technology has been proceeding.

Once in the Oval Office, Ronald Reagan reversed Carter on the B-1. Reagan decided the people of the United States should finance the $4- to $8-billion project, and Stealth, too.

Still, it has seemed moderately reasonable that if the radar-invisible bombers could be made operational relatively soon, it might be an error to spend so vast a treasure on the B-1 — especially since Defense Secretary Caspar Weinberger once told congresspeople the B-1 probably would not have the ability to master Soviet land defenses after 1990. (He subsequently recovered from the truth-telling.)

Now the press has discovered that on Feb. 24, the director of research for the Pentagon, Richard D. DeLauer, advised a Senate Armed Services subcommittee that the Stealth aircraft is on a timetable for operational status in 1991.

The press knows this because the Pentagon has undertaken an urgent effort to classify and consider secret what DeLauer had said in an open, public hearing.

Washington Post reporter George C. Wilson said that "for the moment, the committee has inked over the 1991 date in the Feb. 24 hearing transcript available to the public."

Given the need for the nation to maximize its military investments (and if you still buy the openly debatable notion we need a strategic manned bomber capable of penetrating Soviet air space), what sense does it make to go gung-ho on the B-1 when the Stealth — a much more advanced strategic weapons system — could be available only five years later?

As to any time "gap," several squadrons of B-52s, armed with nuclear cruise missiles, should be on station well before the next presidential election or before the first B-1 flies.

DeLauer's disclosure of Stealth's availability raises new questions about spending all those billions on the B-1.

THE RICHMOND NEWS LEADER
Richmond, Va., July 20, 1983

Congressional debates about defense tend to cover familiar ground. The antis argue that the U.S. should spend its money on the weapons system just down the street — not the one available now. Say the pros: Go with what you've got.

So it was during the latest senatorial joust over the B-1 bomber. Opponents, led by Ted Kennedy, contended that the B-1 never would be able to penetrate Soviet defenses by the time it reaches full production; Kennedy called the B-1 a "supersonic albatross." Kennedy and his allies believe the U.S would be better served by working on the Stealth technology, which would make an aircraft extremely difficult to pick up on radar. Proponents of the B-1 disagree.

Additionally, there is no guarantee that Stealth will be ready by the early 1990s, or that it will do what it should. The B-1 could perform other tasks short of penetrating the Soviet defense, and it could perform them now. It could be fitted for cruise missiles. This time around, the Senate agreed with proponents, voting to spend $2.6 billion to begun replacing the Air Force's ancient B-52s with the B-1s.

The debate over the B-1 (and the MX) leads to questions that seem to recur during defense-procurement debates.

(1) When and if Stealth ever nears an operational state, would the present opponents of the B-1 then oppose Stealth, in favor of some even newer, even more exotic technology — the system down the road? The B-1 hardly can be considered the ultimate weapon, and there may be developments beyond the dreams of today's science. Perhaps congressional Liberals who support the President on such issues as the B-1 and MX do so with this in mind. Congressman Les Aspin, for one, says (a) the U.S. needs some sort of land-based missile and (b) Congress has fiddled with the MX interminably. Writes Aspin: "How do we get the Soviets to negotiate seriously about their ICBMs if we can't make a decision about ours? How do we get the Europeans to face up to their difficult weapons-deployment decisions if we can't face up to ours?" Go with what we have, says Aspin.

(2) Has the Reagan administration's plan for rebuilding American strength led it to a contract of sorts between it and congressional Liberals? Do Liberals — such as Aspin — go along with Mr. Reagan on arms decisions provided Mr. Reagan concedes on arms control? There are many points within the procurement process where programs can be delayed or halted by balky Congressmen. And just who decides where the President has shaped up on arms control? Those same Congressmen.

(3) Certainly the U.S. decision on the B-1 (and MX approval) would send the proper message to the Soviets and the Europeans. Yet arms control talks do not occur in a vacuum. The Soviets can continue deploying their own missiles while fueling the anti-American "peace" movement in Europe, and wait to see who appears on the other side of the negotiating table in 1985. Why should the Soviets give President Reagan an arms-control triumph which could help mightly to re-elect him, while disarming his critics on the Left?

Technology remains cumulative. There is a straight line between the Wright brothers' contraption and the most modern of aircraft. There is quite a progression between the drawing board and the flight line. Yet the U.S., during the Carter administration, developed the habit of postponing or halting promising military programs — a unilateral disarmament of sorts. The B-1 bomber prospectus was eternally fiddled with, much in the way Congress has fiddled with the MX.

Yet the B-1, like the MX, remains necessary from a military standpoint, and as a building block for advances not yet imagined and perhaps not yet imaginable. The Reagan administration has been correct in proceeding with the B-1. May it be successful also with the MX.

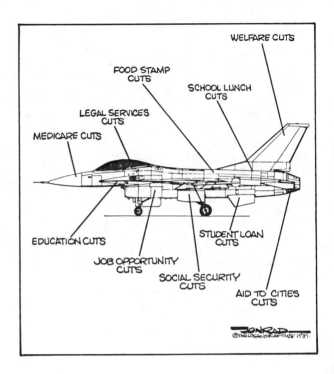

Los Angeles Times
Los Angeles, Calif., July 20, 1983

It looks as if the Senate will give President Reagan most of what he wants in the $200-billion defense-authorization bill. Last week the Senate voted overwhelmingly in favor of the B-1 bomber. Although the vote will be closer, it seems inevitable that the Senate will follow up with a vote authorizing the Pentagon to proceed with the controversial MX missile.

Fortunately, that isn't the whole ball game. Even if the President fares equally well with companion legislation in the House, which seems far from certain, there will still be time for congressional second thoughts, because the big weapon projects must run the gauntlet all over again in the follow-up defense-appropriation bills.

And second thoughts are what the country very badly needs.

The Senate bill includes a $4.7-billion authorization for the MX—money that would, among other things, be used to build 27 of the big missiles, each of which would be armed with up to 10 warheads. Pentagon plans call for the ultimate deployment of 100 MXs in silos now occupied by Minuteman missiles.

The biggest thing going for the MX, in terms of congressional support, is that it is part of a deal between Reagan and key figures on Capitol Hill. In return for their support on the MX, the President agreed to change his negotiating strategy in the strategic-arms talks to emphasize limits on warhead numbers instead of missile numbers. He also agreed to the development of single-warhead "Midgetman" missiles that would become the mainstay of the land-based U.S. nuclear deterrent in the 1990s.

The fact remains that the MXs would be just as vulnerable as the Minuteman missiles that they are designed to replace, and would be more attractive targets. Beyond that, the more MXs that are built, the more difficult it will be to achieve the goal of emphasizing warhead limits in arms negotiations; at 10 warheads per missile, 100 MXs would leave little scope for the single-warhead Midgetman under any reasonably small ceiling.

The MX should be abandoned; some of the savings should be used to accelerate work on the Midgetman.

The $6.8-billion B-1 item approved by the Senate last week would authorize the Pentagon to begin purchasing B-1 bombers to replace the aging fleet of B-52s. The Air Force wants to buy 100 B-1s at an estimated cost of $20.5 billion in 1981 dollars. Critics believe that the final bill would run much higher.

The prospective new bomber, as now designed, is vastly improved over earlier versions. Even so, in case of war the B-1 could not be depended on to penetrate Soviet defenses beyond the 1980s. It would revert to being primarily a carrier of cruise missiles to be fired from outside Soviet airspace. The penetration role would pass to the "stealth" bomber, now under development; it would be much more resistant than the B-1 to radar detection.

This country cannot afford two new bombers. The Air Force should be required to choose one or the other. The stealth program is shrouded in secrecy. But if it can be developed within a reasonable time and at affordable cost, an accelerated stealth program makes the most sense.

It is important to note that the survivability of the B-1 as a penetrating bomber has been brought into greater question by the decision to phase out production of the current-model cruise missile earlier than planned. Production of a new version more capable of evading radar would be phased in.

If current cruise missiles are seen as increasingly vulnerable to Soviet air defenses, it follows that the much larger B-1 would be more so, despite the great progress that that has been made in reducing the bomber's visibility on enemy radar.

If Congress is irreversibly sold on the merits of the bird in hand, a case can be made for abandoning the stealth and relying on the B-1 as a carrier of radar-evading cruise missiles that would be counted on to hit Soviet targets.

From the standpoint of fiscal responsibility and the nation's long-term ability to support a strong defense establishment, a choice must be made one way or the other. It is time that Congress looked that fact square in the face.

ARGUS-LEADER

Sioux Falls, S.D., February 6, 1983

President Ronald Reagan faces many budget questions about the proposed MX missile and whether it should even be built. However, he shouldn't have any serious questions challenging $6.2 billion in his budget to increase production of the B-1 bomber.

The new bomber is badly needed, as shown by three major accidents in the last two months involving B-52 bombers which are showing their age.

Two of the accidents claimed 14 lives. Five airmen died Jan. 27 when a B-52 exploded during maintenance at the Grand Forks, N.D., Air Force Base. Nine crew members died Dec. 16 in the crash of a B-52 at Mather Air Force Base in California. Two weeks earlier, a crew escaped from a B-52 which caught fire just after landing near Merced, Calif.

The plane lost at Grand Forks was built in the late 1950s. The last B-52 — of which 300 are still flying — came off the Boeing production line in October 1962. All the planes have been extensively renovated and rebuilt to lengthen their life expectancy. More modernization for B-52s is scheduled through 1990.

In comparison with other military planes, the B-52 is one of the safest and most durable ever built, according to accident statistics kept by the Air Force. Even so, this safety record has been maintained in recent years by meticulous attention to maintenance and flying procedures.

As Capt. Jon Rosell, Ellsworth Air Force base officer said following the Grand Forks mishap, in order to avoid accidents, "you follow safety procedures, you follow technical data to the letter and you avoid making mistakes."

No other military plane, except the C-47 transport, has had longer service in the U.S. Air Force than the B-52. The C-47 was the Douglas DC-3 airliner in military dress. It served 31 years — finally as a gunship in the Vietnam War — until it was retired in 1971. The B-52, which will be flying into the mid-1990s, is expected to beat the C-47's record. The B-52, which was designed in 1946, has been flying since 1955.

Air Force personnel should not be expected to fly the B-52 any longer than is necessary.

Fortunately, Reagan's new military budget, which is excessive in some respects, is correct in seeking $6.2 billion to increase production of the B-1 bomber from the present seven aircraft a year to 10 in Fiscal 1984.

Research, testing and other funds sought for the new bomber would bring total B-1 funding to $6.9 billion. The effect is to provide $2 billion more in next year's budget for the B-1 than is being spent this year. The B-1 is scheduled for deployment in 1985.

Ellsworth Air Force Base at Rapid City has 19 B-52s, flown routinely week in and week out. As Rosell said, "They're a good airplane. They're a stable airplane. They've performed admirably, but everyone is looking forward to getting new equipment so they can do their job better."

Congress should make certain that Reagan's B-1 budget is kept intact. It's a signal to the U.S. Air Force that major help is on the way in replacing the veteran B-52.

THE BLADE

Toledo, Ohio, March 16, 1983

IT is difficult to fix a bird's broken wing so that it can fly again, especially an old bird. In the case of the aging B-52 bomber the task is becoming equally hard.

A photograph on page one of The Blade last week graphically illustrated the advancing age of this country's long-range bomber force. It showed a B-52 on the ground at Mather Air Force Base in California with a broken wing.

The crew was lucky; the plane had not crashed. The wing snapped as the aircraft was being refueled in preparation for a training flight.

It does not take a great mind to deduce that these airplanes, the first of which went into service 28 years ago and which are still entrusted with a vital part of U.S. military defenses, just about have run the course and should begin to be replaced.

The latest incident follows at least seven previous ones over the past eight years in which B-52s have exploded on the ground or in the air or have crashed for some other reason. The death toll in these accidents has reached 38 crewmen, and several others have been injured. A few escaped with their lives.

The B-52 unquestionably has done yeoman work in its lifetime, but even the best aircraft can be maintained efficiently for just so long before fatigue sets in, as it has in this case.

Defense planners believe long-range bombers will play a military role for several decades in the future, and there clearly is a need to begin replacing the B-52 with modern and more reliable planes, notably the B-1 now going into production. That would enhance the safety of the men who man the U.S. bombing fleet as well as the defense of the nation itself.

RAPID CITY JOURNAL

Rapid City, S.D., July 25, 1983

As the result of recent U.S. Senate action, it now appears Strategic Air Command will get the new manned bomber it's been seeking for so long.

By voting down a move to deny any money to build the B-1B bomber and then killing a proposed amendment to the defense authorization bill to cut B-1B production funds by $888.7 million, the Senate virtually cleared the way for the new bomber to go into production as scheduled.

Further funding challenges in Congress are not expected to be formidable.

The B-1 was conceived about 20 years ago as a replacement for the B-52, the early models of which already were showing their age.

With military budgets strained by the Vietnam War in the 1960s and early 1970s, the proposed bomber was forced into a low position on the priority ladder. But research and development activity continued through the Vietnam years and during the bitter aftermath of that conflict.

Three prototype aircraft had been built for testing and a fourth was being assembled when Jimmy Carter assumed the presidency. Carter reversed a Gerald Ford decision to equip SAC with the new plane. However, with congressional approval, Carter allowed the Air Force to continue testing the prototypes.

Rockwell International, the principal contractor, retained most of its B-1 machine tools. Also, by assigning them to other projects, the firm kept the nucleus of its B-1 management team on the payroll. As a result, after President Reagan decided that the B-1B, an updated version of the 1970s design should be built, lead time on full-scale production was minimized.

Actually, the B-1B already is being built. The first production aircraft is being assembled and, according to Rockwell, it will roll out of the factory late next year, more than three months ahead of the timetable established by the company and the Air Force.

A succession of SAC and Air Force commanders have insisted a new bomber is needed to replace the old and tired B-52 which is the mainstay of the manned bomber component of the strategic triad.

But even with B-1B production assured for several years as the result of the recent action in the Senate, the B-52 will continue to carry the load because it will be late in this decade before SAC has a full fleet of 100 of the new bombers.

The long wait isn't over yet.

Reagan Abandons Mobile MX in Strategic Weapons Program

President Reagan announced his long-awaited plan for modernizing and strengthening the U.S. strategic nuclear arsenal on Oct. 2, 1981. In that portion of his five-pronged plan dealing with the hotly debated MX missile system, Reagan proposed canceling all plans for the mobile basing system in Utah and Nevada, frequently referred to as the "shell game," which had been proposed by former President Carter. Instead, he recommended that 100 MX missiles be built, 36 of them to be deployed in existing Titan missile silos beginning in 1986. The silos, under the President's plan, would be "super-hardened," or reinforced with concrete and steel, to better withstand the blast effects of nuclear weapons. Meanwhile, research would continue into the best method of deployment for the 64 remaining 10-warhead missiles. In the main, congressional reaction to the curtailed plan for MX deployment reflected relief that the controversial and expensive land-based system of shuttling hundreds of the missiles between thousands of shelters had been dropped. Typical of the general reaction was that of Rep. Patricia Schroeder (D, Col.), a member of the House Armed Services Committee, who said: "There's a little sanity showing through." Some conservative strategists, however, including Sen. John Tower (R, Texas), chairman of the Senate Armed Services Committee, argued that it was questionable whether the MX missiles could survive a direct hit in existing silos.

ST. LOUIS POST-DISPATCH
St. Louis, Mo., October 12, 1981

Because there are aspects of the MX mobile missile system that directly increase the possibility of nuclear war, President Reagan's decision to build and deploy the weapon could well prove to be one of the most important ones of his presidency.

The MX is unlike any other American nuclear delivery system. Earlier systems all had technical problems that limited their military utility against targets such as missile silos and hardened command posts. Manned bombers were slow and could be shot down. Earlier land- and sea-based missiles were accurate enough to destroy cities but not missile silos. But the MX, with its designed ability to land 10 nuclear warheads within 100 yards of their targets, is accurate enough to attack silos. Indeed, that is its principal mission.

Since roughly 75 percent of the Soviet Union's strategic nuclear warheads are deployed on its land-based ICBMs — as opposed to just 25 percent for the U.S. — the MX deployment creates an immense "window of vulnerability" for Moscow. Hence, the MX threat against Soviet ICBMs would encourage Moscow to adopt a first strike strategy — sometimes called the "use them or lose them" doctrine.

Another problem with the MX is Mr. Reagan's basing plan. In his speech outlining his new strategic program, Mr. Reagan correctly identified the fatal flaw of President Carter's plan to deploy, as in a giant shell game, 200 MX missiles among 4,600 shelters, when he declared that "No matter how many shelters we might build, the Soviets can build more missiles, more quickly, and just as cheaply."

But in the very next sentence he announced that the U.S. was going ahead with the MX anyway and will initially deploy it in redesigned Titan and Minuteman missile silos. It was as if Mr. Reagan had not listened to the logic of his own argument. If 200 MX missiles deployed among 4,600 shelters are vulnerable to a Soviet first strike, then it follows that deploying 100 MX missiles in single silos would make them even more so. Because of its capability for destroying Soviet missile silos, the MX would be the most important target in the U.S. And because the missile would enhance the threat of a Soviet first stike, the U.S., in turn, would be under pressure to launch its MXs upon warning of an attack. A launch on warning doctrine places a hair-trigger on the first use and early use of nuclear weapons in a crisis.

Mr. Reagan justified the single silo basing plan on the ground that more research is needed on other basing modes. But even here there are serious problems. The three alternatives that most often are cited are: (1) placing MXs on long-endurance aircraft (the so-called "Big Bird" plan); (2) deploying the MX in super-deep silos (2,000 to 3,000 feet underground) and (3) deploying an anti-ballistic missile system to protect the MX bases.

The Air Force has continually rejected the air-mobile idea as being too costly and too vulnerable to attack. The super-deep silos are technologically unproven and may well be too expensive. So it would appear that the anti-ballistic missile system will be the most likely method to be chosen. But if that is the case, it means tens of billions of dollars for a new ABM system that may, in fact, not work, the abrogation of the ABM-limiting SALT I treaty and a dangerous escalation of the nuclear arms race.

The administration's case for its MX program is unpersuasive. Unless it is strengthened in ways that lessen the dangers of nuclear war, instead of enlarging them, Congress should reject the proposal.

THE MILWAUKEE JOURNAL
Milwaukee, Wisc., October 6, 1981

President Reagan has threaded the needle in his strategic weapons policy. He avoided the worst of the available choices, we think. Junking the misbegotten "shell game" scheme for the MX missile is a significant accomplishment — if it can be kept junked.

Had the president decided on a "multiple protective shelter" deployment for the MX, it could have been an appalling stimulus to the arms race. As it is, the announcement that the US will build 100 of the powerfully accurate missiles and initially base about 36 in existing, but additionally hardened, ICBM silos might reduce the flame a degree under the nuclear-weapons pot. Scattering MX missiles in thousands of guess-which shelters could have led to a feverish process in which the US constructed ever more shelters as the Soviets accumulated ever greater numbers of warheads to overwhelm them.

The premise of the Reagan plan is that a "window of vulnerability" threatens the US during the middle 1980s. This "window" is doctrine or dogma, depending on one's geopolitical view. To what degree it really exists and to what extent the president's plan narrows it will properly dominate the congressional debate. Reagan could well be a captive of his earlier supercharged rhetoric about the dimensions of the Soviet threat.

In any case, Reagan will be under assault from both the hawkish right (which believes he is proposing too little to close the window) and from the dovish left (which feels his program — costing $180 billion over five years — vastly overestimates US vulnerability).

Reagan's intention is to strengthen the traditional triad of land, sea and air deterrents. The Navy will get a more muscular submarine missile-capability that should enhance the "blue water" option — the least vulnerable leg of the triad. The Air Force gets only half of what it wanted, 100 MX missiles instead of 200, with a decision on how permanently to base that force deferred until 1984.

To keep the Air Force generals from getting too edgy, however, they'll also get two bombers — the B-1 and the "Stealth" aircraft. We are dubious about concurrent bomber development programs, especially with the 100 B-1s costing about $200 million a copy. The administration contends the B-1 is necessary to fill a gap between a geriatric B-52 fleet and the advanced-technology Stealth in the 1990s. There are technical and operational "uncertainties" about getting a Stealth bomber in the air by the time it will be needed. Yet couldn't a "stretch-out" of a modernized B-52 fleet, now being equipped with cruise missiles, fill that expensive gap? We hope the congressional debate will sharpen this focus.

As another element of the administration's "short term" strategic policy, research on sophisticated anti-ballistic missile technology will be accelerated — which could involve renegotiation of the 1972 ABM Treaty — and an improved "command and control" network will be put in place.

The worrisome B-1 aside, we're inclined to think that much of Reagan's policy is reasonable — to the extent reasonable can be used in the bizarre context of nuclear logic. But the essential point in this entire drill is to get to the arms-talk table — to obtain reductions, not just ceilings, on the awful destructive capacities of the superpowers. That does require "bargaining chips." The crucial question is: How many at what cost?

AKRON BEACON JOURNAL
Akron, Ohio, October 6, 1981

PRESIDENT REAGAN'S plan for revitalizing the nation's strategic deterrent is a mixed bag. In some ways it is more restrained than what was expected. But it also raises questions about whether his ideas represent the wisest use of the nation's defense dollars.

The Congress should examine the President's proposals closely and work out changes where appropriate.

The issue here is not whether the country should be spending more money to improve its defenses against a Soviet attack. Clearly it should. Rather, the issue is whether the plan put forth by President Reagan makes the most sense.

Mr. Weinberger

In particular, the President's recommendations for basing the new MX missile, while less expensive and less prone to trigger increased Soviet defense spending than some others under discussion, seem to lack persuasive logic at this point. Indeed, they appear to be little more than an interim solution, as the President more or less concedes, and a curious one at that.

After all, the plan introduces no new guesswork into the picture for the Soviets, as would have happened with suggestions to rotate a modest number of the missiles among a large number of new shelters in Idaho and Nevada or to keep a supply of the missiles continuously aloft.

By putting the MX missiles in the silos constructed for the Minuteman and Titan missiles, the nation would be saying to the Soviets: "You may know where the MXs are located, but we still don't think you can knock them out, at least for a few years until we figure out another way to base them."

The key to that strategy, if there is one, lies in the President's plan to reconstruct existing silos to add more steel and concrete to help withstand nuclear explosions. But Pentagon experts say that even if the hardness of the silos were doubled, Soviet missile accuracy would have to improve by only 25 percent to be able to destroy them anyway. Those experts say it would not be difficult for the Soviets to step up accuracy to that level.

So what would be accomplished? Only that the more powerful and more accurate MX would be in place. And that the huge expense and environmental damage of the shuttle plan advanced by former President Carter and others would be avoided, a result not without a lot of pluses.

But whether the nation will be any more secure until new basing schemes for the MX can be tested and put into operation is doubtful.

Even Defense Secretary Caspar W. Weinberger himself appeared to recognize that when he testified in his confirmation hearing:

"I would feel that simply putting it into the existing silos would not answer two or three of the concerns that I have; namely, that these are well known and are not hardened sufficiently, nor could they be, to be of sufficient strategic value to count as a strategic improvement to our forces."

The Congress and the nation will want to find out what caused Mr. Weinberger to change his mind.

Questions also remain about the wisdom of building a modified B-1 bomber, especially since hardly a decade is expected to pass between its deployment in 1986 and that of the new advanced technology, or Stealth, bomber in the 1990s.

The Congress should look carefully at suggestions to rely on the B-52 bomber until the Stealth is ready to go.

For whatever faults and shortcomings the President's program may have, at least he has seen through the folly of more expensive MX proposals and their potential for undue escalation of the nuclear arms race. For that he deserves credit.

ARKANSAS DEMOCRAT
Little Rock, Ark., October 7, 1981

President Reagan's announcement of his grand design for future U.S. defense is only the opening gun of a long battle with Congress over what new weapons systems should be built and how any new land-based part of the whole can be most securely deployed.

The President wants to build the MX missile, the "invisible" stealth bomber and the B1 bomber over the next six years. He will probably get only the first two. But the first big debate, already begun, is over how we can best make secure the first three dozen of the MXs, which will be built over the next five years during a period of "vulnerability" to Russian attack.

Jimmy Carter wanted all MXs permanently shuttled between thousands of shelters in the Western desert. Mr. Reagan favors temporarily deploying the first batch – not due till 1985 – among existing but improved Minuteman and Titan silos in Arkansas, Arizona, Kansas and the Dakotas. He is also considering defending the hardened emplacements with anti-ballistic missiles – ABMs – which would intercept and destroy incoming Russian missiles.

All that's first phase and by no means settled, since Congress has veto power.

But what's this "vulnerability" business? The phrase "window of vulnerability" originated in the Defense Department during the Carter years. It expresses the belief that the Russians during the mid-'80s, perhaps starting next year, will have enough missiles of sufficient accuracy to all but destroy most of our Minutemen and Titan ICBMs in their silos. That capability isn't widely disputed. And among those who feel the Russians might indeed attack there's little dispute about what should be done – build more missiles and warheads and deploy them either so securely or so confusingly that we'd have plenty left for a response if the Russians let go at our entire land-based armory.

Building 100 MXs – 10 warheads to the missile – would quickly add 1,000 new warheads. But are silos better than the Western shuttle? President Reagan says yes – that the shuttle-system wouldn't protect the MXs any better than silos, and that the Russians can build new missiles more quickly than we can build the shelters. Defense Secretary Caspar W. Weinberger says the strengthened silos would be 10 times as strong as the shelters.

But Carter's shuttle-shell deployment still has its champions, both in Congress and the Pentagon. Senate Armed Services Chairman John Tower thinks the silo method leaves the "window of vulnerability" more wide open than ever. General David Jones, chairman of the joint chiefs, agrees. They argue – and we think they're right – that to blanket a shuttle deployment the Russians would need to fire practically all their accurate missiles, around 10,000. Silos, however strengthened, are certain targets and would require fewer missiles. And since Congress rejected the ABM in the Nixon years, it's not likely to figure as an added defense.

We'll hear it all over and over again and see it all fought out in detail. What matters is that Mr. Reagan has announced the beginning of a trillion-dollar rebuilding program. We need it.

The News and Courier
Charleston, S.C., October 9, 1981

The Senate is now hearing testimony on key elements of President's Reagan's proposed buildup of strategic forces. If the reader is confused by the day-to-day, shifting winds of commentary blowing from Capitol Hill, there's good reason. There's more than one "shell game" involved in determining the eventual shape the six-year, $180.3 billion strategic modernization program will take.

The two largest components of the strategic package involve construction of a manned bomber and the deployment of a new ICBM — the MX. A look at the MX basing mode controversy is a good example of the reigning confusion.

The administration's basing recommendation was more of a compromise than a clear cut decision — to build, in the interim (translated, that means "after the 1984 elections"), about 100 MX missiles and put about three dozen in reinforced underground silos now occupied by Titan missiles. This delicate balancing act mollifies the many vocal opponents of land basing the MX in a so-called "shell game" of desert shelters constructed throughout the Great Basin of the Midwest. It also apparently leaves a wisp of hope for proponents of basing the MX at sea or in airborne "Big Birds."

It's the varied reactions that cause the confusion:

— Republican hawk Barry Goldwater supported the compromise recommendation, saying "I never thought the Russians were so stupid they couldn't figure out the shell game in a matter of hours."

— Fellow Republican hawk John Tower derided the plan, calling it "silo stuffing."

— Democratic leaders were quick to condemn it for partisan reasons, calling it politically motivated and not based on "national security factors."

— Not surprisingly, Defense Secretary Caspar Weinberger supported his boss Ronald Reagan, although last month he tried to sell him the air-based mode and lost.

— Weinberger's top uniformed advisor, Air Force General David Jones, who for parochial reasons was also a proponent of the air-based mode, suddenly switched horses, disagreed with his boss, and called for the original shell game plan.

Is that not sufficient reason to think that perhaps there's another shell game going on in the hearings? Assume the sea-based proponents, of which we are one, are now in a minority. If it appears the military strongly endorses a plan that would in the long run, desecrate the American West, would not the acceptable alternative ultimately put the MX back in the "Big Bird"?

Sound too Machiavellian? But don't you have to be something of a Machiavelli to get over all the hurdles and around all the roadblocks put up by conflicting interests lobbying and pressuring the decision-makers in the national capital?

THE RICHMOND NEWS LEADER
Richmond, Va., October 5, 1981

He has done it again. Once again President Reagan has defied the predictions of experts who told the public what he planned to do. And once again he has taken firm action to restore America's military capabilities. In announcing plans to deploy 100 MX missiles and to build 100 updated versions of the B-1 bomber, Mr. Reagan made perhaps the most far-reaching strategic decision in decades.

The MX decision is, in a word, a masterstroke. The U.S. needs a new missile system. Its arsenal of Titan and Minuteman missiles grows more vulnerable to a Soviet first-strike each day. That the President would select a new missile was not in doubt. The only question was the deployment system he would pick.

In typical fashion, Jimmy Carter waffled on the MX. Although his administration failed to make a final decision, Carter favored the so-called "race-track" basing system in which the MX missiles would be moved secretly on underground tracks from silo to silo, thereby confounding Soviet detection efforts. The race-track mode cost too much and seemed strategically dubious. And it inspired considerable opposition in the Western states in which it would have been built. Even such defense stalwarts as Utah Senator Jake Garn questioned the wisdom of basing the MX in the desert.

Mr. Reagan finessed the issue. He decided to deploy the MX in existing silos. Thus Mr. Reagan not only approved a missile the U.S. hugely needs; he defused potential political problems as well. The Reagan political touch remains golden. (Two days before Mr. Reagan announced his decision against building a massive new MX complex, a network news reader breathlessly informed his viewers that the President had opted for a "race track" in Nevada.

Thus, once again, the risks of predicting Ronald Reagan.)

The B-1 decision is no less crucial. In one of the worst blunders in his error-prone administration, Mr. Carter grounded the B-1 in favor of continued reliance on the B-52. The B-52s have ably filled their function as the nation's principal strategic bomber. But they are the products of 30-year-old technology, and they are becoming increasingly obsolete. Many of the planes are older than the pilots who fly them. As planes age, repair costs soar. And dramatic advances in anti-aircraft technology make the B-52 vulnerable to Soviet countermeasures.

The B-1 is the world's most sophisticated bomber. The Soviets have nothing like it. It can carry awesome payloads. And it flies so low that it can avoid enemy radar. The pilots who may be called upon to fly missions in strategic bombers surely ranked among the first to cheer the Reagan decision.

More than any other issue, defense ought to remain the primary concern of the national government. Protecting the nation — its people, its territory, its liberty — is government's most important task. Yet for too long defense has not received its share of the federal budget. Defense needs cannot wait; they cannot be postponed. If a country dithers until war breaks out, it will be too late. New weapons systems take years before they become operational. For example, Mr. Reagan's first term will end before the MX and the B-1 go into full service.

Mr. Reagan recognizes defense's primacy. In both word and deed, he has signaled an end to the days when defense rode in the back of the budget bus. His approval of the MX missile and the B-1 bomber is welcome news. He clearly comprehends that defense is a nation's life insurance policy. We can't afford to be second best.

THE ARIZONA REPUBLIC
Phoenix, Ariz., October 6, 1981

CRITICS of President Reagan's decision to deploy 100 MX missiles in hardened existing silos have yet to come up with a better alternative.

There isn't any.

Admittedly, the silos will be vulnerable to Soviet Russia's ICBMs, if — and this is a very big if, indeed — the Soviet ICBMs are as accurate as the critics claim.

However, *any* system of ground-based missiles would be equally vulnerable, including President Carter's "race-track system."

Carter proposed digging 4,600 silos in Nevada and Utah and shunting 200 MX missiles from one to another.

The Soviets, he reasoned, would never know where the missiles were.

This sounded like a great idea until missile experts pointed out that it would be a simple matter for the Soviets to put enough warheads on their ICBMs to hit all 4,600 silos at once.

Defense Secretary Caspar Weinberger had the idea of deploying the missiles in submarines and aircraft.

The Air Force quickly objected that it wasn't technically feasible to carry them in aircraft.

Secretary of State Alexander Haig raised another objection — the United States couldn't very well expect West Europeans to accept land-based missiles unless it, too, deployed them.

Some day, some one may figure out a way of deploying the MX that will make it invulnerable, but, in the meantime, Reagan's idea of putting them in existing silos and hardening the silos is the only practical one.

The president is also on solid ground in ordering production of a limited number of B-1 bombers and continuing work on the development of the Stealth bomber.

There are those who say he should cancel production of the B-1, and wait until all the problems in building the Stealth, a plane that will be invisible to enemy radar, can be worked out.

Unfortunately, that may be years from now. It may be never.

The Morning News
Wilmington, Del. October 8, 1981

President Reagan hadn't finished explaining his $180-billion defense plan to close "what I have called the window of vulnerability" when it was already being denounced by prominent senators as not enough. His program includes modernization of strategic bombers, including production of the B-1 and Stealth bombers; deployment of new submarine-launched missiles; strengthening of strategic defenses; upgrading of electronic and satellite communications, and construction and deployment of the MX missile.

The uproar was prompted by his decision not to proceed with Multiple Protective Shelter basing for the MX missile, the Carter administration's plan to conceal MX missiles by moving them among thousands of shelters in Nevada and Utah. It would have been the $41-billion equivalent of a subway system in which the trains constantly move their MX passengers from one station to another in the hopes of confusing the enemy, i.e. the Soviet Union.

Mr. Reagan's reasoning was simple. The Multiple Protective Shelter plan was abandoned because "a program to deploy 100 MX (missiles) in 1,000 shelters would not be survivable against today's threat, much less the Soviet forces that are likely to be deployed by the mid-1980s." (The MX is scheduled to go into production in 1986.)

The administration also decided against the more ambitious proposal to deploy 200 missiles in 4,600 shelters because it "has only one significant difference from the 100 in 1,000 plan: It is more expensive (but no more survivable)."

The most-chilling word used by Senate opponents to the president's decision is "survivability." It must be understood that they apply the word not to the nation's civilian population but to its ICBMs, currently Titan and Minuteman missiles in fixed silos, 100 of which would be replaced by MX missiles in strengthened underground silos as quickly as possible after MX mass production began. The senators are unwilling to countenance a so-called nuclear deterrent in which 100 ICBMs are presumably sitting ducks to a Soviet nuclear first strike.

They profess that the accuracy of Soviet missiles is so high that the entire ICBM system might be obliterated in a first strike. What are they suggesting? Are we to believe that any Soviet first strike of sufficient magnitude to wipe out those land-based missiles would go undetected by this nation's early warning system? Are we to believe that if such a massive strike were detected by the United States the president would sit idly by until all the Soviet missiles had hit their targets?

What of the other two vaunted legs of our highly acclaimed Triad defense system, strategic nuclear bombers for aerial penetration of Soviet territory and far-flung Trident submarines with nuclear missiles targeted for vast areas of the Soviet Union? Are they no longer the deterrents we were assured they would be when their vast expenditures were debated and approved?

President Reagan proposed his five-part defense program on the grounds that it would upgrade the nation's defenses quickly enough to match improvements in the Soviet nuclear arsenal and at a cost this nation can afford. The package includes several elements, particularly the B-1 bomber, that are far more questionable than his sensible modifications on the MX system.

Unfortunately, all that is obscured by the noisy debate over the sufficiency of anything less than a multi-billion-dollar investment in an underground shell game. And the detestable result of these prophecies of doom for national security is increased fear and insecurity for uninformed Americans who, unlike some of their elected officials, still find nuclear war unthinkable.

DESERET NEWS
Salt Lake City, Utah, October 3, 1981

The appropriate reaction to President Reagan's announcement Friday on the MX missile is the one that's already generally apparent — a collective sigh of relief.

But it's a reaction that should be tempered somewhat because more complex and controversial decisions still must be made, decisions in which this nation's security and survival are at stake.

The sigh of relief is appropriate not just because most — but not all — Utahns and Nevadans were most reluctant to see MX missiles deployed in the western desert unless it was absolutely necessary.

Rather, such a reaction is in order because the White House's decision reflects what is decidedly prudent from the standpoint of getting the best defense system in place as quickly as possible without bankrupting the country.

The decision, of course, is to abandon the race-track or shell-game mode for deploying MX, use the money saved to produce B-1 bombers, and start putting up to 100 MX missiles in hardened, refitted Minuteman or Titan silos. Meanwhile, the Pentagon will study other options for the MX. Those options include placing the missile aboard aircraft, defending it with an anti-ballistic missile (ABM) system, or locating it in nearly invulnerable sites deep underground. A final decision is supposed to be reached no later than 1984.

This approach amounts to putting fewer eggs in more baskets while correcting the mistake that was made when the previous administration cancelled production of the B-1 bomber. As this page noted at the time, the cancellation of the B-1 was a serious error because it left the U.S. with an aging complement of B-52 bombers and substantially weakened the air leg of America's defense system, which depends on a workable balance of sea, ground, and air forces.

The Reagan approach reflects the extent to which even some of his closest advisers, including the prestigious Townes Commission, were sharply divided over how to deploy MX.

It reflects, too, the conclusion recently reached by the agency that advises Congress on technology. The Office of Technology Assessment found that there is no way to base the MX missile that is free of serious risks.

This finding is just a sample of the important challenges still facing the administration as it pursues the new defense plans outlined Friday.

To begin with, the Pentagon seems to have been so firmly wedded to the race-track plan that there's room for wondering if it can study the other options and still come to an objective, expeditious conclusion.

If a conclusion on the merits of the airborne, underground, and ABM options isn't reached expeditiously, the final decision could easily drag into 1984, when election-year politics could divert the White House's attention and add to the controversy over MX.

There's already plenty of controversy over the ABM and airborne options. Putting the MX aboard large transport planes would make it easier for the missile to survive an attack — if those planes took off immediately upon warning. But if attackers destroyed the airfields where the planes could refuel, the U.S. would have to use or lose these MX missiles within the first few hours of conflict. As for the ABM, it might force attackers to use two missiles where otherwise just one would do. But the ABM system may not work and would require the U.S. to amend or cancel its 1972 anti-ABM treaty with Russia. The other option, putting MX deep underground, would be expensive and just might bring the missile to Utah and Nevada. We should never lose sight of the fact, also, that Utah, with its heavy defense installations already here, will no doubt continue to be a prime military target for the enemy.

One final question: Over how wide an area are the MX missiles to be scattered when they are fitted into Minuteman or Titan silos? That point, judging from Friday's news conference by President Reagan and Defense Secretary Caspar Weinberger, still seems to be unsettled. A fairly tight configuration will make it easier to control MX. But such a configuration could also concentrate the adverse social, environmental, and other impacts that were the basis of much of the opposition to the race-track plan for MX in Utah and Nevada.

If nothing else is clear from the new defense plans outlined Friday, it should be the increasingly urgent need to pursue negotiations for a workable arms control agreement just as vigorously as we are striving to fill some of the chinks in our armor.

Silo-Reinforcing Plan Scrapped in Second Revision of Basing Plan

The Reagan Administration announced in February, 1982 that plans to harden Minuteman silos to hold the MX missiles had been dropped. The announcement marked the second revision in basing plans for the MX since the President's October, 1981 decision to harden Titan II missile silos. (In December, 1981 it was decided to use existing Minuteman silos.) A Defense Department spokesman said the decision not to harden existing silos had been made because both congressional leaders and the Administration felt that "hardening on an interim basis wasn't necessarily worth the money." It was estimated that $3 billion would be saved as a result of the decision.

Nearly $4.5 billion had been set aside in Reagan's new 1983 budget for the MX missile, much of it earmarked for research on different basing modes. Among the possibilities for deploying the missiles were placing them aboard airplanes in continuous flight; basing them in deep underground silos, under the so-called "Citadel" plan; or placing them in bases protected by an antimissile defense system of some kind, an increasingly popular alternative.

THE SACRAMENTO BEE
Sacramento, Calif., February 25, 1982

During the 1980 presidential campaign, candidate Reagan attacked the Carter administration for its plan to deploy the new MX intercontinental ballistic missile on moving trains in the Western desert. Nine months after taking office, Reagan's team of experts came up with a plan to put 40 of the 100 still-to-be-built missiles in silos now occupied by the aging Titan II missiles and to "superharden" these silos to protect them from a potential Soviet attack. Two months later, they changed their minds and said they would put the MXs in silos now occupied by Minuteman missiles and superharden *them*.

Now it seems the Pentagon has changed its mind again and will not, in fact, superharden anything. This decision, or rather indecision, derives partly from congressional grumbling about the program, but the principal cause for hesitation appears to be serious doubts within the Pentagon as to whether the MX can be sufficiently protected from attack, or, if so, whether it can be done without budget-busting cost overruns.

There is a real danger, though, that the Kremlin may not view these changes in direction merely as a reflection of an incoherent defense strategy in Washington. Instead, Moscow may see it as "proof" that the Reagan administration never intended to shield the MX from attack but planned it all along as a potential first-strike weapon. This suspicion would be strengthened by the ultimate deployment of the missiles in existing, and vulnerable, Minuteman silos.

The Pentagon claims development of the missiles is moving along "smashing well." How it will be deployed, however, remains as much an unanswered question as when the Carter administration conceived its "shell-game" strategy that evoked so much derision and protest. Probably the only intelligent "deployment" of the MX would be as a bargaining chip at the negotiating table. The current Geneva talks on medium-range missiles in Europe need to be augmented as soon as possible by a new round of strategic-weapon talks. Call it SALT III, START I or anything you like, but get it going.

Arkansas Gazette.
Little Rock, Ark., February 22, 1982

Some excitement is circulating in Arizona these days about a plan, called the "Mesa Concept," that would bury the new MX missiles deep underground beneath desert mesas, which are those flat-topped benches, with steep sides, that moviegoers have seen in thousands of Western films. The Air Force and the Pentagon have confirmed that the plan is one of three for MX basing that are actively under consideration. A recommendation to President Reagan is due in July 1983.

There is still reason to question the need for the MX regardless of the method of basing, but of the three methods under study, the "Mesa Concept" could well be the least vulnerable and therefore the most effective. One method of basing would have the MX placed, at least temporarily, on launching platforms, protected by anti-ballistic missiles. Another would place the MX in modified Minuteman silos.

The mesa plan would have the MX stored deep inside the mesas in such a way that the missiles could be moved around. They would not be poised for immediate launch. Instead, launch would have to await the drilling of a hole, using special equipment, for the MX to pass through. It is an exotic plan, one that on closer examination might be shown to be as faulty as an earlier plan to shuttle the missiles among 4,600 shelters connected by rail tracks.

It is becoming increasingly apparent, in any case, that no land-based system can make the MX invulnerable to a Soviet first strike. Effectiveness of any system will have to be measured in relative terms only. By this measuring stick, the "Mesa Concept" may turn out to be the best method, although the fact remains that should world tensions ever reach the point that either side was firing strategic nuclear weapons, the world would hardly be worth living in anyway.

The Honolulu Advertiser
Honolulu, Ha., February 16, 1982

It's back to square one. That's the effect of the Reagan administration's decision to scrap the "silo hardening" plan to base the MX missile. In doing so, the administration now must reconsider the same options it agonized over last summer.

The silo hardening option was apparently dropped because of Congressional skepticism that it would not adequately protect the MX, and increasing doubts such a move would be cost effective.

The administration has given itself until July 1983 to come up with a new plan. The first MX should be ready three years later.

IT'S HARD to see how the decision making process is going to be any easier the second time around. The main options remain:

● Carry the MX in a new aircraft capable of soaring for days on end. The scheme would be very expensive, require special airfields, and it isn't certain the plane would be ready in time.

● Deployment on special submarines is still a possibility, but a remote one. The subs would have a limited cruising range, and thus be more vulnerable.

● Something similar to the racetrack scheme that President Carter proposed. The Air Force wants something on a smaller scale, but either plan would have major political and environmental consequences.

● Dig silos 3,000 feet below the surface — the so-called "Citadel" plan. It's major drawbacks are the length of time required to get a missile out, and uncertain environmental-related problems.

● Build silos guarded by anti-ballistic missiles. To do so would be repudiation of the 1972 treaty which banned ABMs. Our Western European allies would strongly oppose such a move, and the ultimate cost of the MX would have to include development and construction of ABMs and their deployment.

OF COURSE there may be some combination of the above. But what's notable is the relatively low-key manner with which the administration is handling this delay.

It wasn't that long ago, after all, that Ronald Reagan was lambasting Jimmy Carter for allowing the United States to face a "window of vulnerability." Reagan criticized Carter for not moving fast enough in deploying the MX.

Now here we have President Reagan putting off final plans for MX basing. And there's been no talk about a window of vulnerability.

CHICAGO Sun-Times
Chicago, Ill., February 14, 1982

The Reagan administration has dropped still another plan for basing the costly new MX intercontinental missile. It will not, as it said it would in December, install the first 40 of the 100 on order in existing Minuteman silos hardened to better withstand the shock of a pre-emptive nuclear strike.

The missiles now will go into the Minuteman silos as they are, because the administration has come to agree with congressional critics that hardening "wasn't necessarily worth the money."

That sounds like an economy. Except for one thing: Pentagon specialists say that an MX in a Minuteman silo is likely to be more vulnerable because it is larger and, thus, will have less "rattle-space," or room to absorb the shock of a nearby nuclear explosion.

So, for a lot more money, we are to install missiles specifically designed to close the alleged "window of vulnerability" in holes where they will be a more tempting target than the Minutemen for a Soviet assault.

It would be laughable, except that President Reagan in his 1983 budget is asking for $4.5 billion in obligational authority to produce just the first nine of the 100 MXs.

The soft-silo deployment would, to be sure, be a temporary thing. As the first MXs are stuck in their interim homes, the Pentagon will be casting about for places to put them more lastingly.

But we have no confidence that sensible basing will be found. Under the Carter administration the MX was to be shell-gamed in a racetrack mode, a concept that was politically and environmentally dead at birth, as Reagan recognized when he buried it. And early Reaganite proposals to carry the things on aircraft in continuous flight were sneered out of consideration in the Pentagon.

There are still potentially viable possibilities—deep underground and/or protected by antiballistic missiles, for example—but these alternatives also are polka-dotted with the ciphers of many billions of dollars.

The real alternative, as we have argued before, is to shelve the MX—now, when we can least afford to produce it. There is no window of vulnerability. Even if the Russians could take out all our 1,000 Minutemen in a first strike, which is highly questionable, we would still have enough air- and sea-launched nukes to destroy them many times over.

THE TENNESSEAN
Nashville, Tenn., February 17, 1982

THE administration still doesn't know what to do with the MX missile, which originally was supposed to run around the western deserts on a race track course to prevent any nuclear strike from knocking the system out entirely.

The race-track idea was abandoned by the Reagan administration as too expensive and too controversial among residents of the western states. Instead, it announced that it would place the missiles on a short-term basis in silos reinforced by concrete and steel to withstand a nuclear attack.

Now, the administration has given up that idea. Instead, the first 40 missiles to be deployed would be placed in existing Minuteman silos that have not been reinforced or "hardened" as it envisioned last October.

In that, it seems to have come around to agreeing with the Congress that the plan was ill-advised and too expensive.

In voting for the Defense Appropriations Bill, Congress also voted for a carefully-worded provision that questioned, but didn't prohibit, superhardening of existing ICBM silos as an interim basing solution for the MX.

The intent of the provision was to concentrate efforts on a permanent basing mode and it directed that the secretary of Defense recommend such a permanent solution by mid-1983.

Supporters of the congressional amendment argued that the MX in existing silos, whether hardened or not, simply are not survivable.

The Defense Department had another problem. In October it announced that the MX missiles would be placed in aging Titan missile silos. But in December it was announced that they would be deployed in Minuteman silos. These are smaller in size, so they would have to be made bigger. In order to make them bigger, it would have required permission from the Soviet Union under the terms of the arms limitation treaty known as SALT I. Although that treaty has expired, the administration is tacitly abiding by its provisions, one of which is that extensive changes in existing missile basing by either side would require approval from the other.

The aim of President Reagan's October decision was to help close "the window of vulnerability" to Soviet attack that he spoke of in the presidential campaign. At the time, Pentagon officials said the Soviet Union would have to improve the accuracy of its missiles by 25% in order to damage a "super-hardened" silo.

The U.S. is not quite back to square one in dealing with the MX. The race track idea was absurd and promised to be awesomely expensive. The super-hardened silo was ill-advised and also prohibitively expensive. Putting the MX in unreinforced silos that are of insufficient size is at best an expedient, but it doesn't guarantee much protection.

So the Pentagon will have to start all over again in trying to figure out what basing mode will work, without being prohibitively expensive. That is a tough one. One way out might be to start new talks with the Soviet on strategic arms limitation and hope the MX wouldn't become necessary at all under a new agreement.

BUFFALO EVENING NEWS
Buffalo, N.Y., February 21, 1982

Last fall, President Reagan decided to scrap the Carter administration's "shell game" plan for deploying the new MX missile in favor of reinforcing some existing missile silos to make them more resistant to nuclear attack. This was an interim plan to bolster U.S. defenses pending studies of other options for deploying the MX. Now the administration has dropped even the reinforced-silo plan, leaving the whole MX question as much up in the air as ever.

The Pentagon will save some $3 billion by not reinforcing the silos — and that is welcome in these deficit-ridden days — but the nation seems no closer to solution of the problem of protecting its strategic nuclear missiles.

That was the purpose of the Carter "shell game" plan, in which the MX missiles would be moved among 4,600 possible launching sites, making them less vulnerable to nuclear attack. The problem has arisen in recent years as Soviet missiles have become more and more accurate and the destruction of the U.S. land-based missile force has become theoretically possible.

Mr. Reagan abandoned the expensive "shell game" plan — partly, no doubt, because of political opposition in Utah and Nevada, where the MX was to have been sited — but he has not come up with any long-term solution to replace it.

The reinforced-silo concept was supposed to tide the nation over for five or six years. Last December, it was decided to reinforce Minuteman silos instead of Titan silos as originally planned, but now this, too, has been dropped.

The Minuteman silos would be more difficult to reinforce, and Pentagon officials eventually agreed with congressional critics that, in view of the short time period of use, the value of the plan was questionable. In addition, alterations to the Minuteman silos would be a violation of the SALT I treaty, which has expired but is still being observed by the United States.

All these shifts in plans are casting serious doubt on the credibility of Pentagon experts. Last December, they felt it was necessary to spend $3 billion to reinforce the silos; now they do not. That sum may not seem like much to the Pentagon, but it works out to $13 for every man, woman and child in the country.

Wisely, the Reagan administration has continued to follow the "triad" concept by which the nation's nuclear defenses are divided among land, sea and air forces. Even if the land-based missiles become vulnerable, those based on submarines or in our strategic bombers will remain on guard. But over the long term, something must be done to protect the new MX missiles as they are gradually deployed to replace the aging Titan and Minutemen missiles.

The whole question is one that has troubled defense officials for years, and there is no easy answer. But it is a question that the Reagan administration must not put off much longer.

Reagan Chooses "Dense Pack" Basing Option for MX Missiles

Calling the MX "the right missile at the right time," President Reagan argued in a nationally televised address Nov. 22, 1982, that its deployment was necessary to counteract what he characterized as virtually an across-the-board Soviet nuclear arms advantage. Reagan renamed the MX the "Peacekeeper," remarking that it "still takes weapons to prevent war." As a result, Reagan said, he had concluded that "it is absolutely essential that we proceed to produce this missile, and that we base it in a series of closely-based silos at Warren Air Force Base near Cheyenne, Wyo."

Under this basing mode, commonly known as "dense pack," the 100 intercontinental ballistic missiles, each carrying 10 warheads, would be clustered 1,800 feet apart from each other in an oblong column of silos stretching 14 miles long and 1.5 miles wide. The basing scheme relied on the so-called "fratricide" effect, which would theoretically destroy incoming bombs in the event of a Soviet first strike. A Defense Department statement explained it this way: "Soviet warheads would hit and destroy some [MX] missiles in their silos, but those explosions would also destroy Soviet warheads coming alongside or behind the first group." According to the "fratricide" theory, still under debate among nuclear physicists, about 70% of the MX missiles would survive a nuclear attack and could then be launched.

The Providence Journal

Providence, R.I., November 24, 1982

President Reagan's choice of a "dense pack" mode for deploying the MX missile places the United States in a position to bargain hard with the Soviets on arms control.

This is the best that can be said about the basing plan that would place 100 of the new, larger and more accurate intercontinental missiles in a 14-mile strip of Wyoming.

Many critics are skeptical of the whole MX concept, a view reflected in the uncertainty about its approval by Congress, where financing of the missile survived by only a few votes as recently as July. But the President argued cogently Monday night in contending that only U.S. determination to build the new weapon system will persuade the Soviet Union to negotiate seriously on a general reduction in strategic nuclear arms.

While the administration has been skeptical itself about Soviet devotion to the arms control talks now under way — the START negotiations — new possibilities were suggested by Mr. Reagan's address and by the speech that Yuri Andropov, the new Soviet leader, made to the Communist Party's central committee. The President made some proposals for strengthening "mutual confidence" such as advance warning of test launches and major military exercises. Mr. Andropov made some positive references to detente and to "honest agreement" based on " reciprocity and equality" in arms levels.

These cautious feelers on both sides will have to be explored thoroughly in the talks at Geneva.

Meanwhile, the old impasse remains, with both sides possessing thousands of warheads that could devastate the other's country and probably much of the rest of the world. The old strategy of mutual assured destruction still holds, despite fears by U.S. strategists that the Russians have or soon will have the capability to knock out most of our land-based missiles in a surprise "first strike" attack.

That is where the MX comes in. Theoretically, the dense-pack array could survive even a heavy Soviet attack, because nuclear bursts from the earliest-arriving warheads would disable later arrivals. This theory is called "fratricide," because an enemy's striking power would be blocked by his own missiles. Again in theory, it would give U.S. authorities time to launch their remaining weapons in a retaliatory strike.

Critics of the proposal make some telling points. They contend that there is no certainty the fratricide theory would work; that the Russians would soon find ways of getting around it if it did work; and that, anyway, the dense pack plan is not needed because U.S. missiles deployed on Trident and other submarines are already available to retaliate against any attack. They point out, too, that the super-accurate MX, able to destroy Soviet land-based missiles in hardened silos, could be interpreted as a potential first-strike weapon.

The new plan, which replaces the Carter administration's "racetrack" basing mode, must pass the challenge of congressional opponents who brand it a reckless waste of billions. And it must then impress the Soviets with U.S. determination to build up defenses now considered inadequate. If it fails to do that, the arms race will only have been ratcheted to a higher and more dangerous level.

ALBUQUERQUE JOURNAL

Albuquerque, N.M., November 24, 1982

President Reagan believes he has found a home on the Wyoming range for a string of 100 MX missiles armed with 10 highly accurate warheads, each 10 times more powerful than the atomic bombs that devastated Hiroshima and Nagasaki.

But Congress might have second thoughts about giving the president ammunition for his Wyoming "Peacekeeper," a $26 billion shooting iron he wants to pack so there won't be a showdown with the Soviet Union.

The decision to deploy the missiles in a 14-square-mile grid is part of the president's $180 billion promise to close the "window of vulnerability" by beefing up the nation's nuclear forces by 1987. The system would help answer administration concerns that the Soviet Union will soon have the capability to wipe out this nation's land-based retaliatory capacity.

Congress, however, will have the last word in deciding if the United States will build the MX Dense-Pack system.

The MX system is designed to preserve into the next century the U.S. nuclear deterrent triad force — land-based intercontinental ballistic missiles, submarine-launched missiles and strategic bombers. It also is designed to replace aging, outmoded Minutemen and Titan missiles.

But when the United States already has at least 7,500 warheads on missiles at sea and on land, why add another 1,000? Strategists argue that additional warheads are needed to hit military targets — such as missile silos — in the Soviet Union. While the first round of incoming warheads might strike those targets, the most obvious consequence will be the killing of millions of people.

The administration believes the Soviets have the capability to use one-fourth of their 2,200 missiles to destroy each of the 1,051 U.S. Minuteman and Titan missiles in silos west of the Mississippi River.

The United States wants the Soviets to believe they can't attack our missiles without a massive retaliatory attack by U.S. nuclear weapons. That includes an assumption that if there is an attack, millions of Russians will be killed and their cities flattened.

Such knowledge should be a much stronger deterrent to launching an attack than an assumption that the other side's remaining missiles will be threatened.

No matter how much effort is spent in developing new tactics for basing and using nuclear weapons, their ultimate purpose remains the same — massive destruction and a reign of terror. Their effectiveness, however, is one of perception. If the Soviet Union believes the United States has the capability to inflict massive casualties and damage, it will be deterred from launching a first strike. The same rationale applies to the United States.

The primary purpose of any MX basing plan is to help the United States bargain from a position of strength in arms control negotiations in Geneva and Vienna.

Proponents of the MX Dense-Pack argue that no one can prove the system won't work. Whether it really works is of little consequence. There is no way to test what will happen when one nuclear warhead explodes on the surface as another falls close to the same target. Later incoming warheads might — or might not — be rendered ineffective. Neither the Soviet Union nor the United States is likely to risk an attack to find out what will happen.

Strategists on both sides have given us thousands of missiles, bombs and other weapons but they have not given us security. Will mankind be any more secure with the president's Wyoming "Peacekeeper"? If not, the administration will be wasting $26 billion at a time when the nation's $180 billion budget deficit is damaging the economy.

Fort Worth Star-Telegram
Fort Worth, Texas, November 28, 1982

The biggest question hovering over the fate of the proposed dense-pack deployment of the MX missile is not whether the weapons system could withstand a Soviet nuclear attack but whether plans for the system will survive the scrutiny of the U.S. Congress.

At least 30 plans for basing the MX missile have been fired off and shot down in the past nine years, and there is a distinct possibility that the dense-pack mode will suffer the same fate.

The opposition to dense-pack includes some who question the theory underlying the deployment mode, some who are generally opposed to any further nuclear arms buildup and others who consider it disgraceful to spend $26 billion on such a weapons system when the nation is experiencing such economic difficulties.

There also are suggestions that dense-pack would violate the principles of the unratified SALT II agreement to which both the United States and the Soviet Union have been more or less adhering.

Of the principal kinds of opposition, the first merits the most serious consideration. Unless satisfactory answers are given to the questions of those who doubt if the system will work, it would be difficult to justify such an expenditure, especially in view of the effect that it could have on exacerbating the nuclear arms race.

The idea is to harden the concrete silos — into which the 1,000 missiles would be inserted — enough to withstand five times the blast that the Minuteman silos can endure in the belief that the first Soviet missiles exploding upon them would destroy those coming afterward or throw them off course. That would leave many MX's operable for a relaliatory strike.

Some military experts and some members of Congress say that is an untestable theory. That is true. But it also is only in theory that an intercontinental ballistic missile can be fired over the North Pole and land on a target in the United States or the Soviet Union. There is no real way, short of war, to test that theory.

It should be incumbent upon the administration, however, to demonstrate that there is at least as high a probability that dense-pack will work as conceived as there is that a missile can be fired over the pole and hit a target. Congress cannot be expected to buy the proposal merely as a "do-something measure" to demonstrate this nation's will to close the so-called window of vulnerability.

Neither should dense-pack be approved only for the purpose of serving as a bargaining chip to be traded away in the strategic arms reduction talks. MX is a good weapon that could serve this nation well if a viable way of deploying it can be found. But it should not be deployed in such manner as to be as vulnerable as the Minutemen or in a way that requires augmentation by an anti-ballistic missile system to protect. An ABM augmentation clearly would set back the strategic arms reduction process.

The guarded optimism expressed by Sen. John Tower about dense-pack appears to be the proper frame of mind in which all members of Congress should approach the proposal. Tower, who described dense-pack as appearing to be "the best option available at the moment," advised his colleagues not to lapse into knee-jerk reactions to the proposals based upon third-hand information.

"There are technical questions that need to be resolved. I can give you my assurance that the Armed Services Committee of the Senate will delve into them carefully and fully and will hear from all sides of the issue and all shades of opinion on the efficacy of the system," said Tower.

The perceived efficacy of the system or lack thereof should determine whether dense-pack is really set in concrete or set aside like the other basing plans that preceded it.

The Pittsburgh Press
Pittsburgh, Pa.,
November 26, 1982

Ever since it was proposed in the early 1970s, the huge, powerful and reputedly superaccurate MX missile has been a weapon in search of a secure base.

Over the years the Air Force considered deploying it on airplanes, on railroad cars, on trucks, on small submarines and on freighters; in 4,600 concrete shelters in the West, and in existing silos that now hold the older Minuteman and Titan missiles.

One by one those schemes were discarded as unworkable, giving rise to the suspicion that land-based missiles are vulnerable and that there is no foolproof method of basing them.

★ ★ ★

Now, threatened with congressional cancellation of the MX, the Air Force has devised — and President Reagan has decided on — "Dense Pack," a plan to place 100 of the missiles in closely spaced fixed silos near Cheyenne, Wyo.

To rebut the objection that tightly bunched missiles are an easy target, the Air Force has constructed the theory of "fratricide" — the first incoming enemy warheads will destroy or deflect those following, so enough MXs will survive to inflict unacceptable damage on the foe.

But missile fratricide is only a theory. It is disputed by some experts, and it cannot be tested in practice.

Hence the American people are being asked to risk immense sums of money and their key deterrent on an unverified hypothesis.

The Air Force says Dense Pack will cost $26 billion. By 1989, when the 100 missiles are to be in place, inflation will have pushed that round figure up to $40 billion.

Then, chances are, we will be told that the MXs are threatened and that a $15-billion anti-ballistic missile system is needed to defend them. Then add $3 billion to dig dummy silos to deceive enemy spy satellites.

All in all, we are talking about a minimum of $58 billion for a weapon that may not work.

What's more, some experts concede that by the mid-1990s the Soviets will have devised ways of defeating Dense Pack. If so, a lot of money will have been spent for only a few years of deterrence.

★ ★ ★

In his television address on the MX, the president urged members of Congress "to listen and examine the facts before they come to their own conclusion."

Amen. This issue is vital, and it deserves Congress's closest scrutiny.

That scrutiny should include the option of substituting the Navy's Trident II missile for the MX.

Trident II can be made powerful enough and accurate enough to perform the MX's mission, and it has the advantage of being virtually invulnerable because it is based on constantly moving submarines.

©1982 MIAMI NEWS

The Philadelphia Inquirer
Philadelphia, Pa., November 24, 1982

Moving along from "missile, experimental" — MX — to operational form, it is to be called the "Peacekeeper." One hundred would be built and deployed in a tightly concentrated arrangement near Cheyenne, Wyo., the so-called dense pack system. The first would be in and ready by 1986. Each would carry 10 warheads about twice as powerful as the largest on the current Minuteman missiles, core of the generation-old U.S. land-based strategic nuclear weapons system. The six-year effort would cost an estimated $26 billion, in addition to $4.5 billion already spent on development.

Those are the nuts and bolts of the proposal put out by the Reagan administration Monday and elaborated by Mr. Reagan in a televised speech. It is, he argued, the cornerstone of his commitment that "nothing would have a higher priority in this administration" than arms control. "The prevention of conflict and the reduction of weapons," he reiterated, "are the most important public issue of our time."

A few hours earlier, Yuri V. Andropov, the new Soviet leader, was saying in a speech of his own that "mankind cannot endlessly put up with the arms race and with wars unless it wants to put its future at stake. The Communist Party of the Soviet Union ... does not want arms and the readiness to use them to become a gauge of the potentials of the social system."

But, Mr. Andropov went on, "Statements in which the readiness for normalizing relations [with the United States] is linked with the demand that the Soviet Union pay for this with some sort of preliminary concessions in different fields do not sound serious, to say the least. We shall not agree to this."

So, standing on either side of the window of opportunity opened by the coming of a new order in the Kremlin, the United States and the Soviet Union are rattling ever-bigger sabers while oozing ever-more-unctuous oratory about the most important single issue on Earth — the avoidance of mutually suicidal destruction.

Mr. Reagan's argument for the new system is, essentially, that the United States must have a powerful bargaining chip to jangle in order to draw the Soviets to a serious level of commitment at the arms-reduction bargaining table. That reckoning, which is not without arguable support in past experience, is based in turn on Mr. Reagan's contention that the Soviet deliverable nuclear might is fast approaching a point of being significantly greater than that of the United States.

The problem with the entire argument is that although modernity in military hardware has an undeniable enchantment, especially among those who do the work on and with it, the two superpowers' arsenals already are so massive that they are capable of wiping all life off the face of the Earth — several times over.

Why not, the skeptics demand, hold firm at present levels — endorsing, if it is politically useful, the idea of a freeze in development — and put all force on a truly substantive arms-control agreement? The assumption that must hold firm if that is to be practical is that the Soviet leadership is as aware as most Americans are of the terrible domestic economic drain of further arms development.

There is much persuasion in that argument. Most or all of it seems to have been cast aside by Mr. Reagan and his advisers. It is far from being ignored or rejected in the Congress.

Whether Mr. Reagan gets his "Peacekeeper" plan will depend on congressional funding. The last test of the MX system, in July, survived in the House by a razor-thin 212-209 vote. The President has made it clear that he will bring every power of persuasion and political influence to bear on the next rounds of votes.

Prudence, in the name of both the survival of the race and the health of, the U.S. economy, demands that he fail.

The Washington Post
Times Herald
Washington, D.C., November 24, 1982

A LOT OF THE critics of Ronald Reagan's MX program, like those who criticized Jimmy Carter before him, argue that *as there is no problem*, the MX is no solution—only a gigantically costly and provocative enterprise. We think they are wrong. There is a problem. But the newly proposed Reagan response does not resolve it. Rather, the so-called Dense Pack MX response may only serve to perpetuate the problem, to take the whole exotic business of who could do what (theoretically) to whom in a nuclear war to a further realm of expensive, but inconclusive, competition.

The problem to which the administration is responding is this: the Soviet Union has developed an arsenal of intercontinental ballistic missiles greatly larger both in numbers and in power than our own, and these have the capacity to destroy most of our own land-based missiles in a preemptive strike. Several administrations have concluded that neither the smaller American ICBMs nor our sea-based missiles or strategic bombers have an equal capacity vis-à-vis the Soviets' land-based ICBMs. The United States could not destroy them in a preemptive strike because we do not at present have enough weapons of either sufficient accuracy or weight to do so. So in this sense the Russians have a clear advantage. Defense critics who have spent the past 15 years arguing that the Russians would not possibly be so spendthrift or so foolish as to develop precisely the kind of arsenal they have in fact developed are singularly poorly placed, we think, to argue now that the Russians probably would be too scared to use it or that it probably wouldn't work or whatever the latest nostrum is.

True, this Soviet capability is theoretical; and the chances of its being exploited are extremely remote. But the problem is no less real for that. We ourselves have no doubt that in a dread nuclear war, the whole preposterous antiseptic "scenario" business (they do this, then we do that, so they do this ... and so forth) would be the first thing incinerated. There are more than enough nuclear weapons on both sides now to guarantee that there would be no winners, and the Russians, unless they are true idiots, must know this, too. But a situation in which a large and central part of one side's nuclear deterrent force is vulnerable, even in theory, to a wipeout attack by the other is a prescription for all that is worst in relations between nuclear-armed states: anxiety, suspicion, bullying, miscalculation, lack of confidence, over-quick responses, now-or-never thinking. It cannot be acceptable for this particular situation to persist.

The Reagan administration, like the Carter administration, now seeks to redress the imbalance in two ways. One is by deploying a blockbuster missile (the MX) that is big and accurate enough to do for the Soviet land-based missiles what their SS18s can do for ours: destroy them in their silos. The other is to make a portion of our land-based ICBM forces, specifically these new MX missiles, safe from such Soviet attack; we will try to bury them in such a manner and configuration that no SS18 can reach or destroy them all. That is what the Dense Pack burial plot is all about. It supersedes the Carter administration's peek-a-boo mobile MX scheme, a different kind of technique for trying to get some land-based ICBMs out of harm's way.

The best that can be said for all this is that conceivably it will have some impact on Soviet conduct as a pressure, as a "bargaining chip." That is clearly the hope some of the MX's adherents have for the new missile itself, a missile whose actual development and deployment after all would only create a world in which both sides, rather than one side, stood poised with weapons that it would pay to fire first. And, even then, even if this rather problematical basing scheme did work, what exactly would that mean? Work for how long and against what countermeasures and at what cost in inevitable further refinements and protections and schemes to dig ever deeper and build ever bigger and more?

There will be much argument now over what kind of walls can withstand what kind of shocks, argument over guidance and impact and explosion effects and the rest. And there will also be much argument, equally speculative, over what the effect of all this will be on Soviet policy. But in a sense these are tactical, short-term concerns that miss the major point. They assume there *is* some practical, economically feasible way of making our land-based ICBM force invulnerable to enemy attack. Everything we know about the subject suggests that this is not true. The history of the past couple of decades has in fact been a history of costly, escalating and eventually doomed efforts to bring about this much desired outcome. When something is pronounced vulnerable, from a carrier to an ICBM, it is somehow forbidden in certain quarters to accept that it is terminally vulnerable and to go on to better substitutes. Instead, the great attempt to add on features of "invulnerability" gets going.

That, it seems to us, is where this country is now in the great MX debate. Bright people (until they go into government, when they shut up) talk about alternatives to our huge land-based missile system, talk about putting more at sea, less on land, talk of developing some residual land-based mobile missiles but giving up this hugely costly and ultimately impractical insistence on protecting an essentially vulnerable stationary system. We do not presume to judge now the technological or tactical merits of the Reagan Dense Pack proposal, the yeses and nos of the smaller arguments to be resolved within the framework of its larger strategic assumption that the land-based missiles can be made secure. We begin somewhere else: we think the basic assumption is mortally wrong.

The Virginian-Pilot

Norfolk, Va., November 30, 1982

President Reagan says that a hundred MX missiles tucked deep inside "hardened" concrete ground silos and arranged neatly within a tidy rectangle one mile wide and 14 miles long will deter the Soviet Union from attacking the United States with its stupendous missile-killing SS-18 intercontinental ballistic missiles (ICBMs). There is no way to prove him wrong.

Many disagree with his characterization of "dense-pack" basing of MX missiles as the right weapon at the right time. But few would dispute that "Peacekeeper" — as the White House calls the weapon — would increase the uncertainties that attend nuclear warfare. These uncertainties have helped prevent a third global war.

Doubts about reliability and accuracy of ICBM forces have been a restraining influence. Neither we nor the Russians know for sure how well great numbers of ICBMs would perform if they were fired more or less simultaneously over the northern polar region. Missiles have been test-fired along the east-west axis, not north-south, and neither side has engaged in mass firings. How confident could a Soviet leader be that missiles sent toward the American land-based ICBM force would in fact destroy their targets, thus compelling a U.S. president to choose (1) surrender or (2) to choose massive nuclear retaliation against Russian cities, thus dooming American cities also?

Supporters of the Peacekeeper say it would protect the nation by assuring that a president could send U.S. land-based missiles to take out Soviet missiles, thereby forestalling an attack on American cities (sea-based missiles are not yet as accurate as land-based ones) and staving off military defeat. In theory, some of the Peacekeeper's missiles would survive a Soviet attack — flying debris from explosions of the first missiles striking the Wyoming target would detonate other incoming missiles in the air. The only way the Peacekeeper defense could be tested, however, would be in a nuclear war, which the Soviet Union, if the theory is sound, would not start.

Nuclear-tipped missiles that could swiftly reduce the superpowers to primitive and powerless states are a restraint on aggressive behavior. Retaining the balance of terror is essential. By deploying hundreds of huge land-based ICBMs, the Soviet Union put the lesser U.S. land-based missile force at risk and tipped the terror balance in its favor.

The Peacekeeper may be, as its critics contend, the wrong weapon at the wrong time. Yet another terribly expensive weapon, an anti-ballistic-missile system, could eventually be seen as necessary to counter a sophisticated Soviet strategy for defeating the Peacekeeper. Moreover, the Peacekeeper is designed to fill a gap scheduled to be closed by deployment of U.S. nuclear-tipped Pershing II missiles in Western Europe and 3,000 nuclear-tipped cruise missiles on bombers and other platforms. So it would be well if the United States could avoid spending billions of dollars for the Peacekeeper project. But Congress rarely disapproves major-weapons requests by presidents. Absent arms-control-reduction agreements that would make the Peacekeeper clearly superfluous, Mr. Reagan is unlikely to be disappointed.

The Boston Globe

Boston, Mass., November 23, 1982

The MX missile system recommended yesterday by President Reagan has only one conceivable purpose: to keep alive the fantasy of fighting "limited" nuclear wars with the Soviet Union.

This missile system has nothing to do with deterrence and nothing to do with defense. Defense implies protecting the lives and interests of the American public. This weapons system will put them at risk. The MX is a "war-fighting" system, plain and simple.

Superficially, the MX is designed to permit high-speed, tit-for-tat nuclear exchanges, with precise selection of targets in the Soviet Union. Given what is known about the effects of fear, time pressure and uncertainty in the human decision-making process, it is inconceivable that the MX missile system would ever be used in such a controlled way.

No US leader, whose ICBM force is as vulnerable to attack as will be the case under President Reagan's dense-pack scheme, will have the cool to fire a nuclear "limited option." Knowing that in about 20 minutes the entire $26-billion-dollar missile field stands a fine chance of being demolished completely, costing 100 missiles and 1000 warheads, he will take a deep breath . . . and shoot the works.

A *deterrent* is a second-strike weapon, designed to be capable of surviving a first strike by the enemy and of being available to strike back. The certainty of that costly retaliation dissuades the enemy from shooting first.

The MX missile based in a cluster is not a deterrent. It virtually *invites* the enemy to shoot first. It creates a giant bullseye, to be located in the southeast corner of Wyoming. Unlike submarine-based missiles, which are true deterrents because they are invulnerable to attack and can be held in reserve, 100 dense-packed missiles will sit on perpetual hair-trigger alert.

For six years the Pentagon has put forth a succession of wildly improbable MX plans. The pretense has been that the key factor in deciding how to deploy the MX was to be its survivability.

Now it all becomes clear. The joke has been on the public. The Pentagon and the Administration do not care about MX survivability. They simply want a tool suitable for attacking "time-urgent hard targets," the other side's military installations and command posts. They want the missile so they can play the counterforce game of toying with high-speed war-fighting scenarios.

The MX missile plan outlined last night is arms control disaster. Virtually all analysts agree that it will lead to construction of an anti-ballistic missile system that will violate the SALT 1 treaty. Futhermore, even as revealed last night, it appears to violate the limits on silos and launchers in both SALT treaties.

There are alternatives to the MX. One is phasing out land-based missiles which are inherently vulnerable. Another is the proposal of Rep. Albert Gore (D-Tenn.) to build a light, single-warhead missile that would not present such an attractive target for the Soviets and would not be suitable for nuclear war-fighting.

Weighing these possibilities will take time. But the responsible course for Congress now is clear: Block production funds for the MX.

The Courier-Journal

Louisville, Ky., November 24, 1982

GEORGE ORWELL would have been proud. Here it is, only 1982, and the voice from the Oval Office already sounds like 1984.

You remember 1984. It was novelist Orwell's horrified look at the future. When the book was published in 1949, many of us thought he was pulling our leg. It could never happen, we thought. We were wrong.

Monday night, President Reagan made the nightmare come true. In describing how he plans to locate MX missiles in a supposedly unassailable cluster, he also said they'll be re-named, "Peacekeepers."

George Orwell knew all about such practitioners of what he called *Newspeak.* The totalitarian ruler in 1984 was constantly filling the airwaves with his soothing message, "War is Peace."

Only the other day, Mr. Reagan was slandering the nuclear freeze movement by suggesting that it's inspired by our enemies. Now he has befouled the word "peace" itself by nailing it on a missile system whose destructive force defies imagination.

And for those who don't think the sound of war drums is a good way to signal peaceful intentions? How naive can they be? As President Reagan in his broadcast patronizingly told those misguided children who have written him to express fear of nuclear destruction, they need not worry. Peacekeeper missiles mean peace.

Unfortunately, children, that's not true.

If Mr. Reagan's strategy is carried out there will be 100 Peacekeeper missiles.

Each missile can carry 10 warheads.

Each warhead can generate a 500-kiloton blast.

In short, children, the 100 Peacekeeper missiles with their 1,000 warheads will have the total explosive power of 500 million tons of TNT.

If this is not the most destructive weapons system in history, it is close. But rest easy, children. Big Brother says it's all for peace.

If you buy that you are as gullible as your elders. They believed the President when he said he was for a balanced budget amendment. What they are going to get is a $200 billion deficit.

They believed him when he said he had a vision of American society as a "city on a hill." But he is leaving us dirtier, weaker, poorer, more diseased and more divided than any president in this century.

President Carter said the main concern of his daughter, Amy, was nuclear proliferation. What we need now are more such little worrywarts. The Reagan White House is leading us straight down the road to nuclear destruction while calling it "peace."

But that's right in line with what George Orwell envisioned in 1984. As he put it: "The Ministry of Peace concerns itself with war, the Ministry of Truth with lies, the Ministry of Love with torture and the Ministry of Plenty with starvation."

House Deletes MX Missile Funds from Appropriations Bill

Congressional unease over the proposed MX missile system was made clear Dec. 7, 1982 when the House of Representatives voted, 245 to 176, to delete $988 million in MX procurement funds from the fiscal 1983 defense appropriations bill. Fifty Republicans joined 195 Democrats in rejecting President Reagan's plan to deploy the missiles in the closely-spaced basing system known as "dense pack." The vote, on an amendment to the appropriations bill sponsored by Rep. Joseph P. Addabbo (D, N.Y.), eliminated funds earmarked for production of the first five MX missiles. The House retained $2.5 billion for research and development of the MX. Opponents of the missile had argued that the missile would cost too much, and would violate the two strategic arms limitations treaties with the Soviet Union. President Reagan reacted bitterly to the House vote, calling it "a grievous error" and a "grave mistake." Saying that the vote would demonstrate to the Soviets a lack of American resolve to rearm, Reagan declared: "Unless reversed in coming days, the vote would seriously set back our efforts to protect the nation's security and could handcuff our negotiators at the arms table. . . We should know from experience that the Soviets will not negotiate with us when we disarm ourselves."

The House action represented the first major setback for the President's $1.6 trillion, five-year plan for building up the nation's military forces. The first congressional vote on defense policy since the November congressional elections, it was thought to reflect a new reluctance among congressmen to continue increasing defense spending. It also marked the first time since World War II that either house of Congress had rejected a President's request for a major weapons system.

THE CHRISTIAN SCIENCE MONITOR
Boston, Mass., December 9, 1982

Let's dispense quickly with the media's stress on defeat for President Reagan in the House's vote against MX production. To use the language of warfare in the national effort to deter warfare is a thoughtless echo of the old politics of conflict when the age demands the new politics of cooperation. When both Congress and the White House are strenuously working for peace and security, the results may be mistaken, as Mr. Reagan says in this instance, or prudent, as they seem to many others. But they should not be read like bulletins from the battlefields all sides should be trying to forestall.

In this light the message from the House of Representatives is not so much surrender as go back to the drawing board. It left $2.5 billion in the budget for research and development of the MX. All it cut was close to $1 billion for missile production, a step that logically has to wait on successful research anyway. The Senate could restore this, leaving reconciliation to a conference committee.

But even such a former strong supporter of MX as Senator Nunn has reportedly shifted to favoring submarine missiles as the main strategic deterrent. The growing accuracy of such missiles is one factor calling into question the need for beefing up the land-based leg of America's traditional "triad" of land, submarine, and airborne deterrents.

Mr. Reagan had met the congressional deadline for an MX basing mode. But his "dense pack" array was different from three modes he earlier had described as most promising. He failed to make a credible case for its necessity, workability, and cost.

By withholding the customary blank check for military expenditures, the House at least gave the President a $1 billion hint that the Pentagon budget is not going to be exempt from scrutiny. Members may have been nudged in this direction by the election and the polls suggesting a public concern about excessive military buildup; its contribution to horrendous federal deficits; and the threat to security from a weakened economy whatever the level of arms. But they also have been learning of the waste and inefficiency in military spending still prey to pork-barreling and duplication among the services. And once more there are predictions of costs rising ever beyond present budget requests.

Republican Sen. Mark Andrews, who describes himself as a hawk, has said he was quite appalled when he dug into the Pentagon budget as an appropriations subcommittee member. He was reported particularly alarmed over a lack of quality control.

It is correctly pointed out that much of the military budget goes for personnel, operations, and maintenance, with presumably little room for reduction. However, even here there should be scrutiny. The pension system, with early retirement encouraging two-career privileges, is one candidate for review.

But still the Reagan administration has called for so much in the way of new weapons — $150 billion out of a $526 billion budget through 1984 — that Congress appears to have considerable opportunity to see whether more than the MX should go back to the drawing board. Through 1987 the requests for weapons production, research, and development total $600 billion.

Among expensive weapons being looked at by those in search of more cost-effective alternatives are the B-1B bomber, the M-1 tank, the F-18 fighter, and two large Nimitz-class aircraft carriers.

Americans do not want to deny their country any defenses genuinely needed. But neither do they, as their representatives in Congress are realizing, want to undercut the national economy with unnecessary military expenditures.

St. Petersburg Times
St. Petersburg, Fla., December 10, 1982

The reasons why the House voted against production of the MX missile were explained succinctly by Rep. Norman D. Dicks, D-Wash. "The gut sense of the American people is pretty strong," he said. "They think we have a real deterrent now, and they don't think the Russians are crazy."

President Reagan either does not comprehend public opinion on this question or thinks he can yet turn it around. Thus his uncommonly harsh attack on the House, which he accused of "sleepwalking into the future." Would he say the same of those three members of the Joint Chiefs of Staff who, it has now been admitted, had advised against proceeding with the "dense pack" deployment at this time?

The fact that the President was determined to deploy the MX notwithstanding the opposition of a majority of the Joint Chiefs raises very troubling questions. Is the MX a matter of military necessity or political ideology? Is it indeed true, as widely believed in the Army, Navy and Marines — the services whose chiefs voted against "dense pack" — that nuclear arms are getting too much money and conventional defenses too little?

THE HOUSE made the right decision and the Senate should do the same. The MX "dense pack" plan is worse than just another costly new system of questionable reliability. The deployment of these powerful new missiles in any fixed, land-based mode would step up the arms race significantly.

Despite Mr. Reagan's pique, the fact is that the House did not kill the MX program; it halted only the deployment in that particular plan while retaining $2.4-billion for research and development. That buys time — time for the United States and the Soviet Union to engage meaningfully in arms reduction talks, and for the United States itself to reconsider whether it needs any new 95-ton missile with 10 warheads under even the most threatening set of circumstances. If the problem is that U.S. Minutemen missiles are becoming vulnerable to a Soviet first strike, why not consider moving the Minutemen? Why not develop, as suggested by Sen. Gary Hart, D-Colo, some small but accurate new missiles that could be moved by truck within the boundaries of our military bases, in such a way that the Soviets could not be confident of destroying them in a surprise attack? Mr. Reagan himself ought to welcome the respite; it was a previous administration that bequeathed him a monster missile for which there seems to be no good use. Though he can't seem to appreciate it, Congress is offering to take him off the hook.

ONE GREAT PROBLEM with the scale of modern defense spending is that projects such as the MX acquire a momentum and a special constituency of their own. There are 13 major military contractors and 135,000 workers involved in the MX project alone. According to Common Cause, the public affairs lobby, political action committees representing 12 of those companies gave nearly $1.2-million to congressional candidates in 1982, almost twice their total in 1980. But for that, might the vote margin against the MX have been even larger?

Such circumstances underscore the truth of President Eisenhower's farewell address to the nation nearly 22 years ago, when he warned Americans to be on guard against the "acquisition of unwarranted influence, whether sought or unsought, by the military-industrial complex . . ."

THE SAGINAW NEWS
Saginaw, Mich., December 9, 1982

The U.S. House voted correctly, in our view, in rejecting funding for production of the "dense pack" MX missile system. But the 245 members who voted no did so for some very bad as well as good reasons.

Objections to the basing method were on target; the missile does little good as a deterrent if there is any question of its surviving a first strike. If President Reagan revives the MX, as he vows to do, he should either resolve the deep doubts on "dense pack," or propose another method.

Complaints about defense spending, in this case, were not appropriate; cost should be the last consideration when it comes to keeping the country safe.

But the worst anti-MX arguments were those which treated the whole thing as a joke.

One congressman dubbed the MX proposal "Reagatomics" and linked it to Reaganomics to explain his no vote. Another dredged up President Carter's plan to put the MX on rails and talked about whether Amtrak trains run on time.

It's not that the jokes were good or bad. It's that we have people in Congress capable, on a crucial judgment affecting the security of America, of reducing the decision to such a level.

The guilty ones all seemed to come from the Northeast. Maybe, for some reason, their constituents like this approach. In that case, the real joke is on them — and it's not funny.

THE BILLINGS GAZETTE
Billings, Mont., December 13, 1982

It's difficult to understand the machinations of foreign policy, and harder yet to comprehend foreign policy and weapons systems.

The two seem to be inextricably linked, and finding a thread of logic there is like looking for the peanut under a con man's walnut shell.

Witness, first, the consideration of the neutron bomb development during the Carter administration.

The neutron bomb was heralded as the ultimate answer to the Soviet Union's heavy weight military force poised over Europe's eastern borders.

The neutron bomb, a limited nuclear weapon if there is such a thing, was believed to be the answer to this Soviet threat.

The neutron bomb is a destroyer of people, not things. And rather than creating landscape that glows in the dark years after the explosion, the effects of the bomb clear up rather quickly.

This one weapon, delivered — that's one of those nice, soft military words — by medium and short-range missiles, and presumably by other means, too, would have offset the vast superiority of Soviet weaponry and men in Eastern Europe.

But the neutron bomb was never developed. The reasons were simple. It is a relatively clean nuclear weapon — if there is such a thing as a clean nuclear weapon — and it is relatively limited in scope. In other words, it could be used without endangering civilians in nearby cities.

Because the possibility existed for its use, it could not be developed.

Think about that for a moment.

We couldn't develop the neutron bomb because we might use it.

Opponents said that if the Russians invaded Europe, we might be tempted to use this nuclear weapon to save our good neighbors there. That possibility could trigger nuclear war of the worst kind, they said.

Just having the bomb might offset the delicate balance in Europe, a balance that military leaders were telling us was tipped too heavily in favor of the Russians.

So we turned away from this limited, defensive weapon and opted for the unlimited, offensive MX missile system.

The Carter administration suggested looping the MX missile system across two western states so the Soviets wouldn't know what target to strike in a nuclear attack.

That idea wouldn't sell.

Then the Reagan administration suggested putting all the eggs in one basket near Cheyenne, Wyo. on the theory that Soviet missiles would destroy each other trying to hit our MX missile silos.

But during the discussion of this new plan other factors about the system surfaced.

Some people say that building the MX missile is an act of war in itself, an economic war that is already being waged against Russia. The theory is that the Soviet economy will buckle under the pressure of trying to match this new weapon system that is viable because we won't ever use it.

Think about that for a minute.

The United States, in the worst recession in recent years, is trying to buckle the Soviet economy by building a weapons system America can't afford.

The only thing that makes sense in this scenario is the House of Representative's decision to scrap MX.

But that decision makes too much sense to find any credence in the world of foreign policy and weapons systems.

TULSA WORLD
Tulsa, Okla., December 9, 1982

TUESDAY'S vote by the House of Representatives deleting from the defense spending bill nearly $1 billion for the MX missile system should serve as a warning to the administration: The time has come for political compromise. The president should accept a delay in construction of the MX missile in return for Democratic help in making further cuts in domestic spending. Such an approach is necessary if the government is to reach consensus on overall federal spending.

First District Rep. James R. Jones recently told columnist David Broder that neither a Republican nor a Democratic budget can pass the House.

"The only hope is a broadly based bipartisan coalition ... or we're going to be in a real mess," Jones said.

The Tulsa Democrat has long argued that defense spending should be subject to the same scrutiny as social spending. A budget proposal which tries to make all budget cuts in one area — either defense or domestic programs — will fail.

Tuesday's action by the House cut $988 million out of a defense budget of $232 billion, and left intact some $2.4 billion in research and development funds for the MX and its basing system. That is a sensible course. Construction of the missiles can easily wait a year without severe harm to U.S. security.

The President says MX is needed to convince the Soviets to get serious about arms reduction. But continuation of the research and development effort should serve notice to the Soviets that now is the time to take serious steps toward arms reduction.

The president could help his cause by accepting the House's action and working toward a compromise budget which will limit federal deficits but still boost the nation's defenses.

Newsday
Long Island, N.Y., December 9, 1982

When the House voted against production funds for the MX missile this week, it gave Rep. Joseph Addabbo a victory on the floor that he hadn't been able to win in the Appropriations Committee or in his own defense subcommittee. But Addabbo knows Washington too well to stop fighting just yet.

"We won the battle, but we haven't won the war," the Ozone Park Democrat said after the House backed the $988-million deletion he had proposed. As a matter of fact, the MX's opponents haven't even won their 1982 campaign. Although the House cut MX production money from the defense appropriations bill, it left in nearly $2.5 billion for MX research and development.

What's more, President Reagan has already indicated that he'll pull out all the stops to keep MX production funds in the Senate version of the bill. Presidents don't like losing congressional votes on major new weapons systems, and the vote in the House wasn't even close; the count was 245 in favor of Addabbo's amemdment, 176 against.

No doubt Reagan will continue to insist that a refusal to fund the MX "will seriously set back our efforts to protect the nation's security." But the claim lost much of its force when the chairman of the Joint Chiefs of Staff testified yesterday that three of the four service chiefs had opposed the administration's "dense pack" plan for basing the missile.

The administration is more or less reduced to arguing that the MX program, while not a *military* necessity, has to be built because the Soviet Union won't negotiate arms reductions without it. The trouble with that argument is that a militarily dubious weapon simply isn't much of a bargaining chip.

The President should make no mistake — to use a favorite phrase of his: The House did not vote Tuesday against a secure United States. It voted against wasting money on a missile that the Pentagon still hasn't figured out how to protect against a Soviet attack. Far from "disarming unilaterally," as Defense Secretary Caspar Weinberger charged yesterday, it was demanding better evidence that arming would improve U.S. security.

As Reagan pointed out after the vote, the United States hasn't built a new land-based missile system in 15 years — and with good reason: The Minuteman system it built in the 1960s has been upgraded repeatedly, and priority has been given to less vulnerable weapons, such as air-launched cruise missiles.

The MX vote doesn't prove Congress won't spend what's needed on defense. It just shows Congress wants its money's worth.

The Seattle Times
Seattle, Wash., December 9, 1982

PRESIDENT Reagan views the MX missile as representing "America's margin of safety" in deterring a war with the Soviet Union.

If the MX and only the MX can provide that margin, then all other aspects of the MX debate are irrelevant. Let's deploy it as quickly as possible, and hang the cost.

But a sizable majority of the House of Representatives does not share Reagan's certitude. Neither do a number of the nation's top defense experts.

It seems likely that the 245-176 vote this week to delete from the budget nearly a billion dollars intended to build the first five MX missiles was prompted largely by two factors — uncertainty over the workability of the "dense pack" MX deployment system chosen by the administration, and a growing feeling that the overall defense budget is top-heavy with big-ticket strategic hardware.

To Paul Warnke, former strategic-arms negotiator, dense pack is a "silly answer to a nonexistent problem." William Perry, former undersecretary of defense for research and engineering, and only recently an MX supporter, maintains that "no fixed deployment, no deployment of missiles at fixed, known locations, is survivable."

Reagan rightly notes that the U.S. has not built a new land-based missile system in 15 years. But this country has made remarkable gains in modernizing the other two legs of the strategic "triad" — in tested sea-based and air-based weapons.

We think Congress should continue to appropriate research and development funds for the MX and its basing mode, while denying production funds until the administration can make a more convincing case.

That conclusion is based in part on the published fears of some of this country's most experienced defense specialists, including three former defense secretaries, to the effect that Reagan's planned $1.6 trillion, five-year, military-spending plan has gone overboard on big-ticket strategic systems, which eventually would put at risk the nation's overall military effectiveness.

The Dallas Morning News
Dallas, Texas, December 13, 1982

THE vote against the MX in the House allows the majority of the honorable members to show that they are strong for peace. Whether it shows that they are as strong for sense is another matter.

Indeed, the author of the amendment to delete funds for the first five missiles described it himself as "a symbol."

In the words of Rep. Joseph Addabbo: "I think in a way it is a message to the administration that the people aren't going to give the Defense Department everything they want."

There's not much doubt that this message was sent. But it may not have been necessary. The administration has already made clear its recognition that no blank checks will be available to the Pentagon. The people so signified in November.

But the people have also signified as strongly, if not more so, that they do not trust the Soviet Union and that they want defenses strong enough to keep their freedoms secure.

The main flaw in this "send-the-White-House-a-message" vote is that it also sends the Soviets a message. Whatever the symbol may be, the substance is that five missiles come off the production line a year later than expected. This kind of vote affects metal, as well as messages.

In the metal line, the Soviets have never ceased upgrading and increasing their nuclear strategic arsenal. Throughout the time when the United States was spending its military budget on the Vietnam war, when the Carter team was killing off or postponing new weapons systems, the Russians steadily added to the number and accuracy of their nuclear weapons. Whatever messages they may have been sending during the 1960s and 1970s, the Soviets have also been turning out actual hardware.

In contrast, consider the actual hardware used by the major part of our own nuclear force, the force we and the rest of the world depend upon to deter Soviet use of their might. Our strategic force is armed with a bomber that was produced during the Truman administration and a missile ordered by Eisenhower.

The members of the House could find any number of items on the defense budget that could be killed for message-sending purposes without vitally affecting the strength of the country. What they did choose was one of the few state-of-the-art weapons we have almost ready for taking off the drawing board and putting into production.

While we are playing "do we or don't we," the Soviets are not only producing city-busters like the SS20 by the hundreds, they are emplacing them in launchers aimed at the major cities of Europe. Their symbols have real warheads.

Judging from the reaction of the Europeans lately, we'd say that the Soviet method sends messages even more effectively and convincingly than does the legislative symbolism favored in the House of Representatives.

Before Congress makes final decisions on what messages it plans to send, how and to whom, it would be wise to think about that.

Reagan Promises Flexibility on Arms Control, Wins MX Funds

The House and the Senate approved twin resolutions May 24 and 25, 1983 to release a total of $625 million in research and development funds for the MX missile system. The vote in the House to unfreeze the funds, to be used for development, basing studies and flight testing, was 239 to 186. The Senate vote of 59 to 39 was made possible by the support of moderate Republicans, many of whom had voted against the missiles in 1982. The positive votes were regarded as a significant victory for President Reagan, who had carried out an intensive lobbying effort to overcome congressional resistance. Part of that effort included sending separate letters to the two houses of Congress, assuring them of his willingness to explore "alternative approaches" in nuclear arms reduction talks with the Soviet Union. This strategy was prompted by the growing movement in Congress to tie the fate of the MX missile system to Administration initiatives on arms control.

The Detroit News
Detroit, Mich., May 26, 1983

Congressional approval of President Reagan's plan to deploy 100 MX missiles is clearly a major victory for the administration.

Indeed, the margin of victory suggests Congress may be returning to some semblance of bipartisanship in matters of foreign policy and national security. If this is so, it would be a far more important development than the procurement of a single weapons system.

In the Democrat-controlled House, the MX plan was approved by a 53-vote margin. Many Democrats, who voted to block funds for the missile last year, reversed their decision after a frantic lobbying effort by the White House.

Mr. Reagan made a strong case for the missile — both as a deterrent and as a bargaining chip in arms negotiations with Moscow. The president made it clear that congressional opposition to his defense buildup was encouraging Soviet intransigence.

Many Democrats in Congress, including House Majority Leader Jim Wright of Texas, were also impressed by the endorsement of the bipartisan Scowcroft Commission, which recommended the basing mode approved by the president.

We only wish the spirit of bipartisanship had prevailed in Michigan's delegation. Unfortunately, all 13 Michigan Democrats who voted on the issue opposed the missile. While most of these votes come as no surprise, we are disappointed that Detroit's Dennis Hertel, St. Charles' Donald Albosta, and Trenton's John Dingell also voted no. All three have in the past expressed support for a stronger national defense.

The tradition of bipartisanship in the conduct of foreign policy is vitally important, not only because it provides a sense of continuity, but because it prevents the issue of national security from becoming a political football.

One of the most disturbing developments of recent years is the tendency of the left wing of the Democratic Party to exploit such issues for political gain. Whether it is a demagogic attack on the president's Central American policy or a simplistic "no nukes" approach to arms control, such ploys damage far more than Mr. Reagan's re-election prospects.

Responsible Democrats, like Mr. Wright and others, have an obligation to steer their party clear of these shoals. They might begin by reminding some of their Sandinista-supporting younger colleagues of the political fallout that might occur if, for example, Communists gain further footholds in Central America.

It was the Left that suffered most when a previous generation asked, "Who lost China?"

Reno Gazette-Journal
Reno, Nev., May 25, 1983

House approval of more funds for the MX missile creates mixed emotions.

It still has no permanent home. After years of debate over improbable basing systems, the MX seems destined for old Minuteman silos, which cannot protect it from sophisticated new Russian missiles.

In addition, many experts say that by the time the missile is produced, it will be militarily outdated.

But, at the same time, the Soviet Union is forging rapidly ahead with its own multiwarhead missiles. Can the United States afford to wait? The president thinks not.

Mutual arms reduction seems mandatory if the world is to avoid a nuclear holocaust. Yet the president argues that the Soviets will not bargain if the United States does not defend itself. Common sense says each side has more than enough weapons — but common sense does not always sway international negotiations. The appearance of power may be as important as power itself.

At the least, one must hope the president was sincere when he told Congress that development of the MX would proceed jointly with arms talks, that it would be used to "reduce the level of nuclear weapons and strengthen the peace."

That must be the ultimate goal, without question.

THE ATLANTA CONSTITUTION
Atlanta, Ga., May 30, 1983

Republican Sen. Dan Quayle of Indiana spoke for a good many tepid supporters of President Reagan's MX plans last Wednesday when he said: "I hope the administration doesn't open champagne bottles today, because the MX debate is just beginning. If something doesn't happen on arms control, (the White House) could eventually lose the MX."

Few congressional votes to approve a major new weapons system have come freighted with as many misgivings as those expressed last week in the House and Senate endorsements of the MX basing plan and authorizations of $625 million for its development and testing. Clearly, these decisions constitute only a skirmish in the continuing struggle over the MX.

Next month the battle will be joined in earnest when Congress takes up the question of authorizing more than $2 billion in MX production funds. In anticipation of continuing lawmakers' resistance, the White House has promised to follow up on its pledges to make public newly drafted proposals for the Strategic Arms Reduction Talks (START) in Geneva, which resume later in June.

These are certain to be countered by attempts from both sides of the aisles to exact new arms-control concessions from the president's men, "to keep their feet to the fire," as GOP Sen. Nancy Kassebaum of Kansas put it.

Knotting the process of weapons reductions inextricably with a frightful and destabilizing engine of destruction like the MX bespeaks both an element of ironic black humor and bipartisan despair over an administration which has seemed bent on attempting the unattainable: strategic superiority over the Soviets at any cost.

Another aspect of the MX debate — its dubious value as a Geneva bargaining chip — was a key to the plan's clearing congressional hurdles last week. But it is problematic whether the Soviets may be more forthcoming when faced with the prospective deployment of this admittedly vulnerable weapon or, instead, will respond by putting more SS-18 and SS-19 intercontinental missiles into service.

With all its warts, it's a wonder and a shame that the MX attracted the support that it did. But President Reagan is now on notice that Congress expects serious and flexible approaches from him and his START bargaining agents — and will exert whatever leverage it can command to keep him toeing the mark.

The Evening Gazette

Worchester, Mass., May 25, 1983

The MX missile will be designed to drop 10 nuclear warheads on 10 different targets 6,000 miles away with unerring precision. Each missile will hit within 500 yards of its target.

One hundred MX missiles will be able to blast 1,000 separate targets to radioactive smithereens. The MX will be an awesome weapon, perhaps the most deadly ever devised.

The problem with the MX missile is that it may be obsolete before it is deployed. The other side also has huge precision rockets tipped with nuclear warheads. An MX missile in a fixed silo would make a tempting target. One warhead fired by the other side could knock out 10 of our warheads.

Some analysts say that the day of the huge, fixed-base, multi-headed rocket is almost over. We should, they say, be developing small, single-headed rockets that could be moved around and would not be such an inviting target.

The Reagan administration agrees with that assessment. So does the Scowcroft Commission, which recently produced a nuclear weapons policy for the U.S. government. But the administration and the commission also want the MX as a "bargaining chip," to use in arms negotiations with the Soviets. That implies that we will threaten to build it but will not actually build it.

At immediate stake is $625 million that the House approved yesterday for MX research and development. Given the size of military budgets these days, $625 million is not a huge amount. But it would be enough to give the MX lobby a foothold.

Instead of starting down that $30 billion road, wouldn't it make more sense to develop the small mobile missile that everyone agrees is needed?

And wouldn't it make even more sense to speed up development and construction of the Trident II submarine and its new D-5 missile? That missile, with up to eight warheads, will be able to target enemy installations from 5,000 miles away, and it will have none of the basing problems that have plagued the MX. It is supposed to be ready for deployment by 1986, about the time when the MX will be.

These conflicting considerations illustrate why it is so hard for even the staunchest supporters of the military to get excited about building the MX missile and putting it in fixed concrete silos that will be vulnerable to a Soviet first strike.

The MX more and more looks like the wrong weapon for the late 1980s and 1990s. It doesn't even look like a heavy bargaining chip.

Los Angeles Times

Los Angeles, Calif., May 29, 1983

President Reagan won a significant victory last week when both houses of Congress voted by substantial margins to keep the MX missile project alive. As 19 Republican senators were at pains to say after the vote, however, the President should not mistake what kind of victory it was.

The Republican senators, in a letter to the President, warned that the favorable vote did not represent a consensus in favor of the MX as such. Instead, they said, the vote reflected congressional willingness "to proceed with a militarily controversial program in exchange for a strong commitment to proceed seriously and immediately" with efforts to reach an arms-control agreement with the Soviet Union.

These members of the President's own party were saying, in effect, that they and other senators will feel free to vote against the MX later if he does not appear to be keeping his side of the bargain.

The missile project can still be blocked by a "no" vote on either the military authorization bill, which comes before the House next month and includes a $4-billion request for the MX, or the follow-up defense appropriations bill.

What the House and Senate did last week was lift an earlier freeze on the expenditure of $65 million for flight testing of the big missile and $560 million for engineering and development.

Considering that the MX appeared to be on its deathbed just a few weeks ago, this is an impressive achievement. It was made possible by the President's acceptance of recommendations made by the Scowcroft commission of experts, and by his stated willingness to accept proposals by several influential members of Congress for new, more innovative approaches to strategic arms reduction.

The Scowcroft commission proposed the deployment of 100 MX missiles, each of which would be armed with up to 10 nuclear warheads, in existing Minuteman silos as a stopgap measure. But the panel emphasized the importance of limiting warheads instead of missiles in future arms-control agreements in order to encourage a movement away from big multiple-warhead missiles.

Consistent with this purpose, the commission also urged the development and deployment of a mobile single-warhead missile.

Reagan endorsed the Scowcroft panel's recommendations. Under pressure from key lawmakers, he specifically promised to alter the Administration's negotiating stance in the START talks, which will resume in. June, to incorporate the new emphasis on limiting warheads instead of missiles. He also embraced, in principle, the "build-down" idea under which both major powers would destroy two old strategic warheads for each new one deployed.

The bargain was struck and, as a result, many members of Congress voted for the MX last week despite misgivings as to the wisdom or need of proceeding with the project.

The Reagan Administration is probably correct when it argues that congressional approval of the MX would strengthen its hand in trying to persuade the Soviet Union to agree to meaningful reductions in both nuclear warheads and delivery systems.

The question is whether the Administration is really willing to use the MX as a bargaining chip. There is considerable concern that the Reagan Pentagon would in fact be very reluctant to bargain the big missile away.

In our view, though, two other objections to the MX are more persuasive:

—At a time when restraints on defense spending are unavoidable as a result of the economic situation, it is militarily more important to enhance this country's conventional, non-nuclear fighting capabilities than it is to build the MX.

—A big MX-type missile, with its multiple warheads, is not the best strategic weapon anyway; this is especially true if the Administration is serious about negotiating warhead limits.

As such things are calculated, the Soviets would need only 200 warheads aboard 20 or 30 missiles to destroy 100 MXs armed with 1,000 warheads. But they would require 2,000 warheads aboard a much larger number of missiles to destroy the same 1,000 American warheads if they were deployed aboard the single-warhead Midgetman missiles proposed by the Scowcroft commission.

Leaving aside the greater ease with which a small missile can be made mobile and thus harder to hit, the arithmetic alone makes the Midgetman more survivable.

The more sensible course would be to abandon the MX project entirely, but move forward with development and deployment of the Midgetman missile on a much more urgent basis than the Scowcroft commission proposed.

The Miami Herald

Miami, Fla., May 28, 1983

FIGURE this one out: On May 4, the House of Representatives voted 278-149 in favor of a negotiated freeze on nuclear weapons. On May 24, the same House voted 239-186 to begin development of 100 MX missiles, which will add 1,000 strategic nuclear warheads to the U.S. arsenal. The two votes are self-evidently contradictory. The MX is utterly without justification, but that didn't stop the Senate from duplicating the House's action the next day, 59-39.

The MX is to be a 10-warhead missile designed to knock out Soviet land-based missiles. President Reagan originally insisted that it was necessary to close the alleged "window of vulnerability." Earlier this year, however, the special commission that Mr. Reagan appointed, headed by Gen. Brent Scowcroft, admitted that there was no "window of vulnerability." So as not to embarrass the President, however, the commission kindly urged building the MX anyway, saying it would be a useful "bargaining chip" in arms-control negotiations.

The "bargaining-chip" rationale for embarking on a colossal new weapons system is the last refuge of intellectually bankrupt hawks. History gives every reason to expect the Soviets to respond to the MX by building new weapons themselves. Rather than being a bargaining chip leading to arms control and reductions, the MX is more likely to be a spur leading to a new cycle in the arms race. Besides, the Soviets face over 9,000 U.S. strategic nuclear warheads already, some 1,000 more than they possess. If that is not sufficient motivation to bargain toward arms control and reduction, why would 1,000 more warheads be?

The MX was intended to replace the Minuteman missiles, which are deemed vulnerable in their silos. But the MX, after years of debate over where they should be based, will be put in the "hardened" old Minuteman silos, where they will be nearly as vulnerable.

The MX will give the United States a new capacity to knock out the Soviets' land-based missiles. Though it is unthinkable that the United States ever might launch a sneak nuclear attack, the MX gives Washington the *capacity* to strike first to knock out most of the Soviet threat. That capacity gives Moscow a new incentive — especially in a crisis — to fire first, before a sneak MX attack could destroy their ability to fight.

During a crisis, because the MX is in vulnerable Minuteman silos, the same kind of "use them or lose them" psychology surely would crop up in Washington. Whether either side intends to use such foolhardy reasoning is secondary to the fact that the MX increases the dangerous possibility of such decisions.

The House vote approved spending only $625 million to begin testing the MX. But $4.8 billion more will be needed this year alone, and eventually the 100 MX missiles will cost at least $20 billion. In an era when Federal deficits menace the nation, when defense spending is exorbitant, spending $20 billion on a vulnerable weapon that enhances prospects of nuclear war surely is a mistake, if not insane.

House, Senate Approve MX Missile Production Funds

The Senate July 26, 1983 approved $2.6 billion in funds for the production of 27 MX missiles. The House July 21 had approved $2.2 billion for the production of 21 missiles. The votes were part of the action in both houses on the defense authorization bill for fiscal 1984. The House defeated, 220 to 207, an amendment that would have deleted funds for MX production. Seventy-three Democrats and 147 Republicans were on the pro-MX side. Eighteen Republicans and 189 Democrats favored the amendment. Twenty House Democrats who had voted in favor of MX testing in May switched sides and voted against production. The most influential of those who changed sides, House Majority Leader Jim Wright, explained that he had grown tired of compromise and of "spending more and more for the military, giving more and more to the wealthiest few." Rep. Albert Gore (D, Tenn), warned the Administration that it would have "to come through with more movement on arms control" or risk losing future Democratic support for the MX. The House and Senate bills would go to a conference committee to resolve their differences.

(In September, both houses passed a bill worked out by House-Senate conferees, authorizing $187.5 billion in defense spending for fiscal 1984. The bill included funds for the initial production of 21 MX missiles.)

The Wichita Eagle-Beacon
Wichita, Kans., July 22, 1983

The administration should see this week's House approval of building and deploying the MX missile in its proper light. The narrowness of the 220-207 vote, and the reservations expressed by many of the members about the whole MX concept, indicate the fight for the multiple-warhead missile is far from over. And unless the administration is able to show some substantial progress in arms reduction talks — tied to its claim of the MX being a "bargaining chip" at Geneva — there's every likelihood enough members will switch their vote to one denying actual construction and deployment money.

One senses that when the House earlier voted the funds for flight testing of the MX, a vote that succeeded only because of the support of several House moderates, the president and his advisers thought the latter were "on board," and their future support was assured. As Rep. Dan Glickman's vote this week showed, that's not necessarily the case.

The Pentagon also must show some seriousness, in the meantime, about the development of the Midgetman, a single-warhead missile that would be far less destabilizing in the U.S.-Soviet missile standoff. Though that was another crucial element of the Scowcroft Commission report that linked development of the MX with arms control, there's been a tendency to neglect it.

So the administration has its work cut out if it's to keep the conditional support it so far has received for the MX. In a very real sense, the final determination may come not in the U.S. Congress, but at the arms control table in Geneva.

The Birmingham News
Birmingham, Ala., July 29, 1983

The Senate was wise and acted responsibly in voting down Sen. Gary Hart's proposal to strip $2.5 billion for the MX "Peacekeeper" missile from the $200 billion defense bill. The House has already approved funding the MX.

Alabama's Sens. Howell Heflin and Jeremiah Denton are to be commended for voting to keep the MX in the budget by voting against the Hart amendment.

President Reagan has thus won another battle in the war to make the Peacekeeper a key element of U.S. nuclear deterrent forces. But the war has not yet been won. Hart warns that he will try again to stop construction and deployment of the Peacekeeper when the Senate considers appropriation measures which authorize actual spending for the missile.

Americans should be well aware by now of the arguments pro and con for the MX. The missile was designed to bring U.S. nuclear forces to a par with the Soviets' and to provide the U.S. with a deterrent against a first strike by the Soviet Union.

The Pentagon and U.S. nuclear control advisers also say the missile is vital to bringing the Soviets around to negotiate seriously. Without the MX, they say, Moscow has no real incentive to bargain, since it already has superior forces.

The new MX is part of the president's overall program to upgrade and modernize all of America's military forces. But it is one of the key parts, intended to provide a shield, the absence of which would make the question of a stronger Air Force, Army and Navy moot.

Mr. Reagan's modernization program is a fulfillment of his pledge during the presidential campaign to strengthen U.S. defense forces in response to public concern that previous administrations had let our military strength deteriorate dangerously.

The Boston Herald
Boston, Mass., July 22, 1983

THE HOUSE placed the national interest above political interest when it approved the spending of $2.5 billion to begin production of the first 27 MX missiles for our defense network.

The 220-207 vote was close, and the fact that it was can be traced directly to the high-powered pressure and arm-twisting to which the members were subjected by diehard opponents of the MX. But though there were defections, enough remained steadfast in support of the missile system to enable it to survive this most serious threat.

The outcome is being saluted as a victory for President Reagan, and to a considerable degree that is correct. There is more to it than that, however, because this was a victory for those who believe in peace through strength.

It is a truism that only those nations whose defenses are either actually weak or are perceived to be are likely to be attacked by their enemies. People who are strong survive.

We are now in a far more dangerous era, confronted by a far more powerful and menacing adversary than we were when the Japanese tried to take advantage of our seeming weakness to attack Pearl Harbor. Had this latest vote on the MX gone the other way, then our Soviet adversary would have been given reason to believe that it can undertake its aggressions without any fear of us, that it can produce, deploy and aim its arsenal of nuclear missiles at the United States, at all the nations of the free world if need be, without running any great risk of retaliation.

That would be a most inviting situation for them, and a most threatening one for us, because it would lead the Soviet military brains to believe that they'd been handed an advantage that would make a nuclear war winnable.

Now, however, they cannot be all that sure. The House has seen to that.

THE PLAIN DEALER
Cleveland, Ohio, July 29, 1983

We the people are soon to be the proud owners of the MX missile, not necessarily because we want it, but because, like automobiles, it seems we need it. Agree or disagree, it makes no difference. We have it, and it appears as though we had better make the best of it.

Are we making the best of it? That is a question of paramount importance, especially since the Senate recently voted $2.5 billion for the deployment of the first 27 multiple-headed, intercontinental ballistic white elephants by the end of 1986.

If you spend $10,000 on a car, odds are you will have it rustproofed to protect it. Even if you hate the idea of owning a car, you are going to protect your investment from the first-strike capabilities of corrosion. But the same does not seem to hold true for the multi-billion-dollar expenditure for the MX missile. It is to be placed in existing Minuteman silos in Wyoming and Nebraska that will be hardened, but nevertheless vulnerable to increasingly accurate Soviet missiles.

If you spend $10,000 dollars on a car, you are going to be sure you are getting not just what you want, but what you need. Again, that is not the case with the MX. There is no guarantee that the MX, poorly hidden, will supply the political leverage Washington needs to further its goals in the European theater, which are (A) to get NATO countries like West Germany to accept deployment of Pershing IIs and cruise missiles, and (B) to get Great Britain and France to upgrade their own atomic arsenals. And there is no indication that the Soviets, although perhaps loosening up a little at the Geneva arms negotiations, are going to take seriously a threat which is vulnerable to first-strike, especially when that threat is from the primary leg of the nuclear triad, the massive and powerful ICBMs.

The Scowcroft Commission contended that vulnerability should be viewed from the context of the full triad—land, water, and air based atomic arms. But stools are like chains, they are only as strong as their weakest part. Hence the commission has it backward: The triad's vulnerability should be viewed from the context of its independent legs.

The Air Force puts together a compelling argument for the MX, saying that counter-military targets in the Soviet Union (their missile bases, communications systems, command bunkers, etc.) have been super-hardened, and that the MX provides the strategic and political threat to those targets that we need. Opponents of the system say that the MX system is escalatory, because the combination of the threat it poses and its vulnerability are inducements to a Soviet first-strike.

Take your pick, it no longer matters. Because we are going to have the MX whether we want it or not. In the heat of surrender, however, we should not dismiss the fact that the MX is alarmingly vulnerable, and that the expense of the system will be staggering. If the government is so intent on buying this car—and in terms of atomic passion, President Reagan has eyes for no other—it should be careful to protect it. That means rethinking both the conclusions of the Scowcroft Commission and the strategic theories of the Air Force.

St. Louis Globe-Democrat
St. Louis, Mo., July 28, 1983

Senate approval of deployment of the first 27 MX intercontinental ballistic missiles represents another significant victory for President Reagan in his program for modernizing and upgrading the U.S. strategic missile force.

By a 58-41 vote, the Senate defeated an amendment by presidential contender Gary Hart, D-Col., to delete $2.5 billion in production and deployment funds for the 10-warhead MX, which is designed to partially offset the Soviet advantage of having more than 600 MX-size missiles already deployed.

Last week, the House narrowly approved authorization funds for developing and deploying the MX by a vote of 220 to 207.

In both the House and Senate, the votes on the MX were largely along party lines, with Republicans voting to produce and deploy the missile and most Democrats opposing MX totally.

Under the plan approved, the MX missiles would be deployed in existing Minuteman silos. Opponents claim that the original plan of the MX was to deploy it in such a manner that it was invulnerable to Soviet attack, and that deploying it in existing silos abandons this concept.

The opposition is correct in this charge, but these critics ignore the fact that the MX is needed as soon as possible, not 10 or 20 years from now, to offset the enormous Soviet advantage. Moscow already has eight-warhead SS-18 and SS-19 super missiles deployed and targeted on U.S. missile silos.

In arms negotiations, the United States must have "bargaining chips" if it hopes to get an agreement for a major reduction in strategic, long-range missiles. If Sen. Hart and others running for the Democratic presidential nomination were to have their way, the U.S. would be in an extremely poor bargaining position because it would have unilaterally abandoned the MX without requiring any similar action by the Soviet Union.

So far President Reagan and his supporters in Congress have been able to beat back the determined Democratic opposition to the MX, the B-1 bomber and other major components of his strategic weapons modernization program. But the partisan attack by Democrats on these important deterrents to nuclear war is certain to become a major issue in next year's presidential campaign.

Democrats such as Hart who may be counting on heavy public support for their continuous opposition to strategic arms modernization could be in for a disappointing surprise.

The Honolulu Advertiser
Honolulu, Ha., July 29, 1983

A majority in Congress agree with President Reagan's premise that America needs the MX missile to meet the challenge of newer and more accurate Soviet multiwarhead weapons, and as a bargaining chip to help negotiators in Geneva.

But in approving production funds for the MX, the Congress is taking a dangerous gamble. Weapons systems have a way of taking on a life of their own. Should the Geneva START negotiations fail or move more slowly than the production schedule of the MX, this country could be stuck with a missile that could increase the likelihood of a nuclear first-strike.

The MX, like the missiles that it is supposed to match, is a huge multiwarhead weapon capable of destroying Soviet launchers in the ground. MX opponents fear that fact could convince Kremlin leaders that a first-strike was necessary to ensure the safety of their missile fleet.

Similarly, opponents are concerned American officials could be tempted to use the MX as a first-strike weapon because the silos it is housed in are not capable of withstanding a Soviet attack.

The irony, of course, is that the MX was developed because of the improved accuracy of Soviet weapons. But so far engineers have not been able to figure out how to develop a silo "hard" enough to adequately protect the missile.

We hope approval of the MX will convince the Russians to negotiate a new arms control agreement. By the same token, the Reagan administration must be willing to take the negotiating process more seriously than in the past.

For if progress is not made in Geneva, MX missiles could be rolling off the assembly lines in the not-too-distant future. And once it is actually deployed, the awesome weapon will be that much harder to get rid of.

THE SACRAMENTO BEE
Sacramento, Calif., July 31, 1983

Once again the House and Senate have caved in and voted for the MX, despite the fact that, to gain these votes, the MX has been turned into a system which no longer meets anyone's criteria for a useful weapon. Enough Republicans in the Senate nonetheless voted for it in order to avoid embarrassing the president in his dealings with the Russians. And enough Democrats in the House — like Sacramento's Vic Fazio — voted for it in the misguided hope that the president would reciprocate by stepping up his arms control efforts. Neither is much of a reason to unleash on the world a nuclear weapon so inherently destabilizing that it will set the balance of terror on a hair trigger.

The MX, in its latest incarnation, will be based in Minuteman silos. In other words, a multiheaded weapon powerful and accurate enough to threaten Russia's strategic forces will be based in silos so vulnerable as to make the MX useless as a retaliatory force. That combination can only provide the Russians with an incentive to strike first and our own military with good reason to adopt a launch-on-warning strategy itself. The danger of an accidental Armageddon is thus multiplied. And in any real political face-off, mutual deterrence would be transformed, by the mere existence of the MX in their silos, into mutual encouragement for pre-emptive action.

Last May, there were Republicans who were willing to risk this to gain a "bargaining chip" that could be traded away in arms control negotiations. And there were Democrats who calculated the risk was worth the deeper commitment to arms negotiations that they thought they'd won from the president for their votes. They were both wrong. And just how wrong should have been obvious by the time the latest MX votes were taken. Secretary of State George Shultz, in the meantime, had said quite plainly that arms control is not the "dominant" concern in relations with the Soviets, and Pentagon hard-liner Richard Perle had acknowledged candidly that the administration intends to push ahead on the MX, the B-1 bomber, the Stealth bomber and the Trident II submarine missile even if an arms reduction agreement is reached.

But Congress voted for the MX anyway. The dwindling contingent of pro-MX Democrats now say they are trading their votes — which have become critical — for Perle's demotion and the dismissal of Ed Rowny, Reagan's current chief arms negotiator who seems to be more interested in preventing than signing an agreement. But while such a change of personnel would be something of a relief, it wouldn't change the administration's underlying priorities or the MX's overwhelming dangers. Those who are still trying to use their MX votes as bargaining chips are playing as fast and loose with global security as those who think the MX itself will be used that way.

There will be one more chance to give the $20 billion MX program the burial it deserves, next month when Congress will be called on to officially appropriate the money for the first 27 missiles that its last vote merely authorized. It's an opportunity that ought to be seized to drop the political game-playing and speak plainly for nuclear sanity.

Pittsburgh Post-Gazette
Pittsburgh, Pa., July 30, 1983

The MX ballistic missile has had a harder time than most weapons finding a justification for its place in the U.S. arsenal. So it wasn't surprising that when the Senate voted for the weapon's deployment this week, members were adopting a major nuclear weapon system that bears no clear relationship to meaningful nuclear deterrence.

Approval of this orphan system was undoubtedly good news to weapons contractors who will earn some $4.6 billion from the missile program, as well as to hawkish types who believe that any weapon automatically adds to national security. Even so, the Senate decision and that of the House earlier were major disappointments for believers in a consistent view of defense doctrine — and prudence in spending defense dollars.

After this decision, it can be argued that Congress has voted for a marginal reduction in the stability of U.S. nuclear forces during any future showdown with the Soviet Union. That is because it is likely that the MX with 10 nuclear warheads would be a target for the Soviets of even higher priority than the remaining force of Minutemen with three nuclear warheads each. Moreover, the MX threat may prompt the Soviets to respond by adding additional warheads to their intercontinental ballistic missiles.

Yet the primary problem with the MX remains the extraordinary difficulty of fitting the MX into the overall scheme of U.S. nuclear defense strategy.

Throughout its long debate, defense officials have promoted MX as the answer to the problem of Minuteman "vulnerability." In theory, the Soviets have sufficient numbers of land-based warheads to cripple the present U.S. ICBM force, and MX in its original conception as a mobile missile was meant to correct that situation.

The problem of vulnerable land-based missiles, however, has defied solution, and weapons designers have been unable to place MX missiles in bases that will be invulnerable to Soviet attack. So when the MXs are deployed, they will be as susceptible to a Soviet "first strike" as are the present Minuteman missiles.

Congress has thus voted $4.6 billion on a missile system that everyone — including the blue-ribbon Scowcroft Commission in a report to the president earlier this year — agrees will not fulfill the mission for which it was originally designed. Worse, though conceived as a bulwark in the American posture of nuclear deterrence, MX may actually detract from it.

After a long, tiresome debate, some members of Congress have taken equivocal refuge in the argument that the deployment of MX missiles will function as a useful "bargaining chip" in negotiations with the Soviets for arms control. But that's a dubious proposition.

The deployed MXs may simply prompt the Soviets to expand the size of their already substantial land-based missile force. Consequently, despite its great cost, MX will probably turn out to be no significant incentive for the Soviets to strike a bargain in arms control — and provide no additional margin of benefit as a nuclear deterrent.

Army Says 6 of 10 Divisions Unready; Skilled Personnel Shortage Cited

A confidential Army report, made public Sept. 8, 1980, revealed that while all six of the Army's combat divisions based overseas were rated "combat-ready," six of the Army's 10 combat divisions in the continental U.S. were rated "not combat-ready" in December 1979. A division consisted of 16,500 to 18,000 soldiers. The "not-combat-ready" rating meant that it would take a unit about six weeks to be completely trained and equipped for combat. According to the report, none of the 10 home divisions was rated fully ready for combat. Officials explained that divisions located in Europe and South Korea had drained manpower and resources from divisions at home. Pentagon officials Sept. 8 said the most recent ratings of the home divisions were still about the same as those in the December report.

While the Army in general had shortages in weapons, equipment and funds, the report said, the primary reasons for the low unit ratings were shortages of personnel. In particular, many sergeants were leaving the service because they could find better paying jobs in civilian life.

Gen. Edward C. Meyer, Army chief of staff, had recently described the home-based units as a "hollow army." Meyer Sept. 5 ordered 6,000 sergeants in Europe and 900 in South Korea reassigned to units in the U.S.

The News and Courier
Charleston, S.C., September 14, 1980

It is possible to find some reassurance in the Pentagon's contention that it is not uncommon in peacetime to have Army combat divisions that are not ready to fight. As Assistant Secretary of Defense Thomas B. Ross says, it is common practice in all armed forces to man units in peacetime at levels lower than would be required in wartime. If, as Secretary Ross says, only a third of the Soviet army's divisions are combat ready, then perhaps there is little reason for alarm over a recently-publicized evaluation that found only 10 of 16 United States Army divisions combat-ready.

Still, the evaluation should not be brushed aside as signifying nothing out of the ordinary, because these are not ordinary times. Tomorrow might be more extraordinary.

In peacetime many Army units are not up to authorized strength because of recruiting problems, funding problems, or other problems. It should be remembered, however, that the readiness of divisions is evaluated on more than manpower. Equipment and training figure in, too.

It also should be remembered that comparison with the Soviet army can be misleading. If only a third of the Red Army's divisions are combat ready, that still means an estimated 33, 34 or so, about three times as many as the United States Army counts as prepared to fight.

It is encouraging, on the other hand, to know that the Army's six divisions stationed overseas are rated combat-ready, despite disturbing reports in the last year or two of drug problems, declining re-enlistment rates, and questions of effectiveness of all-volunteer units.

It is essential that divisions overseas that would go on alert first in event of trouble be in top shape. It is essential that those units at home selected for rapid deployment be ready also, but two of the three are not, according to the latest Army evaluation, which wasn't announced, but leaked out.

The Cleveland Press
Cleveland, Ohio, October 2, 1980

Had the Iraqi-Iranian war escalated last month into a crisis requiring some kind of U.S. military response, it's problematical how the Navy — which is the front-line force in that area of the world — could have performed.

A "fleet readiness report" for September found that only six of the Navy's 13 aircraft carriers and only 94 of its 155 air squadrons were rated ready for combat.

One of the carriers, the John F. Kennedy, which has been buzzed by Libyan planes in the Mediterranean recently, was rated combat-ready with major deficiencies.

The September figures continued a trend of steadily worsening readiness levels over the past year.

The Air Force seems to be in better shape. Other reports showed that 111 of the 123 squadrons in the Tactical Air Command were combat-ready last month. But six of 10 Army divisions in the United States were not ready for combat.

In the Navy's case, the problem is not a deficiency of equipment but a shortage of experienced technicians. The lure of better-paying civilian jobs and a normal home life are causing what Adm. Thomas B. Hayword, chief of naval operations, calls a "hemorrhage of talent."

In the other services, "hardware" seems to be more of a factor. Because of the cost and scarcity of missiles, for example, Air Force pilots may go for years without firing one in practice.

It is currently politically popular to talk about pumping up the nation's military might with such big-ticket items as "Stealth" bombers and MX missiles.

But some of the billions for defense both parties are promising to spend had better be devoted to the unglamorous fundamentals of upgraded pay, equipment maintenance and weapons practice.

Otherwise we could find ourselves with the ability to destroy the world, but powerless to put out a brushfire war.

The Union Leader
Manchester, N.H., September 16, 1980

Did you know the U.S. Army is a "Hollow" shell?

Despite all the hoopla about President Carter hiking defense funds, six of 10 combat divisions in this country were not combat ready last December.

This startling disclosure is made in a secret Army report in the New York Times.

Army Chief of Staff Gen. Edward C. Meyer told Congress it all added up to a "hollow Army."

Believe it or not our Army forces around the world are "sharing" the shortages in personnel.

Some 6,900 sergeants serving in Europe and Korea were reassigned to U.S. units. Despite all this, Secretary of Defense Harold R. Brown asks for further cuts for recruiting and training in the 1982 Army budget.

No wonder the Communist world laughs.

BUFFALO EVENING NEWS

Buffalo, N.Y., October 3, 1980

When only six of the Navy's 13 aircraft carriers are considered ready for combat, and when about a quarter of the nation's tactical fighter squadrons are reported unfit for combat, it is past time to ask how our defense forces could have been allowed to drift into so perilous a condition.

Assistant Secretary of Defense Thomas B. Ross, the Pentagon's chief spokesman, insists that the overall condition of the nation's armed forces today is better than it was five years ago, with the exception of personnel.

But that exception, of course, is a key element in the alarming picture of a military establishment all of whose services — the Army, Navy, Air Force, Marines and Rapid Deployment Force — would face severe handicaps in sustaining any actual military action.

In the Army, according to a New York Times survey, most of the 11 divisions in the United States are well below full strength. Training has been cut back because of a shortage of men, money and resources. Constraints on the use of fuel and delays in replacement of ammunition and parts greatly limit training in the use of weapons.

While the Navy's fleets and submarine forces may remain generally superior to those of the Soviet Union, senior officers fear that shortages of key personnel have dangerously weakened the Navy's ability to man all its vessels in a crisis. In only three years, the retention rate for men trained to operate nuclear reactors, for example, has dropped from 57 to 25 percent.

The Air Force is little better off. Shortages of spare parts, lengthened delivery times for crucial items and dramatic drops in reenlistment rates raise serious doubts about the Air Force's ability to sustain any combat. Since 1955, the reenlistment rate for crew chiefs, who oversee aircraft maintenance, has dropped from 72 to 51 percent.

Similarly, the nation's new deployment force, its commander acknowledged, could not "go to the Middle East right now and defeat a Soviet force equivalent to what they have in Afghanistan," about 80,000 troops.

The lagging state of the nation's defense forces is attributable to various factors, but chief among them is the loss of trained specialists and sergeants because of low pay and allowances. Many soldiers are eligible for food stamps, and many non-commissioned officers are said to moonlight on second jobs to maintain their families. Low pay and family instability are chief causes of the Navy's deplorable retention rate.

The Pentagon's latest readiness figures reflect conditions that have been developing since the early 1970s, when America ended its involvement in Vietnam. Today's Army consists mainly of new and inexperienced soldiers and officers. Moreover, nearly half of the enlisted recruits entering the Army under the all-volunteer program score in the lowest intelligence grouping that can be accepted for service.

* * *

Yet only recently has the Carter administration begun to recognize the urgency of military manpower problems, and its relief measures have fallen short of what is required to keep qualified persons in the service. Some senior Army commanders, blaming congressional committees as much as the White House, contend that military dollars have been spent on misplaced priorities. They say funds for costly new weapons procurement gobble up the resources available for maintenance of existing weapons and retention of men with qualified skills.

Whatever the reasons for the weakened state of the nation's combat readiness, no task facing the next president and Congress is more crucial than that of ensuring that planes don't have to be grounded or ships kept in dock for lack of adequate manning. A nation that cannot properly man its weapons is a nation ill-prepared to back up its allies and vital interests around the world.

Los Angeles Times

Los Angeles, Calif., September 14, 1980

Three facts stand out in The Times' in-depth assessment of U.S. defense preparedness as reported in a series of articles during the past week: (1) This country's armed forces are marginally capable, at best, of meeting U.S. defense commitments that are vital to our own security and that of our allies; (2) to overcome the deficiencies, defense spending will have to increase; (3) spending more money is not by itself the answer—it is also necessary to spend defense dollars on the right things.

The Soviet Union's massive buildup of strategic nuclear forces is a cause of genuine concern, but can be dealt with through a prudent mix of arms-control measures and deployment of new missiles in the next few years. Deficiencies in America's conventional, non-nuclear military capability will be harder to correct.

By the peacetime standards of the past, this country has awesomely powerful defense forces. But so have the Russians.

The U.S. armed forces would be hard put to carry out President Carter's pledge to resist Soviet aggression in the Persian Gulf area or, for that matter, to stop a non-nuclear Russian thrust into Western Europe without triggering an all-out atomic war.

To a substantial degree the deficiencies in the armed services are an inevitable result of allowing the Soviet Union to outspend us for most of the past two decades.

According to American intelligence analysts, military spending in the Soviet Union is 35% to 50% higher than in the United States—and has been for years. At the same time, the end of the draft has forced this country to allocate more of its military budget for pay and benefits in order to attract volunteers, and less to the actual development and procurement of military hardware.

One result has been to accentuate the instinctive American reliance on technology to offset the numerical Soviet advantage in many areas of military power. And, indeed, the U.S. defense industry has developed remarkably accurate "smart bombs" and missiles, and is working toward a virtually computerized battlefield.

Many U.S. military men are worried, however, that this country's military hardware is becoming too complex for our own good.

Field commanders complain that Pentagon planners are too inclined to "gold-plate" new weapons—to keep deferring actual production and deployment in order to get the latest technology. In effect, the United States is always preparing for a war some years hence at the expense of its ability to fight a come-as-you-are conflict right now.

In an era of tight budgets, a side effect of the emphasis on ever newer, ever more expensive technology is scrimping on spending for spare parts and maintenance, with debilitating effects on combat readiness.

Air-to-air rockets and antitank missiles are far more effective than old-fashioned machine guns and bazookas—when they operate properly. But their cost is so high that fighter pilots and tank crews get appallingly ittle practice in firing the weapons that they would be expected to use in combat.

Compounding the situation, many military men worry that there is a dangerous gap between the growing complexity of American weaponry and the educational level and skills of the soldiers and sailors who will operate them.

Army generals, in particular, fear that it may be discovered, too late, that overly sophisticated weapons won't actually work under battlefield conditions of dirt, smoke, bad weather and possible radioactivity.

Meanwhile, in order to avoid scaring off peacetime volunteers, basic training in the combat arms has been shortened and softened; when the weather gets too hot, for example, strenuous activity is curtailed.

Finally, this country's airlift and sealift capabilities are insufficient. Despite the Administration's hoopla about the "rapid-deployment force," for example, it would take two months to move all three brigades of the 82nd Airborne Division overseas.

The Carter Administration, shocked into awareness by the Soviet invasion of Afghanistan, has begun trying to correct what's wrong with the U.S. armed forces. But it will take time, money and a greater wisdom and consistency of purpose both in Congress and the Pentagon than have been evident in recent years.

However, the fact that the problems are finally receiving critical attention in Congress, the press and the military establishment itself is a hopeful sign.

The Honolulu Advertiser

Honolulu, Ha., September 15, 1980

At a time when battlefield weapons have become so sophisticated that computer training is needed to operate many of them, the most important link in America's military forces remains the men and women who serve in uniform.

That point finally appears to be hitting home in Washington, though the pressure of an election year probably has as much to do with official receptivity as concern for our defense posture.

Congressional passage and President Carter's approval of an 11.7 percent pay hike and improved benefits package for military personnel is a needed step to insure better retention rates in the armed services.

INDEED, ONE OF the most serious problems faced by the military is the loss of experienced enlisted personnel and officers.

The Navy, for example, is short 21,000 chief petty officers and capital ships are being found "not combat ready" because of manpower shortages.

And this problem is not limited to the Navy. In all of the services, men and women with critical skills — technicians, pilots, electronic specialists and the like — are leaving in large numbers for better paying jobs in the private sector.

A recent American Enterprise Institute report found that perhaps as many as 275,000 military families live below the official poverty level.

The report also found that over the past eight years service pay has increased 11 percent slower than the inflation rate, and has actually fallen 20 percent behind comparable civilian pay.

Given those statistics, it is not surprising that about 32 percent of all servicemen and servicewomen earn less than the minimum wage.

THOSE GRIM figures should improve somewhat with the passage of the $790 million pay bill.

An important element in it is the Nunn-Warner amendment, named for the Senate sponsors Sam Nunn and John Warner.

Their benefits package increases sea and flight pay, improves subsistence allowances and increases housing allowances and gives the Pentagon authority to increase reimbursement rates for moving expenses.

Behind this optimistic news, though, is the necessity to eventually bring military pay and benefits to roughly par with civilian wages.

That was one of the original aspects of the all-volunteer military, but over the years the concept was found to be politically expendable.

It has taken a presidential election, and a heated debate over our defense readiness, to resurrect the idea.

PERHAPS the biggest defense challenge of the coming years will be to maintain that impetus. After all, the most elaborate and sophisticated weapons are of little value if there are not enough talented and trained personnel to operate them.

And they will not remain in uniform unless they are assured of adequate pay and benefits.

ST. LOUIS POST-DISPATCH

St. Louis, Mo., September 30, 1980

Following closely behind the revelation that only six of the 10 Army divisions in the continental United States are fit for combat, the disclosure of a confidential Navy report that only six of the fleet's 13 aircraft carriers are ready for battle is further unsettling evidence of the military's deteriorated state of preparedness. An exhaustive analysis of the Pentagon's readiness to wage war, appearing last week in the *New York Times* presents a corroborating picture of the services: depleted in essential equipment, starved for replacement parts and losing essential personnel at an alarming rate.

Of the nation's ability to respond to an all-out military challenge from the Soviet Union, the commanders interviewed by the *Times* remain confident that the forces at their disposal are adequate. Certainly, no nation could embark on nuclear war against the U.S. and hope to survive. But the ability to fight protracted conventional wars in more than one theater is something about which the generals and admirals are considerably less certain.

Only a few representative statistics are necessary to demonstrate the truth in one admiral's description of the manpower loss as a "hemorrhage" of skilled personnel. In the Navy, for example, the retention rate of skilled petty officers and pilots is now 30 percent. It retains just a quarter of the men trained to operate the nuclear reactors that power more than 100 ships. The Air Force retains just 25 percent of its pilots and navigators — far below what it needs to remain strong — and re-enlistments of crew chiefs, electronic technicians and other specialists are similarly depressed. The reasons are not difficult to fathom. In one case described by the *Times*, an enlisted man making $8,000 a year was offered a comparable job by a civilian firm that would pay $30,000. A pilot, as a captain, earns $25,000 to $28,000 in the Air Force. For an airline, his salary would be several times that amount.

Beside these findings, what passes for a discussion over defense among the presidential candidates sounds both shrill and irrelevant. While the accusations, boasts and recriminations fly over such nonissues as the Stealth bomber, the alleged vulnerability of the U.S. to nuclear blackmail and who is to blame for the Persian Gulf war, the real defense questions go unaddressed. The blame for the decline in readiness cannot be laid at the doorstep of any single administration or Congress.

Recall, if you will, the leading national debates over defense over the past dozen years. (We exempt here for obvious reasons the one pertaining to the prosecution of the Vietnam War.) All concerned expensive and glamorous weapons projects, reflecting the misconception that greater expenditures on hardware would result in greater national security. As Congress and administrations argued over the antiballistic missile system, the Trident submarine, the C5A transport, the B-1 bomber, the cruise missile, the supercarrier, the MX missile and so forth, readiness was slipping away.

Surely, it is not too late for a more informed, more relevant defense discussion to begin. Given the reality that the military will never be able to match civilian salaries in highly specialized fields, how can the decline in re-enlistments be halted? How can an aging and inefficient industrial base be made to furnish spares in needed quantities? How much money should be dedicated to operations and maintenance to assure adequate training and unit combat readiness? And most important, what are the nation's realistic overall defense requirements? What do the candidates have to say about these matters?

THE DAILY OKLAHOMAN

Oklahoma City, Okla., September 12, 1980

THE startling disclosure that seven of the 10 U.S. Army divisions stationed in this country are not rated ready for combat — the result of painstaking research and journalistic enterprise by The Oklahoman's Jack Taylor — is more than just another alarming commentary on the state of our defenses.

The exclusive information first revealed in Taylor's articles, documenting manpower, training, maintenance and spare parts deficiencies, has become the basis for subsequent commentary by other major news media and wire services. Thus the true story of our military weakness is being brought home to all Americans in the midst of a presidential election campaign.

Obviously, the subject is a key issue in that campaign. But the importance of the issue goes far beyond who is elected president in November.

It is the world situation and growing Soviet strength which make it imperative that the United States be perceived abroad as a strong power, capable of using military force to deflect any threat to its national interests.

Among the more disturbing aspects of the decline in our combat readiness is the marked deterioration of preparedness of all 10 Army divisions based in the continental United States. In December, 1977, all 10 were rated fully combat ready. Two years later, none was.

The 82nd Airborne, part of the vaunted Rapid Deployment Force now being assembled, slipped only from fully to substantially ready. But the 1st Infantry and 4th Infantry (mechanized) slid to only marginally ready (indicating major deficiencies). All the others, including the other two divisions of the RDF, were rated "not combat ready" as of last December.

There is no way President Carter and his administration can escape ultimate responsibility for this shocking mess. Carter's recent conversion to advocacy of increased defense spending came after he spent the first three years of his term cutting the Pentagon's budget and can-

celing or postponing programs recommended by the Joint Chiefs of Staff.

Yet it was Carter himself who, as recently as last February, stated the importance of our defense preparedness in these words: "Military readiness may be the best guarantee that military force need never be used. Even in the nuclear age, we must be prepared for conventional conflict — and deterring such conflict may depend on the timely availability of our forces."

Our history is replete with examples of the cost of being unprepared. Until a U.S. naval force could be built and deployed to the Mediterranean by President Thomas Jefferson, this country was forced to pay ransom to secure the release of Americans held prisoner by the Barbary Coast pirates of North Africa. In modern times, World War II could have been ended much sooner had this country not been so ill-prepared on land, sea and in the air when we were swept into that global conflict.

The present world situation does not permit a great nation the luxury of ignoring its military readiness to deal with whatever contingency it may confront on short notice. The widespread view that the United States is a paper tiger, a nation once respected but now ridiculed, makes its own perils to peace.

Our Army is small in numbers by comparison with those of the Communist bloc and must rely on superiority in equipment, training, tactics and the historic initiative of the American soldier. But that very ability to improvise, which has turned the tide so many times in the past, itself comes from familiarity with military equipment and with the tactics by which it may be employed.

More than ever before, today is a time when this nation simply cannot afford to ignore George Washington's counsel in his farewell address, when he warned his countrymen to take "care always to keep ourselves by suitable establishments on a respectable defensive posture."

The Seattle Times

Seattle, Wash., September 16, 1980

IT IS MORE than a little disturbing for the U.S. Defense Department to report that six of its 10 Army divisions are not prepared for combat here in the United States. It renders the word "defense" rather hollow.

Nor is it soothing for an assistant secretary of defense to ho-hum that American intelligence agents estimate that two-thirds of all Russian divisions are below combat strength as well. After all, the Soviets have America outmanned five to one.

There is a ray of encouragement in the Pentagon report that all of the Army's six divisions deployed overseas are fit and ready for combat. Four are stationed in Europe, one in Korea and one in Hawaii.

U.S. Rep. Samuel Stratton, chairman of the House Armed Services Committee, put the matter succinctly when he said that the situation "means we are going to have trouble projecting our power in any area where there might be a challenge."

The Dispatch

Columbus, Ohio, September 12, 1980

DEFENSE Secretary Harold Brown's explanation for those Pentagon ratings that pronounced six of the Army's 10 domestic combat division unfit for battle was classic military gobbledygook:

"As the balance goes," Brown said, "you have to give some on the reinforcement capability to please the training capability. I think it is inevitable that this mixture of functions will cause you to have some units less ready than others."

Translation? Army divisions based in this country serve both as a source for reinforcements to the six divisions overseas, and as training units for new soldiers.

That makes it "inevitable," to use Brown's word, that some domestic divisions would be shy on, say, the number of non-commissioned officers called for in tables of organization.

The secretary also was critical of the criteria used to measure combat readiness. As far as Brown is concerned, those standards may be too strict. And he hastened to add that all of the Army's overseas divisions (in Europe and in South Korea) have met the requirements and have been pronounced battle-ready.

Nonetheless, we find the whole affair far from reassuring. If Brown's tortured explanations for the reports that captured headlines across the nation last week are taken at face value, the American public is left with yet another question: If the Pentagon's fitness reports are all that meaningless, why hold the evaluation tests in the first place?

Recruitment, Retention of Personnel Weighed in Military Pay Raise Bills

One of President Reagan's campaign promises had been to increase the pay of military personnel sufficiently to give the all-volunteer military a better chance of survival. In his defense requests presented to Congress in 1981 Reagan included a July 1 increase of 5.3% and a regular cost-of-living increase of 9.1% already scheduled for Oct. 1. When added to the 11.7% pay boost already effected in 1981, the pay raises would total over 25% in less than a year.

The Reagan Administration wanted the July pay raise to apply equally to all military personnel regardless of their rank, in order to aid recruitment and show national support for the military. Congress split over this issue, however, with the House bill setting a 14.3% across-the-board pay hike and the Senate passing pay raises for enlisted personnel ranging from 7% for recruits up to 22% for senior sergeant majors. (Both houses eliminated the additional July pay raise.) Proponents argued that a graduated pay raise would provide incentive for junior personnel to seek promotion and for senior personnel to remain in the service. These lawmakers argued that retention rather than recruitment was the major problem facing the armed forces. Others feared that the lower pay accorded to new recruits in the Senate bill would force a return to the draft, or that the quality of the new recruits would suffer. In the final bill, officers were given an across-the-board 14.3% raise and pay raises for the enlisted men ranged from 10% for recruits to 17% for senior enlisted personnel.

The Seattle Times
Seattle, Wash., March 23, 1981

IT WOULD be a mistake for President Reagan to support a Pentagon proposal to use tax forgiveness as an incentive to attract and keep top-caliber military personnel.

Obviously a strong military requires skilled, highly qualified personnel. But in recent years low salaries, unchallenging work, low morale among the troops, and a variety of other factors have combined to drive many of the best-qualified soldiers back into the private sector.

Recruitment levels are up, but the dropout rate among military men and women remains a matter of concern. Salary levels apparently bear a significant share of the blame for depletion of the services. Many low-ranking military people qualify for public assistance. Service in the nation's armed forces should be rewarded with more than food stamps.

Still, Defense Secretary Caspar Weinberger's recommendation that the first $20,000 of a military person's salary be tax-exempt would set an unfortunate precedent that could spark similar requests from thousands of other government workers. The exemption could also weaken the nation's tax base and further distort the tax burden on individual citizens.

New steps must be taken to make military service more attractive. But they should be in the form of direct incentives, including higher salaries.

The Washington Post
Washington, D.C., March 25, 1981

DEFENSE Secretary Caspar Weinberger's suggestion to exempt the first $20,000 of military pay from the federal income tax is the first such proposal to surface in this administration, but it may not be the last. Rather than appearing on the budget ledger as higher spending, this way of increasing military take-home pay would appear as lower taxes. Tax exemptions, moreover, do not translate into higher pensions.

But beware. Offering subsidies through the tax system entails hidden costs. One of these is that removing things from the spending side of the budget tends to remove them from public scrutiny. Debate is sharp on spending programs for day care and health. But when did you last hear discussion of the subsidies provided by tax credits and deductions for child care and health insurance?

Tax subsidies are also unlikely to hit the right target with the right amount of fire. House Budget Committee Chairman James Jones has already indicated his well-founded hesitation to use across-the-board military pay increases to deal with the selective problem of attracting and holding people with scarce skills. Tax subsidies are an even clumsier tool.

Because the tax system is progressive, moreover, uniform exemptions favor those who need them less, other things being equal. Excluding the first $20,000 of pay from income tax would be worth little or nothing to the lowest paid personnel or to those with large numbers of dependents. The Congressional Budget Office estimates, for instance, that with the two pay increases proposed by the administration for this year, a sergeant who has six years' experience and three dependents and who takes home $15,995 (including allowances and after taxes) would save only $530, his current income tax liability, through a tax exemption. But a brigadier general taking home $44,886 would save $7,880. The exemption would be worth even more to personnel with working spouses or outside investment income.

If there are reasons to increase salaries proportionately more in the higher grades, they should be argued and pay scales adjusted accordingly. We do not happen to recall anyone claiming that generals were leaving because of the pay. In any event, there is no call to make such changes through the tax system.

The Charlotte Observer
Charlotte, N.C., January 29, 1981

Americans are increasingly concerned about the quality of the United States' armed forces. One way to improve that quality would be to bring military pay scales and retirement policies into the last quarter of the 20th Century.

A study released this week by the Brookings Institution points out that the military's compensation system is outdated. Today's soldiers are paid essentially the same way foot soldiers were paid in the late 1700s — by rank, rather than by occupation. And today's soldiers can retire at half pay after 20 years of active duty, just as soldiers did 30 years ago.

As a result, some servicemen and women are overpaid for what they do; others, woefully underpaid, particularly when compared to what they could make in similar civilian jobs. It's little wonder that quality personnel aren't often attracted to the armed services; and smaller wonder still that, having served for 20 years, few of them stay in.

Last year, a commission created by the Carter administration studied military retirement pay and recommended changes. The recommendations were virtually ignored. But the commission was on the right track by tackling retirement pay first. "20-And-Out" enables — in fact, encourages — someone to retire at age 38 or 40, when he is most experienced and useful, and after the military has spent a lot of money training him.

If Congress raised the requirement to be more in line with private business — say, to 30 years —it would save the military money which could then be applied to people on active duty. Some people might argue that abolishing "20-And-Out" would remove a major incentive for joining the military in the first place. But we believe paying fairer salaries would be a more effective recruiting inducement.

Fearing the wrath they encounter any time they suggest restructuring federal pensions, members of Congress have, in the past, sidestepped the changes needed in the military pay system and simply raised salaries.

Yet we believe Congress could find plenty of public support for such reform. With Soviet troops in Afghanistan, unrest in Poland, and the sense of impotence that lingers from the crisis in Iran, American taxpayers surely will approve any reasonable effort to upgrade the quality of our armed forces.

Rocky Mountain News

Denver, Colo., April 12, 1981

DEFENSE Secretary Caspar Weinberger's proposal to exempt military personnel from federal income taxes is getting the chilly reception it deserves.

Even though his motive is commendable — to induce more soldiers and sailors to stay in service and others to join — it would be bad policy to set one group of taxpayers apart from the rest.

Tax laws already are loaded with special breaks. In the interest of fairness to all taxpayers, the aim should be to strip away the favors rather than add to them.

Weinberger wants to exempt the first $20,000 of military pay from taxes. Other taxpayers undoubtedly would resent that, and rightly so. Why should a person in the armed services making $20,000 a year pay no taxes while a civilian making the same amount is socked with a big bill?

And think of the bonanza such a break would be to generals, admirals and other high-ranking military people, who need no incentive to stay in service.

Besides, paying taxes to provide for the general welfare of the nation is a duty that all citizens should share. Although their role is unique, military personnel still are a part of American society.

It is abundantly clear that the armed services have a problem in recruiting and retaining qualified personnel. The Navy, for example, doesn't have enough skilled men and women to man the ships it has, let alone the new ones that will come along under President Reagan's proposed big military buildup.

To be sure, money is a major cause of the problem. But the solution is to pay military people what they're worth, not bend the tax laws to achieve manpower goals.

The Knickerbocker News

Albany, N.Y., May 5, 1981

From the Brunswick, Maine *Times Record:*

Secretary of Defense Caspar Weinberger suggested recently that the first $20,000 of military salary be exempt from federal income tax (as a) means of halting the exodus of skilled personnel from the armed services.

The military brain drain is an acknowledged, and serious, problem. But Weinberger's answer is no solution. The most severe personnel problem facing the military is the loss of highly trained, highly skilled noncommissioned officers, who often are lured away from the military in mid-career by substantially higher civilian salaries.

But many military men and women, especially those in critical technical jobs, do not earn anywhere near $20,000. Consequently, the amount gained by exemption from federal income taxes would be relatively small. Whatever the gain, it would not come close to the much higher salaries paid by civilian employers.

. . . A much better plan was proposed earlier this year by the Brookings Institution, a private think tank. It suggested that different pay schedules be established for different military occupations. Currently, servicemen and women are . . . paid according to rank and years of service.

THE CHRISTIAN SCIENCE MONITOR

Boston, Mass., March 12, 1981

In seeking to upgrade military pay by proposing an unusual 5.32 percent salary hike costing $2.2 billion in July and a likely hike (with the amount yet unspecificied) planned for next October, President Reagan is taking an important first step in revitalizing America's volunteer military establishment. The pay boosts come on top of an 11.7 percent raise last October. Despite these raises, specialists question whether such short-range steps alone will be enough to redress the manpower shortages increasingly evident in US force levels.

Whatever the social and economic advantages of relying on a volunteer military, the United States is definitely out of step with most of its NATO partners. Belgium, Denmark, France, West Germany, Greece, Italy, the Netherlands, Norway, Portugal, and Turkey, all rely in part on conscripts. Although terms of service vary — ranging from eight months to about two years — the principle of "citizen service" is well established, and the result has been that those armed forces basically reflect the socio-economic makeup of the nations themselves.

By contrast, the US volunteer military, despite some decided strengths, is increasingly made up non-high-school graduates with minimal skills, as well as disproportionate numbers of minority groups in combat units where there is the greatest likelihood of facing enemy fire. Yet all this is occurring at a time when the American military machine comprises an array of super-sophisticated technological weaponry. While society at large is demanding that its work force become more skilled to man the space age technologies of US industry, the military is asked to muddle through with whatever manpower it can muster.

For reasons such as these, the Reagan administration's long-range military plan, while committing billions of dollars to new weapons systems, does not sufficiently address the manpower question. In fairness, it must be said that Mr. Reagan is at the outset of his administration ratcheting pay and compensation levels sharply upward, something that the Carter administration was slower in undertaking. Yet the "manpower gap" — the shortages of skilled personnel and noncommissioned officers (NCOs) — is perhaps the most pressing military issue that must be resolved by the public. Reserve forces, too, have been troubled by manpower shortages.

Recruitment and retention problems under the volunteer concept could actually worsen during the 1980s. The reason? According to demographers, the pool of available young men and women of military age is expected to drop sharply. That means that the Pentagon will be under mounting pressure to compromise recruiting standards.

Overriding the Pentagon's difficult recruitment problem is its difficulty in retaining current forces. The flight from service is particularly severe in middle-officer and NCO ranks, where personnel often have young families, and where the effects of inflation are pummeling household budgets. This flight from service is having profound impact on programs. Case in point: Mr. Reagan has proposed sharp increases in the Navy in the 1982 budget, including restoration of two battleships and development of a new nuclear carrier. Yet, the Navy is already short 20,000 petty officers.

The US thus seems to face an inescapable and difficult choice:

1. If it chooses to retain the volunteer military system, compensation will have to be hiked even more substantially over the years ahead, especially for mid-level career personnel, where salaries are greatest.

2. Alternatively, the US could return to some form of universal conscription.

Universal conscription, assuming that deferments were granted only under the most unique cases (unlike the situation during the Vietnam war when thousands of college-age youths escaped service, while blacks and less-affluent whites were drafted) would obviously go far in expanding manpower in the lower ranks of the military (and into reserve forces), while also ensuring a steady stream of skilled recruits. But at the same time a draft may have only marginal impact in ensuring that middle-level officers and noncoms reenlist. The most pressing shortages, it must be emphasized, occur not at the entry (private) level, but in middle ranks. Yet these mid-level positions are usually filled by second-, third-, or fourth-term personnel.

That is why, in the final analysis, the compensation question becomes so important. Payroll costs continue to spiral, now eating up half the entire Pentagon budget. Yet there is little dispute that pay for most servicemen has lagged behind inflation. According to Senator William Armstrong, regular compensation (base pay along with housing and food allowances) has dropped 20 percent relative to the cost of living over the past eight years. For the most technical positions military pay is totally uncompetitive with comparable civilian jobs, which explains why the Air Force and Navy have such difficulty retaining pilots. In updating benefits levels, Congress might also want to consider restoring the education benefits of the GI Bill, dropped in 1976.

Should the US scrap the volunteer military outright? That depends on one's reading of the effectiveness of the volunteer force itself. Opinions vary widely. Many professional military men argue that a draft is needed not only to fill ranks with adequate numbers of skilled personnel, but to demonstrate America's resolve to defend its interests in the world. Also, at a time when many young people seem to be drifting aimlessly, there is something to be said for the sense of purpose that military service can instill — each individual doing his or her part to support the nation for a short period of time.

President Reagan, for his part, has indicated strong support for the volunteer military concept. Advocates of the volunteer forces in general note it is a remarkable accomplishment that the US has been able to build a military establishment of over 2 million persons on a volunteer basis to begin with. Returning to a conscript military, it is argued, runs the risk of a return of the strident disruptions that wracked the nation in the late 1960s and early 1970s, when much of the public, and young people in particular, expressed hostility to the military. Since that time, in large part because of the concept of volunteerism, the Pentagon has once again been able to garner strong support from the public at large. That is probably one of the most important strengths of the American military at this time. The effect of perhaps destroying that national consensus must therefore be carefully weighed.

One point seems clear. President Carter was both correct and courageous in reinstating registration so that in case of national need the US could move quickly toward a draft. Registration should be continued, and in fact, Congress should ensure that a more formal selective service mechanism (such as the old board system) rather than the current relatively informal process is put in place throughout the country.

THE LOUISVILLE TIMES

Louisville, Ky., May 29, 1981

With a lifetime at center stage, President Reagan knows how to play to an audience. The problem, as his address to the graduating class of the U. S. Military Academy Wednesday showed, is that nowadays he seems to forget who his real audience is. When the President of the United States rattles a saber or jingles a money bag in West Point, N.Y., it is heard all over the world.

There are also signs, however, that a growing number of people, including some influential ones in Congress and the Pentagon, are beginning to worry that we are all hearing too much of it.

Mr. Reagan rattled and jingled aplenty Wednesday. He linked his administration's drive for the most massive peacetime defense spending in our history with "a spiritual revival." He mentioned treaties and arms reduction negotiations only in a disparaging way. And he promised to try to shower higher pay and benefits on the military, suggesting it may be an incentive to a volunteer force that will forestall a draft.

Meanwhile, Gen. Bernard W. Rogers, commander of NATO forces in Europe, was telling another audience in Chicago that sticking with an all-volunteer force and our present reserves would mean defeat for us if Warsaw Pact forces ever invade Western Europe. His solution is a limited draft, without exemptions.

In an article for *The Wall Street Journal* Tuesday, retired Gen. William Westmoreland, former Army chief of staff, agreed. He suggested that the administration plan "to throw more money at the problem" would "foul up the system."

Throwing money certainly seems to be what the administration has in mind. Although military pay lagged behind in recent years, an 11.7 per cent raise was effective last October, 9.1 per cent is scheduled for next October, as well as 5.3 per cent Mr. Reagan had wanted to take effect July 1 of this year. Defense Secretary Weinberger also has proposed exempting the first $20,000 of military income from federal taxes.

But such plans, plus others even more generous, are alarming some of the staunchest backers of the Pentagon in Congress. "We got enough men in uniform now," but not the skilled ones the services need, said Sen. John Stennis.

Texas' John Tower, Sen. Stennis' successor as Armed Services chairman, and Sen. Sam Nunn, D-Ga., told a *Washington Post* reporter last month they fear the pro-defense constituency could fall apart a lot quicker than it was built if the public becomes convinced the money is being wasted.

Merit raises and bonuses aimed at retaining an experienced cadre of technically trained men and officers have been suggested as more cost efficient than general raises for everyone in uniform.

But the administration's military plans are so ambitious there is doubt whether even that approach is affordable. The plans call for up to 250,000 more uniformed personnel over the next six years, a 12 per cent increase, during a period when the pool of 17- to 21-year-olds is dropping quickly because of declining birth rates. And if the administration's predictions of a civilian boom from its economic program come true, it will be even harder to attract enlistees.

Of course, if the predictions don't come true, recruiting sergeants may have to beat them away with sticks.

DESERET NEWS

Salt Lake City, Utah, June 3, 1981

The U.S. simply can't afford to let inflation keep eroding the paychecks of the armed services if the military is to retain enough manpower.

Worse yet, it's grossly unfair to pay service personnel so miserably that several hundred thousand service families must resort to food stamps and moonlight jobs.

Even so, there are sharp limits to how far Congress should go in raising military pay, particularly when all Americans are being asked to sacrifice and social services face substantial cuts.

Some of those limits were outlined this week by the General Accounting Office to a congressional committee considering a 14.3 percent pay raise for the military.

While the committee heard the Pentagon insist that the raise is needed to improve military readiness, an increasing number of observers insist the job can be done only by scrapping the all-volunteer army and returning to the draft.

If there's another war or the immediate threat of one, there is little doubt the draft will and should be reinstated. Meanwhile, calls for reviving the draft are premature, as is demonstrated by the GAO's report on military pay and manpower.

Despite the widespread impression that enlistments are low, the report notes, the active duty enlisted force has been stable and close to authorized levels during the eight years of the all-volunteer force.

Instead, the problem is in holding onto servicemen in desired categories such as senior non-commissioned officers and getting people to fill certain jobs that are highly competitive with the private sector.

For instance, the GAO observes, people with highly marketable skills, %such as aviation-related work, might not stay in the military even if they receive more money than the proposed new pay raise would provide.

Another limit on how far the U.S. can afford to go in raising military pay was recently noted by Utah Sen. Jake Garn. While the U.S. already spends 57 percent of its defense budget for military manpower, he reported, Russia devotes only 25 percent of its military budget for personnel. That means Russia can spend that much more on hardware. Our NATO allies spend about as much of their defense budgets on personnel as does the U.S.

By all means, let's make sure that U.S. military pay at least keeps up with inflation. But clearly we must compete with Russia not only in terms of stepping up defense spending, as the Reagan administration is seeking to do, but also in terms of making our military machine as lean and efficient as possible.

When it comes to military manpower, defenders of the all-volunteer system say some problems can be overcome not just by pay raises but by recruiting more women and civilians for non-combat roles, lowering mental and physical standards where appropriate, and reducing personnel turnover. In fact, President Reagan says enlistments already are starting to rise and many who left the service are now returning.

Moreover, at least one recent study suggests that many of the army's problems stem from a single fault — the belief that future wars will involve protracted battles requiring heavy firepower and large combat units. Instead, the study recommends that the emphasis should be on smaller fighting units trained for impact — bigger bang for the buck.

Meanwhile, as long as the U.S. relies on an all-volunteer force, manpower costs are bound to account for a big part of the defense budget. The challenge is to make sure the paymaster is fair without turning the military into what the GAO warns could become a "privileged class."

FORT WORTH STAR-TELEGRAM

Fort Worth, Texas, June 9, 1981

Pay increases for military personnel will be a vital part of the expanded defense budget that will come under congressional scrutiny before long.

The Defense Department is seeking $4.5 billion to fund a 14.3 percent pay raise in the fiscal year beginning on Oct. 1. President Reagan, after originally favoring a two-part, phased-in military pay increase, has indicated more recently that he would go along with the push for a single 14.3 percent jump.

Any doubts that a substantial pay boost is justified should have been laid to rest by testimony offered by Maj. Gen. R. Dean Tice, deputy assistant defense secretary for personnel policy, before the House Defense Appropriations subcommittee last week.

Tice produced statistics showing that the 14 men killed when a plane crashed on the deck of the aircraft carrier Nimitz during night maneuvers recently were making about $1.10 an hour, which is slightly less than a third of the civilian minimum wage.

He said further that the highest-ranking casualties in the Nimitz accident averaged only $3.19 an hour, still below minimum.

One of the major problems encountered in the military is the number of hours in the normal work week. The 40-hour week, common among civilian pursuits, is rare in the armed forces, and military personnel don't draw overtime pay for their 50 and 60-hour weeks.

The Reagan administration has made the strengthening of the American defense position a high-priority item on the national agenda, and as a result, billions of dollars will be spent on military hardware.

The 14.3 percent pay raise being sought for the people who will use that hardware may be the biggest bargain in the whole package. Congress should give it swift approval.

ST. LOUIS POST-DISPATCH
St. Louis, Mo., June 19, 1981

Congress will be taking an important step toward solving the military's problems in recruiting and retaining people with special skills if it goes along with the recommendations of Senate and House subcommittees. Both groups said that the military pay increase should include extra amounts for those with critical skills — aircraft mechanics, for example — or in key leadership posts — Navy petty officers, say.

Instead of the 9.1 percent across-the-board increase for all 2 million military personnel recommended by the Reagan administration, a Senate subcommittee on military manpower has proposed a general increase of 7 percent and increases of up to 22 percent for specialists and certain other categories. The House subcommittee on defense appropriations concurred. In the private sector, people with special skills or who are especially competent are paid more than others, and it only makes sense to do the same in the military.

Strangely, the administration and the Pentagon oppose the proposal for targeted increases, though the president seemed to endorse that approach in his speech last month to graduating cadets at West Point. It is not as though over-all pay levels have been neglected. The subcommittees' recommendation for an across-the-board raise of 7 percent would follow by just a year a general 11.7 percent increase.

The subcommittees' proposal would add between $4 billion and $4.4 billion to the 1982 budget, compared with the $5 billion cost of the White House proposal. Thus, the plan for targeted increases is not only a little less costly but by better assuring that the services would retain key personnel it would make a greater contribution to military readiness.

THE ATLANTA CONSTITUTION
Atlanta, Ga., July 26, 1981

A YEAR AGO America got some bad news about its Army. Six of the 10 divisions based in this country were rated not ready for combat; so many non-commissioned officers were leaving the service that training and fighting capacity were seriously impaired; and the percentage of recruits without decent education was dangerously high.

Now, though, things are remarkably different, according to the Army's chief of staff, Gen. Edward C. Meyer. In an interview with the Associated Press, Gen. Meyer said all but one of the U.S.-based divisions are at proper readiness levels; the shortage of non-coms has been cut by two-thirds (although there are still 2,900 fewer than needed) and young men and women with high school diplomas now make up 70 percent of recruits, rather than 40 percent or less.

If these things are real, and not the result of shuffling people around and massaging statistics, then the Army command deserves high praise for engineering such a rapid and dramatic turnaround. As we have noted before, all the defense spending for sophisticated new weapons systems won't do America much good if our soldiers aren't capable of using them and prepared to fight. The picture painted by Gen. Meyer is encouraging, because it suggests the men and women of the Army are well on the way to being capable and prepared. If that picture holds up, then he and others in charge deserve a salute from all of us for their work.

THE PLAIN DEALER
Cleveland, Ohio, June 13, 1981

Americans feel uneasy as they watch the Soviet Union's arms buildup and creeping expansion. Cuba, Africa, South Asia — where next? And not a show of U.S. force to stop it.

No wonder the Reagan administration can plan to pour a massive $1.5 trillion into defense outlays over the next five years. Americans want to get back into first place.

They want clear superiority over the Soviets and they are willing to throw carloads of money into buying it. But just unchecked spending may not attain the goal.

There is a national consensus in favor of lavish Pentagon arms purchases and increasing military strength. But even Defense Secretary Caspar Weinberger says that consensus is "fragile." Signs of waste or extravagance would shake it apart.

More serious than that, rigging up expensive, new smart weapons — the 200 MX missiles in their labyrinthine tunnels, an improved B-1 bomber, big-deck carriers and all that — will require a bigger military force. Manpower would have to be expanded 200,000, and those would have to be smart, skilled and enthusiastic if the sophisticated weapons are to work right.

An all-volunteer military, which President Reagan has supported repetitiously, simply cannot meet the requirements. People who demand American military superiority will have to demand a return of the draft. Just being healthy will not be enough for the future U.S. forces.

Former Defense Secretary Melvin Laird says the quality of recruits has declined.

If Reagan is going to build the Navy up to 600 ships from its present 450, that will mean more skilled manpower. If four more Army divisions are to be built, that will need still more. If five new Air Force wings are to be created, still more will be demanded.

The public is growing skeptical. "There are serious warning flags being raised," says Sen. John C. Stennis, D-Miss.

Out of the research labs and think tanks come marvelous war toys. Some of them are wonder weapons, gold-plated and sure-fire. But those might be better delayed until America decides how it will man those war tools and muster the spirit to make them work successfully.

THE ARIZONA REPUBLIC
Phoenix, Ariz., June 26, 1981

ALTHOUGH President Reagan still is committed to maintaining the all-volunteer army, there is a growing consensus among defense experts that simple arithmetic eventually will force him to change his mind.

The president cannot possibly achieve his defense goals without reinstituting the draft, they say.

Those goals include creating four additional Army divisions and five additional Air Force wings, and expanding the Navy by 150 ships.

This will require a minimum of 200,000 additional servicemen and women, an increase of 10 percent.

The armed forces are barely able to meet their present manpower quotas. In order to meet their recruiting goals, the Army and Navy last year lowered entrance standards.

These standards are now so low that many recruits are unteachable. The armed forces have rewritten manuals to a sixth-grade reading level, and still many recruits find them incomprehensible.

Raising pay will help, but there is another problem the armed forces face that no amount of money can solve — the number of men reaching the age of 18 is falling year by year.

By 1990, it will have dropped 25 percent.

Money can't solve the problem of the National Guard and the Reserves, either.

As long as they were an alternative to being drafted, they had no difficulty in remaining at full strength.

With the draft gone, they are shrinking. There's no way to stop them from continuing to shrink except bringing back the draft.

The nation can't have it both ways. Either Reagan must trim his goals, or else he must call for bringing back the draft.

The arithmetic says so.

The News and Courier

Charleston, S.C., July 28, 1981

Having tried, with minimal success, to minimize an evaluation last September that six of its 16 divisions were unready for combat, the Army now is saying that all divisions save one have shaped up. On the face of it, that is good news. Most civilians, however, are not in position to make informed assessments of military preparedness. They'll have to take the Army's word for it, and hope.

There are, nonetheless, points to ponder in the assurances given the other day by Gen. Edward C. Meyer, the Army chief of staff, that combat readiness has improved markedly in units formerly found wanting.

A key factor in the improvement, according to Gen. Meyer, has been the ability of the Army to overcome to some extent a shortage of non-coms. More non-coms are staying in because of pay raises granted last year and further increases in benefits supported by the Reagan administration this year.

Another important factor has been the gradual reassignment of seasoned non-coms from overseas commands to the United States to strengthen training programs. The more experienced instructors, combined with a longer and tougher basic training course, is credited with enhancing combat readiness in five divisions.

The turnabout in readiness the Army says has taken place thus emphasizes once again the importance of the non-coms' role — and emphasizes, too, what must be done to keep experienced non-coms in the ranks.

Beyond the training and the trainers, Gen. Meyer touched in an interview on another factor relevant to greater combat readiness. The quality of soldiers, the general said, has been improving. The percentage of male recruits who are high school graduates has risen from 40 to 70 within the last year.

To be fit to fight these days, soldiers must not only be physically able, they must also have the capacity and the training to handle weapons and equipment steadily growing more complex.

St. Louis Globe-Democrat

St. Louis, Mo., July 27, 1981

It is a relief to receive some good news for a change on U.S. military preparedness. There's been too long a spell of nothing but bad reports.

Gen. Edward G. Meyer, Army chief of staff, reports that less than a year after six of the Army's 10 U.S.-based divisions were found unfit for combat, all but one have been brought up to full readiness.

Meyer said a key factor in the Army's improved readiness was the successful campaign to reduce the serious shortage of non-commissioned officers who are vital to training. That NCO shortage has been cut by about two-thirds since last December and now totals about 2,900.

The chief of staff attributed gains in retaining seasoned non-coms — and recruiting new soldiers of higher quality — in part to pay increases voted last year by Congress and further boosts in benefits recommended by the Reagan administration this year.

A longer and tougher basic training course put into effect by Meyer last fall also is credited with improving combat readiness. Greater resources also are being applied to maintaining weapons and other equipment.

Indicative of the marked improvement in attracting higher caliber soldiers is the fact that the percentage of male Army recruits with high-school diplomas has climbed to about 70 percent from below a 40 percent level in 1980.

General Meyer concedes out there still is a long way to go. He didn't elaborate but one is his concerns undoubtedly stems from the fact that the major increases in Army forces planned by the Reagan administration in the coming years, to fill out such large new units as a Rapid Deployment Force, are going to put a very heavy strain on the All-Volunteer Force concept.

The new strategy announced recently by Secretary of Defense Caspar W. Weinberger, requiring the capability to fight two major wars simultaneously on a sustained basis — as opposed to the recently discarded strategy of being prepared to fight only one major conflict and a smaller (half) war at the same time and only for a few months — will require the Army, along with the other services, to shift gears. There will be a need for larger numbers of high quality, skilled soldiers to carry out new missions calling for much more mobile, flexible responses than were deemed necessary in the past.

But it is reassuring that the Army has been able in a relatively short time to make such progress in putting its U.S.-based divisions in a much higher state of combat readiness. It is a tribute to General Meyer, a first-rate, dedicated career officer, and to the much better support being given to our Armed Forces by the Reagan team and Congress.

The Washington Star
and Daily News

Washington, D.C., July 20, 1981

The all-volunteer force was flawed at conception, and nothing in its existence so far suggests that the defects can be accommodated to the necessities of a sound national defense. It does not matter, from today's perspective, that principle and expediency were intimately mixed in President Nixon's initiative to end the draft. The question that must be faced is: How long dare we continue to pay the price of a critical misjudgment?

There are signs, faint as yet, that the all-volunteer experiment may be dispatched to the archives of libertarian dreams, its proper repository. The White House has appointed an interagency task force to ponder how to "increase the effectiveness of the active and reserve all-volunteer forces" — looking into pay, educational benefits, enlistment standards and the like. That marching order would seem to diminish, if not demolish, our hope that the fascination with a voluntary soldiery is waning, particularly in the light of President Reagan's opposition to resumption of the draft.

But the writ of the interagency task force is sufficiently broad that it can venture beyond how to "increase the effectiveness" of the AVF. Indeed, given as its premise the Reagan defense agenda, how can it avoid considering revival of the draft? "The task force could make that judgment," a senior Pentagon official said. "We aren't prejudging anything." That is encouraging.

There are those who suspect that the expressed opposition to conscription by the president and top members of his administration — notably Defense Secretary Caspar Weinberger and Pentagon manpower chief Lawrence Korb — is but a stratagem to camouflage a decision already, if reluctantly, conceded — to crank up Selective Service at some point down the road. It would require, however, ether a fool or a saint to rush into an area of such remarkable volatility without assembling a persuasive brief that it is essential.

In other words, we don't think the manpower study is loaded in favor of the draft. But we would not be astonished if the task force finds compelling evidence for revival — notwithstanding the opposition in principle by Messrs. Weinberger and Korb, and the prominent membership on the task force of presidential assistant Martin Anderson, a key staffer on the Gates Commission, the group that in 1970 provided the institutional rationale for the all-volunteer force, along with some projections that have proved dolorously imprecise.

The framework of the task force's deliberations is an administration defense policy that will require substantially greater manpower — an increase in the active-duty military by mid-decade of about 200,000, or 10 per cent over present force levels. Even aside from the thorny debate over the quality and demographics of enlistees today, that demand will coincide with a shrinking population of eligible males. There might be various ways of jiggling bodies to assure that 200,000-person increment, turning to civilian employees for some of the new positions or contracting with outside firms to do work now done by GIs.

So jerry-rigged a manpower structure, patched on the AVF fabric, would beg an almighty number of questions, however. Neither the variety of pay schemes that have been suggested to attract a cross-section of population to the armed services and retain careerists, nor the various benefit proposals (e.g., a revived GI Bill), would wring out the pernicious problem of a "civilianized" military force.

The notion of soldering as merely another job, and the pattern of a managerial, ticket-punching officer corps cannot be ameliorated so long as the all-volunteer concept permits a major segment of the population, the middle class, to ignore if not to disdain military service.

It will be a supremely difficult political decision to advocate that the draft be resumed. There is no doubt in our mind that an equitable Selective Service formula can be fashioned. The interagency task force and the man who appointed it cannot wait too long to confront those crucial challenges.

CHARLESTON EVENING POST

Charleston, S.C., August 31, 1981

Earlier this summer, two key congressional subcommittees turned a deaf ear to a Pentagon plea for across-the-board military pay raises and voted instead to give high selective pay raises to certain specialists and middle management officers, while depressing the raises for both junior and very senior officers and enlisted not employed in critical skills. We think the Congress made a big mistake.

There exist today, highly complex procedures that determine, for enlistment and reenlistment bonus purposes, which of the many skills offered by the services are considered "critical." The bonus money is used to channel the flow of people with the right skills into the right jobs. Not all "critical" jobs require working with highly sophisticated equipment. For example, the Army tries to attract men into the combat arms branch — foot soldiers or infantrymen. One of the Navy's critical shortages is in the Boilertender rating, the men who work in hot boiler rooms. When the bonus money attracts or retains enough people in one critical skill, then the system reduces the amount of bonus money offered there and raises that offered in more critical rates. The monthly pay scales, however, are set by pay grade and time in service.

Congress has now introduced a new variant to the pay scales. Some officers and enlisted men could get substantially higher pay raises than others. It's possible that some middle management officers might have to take a paycut when promoted out of the "middle management" class.

When Congress starts putting these plans into law, then the flexibility of the bonus plan is lost, the services end up with an administrative nightmare for paymasters, and with service by some less equal in terms of pay than service by others. The bonus machinery is a necessary management tool. Proposed pay discrimination is not.

The Houston Post

Houston, Texas, July 19, 1981

President Reagan has consistently opposed revival of the draft to meet the nation's military manpower needs. But administration plans to beef up the armed forces will require the addition of 200,000 more personnel by the mid-1980s. Will the present all-volunteer system be able to recruit that many qualified young people?

The president has appointed a special task force of his top advisers to study this and related questions, and recommend ways to fill the ranks of the armed services. The task force begins its work against the background of an Army report assessing its ability to attract the nearly 100,000 troops it will need to bring the Army's strength to 870,000 by 1987. The report doesn't mention the word "draft," but Gen. Edward Meyer, the Army chief of staff, recently recommended that the draft be resumed by the mid-'80s. Army Secretary John Marsh rejected the proposal.

Though Reagan and Defense Secretary Caspar Weinberger oppose conscription as an interference in citizens' lives, they have said they would recommend its reinstatement if the all-volunteer system failed to produce enough manpower. The new presidential task force's first priority is to study military pay levels, fringe benefits and recruiting standards. But a Pentagon official points out that if it concludes manpower needs cannot be met by recruiting, it could recommend a return to the draft.

The administration hopes to fill the expanded ranks of the Army, Navy, Air Force and Marine Corps by raising military pay and possibly using reserves and civilians for some jobs. Yet the slowdown in the nation's population birth rate will shrink the pool of young people eligible for military service later in this decade. That, if coupled with an expanding economy, could make it increasingly difficult to meet recruiting requirements.

Most of our allies and adversaries, as well as neutral countries such as Sweden and Switzerland, draft their young men for military service. Only three of our NATO allies, Canada, Britain and Luxembourg, have all-volunteer armed forces. The Soviet Union and its six Warsaw Pact allies also use the draft to meet their military manpower needs. When we exhort those of our allies who draft to do more for the common defense, they can cite the fact that we have no more than standby registration for our 18- to 20-year-old men.

The draft in this country was a casualty of the Vietnam War. In extracting ourselves from that bitterly divisive conflict, we adopted the all-volunteer system. In doing so, we hoped that we could provide the manpower needs of the armed forces from among those who wanted to serve and possibly make the military a career. But the all-volunteer concept has been costly in practice and evidence of its shortcomings is mounting. Despite administration opposition, revival of selective service may be the only practical way to achieve the 10 percent expansion of the armed services the president wants in the next five years.

THE INDIANAPOLIS NEWS
Indianapolis, Ind., September 21, 1981

For reasons which are doubtless sound to him, Rep. Adam Benjamin, D-Ind., has cast the one negative vote in the House against a pay raise for all military personnel.

But 396 congressmen voted this week to raise military pay, across-the-board, 14.3 percent.

The issue will now go to a House-Senate conference committee that will try to work out a compromise on the pay increase, set now for Oct. 1.

The pending argument is related to how to use the raises — using them to encourage experienced personnel to remain in the service or to reward everyone who enters the service. A Senate bill passed last week places the emphasis on retaining non-commissioned officers and provides less than the 14.3 percent increase to two-thirds of all military personnel.

Critics of the Senate package say that the lower enlisted grades would receive less, thereby making recruiting more difficult. Both bills, however, provide increased special pay and bonuses for personnel in hazardous duty or critical skill areas and improved travel and transportation allowances to ease the cost of transfers.

The Reagan administration favors the across-the-board increases, as do we.

Under the pressures of maintaining the military forces on a volunteer basis, it is imperative that salaries and benefits be increased.

Workers in the public sector — postal, air controllers and others — have emphasized the justice of paying public employes on levels comparable to civilian employes. In all areas except the military, most salaries have raced ahead of the civilian levels.

The fact is that pay for military work — much of it highly skilled — is disgracefully low. The time for raising it is long overdue.

AKRON BEACON JOURNAL
Akron, Ohio, September 22, 1981

THINGS ARE looking up for the all-volunteer military these days. A look at recent figures of recruits coming into the military and retention rates of enlistees is encouraging.

But the defense buildup planned by the Reagan administration will put even more pressure on the armed forces to recruit and hold added personnel. Today's all-volunteer force of 2 million will need to be expanded by perhaps 260,000 or so over the next several years to meet higher manpower targets of the Air Force, Navy and Army, according to Defense Secretary Caspar W. Weinberger.

Congress is now in the final stages of a debate over a military pay bill that has broad implications for how well the armed forces meet their manpower needs in the future and whether the nation will have to return to a military draft.

Both the House and Senate have approved separate versions of a pay bill, each with a price tag of $4.5 billion in the year that begins Oct. 1. But there the similarity ends.

The House bill proposes to distribute the money primarily in an across-the-board pay increase of 14.5 percent. The Senate bill gives fatter increases to non-commissioned officers in an effort to stop the exodus of highly trained individuals to better-paying civilian jobs. Senators voted to give recruits as little as 7 percent more and non-commissioned officers as much as 22 percent.

The differences are important and bear heavily on whether the $4.5 billion will be used primarily to recruit or retain. But aside from that argument, the Reagan administration, which supports the House proposal, and the Congress are on the right track in recognizing the need to make the all-volunteer military work better and to attract additional manpower to staff and operate the new weaponry the Pentagon intends to acquire.

But back to the key question that a House-Senate conference committee is attempting to solve.

Now seems to be the time to zero in on the problem of skill shortages in the military by using pay incentives.

Pentagon officials say the Navy has a shortage of 20,000 senior enlisted personnel and the Army about 5,-000. In an era of high-technology weaponry, the military can ill afford not to be competitive with civilian employers seeking skilled individuals.

Recruiting is likely to remain less of a problem as long as the economy is depressed and unemployment runs above normal. Moreover, as one Senate staffer said recently, "when you're in basic training, the last thing you're thinking about is how much you make a month. You're thinking about survival."

The differences between House and Senate versions seem less impressive than they very likely will to an NCO deciding whether to stay or leave. For example, a sergeant major now receiving $1,659 a month would draw $1,897 under the House bill beginning Oct. 1 and $1,975 under the Senate. A buck private now drawing $501 would get $573 under the House bill and $536 under the Senate.

If Congress ultimately settles on an across-the-board increase, it at least should give President Reagan limited discretionary authority to divvy up some of it in a way that helps alleviate skill shortages.

The Morning News
Wilmington, Del., September 17, 1981

Their leaders are claiming, proclaiming and complaining that the raises most civilian federal employees get next month are niggardly. The spokesmen say the increases, basically 4.8 percent, will widen a gap that, according to them, exists between federal workers and those in the private sector.

Columnist Mike Causey of the Washington Post Service, who specializes in federal workers' concerns, cites an average salary for federal bureaucrats in the District of Columbia area of more than $26,000 a year after the raise.

Mr. Causey cautions that "averages" are tricky things to work with, and he is right. It is fact, however, that many private sector workers — skilled workers with vast seniority — will read that $26,000 figure enviously.

Be that as it may, it only introduces the topic of a gap whose existence hardly anyone disputes: the gap between what civilian workers — private or governmental — are paid and the pay of most members of the armed forces.

On Tuesday, the House approved an across the board 14.3-percent increase for the military.

Its basic public purpose is to allow the armed services to recruit and retain personnel to bolster the real backbone of our defense system: its people.

Without pay scales comparable to those in the *civilian* sector — private and public — this recruiting and retaining is hardly possible. "Service to country is noble," recruiters are told, "but I can do better with my skills — even if I did acquire them in an early enlistment in the military — outside the service."

That is the real public and social concern for members of the U.S. Senate to bring now to their conference with the House members.

The Senate voted for a raise that would favor the higher uniformed grades. Its delegates should go to the conference prepared to accept something very close to the House bill.

Associated Press figures show that an Army master sergeant with 20 years of service would make $20,000 a year (base pay) under the House approach. At that grade and service this non-commissioned officer would, of course, make out quite a bit better under the Senate plan.

An Army recruit's pay would soar to $6,800 a year under the House formula, but senators would have given only $6,400. This is the person we want to enlist and remain in a service that subjects its people to stern discipline and whose officers can order them to put their lives on the line at any time.

Let Pentagon budget cutters assiduously slash costs — or scope — of such weapon systems as the MX, or the submarines or the tanks and planes. The recruiting and retaining of people — and letting them live decently — are other issues entirely.

And let the folks who are in Washington Saturday for the Solidarity Day protest against a Reagan budget they feel gives too much to the military at the expense of "social programs" take it easy with this one. It *is* a social program.

THE MILWAUKEE JOURNAL
Milwaukee, Wisc., September 20, 1981

The House has passed a military pay bill that will cost $4.5 billion. The Senate has passed a military pay bill that will cost $4.5 billion. But the manner in which the two would target pay increases is significantly different, a difference that embodies divergent military manpower policies.

The House voted 232 to 170 to provide a 14.3% pay raise, across the military board. This is what the Reagan administration wants.

The Senate by unanimous vote canted the pay increases toward encouraging experienced personnel — senior sergeants and petty officers, for example — to stay in the service. The Senate bill would raise the pay for these servicemen up to 22%, depending on rank and length of service. It would raise pay for junior enlisted men and women and for recruits by only 7%.

That, we think, is the thoughtful approach. It seems more sensible to proportionately reward career soldiers and sailors whose experience is vital in an increasingly technological military establishment, and whose cultural influence, if you will, is the bedrock of a disciplined, efficient military.

Proponents of the across-the-board House bill contend that the most severe manpower problem right now is recruitment, particularly of young men and women of sufficient capacity to keep afloat the experiment with an all-volunteer military force. The proponents argue, and the administration continues to concur, that higher pay is essential to keep the recruits coming.

We question whether pay, either alone or primarily, attracts the best and the brightest among the young. But that is a discussion that assumes almost theological tones. Of more practical concern, in a time of scarce federal resources, is the alarming fact that an enlistee already is being paid $16,000 a year (total compensation) to try out the Army. It is more alarming when you consider that only roughly one out of every three recruits in recent years has completed first enlistments. That's like paying for a bottle of beer with a $20 bill and telling the bartender to keep the change.

The two pieces of legislation now go to a conference committee to have their differences reconciled. We hope the Senate is able to retain the principle, if not the precise scales, of differential military pay. Rewarding those who have committed themselves to a military career and developed both the pride and the skill of professionals is one way of emphasizing that soldiering is more than just a job.

The Pittsburgh Press
Pittsburgh, Pa., September 24, 1981

Whether Congress adopts the Senate's military pay bill or the House's version, the armed forces are in for a sizable pay increase.

The question is whether the money package should be tailored toward attracting recruits or toward retaining skilled personnel.

The House bill provides an across-the-board increase of 14.3 percent, offering the same raise to a recruit as to long-term people.

The Senate bill proposes raises for enlisted men and women ranging from 7 percent for recruits to 22 percent for senior non-commissioned officers. The range for officers would be from 9 percent for junior members to 17 percent for the most senior.

The Senate bill is preferable. For the more pressing problem is keeping trained personnel.

These skilled men and women are the backbone of the armed forces. They are depended upon to keep the services at top readiness. But they are leaving in droves because their skills can command higher pay in the private job market.

The military has recruiting problems, to be sure. Without a draft, it is not easy to find enough qualified young people to fill all the spots. And this problem may increase as the armed services grow under the Reagan program to expand military preparedness.

Nevertheless, the Navy, Air Force and Marine Corps have managed to fill their quotas so far this year, and the Army has come within 1 percent of its goal.

★ ★ ★

The Senate's 7 percent pay increase at the bottom would raise the base salary of a first-class private to $715 a month. That, plus room, board, medical care and a chance to learn a useful skill, is not to be sneezed at.

Once the recruit is enlisted, the Senate's bigger pay bulge for experienced personnel is more likely to encourage the desired re-enlistment.

Oregon *Journal*
Portland, Ore., September 19, 1981

The Senate came up with a commendable idea the other day, and it's too bad the House didn't go along with it. The Senate proposed directing most of the military pay raise to experienced noncommissioned and middle-grade officers.

With the volunteer Army, the veteran noncoms and seasoned officers are the ones who should be retained but often aren't because the pay is too low. The recruits and new officers come for the experience and education. The older officers stick around for the retirement benefits.

The pay raise is healthy. The House voted for a 14.3 percent pay increase, $4.5 million to be spread across the board. The Senate proposal would provide raises of 7 percent for new recruits and scales ranging up to 22 percent for top sergeants and chief petty officers. The bill has been sent to a conference committee in search of an agreement.

The Pentagon and Congress have managed to make a snafu of military spending. They spend for exotic strategic weapons to counter nuclear war, or make it more probable, while ignoring the much more likely threat of conventional war. If the U. S. is sucked into a war, it most likely will be one involving the same type weapons used in Vietnam — not MX missiles or B-1 bombers.

The heart of U.S. defense needs is dependable, well-maintained weapons and trained personnel. But large numbers of technical jobs remain unfilled because the young soldier or sailor can earn more money in private industry. The middle ranks, the experienced individual with an option to leave the military for better pay, is where the bulk of the pay raises should be spent.

THE KANSAS CITY STAR
Kansas City, Mo., September 17, 1981

The House has approved a military pay raise bill of 14.5 percent across the board. It is better than the Senate version, passed last week, which would have put bigger increases in the upper enlisted ranks.

The more senior noncoms have suffered longer under sad conditions, and many are in important jobs from which service personnel have been fleeing. The primary reason for better pay is to keep specialists in the technical jobs who have been leaving in droves for more money on the outside. So a case could be made for slanting the increases toward the senior people.

But we must assume in this instance that the Pentagon has some knowledge of what is in its own interests. And the House version is what the professionals and the administration want. They believe that across-the-board hikes, along with other recent improvements in pay and benefits for housing and education, will emphasize the fact of general, uniform progress and momentum.

Morale at all service levels has been wretched as the cost of living continued to eat into pay and benefit levels, and often wiped out entirely the improvements of a few years back. The story of service families on food stamps is familiar. Not so well known are the misery of families forced to dig deep into savings to pay moving expenses dictated by routine and frequent job changes; of wives, husbands and often children working at one or even two civilian jobs at night and on weekends to meet ordinary bills. It's a big price to pay for the privilege of getting shot at first, or staying at sea for months at a time.

This is an intolerable way for the country to treat its military people, and there is no excuse for it. Simple justice requires something a lot better, and necessity demands it. Tens of thousands have not been re-enlisting, often leaving at a point of optimum experience and value. Those who love the service were being forced out by the immutable mathematics of what is needed to survive as a family.

Things are getting better. Things have gotten better before. Why not keep things on an even keel? Surely the least the civil authorities—that is, the Congress and the White House—can do is to make every effort to see that fair and conscientious support of the military ceases these crazy, costly, roller-coaster rides. No one picks the military life as a way to riches. But no one should enter it with the expectation of becoming poor.

Lincoln Journal

Lincoln, Neb., October 9, 1981

Still trying to make the all-volunteer defense force work, Congress has produced a new military pay bill which seeks to accommodate two competitive elements.

A flat 14.3 percent raise is carded for all officers, from gold bar to flag rank. For enlisted personnel, there's to be a range, from 10 to 17 percent, with the highest awards to the senior personnel.

It's probably as good a measure as politically could be packaged to meet the different, and not necessarily compatible, objectives — attractiveness of service for recruits, and retention of careerists.

Nebraskan J. J. Exon provided floor leadership in the Senate to secure a spread in increases, granting veteran non-commissioned and petty officers considerably more of a pay boost than either rookies or the officer corps.

That, to him, and to this newspaper, was Priority No. 1. The compromise doesn't give Exon all he desired.

But there was enough of the differential proposition left to allow Exon to hail the act as "a significant change in the way we pay our military personnel."

Of the change, no question; of its long-range significance and efficacy, we'll have to wait and see.

Regardless, the Journal would press Exon and other Nebraskans in Congress to be sympathetic toward bills requiring the exposure of all American youth, male and female, to a period of national service. That service could be in the military, or in other areas.

The Detroit News

Detroit, Mich., October 7, 1981

Anyone who has been in the military knows that national defense depends largely on the retention of senior non-commissioned and line officers.

The Senate recognized as much when it recommended that a 14.3 percent pay raise for servicemen be scaled to reward skilled personnel, who too frequently abandon the military for better paying civilian jobs.

The House disagreed, maintaining that an egalitarian pay raise will strengthen the all-volunteer concept by attracting greater numbers to the ranks. Now the measure will be resolved in a conference committee.

The Navy is already short 22,000 petty officers and must juggle crews in order to put a fleet to sea. The absence of trained USAF technicians is so critical that aircraft are often grounded during extended periods for want of maintenance.

Recruiting, by contrast, is hardly a problem. All of the services have either met or exceeded their recruitment goals for the year. And while the quality of some recruits is questionable, there is no evidence to suggest that money is at issue.

To the contrary, Department of Defense studies show that youngsters enter the military primarily in search of a skill. The irony is that once they have acquired a specialty, their paycheck discourages them from remaining in uniform. Consequently, the military repeats the expensive training process and the middle-management drain continues.

The most sophisticated weapons system is worthless without qualified personnel to operate it competently. A pay increase that recognizes and rewards skill and experience would help the services keep the people they most need to accomplish the strategic mission.

Los Angeles Times

Los Angeles, Calif., December 21, 1981

The Pentagon is counting 1981 a good year for the all-volunteer armed forces. Manpower quotas have been met, and the percentage of first-time enlistees who have high-school diplomas has recently shown a rise. That means that the services, and particularly the Army, have been able to be somewhat more selective in their enlistments. If high-school diplomas mean anything, the services' enlisted ranks are today brighter and better motivated than they were a year ago.

It would be a mistake, though, to infer too much from this, least of all to assume that the experience of 1981 will necessarily be repeated. Military enlistments tend to correlate with conditions in the civilian economy. When jobs are plentiful, the armed forces do not have an easy time of it in attracting skilled or better-educated young volunteers. This year has seen a deepening recession in the civilian sector. Overall unemployment is edging toward 10%. White teen-age unemployment is close to 20%; for blacks, the figure is more than 40%. In these circumstances, the military naturally gains in appeal as an employer—if only an employer of last resort.

But as economic conditions improve, the quality of service enlistments is once again likely to decline, to the detriment of the forces. Personnel quality has a direct bearing on military performance. Since its inception, the all-volunteer system has tended, for obvious reasons, to attract a disproportionate percentage of the poorest and least skilled of the nation's youth. In some years, close to 40% of all new recruits fail to complete their term of service. That is an expensive, wasteful and demoralizing dropout rate.

None of this was foreseen, at least officially. The Gates Commission, whose study and recommendations President Nixon accepted in 1970 when he set in motion the shift toward all-volunteer armed forces, concluded that "an all-volunteer force will not differ significantly from the current force of conscripts and volunteers." The differences have in fact been enormous, most obviously in education levels. In 1964, before the Vietnam draft began, 17% of draftees and 14% of enlistees had some

college education. Last year, only 3% of those who joined the volunteer Army had ever been to college.

The fact that the nation's armed forces are no longer broadly representative of the nation's population is bad for the services and bad for the country. The services, for their own benefit, ought to have a more balanced social and educational mix, reflecting not just practical need but also the responsibility of all segments of society to contribute to national defense. Someday—and soon, we think—that balance will have to be restored.

For now, we are left with the all-volunteer force, and with the minimal program of standby draft registration for 18-year-olds. Even the survival of that quasi-preparatory system is in doubt. President Reagan must decide by the end of the year whether to continue standby registration. In his campaign for the White House, he opposed it. Since then, closer acquaintance with the realities of the military-manpower problem may have changed his views. But that is by no means certain.

In the current fiscal year, the United States plans to spend just under $200 billion on defense. It would be ridiculous, given the firmness of national purpose that this huge expenditure is in part intended to convey, for the President simultaneously to take the backward step of eliminating standby registration.

It would be similarly shortsighted if the nation's political and military leadership did not begin urgently to consider alternatives to the all-volunteer force. That could involve a return to the lottery-based Selective Service system, with no exemptions allowed. It could mean some form of short-term universal military training, a prospect that will become more affordable as the pool of young people of military age shrinks in the mid-1980s. It could involve a two-tier pay-and-benefit system, with desirable longer-term volunteers being better rewarded than short-term draftees.

Whatever the approaches chosen, a primary aim should be to assure that the armed forces once more truly reflect the society that they represent.

Reagan Reverses Stance on Draft Registration

President Reagan Jan. 7, 1982 announced his decision to resume the registration of 18-year-olds for a possible military draft. In a statement read to reporters, Reagan reversed his campaign position on draft registration, a practice he had described as "ill-considered" and destructive of "the very values that our society is committed to defending" in May 1980, after President Carter had announced the inception of draft registration. Declaring that "continuation of peacetime registration does not foreshadow a return to the draft," Reagan maintained in his statement: "We live in a dangerous world. In the event of a future threat to national safety, registration could save the United States as much as six weeks in mobilizing emergency manpower." Those who did not register would be prosecuted, presidential counselor Edwin Meese 3rd said, but he added that there would be a grace period "in the nature of" 30 to 60 days for those who had not done so to register with impunity.

Chicago Sun-Times

Chicago, Ill., January 10, 1982

Ronald Reagan in 1980 fiercely cut up President Jimmy Carter for resuming registration for the draft, citing "moral" objections and charging that the action was "ill-considered" and violated American "values."

President Reagan has reversed candidate Reagan and decided to continue the registration—not actual conscription—having recognized that "we live in a dangerous world."

The world probably is no more dangerous now than it was in 1980, so the hypocrisy lies in the original opposition, voiced as it was by a Reagan determined to "re-arm America."

The presidential position is the correct one. The world *is* dangerous, scrapping registration would contradict the signal Reagan has sent to the Kremlin by imposing economic sanctions over the Polish crisis and the advance signup would knock six or so weeks off the time required to mobilize the nation in case of an emergency.

The American Civil Liberties Union has responded hysterically, saying that Reagan has "precipitated a law-enforcement catastrophe." We prefer to think that the president was closer to truth when he said "that this generation of young Americans shares the sense of patriotism and responsibility that past generations have always shown."

All it takes now is a name, address and Social Security number. If more is required in the future, the need should be obvious. If it isn't obvious, then will be the time to drag heels and cry, "Hell no, we won't go."

Pittsburgh Post-Gazette

Pittsburgh, Pa., January 13, 1982

Much of the instant reaction to President Reagan's recent decision to continue standby registration for the draft took one of two forms: glee at Mr. Reagan's discomfort in having to go back on a campaign promise, and apocalyptic warnings that a full-fledged draft is now inevitable. Both reactions miss the point.

A president who casts aside campaign promises left and right will acquire, and deserve, a reputation for capriciousness. But since such promises are often made in haste and with an eye on the polls rather than the facts, a few second thoughts are not only permissible but desirable.

In the case of Mr. Reagan and draft registration, a change of heart was widely predicted even in 1980. The resounding — and dogmatic — condemnations of draft registration that are now being quoted back at the president were music to the ears of one part of Mr. Reagan's conservative constituency, so-called "libertarians." Not coincidentally, they also provided the Republican candidate with one issue on which he could appear more "pro-youth" than his Democratic opponent, President Carter.

But even at the time of Mr. Reagan's earlier statements, most conservatives cared less for libertarian dogma' about personal freedom than about military readiness and toughness on the Soviet Union, the twin justifications for standby registration. The advisory commission that supposedly persuaded President Reagan to change his mind about the preparedness value of registration is, in Ted Kennedy's phrase, a transparent fig leaf over what was probably an inevitable conclusion that dismantling registration would send the wrong signal.

Does it follow that, having reversed himself on registration, the president is likely also to press for an actual draft?

Such is the prediction of the anti-draft movement which, in what often seems an exercise in '60s nostalgia, insists that the Pentagon is scheming to acquire cannon fodder for new Vietnams. But, while there remains strong sentiment in the military for resumption of conscription, a draft would present enormous problems of politics, equity and logistics.

More to the point, as Mr. Reagan pointed out, the all-volunteer services lately have been doing a better job of recruiting qualified personnel. That fact should make it easier for the president to allow standby registration to serve the symbolic purpose of demonstrating U.S. resolve and the practical one of facilitating mobilization in a real military emergency.

There is a final criticism of the president's action: that standby draft registration is unenforceable, except in a selective and therefore unfair way.

The lackadaisical response of many young men to registration is troubling. But to some extent it probably reflects the uncertainty created by Mr. Reagan's well-publicized opposition to the registration system. That uncertainty has now been dispelled by the president's sensible second thoughts.

ARKANSAS DEMOCRAT

Little Rock, Ark., January 12, 1982

President Reagan has done an about face on the subject of the draft, deciding to continue the Carter legislation of last year, which requires registration but no actual military service as yet. The decision won't be universally popular, but it is the right one.

Though, as a campaigning conservative, Mr. Reagan last year opposed the draft — conservatives think people should voluntarily defend the country — his military preparedness program would be only a half-plan if it did not include a standby readiness to reinstitute the draft.

An adequate ground force is the symbol of preparedness for conventional war, and the present voluntary system isn't getting the job done. We have nothing to match Russia's giant land force, which is routinely used as a tool of foreign policy, especially to bully Western Europe.

Mr. Reagan's decision is important for yet another reason — the fact that the draft-aged have engaged in wholeale evasion of the registration law. An astounding 800,000 men or more have failed to sign up — largely, we'd guess, for 2 reasons. First, the expectation that Mr. Reagan, if elected, would drop the law and, second, because Jimmy Carter was such a quick man with amnesty for evaders of the Vietnam War. Forgetfulness was the word he used to describe his chosen approach of asking them to come home, turn themselves in and receive absolution.

The response wasn't what he expected. Some evaders chose to stay outside the country, but many others have probably returned from Canada (or from Sweden and other parts via Canada) without bothering to go through the official amnesty process, either out of distrust or unconcern.

Because of his past opposition to draft registration, Mr. Reagan can't very well breathe fire at today's delinquent registrants, but he is making it plain that after an as-yet-unspecified grace period (of 30 to 60 days) any holdouts will be subject to heavy fines and up to 5 years in prison, as provided by the registration law.

That announcement will probably fetch most of the delinquents, but the fact that they represent about a sixth of the draft-aged suggests yet a third reason for the widespread evasion — the growing "peace movement."

Since it can be taken for granted that draft registration points ultimately toward military service, its renewal may well give the peace movement new ammunition among militants. The fact is that a prospective draft is — next to rebuilding defense and instituting an actual draft — the best insurance for peace there is. In fact, we think that enforcement of registration ought to be followed up by the draft itself. Mere registration can never be a real deterrent to Russia's adventuristic use of her vast ground force to get what she wants short of nuclear war.

Having stepped out for registration, Mr. Reagan should before too long urge reinstitution of the draft. That's a matter for Congress, of course, but Congress has shown a willingness to rearm and it can't disregard the draft as an essential part of rearmament — especially now that it has been settled that women won't have to serve..

The Pittsburgh Press

Pittsburgh, Pa., January 10, 1982

Risking embarrassment with a 180-degree reversal in policy, President Reagan has decided to continue registration of 18-year-old men for a possible military draft.

Actually, the president had no choice but to eat the words he uttered on the 1980 campaign trail when he promised to end draft registration. For to do otherwise would have signaled to Moscow national weakness and irresolution in the midst of the Polish crisis.

★ ★ ★

President Carter ordered resumption of registration in February 1980 as part of his reaction to the Soviet invasion of Afghanistan.

Mr. Reagan's opposition to the move came out of his political persona at the time: He disapproved of everything Mr. Carter did, including how the guy tied his shoelaces.

Mr. Reagan also had been told registration would speed mobilization in an emergency by just a few days. Now he has been advised, by a commission he appointed, that registration could save six weeks if a draft had to be used.

Mr. Reagan remains opposed to an actual draft, as he should be, except in the event of "the most severe national emergency." But he recognizes that "we live in a dangerous world" — so pre-registration is prudent.

Having made his decision, the president now faces the problem of what to do about an estimated one million young men who have failed to sign up since the draft registration began.

It's impossible to prosecute so many persons, a fact that draft-resister groups are counting on as they counsel defiance. Yet it is unfair to the 6.6 million youths who have registered to let the others off scot free.

★ ★ ★

Many among the missing million may have skipped signing up because they expected Mr. Reagan, based on his campaign rhetoric, to scrap the system. They now should be given a chance to fulfill their civic duty.

As for those who don't sign up, the president has some effective tools to see that the law is observed and to make the point that youths have not only privileges but also duties.

The simplest way is to require any young man in the draft-age group to show his registration card when applying for a government job, a student loan, food stamps, welfare or any other federally supported benefit.

Mr. Reagan could require some of this by executive order. Congress should do the rest.

It is important to demand respect for all laws and not allow anyone to pick and choose those they will obey.

The Detroit News

Detroit, Mich., January 10, 1982

President Reagan has agreed to continue draft registration, finally yielding to the blandishments of Defense Secretary Caspar Weinberger, Secretary of State Alexander Haig, the Joint Chiefs of Staff, and a presidential commission on military manpower.

Mr. Reagan criticized former President Carter for reinstituting registration in 1980, calling it a meaningless gesture of protest against the Soviet invasion of Afghanistan. And White House spokesmen are trying to deny a parallel between Afghanistan and the Polish crisis, but they aren't very convincing.

The president has bumped into one of the realities of public office — circumstances change and campaign promises can't always be kept. Mr. Reagan did try to balance the announcement by saying that draft registration doesn't foreshadow conscription. But why register for a draft that isn't contemplated?

We believe the draft will be necessary to meet the huge manpower requirement mandated by the expanded defense budget. Indeed, the Pentagon says the three services must have 200,000 more men — a goal that can't be met by voluntary enlistments.

The question is not whether, but *when* the draft will be resumed, and how it will be organized to insure fairness.

A new draft must not, for example, offer educational deferments to middle and upper-class men, as the previous draft did. The term of service should be changed, to minimize the inconvenience to all draftees. An active-duty period of six to 12 months ought to be sufficient for basic instruction. Then the draftee should be transferred to the reserves to participate in regular drills and attend summer camp.

Congress has accepted the need for Mr. Reagan's military buildup, and Mr. Reagan must accept the need for conscripted manpower. Friends and foes will never be entirely sure of America's determination until military service is once again a compulsory obligation.

The Virginian-Pilot

Norfolk, Va., January 12, 1982

Candidate Ronald Reagan jumped all over President Jimmy Carter in 1980 for ordering young men to register for the draft. "Perhaps the most fundamental objection to draft registration is moral," Mr. Reagan preached back then. "Only in the most severe national emergency does the government have a claim to the mandatory service of its young people. In any other time, a draft or draft registration destroys the very values that our society is committed to defend."

Two other presidential hopefuls — Sen. Edward M. Kennedy, D-Mass., and former Rep. John B. Anderson, R-Ill. — were equally critical of peacetime draft registration, as were other congressmen; to approve funding for the program, the Senate had first to overcome a filibuster by registration foe Mark O. Hatfield, R-Ore. Not so long before, Mr. Carter himself had opposed registration. But the takeover of the U.S. Embassy in Tehran and the Soviet Army's invasion of Afghanistan had turned him around.

Now President Reagan, like his predecessor, has had a change of heart. The military crackdown in Poland doubtless figured in the conversion. "We live in a dangerous world," he said in justifying the continuation of registration. "In the event of a future threat to national safety, registration could save the United States as much as six weeks in mobilizing emergency manpower."

Well, the world is indeed dangerous, and could easily become more so if the leaders of the Soviet empire escalate tensions to divert their restless subjects' attention from substantial grievances. And surely some time would be saved during a national emergency by having the names, addresses and Social Security numbers of millions of young men tucked neatly into federal data banks, although how much would be saved is hotly disputed.

In any event, no one can rule out a genuine national emergency demanding a swift expansion of the armed forces. Although the superpowers' vast arsenals of nuclear weapons tend to deter rashness by either East or West, it cannot be said that perilous confrontations between Washington and Moscow ended with the Cuban Missile Crisis. Draft registration is thus a prudent precaution — and a signal of sober intent to defend U.S. interests.

The draft has rarely been popular in America — the enthusiasm with which Americans took up arms in World War I was exceptional. Extension of the Selective Service Act came within one vote of being defeated in the House of Representatives in the months before Pearl Harbor, and when American boys were summoned to serve in World War II, they responded cheerlessly to the call and welcomed discharge when the shooting ended.

Sending American draftees to defend South Korean territory in the Fifties was criticized at the time and contributed to the less-than-satisfactory outcome of the Korean "police action." And fighting the Vietnam War with conscripts — most of whom came from the lower economic strata — proved the undoing of the postwar Selective Service program and the start of the All-Volunteer Army.

So the draft is dead for now. President Reagan expressly denies that registration presages a revival of Selective Service short of an emergency. But many are understandably skeptical, seeing in the move a start down the slippery slope. Many others deplore retention of a law that more than a million young men have defied, and punishing the scofflaws could be both expensive and embittering.

Even so, the nation should be poised to tap the manpower pool if circumstances warrant. On a scale of 1 to 10, draft registration, as opposed to the draft, is a minimal — and not immoral — demand.

Newsday

Long Island, N.Y., January 11, 1982

It was mildly surprising last week when the Defense Department came out in favor of retaining the Selective Service System. After all, Ronald Reagan had campaigned not only against the draft but against registration as well, on the ground that both undermined basic American freedoms.

So it was even more surprising Thursday when Reagan himself announced that registration would be continued.

Since the President has shown himself alert to the hazards of reversing political pledges, this decision couldn't have been easy. But we think it was the right one.

Reagan said he was still dead set against a peacetime draft, as he should be; fortunately, Washington is having more luck lately filling the services' personnel needs with volunteers.

But there's no guarantee that a peacetime Army would be strong enough to handle every wartime eventuality. To be a credible force, the military must be able to expand quickly. And without Selective Service in place, expansion would be dangerously time-consuming.

The President *could* have said that ending registration would have sent the Soviet Union misleading signals of weakness just when Washington wants to take a strong stand on Poland. But policy shouldn't be made to meet each day's crisis.

Reagan's announcement that the million or so 18-year-olds who have failed to register will be given a grace period in which to do so may have been motivated by necessity; chasing them down would be prohibitively costly. But it was also a sensible way to get the program rolling again.

San Francisco Chronicle

San Francisco, Calif., January 11, 1982

THE REAGAN GOVERNMENT, like the Carter administration before it, is apparently determined to avoid all talk or consideration of a military draft. In reaction to Afghanistan's invasion by the Soviets, Jimmy Carter instituted draft registration for 18-year-olds, which he regarded as a message to Moscow asserting our firm national will. Running for president against him, candidate Ronald Reagan rejoined by saying that "registration will do little to enhance our military preparedness," and found "the most fundamental objection" to be a moral one. That, we thought, was political twaddle and we are happy now, two years after Afghanistan, to see President Reagan come about 180 degrees. Evidently he'd rather switch than fight his own defense advisers, who have urgently recommended that he continue the draft registration machinery.

Carter started up draft registration in February 1980, seven years after Nixon dropped it in 1973. Early on, the response was overwhelmingly favorable, but under Reagan the signup has fallen off rather distressingly.

WHAT MEASURABLE BENEFIT to the military services can be expected from continuing the registration process without resorting to any form of conscription we would be hard put to say. It is possible that the act of having to go to the post office to sign up concentrates the minds of some 18-year-olds on the advantages of enlistment to them for their future careers, and thus helps build up the All Volunteer Force. But not all manpower experts who have been studying the question believe volunteerism is going to be enough. A group of these who met at the American Assembly in Mt. Kisco, N. Y., last September framed the issue this way:

"We face a fundamental national decision to determine whether we will attempt to deal with this problem through purely voluntary measures, through a return to some form of compulsory service, or through some combination of measures involving elements both of inducement and compulsion."

AND THERE THE ISSUE stands, unsettled, with Reagan opposed to any form of compulsion. For ourselves, we see registration as a message to the Soviets of an American national will and mind only half made up. A draft of the talents that the services so desperately need and are so conspicuously losing under the volunteer system would be a much stronger message.

ARGUS-LEADER

Sioux Falls, S.D., January 14, 1982

One point on which President Jimmy Carter was correct and candidate Ronald Reagan was wrong was retention of draft registration. President Reagan has now changed his mind and favors retaining the registration system.

Reagan essentially used Carter's argument. Reagan said that "in the event of a future threat to national safety, registration could save the United States as much as six weeks in mobilizing emergency manpower."

The president commented that "we live in a dangerous world," certainly an understatement.

Sooner or later — and especially if the Reagan program for increasing and improving the nation's defenses continues, the United States will find it necessary to return to a draft of able-bodied young men.

Too large a burden has been placed on the volunteer to fight the country's battles if war should come. The volunteer concept has brought very high monetary costs and a defense force which does not reflect a representative cross section of the nation's population.

If the United States returns to the draft, it should apply to all young men on a lottery basis with deferments granted only for extreme hardship. The system during the Vietnam War in which deferment was gained by going to college was one of the nation's most inequitable practices and should not be repeated.

Cancelling draft registration would have been the worst kind of message to send to President Leonid Brezhnev and his colleagues in the Kremlin. It would have demonstrated weak will on the part of the United States at a time when a Polish military regime, using martial law, and their Russian sponsors are taking advantage of the people in Poland.

We are no longer the world's policeman — as we were for two decades after World War II. However, no one else in the free world can take our place. If this country doesn't use its moral persuasion, backed up by strength instead of weakness, who will?

We don't recommend a military solution for Poland or other world trouble spots. Neither do we recommend strong talk with no resolve to back it up. Hopefully, this country's firm stand will help the Poles, dissuade the Russians from further military adventures and also convince U.S. allies throughout the world that the United States stands by its commitments.

No major country, the United States included, can rely solely on paying volunteers to be ready for an emergency. Retaining the registration system was a prudent step.

We commend Reagan for changing his mind.

"SURE, REGISTRATION IS AN INTRUSION, BUT IT'S ONLY IN CASE THE U.S. HAS TO BE DEFENDED...."

Herald News
Fall River, Mass., January 11, 1982

President Reagan has ordered the registration of young men for a possible future draft to continue. His decision, even though it involves a reversal of his earlier opinion about the registration, is certainly correct.

The registration for a possible future draft was ordered by President Carter after the Soviet takeover of Afghanistan. It was widely viewed as a response to the Russian aggression and a veiled warning to the Kremlin that it was pursuing a perilous course.

Congress endorsed President Carter's decision, although the early period of registration was confused by the question of its constitutionality raised by those who opposed it because it did not include women as well as men.

When the Supreme Court ruled the registration was constitutional, it proceeded without untoward incidents, and at last reports, about 94 percent of the young men legally required to do so, have registered for a possible future draft.

Without President Reagan's decision, however, it would have come to an end. The President was apparently persuaded by the arguments of the Secretary of State and the Secretary of Defense, especially by the report from the Pentagon that without the registration, any future mobilization would be delayed.

He is also reported to have been swayed by the argument that ending the registration now would be interpreted as a weakening of the country's resistance to Soviet aggression. In the light of the Polish crisis, the argument was sound. There should be no doubt about the nation's resolve.

The registration will therefore continue. It obviously reflects the heightened international tension, but the tension has clearly not decreased since President Carter's decision following the invasion of Afghanistan.

President Reagan's reversal of his former position simply accepts the necessity to be prepared for a possibly dangerous future. It does no more than recognize the realities of the international situation at the present time.

For him to have let the registration end would have been a mistake, and it is heartening to find that he did not allow the fact of his earlier opposition to force him to make that error now.

The Wichita
Eagle-Beacon
Wichita, Kans., January 10, 1982

It's true that Ronald Reagan, as a candidate, said he saw no sense in peacetime draft registration. Now, as president, Mr. Reagan, facing up to world realities, has changed his mind and ordered the registration continued.

He still says he has no intention of actually ordering any registrant's call-up except in a true national emergency, but recognizes that, should such an emergency ever occur, having available a registry of draft-age young men could speed up mobilization of needed manpower by six weeks.

Thus, registration by 18-year-old men, first ordered by ex-President Carter in response to Mideast troubles, must continue. To encourage the enrollment of those who have passed their 18th birthdays but did not comply, a grace period for late registrations has been ordered.

We still think that, as we have said on several occasion, a universal registration of youths for public service — both civilian and military — would be preferable to registration for military draft only.

Mr. Reagan's recent decision apparently is based somewhat on what he perceives as a means to help ensure the nation's safety "in a dangerous world" recently made even more perilous by the crisis in Poland.

But rather than endorse what seems to be the most obvious answer, the president and Congress should be encouraged to research the possibility of instituting a more forward-looking, productive alternative to the military draft, in the form of a universal national youth service program.

Detroit Free Press
Detroit, Mich., January 11, 1982

WHEN PRESIDENT Carter called for the registration for an as-yet non-existent draft, we supported it as a necessary precaution in response to the Soviet Union's move into Afghanistan, to the Iranian crisis and to other perceived threats to world peace. That remains our view: that the registration of young people for the draft would save time if a military emergency did occur.

President Reagan, in his campaign, opposed the restoration of the draft and said he would not enforce the registration requirement. We did not believe then that the restoration of the draft was imminent. We did believe that the United States did need to communicate its willingness to challenge overt Soviet aggression as best it could.

Now, with the declaration of martial law in Poland, Mr. Reagan finds himself reaching for the same gestures, at least in principle, that Mr. Carter did: sanctions against the Soviet Union, though not a restored grain embargo, and now the enforcement of the requirement of registration for the draft. His own dismissal of them as meaningless and avoidable before makes them less palatable and less credible now.

The Reagan foreign policy has thus far consisted of some fairly bombastic talk and some fairly restrained action. What is troubling about having our sons register for the draft, and supporting government enforcement of that requirement, is that it may become a part of reconciling rhetoric and action, and it may involve risk-taking with the lives of another generation of Americans.

In time of war, we believe a draft represents an attempt to equalize the sacrifice. Without it the military tends to be a mercenary army, made up, far too largely, of those who cannot find other work. It becomes an army of the sons of poor families. In such a context, we believe a draft is a necessary evil, both from the standpoint of national defense and of social equity. Would Lyndon Johnson have been able to carry the country as deeply into the Vietnam quagmire as he did if the first units sent to Vietnam had not been carefully composed of all-volunteer units? We ought not to slip into a warlike situation because the middle and upper classes are complacent in the knowledge that an all-volunteer army will permit their sons to escape service.

President Reagan's reversal suggests a larger concern: that his attempt to sustain the all-volunteer army has failed and that this is a forerunner to full restoration of the peacetime draft. It is a pity the government will not be forthright if that is indeed the case.

In any case, it is a reminder that the ultimate risk of any foreign policy is that the execution of it, or the response to its failures, may deprive us of our sons and possibly daughters. If that does not arouse the broad middle to a concern about the risks of adventurism in foreign policy, we don't know what will. The danger to our children is always there. What Mr. Reagan has shown us, once again, is how foolish we are to believe that the campaign promises of any politician offer us any sort of selective protection.

The only real protections are restraint and wisdom, rather than some pattern of posturing, in the conduct of our foreign policy.

The Cleveland Press
Cleveland, Ohio, January 10, 1982

Risking embarrassment and making a 180-degree reversal in policy, President Reagan has decided to continue registration of 18-year-old men for a possible military draft.

The president was right to eat the ill-considered words he uttered on the 1980 campaign trail and to keep draft registration. To do otherwise would be to signal weakness and irresolution to Moscow in the midst of the Polish crisis.

President Carter ordered resumption of registration in February 1980 as part of his reaction to the Soviet invasion of Afghanistan. Reagan's opposition to the move came out of his political persona at the time: he disapproved of everything Jimmy Carter did.

In addition, Reagan had been told that registration would speed mobilization in an emergency only by a few days. Now he has been informed by a commission he appointed that registration could save six weeks if a draft had to be used.

Reagan remains opposed to an actual draft, as he should be, except, "in the most severe national emergency."

Having made his decision, the president faces the problem of what to do with the estimated 1 million young men who have failed to go to post offices or Selective Service offices to sign up within 30 days of their 18th birthday.

It would be impossible to prosecute so many persons, a fact that draft-register groups are counting on when they counsel defiance to young men. Yet it would be unfair to the 6.6 million youths who did register to let the others off scot free.

Many among the million missing did not bother signing up because they expected Reagan, based on his rhetoric, to scrap the system. Most of these now will perform their civic duty.

As for the rest, the president has effective tools to see that the law is observed and to make the point that youths not only have privileges but also duties. The simplest way is to require a young man to show his draft registration card when applying for a government job, student loan, food stamps, welfare or any other federally supported benefit.

Reagan can do some of this by executive order. Congress should do the rest.

The Times-Picayune
The States-Item
New Orleans, La., January 9, 1982

The draft is back in the news again as President Ronald Reagan decides to retain the present draft registration system. President Jimmy Carter reinstated registration, and candidate Ronald Reagan opposed it. Now President Reagan's top foreign affairs and military advisers — Secretary of State and former General Alexander Haig and Secretary of Defense Caspar Weinberger — urged him to keep it.

It is a hot issue that should be a non-issue. It is hot because "draft" — even simply registering for a draft that might be called at some possible future date — is a buzz-word, a symbol created during the anti-Vietnam war days that stands for militarism — old warmongers sending young men off as cannon fodder in immoral foreign wars.

It should be a non-issue because there is nothing at all remarkable about a nation's sensible preparations for an emergency. The present system does not draft anyone into the armed services. It simply requires service-eligible men to register. Should a military emergency arise and Congress authorize a draft, it could begin immediately because the registrations would be on file.

Mr. Reagan's opposition to draft registration derived from his support of voluntary armed forces and his use of the current politics of the issue. But the two matters are quite independent. Simply registering the draft-age male population has no effect on the present volunteer force one way or the other.

If draft registration is to be used as a symbol, it should be as one of national readiness to act in the national interest. We are building up our military forces to respond to a long-standing Soviet buildup and to the challenges of Soviet sallies worldwide. Refusal to do such a basic thing as develop a registry of potential military manpower would be interpreted as a softness in action that belies the firmness in words that we mean to be taken seriously by our adversaries.

The opponents of registration warn of a passive resistence that will embarrass the government by making it seem to be at war with its own population. But since registration was reinstituted in 1980, more than 6 million men in the eligible 18-20-year-old population have duly registered. Those who haven't number some 800,000 — a decided minority. Their motives are doubtless quite varied, and it is proper for the Justice Department to announce a grace period for their signing up and then to move to enforce the law.

New Army Chief Says Military is Stretched Thin

Gen. John A. Wickham Jr., the new Army chief of staff, Aug. 8, 1983 told reporters in Washington, D.C. that current U.S. military commitments were stretching thin the nation's armed services. Wickham, citing the Administration's growing commitments to Central America, Chad and the Persian Gulf region, said that the "range of contingency needs" was "probably" exceeding military "force capabilities." The general, however, praised the volunteer Army, saying there was no "need of a draft now" because the current soldiers were the best he had seen in his 33 years in the Army. "They'll fight," he said, "and they are as patriotic as you or I. They follow orders and they die."

Wickham's comments reflected a growing concern that the armed forces would not be able to meet the demands of the Reagan Administration's foreign policy. If the U.S. continued to send forces wherever it had defensive commitments or whenever its perceived strategic interests were threatened, analysts warned, the defense budget might grow so large as to topple the U.S. economy.

THE TENNESSEAN
Nashville, Tenn., August 12, 1983

THE United States has commitments virtually around the world and it has taken on some new ones lately that threaten to overtax the abilities of the military to be in several places at once.

Gen. John A. Wickham Jr., the Army's chief of staff, has called attention to the problem. "Traditionally," he said, "we've had a range of contingency needs that probably exceed the force capabilities that we've been able to generate. That probably applies now."

At present 43% of the Army is deployed abroad, from West Germany to South Korea, with detachments in Honduras, Egypt and the Sinai Peninsula. The Navy has five of its 12 aircraft carriers in foreign waters. Marines are in Lebanon, guarding the streets of Beirut. From the Air Force, 14 of a fleet of 30 AWACS planes are overseas.

The Reagan administration has just committed U.S. land, sea and air forces to Central America for six to eight months. Now, there seems to be some sort of commitment to Chad. That started small with shipments of missiles and three sergeants to train Chadian soldiers. But more military assistance has been announced by Washington.

Five and a half divisions of the Army are on duty in Europe, another in South Korea and a brigade in Panama. Several battalions are in Egypt as part of an exercise known as "Bright Star." Smaller units will do similar training in the Sudan and Somalia.

Last month, a unit of 3,500 soldiers finished maneuvers alongside Thai troops. Next month, 17,000 soldiers will be flown to West Germany for the annual Reforger movement. Some 900 soldiers will train with Japanese ground forces in October.

That is an indication of the widespread dispersal of American troops around the globe. Sen. Sam Nunn, D-Ga., a member of the Armed Services Committee, has said that, "Despite expanding obligations, U.S. force levels have remained essentially static...In short, our military strategy far exceeds present capability and projected resources."

The U.S. can't be a policeman to the world, or a fireman for all the brushfire wars that go on in that world without substantially increasing its armed forces. President Reagan's military buildup concentrates largely on missiles such as the MX and Pershings, plus big ticket items such as the B-1 bomber and various exotic weapons systems.

In terms of manpower for the services that factor has been downgraded against other things. But there is one thing that stands out in the present, and it is that commitments are straining capability. At some point, the U.S. may be tested and found wanting. It should either reduce its commitments or rethink its strategy and manpower situation.

The Knickerbocker News
Albany, N.Y., August 11, 1983
Even our military experts are concerned now.

Recent U.S. commitments in Central America, Chad, and the Persian Gulf have resulted in a situation in which our forces and strategy are mismatched, according to military officials.

Forty-three percent of the Army is deployed abroad, 14 of a fleet of 30 AWACS electronic surveillance planes are overseas, and five of the Navy's 12 aircraft carriers are in foreign waters. Not to mention the Marines in Lebanon.

Gen. David C. Jones, retired chairman of the Joint Chiefs of Staff, says the mismatch between our military forces and strategy "is greater now than it was before because we are trying to do everything."

And Sen. Sam Nunn, D-Georgia, a member of the Armed Services Committee, says "in short, our military strategy far exceeds our present capability and projected resources."

Even in Chad, where President Reagan accuses Libya of attempting to "substitute its own surrogate." Now, there's the possibility American AWACS may fly over Chad, at that country's "invitation," risking attack by Libyan warplanes.

The White House recently chided the news media and U.S. churches for opposition to the administration's strategy in Central America. Now, after its abrupt re-entry into African operations, the confusion grows even more over U.S. foreign policy and military commitments.

The U.S. should know by now it cannot be the world's policeman.

Former U.S. Rep. John Dow, who now heads a local disarmament group, says, "We should leave those countries like Chad and El Salvador alone to solve their own destiny. The small nations should be solving their problems in the United Nations."

That is unrealistic in today's world, but there's a middle road which we fear is being ignored.

Khadafy's ambitions may well be a direct threat to Sudan and Egypt, and to the Middle East, in general. While some U.S. action may be justified, we would feel better if it were done in coordination with our allies, who have a large stake in the stability of the area. We can't help but fear Mr. Reagan's simplistic approach: Wherever there's trouble, automatically deploy military forces.

As the administration pushes for more weapons, many of them legitimate, some horrendous (nerve gas), the American public has a right to be skeptical.

The Register

Santa Ana, Calif., August 15, 1983

Perhaps, just perhaps, the new Army chief of staff, Gen. John Wickham, has brought into the open the problem that will engender a national discussion of military and foreign policy that will get down to the nitty-gritty.

In an interview last Monday Wickham suggested that worldwide U.S. strategic and military commitments are dangerously close to outstripping U.S. military capacity. Other military leaders have echoed this view. Gen. David Jones, who recently retired as chairman of the Joint Chiefs of Staff, recently said that the mismatch between U.S. forces and strategy is "greater now than it was before because we are trying to do everything."

The situation is not hard to grasp. Forty-three percent of the Army is deployed abroad, from West Germany to South Korea, Honduras, Egypt and the Sinai Peninsula. There's an Army brigade in Panama and rotating battalions of Marines in Lebanon. Joint exercises with Thailand, Japan and West Germany are regular events, and special exercises in Egypt, Somalia and Oman are planned in the near future.

All this is in addition to conflicts that threaten to become active in which the government has chosen to involve itself. Trainers, weapons and money have been sent to Chad to counter the Libyan-backed insurrection. More may be "required." More then 5,000 Americans will be on "maneuvers" for nine months (!) in Honduras, where outright hostilities may be imminent.

This scattering of U.S. forces is a logical outgrowth of the "bipartisan" foreign policy the U.S. has followed since the end of World War II. The policy consists of a complex web of forward alliances and commitments to come to the aid of innumerable friends and allies around the globe in the event of various kinds of troubles, along with the stationing of U.S. troops in numerous foreign countries.

As Gen. Wickham has pointed out, such a policy requires a very large military establishment to make it credible. Wickham believes U.S. forces are dangerously thin, given U.S. commitments. He may be right.

The question that should present itself is, however, are U.S. forces spread too thin or are U.S. commitments spread too thick?

The U.S. economy may be in a period of relative recovery, but there are serious doubts about whether it has the resources for the renewal or revitalization of its industrial base or a transformation to the service-oriented economy many futurists believe is the next logical step. Federal government spending now seizes a crushing 25 percent of GNP. Even higher military spending, especially if financed by credit-consuming deficits, could put the economy in a permanent tailspin.

And make no mistake, the kind of spending needed to back up foreign policy commitments would be crushingly expensive. In military spending, strategic nuclear forces may get the headlines, but "conventional" forces get the money. Analyst Earl Ravenal, a former Defense Department official who is professor of international relations at Georgetown University, has estimated that in fiscal year 1983 military budget authorizations (actual outlays are usually higher) for strategic nuclear forces cost about $54 billion, or 21 percent, while general purpose forces cost some $204 billion, or 79 percent.

Ravenal also estimates that defending Europe will cost U.S. taxpayers about $129 billion this year, about half the military spending total. The defense of Asia, including Japan, will run about $39 billion.

Is it necessary for U.S. taxpayers to pay so much for the defense of Japan and Western Europe when those countries are at least as prosperous as ours and some significantly more prosperous? Is it necessary to have a Rapid Deployment Force to defend the Persian Gulf when the U.S. gets only 8 percent of its oil from that region and the RDF's effectiveness in an emergency is highly questionable? Is it really necessary or advisable to defend Chad (the "rebels" were the U.S.-approved government two years ago), though all would agree that the madman Khadafy is distasteful and dangerous?

In short, can the U.S. sustain the function of global defender, peacekeeper and intervenor wherever there's a danger that local circumstances and conflicts may turn out unpleasantly? There's a certain nobility in wanting to defend others from the bad guys, but is the U.S. capable of translating good intentions into good results throughout the world? Can U.S. taxpayers sustain the effort, however it may turn out?

It's time to face the possibility that the structure of alliances erected following World War II is outdated and becoming dangerous. Since the Soviets have achieved nuclear parity, the U.S. commitment to NATO to respond to a Soviet threat to Western Europe with nuclear weapons lacks credibility, since it could lead to an attack on the U.S. Furthermore, U.S. troops and commitments in Europe may be more destabilizing than not in the present era.

In a real sense, this is a debate about the soul of America. Do we wish to take the steps and make the commitments that will make us an empire or a free republic in years to come? If we act like an empire, the costs in taxation (to say nothing of possible conscription and other limitations on personal freedom) can't help but undermine liberty at home.

A great Republican of an earlier era, Robert Taft, said: "We cannot assume a financial burden in our foreign policy so great that it threatens our liberty at home." How many Republicans today would agree?

Gen. Wickham has kindly clarified the issues. Let the Great Debate proceed.

The Houston Post

Houston, Texas, August 21, 1983

Army Chief of Staff John A. Wickham has added his voice to those of other U.S. military leaders warning of the widening gap between our global defense commitments and our armed forces' ability to fulfill them. Though more cautious in his assessment than some of his colleagues, Wickham points out that our involvement in such far-flung places as the Mideast, Africa, Central America and the Pacific threatens to spread our defense resources dangerously thin. A former chairman of the Joint Chiefs of Staff, Gen. David C. Jones, goes further, describing the imbalance between our global strategy and our military strength as "greater than it was before because we are trying to do everything."

Jones' warning is echoed by Sen. Sam Nunn, one of the best informed members of Congress on military affairs. The Georgia Democrat, a member of the Senate Armed Services Committee, says that while we have taken on a lengthening list of military obligations around the world, the armed forces have not expanded to meet them. Marines in Lebanon, AWACS radar planes and military supplies for Chad, large-scale maneuvers in Central America and Egypt are the most recent missions requiring large numbers of military personnel and large amounts of equipment. These are in addition to our long-standing commitments in Europe and the Pacific and, since the Iranian revolution, in the Persian Gulf-Indian Ocean area to protect the Mideast oil pipeline.

Nearly half of the Army's strength is now deployed overseas; five of the Navy's 12 aircraft carriers, with their support ships, are in foreign waters; and 14 of our 30 AWACS aircraft are also based outside the country. Five and a half of the 16 Army divisions are in Western Europe, another is in South Korea and smaller units are assigned to nearly a score of other countries. Still others have recently been or will soon be involved in maneuvers in such widely separated parts the globe as Thailand and Honduras.

Small wonder that our military people and those in Congress most familiar with our foreign and security policies are concerned about the scope of our worldwide defense duties and our ability to discharge them. That confronts us with a hard choice: beef up our armed forces to handle the increasing burden of commitments or reassess and reduce those commitments. It has often been said that the great lesson of our involvement in Vietnam was that we cannot be the world's policeman. Yet time has a way of dulling such painfully learned lessons of history. Once again it seems, as Gen. Jones says, we are trying to do everything.

The danger in spreading ourselves too thin militarily is that our pledges of aid to our friends and allies in case of trouble could lose their credibility. The more overextended we are, the greater the risk that we will have our hand called, that the American shield will lose its deterrent power. We must re-examine our global strategy and devise a set of priorities that we can realistically meet. At the same time, we must impress upon our allies how vitally important it is that they assume a larger share of the common security burden.

San Francisco Chronicle

San Fransisco, Calif., August 15, 1983

THE CURRENT MODEL of a four-star general (chief of staff division) seems a cut more independent and outspoken that the big brass of yore. While still part of the dutiful Army breed, they are also imaginative men not averse to unconventional thought.

Back in June, the departing chief of staff, General Edward C. Meyer, said he would oppose sending U.S. combat forces into El Salvador because Americans would not support them and the Salvadorans were not fully committed to defeating leftist insurgents. This former field officer drew a parallel with Vietnam: "I was a bit confused myself as to why I was over there."

Now General Meyer's successor, General John Wickham Jr., has warned that new commitments in Central America, Chad and the Persian Gulf threaten to stretch the Army and other armed forces thin. That kind of talk may sound like heresy coming from a man in uniform. But it has considerable support from Democratic Senator Sam Nunn of Georgia and the Armed Services Committee.

"DESPITE EXPANDING obligations, United States force levels have remained essentially static," said the senator recently. "The inevitable result has been a widening gap between forces on hand and forces needed to achieve our military strategy. In short, our military strategy far exceeds our present capability and projected resources."

General Wickham's position drew what amounted to disagreement from his commander-in-chief, Ronald Reagan, who felt he had to reinterpret the general's words at his press conference. "The world has grown more interdependent," said the president, requiring a variety of peace time commitments. But he added the forces would only be strained if they were "called into action in all those places at once."

So General Wickham's thoughtful proposition resulted in an interesting clarification, if it can be called that, from the president. The general's other major point — that poor performance of arms and equipment in the Army largely results from deficiencies in quality control by American industry — is something that had long needed to be stated. One hopes that, once again, he will gain a few listeners.

FORT WORTH STAR-TELEGRAM

Fort Worth, Texas, August 12, 1983

Looking to the future. That is what U.S. defense planners have to do. And that concern for defense needs five years from now, 10 years from now, even 20 years from now, may demand some rethinking.

This week, Defense Department spokesmen revealed a school of thought within the Pentagon that the Army should be allocated a larger share of defense funds.

At almost the same time, Army Chief of Staff Gen. John A. Wickham Jr. and former chairman of the Joint Chiefs of Staff Gen. David C. Jones expressed concern that American military commitments worldwide far exceed U.S. military capability.

In terms of available ground forces, especially, we already are spread thin and we are unable to cover all bases. That is also true of certain naval elements and Air Force support units. If the United States has to tend to business in one area, it must take away from another area.

The Defense Department, looking ahead, wants to equip one new Army division a year from 1985 through 1989.

All of this refers generally to conventional arms — soldiers, guns, planes and vessels to transport them, AWACS jets to provide intelligence — rather than strategic nuclear weaponry.

Given the necessity to fund not only defense requirements but domestic programs, our military obviously cannot have everything it would put on a Christmas "wish list." That's where planning for known needs as well as contingencies comes in.

Defense thinkers are probably right that more (and more up-to-date) conventional forces are needed. Down the road, it is the hope of Americans that the threat of world holocaust can be diminished through a decrease in nuclear arsenals and greater control of nuclear arms in general.

These strategic arms have played a role in preventing a destructive world war. For the foreseeable future, they will continue to be needed, in whatever numbers, for that purpose.

But it becomes clear that nuclear warheads do not deal with brushfire situations, many of which are of vital national interest to the United States and many of which require our military to be at the ready.

Our obligations do extend beyond our conventional capabilities, and as we are able to move toward a lessening of nuclear tensions, there will be even greater strain placed on conventional arms.

If that is what the defense planners have on their minds, the American people should applaud their thinking.

And soon, both those defense planners and the public must make some basic decisions based on these considerations.

Part III: The Military-Industrial Complex

It is unsurprising that the cost of nearly every weapons system skyrockets between the time of its conception and its delivery. A premium is placed by the Department of Defense on the promised technical capabilities of a new weapon. The major defense contractors—of whom there are relatively few, in part because even the plans and prototypes for a weapon before it is contracted may run into millions of dollars—try to outdo each other in producing a blueprint for the most advanced weapon to fit the need. The contract is often won, on the basis of promised performance, with an unrealistically low price tag attached; this is known as "buying into" a project. Once a weapon is in production, there is seldom any threat of competition to pressure the contractor into delivering as promised. Usually, the weapon will undergo a series of design changes in the course of its development that drive up its price, in addition to delaying its delivery. Even the testing of a new weapon is often carried out by defense officials who have the most to gain from its production, and places more emphasis on the weapon's optimum performance than on problems that might interfere with that performance in the field.

This system of purchasing, which ignores all the usual rules of the marketplace, has evolved in part because of the close relationship that exists between the Pentagon and private contractors. A great number of defense officials look to private industry to provide them with a second career when they retire from the military. (A lesser number move from contracting firms to the Pentagon.) There is thus a great disincentive for military personnel to find fault with the contractors, or to insist that they adhere to contractual promises. The common interests shared by the "military-industrial complex," as this network of government and business defense officials has been dubbed, are conducive to a tendency to disregard escalating costs or delays in production. Every so often this tendency becomes glaringly apparent, as in the "spare parts" scandal of 1983, and the public reacts with horrified indignation to accounts of the purchase of screws at $92 apiece. The case histories, included at the end of this section, of three particularly trouble-ridden weapons—the XM-1 tank, C-5 cargo plane and F-18 jet fighter—illustrate the worst problems of the military-industrial complex.

Arms Buildup Sparks Debate on Industrial Preparedness

As the nation's attention turned in 1981 to the Reagan Administration's plans for a massive military buildup, one topic that began to recur in newspaper editorials was the ability of America's industrial base to handle the influx of funds for the development and procurement of arms. Although less obvious than the "guns-vs.-butter" budget issue, this was a crucial question for strategic planning. Would it be possible, analysts asked, for the defense industry to gear up quickly enough, in the event of a major armed conflict, to provide U.S. troops with the equipment they would need? The question applied not only to large-ticket items such as the MX missile, but to all the spare parts needed for the operation and maintenance of these items. Production times and costs for major weapons had grown considerably in the decades since World War II, not only because of the increased complexity of the weapons but also because of a reduced number of defense contractors, part suppliers and skilled laborers as well as a growing dependency on foreign sources. Other areas of concern were the condition of the manufacturing equipment that would be needed for a surge of industrial mobilization, and the dwindling stockpiles of strategic raw materials that would be tapped. In testimony before congressional committees, defense analysts warned repeatedly that the so-called "military-industrial complex" might take longer to warm up to full production capability than the next war would last.

St. Louis Globe-Democrat
St. Louis, Mo., January 6, 1981

It probably is assumed by most Americans that in the event of a major war the United States could gear up to turn out the necessary tanks, planes, ships and other weapons as rapidly as it did in World War II.

It comes as a shock, therefore, to learn that this invaluable industrial "surge" capability is gone, principally due to very bad government policies in the last 20 years.

A special panel of the House Armed Services committee headed by Rep. Richard H. Ichord, D-Mo., after conducting an extensive investigation, has concluded that the U.S. is in jeopardy because our defense industry doesn't have the ability to respond to the needs of even a short war.

"Our troops are outmanned and outgunned at almost every turn. Plainly and simply, we are not prepared. Our defense production base is ailing, and in the event of a crisis we do not have the staying power to sustain us until that base could come into play," said Ichord.

The investigation disclosed that many plants necessary for expanding defense capabilities rapidly have been closed. Existing defense facilities and equipment are old and outdated. Productivity has declined sharply. Lead times for weapons systems have lengthened unbelievably. Skilled labor shortages plague many plants, and defense budgets consistently have not provided enough funds to keep the industrial base healthy.

Another alarming disclosure is that the nation has become dangerously dependent on imports for some 40 strategic minerals, in many cases from 50 to 100 percent of them coming from unstable nations in southern Africa. To aggravate this problem, the national stockpile of strategic minerals has been mismanaged. It now has

so many shortages that 60 percent of the critical materials stockpiled don't meet established goals.

A key witness during the hearings was Gen. Alton D. Slay, commander of the Air Force Systems Command. Slay said one reason for the sad state of the nation's industrial "surge" capability is the closing of "literally hundreds of foundries in the mid-1970s as a result of very ambitious OSHA/EPA rule making."

Today there are only three remaining U.S. suppliers of large forgings such as those needed for aircraft landing gear and components, said Slay. Thus the lead time for large titanium forgings in just two years increased from a little over 9 months to well over 2 years.

The net effect of these multiple shortcomings in the U.S. industrial base, said Slay, is that "even if we go all out for mobilization of our resources, we won't be able to deliver significantly larger aircraft quantities in the first 24-month period. A chilling example is that after nearly 18 months under surge conditions, we could only expect to get an aggregate of 22 more A-10s and no additional F-15s and F-16s than already exist on the currently contracted delivery schedule."

"Obviously, with proper funding, we could greatly increase the output of these aircraft, but we would not begin to see significantly larger numbers flying for at least three years or more," Slay observed.

Patently the restoration of U.S. defense industry's "surge" capability has to have first priority. Without this capability, the United States wouldn't have the ability to defeat an enemy capable of launching a sustained attack. In fact, the war could be lost before the necessary new weapons could be produced.

The Houston Post
Houston, Texas, January 13, 1981

The decline in U.S. industrial productivity not only threatens the economic health of the nation, it also jeopardizes national security. So concludes a special panel of the House Armed Services Committee after a study that disclosed what its chairman, Rep. Richard H. Ichord, D-Mo., described as a "shocking picture" of weakness in the industrial complex we depend on for our arms.

The panel report questions the ability of our weapons industry to expand rapidly enough in event of war to sustain a prolonged conflict. It cites obsolete plants and equipment, shortages of critical materials and skilled labor, and burdensome government regulations as major crippling factors. Among the panel's recommendations to reverse this deterioration of our defense industrial base: Change government defense contracting and procurement procedures to permit more efficient purchases of arms and other material, allow faster tax writeoffs of new plant and equipment and revise the tax laws to encourage greater investment in advanced technology and facilities.

Some of these proposals parallel recommendations made by the congressional Joint Economic Committee and others to boost productivity and revitalize the economy generally. In the case of the defense industry, however, the government is the chief customer, writes the specifications for what is manufactured and controls procurement procedures. That puts it in a far stronger position to influence directly what happens in the industry than it will ever bring to bear on the economy as a whole.

In both World Wars I and II, our industrial centers were spared attack and we had enough time to transform the nation into the "arsenal of democracy" so vital to victory in both conflicts. Distance no longer insulates us from attack and we cannot expect the luxury of sufficient time to tool up for a future war. The complexity and cost of modern weapons require long lead times for their development and production. As sophisticated as World War II's weapons were, they were relatively simple compared to many of today's arms, with their ultrasensitive electronic systems and computer controls.

Because of the demands modern warfare would make on any defense system, we cannot permit the continued erosion of our defense industrial base. It must be put in a state of readiness to expand on short notice, and it must be kept that way. The new Congress should give the House Armed Services panel's recommendations the high-priority attention they deserve.

The Seattle Times
Seattle, Wash., January 9, 1981

A DAMNING report on the Defense Department procurement policies that have been allowed to develop under the Carter administration and its immediate predecessors was made public this week by a special panel of the House Armed Services Committee.

A steady decline in the defense industry has reached the point of seriously jeopardizing the national security, the report found.

The panel, under the chairmanship of Richard Ichord, Missouri Democrat, has no political ax to grind. Its findings reflect many years of experience in defense affairs.

In summary, the 10-member panel painted a picture of "an industrial base crippled by declining productivity growth, aging facilities and machinery, shortages in critical materials, increasing lead time, skilled-labor shortages, inflexible government contracting procedures, inadequate defense budgets, and burdensome government regulations and paperwork."

According to Ichord, "we are not buying the required ammunition, equipment, and weapon systems to fight even a short war . . . Our troops are outmanned and outgunned at almost every turn. Plainly and simply, we are not prepared."

Here is must reading for Caspar Weinberger, the incoming secretary of defense. The picture is alarming. But the recommendations indicated would appear to be well in line with the Reagan team's thinking.

This includes an overhaul of Defense Department procurement policies and practices that discourage higher productivity and new capital investment in the defense industry.

Houston Chronicle

Houston, Texas, May 26, 1981

A nation's might is determined by the number of planes, ships, rockets and tanks at its command. That isn't much different from the days when emperors counted swords, chariots, spears and shields.

Also unchanged is the fact that the weaponry has to flow from an industrial base, whether it be an automated factory or a crude forge. Without that industrial strength, no nation can protect its borders and exert influence in the world.

In recent congressional hearings, the testimony was that the industrial base of the United States is inadequate. That assessment has serious implications.

Gen. Bryce Poe II of the U.S. Air Force told the House Armed Services Committee that U.S. industry now is not capable of satisfying both the commercial and military needs. The result is it takes longer to fill orders for basic equipment. He said there is a shortage of skilled labor in some sectors of the electronics industry and the toolmaking industry is being eroded by foreign competition. Our steel industry is losing capacity because its aging facilities are unable to compete with foreign industry. The semiconductor industry is dominant but is facing intense competition with Japanese and European producers. In addition, the United States is dependent on foreign sources for more than 50 percent of the 40 minerals which are essential to our economy. It was not a reassuring picture he painted then or during talks he made during a Houston visit this month.

Not just the generals are concerned about our industrial base. Industrialists and bankers are worried about the need to rebuild our plants and strengthen our economy. A leading banker, Thomas G. Labrecque of Chase Manhattan, recently cited the advice from Satchel Paige: "Never look back; something might be gaining on you." He added that in far too many industries, we've already been overtaken.

Both the general and the banker say that in order to turn the situation around there is going to have to be a different emphasis, a different attitude. Growth must be encouraged. There must be reason to save and invest. Taxation and regulation must favor industrial expansion, not bring it to a halt.

An example: To encourage capital investments in industry, Japan has a policy which offers the equivalent of up to 193 percent depreciation on machinery and equipment in the first year. The United Kingdom allows 100 percent depreciation in the first year and Canada and Switzerland allow 50 percent. The United States allows only 28 percent depreciation. Those figures are one reason U.S. industry has not kept pace with modernization.

Whether they were counting aircraft carriers or sailing ships, leaders of nations have always taken into account the will of their people, their patriotism, their discipline and determination.

For some time in this country, there has been at large a feeling that big is bad, industry is bad, growth is bad, strength is bad. Now more people are coming to realize that the consequences of weakness — in industrial base or in moral fiber — are even worse.

This nation can either rebuild its factories, put its people back to work, regain its pride and hold its principles high — or it can drift into tragedy. And most of us understand that, even without a general or a banker to remind us.

The TENNESSEAN

Nashville, Tenn., May 31, 1981

SOME of the problems facing the Reagan administration in its program for added defense capability are illustrated by the expensive reality of new weapons.

According to administration sources, for instance, the Air Force has informed the administration it will cost approximately $26 billion to build the modified version of the B1 bomber, recently recommended by a Pentagon study panel.

That means that each airplane would cost more than $200 million, twice the cost of the B1 canceled by President Carter. That could wreak havoc on other parts of the military budget.

Other than the bomber, the administration plans to increase the production rate of fighter aircraft such as the F14s and F15s. The M1 tank project and several others are to be expanded.

The Navy's shipbuilding program would be increased, practically doubled. And President Reagan has called for new missiles, more aircraft carriers and battleships and increased military pay.

A military buildup of this kind faces not only the problem of skyrocketing costs but also that of insufficient production facilities of the size to do the job.

There are only two tank production lines in the country, only two Navy shipbuilding yards capable of making nuclear submarines, and only one with the capability of building a nuclear carrier.

The aircraft building companies that flowered during World War II and the Korean conflict have dwindled to a few. Many of the plants have been shifted to other kinds of production.

So, a major question is how to solve the production bottlenecks that exist now. For a rearmament program such as that envisioned by this administration, billions of dollars would have to be invested in new plants, in re-tooling, training and in attracting subcontractors who make components. Like the major plants, many subcontractors to the military have cut back, or shifted to other lines of work.

Mr. Reagan seems to be talking in terms of a buildup that is comparable to that of wartime and it cannot be done inexpensively or overnight. The administration has a wish list, but it does not yet have a list of its defense priorities.

The President will have to decide soon on the bomber to replace the B1, at $26 billion. After that he will have to make a decision on how and where to base the MX missile, at a cost of about $33 billion. The MX is already embroiled in controversy with the Western states over any kind of "race track" deployment of the intercontinental missiles.

The MX scheme is dubious at best and its estimated cost is not likely to be close to what the real cost will be when and if it is put into operation.

But the White House and the Pentagon are going to have to have a list of priorities. Even if programs are started out at a relatively low cost, those costs over three or four years are going to go through the roof.

If defense spending is to grow by the amounts projected, there will have to be an economy vigorous enough to support such expenditures. Suppose it does not regain its vigor as fast as necessary. In that case defense expenditures only add to inflationary pressures and to certain large and painful deficits.

Mr. Reagan seems to have something of a consensus in the country for putting the defenses of the nation in order. But the plain, hard fact of the matter is that the administration is going to find out that it cannot do everything it wants to do. The cost will be too astronomical. It had better decide now what it can do and proceed with the possible.

THE INDIANAPOLIS NEWS

Indianapolis, Ind., July 28, 1981

Preparing for an emergency is something people don't like to think about — particularly when that emergency could be a war.

Nonetheless, the capacity to arm and mobilize quickly often determines a nation's defense readiness. The United States emerged as a great military power in World War II precisely because it could mobilize quickly.

Now, however, many people connected with the defense industry argue the United States couldn't respond to a national emergency. Perhaps the most articulate of these is Dr. Allen Puckett, chairman of the board of the Hughes Aircraft Co. Puckett told the U.S. Senate Small Business Committee the United States' "defense industrial base is in danger."

Puckett cited familiar reasons for the dilemma of the industrial base, including the chief one — Federal inefficiency. He illustrated: "Small firms in particular claimed they received orders for the same parts for a single program as often as four, five, and six times within a single year. Much of these repetitive procurements are a result of how government releases funding to the prime contractor. A small subcontractor finds this kind of ordering devastating."

In addition, Puckett fired upon the chief product of the Federal government — mountains and mountains of papers typed in triplicate. "Perhaps no other single issue generates more heated discussion among businessmen and women than the belief that industry is swamped with burdensome government paperwork which does nothing to enhance productivity."

Whatever the reasons, and there are many more, Puckett's analysis of industry's capability to respond to an emergency is chilling. In the event of war, industry's response to extra demands placed upon it would have the momentum of a melting snowball thrown by a 2-year-old — it would be little and long in coming.

"If an emergency arose requiring an increase or 'surge' in our output of defense hardware, our ability to respond would be limited by the availibility of our suppliers. We do not believe that such a capacity exists," Puckett judged.

The support for his gloomy analysis is certainly present. Hughes was able to deliver airborne radar systems within 12 to 14 months in years past. Now it requires 24 to 27 months. The time required for aircraft deliveries climbed to 45 months from 32 months.

That's nearly four years — a duration longer than all but three of America's wars.

That list need not be confined to Hughes, either. The M-1 Abrams tank languished for nearly a decade in development and it's far from ready now. Among its current flaws are a 50-millimeter cannon almost impossible to aim. In addition, a teen-ager with a good right arm can pitch rocks through a hole between the fenders and hit the driver, disabling the vehicle. It's still not combat ready — after a $19 billion investment.

These facts, coupled with the distressing state of the military, as was documented in an editorial series in *The News* in early May, make Puckett's testimony alarming. Clearly, not only the nation's defense itself, but the defense industrial base, is in need of more attention than it has been receiving.

Puckett's suggestions are simple. He said that the Federal income tax laws should be revised to permit rapid recovery of capital investment, and he supports legislation permitting multi-year procurement to reduce herky-jerky purchases and production.

Finally, he suggested the Federal government should remove all excess regulations and requirements which are nonproductive. There's nothing to argue with there.

One of the reasons Puckett's suggestions make sense is that he recognizes national defense is more than a government responsibility. More must be done to allow the private sector to shoulder its portion of the responsibility — and it should be done soon.

THE MILWAUKEE JOURNAL

Milwaukee, Wisc., September 17, 1981

Even if the Reagan administration lowers the amount it wants to spend on defense, it still faces some subtle but far-reaching questions. The administration has talked about the largest peacetime buildup in American history, and it's not unreasonable to ask: Is the nation's defense industry up to it? The evidence is less than reassuring.

In the past 15 years, many traditional defense suppliers have either gotten out of the business or turned their attention elsewhere. Fluctuating defense budgets, rigid government regulation and bureaucratic red tape have all taken their toll.

Moreover, many of the same firms that gave the nation a strong defense industrial base in the Vietnam era are in a state of disarray today. A congressional study completed in the last year said that the nation's industrial base was troubled by outdated plants and machinery, declining productivity, certain manpower shortages and growing dependence on foreign suppliers for raw materials. How ready is the nation's economy for a surge in defense spending?

Defense experts agree that the prime contractors — companies such as Lockheed and Boeing — probably could absorb much more work. But they also quickly note that these companies are dependent on a dwindling number of smaller suppliers. The number of firms involved in aerospace production, for example, is down 40% from 1967, from 6,000 to about 3,500.

Meanwhile, there is only one company in the whole nation that makes precision ball bearings for military aircraft, and only three companies make aircraft landing gear. On other fronts, only one company makes turrets and hulls for the M-60 tank; only two can make Trident submarines. The overall lack of competition is likely to mean higher costs and less efficient products.

And how will the administration's pursuit of greater defense capabilities affect the non-defense sectors of the economy? Many skilled technicians — already in short supply — probably will be lured back to the defense industry. How will this loss affect our ability to compete with Japan's high technology in producing consumer goods?

It behooves the administration to widen its lens as it examines the nation's defense needs. The various armament proposals under study, from an advanced manned bomber to the MX missile, call for massive outlays. In scaling its program to fit reality, the administration should worry more about whether the defense industry, as well as the nation's economy, is up to the task.

TULSA WORLD

Tulsa, Okla., September 23, 1981

DESPITE Defense Secretary Caspar Weinberger's intense lobbying to the contrary, the Reagan budgetcutters could — and should — reschedule the military's spending program without slowing the rearmament process a bit.

The reason is that the highly-vaunted U. S. "military-industrial" complex is not prepared to immediately launch the kind of manufacturing program contemplated by the Reagan budget.

Neither is the military procurement machinery geared up to award and administer the kind of contractual load that would be required in the early years of the Reagan plan.

In short, if the military gets the kind of money outlined by the Reagan budget, we can expect a hurried, wasteful attempt to spend the money. That's the last thing the country needs in its present economic and political climate.

Because of the decline of military procurement in recent years, armaments companies simply don't have the plants, equipment and tooling at hand to quickly reverse field.

Given this, Reagan and Weinberger can easily reduce the amounts targeted for defense spending in the opening years of the rearmament process without slowing the total effort.

It ought to be done to help the President reach the level of new budget cuts needed to avoid the kind of deficits that threaten to wreck his entire economic program.

The Birmingham News

Birmingham, Ala., December 1, 1981

Defense is not manpower alone. It is also guns, tanks, personnel carriers, airplanes, rockets, boots and parachutes. A modern military force must have thousands of items of equipment before it can be considered battle-ready. For that reason the capacity of a nation's defense industries is vital to overall security.

Since the end of World War II, despite the war in Korea and Vietnam and sales of military equipment abroad, the U.S. defense industry has slowly shrunk until it reached alarming levels during the Carter administration. In order to increase the number of firms which could and were willing to make military hardware, President Carter spent some $735 million.

Congress and the Reagan administration do not feel that amount is sufficient to turn things around and have allocated $1.2 billion for industrial preparedness next year. That is a good start but it should be increased over the next four or five years, since the number of firms in the defense business is deplorably small.

As a matter of fact, American industry is in no shape to fight a war of longer duration than perhaps 30 to 90 days. The decline dates back to the hostility defense faced in the '60s and '70s. It has also endured a damaging bombardment of federal regulations and tax policies.

Now the basic steel industry is battling for its very life, unable for the most part to finance needed modernization; automakers, who supply some of the heaviest components for military preparedness, are struggling to stay afloat; the non-ferrous metals industry already operating at near capacity, lacks the money needed for expansion. At one point, the country had only one firm capable of manufacturing turrets for tanks. Others had been put out of business by their inability to meet pollution standards.

Despite recent progress, a huge backlog for machine tools, many specialized for defense-related production, now requires nearly two years for delivery of new orders; the defense sectors of the aerospace and aircraft industry, operating at about three-quarters of capacity are dangerously limited by an acute shortage of skilled labor and have little margin for expansion.

Moreover, because of hostile attitudes by some segments of the public and wavering government policies, private industry has been reluctant to tie up scarce capital in defense-related facilities and specialized machinery. In the not-too-distant past some firms have spent millions tooling up for defense items only to have Congress spend the money elsewhere, leaving them high and dry.

Even with the $1.2 billion the administration plans to spend, the task of strengthing our defense-related industry will be enormous. Some figures tell the story: During the '50s, the United States spent 10 percent of the GNP for defense. But in the '60s and '70s, spending was hardly 5 percent of the GNP. In 1956, 24,000 firms were listed with the Defense Department as being capable of producing defense items. As recently as 10 months ago, only 8,000 were listed as possible suppliers.

The Reagan administration's objective is to reverse 10 years of hard neglect by beginning to break existing bottlenecks in weapons production and by planning for several scenarios that would require industrial mobilization. So next year, the government will spend $232 million to improve weapons production and technology, $633 million for modernizing and expanding government defense plants, $145 million for maintaining and reactivating other plants and $65 million for industrial preparedness planning.

Much of the impetus for upgrading the defense industry has come from Fred C. Ikle, undersecretary of defense for policy, who declared two years ago that it was "an open question whether our economy could accomplish an industrial mobilization comparable to that after Pearl Harbor within only two years."

Obviously, the Reagan administration with Congress' blessing must pursue rehabilitation of the defense industry with determination, if the U.S. is be-effective in efforts for peace.

Chicago Tribune

Chicago, Ill., September 14, 1981

In the great arms debate that will rage in the nation's capital for the next few weeks, there is a significant if seldom considered reality that ought to anchor the arguments of both sides.

The chief limitation on arms spending in the next decade will arise not from demands for social services, congressional vetoes, rising budget deficits, or fears of inflation. It will come from the fact that the United States simply is not prepared to manufacture that many more weapons.

Since the Viet Nam War, the productive capacity of the American defense industry has atrophied at an alarming rate. This results in part from the anti-militarism and consequent decline in defense spending that followed the Viet Nam War. It has also been caused by high-technology firms turning to consumer products and the manufacture of computer and automation equipment.

It is in very large part the result of companies turning away from the defense because of government indecision, mind-changing, and lack of long-range planning, particularly during the Carter administration.

But it's a fact. The Reagan administration is contemplating an arms build-up that, even in terms of 1965 dollars, far exceeds that for the Viet Nam War. Yet the American defense industry will not be able to deliver. That is why White House economist Murray Weidenbaum, among others, wants the defense budget cut.

According to the Morgan Guaranty Survey, the number of military aircraft subcontractors in this country fell by 35 per cent between 1968 and 1975. U. S. News & World Report found the number of Navy suppliers reduced by 25 per cent since the war. Aerospace contractors have fallen from 6,000 in 1967 to 3,500 today

There is only one company in the entire United States that makes precision ball bearings for military aircraft and only one that makes turrets and hulls for the M60 tank. Only three companies manufacture aircraft landing gear. Only two companies can make Trident submarines. Disgusted with performance, Navy Secretary John Lehman started talking about having the subs built in Europe.

Already, some 90 per cent of our radar, underwater surveillance, and missile guidance systems depends on components assembled in the Far East.

The American defense industry is suffering from a shortage of raw materials. A lack of lightweight titanium for F-15 and F-16 jet engines has doubled production time. Chromium, vital for M1 battle tank engines, is scarce. The price of Zairian cobalt has gone up 246 per cent since 1978. Our quartz supply for navigation instruments is down to near zero.

A more severe problem is the shortage of skilled workers. American defense industries reported a shortage of 30,000 aerospace and electrical engineers in 1979. They recruit only three-quarters of the new machinists they need every year, and there's expected to be a 250,000-man machinist shortage in 1985. Shortages of computer specialists and statisticians are running at more than 50 per cent. Some 15,000 skilled workers would be needed to start work on the B-1. Where would they come from? Where and how quickly would they be trained?

Moreover, the industrial plant of the defense industry is aging. According to the U. S. News survey, 20,000 of 26,000 government-owned machine tools are more than 20 years old. Sixty per cent of the machinery used to build aircraft is more than 20 years old. And the machine tool industry is running at almost full capacity. A U. S. Maritime Administration study found that American shipyards lag in more than half of the new technologies used in modern warship building.

Shoving tons of money and tons of orders into the intake funnel of the American defense industry in a hurry will not improve matters. It will only clog the funnel.

It will cause increased delays, and delays and cost overruns have already made the defense industry a major factor in our deficit and thus in inflation. As it is, the average cost of the 47 major weapons systems now being manufactured for the Pentagon rose 20 per cent in 1980, while the inflation rate for the entire economy came to just 9.3 per cent.

At the same time, that sort of pressure for so many weapons so fast is going to produce shoddy goods.

The only immediate source of new skilled workers for the defense industry is in the civilian sector. Hiring them away at the higher pay scales required by the Davis-Bacon Act will drive inflation higher and bring about a decline in American-made consumer goods, reducing productivity and the gross national product and kicking inflation even higher.

The White House will soon have to decide whether it is politically possible to ask for the kind of consumer sacrifice necessary to engage in an all-out strategic and conventional arms race with the Soviets. The manpower, material, and plant capacity shortages suggest that the United States is not now capable of engaging in such a race anyway.

Defense spending must become the art of the possible. The Reagan administration should be taking the longest, hardest, and most dispassionate of looks at what our true defense needs are, at how much we can really afford to spend, and at how much we are honestly capable of building.

It should give as much priority to the careful rebuilding of our defense plant as it does to the procurement of new weapons, and it should do so on the basis of sound, long-range planning.

It is fine for the generals and admirals to barge into the restaurant throwing money around and ordering everything on the menu. But if there's only one cook in the kitchen frying hamburger, that's all they're going to get.

Complexity of Arms Seen as Counter-Productive

Each year sees the introduction of more technologically sophisticated weapons into the Pentagon budget, such as the "smart" missiles that can be redirected to new targets after launching, or the radar-evading Stealth bomber. The cost of producing these complex weapons means that fewer of each of them can be afforded. According to several reports by the General Accounting Office and military analysts in 1981, it also meant that the new weapons were more prone to breakdowns; there was, quite simply, more that could go wrong with these weapons than with their simpler predecessors. Many of them were more expensive not only to build but to operate, and as a result the men who would have to use them were getting insufficient "hands-on" training. Maintenance budgets, it was argued, were not large enough to keep such weapons in operable condition.

Against these considerations were heard the assertions of Administration officials that each new weapon was necessary if the U.S. was to meet the threat of Soviet arms capabilities. If a new plane was 10 times more effective than its predecessor, the argument went, fewer of them would be necessary in combat. This basic difference in outlook also tended to separate adherents of more conventional arms from those who favored building strategic nuclear weapons. The question remains unresolved in 1983. Secretary of Defense Caspar Weinberger, addressing the Air Force Association in September, declared; "Critics who would have us do without this modern equipment—make do with cheaper, less sophisticated, easier-to-maintain technology—don't consider really the value of human life. . . I don't want to send our men out to fight in equipment that I know is inferior to the Soviets'."

The Salt Lake Tribune
Salt Lake City, Utah, February 3, 1981

Laymen who have done battle with "the computer" will have no difficulty understanding a critical Pentagon report which concludes that multibillion dollar investment in increasingly complicated weapons is beginning to boomerang on the armed forces, undermining America's combat readiness.

Boiled down to essentials, the report emphasizes that the more "advanced" a weapons system is, the more apt it is to break down. Further, the highly complicated weapons require equally highly trained technicians to operate them. All this takes time and costs money which the national security cannot spare.

A news story in Monday's Tribune noted that the Air Force is wooing back ex-pilots from the commercial airlines as one way to man its fleet of sophisticated combat aircraft. The story noted that it costs the Air Force $1 million to train one pilot to fly such craft as the F-15 fighter. It also takes several years.

One F-15 costs $27.8 million yet, according to a report by former Secretary of Defense Harold Brown, the Air Force's F-15s were "out of commission" 44 percent of the time because of mechanical malfunctions.

The Pentagon study critical of growing reliance on highly technical equipment was alluded to by Sen. Sam Nunn, D-Ga., during a meeting of the Senate Armed Services Committee. It has not been officially released by the Defense Department. The senator told new Defense Secretary Caspar Weinberger that the study "basically shows that the increasing complexity in almost all of our weapons systems has led to certain disastrous developments" which he then listed.

Attacking U.S. technical advances in weaponry is akin to questioning the character of Abraham Lincoln. Reliance on superior technology is a central tenet of U.S. defense policy. American superiority in weaponry is supposed to compensate for disadvantages the nation might face in manpower on the battlefield. But if the super weapons are too expensive, not reliable and require more highly trained operators than can readily be found, then the basic concept is greatly suspect.

That doesn't mean that faith in technology must or should be drastically curtailed. But it does argue for a reappraisal of the way in which technology is evaluated. It means that instead of contracting for a new gun that can shoot around corners simply because technology can produce it, the Pentagon must take into consideration other factors such as how often the trigger mechanism breaks down and whether it is militarily worth it to spend millions to shoot around corners in the first place.

The Houston Post
Houston, Texas, March 24, 1981

Are U.S. defense planners relying too heavily on weaponry so technologically complex and delicate it may be impractical in battlefield use? The question has been raised in two recent reports and is likely to figure prominently in the forthcoming debate on the hefty defense spending increase sought by President Reagan.

An internal Air Force study, smoked out by congressional pressure, terms the growing dependence on high-technology weapons "a form of organizational cancer" that eats away at defense budgets while supporting fewer and fewer planes, ships and other arms. Another study by the General Accounting Office, the research arm of Congress, concludes that the Pentagon brass is so enamored with high-tech wonder weapons it overlooks the possibility that they may not be rugged enough to perform reliably in combat.

The GAO cites numerous instances of planes, ships and other weapons impaired by the failure of key electronic parts. A few examples: The Air Force's F-15 fighter planes are frequently grounded for repairs, particularly of the engines, from which the Air Force has demanded extremely high performance. The antitank missile system on the Army's Cobra attack helicopter averages a failure every 100 hours. The Navy's advanced electronic weapons-control system was usable only 60 percent of the time in 1979. The report says that when the system fails "a ship is virtually defenseless."

Critics of the present trend toward increasingly complex weapons systems contend that we should adopt simpler weapons and put less emphasis on attaining narrow edges of superiority over Soviet weapons. They argue, for example, that we paid dearly for the new M1 tank's 5 percent advantage over the first-line Russian tanks. They further contend that the Soviets have developed their weapons at a steady pace, progressing from one model to the next with a series of gradual improvements.

Defenders of the present practice of buying weapons systems incorporating more and more high-tech features reject the argument that we should return to simpler systems. William J. Perry, a former undersecretary of defense who supervised development and procurement of new weapons, says the simplicity of Soviet arms is a myth. Perry, who has been temporarily retained as a consultant by the Reagan administration, points out that late-model Soviet weapons are every bit as complex as ours, some even more so. While conceding some mistakes in high-tech weapons development, he contends that advanced electronics is making weapons simpler, more reliable and easier to repair. Most of the failures, he says, involve electromechanical systems that are 15 to 20 years old and need to be replaced.

Perry also points out that for the past decade the Soviets have outspent us in weapons development. Even though they lack our technological expertise, he says, that long-term investment has begun to pay off. The Army's M1 tank, he believes, is superior to any the Russians have, but we are just getting into production while they have thousands of tanks ready for combat.

Lt. Gen. Kelly Burke, the Air Force weapons research director, makes perhaps the most telling point in the weapons technology debate when he says: "To send a young American over to Europe in an F-5 (the fighter preceding the F-15) against a MiG-23 is to make cannon fodder of him." That, after all, is the bottom line. Ways must be found to improve the reliability and readiness of our technologically advanced arms. Their failure to function can also cost lives. But we should not be gulled into building weapons inferior to those they might confront on some future battlefield.

The Boston Globe

Boston, Mass., May 11, 1981

Most attention during the House budget debate last week was focused on the end of the liberal era. However, the most interesting question raised by the budget is how the military portion will be ultimately spent. It was increased to $188 billion from the $159 billion proposed by President Carter, and how all that money is spent will be a major test of the Reagan Administration's political strength and management skills.

Reagan has, since the early stages of his campaign for the White House, stressed his belief that the American military program has been shortchanged. To cure that problem, he endorsed reductions in social programs to free funds for military spending. He has won the political battle for the cuts but only begun the job of setting priorities for the Pentagon.

Most of the early rhetoric has concentrated on the spectacular: Restore the B1 bomber in a modified form; build another nuclear supercarrier; step up the pace of the MX missile program; prepare the way for a three-ocean Navy; buy more Mach 3 fighter-bombers.

Programs like these are the show-biz of American military power. They may not be worthless from a military point of view, although there is increasing criticism of oversophistication in American armaments. They have the political advantage of being highly popular with a Congress that often prefers the spectacular to the mundane in military programs.

The problem with hypersophistication is that it fails to address much more serious shortcomings of the military, concentrated largely in the areas of personnel, maintenance, supply and orderly procurement.

It does relatively little good to have a lot of fancy new machines if there are inadequate numbers of inadequately trained people to operate them. Even now, the US military is hard pressed to fill all of its authorized posts.

The Administration, to its credit, has begun to address some of the issues. Last month some Pentagon review groups sketched new systems for more orderly procurement of weapons systems to avoid start-stop buying patterns that make planning very hard for suppliers.

Even this review, though, reflects a hardware-oriented set of priorities rather than a people-oriented set. Unless the Reagan Administration can come to grips with the fundamental need to run the machines it buys, and keep them in good operating order, it will have lost the battle it seemed to have won on the floor of the House on Thursday.

Sentinel Star

Orlando, Fla., February 10, 1981

JUST AS he is beginning to address the problems of America's military strength, Secretary of Defense Caspar Weinberger has received an unsettling report from the General Accounting Office, which says that too many complex new weapons systems are just that: too complex.

Among the particulars, the GAO notes:

● The new Navy systems controlling the guns and missiles on the Navy's newest combat ships suffer from chronic breakdowns, rendering the ships "virtually defenseless."

● The turret on the Army's $600,000 battle tank is "fantastically complex" and has had a "long history of unreliability."

● The fuses on cannon shells used by U.S. ships on NATO duty were designed with such close tolerances that they "would not fire from a gun that was not perfectly maintained, a near-impossible task in a shipboard environment."

CAUTION: SYSTEM FAILURE

● Some of the problems of the F-15 fighter stem from complex but failure-prone electronic test equipment that was intended to minimize F-15 maintenance problems in the field.

Although not specifically mentioned in the report, another factor has to be the emphasis the American military has always placed on technology to make up for personnel shortages. Complicating this still further are the swelling lines of departing skilled technicians — non-coms who make up the backbone of a highly technical military machine — who are leaving for a variety of social, pay and other reasons. Perhaps the single most serious question the military faces today is, Who will work at making the machine work?

There also seems to be far too little recognition of the basic tenet of the grunt, the seaman or the line airman: "If something can go wrong, it will go wrong," and of its corollary, that "it will usually go wrong at the least opportune time."

Before spending billions of dollars on new weapons, President Reagan must address the reliability factor and copy the Soviet Union, which stresses simplicity and reliability above all else.

An operational F-15 is the world's most advanced aircraft. Grounded for a system failure, it is a piece of junk.

The Oregonian

Portland, Ore., February 23, 1981

The risk the United States runs in beefing up its defense system is that it will follow the Soviet lead and try to substitute numbers and muscle for brains and superior technology. Such a course would prove fatal in the long run and ruinously costly in the short term.

So far, the debate over America's defense expenditures has centered on how much money should be spent rather than on whether an effort to sustain technical advantages should be eclipsed with a greater emphasis on mass, muscle and numbers.

William Perry, the retiring chief of research and development for the Department of Defense, firmly believes ingenuity, "smart weapons," new ideas and the nation's ability to produce sophisticated gadgets would win over the ponderous Soviet approach. The most difficult task the new administration will face, he recently reported in Science, will be in convincing the public to put its faith in basic research and advanced technology as the security backbone of the nation.

Perry said electronic technology is about to give birth to a new generation of precision weapons, relying on natural microwaves rather than on wire-guided and laser targeting. The new munitions won't even require human beings to spot-guide them. In his opinion, they make it inconceivable the Russians could carry out a successful invasion of Western Europe.

The public has worried that the hardware of war has become overly sophisticated, far too costly (gold-plated) and probably unreliable when used in actual combat. It is reassuring that some experts believe the new revolution in weapons will produce more reliable and less expensive hardware too difficult for the Soviets to copy, as Perry insists.

While it has not been the policy to match the Soviets tank for tank, missile for missile, sub for sub, there is a danger, if the quantity gap gets too wide, as many believe it now is, or if weapons are built only for engineers and not soldiers, that technical excellence could be overcome with brute power. Knowing precisely when brawn will overwhelm brains will prove difficult; thus, the margin cannot be cut too fine, as it may be at the present time.

In dealing with strategic systems, such as the MX, Perry believes either a land-based or submarine system can pass technical tests. But he said, "Deterrence exists as much in the minds of your opponents as in your technical capability." He added, that a proposed MX compromise — putting the MX in old silos — would be "The worst of all possible solutions," as it would increase Soviet interests in striking first, forcing the United States to adopt a policy of "launching on warning." That amounts to turning the start of World War III over to a computer, he said.

In the end, the United States has no real choice but to bank on brains over brawn. The efforts of those, like Perry, who were able to reverse a 12-year trend of cutting defense research funds, thus trying to make smart weapons even smarter, should not again get lost in an enriched defense budget.

THE PLAIN DEALER
Cleveland, Ohio, May 24, 1981

America's decline militarily is now recognized. Dramatically higher defense spending — at least $25.8 billion more — is in store for fiscal 1982. Yet, one major problem remains — the Defense Department's deserved reputation of being wasteful and of preferring to plan and buy ever more expensive and complicated military toys.

Certain military needs are clear. The military forces are short on ships, planes that are ready and useable and other equipment and material. The military is plagued with problems of retaining qualified and highly skilled personnel. The nation's forces are hardly combat ready. The means for rapid deployment are lacking. Morale and discipline are not up to proper standards.

Fortunately, the Reagan administration is taking steps to improve the pay of military personnel and to provide other incentives to retain qualified personnel. Recruiting procedures, particularly for the Army's all-volunteer force, are being changed to emphasize quality, not quantity.

Higher defense spending to meet these needs and on conventional equipment to improve the military's readiness is justified. But what continues to worry many Americans, and us, is the Pentagon's propensity to spend billions of dollars in search of somewhat mystical new weapons systems.

The Pentagon's planners should concentrate first on solving the structural problems of the military's forces. Defense procurement practices have placed too much emphasis on highly complex weapons systems which can prove to be obsolete by the time they are ready. Consider the B-1 bomber proposal. It is a costly weapons system that by the time of its readiness would have been too vulnerable to destruction by sophisticated missiles.

The Reagan administration has a unique opportunity to restore the nation's military position in the world. It must not lose the support of the American public by allowing the Pentagon to go on a spending spree that poses the threat of more wasteful spending and more inflation.

Secretary of Defense Caspar W. Weinberger promises a fight against traditional waste and inefficiency. He says the administration desires the maximum improvements in defense capabilities for every dollar spent. The defense secretaries of other administrations have uttered the same noble promises — only to fail. But Weinberger's background as a no-nonsense budgetary conservative is reason for hope.

Retired U.S. Army Gen. Maxwell D. Taylor recently advised the Reagan administration to display "toughness in examining the military policy recommended by the Pentagon." Taylor said the Defense Department should be required to present strong evidence of precisely how its major military requirements "relate to the protection of specific national interests and to the support" of the president's foreign policy.

The former Army chief-of-staff and chairman of the Joint Chiefs of Staff offers sound advice. The Reagan administration, if it is to spend defense dollars wisely, needs to shape a new doctrine that defines in a rational manner to what extent the nation will go to deter Soviet expansionism. Critical to such a doctrine is support of the American people, which will require choosing weapons systems cautiously and wisely.

THE INDIANAPOLIS STAR
Indianapolis, Ind., May 27, 1981

Top military brass is talking of putting super-secret United States defense data into a computer system where — so it is said — it will be safe.

That should make people who work with computers shudder with disbelief.

Safe?

Data — whole stories and big hunks of them, research and notes and information of all sorts — disappear in computers never to be seen again.

No one seems to know exactly why, although as with UFOs just about everyone has a theory.

The operator will punch a terminal keyboard with coding as familiar as the palm of his hand. The computer, for reasons which only it fathoms, responds: "No such queue."

Or an operator bats the equivalent of six pages of copy into the blooming computer and — all at once — there is a "bleep" and the whole thing aborts, as they say.

Suppose the generals fall for this blinking idea and super-secret defense data is entrusted to these mercurial, dandy gadgets.

It would be only a matter of time before some alarmed, bright-eyed young colonel in a secret lair in some hollowed-out mountain springs up and blurts:

"General, the enemy is approaching our shores and the skies are full of missiles. What do I do?"

Says the general: "Punch Redeye Hot Dog Niner and activate Plan D."

The colonel sits down at the computer terminal and pecks away.

The screen flashes back: "No such queue."

There's no time for arguing or fiddling around.

What next?

Maybe the generals should stick to old-fashioned ways. When we've had to we've won a lot of wars with them

'No 220 outlets!?!! What the heck kinda battlefield are you running here, soldier!?!'

Rockford Register Star

Rockford, Ill., July 13, 1981

"A billion here, a billion there," the late Sen. Everett McKinley Dirksen once said, "and pretty soon you're talking about real money."

That's what concerns critics as President Reagan plans massive new military spending which threaten to scuttle hopes for a balanced federal budget, endangers the fight to control inflation and offsets the fiscal gains from his billions of dollars in social spending cuts.

Reagan plans the greatest peacetime military spending spree in the nation's history, escalating costs into the trillions of dollars. And what does the nation get in return?

THE MILWAUKEE JOURNAL
Milwaukee, Wisc., October 4, 1981

The world seems transfixed by fancy weapons that operate on the frontiers of technology. Call it the "macro-military" focus.

Meanwhile, on the "micro-military" front, remember the Iraq-Iran war? Despite a generally static battle line, thousands have perished — their deaths largely unnoticed by the rest of humankind. There's a topic for the political philosophers: Is it any less awful when Tennyson's "blood-red blossom of war blooms in the far crevices of the world"?

The dug-in Iraqi forces and the Iranian troopers across the dusty way have been dying right along from sniper fire, from tank and artillery exchanges and in fierce small-unit clashes. If their war has dropped from headlines and television, it exemplifies what we tend to forget in intense debate over MX, theater nuclear forces and the like: that war, finally, is carried on by men whose names will never be known; it is pursued by isolated groups of individuals in profound uncertainty whether they will be alive a millisecond hence. No matter their uniforms, language or the vagrant circumstances that bring them to combat, individuals pay their nation's brutal bill of war.

If by some supreme act of imagination, people were able to keep constantly in mind the image of a mangled 19-year-old infantryman — of whatever nationality in whatever exotic conflict — they would natter less casually about asserting national power.

That sentiment does not denigrate those who choose the hard calling of arms. Nor does it evade the fact that preserving a country's values can require force. But reflection from time to time on the grotesque nature of war should increase appreciation of the selflessness of those who respond to duty's often ambiguous summons. It was the frequent denial of such appreciation that still sears veterans of the Vietnam War.

The Iraq-Iran conflict is likely to continue inconclusively, neither side able to marshal the combination of political will and military resources for conquest. In the renewed fighting around Abadan, the Iraqis conceded they had been forced into a withdrawal — but, they said, at a cost to the Iranians of 2,700 casualties. That's two thousand seven hundred men.

According to many knowledgeable experts, including some within the military, the nation just might get a military force even less equipped to cope with today's problems.

Some specific examples of what this spending is apt to produce are emerging.

WE WOULD, FOR EXAMPLE, get very little improvement in the nation's now-inadequate tactical strike force, so necessary in the limited confrontations of the last decade. Instead:

—We would get 20,000 new civilian employees on the Pentagon payroll by the end of 1982.

—For $54 billion we would get 250 new bombers to replace today's 375 B-52s and FB-111s.

—For $30 billion we would get a nuclear aircraft carrier task force which has been called "a large floating target for advanced Soviet missiles."

—For $26 billion we would get 13 new Trident submarines, armed with 24 missiles each, to replace the 41 Polaris and Poseidon subs and their 656 missiles now at sea.

—For somewhere between $43 and $82 billion we would get the MX missile system which will destroy thousands of square miles of productive rangeland in Utah and Nevada, but which either isn't needed or has no hopes of growing fast enough to assure it would survive a Soviet first strike — depending on which "expert" evaluation of Soviet missile capability you believe.

That is, the nation would get these weapons eventually if present massive design problems can be overcome. Even under the most optimistic forecasts, some of these weapon systems could not be available until the year 2000.

In short, for $1.3 trillion in defense spending over the next five years (about $5,800 for every man, woman and child in America) the nation could get a smaller, but more technical military arsenal sometime within the next two decades.

THIS COMPLETE RELIANCE on high-technology weapons has come under massive attack on many fronts. New Hampshire Sen. Warren Rudman, a member of the Defense Appropriations Subcommittee, may have best expressed this opposition when he said:

"Nowhere is the gap between prudent strategic planning and force procurement policy more pronounced than in the services' seeming fascination with high-technology weaponry. If simply acquistion of ever more complex and less reliable systems substitutes for the well defined strategic thinking which should guide their use, then our most grievous military setback will be largely self-inflicted. The spending of dollars alone, the failure to realistically evaluate the threats that we face and the surrender of our intellect to simplistic solutions will not lead to America's return as the preeminent military force in the world, but rather to our continuing decline."

There are specifics to site, including:

—The Navy's newest high-technology radar system is effective only 60 percent of the time.

—A prized new Army tank which is laden with sophisticated electronic equipment, but cannot survive dust and dirt.

—The Navy's new F-18 fighter plane, at $30 million each, cannot match the performance of the much less expensive F-5 in actually combat-type exercises carried out by Navy pilots.

—The B-52 bomber, just now being converted to carry what may be our most potent strategic weapon, the cruise missile, would be replaced with fewer B-1 or "Stealth" bombers which would not carry these pilotless long-range missiles.

—High-performance short-range Sidewinder missiles would be replaced by Sparrow and Phoenix missiles which cost up to 100 times as much, but do not perform as well.

—Our 41 Polaris and Poseidon subs, the one missile-launching system guaranteed under today's technology to survive any Soviet first strike, would be replaced by a handful of Trident subs which already are two years behind schedule. Just this month, the first sea-tests of the first $2 billion Trident were launched and there is a serious question about the manufacturer's ability to meet any construction schedule. The United States already has, right now, fewer nuclear missile subs at sea than at any time since the 1960s. Conversion to Trident submarines would further reduce this most critical of all nuclear-deterrent weapons.

But the most questionable spending plan of all involves the MX missile system, a program under which missiles would be shuttled among concrete-and-steel shelters so the Soviets would not know where they were. Costs would range from 200 missiles at 4,600 sites for $43.3 billion to 550 missiles and 12,500 sites for $82.6 billion.

A RECENTLY-RELEASED study by the Office of Technology Assessment (OTA), Congress' research arm, says this system could not possibly be built or expanded faster than the Soviet's ability to locate the sites and target individual missiles for every possible site in any first strike.

The OTA looked at 11 possible methods of launching intercontinental ballistic missiles and said only submarine-launched missiles would have any chance of surviving a Soviet first strike. "No existing technology and no technology believed to be on the horizon," the report says, "offers any promise for permitting an effective Soviet attack on a fleet of small MX-carrying submarines." That agrees completely with military claims that a defense system based on nuclear deterent can best be provided by a large number of rather small submarines.

Such a defense system has no room, nor any need, for bigger — but fewer — submarines, billion-dollar bombers or massive ground-based missile systems. Yet the record spending being urged today by the Pentagon would spend more than a trillion dollars on such weapons, while seriously reducing the number of American subs — and the number of submarine-launched missiles — available.

Former Secretary of Defense Melvin Laird once warned: "The worst thing that could happen is for the nation to go on a defense spending binge that will create economic havoc at home and confusion abroad and that cannot be wisely dealt with by the Pentagon."

That is exactly what the Reagan administration is proposing.

Sentinel Star
Orlando, Fla., July 27, 1981

AMERICA has always trusted machines to do its work: machines to sow and reap, machines to make cars and clothes, machines to destroy men and other machines.

During the last 30 years America's predilection for things mechanical has also assumed a dominance in our national defense posture. It is a disturbing inclination to overemphasize technology — complex machinery — at the expense of the human factor.

It is a trend that has touched off a national debate among defense experts. And those soldiers whose lives will be on the line if hostilities erupt are even more pessimistic about the shift to more complex weapons. Front-line soldiers know better than anyone the truth of the adage, "If something can go wrong, it will go wrong." And the older hands add, "And it will always go wrong at the worst possible time."

For the past four weeks, in this continuing series of editorials, we have examined this country's urgent need for a return to the draft, the necessity of a clear decision on the MX missile and the disturbing lack of cohesion in NATO. Yet, within the ranks, there may be no greater concern than the reliability of the highly technical weaponry that is rapidly becoming an American military staple.

In his rush to revitalize America's military, President Reagan must address the question of just when reliance on technology surpasses the point of peak efficiency and becomes too expensive and too complex for the country's good.

Consider some contemporary examples:

● The U.S. Army, whose 11,500 tanks face 48,000 Soviet tanks, relies on wire-guided missiles to improve the odds of winning on the battlefield. But the TOW and Dragon rockets are so expensive that the men assigned to shoot them at onrushing Soviet tanks never get to launch more than one a year.

● The Navy's Phoenix missile is said to be the state of the art in air-to-air missiles, and yet, at a cost of $2 million each, it is almost never fired in training. The pilots have to assume the missiles will work as the engineers say they will when a Soviet Foxbat is zooming in for the kill.

● The Air Force is putting all of its air-defense chips on the sleek back of the F-15 Eagle. But the aircraft is so complex and the parts so costly and in such short supply that the F-15 shows only a 15 percent readiness. This is for an airplane that costs $20 million a copy.

This emphasis on high technology got its greatest boost from Robert McNamara, whose zeal for efficiency was matched only by his faith in technology. Perhaps no greater monument exists to the problems with this philosophy than the now-forgotten "McNamara line." Consisting of thousands of listening devices, "people sniffers," and seismic sensors designed to look like palm trees, the line was conceived by the then-secretary of defense to impede North Vietnamese movement across the "demilitarized zone" separating the Vietnams. It cost hundreds of millions of dollars and hundreds of American lives to install and monitor. Its effectiveness speaks for itself.

It is a little ironic that the leftover sensors, still disguised as palm trees, are now in northern European supply depots awaiting deployment behind Soviet lines in the event of a war.

It seems to many Americans directly involved in defense — pilots, tank commanders, deck officers — that their needs are given only lip service by the engineers who design weapons and by the generals and civilians who buy them. A defense expert recently said the military was guilty of "consciously subordinating warfare priorities to bureaucratic priorities ... by layers upon layers of engineering officers" who "don't understand strategy and operations, only engineering."

And the cost of pursuing what engineers say will work as opposed to what the grunts know will work is becoming prohibitive. As a rule of thumb, the Department of Defense says the cost of tanks has escalated 10 times since World War II, airplanes 100 times and anti-tank and aircraft missiles 2,000 times.

Indeed, a defense expert recently noted that the simple arithmetic progression of jet fighter costs is such that "if the trend continues, in the year 2054, the entire defense budget will purchase just one tactical aircraft."

We cannot abandon our reliance on our technological edge. But if we are to survive, neither can we allow our fascination with machines to override the critical, basic need for weapons that work and weapons that we can afford.

DESERET NEWS
Salt Lake City, Utah, August 10, 1981

Is America really getting the "biggest bang for the buck" out of its military expenditures? Or is much of that money being lost in the increasing complexity of military hardware?

Those questions are important because the Pentagon is now calculating total costs for a five-year military buildup intended to meet the Russian challenge. Those costs are staggering. In a report released last week, the Defense Department announced a record five-year budget program costing more than $1.6 trillion for fiscal 1983 through 1987 — $4 per day for every man, woman and child.

Not only are weapons systems growing more costly, but more complex as well. And the military's demand for the "latest" technological advances is adding to both cost and complexity, but not always to combat efficiency.

Costs of individual weapons systems are escalating at a dizzying pace. The MX system, it is estimated, would cost $60-$100 billion before it is finished and operational. The proposed B-1 manned strategic bomber comes with a $20 billion price tag.

But even high cost does not mean good serviceability, even under peacetime conditions. Avionics packages are now so complex on some advanced fighters that the "down time" when they're undergoing repairs is cutting their combat effectiveness.

The F-15 Eagle, for example, contains 45 black boxes that control guidance and weapons systems, navigation, and other components of the plane. Cockpit indicators allow the pilot to know when any of those boxes is malfunctioning. It's a simple job to remove the defective box and snap in a new one.

But for repair crews, it takes from three to eight hours for each avionics expert to check one black box. Imagine the nightmare of trying to maintain more than 3,000 black boxes for a typical tactical wing with about 72 F-15 fighters.

Author James Fallows, in his book on "National Defense," maintains that our defense establishment is mesmerized by costly and complex weapons systems that end up providing less, not more, military security. He cites the M-16 rifle and F-16 jet fighters as examples of simple, efficient designs that have been complicated into combat unworkability by requested changes.

The helicopter malfunctions during the Iranian hostage rescue mission, the sorry performance of the Army's new main battle tank, the recent breakdown of the USS Guam in the Philadelphia River after a $23 million overhaul ... all leave a certain uneasiness about the state of the military arts. Money, regardless of how many billions, will not procure an efficient defense establish-

The Virginian-Pilot

Norfolk, Va., December 20, 1981

Georges Clemenceau asserted that war was too serious a matter to be entrusted to the military. And the bipartisan Military Reform Caucus, which Second District Rep. G. William Whitehurst co-founded with Sen. Gary Hart, D-Colo., is saying that defense is too serious a matter to be entrusted entirely to the Defense Department. The point is well-taken.

The battle readiness of America's far-flung military forces is of concern to all Americans. Thoughtful men inside and outside of the defense establishment have been asking hard questions about American military preparedness for several years. They are troubled because more dollars are buying less defense. That's because the Pentagon persists in ordering gold-plated tanks, aircraft, naval vessels and other military hardware in its pursuit of "the magic weapon," as the Atlantic magazine's Washington editor put it, "the weapon that will make victory automatic, that will give ten men the power of ten thousand."

Alas, as weapons become more costly and more complicated, the military buys fewer of them. It then devotes more and more dollars to maintaining them because of their vulnerability to mechanical failure. Observing that aircraft costs "have been increasing by a factor of four every ten years," a Martin Marietta Aerospace official projected, tongue in cheek, that "in the year 2054, the entire defense budget will purchase just one tactical aircraft [which] will have to be shared between the Air Force and the Navy, three and a half days each per week."

The Capitol Hill reaction to this trend — manifest in the emergence of the Military Reform Caucus — is, if anything, overdue. But now congressional judgments that U.S. defenses have been weakened by a slavish devotion to technology underlie the recent demand by the House Appropriations Committee that the Army consider buying armored infantry carriers instead of the expensive M-2, and that the Navy consider augmenting its nuclear-powered submarine fleet with diesel-powered submarines. It also explains the adoption of an amendment (offered by Sen. Sam Nunn, D-Ga., a steadfast support-

er of a strong military) directing the Pentagon to notify Congress whenever the projected cost of a new weapon rises more than 15 percent — the costs of 14 weapon systems studied by the General Accounting Office rose by 30 percent last year.

Not long ago, Deputy Defense Secretary Frank Carlucci told the Senate that the Pentagon had subordinated military readiness "to hardware procurement and deployment." That remarkable admission confirmed the darkest suspicions of military commanders whose units have been starved for essential operation and maintenance funds to pay for exotic new weapons.

In his farewell address in 1961, President Eisenhower noted that the "conjunction of an immense military establishment and a large arms industry is new in the American experience." He warned his countrymen to "guard against the acquisition of unwarranted influence, whether sought or unsought, by the military-industrial complex." That the nation's defenses have been jeopardized by that influence probably would not have surprised him at all.

THE SACRAMENTO BEE

Sacramento, Calif., July 20, 1981

For years the Pentagon has confused weapons sophistication with military strength, and spending with problem solving. According to the most recent analyses of American military power — based largely on criticisms coming from inside the Defense Department itself — the results could well be disastrous if this is allowed to continue.

Sophisticated weapons systems that break down repeatedly and are too complicated to easily repair obviously undermine America's military position. Yet as the Government Accounting Office and the Defense Department have documented, such failures have become endemic in the military without changing weapons planning at all. M-16 rifles are still being bought although they were so troublesome in Vietnam that enemy troops wouldn't even take them from dead soldiers; the new M-1 tank lasts an average of 34 miles between breakdowns, and that in non-combat conditions; the radar and firing system on the Navy's most advanced ships works only 60 percent of the time because of random failures among its 40,000 parts; at least one-third of F-15 fighter planes are grounded at any one time, and their maintenance depends on three diagnostic computers which themselves are out of commission 20 percent to 50 percent of the time.

The new critics are even more concerned, however, with the subtler problems created by the military's continuing quest for superiority through complexity. As weapons get fancier, we can afford fewer and fewer of them, and fewer manufacturers develop the capacity to produce them. We thus fall perennially further behind the Russians in the one area — number of armaments — that is continually used to justify new spending. And we lose, as well, the capacity to increase produc-

tion dramatically in an emergency.

Moreover, because the new weapons are so expensive to build, use and maintain, the military is reluctant to test them or use them in training. Not only does readiness suffer as a result, but the weapons themselves are rarely judged in battle conditions. This brings us such notable absurdities as the Pentagon's newest anti-tank weapon, which is remarkably accurate but can only be fired by a 5-foot-5-inch, 225-pound soldier, who must expose himself to enemy fire for a full 10 seconds in order to aim the weapon. Similarly, the newest jet fighter system allows pilots to shoot down planes they can't see, but since they can't tell friend from foe without looking at him, pilots in Vietnam were ordered not to use the new system at all.

The Reagan administration's military goal is to develop the capacity to show power on any and all fronts. With this kind of strategy, it makes no sense to concentrate production on a limited number of expensive weapons. Indeed, even without the grand pretensions of such a strategy, America's broad and changing interests in a volatile world suggest placing a premium on military flexibility and mobility.

Yet flexibility is precisely what has been sacrificed by spending vast sums on gadgetry that loads down our air, land and naval vessels and requires them to travel in tandem with enormous and complex support systems. And because of the long lead-times and high costs associated with the unadaptable new super-weapons, we will be stuck with them long after the particular tactical and policy needs they were designed for have disappeared.

For the past 30 years, the new military critics point out, defense planners have consistently overestimated the funds that will be

available to them several years down the road, and this has compounded the risks of relying on a few very complicated and expensive weapons. Building state-of-the-art equipment inevitably involves cost overruns; combined with tighter-than-expected budgets, this has left the military perpetually short of funds for maintenance and operation — and with continually fewer baskets for its eggs.

The Reagan administration says it will increase defense spending enough each year to avoid these problems. But even if such enormous defense budgets made sense for the American economy, they are not to be counted on politically. No past administration has succeeded in sustaining increases of the size Reagan has promised, even during the Korean and Vietnam wars. When the Reagan team budgeted for a 35 percent increase in purchases and construction over the next two years and only a 4 percent increase in support costs — saying it can always pay for upkeep in the future — it was as if the lessons of 30 years, of grounded fighter jets and of unoutfitted Army units had never been learned.

The Defense Department's answer to its internal and external critics is that it has no problems money can't fix. But money obviously can be — and has been — spent without improving American battle readiness, the logic of military plans, the morale of the troops, or even the American position vis-a-vis Russia. Indeed, a better-funded continuation of the military's ethos of giantism and its nearly mindless faith in technology threatens to aggravate all these problems rather than solve them.

The administration is in an excellent position to insist on changes in traditional military planning. But first it has to stop thinking bigger and start thinking better — and simpler.

Quality Control, Lack of Bidding Blamed for Arms Deficiencies

W. Paul Thayer, Deputy Secretary of Defense, told a meeting of military contractors in June, 1983 that they could eliminate between 10% and 30% of their costs by simply making weapons and equipment right the first time. Thayer urged the executives, who were gathered in Washington, D.C., to take personal responsibility for quality control. A few weeks later, Rear Adm. Frank C. Collins argued that Thayer's estimate was conservative. Collins, the chief of quality assurance at the Defense Logistics Agency, contended that inferior workmanship added 50% of the cost of weapons and equipment. Their voices were added to a chorus of criticism of defense contractors for shoddy workmanship that inflated cost overruns.

Equally expensive was the failure of purchasers to seek competitive bids from defense contractors and parts suppliers. A study released in July criticized both the Air Force and Navy for negotiating contracts that allowed contractors to raise their prices repeatedly, and for awarding contracts at excessive prices without checking to see if another supplier would provide the items more cheaply. The lack of competition among contractors, critics said, resulted in poor quality and high prices.

THE COMMERCIAL APPEAL
Memphis, Tenn., June 5, 1983

THE PENTAGON is living proof of the adage, the bigger the organization, the bigger the problems. One of the Defense Department's problems is that it pays too much for weapons that don't work. Never fear, though. Our hard-working defense officials are on top of the problem.

Why, the Army is looking for a light antitank weapon that is accurate, works when fired and doesn't cost too much. It has been looking for one since the Korean War, actually, and is determined to find one, by golly. And the Navy, after a decade of trouble with unreliable shipboard radar, is still looking for a system that works.

Those are just two of the stories that have come out of a recent conference called "Bottom Line II" at the Industrial College of the Armed Forces in Washington. Pentagon officials talked about how wasteful it was to buy weapons that don't work. Deputy Secretary of Defense Paul Thayer told contractors they could cut between 10 per cent to 30 per cent from their costs if they didn't rework or remake weapons that were already on assembly lines.

Thayer sounds like a parent admonishing a child to do it right the first time.

The conference participants agreed that only a change in attitude that insisted on quality from design to production would make a difference. The chairman of the board of Lockheed said corporations don't pay enough attention to quality control and said they need "the overriding dedication of top management to quality and reliability for the long term."

This advice is common sensical, but still seems a bit otherworldly. Here we all thought the essence of capitalism was its ability, through competition, to produce high-quality products at reasonable costs. Well, the rules don't seem to apply when it comes to the military.

FOR ONE thing, the military is mesmerized by high-tech gadgets. This fascination causes the military to buy sophisticated systems, some of which actually cost more to maintain than to buy. Generals and admirals, jealous of competing services, rush into buying weapons without being specific about what it is they actually want.

And there isn't a lot of competition among defense contractors. A few firms dominate the field. There are few incentives to hold costs down. Once costs soar, no one is willing to take a hard look at particular systems because so much already has been sunk into them.

"Bottom Line II" is at least a start. Defense officials saying "Please, guys, be good" is marginally better than nothing.

The Houston Post
Houston, Texas, June 18, 1983

Leaders of the military-industrial complex let their hair down the other day and admitted that poorly made weapons and other equipment were adding billions to the cost of defense. Deputy Defense Secretary Paul Thayer told a meeting of major defense contractors that outlays to replace or repair defective military hardware total as much as $16.5 billion annually. He said the contractors could save 10 to 30 percent of their manufacturing costs by reducing waste and inefficiency.

If this order of saving could be achieved, the Reagan administration's proposed $94 billion military procurement budget for fiscal 1984 could be cut by $9.4 billion to $28 billion without sacrificing a single weapon. It is the very size of the defense budget that has focused fresh attention on the price the Pentagon is paying for armed forces materiel. Thayer warned the arms-makers, "Every time there is a story about hardware that doesn't make the grade, our credibility is eroded."

A former chairman of LTV Corporation, an aerospace and defense contractor, Thayer spoke from practical experience as a Pentagon supplier. He was joined by military brass and civilian experts, who cited various factors contributing to the high cost of military equipment. Rear Adm. Frank C. Collins Jr., director of quality assurance for the Defense Logistics Agency, which sponsored the meeting of contractors and defense officials, criticized the quality of both military and civilian goods produced by this country. Other officers said the Pentagon sometimes failed to communicate its needs to contractors or insisted that weapons be produced before they were fully developed.

Joseph Juran, a quality control consultant, said some electronic equipment bought by the military was so poorly made the annual cost of maintaining it was greater than the purchase price. He also pointed out that some U.S. industries operated on the assumption that 10 to 15 percent of their production would have to be scrapped as defective. He said the Japanese, by contrast, accepted a scrap rate of only 1 percent.

Juran blamed this waste, in part, on inadequately trained workers and poorly manufactured materials, such as metals that cannot be machined to close tolerances. But both Pentagon experts and the defense contractors agreed that top management bore the final responsibility for plant efficiency and product quality.

This critical self-examination by the makers of military hardware and their Pentagon customers is encouraging. But pinpointing the problems is only the beginning. Vigorous steps should now be taken to remedy them. Both the taxpayers and military personnel are entitled to the assurance that defense dollars are buying sound, reliable equipment, not being wasted by inept, indifferent management. As Marine Gen. Paul X. Kelley observed, "A money-back guarantee is of little comfort to a Marine whose rifle jams."

The Pentagon must bear a major share of responsibilty for seeing that we get our money's worth for the arms and equipment bought in our name. One way to do that is to let companies know that if they perform poorly on one contract, it will not be forgotten when they are considered for future contracts. The threat of "capital punishment" could go far to improving the quality of our military hardware.

The Detroit News
Detroit, Mich., August 2, 1983

Economic competition is a basic principle of American democracy. Why, then, is the federal government loath to practice it? Only a little more than one-third of the billions of dollars worth of federal contracts are awarded each year on a competitive basis.

The government's preference for noncompetitive, sole-source contracting is unfair to small business and new entrants to federal contracting. It increases the risks of waste, overpricing, and fraud.

A lot of money is involved: In fiscal 1982, federal contract actions totaled $159 billion, $125 billion for the Department of Defense alone. Some 63 percent of the total were sole-source contracts.

Why are so few contracts decided on a sealed-bid basis? One reason is the large number of exemptions to requirements for sealed-bid procurement. The Armed Services Procurement Act alone contains 17 exemptions.

Thus, Sen. Carl Levin has sponsored a bill that would increase competition for federal contracts by narrowing exemptions. The legislation would provide exceptions to competitive bidding in six instances, such as availability from only one source, national security, and urgent need.

Congressional conferees have already approved two other Levin procurement reform goals. One bill requires advance notice of planned procurement actions worth $10,000 or more, a 30-day period for competitive bidding after solicitation, and a 30-day notice of a sole-source procurement. Another lowers the threshold value at which sole-source contracts require approval by the agency's top procurement official.

The reforms are long overdue.

Los Angeles Times
Los Angeles, Calif., July 3, 1983

The Pentagon is starting to make public its longtime private complaints about the billions of dollars that are wasted each year because too many defense contractors do bad work. A few weeks ago one high Defense Department official estimated that slipshod production is adding as much as 30% to the costs of weapons and equipment. Now Rear Adm. Frank C. Collins Jr. of the Defense Logistics Agency suggests that the situation may be even worse. In some cases, Collins says, product costs are 50% higher than they should be because of contractors' failures to get things done right the first time.

The 1984 defense budget proposed by President Reagan allots $94 billion for military procurement. If the Defense Department officials are right, and there is no reason to think that they are not, tens of billions of those dollars may be spent simply on making up for mistakes and wastage.

The worst offenders, according to Collins, are producers of electronic equipment. Only 30% to 40% of what the industry makes for the military is acceptable. The rest has to be redone or discarded. Builders of submarines and cruise missiles also have poor quality records. So do makers of uniforms, of all things. On the other side of the ledger, manufacturers of aircraft, diesel engines and trucks have low rates of waste.

Collins cites several reasons for the waste problem in defense procurement. Some executives of contracting companies, he says, simply lack integrity or don't care about producing quality work—an attitude that quickly enough gets communicated to factory workers. In other cases workers are inefficient because they are poorly trained to begin with. The Defense Logistics Agency, which among other things monitors quality control, has 6,450 inspectors assigned to defense production plants. But, with 280,000 defense contracts to supervise, the inspectors are spread thin. "It's physically impossible," Collins says, "to catch everything if the contractor wants to beat you out." Plenty of contractors apparently want to do just that.

Defense contractors on their part contend, and the Pentagon is now starting to concede, that industry alone is not to blame for the shoddiness and inefficiencies that may lead to massive cost overruns. Weapons are sometimes designed and approved without adequate thought as to how efficiently they can be produced. Rigid deadlines imposed on contractors may lead to corner-cutting that affects durability and performance. In other cases equipment is rushed into production without sufficient testing. "Sometimes," Collins notes, "I feel that we are so in love with the state of the art that we really don't wait to see how to make it right."

Waste can also be created when the Defense Department insists on overly precise specifications for the products that it buys. Harold Brown, who was the defense secretary in the Carter Administration, has proposed one answer to that problem. Brown would have weapon-system contractors meet performance specifications (this is what we want achieved) rather than detailed technical specifications provided by the Pentagon (this is how you must do it). Brown also notes in his recent book, "Thinking About National Security," that close congressional and bureaucratic oversight in systems development, while often necessary, can have cost-raising drawbacks. It is an example of too many cooks seasoning the soup. Brown thinks it is no accident that some of the most innovative, successful and cost-effective additions to defense capabilities, including the U-2 and SR-71 reconnaissance planes and "stealth" technology, have been developed secretly and with minimal outside supervision.

Quality problems between the armed forces and their suppliers, involving everything from boots to food to shot and shell, have always existed. The very word "shoddy," in fact, derives from an inferior quality of wool that was used to make Union Army uniforms during the Civil War. But never before have the problems in military procurement been so costly, or the opportunities for reform so great. Last week, for example, a presidential advisory group reported that the military services could save billions of dollars annually if they did nothing else but improve management techniques in their acquisition programs.

What is needlessly eating into the budget of the Defense Department is also imperiling the nation's security goals. What it comes down to is that the armed forces are being shortchanged and the taxpayers are being ripped off as a result of ineptitude, dishonesty and bureaucratic rigidity in defense contracting. The Pentagon has many priorities. Cleaning up the mess in procurement ought to be put close to the very top.

DESERET NEWS
Salt Lake City, Utah, July 11-12, 1983

The Pentagon handled $125 billion worth of contracts in 1982, or 79% of the total federal contracts awarded that year. Of those defense contracts exceeding $10,000, only 35% were awarded by competitive bidding. Yet competitive bids, according to the General Accounting Office, could have saved 10% to 50% on each contract.

That's why Congress ought to approve a bill introduced by Sen. William Cohen of Maine that would restrict the use of non-competitive federal contracts and establish a clear preference for competitive procedures in awarding federal contracts.

It's also why the lawmakers should resist the efforts of the Pentagon to weaken this bill with 15 amendments, including one that would let officials use non-competitive procedures whenever it is deemed necessary and "not inconsistent with the public interest." Such an exeption is so sweeping it would make the Cohen bill meaningless.

But the savings that could be achieved by this measure, substantial as they are, are not much greater than the money that could be saved if Washington would get tougher on defense contractors after the contracts are awarded.

A few days ago, Deputy Defense Secretary W. Paul Thayer told a conference of private contractors that their shoddy work costs the taxpayers 10% to 30% more than they should be paying for weapons and other military equipment. The contractors, he said, are wasting money by having to remake military hardware that should have been made right the first time.

If this waste were eliminated, the Reagan administration could save up to $28 billion on its $94 billion budget for arms and related equipment.

But the Pentagon should do more than just give the contractors a tongue-lashing. It should also insist on quality control. And if it doesn't get it, the Pentagon should stop doing business with careless contractors and stop paying for shoddy work.

In any event, between the savings to be made from competitive biddings and from getting tough on sloppy defense contractors, it's hard to buy the administration's argument that the military budget can't and shouldn't be cut.

The Chattanooga Times

Chattanooga, Tenn., July 5, 1983

Wise consumers shop around for their purchases, searching for the best buy they can get. It's a practice that pays off and makes undeniably good sense. One would hope that when federal bureaucrats are spending taxpayers' money they would exercise that same wise discretion, but this is not the case.

The federal government routinely awards non-competitive contracts for goods and services which can easily be purchased on the open market. But Sen. Bill Cohen, R-Maine, is pushing a bill that would change that costly habit of sole-source contracting by requiring officials to justify their use of non-competitive procedures. The bill is a good one and deserves to be enacted.

Demonstrating the breadth of the problem, government statistics show that federal expenditures for goods and services last year totalled $158 billion; *less than half* the amount was spent on contracts let with the benefit of competitive bidding.

And getting down to specifics, reports have documented such ludicrous abuse of non-competitive contracting as this: In 1980 the Defense Department paid $1,676 each for 71 aluminum ladders. Three months previously the Air Force had paid $586 each for a number of the same ladders, ladders which could have been purchased at a Washington, D.C., retail store for $160.

It is the taxpayer, obviously, who is being ripped off.

Sen. Cohen's bill would apply not only to the defense establishment, but government-wide. "The bottom line," he has said, and rightly so, "is that competition among suppliers is necessary to maintain integrity in the expenditure of public funds by insuring that the good or service to be acquired is of the best quality and the lowest possible cost ... and that government contracts are awarded on the basis of merit rather than favoritism."

In an analysis of the legislation's potential effects, the Congressional Budget Office estimated more than $2 billion could be saved annually by competitve contracting. This magnitude of waste through foolish procurement practices is indefensible. Passage of Sen. Cohen's bill would be a step toward making a dent in the spectacular federal deficit without affecting tax rates or diminishing programs.

The legislation has been endorsed by both the Governmental Affairs and the Armed Services committees in the Senate and by the congressional watchdog of fiscal affairs, the General Accounting Office. It is expected to come to a vote on the floor of the Senate early this month; from there it will move to the House. There should be no controversy over this bill, and no delay. It is clearly in the public interest.

The Hartford Courant

Hartford, Conn., June 28, 1983

If you don't believe there is plenty of fat in the defense budget, just ask around the Pentagon.

The cost of some weapons could be reduced by 50 percent if military contractors improved their workmanship, Rear Adm. Frank C. Collins Jr. recently told the New York Times. He contends that Defense Department estimates of cost overruns are in some cases "conservative."

Earlier this month, senior officials claimed the Pentagon procurement budget could be reduced 10 percent to 30 percent annually without a loss of firepower. That would translate into a savings of $9 billion to $28 billion, based on present procurement outlays. If Adm. Collins' estimate is accurate, the potential savings are even greater.

The estimate of the cost of shoddy work and waste is startling — especially at a time of record increases in defense spending, and while Congress and President Reagan sometimes differ by only fractions of a percent in trying to come to terms on military spending.

Still, the administration, with its reputation for being soft on voracious Pentagon spending habits, could be credited with exposing the cost overruns. The problem was disclosed at a conference of military contractors and Pentagon officials.

The waste comes from manufacturers having to remake weapons and other equipment done wrong initially.

Senior officers said part of the fault was the military's for not being specific enough about the kind of weapons it wants, and then demanding the finished product before it has been adequately tested. Executives admitted to setting low production standards, insufficient worker training and not having enough commitment to excellence at top management levels.

The dialogue was both hopeful and frightening.

It's hopeful because the contractors and military officers presumably speak one another's language. Their admitting to waste in procurement is more likely to lead to cost reductions than criticism from "anti-defense" members of Congress.

Hearing talk about shoddy workmanship coming from the people who make the stuff and the people who buy it is frightening for the obvious reasons. What kind of quality are the taxpayers getting for their record defense outlays? If management lacks commitment and workers are not adequately trained, what certainty is there that hardware will work as well as it should even after being remade?

The security aspect of the procurement issue is as important as the debate over costs. A president interested in the public "getting our money's worth" should be riding herd on procurement officers and contractors.

Portland Press Herald

Portland, Maine, July 13, 1983

There's so much waste in military spending these days that even the Pentagon has expressed alarm. It *must* be pretty bad.

A draft report prepared by the Pentagon's internal watchdog agency says military purchases are out of hand largely because buyers are not going through the competitive bidding process. Instead they are handing out contracts to single-source suppliers.

One result, the report says, is that the cost of thousands of spare parts for military aircraft have more than quintupled over a three-year period under the system.

It's just one more argument in favor of a bill sponsored by Maine's Sen. William S. Cohen to increase competition in bidding for government contracts, military and otherwise.

There's simply no good reason why the government shouldn't shop around for the best buy, just as the rest of us do.

More than half the $158 billion in goods and services purchased by the government last year were bought without competitive bidding. It's a system which virtually invites inflated prices, cost overruns and other unnecessary waste of our tax dollars.

The Senate's Government Affairs and Armed Services committees have unanimously endorsed the Cohen proposal. Let's hope the full Senate demonstrates equal enthusiasm for this thoroughly sensible plan to promote efficiency in government spending when the bill comes up for enactment sometime next month.

Weapons Testing Assailed; Senate Backs Independent Office

Another area of weapons procurement that was the target of widespread criticism in 1982 and 1983 was weapons testing. The General Accounting Office reported in June, 1983 that the Defense Department was spending billions of dollars on weapons systems that had not been adequately tested. The study maintained: "Field commanders are operating weapons with unknown, perhaps dangerous, limitations." The GAO, while acknowledging the technical problems associated with weapons testing, contended that the Pentagon had worsened the situation by failing to give testing suitable priority and financing. The report also noted that many Defense Department officials were in charge of both developing and testing weapons. Included among 10 weapons systems cited in the report whose "safety, reliability and combat readiness remain unproven" were the avionics electronic system for use on B-52 long-range bombers, and antiaircraft and antimissile missiles.

When the Senate passed its fiscal 1984 defense authorization bill in July, 1983, it included a provision for the establishment of an independent office to oversee the testing of new weapons systems. An amendment, passed by a vote of 91 to 5, would create an agency to monitor and evaluate weapons tests. The agency would be headed by a civilian subject to Senate confirmation. The Reagan Administration strongly opposed the amendment, arguing that it would merely create another layer of bureaucracy within the Defense Department. (Although not included in the House bill, the amendment was included in the final compromise bill hammered out by conferees in August.)

FORT WORTH STAR-TELEGRAM

Fort Worth, Texas, August 11, 1982

Some members of Congress are saying that the ancient wisdom concerning the judging of pudding also applies to military hardware.

Their utterance on that score is not new. Concern about the failure of weapons systems to perform up to expectations during combat has been a recurring theme since World War II. The increasing expense of weapons and sophisticated weapons, however, is triggering calls for more realistic testing before those weapons go into full-scale production.

Some members of Congress believe that the way to provide for such testing is to create a branch of the Pentagon, headed by a civilian, that would be responsible for operational testing and evaluation. They argue that weapons are now tested by the Pentagon under laboratory conditions which provide little assurance that they will perform under combat conditions.

"Defense experts have been telling us for more than a decade that operational testing ... has been the most sadly neglected activity in the weapons procurement process," says Sen. David Pryor, D-Ark.

The critics of current weapons testing procedures cite numerous instances of weapons that performed well in laboratory settings but proved to be major disappointments in combat situations, including the M-16 rifle, the Sheridan M-551 tank and the F-111 fighter bomber. Such misfires occur, they say, because the personnel involved in the testing are usually more highly skilled than the personnel who are to use the weapons, maintenance during testing often is performed by civilian contractors and failures during testing often are deleted from the Pentagon's final test results.

They point to a recent General Accounting Office survey that revealed "incomplete, misleading, or inaccurate reporting" on testing of 20 out of 27 weapons systems. The biggest problem, they say, is the institutional momentum a weapon system gains as it goes through the procurement process. There is a built-in tendency to keep pushing a system, despite evident shortcomings, in the belief that the problems can be corrected later.

While a good case can be made for the needed for improved operational testing and evaluation, it does not necessarily follow that the imposition of another layer of bureaucracy at the Pentagon is the best approach. It is a concept, however, that is worth exploring. It is well that Sen. John Tower, chairman of the Senate Armed Services Committee, who is opposed to the idea, is willing to hold hearings on the proposal.

The Washington Post

Washington, D.C., September 27, 1982

HOW GOOD are the multi-billion-dollar weapons the Pentagon plans to buy? That subject was stirred up again the other day by public release of a year-old Army report on field testing of the controversial M1 tank.

Whether or not the tests show that the M1 is a wise investment for the $20 billion involved, it's the general question that is more interesting: is defense decision-making sufficiently open to the possibility that, no matter how much money has already been spent, experience may show that some weapons ought to be junked—or greatly modified—before more money is wasted?

For some years now, the General Accounting Office, special defense advisory panels and academic critics have asserted that weapons testing within the Pentagon is not rigorous enough. Test findings are ignored or explained away in the powerful drive within the bureaucracy and the defense industry to move weapons systems into full production as quickly as possible.

Realistic field tests are not normally conducted until after the decision to start weapon production has been made. Testing organizations within each of the services and at the departmental level have independent access to the people who will make the decisions, but by the time their tests are completed, much time, money and prestige have already been invested in the project. At that point, test advisers can't do much but insist on certain modifications, even if their findings call the whole weapons project into doubt. Reagan administration moves to give more control over weapons development to the individual services—where the commitment to particular weapons is traditionally strongest—may further reduce the testers' influence.

Pentagon managers argue that the system has a strong built-in check: the weapons it produces must ultimately be used by its own forces. But the actual field deployment of a weapons system in combat is far removed in time and responsibility from the decision-makers who guide the budget process. In any case, making sure that, for example, a tank won't burn up its occupants is only one aspect of determining that the best possible weaponry is being bought for the available money.

One frequent proposal, soon to be introduced as legislation by Sen. David Pryor, is to set up a test office totally independent of the rest of the Pentagon bureaucracy. That might help raise the visibility of testing, but it's not likely in itself to produce better decisions. What's really needed is a commitment by congressional committees and top Pentagon officials to ask tough and thorough questions at the right time and, further, to be prepared to accept inconvenient or disagreeable answers. That, of course, also means not worrying about how much money has already been misspent or whose reputation is on the line or whether the Pentagon won't get as much money as it hoped for next year.

The San Diego Union

San Diego, Calif., August 7, 1983

When in doubt, create another department. This has been the maxim of American government for decades, guiding policy on everything from energy to education. True to formula, Congress has come up with a novel answer to waste in the Pentagon: Create an independent test agency to evaluate and report on the Pentagon's weapons programs.

Weapons programs managers must already report to six congressional committees; the General Accounting Office, Congress' investigative arm; the State Department; the National Security Council; the Arms Control and Disarmament Agency as well as an army of inquisitive think tanks, and skeptical reporters.

Does this broth need more cooks?

Congress held no less than 407 separate hearings on the military between Feb. 8 and Sept. 30 in 1982, according to the *Armed Forces Journal*. During that time, more than 1,200 Pentagon officials paraded down to Capitol Hill, spending more than 5,000 hours testifying, perhaps 50,000 preparing. After one hearing, a Defense Department received a series of followup questions. The questions ran 150 pages.

The new testers, presumably, will be selected from the rather limited pool of experts that work for the military. They will be no more independent than they could be elsewhere in the military-industrial, journalistic-congressional complex right now. But they will be less responsible for failure.

When a weapon flops, Pentagon programmers will blame the procedures of the independent agency. When a weapon approved by the agency fails in the field, the agency will say soldiers weren't trained correctly. Etc.

By adding yet another review layer, moreover, Congress will slow down the procurement process by at least one year, probably two. It already takes the country more than a decade to put a major weapon on line — about 17 years in the case of the MX missile. This dynamic of political indecision and delay, and not the purchase of an occasional $25 paperclip, is the major source of military waste.

For each added year it takes to put a weapon in the field, inflation and re-testing and re-engineering costs drive the cost up another 25 to 30 percent, according to a GAO study.

Weapons testing can be improved. More tests, for example, should be conducted by soldiers who must use a weapon in the field. "You just try to find a test pilot," one procurement officer puts it, "who minces words about an aircraft he is evaluating."

Effective military reform, though, implies greater military autonomy, less congressional meddling. The idea of fighting bureaucracy with bureaucracy has been under test since the 1960s. And it has flunked.

The Chattanooga Times

Chattanooga, Tenn., July 11, 1983

It costs a lot to underwrite the defense needs of the United States, nearly $250 billion this year and a requested $268 billion for 1984. And while Americans generally think they are overtaxed, most properly regard national defense as a crucial budget item to help ensure the nation's survival in a hostile world. But that responsibility cannot be met if the weapons don't work properly.

The General Accounting Office published a study the other that criticized the Pentagon for spending billions of dollars on new weapons before they are adequately tested. The Defense Department, said the GAO, is "fielding weapon systems without sufficient knowledge of their ability to survive or function in combat." It hardly needs be said that soldiers faced with a weapon that breaks down when they need it most would be effectively disarmed.

Lack of time and money, the GAO said, are two reasons for the Pentagon's failure to test the weapon systems properly; bureaucratic foulup and poor management are also important factors. But the Pentagon's fascination with super-sophisticated weaponry is perhaps the root cause of its problem. Many of the weapons the GAO says have been inadequately tested are complex and highly expensive — but they are also the ones on which the armed services would rely heavily in case of war. Among them: the Navy's AEGIS guided-missile cruiser and the Phoenix air-to-air missiles, the sophisticated electronic warfare equipment on the Air Force's B-52s and the Army's Patriot anti-aircraft missile.

Legislation has been introduced to require a new independent test and evaluation unit at the Pentagon. But Defense officials and armed services chiefs say it is unnecessary to add what would amount to nothing more than another layer of bureaucracy. They are probably right; more bureaucracy would probably make the problem worse. But the present system clearly isn't working in the nation's best interests. If the Pentagon doesn't want another agency looking over its shoulder, it ought to make the testing and evaluation system it has now much more effective.

The News Journal

Wilmington, Del., July 16, 1983

WHILE everyone in Washington was scurrying about looking for tapes of various recreational activities, the U.S. Senate rabbit-punched the Pentagon.

The brass never knew what hit them as senators approved, 91-5, an independent agency to detect unsafe or ineffective "weapons flops."

Generals and admirals, taken a little aback by the swift Senate action, can be expected to regroup to oppose the measure, part of a $200 billion military spending bill.

The plan was cosponsored by Sen. William V. Roth Jr., who branded Defense Department monitoring of its own purchases a "conflict of interest." It would create a civilian director of the new office. Naturally, this director would require a little help.

His office may not rival such agencies as the Pennsylvania Avenue Development Corp. — approximately one filing cabinet, one coffee maker — but it will need expertise.

Much attention in debate over armed forces purchases has centered on such dramatic examples as a 4-cent diode for which the Navy apparently paid $110, and a 3-inch bolt, originally priced at 67 cents, which cost the Defense Department $17.59.

A case other observers cite is the F-18, designed to be a simpler replacement for the F-14 and to be used, among other functions, in carrier operations. The Navy allegedly has added so many boxes of tricks that the cost in four years has run $310 million over budget. Also, as the plane gained weight, its range dropped.

Pilots landing on the pioneer carrier Langley pointed their wood and fiber airplanes at the deck, exhaled and prayed. Later, flight deck arresting gear was developed; if you missed the wires, you pointed your Hellcat at something substantial, like a crane, and hoped. The $3 billion floating theme parks in today's line of battle have more sophisticated systems, but to use sophisticated systems you need a sophisticated flying machine.

The new agency's director, or an assistant, might well try flying an F-18 off of and onto a carrier deck before deciding if the additions to the original plan were justified. Acquiring such expertise, and knowledge about diodes and bolts, will cost money, but taxpayers could net a worthwhile overall saving.

If the Pentagon wants $200 billion a year to deter aggression, and wants to stave off further curbs on its cherished independence, it might now turn its attention to an even more basic problem than testing. It might hasten its efforts to reform a procurement system which encourages delays in deliveries and the billions in cost overruns which those delays generate.

The Cincinnati Post

Cincinnati, Ohio, July 21, 1983

In a stinging rebuke to the Pentagon for buying weapons that fail to work, the Senate has voted 91-5 to create an independent office to test new military equipment and report to Congress on its performance.

The overwhelming vote reflected the Senate's anger over the recent flood of reports about expensive aircraft, tanks, guns and missiles that do not meet specifications but are purchased anyway.

Congressional frustration with procurement foul-ups is understandable, but it is doubtful that an independent testing office—really a new level of bureaucracy in the Defense Department—is needed.

All the horror stories about FA-18 fighters that lack range and M-1 tanks that break down originate with tests performed by the armed services and an existing testing office in the Pentagon.

This suggests that the problem isn't testing but management. Defense Secretary Caspar Weinberger has relieved one naval officer of his command for paying excessive prices for spare parts. Things would improve greatly if he would make it a practice to fire brass hats and civilian officials whose design and procurement blunders are sapping the national defense.

Things would also improve if major weapons systems that display grave flaws were simply canceled. This never happens. One reason is Pentagon inertia. Another is Congress. Every military turkey seems to be manufactured in the district of an influential congressman.

President Reagan must share the blame. He was most effective in convincing the nation of the need for a military buildup and extracting the money for it from Congress. He has been ineffective in seeing that the country gets its money's worth for its defense dollars.

Of course Reagan has other things on his mind and has delegated supervision of the Pentagon to Weinberger and others. But when the military pays $110 apiece for electronic parts that cost 4 cents each—as the Navy did to the Sperry Corp.—it is clear that supervision has broken down.

After more than two years in office, Weinberger should have passed the learning stage. It is his duty to get waste under control and to buy cost-effective weapons. Or to resign and let someone else do it.

ST. LOUIS POST-DISPATCH

St. Louis, Mo., June 28, 1983

The General Accounting Office, Congress's fiscal watchdog, has confirmed what many have suspected — the Pentagon is buying billions of dollars worth of new weapons before they are fully tested.

According to the GAO, the Defense Department "is fielding weapon systems without sufficient knowledge of their ability to survive or function in combat." This means, as the GAO further charges, that "field commanders are operating weapons with unknown, perhaps dangerous, limitations."

The failure on the part of the Pentagon to test these new arms properly is a result of time and budgetary constraints and, in a number of cases, just plain bad management. The GAO also suggests that some of the problems may be bureaucratic.

Among the weapons that the GAO says have been poorly or under-tested are some of the most expensive and complex ones in the U.S. arsenal. They are also weapons in which the armed services have placed a great deal of faith, weapons that would be critical to U.S. forces in wartime. The list includes the Navy's AEGIS guided-missile cruiser and the long-range Phoenix air-to-air missiles, the Army's Patriot anti-aircraft missile and offensive electronic warfare gear on Air Force B-52 bombers.

The Senate's Governmental Affairs Committee under Sen. William Roth is currently holding hearings on this issue and is also considering a bill that would require a new and independent test and evaluation agency within the Pentagon. Many top officials at Defense, however, are strongly opposed to this move and argue that it would only add another layer of bureaucracy.

That may be so, but as the GAO report so clearly points out, the present arms testing procedure has too many holes. At the very least, a major repair job is needed.

St. Louis, Mo., July 19, 1983

In an overwhelming show of bipartisan concern, the Senate voted 91-5 last week to establish a new, independent arms testing agency within the Pentagon.

The action was long overdue. Republican Sen. William Roth has held a number of recent committee hearings that have documented some of the costly abuses and shortcomings of the weapon testing system currently used by the Pentagon. Critics argue that the present system basically allows the weapon development groups in each of the armed services to do its own operational testing. This creates a conflict of interest, critics charge, since many of the tests are liberally structured to allow for human or machine errors that are not always counted against the weapon. The General Accounting Office, Congress' fiscal watchdog, found that $33 billion worth of arms now going into service have been inadequately tested.

Under the new system, a civilian director of operational testing and evaluation would oversee the independent testing of the arms before they are procured.

Pentagon defenders of the present testing procedures do have a legitimate criticism that this new testing agency could merely add another layer of bureaucracy to an already hopelessly complex system. Rather than streamlining the process, it is said, the agency could make matters worse.

There is a danger of that, but good planning and hard effort on the part of officials can avoid that pitfall. However, what is known is that the present procedures are not working, and that has to change.

The Courier-Journal

Louisville, Ky., July 19, 1983

CONGRESSIONAL exasperation with expensive weapons that don't work as advertised is finally producing results. The Senate, over the Pentagon's strenuous but illogical objections, last week voted 91-5 to establish an independent office to oversee testing of new weapons and report back to Congress on their performance.

If the House follows suit and President Reagan doesn't invite a rebellion on Capitol Hill by vetoing the bill, the Senate measure would end the Pentagon's curious practice of having weapons tested by the same people who develop them. This practice has led, unsurprisingly, to all sorts of test rigging. Performance standards are lowered until a given weapon — the Navy's F-18 fighter, for instance — can pass, even if it doesn't perform anywhere near as well as originally expected. Invariably, costs rise even as the standards are dropping.

Undersecretary of Defense Richard DeLauer lobbied hard against the Senate bill, arguing that it would just add another layer of bureaucracy to an already cumbersome arms procurement process. But the salaries of a few dozen more bureaucrats couldn't possibly be as costly as spending billions for tanks that break down twice as often as expected, or planes that fly only half as far as anticipated on a tank of fuel, or missiles that can't find their targets.

A truly independent testing agency would have no stake in a particular weapon, beyond making sure it works. If performance fell below expectations, Congress would have solid information on which to decide whether to halt development. The military brass would still be able to argue that the weapon, though disappointing, was necessary. But they wouldn't be able to delude lawmakers by offering phony test data.

In the long run, these and other reforms are essential to maintaining public support for the U.S. defense effort. While the country may be divided over the affordability and wisdom of the Reagan military buildup, everyone agrees that the taxpayer should get his money's worth. Defense Secretary Caspar Weinberger conceded as much when he chastised the Navy last week for paying $110 apiece for electronic diodes that cost the manufacturer only 4 cents each to produce. The wonder is that Mr. Weinberger, recognizing that sort of rip-off, didn't welcome the independent testing agency with open arms.

THE INDIANAPOLIS STAR

Indianapolis, Ind., July 26, 1983

Angered by a flurry of costly weapons errors, the Senate has voted to create an independent office to test new military equipment and report directly to Congress on its performance.

This break with Pentagon channels was precipitated by monumental cost overruns for poorly designed weapons that underwent one expensive retooling after another and then were finally approved even though they didn't meet specifications.

There have been fighter planes that lack range and that operate efficiently only in ideal weather conditions; new tanks that break down too easily, that can't take rough terrain and require twice the amount of fuel; missiles with faulty guidance systems etc. There have been enough gosh-awful snafus in the past year alone to keep the Kremlin smiling for years.

But is an independent testing office the solution for all this disastrous nonsense? Probably not.

What the Senate is doing is creating yet another bureaucracy, adding more paperwork, more staff, more consultants, more experts to the federal payroll. That has rarely solved problems.

And what is the Senate going to do when this "independent" office determines that some costly weapons system is too flawed to salvage and recommends scrapping it — but development of the weapon is providing a significant number of jobs in the home state of a Senate committee chairman and another committee chairman is counting on getting a hefty production contract for his district somewhere down the road?

J. Peter Grace would probably say the Senate will opt for business as usual and just order more design changes. Grace, chairman of the President's Private Sector Survey on Cost Control, a panel of top business and labor executives who have spent the past year studying government waste and efficiency, doesn't think much of the bureaucracy's ability to discipline itself.

One of the troubles with those in government, Grace said in an interview with U.S. News & World Report, is that "nobody wants to take any flak, nobody has any guts. They say: Life's too short, so let's punish the taxpayer."

And most of that punishment is dealt by the Congress, which Grace blames for the majority of waste and abuse. "I blame them because we have 160 committees in Congress. Congress has been codified basically along special-interest lines. It's a club. The city people vote for food stamps; the farm people for farm spending. These things are traded off."

Sorry to say, Defense Secretary Caspar Weinberger also seems to lack the guts Grace talks about, the guts for hard decisions that he promised to bring to his job. He is the president's point man, the one most responsible for curbing the monumental waste of the military establishment and providing the nation with cost-effective, combat-worthy weapons. Yet his two-year record has been sorely disappointing.

He hasn't fired civilian or military officials whose development and procurement blunders have damaged the nation economically and strategically. He has tolerated the traditional excesses of defense big shots, whether it's Persian rugs on the office floor or the misuse of military rank and property.

In fact, Weinberger was among a handful of Pentagon officials who just happened to schedule a short tour of a Navy supply center in California on the same weekend that the famous Bohemian Club was having its annual outing nearby. The finagling let the trip West go on the books as a defense department expense.

That's the kind of thing that makes cynics of taxpayers and of cost-cutters like J. Peter Grace, who would do well to ask if the people have the guts to put a stop to it all.

Pentagon Spare Parts Scandal Unfolds

The scandal emerged in a report made public in July, 1983 by the inspector general's office of the Defense Department. Several defense contractors, the report said, had routinely raised their prices for spare parts by 100% or more over a three-year period. Among the specific instances cited were prices of $17.59 each charged to the Air Force by Pratt & Whitney Aircraft Group for bolts that had a projected cost of 67 cents each; a Navy purchase of diodes from Sperry Corp. at a cost of $110 each, when the same parts were available from the Pentagon supply system at four cents apiece; and the provision of screws to the services by Bendix Corp. at a cost of $92 apiece. Secretary of Defense Caspar Weinberger July 18 revealed that disciplinary action had been taken against a naval officer and several civilian Pentagon officials for buying military spare parts at grossly inflated prices. In the wake of the adverse publicity surrounding the scandal, President Reagan praised the Defense Department for taking strong actions against waste and fraud. "What is missing or buried in all those stories about waste is who provided the information for all those horror stories," he said. The President promised to "keep on exposing these abuses."

THE DENVER POST
Denver, Colo., July 15, 1983

ONE OF THE most durable inequities in the Reagan administration's concept of government is in its approach to spending for social and military programs. Social programs have grown soft and flabby, the line goes, but our military effort has grown weak.

The administration's litany attempts to justify drastic surgery in human services — there is, after all, a budget deficit that threatens to exceed $200 billion — but it urges fiscal indulgence to fortify national security.

Lately, however, come significant reports of unhealthy excess and bad habits in the military's fiscal practices. An internal investigation has found widespread overcharging by defense contractors for aircraft engine parts purchased by the Air Force and the Navy — several cases amounting to 500 per cent increases in a six-month period.

It should be emphasized that this is only one specialized — though important — aspect of defense spending. If there is such evidence of fiscal mismanagement in this one small area, how much more of the administration's proposed $240 billion defense budget is similarly infected? One gets the uncomfortable feeling that those within the military establishment believe they can get away with almost anything.

It's admirable that the Defense Department says it will reassess its profligate lifestyle. But it also makes one marvel at what other fiscal horror stories have yet to be uncovered. And, considering the specter of a $200-billion-plus budget deficit, it makes one wonder what it will take to make the administration concede that there is room for some serious trimming in military budgets, too.

THE ATLANTA CONSTITUTION
Atlanta, Ga., July 13, 1983

ITEM: Government specialists have concluded that a small plastic part that cost the Air Force $916.55 two years ago could be bought for about $10 now through competitive bidding. The Associated Press, May 11.

ITEM: The Navy paid the Sperry Corp. $100 or more last year for several simple aircraft simulator parts available for a nickel or less in the government's supply system. United Press International, July 11.

ITEM: A simple 3-inch bolt, originally priced at 67 cents, cost the Defense Department $17.59. Military procurement officers paid $57.52 for a small bushing that had originally been priced at $2.83. The New York Times, July 12.

Terrible? Yes. Shocking? Not really.

While remarkable, these instances of military waste, costing taxpayers millions each year, have been with us for a long time.

One of the problems endemic to any mega-bureaucracy is waste, fraud and poor judgment. No sooner do government auditors staunch a dollar drain in one spot than new leaks spring up somewhere else. The green-eyeshade brigade can't be everywhere at once, but of course, it should try.

In the Reagan administration, though, a double standard is evident. On the one hand, it uses fraud and abuse as partial explanation for axing social programs. We've heard plenty in recent years about "welfare cheats" and college students on food stamps.

On the other hand, while there is abundant evidence that the military faces a similar problem of misused money, nobody in the administration is talking about cutting that budget as an outraged response. Far from it.

No, waste should not be condoned — whether for welfare programs or spare parts on military planes.

But to judge one set of programs by its aberrations and another by its overall performance makes little sense. The goal of efficiency should be applied equally to all facets of government.

The Burlington Free Press
Burlington, Vt., July 13, 1983

American taxpayers are shelling out billions of dollars a year in inflated costs for spare parts for the the Defense Department, according to a Pentagon report which was made public Monday by the Project on Military Procurement.

Cited as examples of exorbitant price increases were purchases of simple three-inch bolts, orginally priced at 67 cents each, at $17.59 and small bushings, priced at $2.83, for $57.52. Perhaps the most extreme case was the Air Force order for eight engine tubes from Pratt and Whitney Aircraft which were priced at $12 when ordered and cost $639.29 on delivery, representing a 5,227 percent price increase.

The Pentagon study said the cost of thousands of spare parts for military aircraft quintupled in a three-year period because purchasing officials ignored directives to cut costs. The report said too many items were being purchased without competitive bidding, even though Defense Secretary Caspar Weinberger issued an order last September calling for use of the procedure.

At seven Air Force and Navy installations, the cost of nearly 65 percent of the spare parts bought more than once during the three-year period rose by more than 50 percent. Over 4,000 spare parts jumped over 500 percent in price during the same period, the report said.

Because purchasing officers neglected rules to buy directly from manufacturers, failed to encourage bidding and did not find new sources for the parts, the government was forced to accept the huge price increases, the report said. Purchasing officers paid scant attention to the costs because their work is rated primarily on completion of paper work, not on prices paid or savings on purchases.

"Increases in material costs or other inflation factors cannot explain the prices being paid by the government for aircraft engine spare parts," authors of the report said.

Such waste in the Defense Department should not go unnoticed by Congress which is asked to approve massive budget increases for the nation's armed forces with the understanding that the money will be spent efficiently and effectively. That such a situation has existed for some time should be enough to prompt some congressmen to demand an accounting from the department. If defense officials can ignore purchasing regulations, it could well be that vast amounts of money are not being spent for legitimate purposes.

Not only should they be held responsible for their negligence but the firms that bilk the government out of billions also should be penalized for their actions.

It is one thing to spend money for items which are considered essential to the nation's defense; it is quite another to ask American taxpayers to pick up the tab for outrageously wasteful spending.

Rocky Mountain News

Denver, Colo., July 16, 1983

IF the local hardware store charged $17.59 for a 67-cent bolt, it would soon be out of business. Customers would shun the place.

Yet, purchasing officers for the Department of Defense line up to buy such outrageously priced items with taxpayers' money.

The department's inspector general has just completed a study of the purchase of 15,000 spare parts for Air Force and Navy aircraft engines from 1980 to 1982. The audit found that over the three-year period, two-thirds of the parts rose more than 50 percent in price, more than half doubled in price, and more than a quarter increased by a staggering 500 percent or more.

The bolt cited above was one example of the ripoffs. Another was a bushing originally priced at $2.83 but for which the military paid $57.52.

How can such things happen? One reason is that the military services tend to buy spare parts from "prime contractors" who originally furnish equipment, in this case aircraft engines, even though most of the parts may not be made by the company that assembles them. These prime contractors mark up the parts as high as they can get away with.

They can get away with plenty because the military purchasing officers aren't graded on how much they save the taxpayers but on how many purchase orders they can process in a given time. Shuffling paper apparently is more important than saving money.

"Sole source" contracts are another reason for high prices. Instead of shopping around for the best prices, the military purchasing agents like to deal with familiar faces.

The inspector general cited an instance in which a company protested that it was being shut out of bidding on "divergent nozzle assemblies" for F-100 jet engines. When the protests got so loud that the competing company finally was given an order, the government got the nozzles for almost half the price it had been paying — $1,395 vs. $2,469.

If Pentagon bigwigs wonder why there is so much opposition to defense spending, they can find some of the answers in the inspector general's report. Taxpayers may not fully understand budgets in the tens of billions of dollars, but they darn well know how much a simple three-inch bolt ought to cost.

Our advice to the Pentagon: Watch your bolts and the missiles will take care of themselves.

The Des Moines Register

Des Moines, Iowa, August 6, 1983

We have an idea that the Reagan administration and especially Defense Secretary Caspar Weinberger and his deputy, Frank Carlucci, are in a mood to celebrate because Congress is taking a month's vacation. Among other things, it means for them that maybe Iowa Senator Charles Grassley will let up a bit.

Grassley is building a reputation by criticizing military costs that soar over their estimates, and the sting of his pre-vacation shot may last until September.

"Son of Carlucci" was the term he used to describe Weinberger's recent 10-point directive on controlling excessive costs of spare parts. It refers to the 32-point directive issued when Carlucci went to the Pentagon in 1981.

"The Carlucci initiatives were to be the be-all and end-all of positive change in the Pentagon," said Grassley. "But they had no teeth. There was no timetable, no accountability and no clear indication that the initiatives were a serious undertaking.

"Now, Mr. Weinberger has given us 'Son of Carlucci,' 10 new initiatives which are even more vague than the first 32. Yet, he claims: 'It is a program with teeth' and it will end cost abuses 'once and for all.'

"The secretary is giving us nothing concrete. No goals, no timetable, no accountability. The real 10 commandments are straightforward: Thou shall not kill. Period.'"

Right on, senator, as we've said before. And don't let up — even for a vacation.

•

Here's an example of the sort of thing Grassley is complaining about:

There is this little plastic cap that fits on the legs of the stools B-52 navigators sit on. Air Force cost analysts place its value at about a quarter. Right now, after switching suppliers, the Air Force is paying $4.

But before switching suppliers, it was buying the gizmos from Boeing for — are you ready? — $1,118.26 apiece. That is no typographical error; that is one-thousand one-hundred-eighteen and twenty-six one-hundredths dollars.

According to Time magazine, this particular gravy train was derailed by an angry Air Force maintenance-crew chief who discovered that the price of a 25-cent chunk of plastic was higher than his monthly take-home pay.

Robbery is not too strong a word for that kind of pricing. Boeing owes the American people an apology and a restitution. The Pentagon owes the American people an apology and an overhaul of its unbelievably sloppy purchasing practices. Don't hold your breath waiting for either.

And yet, if enough voters and members of Congress eventually get angry enough about comprehensible small-dollar scandals like this, perhaps progress can be made on the truly big ones. Those don't seem to bother people as much, probably because most of us have no idea what an entire bomber or nuclear submarine really ought to cost. (More than likely, a lot less than is being paid for them, though.)

FORT WORTH STAR-TELEGRAM

Fort Worth, Texas, July 16, 1983

Much of the continuing congressional debate over the nation's defense budget is partisan in nature, and many of those participating in that debate — on both sides of the aisle — are seldom guilty of allowing facts or logic to sway their judgment.

There is one issue, however, on which lawmakers on both sides of the defense budget fence can — and should — come together in harmony. That is the issue of waste within the military establishment. It is to the advantage of each side — not to mention the average taxpayer — to keep as tight a rein as possible on the Pentagon's purse strings.

That is why both proponents and opponents of President Reagan's defense spending goals should insist that the Pentagon keep its word to take "fast and immediate action" to put a stop to widespread overcharging by defense contractors uncovered in a recent Department of Defense investigation.

The DOD's inspector general's office issued a report outlining millions of dollars in overcharges for spare airplane parts. The cost of thousands of such parts rose more than three times in a three-year period because purchasing officers ignored a directive to cut costs, the report said.

Inspectors found that many items were being purchased without competitive bidding, despite a directive issued last September by Defense Secretary Caspar Weingerger ordering that competitive bids be taken.

The study concentrated on seven Air Force and Navy facilities that purchased $1.2 billion worth of spare parts during fiscal 1982. Investigators found that the cost of nearly 65 percent of spare parts bought more than once during a three-year period increased by more than 50 percent. During the same period, more than 4,000 spare parts increased in price more than 500 percent.

"Increases in material costs or other inflation factors cannot explain or justify prices being paid by the government for aircraft engine spare parts," the report said, adding that 61 percent of 357 items studied by DOD auditors were purchased without competitive bidding, which resulted in a 100-percent price increase.

Some specific examples pointed out included bolts that cost 67 cents being purchased by the government for $17.59 each and a tube that cost the manufacturer $12 being sold to the Air Force for $639.

Deputy Defense Secretary Paul Thayer, quizzed about the report, said that it "appears there has been some negligence." That is an understatement of generous proportions. Both those who support and those who oppose the president's defense-spending goals should join forces to ensure that the Pentagon act swiftly — even ruthlessly, if necessary — to stop this shameful waste of the taxpayers' money.

The Washington Times

Washington, D.C., July 20, 1983

Should there come a time when our spears are forged into plowshares, we suggest that jewelers be employed in the transition. Recent findings by a government inspector show that some of our shiny new weapons could hardly be more valuable were they made of gold.

Take those small plastic leg tips for navigators' stools. At $1,118.26 each, the parts seemed a bit overpriced to Staff Sgt. Charles K. Kessler, whose monthly base pay is $1,102.80. He inquired as to how this could be, and indeed it was revealed that the plastic in the tip was worth about 26 cents, and that the items could be purchased on bids for about $10 each.

Quite a difference, most will note. The problem in this price war, however, was that the side inflicting the greatest damage to the taxpayers' purse was winning, seemingly by design.

Consider the report by the government inspector, who found that prices for many spare parts for Air Force and Navy jets had increased more than 500 percent over a three-year period. Accusing fingers jabbed, most furiously in the direction of Air Force officials who dealt with the Pratt & Whitney Aircraft Corp., the major supplier of jet engines for military aircraft.

How can such a thing happen? Well, there is what is called an "approved" list, which means a contractor gets "automatic approval" for contracts. Something seems missing here, like a review that might discover a better deal from another source. With automatic approval, the poor contractor finds himself on the receiving end of a dangerously raging cash flow.

Laxity by procurement officials is the official explanation for this mess. Not an official explanation is the fact that many high Air Force officers have gone to work for Pratt & Whitney in recent years. Cap Weinberger, among others, hopes that this transfer will indeed result in more efficient procurement. We trust he means of parts, not cash.

This week, Pratt & Whitney was removed from the "approved" list, a Navy commander was removed from his post, and reprimands were issued to several civilian procurement officials. Certainly, a toast is in order. Yet with the waste from noncompetitive contract approval said to run between $2 billion and $4 billion a year, most of the cheer remains in the bottle.

A cleanup of this cash spill is certainly in order. How about starting with something called competitive bidding, or is the door to the cannon works closed? We know one official who should interest himself in the project — the commander in chief. Unless Henry's interested.

The Orlando Sentinel

Orlando, Fla., July 22, 1983

Defense Secretary Caspar Weinberger made a big deal of firing an officer in the purchasing program at the Orlando Naval Training Equipment Center earlier this week. Indeed, paying $80,000 for parts that should have cost about $3,600 is outrageous and someone deserved to be fired.

But the real problem isn't in Orlando, it's in Washington. And it won't be solved just by punishing middle-level career officers and civil servants. If Mr. Weinberger thinks it will, he has lost sight of a lesson drilled into all young officer candidates: "You can delegate authority but you can't delegate responsibility."

The problem is that Mr. Weinberger and apparently President Reagan just don't think that waste in the military is something to get all hot and bothered about. The result is a scandal in military spending.

Consider events of the last two weeks. Last week, the Defense Department's inspector general blistered the Navy and the Air Force for the way they buy parts for jet engines. The report named names and cited specifics. Tuesday, Mr. Weinberger announced the firing.

Right away the cynics started muttering "scapegoat, scapegoat," and they were right.

Even as Mr. Weinberger's office was announcing the disciplinary action, across the hall another cog in the Defense Department was announcing that it is adding $9.8 million to contracts for spare engine parts. The supplier? Pratt & Whitney.

That is one of the companies roasted by the inspector general a few days before. It is the same company from which the Air Force said it is withholding $1 million in contested payments. It is the same company that is the subject of a federal grand jury investigation for its pricing policies.

And what was the Air Force's explanation? The Air Force had decided that the previous price was insufficient — even though that previous "price had yet to be negotiated." Air Force officials insisted on saying they had a "firm, fixed price" agreement but that, of course, the prices wouldn't become "firm and fixed" until "they were agreed upon."

That shows a little something about what is wrong with military spending. The Pentagon's inspector general has a lot more examples: Military officials were paying $176 for engine brackets worth 67 cents, $92 for $19 screws and $17.59 for 67-cent bolts.

The administration seems only casually concerned. In fact, the president at first opposed having an inspector general at the Pentagon, then failed to fill the post for nine months after Congress created it. Now he seeks only $46 million to fund the operation, a mere $2 million more than a similar operation at the Agriculture Department — despite the vast difference in workload.

This is the stuff of shame. It is hypocrisy for the Reagan administration to ignore such problems when getting more bang for the defense dollar was once its top priority. Mr. Weinberger earned the moniker "Cap the Knife" for his trimming of the fat during earlier tenures as budget director and as head of the Department of Health, Education and Welfare. Where is his knife? Does he care?

If Mr. Reagan wants to wake up the Defense Department, he should start at the top.

Rockford Register Star

Rockford, Ill., July 18, 1983

We will stop short of suggesting people who work in five-sided buildings may be untrustworthy. But we will say those who toil in the Pentagon, this nation's citadel of military genius, demonstrate an appalling indifference to expense and frugality.

Evidence of the military's cavalier attitude toward the public till has at least two immediate effects on us as payers of Pentagon's bills — in this order:

● It makes us purple-veined angry.

● It makes us question the soundness of a multibillion dollar defense budget as well as the soundness of motives among the administration's military advisers.

We can fully understand the squirming discomfort of Sen. John Tower, R-Texas, chairman of the Senate Armed Services Committee, as the Senate plods each maddening step by step through a $200 billion defense bill. First, the Senate must accept the astonishing fact that $200 billion in new defense spending was "found" due to the administration's fortuitous overestimation of inflation's effect.

Then there's the discomfort of Senate Majority Leader Howard Baker, who has become so uncomfortable with the Senate's desultory deliberations he threatened to schedule night and weekend sessions.

But the long, hot summer only gets longer and hotter for the Pentagon's champions. Neither the auditors of military expense nor the brass hats themselves will maintain the decorum needed to reduce heat on the defense spending bill.

For example, there is an embarrassing Pentagon audit of showing:

● The Navy paid more than $100 each to Sperry Corp. for aircraft simulator parts available for 4 or 5 cents from the government supply system.

● For radar parts from McDonnell Douglas Corp, the Navy paid $417,000 more than the federal supply system price.

● The Navy splurged $511 for a 60-cent light.

● The Air Force this is being charged $36.77 each for a Minuteman II machine screw that cost $1.08 last year.

● A defense firm charged $21,797 for making a phone call requesting a delivery from a manufacturer to the Navy.

Waste? Inefficiency? Our Defense Department commanders have more pressing concerns. They're busy covering their respective posteriors in a squabble over an Air Force proposal for a unified military space command.

The command would be responsible for operating the vast networks of communications, weather and intelligence satellites. It would include the new laser defenses against missiles, anti-satellite operations and military aspects of the space shuttle.

That sounds like a reasonable approach to a four-service involvement in space. But no, says the Navy, whose admirals' argue seagoing units are more dependent on satellite communications than the Air Force or the Army. "We don't see the need for it now," says an articulate Vice Adm. Gordon Nagler. The situation might change in five or six years, he said, but for the present, "It's working fine. Why fix it if it ain't broke."

What is broken, we'd like the Pentagon denizens to know, is their purchasing system. Also broken, therefore, is our confidence in their ability to advise the president in his defense policy. All of this is in urgent need of fixing — now.

The Boston Herald
Boston, Mass., July 25, 1983

THERE IS inevitably some waste in a budget as large as that which our Department of Defense spends year-in and year-out. But there is no excuse for the dumb-bunny decisions and laxity in military procurement which have been coming to light for the past several weeks.

Who, for example, was responsible for paying the Sperry Corp. $110 for a part that could have been bought elsewhere for four cents? Or paying Pratt & Whitney $57.52 for an engine bushing for which it originally agreed to pay $2.83? Or paying $1 each for rivets worth less than a quarter? And what is most incredible — or awful — is that a branch of government which employs no fewer than 18,000 auditors and inspectors let these overpayments get by.

Examples such as these abound, and if there is any encouraging feature about them it is that in many cases the waste has been uncovered and blasted by senior officials and advisers of the Reagan administration.

One, Deputy Defense Secretary Paul Thayer, laid it right on the line to defense contractors, saying that procurement costs of weapons and other military equipment could be cut 30 percent if they were made correctly the first time.

Another, J. Peter Grace, chairman of the president's Private Sector Survey on Cost Control, came up with his own list of horror stories and predicted that his group will be able to show the Pentagon how and where to reduce costs by about $25 billion — without any cuts for major weapons systems.

There's no cheapskate or bargain basement way to build a strong national defense. Developing and maintaining military hardware comes high; there's no escaping it. But because it does, and because the nation is staring at a deficit guessed to be somewhere in the neighborhood of $200 billion, every effort ought to be made to cut waste to an irreducible minimum. If the stories out of Washington are evidence that it is about to happen, in earnest — it comes none too soon.

Wisconsin State Journal
Madison, Wisc., August 4, 1983

More than $1,000 for a small plastic cap worth less than $1? Nearly $700 for a single washer? Nearly $440 for a $10 measuring tape?

Those are among the examples of ridiculous waste in military spare-parts purchases that have been disclosed recently.

According to auditors at the Pentagon, the military has been overcharged hundreds of millions of dollars for parts available for a fraction of the price at any hardware store.

A few hundred million dollars may be peanuts compared to the billions of dollars in cost overruns cited for various weapons systems, but the so-called "spare-parts scandal" is a political bombshell.

Taxpayers may not understand Pentagon procurement policies nor comprehend billions of dollars of waste, but they *know* something's seriously amiss when the military pays $1,118.32 for a small plastic cap that covers the leg of a stool.

Defense Secretary Caspar Weinberger, embarassed because these latest revelations of waste contradict his past assurances

that all the fat had been cut out of Pentagon spending, has issued a list of reforms for tighter control of spare-parts buying.

Among them are incentives within the bureaucracy for military officials to pay less for parts. The Pengaton is talking about clearer coding on its computerized parts list so clerks know what they're paying for an item before ordering it.

Well and good. But the list of reforms also should include competitive bidding by companies that wish to sell common tools, parts and equipment to the military.

Such bidding may not be practical for highly specialized weapons parts, but it makes sense for measuring tapes, washers and the like. Suppliers of such goods should be willing to offer sizeable discounts to win a client as big as the armed forces.

Further, Weinberger should take steps to recover the millions of dollars paid out already in ludicrous overcharges for spare parts. Any company that refuses to refund these excess profits should be blacklisted from further business with the government.

TULSA WORLD
Tulsa, Okla., July 26, 1983

IT'S A SMALL victory for American taxpayers, but perhaps it's a start.

The Secretary of the Navy has asked Sperry Corp. for a refund on the $109 the company charged for a 4-cent diode.

Secretary John F. Lehman Jr. has written Sperry's president requesting the refund and, asking that whoever was responsible for the overcharge be disciplined. Lehman said the navy has taken steps to discipline defense officials who allowed payment of the $109.

A Defense Department auditor told a congressional subcommittee earlier this month that the Navy paid Sperry the $109 for diodes available in the government's own inventory for 4 cents because it wanted to save time in building a flight simulator for the F-18 fighter. Altogether, the navy spent some $80,000 for

parts worth $3,000, the auditor said.

Lehman's action is a valiant effort, but a classic case of closing the barn door after the cow's gone. Lehman ought to propose that Sperry and any other company found gouging the Pentagon on parts be banned for good from bidding on government projects.

The military also bears much of the blame for these outrageous parts prices and cost overruns on Pentagon projects. Military officials often pay ludicrous prices in order to speed defense projects.

The situation points out again the dangers inherent in President Reagan's proposal to spend a trillion dollars on national defense over three years. Can the Pentagon spend that much money efficiently? Without far better oversight, the answer is a clear "no."

CHARLESTON EVENING POST
Charleston, S.C., August 3, 1983

The Reagan administration has been trying to get some political mileage out of recent "horror stories" from Washington on cost overruns in defense spending — an embarrassment to the Pentagon. The president's men are saying that the administration is responsible for ferreting out the overruns and overpayments, that the disclosures are but fulfillments of promises to reduce waste in government.

The taxpayer, of course, is less interested in who takes credit for controlling military spending than he is in being assured that watchdogs are on the job. He would like to believe corrective action is being taken in such areas as spare parts purchases. He would like to believe the Navy no longer is paying $44 for a light bulb that could have been had for 17 cents; that the Air Force no longer is paying hundreds of dollars for plastic tips for table legs that it could buy for pennies.

Taxpayers worry as much, or more, about that kind of overspending than they do about overruns of $20 million in weapons systems. They worry more because they can relate better to a $150 overcharge by a manufacturer of a 79-cent item than they can relate to overruns in the millions. They are not accustomed to dealing in big figures, but they are wise enough to suspect that when they read that the Pentagon is paying $17 dollars for a bolt it could get for 67 cents, they are reading about only the tip of an iceberg.

If it wants to increase its political mileage from the military overspending issue, the Reagan administration could make clear an intention to lean equally hard on the buyer and the seller; replacing purchasing agents who exercise poor judgment and cancelling contracts with manufacturers who gouge. Taxpayers can appreciate firm actions which save money and right wrongs.

DAYTON DAILY NEWS
Dayton, Ohio, July 30, 1983

Americans are used to reading about waste and inefficiency in the Pentagon. Hardly anything surprises them anymore or is likely to in the future.

A whistle-blower reported that one-inch square, plastic caps used on the legs of Air Force stools were produced by Boeing for about 25 cents but cost the government $1,118.26 apiece. That's right, $1,118.26.

Something like this cannot be happenstance. Not even in the armed forces. There has to be some deeper meaning.

Maybe the Pentagon does these preposterous things because it knows the public likes to read about bureaucratic snafus. They brighten our day. We pretend to be horrified but we chatter about it over the back fence, eagerly share the news at the drinking fountain, and write soul-satisfying letters of dismay to the editor. Since none of this affects the Pentagon's appropriations by one thin dime, why not give the taxpayers some fun for their money?

But this explanation won't do for those plastic caps. An example of waste so colossal, so spectacular, so — there's-no-word-for-it — could only come about by design.

How about this scenario? Even though public sputtering about military waste has never hurt the Pentagon yet, there is always the lingering fear that sometime it will. If it can finally exhaust the public's capacity for even simulated indignation by waste like this, maybe the public would hereafter take in stride whatever incredible incompetencies and extravagance the future brings.

The Pentagon knows Caspar Weinberger will not blink, no matter what it does. Now, if it can get the voters so numbed and immobilized by waste so galactical — that's the word! — that all future examples will be anticlimactic, they will have us where they want us. Those plastic caps may do the job.

Smart folks, those generals.

St. Petersburg Times
St. Petersburg, Fla., July 24, 1983

The Air Force paid Boeing $1,186.26 for a single plastic cap like you'd put on the leg of a kitchen stool. It paid Pratt & Whitney $3,033 for turbine seals that had cost $16 the year before. The Navy, meanwhile, paid Sperry $110 per copy for diodes already in its own stocks at 4 cents each.

In politics, it's the little things that get you. Disclosures such as these are finally prompting action of sorts at the Pentagon, where for years defense secretaries and brass hats have only yawned at overruns of megabuck proportions.

So Defense Secretary Caspar Weinberger held a press conference last week to announce that a Navy officer had lost his command and civilian officials had been reprimanded for paying too much for spare parts. He also told Navy Secretary John F. Lehman Jr. that he was "extremely displeased."

That's not enough, of course, even if it is the first time anyone in the defense establishment has been punished for overspending. Making examples of a few spendthrifts won't cure the institutional waste that subverts the U.S. defense effort. If Weinberger were serious, he'd start holding contracts in default. He'd refer some cases for prosecution. And he'd tell the brass to get behind pending legislation that could do some lasting good.

ONE BILL, by Sen. Charles E. Grassley, R-Iowa, would require more competitive bidding on military hardware, only 6 percent of which is now subject to competition. Another, by Sen. Mark Andrews, R-S.D., would require manufacturer warranties — like the ones on your new car — so that the taxpayers wouldn't be stuck when, for example, brand-new tank engines break down. And to make sure that new weapons systems will do what's promised for them, there's a bill by Sens. William Roth, R-Del., and David Pryor, D-Ark., establishing an independent testing office to report to Congress as well as to the secretary of defense; the Senate passed it 95-1 two weeks ago. The collective purpose of those three bills is to get better, cheaper, more reliable goods for the national defense. Yet the Pentagon opposes all three.

One reason is that Weinberger, much feared as "Cap the Knife" when he was budget director years ago, is acting like a dud at the Department of Defense (DOD). Beyond that, institutional defects run deep.

✔ Parts procurement officers are rated according to how fast they fill orders, not how economically.

✔ The careers of systems development officers depend on how much money they can get from Congress, not how much they save. (With no wars under way, systems management is presently the glory road to promotion.) One result: The costs of new weapons systems are almost always underestimated, which means Congress eventually must spend more or buy less than it planned.

✔ Pentagon practices encourage prime contractors to retain control over spare parts. Once it's in the contractor's blueprint, it's "proprietary," even if it can be bought off any hardware shelf. That's how taxpayers come to pay $103 for a common wood screw.

✔ Officers angling for cushy retirement jobs are unlikely to police defense contractors — just like the DOD political appointees from those companies.

✔ The DOD's obsession with expensive, exotic new hardware is depriving forces in the field and stripping the nation's defenses. Examples: The Navy is retiring 22 ships this year, 15 of which were overhauled within the past three years, to afford the construction of six new ones. In its haste to acquire the temperamental, unreliable M-1 tank, the Army accepted 60 of them without engines. And at one point this year, 10 percent of the engines arriving from the factory needed major repairs. The Army could have six M-60 tanks in the field for the time and money it takes to build one M-1 and keep it operational.

THE CONGRESS not only tolerates the waste but shares in the spoils. With the Pentagon's avid cooperation, the defense industry spreads subcontracts widely, hoping to point to job creation in nearly everyone's district. The B-1 bomber, for example, is being manufactured in every state but Alaska and Hawaii. Swallowing the bait, Congress considers projects not on their military merits but as pork.

Grassley, a conservative who is spearheading the military reform movement in Congress, estimates that up to 40 percent of the current $94-billion procurement budget is wasted. The rear admiral in charge of quality assurance for the Defense Logistics Agency says that up to half the cost of some products is wasted because of shoddy work by contractors. An enemy intending harm to the United States scarcely could have done more to exhaust its treasury and cripple its defense. It will take more than a few sacrificial firings and expressions of "extreme displeasure" to set things right.

THIS IS A SPARE PART...

IT SHOULD COST 2¢. BUT THE DEFENSE DEPARTMENT PAYS $15,127.95 FOR IT. THAT'S BECAUSE IT'S USED IN A VERY SPECIAL WAY...

TAX-PAYER

Mike Keefe, THE DENVER POST 83 FIELD SYNDICATE

The Army's XM-1 Battle Tank

Full-scale production of the Army's new, sophisticated XM-1 battle tank was approved in January, 1980, although it had encountered some engine and track problems. President Carter requested $1.15 billion for 569 of the battle tanks in his fiscal 1981 budget. President Reagan, in his economic recovery program, raised the figure to $1.64 billion for 569 tanks in 1981; for 1982, he requested more than $2 billion for 720 tanks. Meanwhile, as the cost of the "advanced" tank continued to rise, a series of tests conducted in 1981 showed that the XM-1 remained beset with serious operational and maintenance problems. A report by two Army agencies, not released until September, 1982, revealed these findings: The average tank was broken or under repair 56% of the time during testing; only 15% of the M-1s could travel 4,000 miles without experiencing an engine, transmission or final drive failure; only about half the tanks remained operational at the end of a rigorous, six-day field mission; and finally, in one test, 27 of 29 drivers required medical attention for severe back and neck pain after driving the XM-1 for several hours with the hatch closed. The Army still planned to purchase more than 7,000 of the tanks over a period of several years, at a cost of nearly $2.8 million each. It had already received 585 M-1s and stationed 174 in Europe. An Army spokesman maintained that a number of changes had been made in the tanks since the completion of the tests.

ST. LOUIS POST-DISPATCH

St. Louis, Mo., July 7, 1981

A new report from the General Accounting Office provides a stern warning to the Reagan administration on the dangers of charging ahead on new weapons programs before all the problems have been ironed out. According to the *Chicago Tribune*, the GAO has raised serious technical questions about the Army's new M-1 tank, which is now going into full-scale production and which has already suffered many serious development and production delays. These problems, and inflation, have driven the production cost up from around $800,000 to $2.8 million per tank. But the Army has argued that these problems have been solved and that the tank is ready for production.

However, according to the GAO, the M-1 still has numerous technical problems that will take billions to solve. Moreover, the GAO says that it is doubtful that the tank will meet all of the Army program standards. In particular, the GAO argues that spare parts and logistical problems are so severe that it makes the M-1 almost impossible to support and repair in the field under probable combat conditions. The agency has charged that in the rush to get the tank into production the Army has wasted billions of dollars by buying cheap spare parts or the wrong spare parts.

The moral of the GAO report is more than "haste makes waste." The danger of the Reagan administration's rush to build more weapons is that without the right spare parts and critical support equipment these weapons are useless. Unless Mr. Reagan develops a more balanced approach to military spending — one that stresses spare parts and maintenance as much as weapons procurement — the Pentagon will continue to waste tens of billions of dollars on broken-down high technology weapons.

The Register

Santa Ana, Calif., July 17, 1981

We just want to be helpful. We're sure the Reagan administration will be delighted with an idea that could save $19 billion.

The Army now plans to spend that amount on new M-1 tanks built by Chrysler Corporation. However, a few problems have already developed.

The probability of drive-train failure in the tanks tested so far is 31 percent higher than specified by the Army. A gap in the fenders permits rocks to be thrown in the driver's face. The treads, which were supposed to last 2,000 miles, are wearing out after only 850 miles. The .50-caliber machine gun is virtually impossible to aim. And, as a crowning touch, the cost, which was initially estimated at $500,000 apiece, is now close to $3 million — per tank.

Chrysler and the Pentagon say that the problems can be worked out. Maybe so. But one must still wonder why we want to spend so much, even if they can get them perfect.

The tank is a useful weapon for countries that face land invasions or that contemplate making land invasions. Though the likelihood of the U.S. facing a serious threat of land invasion is pretty low, it might be a good idea to have a few of them around.

However, the M-1 tanks will, for the most part, be deployed in Germany. Last time we checked, Germany had a higher per capita income than the United States. The Germans also produce a fine tank — the Leopard — which is often sold to other governments in need of military hardware. Why does the United States continue to provide military welfare to Germany?

Few dispute the need to cut the budget. Defending Europe, which has become in many ways more prosperous than the United States, seems to have become a tradition since World War II. Traditions tend to develop inertia, to become virtually immune to questioning. We've been stationing troops and tanks in Europe ever since we can remember, due to some postwar vision of the national interest. It's a policy that's due to be questioned.

The Salt Lake Tribune

Salt Lake City, Utah, August 8, 1980

Where, it ought to be asked, is the new 60-ton XM-1 tank going to be used in battle?

Better yet, it might be questioned whether the tank will get into battle at all.

The old adage that battles are won by those who "get there firstest with the mostest" was apparently forgotten by the super tank's designers.

According to Congressional Quarterly's report on the Senate defense spending bill, the XM-1 is so heavy that ships which can carry sufficient quantities of them move too slowly to get them there (the battlefront) in time. U.S. cargo aircraft, on the other hand, can carry too few. A C-5 aircraft, for example, can lift only one XM-1 tank.

Mobility is one of the tank's chief military assets. But that advantage cannot be applied unless the armored vehicle can get to the scene of the action in time to fight.

The Chattanooga Times

Chattanooga, Tenn., July 11, 1981

Anyone who has ever decided not to buy a new product until it has been improved with understand the General Accounting Office's warning to the Reagan administration regarding purchases of new weapons systems before all the "bugs" have been worked out. It could save billions of dollars in defense costs — that is, if the Pentagon is interested in saving money.

The Chicago Tribune reported last week that the GAO report deals especially with the Army's new M-1 tank. The armored vehicle is just now going into full-scale production after having suffered numerous development and production hang-ups. Along with inflation, the problems have ballooned the tank's production cost from $800,000 to about $2.8 million each. Acknowledging the increases, the Army nevertheless says the problems have been solved and production should begin.

But, the GAO argues, the M-1 is still plagued by many technical snags that will cost untold millions more to solve. And even if they are, it says the M-1 probably won't meet the Army's needs. For example, the report points out that problems of spare parts and logistics are so serious that it will be virtually impossible to support and repair the M-1 under combat conditions in the field. By trying to rush the tank into production, the GAO says, the Army has wasted billions of dollars buying cheap or unworkable spare parts.

The GAO report, which in effect warns that haste makes waste, underscores a point that bears repeating as the Reagan administration orchestrates a dramatic increase in defense spending, including orders for new weapons systems. Those weapons are remarkably efficient — until they break down. Lacking the right spare parts or necessary support equipment, they become expensive junk. The administration has a responsibility to develop a more balanced military spending program. And unless that program emphasizes the importance of proper maintenance and spare parts supply, the probable result is that the Pentagon will waste billions of dollars on sophisticated — but unworkable — weaponry.

The Birmingham News

Birmingham, Ala., April 23, 1981

There are big problems with the Army's new M1 tank. According to a report in *The Wall Street Journal* based on still confidential test findings, the new tank (which used to go by the designation MX1) is lagging badly in several areas of performance even as the Pentagon presses for rushed-up mass production of the M1.

Among the problem areas: There is a 70 percent possibility that the engine or drive train of the tank will need major repairs in less than 4,000 miles (as against the 50 percent top-line ratio set by the Army originally); treads, which are supposed to last at least 2,000 miles, are averaging just 850 miles of life; the engine is getting considerably less than the .5 miles per gallon specified — under battle conditions, the tank's 500 gallons of fuel will carry it only 130 miles.

The tank's principal machine gun is "almost impossible to aim," according to field reports, and crew members complain that portions of the interior design are inefficient.

All this, with a tank now estimated to cost $3 million per copy.

Developmental problems with a sophisticated weapons system are nothing new, and the Army brass, long-range, may well be justified in their praise of the M1. All that, however, does not mean that the Pentagon should bull ahead with a crash building program just to get numbers in the field.

Numbers are a problem — the Soviets currently hold a 4-to-1 advantage in tanks — but it would seem the wiser course to rely on less sophisticated models, including modernizations of current tanks, rather than to rush M1 development. It certainly beats the alternative of a billion-dollar M1 armada, composed of tanks which don't work — or at least don't work as they should.

The Philadelphia Inquirer

Philadelphia, Pa., August 6, 1981

The U. S. Army's new M-1 tank is a wonder of modern technology. Its accuracy in hitting a target while moving is unsurpassed, according to recent tests. There's just one problem. The tanks tend to break down rather frequently. As often as every 30 miles or so. That's not a particularly admirable performance record for a vehicle that costs about $3 million.

Back in 1974, the Army announced plans to buy 7,058 M-1 tanks to bolster its readiness for tank warfare in Europe. When finally delivered the tanks will cost about $19 billion, or $5 billion over budget. That doesn't include the $800 million "product improvement" program everybody agrees is necessary. Nor does it include the cost of ammunition or fuel, which is burned at the rate of four gallons to the mile.

Recent testimony before Sen. William Proxmire (D., Wis.) produced some more bad news about the tanks: They probably are far less reliable than the tanks the Army already has in Europe. Walton H. Sheley Jr. of the General Accounting Office told Sen. Proxmire that, unless the M-1's problems can be remedied, "we've got a lemon."

Mr. Sheley said he hoped a final analysis of the M-1 tests would show that the "combat mission reliability" goal set by the Army can be met or exceeded. That goal is an average of 320 miles between failures. On the other hand, he said he is "virtually certain" that the goals for durability of the drive train (4,000 miles without replacement of the turbine engine or transmission) and for maintenance (1.25 man-hours of maintenance for each hour of operation) "will not be achieved."

In light of this information, it is worth noting that another piece of equipment critical to the nation's defense is being tested now by the Army with some reassuring results. Since May, 31 soldiers have been walking as much as 15 miles a day at the Aberdeen Proving Ground in Maryland testing a new style combat boot.

Although the test has many more miles to go, the "combat mission reliability" seems to be unquestioned. The participants have not experienced any breakdowns, only a few blisters. And as any GI out in the field will tell you, fancy weaponry aside, the best line of defense is a soldier's feet.

The Houston Post

Houston, Texas, July 18, 1981

The Army's new M-1 tank, formerly the XM-1, has been a high-profile target of criticism almost since its development began a decade ago. The M-1 has had to bear the stigma of the disastrous MBT-70 program, the joint U.S.-West German effort to build a supertank. That collapsed in 1970 amid bitter disputes and huge cost overruns. But the M-1 has had its own problems, as a recently completed draft report by the General Accounting Office emphasizes.

The report by the GAO, the investigative arm of Congress, is now being circulated for Pentagon comment. If accurate, it is a horror story of poor planning and procurement ineptitude involving one of the nation's major weapons systems. But it is by no means the only example of the Pentagon's shortcomings in buying arms and equipment. The M-1 is being built by the Chrysler Corp. as the Army's main battle tank. The Pentagon is planning to buy 7,000 at a total estimated cost of $20 billion. But GAO investigators say the cost could be much greater because of high maintenance expenses and lack of attention to the weapon's support needs.

The GAO study found that the new tank is prone to breakdowns and virtually impossible to repair in the field. Its report also faults the Army for not providing enough repair kits, tools and instruction manuals, and says the manuals contain unclear and inaccurate information. So eager was the Pentagon to make the M-1s operational, says the GAO, that it has not ordered enough fuel, ammunition and transport vehicles to service them.

Some 350 of the M-1s have been assigned to tank units at Fort Hood in Central Texas and to Fort Knox, Ky., for field trials. They are scheduled for deployment in Europe next year. In all fairness, they are the top of the line in modern armor — when they perform as they are supposed to. Weighing 60 tons, they can race over rough ground at speeds over 30 mph. Their 105-millimeter guns can be fired accurately on the move with the aid of electronic aiming devices, even at night or on a battlefield obscured by smoke.

At $2.8 million apiece, it can be argued, the M-1s should be top performers. But the GAO cites the new tank's failure to pass many of its tests, including an Army requirement that it travel 4,000 miles without maintenance at a depot. The average life of the M-1's treads, says the GAO, is about 850 miles instead of the required 2,000 miles.

Even before the GAO report, Pentagon officials acknowledged some deficiencies in the M-1 program. As the GAO pointed out, the Army expected to correct maintenance problems in the field. Yet many of the M-1 program's problems appear to be the kind that the Defense Department should solve before they cost taxpayers extra billions.

The Carter administration asked Congress for substantial increases in defense spending. The Reagan administration is asking even more. We face a trillion dollars in military outlays over the next five years in an effort to catch up with the Soviet Union, which has been consistently outspending us on arms. U.S. public opinion supports greater defense spending. But continued disclosures of poor Pentagon stewardship of tax money could disillusion the public with ever larger defense budgets to the detriment of national security.

TULSA WORLD
Tulsa, Okla., February 21, 1982

YOU'VE been reading a lot about the M-1 tank recently. Columnist Nick Thimmesch writes about it elsewhere on this page and there may be other references elsewhere in today's paper. The reason is that it raises a pertinent question: How can the U.S. Defense Department effectively spend $1.6 trillion over the next five years?

The tanks are estimated to cost almost $2.7 million each. The transmission is so fragile the machine cannot be equipped with a bulldozer blade. So it can't dig itself into a hull-down position on the battleground. Instead, high-speed armor-covered bulldozers — cost $1 million each — will be assigned to each tank company to handle the digging chores.

Also, the Army belatedly noticed that the tank gets one mile per 3.8 gallons of gasoline. So the Pentagon is hastily shopping for extra tank trucks to follow the tanks.

The case of the M-1 tank should convince President Reagan to some of the cost-cutting pressure to the Pentagon that he has applied to non-military waste.

Meanwhile, someone ought to find out if Japanese automakers have got anything in a small, fuel-efficient tank.

The Oregonian
Portland, Ore., March 17, 1982

When it acts on the record Reagan defense budget, Congress should put on hold continued production of the multiflawed M-1 main battle tank until the Army can prove it can be made to perform as advertised.

In addition to their soaring costs — from an originally estimated $600,000 each to $2.7 million a copy today — the tanks are beset with engine, transmission and track problems. They break down frequently and use a flammable transmission fluid that critics say could make them a rolling death trap in combat.

The tank is supposed to go 4,000 miles without a major breakdown, but of the 40 M-1s tested last year, only 37 percent achieved that standard. Although the Army says otherwise, critics of the tank program claim they have Army documents that show the test results were padded and that in the final phase of operational testing only 15 percent passed.

The M-1 replaces the supposedly outmoded M-60 tank, but according to Sen. Warren Rudman, R-N.H., a member of the Senate Appropriations subcommittee on defense, updating the M-60 with a laser range finder and guns similar to the M-1 would produce a tank that would work just fine in Europe, where the major tank battles are expected to be fought, and for a lot less money.

The M-1 fleet's price tag is a staggering $19 billion for 7,058 tanks. Costs during operational life are projected at $27 billion. This year the Army is spending $1.7 billion for 665 of the tanks. It wants another $2 billion for 776 more of them in fiscal 1983.

Congressional critics of the M-1 program want 1983 funding cut by at least $400 million. Others say the Army has so much invested in the M-1 that it cannot stop building it. That is nonsense. Production should be delayed until the tank performs to specifications. Putting American soldiers into a weapons system that is dangerous and subject to breakdown is a treacherous disservice to them and the nation.

The Pittsburgh Press
Pittsburgh, Pa., February 16, 1982

In 1972 the U.S. Army conceived its main battle tank of the future, the M-1.

Compared with existing tanks, it was to be faster, more agile, better armored, and able to fire accurately on the move. It was to cost about $500,000 apiece.

The M-1 now is coming from Chrysler Corp. plants, and it is capable of doing many of the things it was designed for. Unfortunately, its price has ballooned to $2.6 million each, meaning taxpayers will be tapped for $19 billion if the Army gets the 7,000 tanks it wants.

* * *

Meanwhile, tests have shown the M-1 to be much less durable than it was supposed to be. Engines, transmissions, power trains and treads have to be repaired or replaced more frequently than specifications call for.

Recently it was reported that the M-1's delicate transmission makes it impossible for the tank to dig itself in on the battlefield to fire or find protection against the enemy. Some earlier tanks had that ability.

Undaunted, the Army thought up a companion vehicle for the M-1, a high-speed armored bulldozer called ACE. This $1.1-million vehicle is to go into combat with the M-1 and dig it in. The Army seeks more than 600 copies of ACE.

Also, because the M-1 is a noted gas guzzler — if it doesn't break down en route it goes 250 miles on a 500-gallon fuel tank — the Army wants 26 additional fuel trucks for each battalion of M-1s.

* * *

If hostilities ever did break out in Europe, can't you just see the M-1s going into action, each one throwing its treads and being followed by its own ACE bulldozer and filling station?

No doubt the Russians would laugh themselves to death at the sight, and the United States would then stand accused of fielding an inhumane weapon.

Seriously, the sad story of the M-1 helps explain why the Pentagon budget now stands at $263 billion — without producing the weapons the nation needs. Overly complex designs, inept procurement and shoddy manufacture are as threatening as any enemy.

THE ARIZONA REPUBLIC
Phoenix, Ariz., February 14, 1982

BEFORE Congress votes another cent for the M-1 tank, the armed services committee of either the House or the Senate should hold a full-scale investigation to determine whether its critics are justified in calling it a turkey.

The Army says the M-1 is the best tank ever built.

Critics say it would be next to useless in combat.

At present, the critics seem to have the better of the argument.

This much the Army concedes:

The M-1 is by far the most expensive tank ever built. Each tank costs roughly $3 million. The Army is asking for 7,058 M-1s at a staggering cost of $22.2 billion.

But that's just the beginning.

The M-1 has such a delicate transmission that, unlike other tanks, it can't dig itself in.

So the Army has designed a companion vehicle, called ACE (Armored Combat Earthmover). This is a fancy bulldozer to dig the M-1 in. Each ACE will cost about $1.1 million.

The Army wants 600. Total cost: approximately $650 million.

And that's not all.

The M-1 holds 500 gallons of fuel. This is only enough to keep it running 250 miles when it's cruising and 150 miles in combat.

To keep a battalion from running out of fuel, the Army says it will need 26 fuel trucks at a cost of $632,000. The number of planned battalions is a military secret, but outside experts say it probably will be about 1,000.

Add $63 million more.

This fantastic expense would be justified, of course, if the M-1 were as effective a weapons system as the Army claims.

Critics say that, on the contrary, it's a death trap.

For one thing, they insist, leakage of the fuel from the hydraulic pumps that stabilize the tank's gun turrets makes the M-1 a "Molotov cocktail."

For another, because of a design fault, the driver cannot see the ground any closer than 27 feet in front of him.

For a third, the tank frequently breaks down because of dust clogging the engine. It needs a new filter every 75 miles.

The critics cite numerous other deficiencies. The Army does not deny they exist, but it says it can remedy them all.

What's more, it maintains, the M-1's capabilities far outweigh its deficiences. With a top speed of almost 50 miles an hour, it can run rings around the M-60. It has accurate shoot-on-the-move capability. And it can survive a land mine or a hit by the new Soviet 125-mm cannon.

The critics could be wrong. The Army could be right. There's no way of telling without a congressional investigation.

Meanwhile, there has been a troublesome development.

Less than a year ago, Army Chief of Staff Gen. Edward Meyer called the M-1 "better than anything the Russians have in service or on the drawing board."

Now the Army says the Russians have developed a tank superior to the M-1, and that it must start right away on designing a successor to the M-1.

LIST PRICE $500,000

XM-1 TANK
YOUR PRICE only $2.7 MILLION

ENGINE BREAK-DOWN EVERY 43 MILES

TREADS LAST AT LEAST 37 MILES

3.8 MPG (MILEAGE MAY VARY DEPENDING ON BATTLEFIELD CONDITIONS AND WHETHER TANK IS RUNNING)

WEIGHT AND SIZE: TOO HEAVY AND TOO WIDE FOR EUROPEAN BRIDGES

©1982 Atseff
SYRACUSE HERALD-JOURNAL

The TENNESSEAN
Nashville, Tenn., March 8, 1982

THE Army assured the Congress last week that its new Abrams M-1 battle tank, while not perfect, and priced at $1.8 million each is a good and cost-effective investment, but not everbody shares that view.

The M-1 has had its share of problems, and now has a new one. Its transmission is so delicate that it cannot do what previous tanks have traditionally done — dig itself in on the battlefield.

So, the Army has come up with a companion vehicle, called ACE. That stands for Armored Combat Earthmover, or what might be termed a high-speed bulldozer. The earthmover costs about $1.1 million each, almost as much as the tank, and the Army wants some 600 of them at about $600 million.

But there is still another problem. The M-1 tanks not only have delicate transmissions, but they guzzle fuel and get only a few miles per gallon. In order to be able to keep them moving, the Army says each battalion of M-1s will need 26 additional fuel trucks and tanks. That will cost $632,000 per battalion. The number of these is not known, but ultimately it probably would be 100. That is $63 million more.

As for the M-1 tanks themselves, the Army wants 7,000 of them, and depending on how much inflation continues to add, at a cost of $20 billion or so. Nobody knows for sure.

Gen. Glenn Otis, commander of the Army's training and doctrine command, said that inflation only has increased the unit cost of the tank from $507,000 in 1972 to $1.8 million in 1983. The Pentagon's budget in 1983 includes a request for $2.1 billion to build 776 M-1 tanks during the year. This year's budget includes $1.6 billion to build 720.

But if one counts the high-speed bulldozers and the fleets of tank trucks to carry fuel, the total in outlays for a new battle tank is enormous, and it still is flawed.

"We recognize the Abrams is not a flawless tank and we have had a number of problems to overcome to get it in the field," said General Otis, adding, "On the other hand, we believe it is the best tank in the world, one in which the soldiers who operate it have great confidence."

It may indeed be a good tank, if all the "bugs" are worked out. But a tank that needs a fleet of tankers and bulldozers to accompany it when it goes into battle seems to be carrying sophistication beyond practicality.

Tanks normally dig in on the battle field either to fire or to protect themselves from the enemy. Older tanks can have a blade attached to do the digging themselves. But according to testimony last year from the Army Chief of Staff, in order to install a blade on a M-1 "you would have to use a different engine, different transmission, supension and make other significant modifications." So a combat earthmover is necessary.

The M-1 is a prime example of problems plaguing the military. Many, if not most, of the new weapons systems are running far beyond their original cost estimates. With respect to the M-1, the General Accounting Office probably has the right idea. In a report issued in December, GAO said production of the M-1 should be limited until the power train can be improved. Otherwise, the tanks may have to be retro-fitted at an even greater cost for each unit. While the budget debate is going on, the limited purchase idea is something the Congress ought to consider.

THE MILWAUKEE JOURNAL
Milwaukee, Wisc., March 19, 1982

The Army proudly proclaims its new M-1 battle tank to be the finest tank in the world. It may be — theoretically. Right now, it is a prime candidate for belt-tightening as Congress considers President Reagan's controversial defense budget.

The Pentagon is seeking $2.1 billion in the pending budget for accelerated production of the tank. Eventually, the brass wants to acquire 7,058 M-1s at an overall cost of $19 billion.

The sticker price on each M-1 is now $2.7 million, compared to the 1972 estimate of $1.4 million a copy. The tank has been bedeviled by problems, and it is not clear that they have been solved — which makes the current $2.7 million per tank a conditional price.

Not to worry, says the Army. Not so fast, says the General Aecounting Office. The GAO warns that it would be "unwise to produce the M-1 in large numbers" until questions about its reliability are resolved.

The questions are substantial. For example, the tank's tracks were supposed to have a life of 2,000 miles, but test models are getting a maximum of 1,400 miles.

The GAO is skeptical also about the Army's reports of its own tests on the tanks. The Army's figures, according to the auditor's report, show the tanks averaging 126 miles between failures, decently above the requirement of 101 miles. But the GAO says that "our analysis showed that the M-1 averaged only about 30 miles" between breakdowns in one set of tests, 32 miles in another and 36 miles in a third.

All of that does not necessarily mean that the M-1 is a lemon. It does suggest that the frantic effort to include the most sophisticated features in the tank — and in other advanced weapons systems — is a guarantee of a relentless chain of problems and ever higher costs.

So what's to be done? The Congressional Budget Office has a suggestion: continue production of the current main battle tank, the M-60, aging but still effective, and slow down the production rate of the new M-1.

If that rate were held to 720 tanks a year, there would be a net savings of $1.1 billion by fiscal 1987. Even that rate might be excessive, however, if the bugs in the new tank are as severe as GAO believes.

Mean decisions such as the one on M-1 tank production will be the main determinant of defense costs in the years immediately ahead, and Congress must make those decisions in the *pending* defense budget. Next year and the year after will be too late.

the Charleston Gazette

Charleston, W. Va., October 30, 1982

THE CHRISTIAN SCIENCE MONITOR
Boston, Mass., March 5, 1982

If one were to pick a "case study " that underscores the Pentagon's tendency to buy complicated weapons — and then fail to ride herd on development problems and production costs — a good candidate might well be the new M-1 tank. The Army is planning to buy 7,058 M-1s, at a cost of $2.7 million each or a total cost of $19 billion, plus another $27 billion for operation and maintenance of the weapons system over its projected 20-year lifetime. Yet enough legitimate questions are now being raised about the safety, vulnerability, and operability of the M-1 as to make some lawmakers and defense analysts wonder whether the public interest might not best be served by a freeze or even total halt in the M-1 production line.

The issue is not one of rejecting the concept of battlefield tanks for the American military. The US definitely needs a battlefield tank. But it must be the right tank — which means it must have a reasonable likelihood of doing what it is supposed to do and at a cost that is not excessive. It would be unconscionable for the Pentagon to push ahead with a massive tank-procurement program if there is sound reason to believe that the M-1 is a dud, or if changing technology has rendered the tank ineffective.

Critics of the M-1, like Sen. Gary Hart and Dina Rasor, director of the Project on Military Procurement, an independent research group, point out that the tank has a pesky tendency to come to a halt for repairs every 43 miles or so; that the engine gets a paltry one mile for each 3.86 gallons of gas; that the hydraulic fluid in the weapon is particularly flammable; that tank drivers tend to have trouble operating the vehicle's complex array of computers and electronics. If this were not such a serious matter, it would be comic. There are also the "backup" problems, such as the fact that each tank battalion must have a large number of service and support vehicles, as if warfare were so tidy that tanks could be easily serviced in the midst of it.

And, if all this were not enough, there is the problem of what the military calls "advanced kinetic-energy rounds." These are long, thin antitank projectiles that the Pentagon says it has discovered can penetrate - guess what? — the M-1 tank. For that reason the Army is now expected to award contracts to two companies this month to build test-model tanks based on the M-1, but without turrets and with a thicker armor. In other words, the Army now says that the $2.7 million M-1s roaring off the production lines are vulnerable. Does that mean then that existing production should be stopped, even temporarily, until the design problems are resolved? Not according to one top Army official, who says, "We can't stop building it." He adds: "The fact that we got surprised, or that something can penetrate it, doesn't mean it isn't a great accomplishment. It can still stop a lot of types of projectiles."

But the point is, can it stop "advanced kinetic-energy rounds"?

The Pentagon may be correct in pressing ahead with the costly M-1. There are alternatives, of course, such as stepping up production of the older and cheaper M-60 ; or refitting even older M-48 tanks. But it would seem incumbent on lawmakers to ensure that whatever tank the Pentagon builds can at least do what it is intended to do — and at a reasonable price to taxpayers.

THE Pentagon continues to speak of it as if it were without flaw. Its critics contend that it is an incredibly expensive turkey. We are speaking of the M-1 Abrams tank which, at $2.8 million a copy, may provide an example to those who contend that "defense spending" doesn't necessarily mean prudent spending.

The Army plans to purchase 7,058 of these tanks for a total cost in the neighborhood of $20 billion. The generals say that the 60-ton tank meets a goal of 101 miles of operation between mechanical failures. This is hardly something to brag about. Moreover, it is something on which the generals are being challenged. The Project on Military Procurement's analysis of the Army documents finds that the Abrams goes only an average of 45 miles before something breaks down.

But even when we accept the Army's own mathematics, we are put into a state resembling astonishment. Would the Air Force be satisfied with an airplane that it could expect to fly only 101 miles before breaking down? Wouldn't the Navy expect better performance from a ship? For that matter, most Americans expect their automobiles to run for 30,000 miles or so before succumbing to mechanical failure.

And what of the terrain over which the Abrams piles up such unimpressive breakdown-free mileage? According to retired Rear Adm. Eugene J. Carroll Jr., interviewed when he visited Charleston recently, the test conditions for the Abrams were stacked heavily in the tank's favor. Carroll, who thinks the tank is a total bust for other reasons, said the tests were carried out over flat ground, not on terrain it likely would find in battle. He also observed that the Abrams gets a mile to four gallons of gasoline and that they must be accompanied into battle by bulldozers. The bulldozers would push disabled tanks out of the way.

Carroll wondered why the Army believes it important to have big tanks like the Abrams. He cited the existence of a newly perfected anti-tank weapon that works beautifully and is part of the arsenals of most of the nations of the world.

We have a sneaking suspicion that the Army's love affair with the Abrams tank may have something to do with the military establishment's penchant for preparing for wars already fought. We recommend a very close look at the Abrams tank before the order has been filled.

Rockford Register Star
Rockford, Ill., March 24, 1982

Pentagon brass, pleased as punch with their new $2.7 million M-1 tank, recently invited newspeople to take a test drive at the Aberdeen (Md.) Proving Ground. They want the world to know their 30-ton, 45 mph cannon-carrier is a sweetheart, even if the sticker price is steep.

Army officers took the occasion to try to contradict criticisms raised over the machine designed to make the U.S. an armored warfare leader through the 1990s.

That's a tip-off up front that the Pentagon will expect, in about a decade, another multi-billion-dollar update of armored vehicles, last deployed effectively in the Arab-Israeli conflicts.

But where there's Army, there's armor, says our brain trust in the five-sided building. And, since the media has been bad-mouthing the M-1, the Army says, here's the straight story:

✔Too expensive? Nonsense: The straight-stick model only costs $1.8 million each, although contracted for at $1 million per. The rest of the cost, up to $2.7 million each, is for research and accessories.

✔Too heavy? It's only 1½ tons heavier that the M-60 which it replaces. It's not too heavy for "most bridges" in Europe, they say. There is no mention of bridge testing in El Salvador, Afghanistan, the Sinai Peninsula or Maryland.

✔Gas guzzler? The military makes a good point here: At 3.5 gallons of gasoline burned for each mile traveled, the M-1 gives us 1½ tons more tank at only eight-tenths of a gallon more per mile than the M-60. Sure, you've got to pump a lot of gasoline for that kind of mileage, the Army admits. But you only need five more fuel trucks for a battalion of M-1s than you needed for a battalion of M-60s.

✔Breaks down too often? Tests show you can go 4,000 miles (14,000 gallons of gasoline later) without replacing a major part, says the Army, conceding durability must be improved.

✔Needs a "nursemaid" M-9 armored combat earthmover (ACE) to be effective? Well, OK, we do, says the Army, but we needed the ACE anyway for "battlefield earth-moving work."

Sen. Alan J. Dixon, D-Ill., and International Harvester would like to remind everybody of a couple of facts on the ACE. Harvester repeatedly has tried to bid competitively on ACE work, but the Pentagon has refused. All of the work has been awarded to one company, Pacific Car and Foundry Co. of Renton Wash.

Dixon said the ACE price tag, estimated at $200,000 in 1978, hit $1.1 million last year and rose another $500,000 in the last six months. He said the Army could have saved millions by allowing other firms a chance to bid on the work.

Dixon notes the failure of Reagan to make good on a pledge to increase competitive bidding in defense contracts: "It is foolish to award any contract on a 'sole source' basis."

"Foolish" seems a pitifully inadequate description for the vast expenditures and the vast wastes taxpayers are asked to accept in defense costs creating a $100 billion federal deficit.

The Pentagon's cheery tank-makers could better serve the bill-payers than its recent media exhibition. The professed pride is in an armored vehicle finally produced at more than twice its estimated cost and still not ready for use in the field — whatever field that might conceivably be.

THE LOUISVILLE TIMES
Louisville, Ky., September 23, 1982

Although the new M-1 Abrams tank has been dubbed "Superlemon" by some, the Army insists that it is making progress in correcting the tank's deficiencies. Last March, the Pentagon told Congress that the M-1 is "the best tank in the world." Given that assurance, Congress turned loose nearly $1.7 billion so that the Army could order another 1,755 of the tanks.

Now results of the Army's own testing of the vehicle, leaked to a Pentagon watchdog group, show that little progress has been made in solving some serious problems, while new ones have been noted. Moreover, those test results were compiled last fall but were not made available to Congress before the authorization vote. The Project on Military Procurement, which made the results public, said it received them from sources within the Pentagon. The watchdog group has been accurate in the past.

The latest tests, including some conducted at Fort Knox, indicate that durability of the M-1 has actually worsened since tests in early 1980. The Army standard requires that at least half of the tanks be able to go 4,000 miles without overhaul or replacement of the engine or transmission. In March, Army officials told Congress that 37 per cent of the tanks met the standard, but the test results show only 15 per cent actually went 4,000 miles in field tests without a breakdown. And in another field test at Fort Hood, only 21 of 39 tanks finished the 178-mile course without breaking down.

One of the documents made public also verified that the M-1 has a serious fire problem because its hydraulic fluid is highly flammable and its automatic fire-extinguisher equipment is not responding as it should. The Army denied both problems earlier this year, but the document warning of the problems was circulated to Army units last October.

Other documents also noted a turret machine gun is susceptible to "accidental firing" and suggested that the turbine engines produce so much heat that the M-1 could not easily hide from Soviet heat-seeking devices. The "operational availability," or average time that the tank is not being serviced was so low — 44 per cent — that it was recommended each tank battalion add seven mechanics just to keep up with maintenance.

The cost of "Superlemon" has already reached $2.7 million a copy, more than five times what Congress originally authorized for the vehicle. The final bill for the 7,058 the Army wants is estimated to be about $19.5 billion.

And that may by no means be the end of it. Each M-1 was supposed to even the odds in Europe by being able to take on two Soviet T-72 tanks, but Soviet army planners have not cooperated. They apparently have modified a heavier, older tank — the T-64 — instead, and it is closer to a one-to-one match for the M-1. The expected Pentagon response, of course, is to demand more bucks to modify the M-1.

The only bright spot in the picture is that the Russians have copied some features of the M-1 so closely in modifying the T-64 that they may have duplicated some of the defects, too. The armor of each tank appears vulnerable to anti-tank projectiles, and each also has overly-complicated laser gunsights and computerized fire-control system. Although the T-64 doesn't gargle three or four gallons of fuel for each mile, like the M-1, it also uses a lot. And both tanks are so heavy that most European bridges cannot support them.

Maybe the real hope for world peace lies in more military ineptitude, not less. Then the Great Tank Battle of the European plain could end with thousands of the behemoths facing each other impotently, broken down or out of gas and abandoned by their disgusted crews, who will have to hitch a ride back to their bankrupt homelands.

THE BLADE
Toledo, Ohio, September 26, 1982

THE Pentagon has a problem. The army wants to buy the new M-1 battle tanks now being produced in Lima, but field tests are still turning up evidence of serious mechanical deficiencies in the 60-ton vehicle.

The new tank has demonstrated speed, quietness, a low silhouette, and maneuverability. Troops like it because they believe those qualities would make the tank more difficult for an enemy to hit or destroy.

But the M-1 has piled up an unflattering record of malfunctions. In one recent field test half of the tanks were forced out of action by mechanical or electrical breakdowns by the fifth day. The tank is functional only about 40 per cent of the time it is supposed to be operating.

The M-1 on the average, according to one evaluating agency, can travel only 44 miles before something goes wrong. And the various problems, from engine breakdowns to treads that come loose, have required a small contingent of mechanics and repair specialists to travel with each tank battalion, simply to keep the M-1 in operation.

In light of these facts, one might think that the army would be cautious about going ahead with the new tank, but that is not the case. The army is actually pushing hard to purchase more than 7,000 of the M-1s at a total cost of $19 billion, not counting cost overruns. That's $19 *billion*, taxpayers.

If the M-1 is the turkey on treads that some observers contend, does it make sense to build 7,000 of them before the bugs are removed? A tank that will travel on average only 44 miles before breaking down would be splendid if the next war is fought in, say, Liechtenstein, which is a country of only 61 square miles. But, alas, Liechtenstein shows no warlike tendencies that would seem to call for the use of these defect-plagued behemoths.

Congress should step in and be absolutely certain that the M-1 works in every respect before it permits the army to load up its arsenal with them.

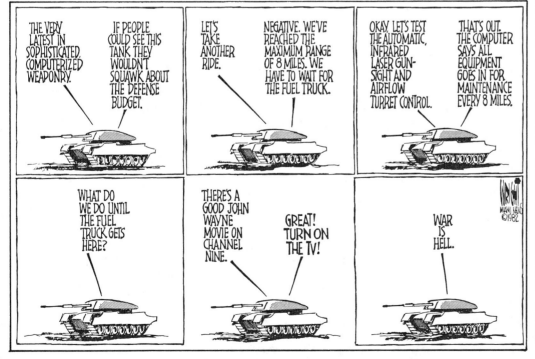

The Air Force's C-5 Military Cargo Plane

A battle between McDonnell Douglas Corp. and Lockheed Corp. was settled in January, 1982 when President Reagan approved a Pentagon recommendation to purchase Lockheed's C-5 transport plane rather than the new C-17 cargo plane designed by McDonnell Douglas. The C-5 planes, long a subject of controversy because of their history of record cost overruns and operational difficulties, were the world's largest cargo planes, with a wingspan of 222 feet and room inside to carry either two of the Army's new M-1 tanks or up to 345 troops. They were intended to provide aerial transport for tanks, helicopters, trucks and artillery to accompany the Rapid Deployment Force. McDonnell Douglas, whose C-17 plane had been chosen by the Air Force as the best model submitted, said the decision made a "mockery" of the competitive process among military contractors.

The Senate defense authorization bill for fiscal 1983 eliminated the C-5, however, in favor of purchasing used Boeing 747s, to be modified as cargo planes. Intense lobbying by both Boeing and Lockheed followed, and the House bill passed two months later included funds for the C-5s. House-Senate conferees agreed in August to fund the purchase of 50 Lockheed C-5s, as the House bill had approved, rather than the Boeing 747s favored by the Senate. This compromise was reached despite the disclosure early in August that production of the C-5 air cargo plane would cost almost 25% more than the April, 1982 "firm, fixed price" of $8.84 billion for 50 planes, and that production would be slower than Lockheed had promised.

Another wrinkle was added to the transport plane problem when the General Accounting Office reported in September that Air Force and Defense Department officials had "violated federal antilobbying laws" by working with Lockheed Corp. to win congressional funding for the C-5. The GAO report stated that the lobbying effort in favor of the C-5 over the Boeing 747 had been "initiated and directed by officials of the Department of Defense and that material but undeterminable amounts of appropriated funds and government resources were spent" to influence Congress.

St. Louis Globe-Democrat
St. Louis, Mo., April 17-18, 1982

The school of thought which holds that a bird in the hand is worth two in the bush is being challenged sharply by critics of the Pentagon's decision to keep buying Lockheed C-5s rather than switch to the McDonnell Douglas Corp. C-17 as the airlift plane of the future. The dissenters make some valid points.

In explaining Defense Department Secretary Caspar W. Weinberger's decision to buy 50 more C-5s instead of waiting for development of the McDonnell Douglas aircraft, Deputy Defense Secretary Frank C. Carlucci said it boiled down to "a proven design vs. a paper airplane." The C-17 is still on the drawing board, but it has passed design tests with flying colors.

The Air Force, along with the Army and Marine Corps, initially recommended shifting to the C-17 for shipping military equipment to world trouble spots. The consensus was that since the C-17 was to be smaller and more agile than the C-5, and thus could land closer to the battle area, the C-17 would be more suitable to military needs.

But a funny thing happened on the way to the Pentagon's decision on what kind of long-distance transport planes it should buy for its Rapid Deployment Force and other units.

Air Force leaders apparently were turned around. As Carlucci explained, "once briefed on the facts as we have them," the Air Force leaders "came back unanimously" in favor of buying the C-5.

There may have been a little sweetening of the Air Force's pot to cause such "unanimity." It has been suggested that the Pentagon's willingness to place more money in the budget for the C-5s helped change some military minds about the C-17s.

The handling of the C-5 affair is viewed as "scandalous" by the Army's second-highest civilian, Army Undersecretary James R. Ambrose. In an internal memo dated Feb. 19 to the Pentagon's chief of research, Richard D. DeLauer, Ambrose said the Weinberger decision means "perpetrating a scandalous situation."

The Ambrose memo to DeLauer said: "Surely you do not expect support for this decision to consist of anything beyond agreeing: (1) Office of the Secretary of Defense has the right to decide; (2) the decision, to which we were not a party, evidently was made in favor of near term long-haul airlift which, of course, is an urgent need. Intra-theater requirements, which are also urgent, remain to be satisfied."

In his memo, which was obtained by the nonprofit organization, Project on Military Procurement, Ambrose called the Air Force's presentation to Congress on the C-17 transport plane "appalling." The presentation, he said, was "one more illustration of the likely and unreasonable fate of adequate airlift in the hands of an Air Force which has its hands full" with other programs like the MX missile and satellites.

On the basis of fair competition, the C-17 has been judged superior to the C-5 and other cargo craft. It deserves far better treatment than it has received at the hands of some in Washington.

Flying to the rescue of the C-17, U.S. Sen. Thomas F. Eagleton, D-Mo., has urged President Reagan personally to review the Pentagon's controversial decision. It is "intolerable," Eagleton said, that the Pentagon's top civilian officials would overrule the nation's "highest military experts." The president should intervene and judge for himself. The C-17 deserves an impartial review at the highest level.

The Wichita
Eagle-Beacon
Wichita, Kans., May 15, 1982

The Senate's decision to give the Defense Department's Rapid Deployment Force 747s instead of C-5Bs for its materiel transportation fleet is good news for Wichita and for Kansas.

It also is good news for the rest of the nation because:

- Taxpayers stand to save at least $4 billion. The Georgia-based Lockheed company had hoped to get an $8 billion contract to build 50 C-5B cargo aircraft. Boeing has offered an equal number of 747s for about half the amount.

- Time will be saved because Lockheed would have to retool production lines that have been down for a decade. Boeing already has 747s ready to go after a little modification and retrofitting.

- The choice of 747s would benefit the financially pressed airline industry if the Pentagon would take off its hands those jumbo jets some airlines had ordered but been unable to take delivery on, and those that have been parked because changing travel patterns and route structures made their operation in passenger service no longer economical.

The Senate's verdict is good news for Wichita workers because much of the work, and especially the retrofitting of existing aircraft, would be done by Boeing Military Airplane Co. Boeing's Seattle division would benefit, too, of course.

The 747s could, in most cases, meet the Rapid Deployment Force's needs better than the C-5, and that the Defense Department already has enough of the latter craft to transport the few types of military equipment more easily accommodated, without disassembly, in the taller C-5 cargo holds.

Sen. Bob Dole, R-Kan., summed things up very well with this statement: "The Air Force will get an efficient aircraft, the aviation industry will get a shot in the arm and the American taxpayer will be saving a few billion dollars."

Now it is up to Rep. Dan Glickman, D-Kan., and other members of Kansas' congressional delegation to help see that the House agrees.

THE ATLANTA CONSTITUTION

Atlanta, Ga., January 21, 1982

It's not official, but it has been "confirmed" that the Pentagon will award Lockheed-Georgia Co. a contract to build an undisclosed number of updated versions of the C-5A Galaxy jet transport. That's wonderful news for Georgia and the Atlanta area. Between 4,000 and 8,000 new jobs will be created for people here. In addition, the wise decision made by Pentagon officials to go with the C-5A will benefit the entire nation.

The Pentagon received considerable pressure to start production of the new C-17 design propose by the McDonnell Douglas Corp. Officials estimated that new jet transports would cost between $24 billion and $25 billion.

It was then decided to study other airlift alternatives, including reactivating the production lines of older military transport planes like the C-5A or using military versions of commercial aircraft, such as the DC-10 and Boeing 747. At a time when the U.S. military budget is considerably above the total budgets of many other countries, it makes sense to look at alternatives when billions of dollars can be saved.

That's where Lockheed entered the picture, since it designed the original C-5A. The Marietta company proposed to build 44 C-5As at a guaranteed price of $4.18 billion out of a total package of 144 planes. Lockheed

officials argued that for the $1.7 billion it would cost to build one experimental McDonnell Douglas C-17, Lockheed-Georgia could build 17 new C-5As, as well as deliver the first of the planes by December 1984.

Lockheed and Georgia may be happy about the decison, but not Missouri Sens. Thomas Eagleton and John Danforth, who are upset that the C-17 project is being abandoned. The C-17s would have been built in St. Louis by the Douglas Military Aircraft Co., a subsidiary of McDonnell Douglas. Naturally, constituents of Eagleton and Danforth would have benefited had the Pentagon gone with production of the new plane. The senators are questioning the legality of the Pentagon's decision, saying McDonnell Douglas was the winner of the design competition to build the C-17s.

One of the major criticisms of the Pentagon involves cost overruns on projects and not considering alternatives to save money to reach the same objective. In this case, the Pentagon has made an effort to answer some of those criticisms. This time, it makes more sense to reactivate production lines at Lockheed.

It was the Pentagon who sought alternatives and not Lockheed. It just so happens that this time Lockheed had the solution to the alternative for which Pentagon officials were looking.

Atlanta, Ga., May 17, 1982

If Democrat Henry Jackson ever wants to give up being a senator from the state of Washington, he obviously possesses the talents for another, similar job. He would be a great snake-oil salesman for a traveling medicine show.

The Senate, thanks in major part to slick lobbying by Jackson, voted last week not to purchase 50 new C-5Bs, but rather to buy used, refitted 747s as giant cargo planes for the U.S. military. The 747s are manufactured by the Boeing Co. in Jackson's home state of Washington.

The C-5Bs would have been built at Lockheed-Georgia in Marietta, and would have meant a $4.5-billion contract providing about 8,000 new jobs at the Marietta facility.

The Defense Department and congressional committees had recommended purchase of the C-5s, but Jackson succeeded in getting the full Senate to reject the recommendations. This he managed, despite Pentagon studies showing that the C-5B would be far superior than the 747 in meeting the military's airlift needs.

But the name of the game was politics and lobbying. Jackson, an influential senator, surely called due some political IOUs from fellow senators. And the Washington senator was joined in his lobbying efforts by airline officials (who have used 747s to sell), by officials of companies who subcontract work from Boeing and by officials of companies who supply materials to Boeing.

Sen. Barry Goldwater, R-Ariz., a supporter of the C-5B, put it perfectly when, after the vote, he said, "We were outlobbied."

There is no question that the C-5B is the superior plane for meeting the military's need of airlifting troops, equipment and supplies, quickly and in great quantities, to various parts of the world. The C-5B can carry much larger equipment than the 747; for example, the 747 cannot carry the Army's new tanks. Numerous other weapons would have to be disassembled before they could be transported in the 747, and then reassembled on the battlefield. Numerous modifications would also have to be made on 747s, whereas the C-5B is already designed for heavy military-airlift purposes.

The 747 forces' main argument was the Boeing plane's considerably cheaper initial price, but Sen. Sam Nunn, D-Ga., argued that the life-cycle cost of the C-5s is just $1 billion more. That is not much to pay, he maintained, if it means the difference on whether U.S. troops waiting on a battlefield will be able to get the weapons they need.

The 747's victory over the C-5B is not yet certain, since the House has yet to act, and there are possibilities of reconsideration in the Senate. Congress surely will come to its senses and permit the C-5B's military superiority to defeat the 747's politics and lobbies.

The Washington Post

Washington, D.C., May 18, 1982

THE SENATE huffed and puffed its way through 20 hours of debate before passing the mammoth defense procurement bill in the wee hours last Saturday morning. Despite, or perhaps because of, this frenzied activity, the Senate left hard decisions on military priorities for another day.

The $178 billion authorized for developing and buying weapons trims $5.6 billion from the administration's initial budget request. That's not enough to meet even the modest defense savings for next year that were agreed upon by the administration and Senate Republicans a week earlier.

The Senate accepted almost all of the decisions made earlier by its Armed Services Committee—decisions that may make it still harder to control defense spending in future years. Despite the spending cuts, the committee was able to find room to make down payments on all the new hardware the Pentagon requested, including two new carrier task forces and resumption of chemical weapons production. It even turned away from most of the savings that Defense Secretary Weinberger had put on the table earlier in the week. These weapon starts put a heavy mortgage on the defense budget in future years.

The only tough choice the Senate actually made had heavy political overtones. It was the decision to buy used Boeing 747 airplanes to bolster airlift capability instead of ordering more new Lockheed C5 cargo planes. Boeing is located in Washington State, the home of Sens. Henry M. Jackson and Slade Gorton, who led the debate in defense of the 747.

Lockheed, of course, is not exactly without regional defenses. It builds its C5s in Georgia, and it had Sens. Sam Nunn and Mack Mattingly to speak for its merits. But the balance was tilted in favor of the Washington State contingent by the bankruptcy of Braniff International—some of the 747s would be bought from failing airlines—and by an alliance with senators from Missouri and Kansas who hope that if the C5 falls from favor, their favorite contractor, McDonnell Douglas, will get to build the new C17 transport.

By moving the defense bill ahead of the budget process, Armed Services Committee advocates of a no-cut approach to defense spending scored an early victory. That success, however, may mean that decisions on defense priorities will be shifted in the budget reconciliation process to the Appropriations Committee—where final adjustments to meet budget controls will be made later in the year. Shaving money from next year's spending in the rush of budget reconciliation is definitely not the best way to ensure that the country's armed forces are ready for action now or in the future.

The Seattle Times

Seattle, Wash., May 21, 1982

IF SENATOR Jackson ever retires from the Senate, began a recent editorial in an Atlanta newspaper, "he could get a job as a snake-oil salesman."

The paper was lamenting the May 13 vote to pass a Jackson-sponsored amendment canceling the Pentagon's planned purchase of 50 new C-5 cargo planes for the military's new Rapid Deployment Force. Fifty new and used 747s would be bought as a bargain alternative.

The vote, which Congressional Quarterly described as "startling," pitted two longtime giants of the Senate Armed Services Committee against each other.

At stake are jobs in Jackson's home state, producer of the 747, or jobs in Sen. Sam Nunn's home state of Georgia, manufacturer of the trouble-plagued, cracked-winged C-5.

The lobbying effort that helped Jackson win involved not only The Boeing Co. but airlines such as United and World Airways, which have surplus 747s.

Boeing can identify 40 surplus 747s available from airlines, meaning that 10 new 747s would be produced under the Jackson amendment.

But the real issue before the Senate, of course, was not which region or companies would benefit, but the national interest.

This week Malcolm Stamper, Boeing president, visited the lions' den, Atlanta, to reiterate that basic issue. He said both the C-5 and the 747 are needed to boost the military's airlift capability.

"The 747," Stamper said, "can carry heavier weights. We can fly it faster and farther without refueling. But a combination of the two planes is what we're selling."

The C-5 would be used to carry oversized loads. The Air Force has about 77 C-5s, quite enough for that task, in its inventory. By filling out the rest of the rapid-deployment fleet with 747s, more than $6 billion would be saved. As Jackson earlier told the Senate:

"What this boils down to is the Pentagon wants to spend an extra $6 billion for the convenience of airplanes with big doors . . . We simply cannot afford the luxury of gold-plated doors."

In Atlanta, Stamper hailed the Senate vote as an economical decision "in favor of the taxpayers."

We trust the House will see it the same way — even without benefit of a "snake-oil salesman."

Seattle, Wash., May 25, 1982

DEFENSE Secretary Caspar Weinberger has written a letter to Rep. Norm Dicks, Democrat from this state's 6th District, assuring him that the Air Force will not buy new Lockheed C-5 cargo planes until the House finishes debate on whether to buy Boeing 747s instead.

Dicks, a member of a House defense-appropriations subcommittee, says he is "delighted" with Weinberger's letter. We are, too — but also puzzled.

We're wondering why such a letter was necessary. The Senate voted by an impressive 60-39 margin May 13 to substitute new and used 747s for the new C-5s the Air Force wants to purchase for the Rapid Deployment Force.

Surely Weinberger was not planning to defy nearly two-thirds of the Senate by going ahead with the C-5 program before Congress has settled the question!

And it is highly unlikely that Republican Weinberger would write to a Democratic congressman just to cast the lawmaker in a favorable light with his constituents.

Whatever the reason for the secretary's "delightful" letter, the reasons behind the Senate vote remain unchanged. The 747s would be available at least three years sooner than the new C-5s the Pentagon wants to buy. They can fly farther and faster than the C-5s. And the 747 plan would save the taxpayers $6 billion, of which $500 million would be saved in the first year of the program.

We trust the House will follow the Senate's lead in seeing the logic of the 747 alternative, as well as seizing a clear-cut opportunity to show that Congress in these tough economic times is not willing to write the Defense Department a blank check.

The Morning News

Wilmington, Del., May 17, 1982

C AS IN C-5 STANDS for controversy, at the moment, but it also stands for constituents in the minds of the senators of three states, including Delaware.

Sens. William V. Roth Jr. and Joseph R. Biden Jr. voiced their disappointment last week when the Senate voted 60-39 to cancel Defense Department plans to buy 50 new C-5 cargo planes for the U.S. Air Force. Sen. Sam Nunn, D-Ga., was unhappy, too. Sen. Henry M. Jackson, D-Wash., was elated.

We elect senators and representatives to make judgments with our interests in mind. So it is commendable when they look even at national issues with the thought, "What's in it for my state?" In this case, 50 new C-5s for the Air Force might have meant for Delaware as many as 25 more of the giant aircraft and 3,400 new jobs at Dover Air Force Base. (It is possible, of course, as Sen. Roth pointed out, that even 747s might be stationed at Dover, thus easing the disappointment for Delawareans.)

For Georgia, it would have meant a major new contract for the Lockheed Corp. in Marietta, Ga. For Washington, it means new production for the Boeing Co., which builds the 747s that the Senate vote substituted for the C-5s.

The Senate's action also would require the Air Force to buy and refit commercial 747s now going unused by the nation's airlines as a result of the recession. Sen. Nunn urged the Senate not to let the problems of the airlines influence a military decision. There is reason to believe, however, that the influence he exerts as a member of the Senate Armed Services Committee helped to let the interests of Georgia influence the Pentagon decision to order 50 C-5s in the first place.

One of the tasks for which the Air Force would use the new C-5s is transport of Army troops and equipment anywhere they are needed. The Air Force preference for the C-5 met stiff Army resistance in the Pentagon. While they were not totally pleased with 747s as alternatives, the generals argued that the landing requirements of the giant, lumbering C-5s severely limit their ability to deliver troops and weapons close enough to where they are needed.

The new C-5s are modified versions of the C-5A, which was plagued with trouble from the time the first aircraft were delivered by Lockheed. Original weight problems forced changes in wing design below contract specifications. But Lockheed told the Air Force it couldn't perform structural tests on the redesigned wings.

Only a month after the first C-5 was delivered, cracks appeared in its wings. But Lockheed was in serious financial trouble, so the Air Force converted the fixed-price contract on C-5s to a cost-reimbursement, fixed-loss contract. It continued to accept delivery of C-5s that it knew to be deficient because it had not had time to collect enough data to determine the modifications that would be necessary.

By the time that information was in hand, the Air Force owned 77 C-5s. The contract on a 12-year program to strengthen the wings of those aircraft went, of course, to the manufacturer. Lockheed argues that it would be foolish to design a new cargo plane more adaptable to the needs of the U.S. Army, or to use the smaller 747, now that newer and better C-5s can be built.

It has always been difficult to separate parochialism from patriotism when it comes to spending for the national defense. It is never easy to subordinate local interest to national interest when millions of federal dollars are involved. That is particularly true when recession has crippled local economies. But it is necessary, particularly when there are growing demands for economy in defense spending.

In the case of the Senate's decision not to buy 50 more C-5s, the most important question is not what's in it for Delaware, or Georgia, or Washington, but what's in it for the national defense. The Senate vote was encouraging but there is still little reason to believe that that question has been satisfactorily answered.

The News and Courier

Charleston, S.C., June 15, 1982

The latest congressional "dip" into the Defense porkbarrel is inexcuseable. Its author is Sen. Henry Jackson, D-Wash., sometimes known as the "senator from Boeing" since Boeing's headquarters are in Seattle.

What the senator proposed is that Defense scrap its planned purchase of Lockheed C-5 cargo planes and substitute a bunch of second hand, surplus Boeing 747s owned by ailing U.S. airlines. Boeing would refit the 747s for military use — at a profit, of course — and the airlines, suffering from fare wars and slumping air travel, would recoup their investment. And it's all billed as a "bargain" for Defense with everybody ending up a winner — Boeing, the airlines and Uncle Sam.

That's nonsense. The C-5s are specifically designed to handle outsized cargo such as tanks, heavy artillery and large helicopters. They would carry the backbone needed for operations by the Rapid Deployment Force. It's the only aircraft that can do it. There's no way the 747 can be refitted to handle that type of cargo.

Boeing's response is to use the current C-5s strictly for that big cargo and the 747s for all else. Maybe that means put the helicopter in one plane and its rotor blades, wheels and spare parts in another. Whatever, it would be a planning nightmare for the military and slow down operations at a time when *rapid* deployment is the key.

The Senate's action last month to force-feed these planes on the military should be reversed by the House. It is a flagrant attempt to bail out Boeing and the airlines while providing a military airlift "on the cheap." Industrial welfare should never be a part of the Defense budget.

Sentinel Star

Orlando, Fla., July 2, 1982

For a telling insight into why the military acquisitions get so out of step with financial and political reality, you need only look at the debate over the Air Force's heavy airlift needs.

The issue seems simple. Civilian and military experts agree that the Air Force is 20 million ton-miles a day short of meeting its airlift requirements. A ton-mile is the space needed to haul 1 ton 1 mile. To fulfill its mission of getting outsized combat equipment wherever it's needed, the Air Force says it needs 50 additional C-5s, its largest plane. It now has 77 of them. Lockheed, the plane's manufacturer, has offered to sell the modified C-5s to the government at a fixed price, eating any cost overruns.

Now comes the politics. Washington state's senators, Democrat Henry Jackson and Republican Slade Gorton, successfully maneuvered a measure through the Senate recently that would order the Air Force to forget the C-5s and to take advantage of those surplus Boeing 747s lying around the country's civilian airfields. They argue that would help the airlines by soaking up their expensive surplus planes, giving the Air Force lots of heavy lift capacity right away and saving the taxpayers $6 billion on the purchase price. Sounds swell doesn't it?

But the equipment the Army would be shipping around the globe in the planes — M1 tanks, for instance — cannot fit into a 747. The Army chief of staff testified that "it would take six times longer to airlift the 101st Airborne Division with 747 aircraft than with C-5s." Nor does the 747 have in-flight refueling, airdrop capability or the ability to operate from unimproved landing strips as does the C-5.

Furthermore, the Air Force says that if forced to buy the 747s, it will have to vastly overhaul its parts inventories and retrain service crews to compensate for introduction of an entirely new aircraft into the system. The Air Force also disputes the $6 billion savings figure, saying that when all the factors are toted up, the difference is not $6 billion in two years but $50 million over a 20-year span.

Oh, one other thing. The major industry in Mr. Jackson's and Mr. Gorton's home state is the Boeing Aircraft Co., which happens to be laying off thousands of employees because of the airline market slump. But of course, no one is suggesting such parochial interests have any bearing on top priority national defense issues.

The Detroit News

Detroit, Mich., June 25, 1982

Members of the House Armed Service Committee are umpiring a nasty little dustup between Lockheed and Boeing over the type of plane the Air Force will buy for hauling heavy cargo. The exercise is instructive because it shows how wrong weapons are sometimes bought.

The Air Force now has 77 C-5As, built by Lockheed in Marietta, Ga. This type is an enormous kite with a high wing, a floor near the ground, and both front and rear doors. Air Force crews know how to fly and fix it, and already have a stock of spare parts.

C-5A clearances allow for hauling "outsize" cargo, including a pair of main battle tanks, or three helicopters, or 10 Pershing missiles with tow and launch vehicles.

The recession is hurting Boeing, and its management thought the Air Force could be conned into buying used 747 airliners, instead of 50 new C-5Bs. Idle 747s would be absorbed — to the great relief of the struggling airlines — and Boeing would keep some people at work refitting them at $12 million apiece.

The issue became a test of wills between two powerful Democrats, Sen. Sam Nunn of Georgia (Lockheed's home state), and Sen. Henry Jackson of Washington (Boeing territory).

There was a blur of numbers, all of which were affected by some strange inflation calculations. Boeing says used airplanes could save the Defense Department $6 billion, while the Pentagon says the difference would be $1 billion during the planes' life cycle.

Sen. Jackson won a startling victory for used Boeings, and his bill is now before the House.

The Boeing deal would be a great mistake. The 747 is a fine civilian airplane, but it lacks air refueling capability, can't carry outsize items like tanks, doesn't have fast roll-on and roll-off capability, and can't land on anything but long, paved, airport runways.

The C-5B is designed to do a military job, while the 747 is great for tourist charters and package freight. The House would be wise to oppose the Senate action.

THE ARIZONA REPUBLIC

Phoenix, Ariz., June 21, 1982

BOTH the Boeing 747 jumbo jetliner and Lockheed's C-5 military transport are huge airplanes able to carry enormous payloads over long distances.

Now both are in competition for a multi-billion dollar contract to enlarge U.S. military airlift capacity.

The Pentagon prefers the C-5, whose cavernous innards can accommodate the largest Army tank, trucks, troops and even other smaller aircraft. With inflight refueling, its range is global, and thus is especially useful for overseas deployment of troops and support equipment.

Its 28 wheels enable it to land on rough-hewn airstrips, and load and unload quickly through an opened nose.

But the C-5 has a tawdry past. The original 80 C-5s cost more than programmed, and subsequent wing cracks cost another $1 billion to repair.

Enter Boeing Aircraft Co., and Sen. Henry Jackson, D-Wash., often called "the Senator from Boeing."

Jackson convinced colleagues to ignore the Pentagon, and instead to buy 48 Boeing 747s, which supporters say have lower maintenance costs, bigger payload capacities and faster turnaround times.

But Senate approval of the 747, whose principal fame is as a luxury airliner, has all the appearances of a tonic for airlines who want to sell their mothballed 747s, and for Boeing, which has suffered cancellations because of a slump in the airline business.

Critics point out that the 747 lacks the onloading, off-loading design of the C-5, the rugged fuselage construction for landing in combat areas and the interior to handle some of the military's outsized equipment.

The debate now shifts to the House, where C-5 supporters hope to prove that airlines stuck with unused 747s are simply looking for relief.

If, indeed, a backdoor airline bailout is behind the Senate's 747 choice, it shows a callous disregard for military requirements.

The Seattle Times

Seattle, Wash., May 15, 1983

ONE of the most bruising defense-procurement battles in recent congressional history was fought last year over whether to buy Lockheed C-5Bs or Boeing 747s as the backbone of the Air Force cargo-transport fleet.

The 747 won in the Senate, but that decision was overturned in the House after feverish lobbying for the Lockheed plane by President Reagan and the Pentagon's civilian leadership under Defense Secretary Weinberger.

The biggest losers in the decision to buy a huge new batch of Lockheeds were the nation's taxpayers, who are footing the bill for an extra $6 billion to $7 billion.

But that's all history. What's of interest now is a sequel to the big battle. As part of the plane-procurement bill that finally was signed into law, the 747 backers were tossed a small bone in the form of funds to purchase three used 747s for tests to determine the plane's utility as a military-cargo carrier.

But the Pentagon, in defiance of congressional wishes, resisted even that concession. There were indications that the administration would seek to shift the 747 money to other programs.

Happily, that last-ditch resistance at last has been overcome. Weinberger informed Senators Jackson and Gorton and Representative Dicks the other day that the Pentagon will proceed with 747 purchase and testing, as directed.

"We are delighted," Jackson commented. "This is the first time the Boeing 747 will be tested for military-airlift purposes. It gives us a toehold in the door, and I believe the test evidence will be hard to refute.

"The 747 is more economical and can fly faster, farther, and with a heavier load than any other cargo plane, including the C-5. I hope this will lead to future purchases of the 747 for military purposes."

We're hopeful, too. But no matter how well the 747 performs, it will continue to encounter the turbulence known as politics.

THE LOUISVILLE TIMES

Louisville, Ky., October, 4, 1982

With the finding of General Accounting Office auditors that Defense Department officials broke the law by spending federal funds lobbying Congress to buy the Lockheed C5B, it is time for the Justice Department to conduct a full-scale investigation, with the aim of prosecuting violators. If the GAO investigators are correct, they could include Deputy Defense Secretary Frank Carlucci and Air Force Secretary Verne Orr.

The GAO not only found that an illegal lobbying operation was initiated and operated by the Pentagon with federal funds, but that Mr. Carlucci and Mr. Orr approved the effort.

Federal law for 60 years has prohibited any use of appropriated funds to lobby Congress, although no one has yet been successfully prosecuted for violating it. Defense Department involvement in the shameless, months-long battle over the Air Force heavy cargo plane contract was so blatant, however, that it could not be ignored.

The Air Force backed Lockheed's entry during congressional hearings early this year, but the Boeing Corp. surprised everyone in May by winning Senate approval for a proposal to use converted civilian 747s instead. Boeing's hard-sell effort broke an unwritten rule among contractors to give up lobbying once the military had made a decision. Moreover, the 747 proposal probably would serve Air Force needs worst of several competing plans.

Nevertheless, the Air Force had no business orchestrating an even more heavy-handed lobbying effort on behalf of Lockheed, leaning on industry subcontractors, as well as congressmen, and even enlisting reservists in the battle. As a result, in July the Lockheed plan rolled through the House, and soon thereafter was chosen by a House-Senate conference committee. It was a classic example of action by "the military-industrial complex," of which President Eisenhower warned in his farewell address.

Disgruntled Boeing backers in Congress forced the matter into the open, and it should not be allowed to slip below the surface again. The Justice Department must fully air it, then make sure any civilian and uniformed violators uncovered are prosecuted. The GAO also urged quick action to prevent an additional outrage — government reimbursement, through other federal contracts, of both Lockheed and Boeing for part of their lobbying costs.

And if that doesn't serve to warn the Defense Department away from interfering with the right of Congress to make spending decisions, the congressmen ought to put a few more teeth into the law.

Los Angeles Times

Los Angeles, Calif., July 30, 1982

It was a close call, but the U.S. House of Representatives made the right decision the other day when it voted to go along with the Air Force proposal to buy 50 new models of the giant C-5 air cargo plane instead of substituting surplus Boeing 747 airliners.

There is widespread agreement that the Air Force needs additional long-haul transport planes to carry men and equipment to potential hot spots in the Middle East or elsewhere. The issue is what kind of planes should be procured to do the job.

The Air Force now has more than 70 huge Lockheed C-5As capable of carrying such large items as helicopters and heavy tanks, in addition to a fleet of smaller, less capable aircraft.

When the need for more airlift became clear with the creation of the Rapid Deployment Force, the generals originally wanted an entirely new plane, the C-17, developed by McDonnell Douglas Corp.

But the Administration refused to approve the proposal, whereupon the Pentagon in January decided that the next best thing was to buy 50 more C-5s—modified to avoid structural problems that plagued the original C-5A version.

However, that decision has been challenged by the Boeing Co. and its supporters in Congress, who argued that its 747 jetliners could be modified to do most of what a new C-5 could do—and for less money. The Senate agreed, and voted in favor of the 747s. With the House going one way and the Senate the other, a conference committee must now choose between the two planes.

There was heavy lobbying on both sides. Boeing, and the airlines and banks that lobbied in support of its case, leaned more on economic than on military benefits of choosing the 747.

As a result of the recession, many airlines are unable to fill all those seats on the big 747 jet airliners, and have been forced to take them out of service or fly them at a loss.

If the Air Force were to take 50-odd 747s and have them modified for military-airlift duty, the airlines would get out from under a lot of debt— much to the relief of the banks as well as the airline managers.

Boeing would benefit both from the fees that it would collect for the modification of the surplus 747s and from the larger market that would then develop for its newer and more fuel-efficient jetliners.

We see nothing wrong with all this. If a military purchase also happens to benefit the airline industry and a company that earns valuable foreign currency for the United States by exporting jet airliners, the American economy as a whole benefits.

But such side benefits, attractive as they are, cannot be allowed to outweigh important military considerations. And the fact is that the C-5s have important military advantages that tip the scales in their favor.

As Boeing officials concede, modified 747s could not carry heavy tanks and other large cargo. And even if you accept the argument that the existing C-5As could carry extra-large or heavy loads, leaving the modified 747s to carry other types of military cargo, the facts still favor the C-5.

The C-5s, designed as military transports, are built close to the ground. Tanks, trucks, helicopters and other cargoes can be rolled down short ramps right onto the ground.

As an airliner, on the other hand, the 747 sits much higher off the ground and has no roll-on, roll-off capability. Even for the smaller cargoes that it would carry, special ground-handling equipment would have to be pre-positioned at airports in the zone of hostilities—an obvious impossibility in many cases.

Obviously, then, the C-5 could get into many airfields that would be impractical for the 747s. And the C-5's quicker turnaround time would make it less vulnerable to enemy action.

The 747s would be cheaper—whether by $1 billion or $6 billion over a 20-year period is disputed by Boeing and the Pentagon—but the C5s have a clear edge in military effectiveness. Besides, the 747s would be only an interim solution; if the Boeing option were chosen, it is anticipated that the C-17 would be built later as a follow-on workhorse of the long-haul military air fleet.

The problems plaguing the airlines are real. But turning all those surplus 747s into military-airlift planes isn't the way to go about helping them.

The Navy's F-18 Jet Fighter

Deputy Defense Secretary Frank Carlucci gave the Navy approval to purchase the controversial F-18 jet fighter, called the Hornet, in June, 1981. He also ordered measures to reduce its cost, which was then the highest of any U.S. fighter—$25.6 million per plane. The F-18 was unusual in that it was designed as both a fighter and an attack plane, operations which usually required two separate aircraft. It had been controversial not only because of its high cost but also because performance flaws had been detected in testing. Its manufacturer, McDonnell Douglas Corp., claimed the flaws had been eliminated.

In October, 1982, the McDonnell Douglas Corp. agreed to reduce the price of the F-18; under the new contract, the Navy would pay a fixed price of $22.5 million for each of 63 F-18 jet fighters. Navy Secretary John F. Lehman declared that, because the contract was for a fixed price, there was "no cost overrun possibility in this thing." Although the contract would have to be renegotiated in one year, Lehman said: "If we find next year the price has grown, we'll go elsewhere."

The Navy disclosed in November, 1982 that pilots who had tested the F-18 had recommended that it not be used as a bomber. A Navy spokesman said that the pilots, in six months of operational testing, had found that the jet's "combat radius fell short of Navy expectations." The pilots who tested the planes concluded that they would be "of limited effectiveness" as a light bomber because of several shortcomings. They found that the jet could not fly the entire 550 nautical miles for which it was designed while carrying a full load of bombs, that the planes took too long to refuel and rearm between missions, that they were too heavy to land safely on aircraft carriers, and that there were possible safety problems with a parachute on the pilot's ejection seat. McDonnell Douglas strongly disputed the pilots' report.

Secretary of Defense Caspar Weinberger ordered an investigation of the F-18 program in January, 1983, after congressmen charged that the Navy had amassed a $500 million cost overrun on the fighter and attack jet program, and had misused appropriated funds in order to cover up the increased cost. Three members of the House Appropriations Committee wrote a letter to Weinberger in which they stated that the Navy had siphoned off funds intended for combat equipment and maintenance costs on the F-18s and used the funds to pay for production of the planes themselves. In addition, the letter said, funds had been diverted from one fiscal year to another to hide the cost increases. It accused Navy officials of being "evasive, and in some cases, misleading" about the F-18 program, and said it would be "impossible" for the committee to consider appropriating further funds for the F-18 until the Pentagon had submitted a "detailed financial audit" of the program and an opinion on the legality of the fund transfers.

The Birmingham News

Birmingham, Ala., July 1, 1981

The Pentagon has announced that the Navy can start full production of the F-18 Hornet jet fighter. However, it wants the Navy to try to cut the cost of the nation's most expensive fighter, and that desire is certainly appropriate. Each F-18 carries a record price tag of $25.6 million.

To get an idea how much that is, its counterpart built during World War II was more than a thousand times cheaper. For the price of one F-18 Hornet, more than 1,000 P-38 fighters could have been built.

The $25.6 million price tag is attributed to inflation, a galaxy of electronic devices, additional fire power and vastly higher wages in the aircraft industry. The Navy wants to contract for some 1,366 F-18s and A-18s for $35.3 billion.

One can hardly blame Deputy Defense Secretary Frank Carlucci for urging the Navy to cut costs. One also wonders if some of the electronic devices are reasonable in view of the expendability of fighter planes.

St. Louis Globe-Democrat

St. Louis, Mo., July 18-19, 1981

It was a banner day for the Navy's F-18 Hornet fighter-attack aircraft and its manufacturer, McDonnell Douglas Corp., Thursday as the House overwhelmingly endorsed continued production of this high-performance plane to counter burgeoning Soviet sea power.

By 306-101, the representatives rejected an effort to kill the $38 billion program under which the Navy plans to buy 1,377 Hornets in the next decade.

Down in flames went CBS, which had tried to undermine the Hornet in a recent series of television programs on national defense by presenting a number of spurious arguments against the F-18. Crashing to earth came Rep. Bruce F. Vento, D-Minn., and Rep. Thomas J. Downey, D-N.Y., who led the drive against the Hornet with claims that the F-18 was too expensive, too sophisticated, etc.

What happened was that when members of the House looked at the facts as obtained from the real experts — the pilots who have flown the F-18, and Navy Commanders who have observed its performance and know what it can do for the Navy — there was no question that the Hornet is the best fighter-attack aircraft the Navy can buy.

In a recent memorandum from the Office of Chief of Naval Operations to Globe-Democrat columnist Maj. Gen. Henry Mohr, AUS, Ret., the office had this to say about the F-18:

The F-18 is a "remarkable, multi-mission aircraft. These qualities have been proven in flight-testing. Specifically, these qualities are its reliability, maintainability, versatility and its predicted survivability in combat."

In reply to the reckless charge that the F-18 is "the most expensive aircraft in history," the Office of Chief of Naval Operations said:

"In fact, any fair economic comparison would place the unit cost of the Hornet at roughly two-thirds of that of the front-line fighter-interceptor aircraft bought over the past decade."

The F-18 is sought by Navy commanders and pilots because it is the best fighter-attack plane that has ever been developed for the Navy and because it is superior to anything the Soviets have. Of necessity, the Hornet has to have advanced technology and a high degree of sophistication because it has to match and surpass Soviet aircraft which are technologically advanced and use sophisticated systems.

The Hornet is designed for two roles — as a fighter and as an attack plane against ships and ground targets. Rep. Robert K. Dornan, R-Calif., a former Air Force pilot who has flown the F-18 and many other military planes, said, "I'll tell you, something, there is no comparison."

Answering the critics who charged the F-18 did not meet all specifications in early testing, Dornan said the Hornet has the unique record of never having killed a test pilot.

The News and Courier
CHARLESTON EVENING POST
Charleston, S.C., November 13, 1982

For years, funding for the defense of the United States was made secondary to funding the many give-away programs initiated by the Great Society promises of Lyndon B. Johnson. When a specific service project was costed out at the action officer level, there would be a built-in fudge factor to accommodate the anticipated slashes at the Defense Department level. As the project progressed up the approval chain, further padding would be added to accommodate inflation added to expected cuts from the Office of Management and Budget and ultimately, the two houses of Congress. By the time a specific project was authorized and funded, anything from two to five years had passed from the time it left the action officer's desk — sometimes a lot longer than that. But the expected cuts added to the effects of inflation had reduced the padding to zero and many times below the minimum funding level required. And the services, playing the parochial role they were expected to play, came up with any number of projects knowing full well that entire projects would be scuttled at the Defense or Capitol Hill levels.

Then came the Reagan administration and Defense Secretary Caspar Weinberger. Most of the service-requested projects are now being forwarded to Congress with little or no paring and Congress returns them approved and fully funded. The once-needed padding has now turned into an embarrassment of abundence causing such a voice of conservatism as The Wall Street Journal to label the Pentagon "an enormously inefficient nationalized industry." The military is devoting more and more of its expanding budget to, as one specialist calls them, "Things people can ride on," — M-1 tanks for the Army, more ships for the Navy and F-16s for the Air Force.

An example of better being the enemy of good enough is the Navy's FA-18 Hornet program. When the first orders were approved in 1978, the entire Hornet project was costed out at $12 billion or roughly $15 million per plane. Today, the program cost is $40 billion and the price per aircraft has escalated to $22.5 million. Certainly, inflationary effects over the past four years cannot account for such a shocking increase.

Cost isn't the only problem with the fighter-bomber. The FA-18 has more weight per cubic foot of volume than any aircraft ever built making it difficult to operate from carriers. In addition, a congressional study concludes that the Hornet's weight problem stems from Navy designers trying to cram all available high technology and weapons into a relatively small fighter.

But the bottom line that the Navy seems unwilling to accept is that it could build larger numbers of the proven F-14 fighter and A-6E light bomber to better fill the missions planned for the Hornet and save billions in the process.

Over the years, we have consistently advocated a stronger defense and have taken strongly to task those who would frivolously tamper with the future security of this country. We must now join the growing chorus calling for more restraint in defense spending. Yes, funding must be increased to meet a mounting threat but throwing money at the Pentagon is a recipe for disaster. The expected duties of a watchful Congress backing up a unified Defense Department's listing of project priorities is now overdue.

Chicago Tribune
Chicago, Ill., November 19, 1982

The Navy's latest wonder weapon, the FA-18 Hornet tactical fighter, is an excellent example of why more defense spending doesn't always mean more security.

The new super aircraft is designed to carry 17,000 pounds of Sidewinder and Sparrow attack missiles and thousands more pounds of electronic defense equipment, including a new laser tracker/strike camera, while operating from carriers. It's supposed to have an out and back combat range of 550 miles, as the Navy specified when it ordered $40 billion worth of the things.

But as the Navy has admitted, the FA-18's first sea trials showed the airplane to be a woeful failure.

Because it is so densely packed with high-tech equipment to perform so many different functions and missions, its maximum combat range is only 440 miles. This is far short of the range from which Russian Backfire bombers can fire missiles at our naval task forces. Worse, it means our carriers would have to sail that much more dangerously close to enemy coastlines to send its aircraft against shore targets.

Also, the Navy found that the new jet is too heavy for the present carrier deck arresting gear used for landings.

A congressional report on the plane called it "a restricted, short-range weapons platform" in which the lone pilot "is a busy man." A group of Navy test pilots completing a five-month evaluation of the new plane called it "not operationally suitable" and suggested the Navy stick with the old combat-tested A-7, which they called a superior aircraft and which has demonstrated a 608-mile combat range carrying the same load as an FA-18.

The first function of an airplane is to fly, preferably without wrecking arresting gear on landing. The principal mission of a carrier force is to project force over a great distance. When these are sacrificed for more and more technology, then someone has it all backwards, as our mounting deficits attest.

THE LOUISVILLE TIMES
Louisville, Ky.,
November 30, 1982

The nation's newest high-tech warplane is the F-18 Hornet. The name fits, for the plane packs a sting. Only so far it has just been financial.

The twin-engine fighter-bomber has somehow evolved into a craft that is slower than other fighters and has less range than a typical small bomber. That has prompted a number of critics, and not just those potentially out to steer business to competing defense contractors, to cry "foul."

Seven years ago, the Navy chose the F-18 for its low cost — about $8 million a copy — and light weight. The Navy saw it as a way to replace many of its aging aircraft with one far less expensive than its top-of-the-line F-14.

Today, the F-18s cost more than $22 million each, with the price likely to escalate in the near future. (In its budget last January, the Defense Department listed the unit price as $31 million, but the Navy got the plane's maker, McDonnell Douglas, to agree to the lower price for this year.)

And they're not the lean machines originally intended to be used primarily as fighters. The F-18 is now as much bomber as fighter; and while it doesn't have as much high-tech gear as its fancier cousin, the F-14, it has more than first intended.

True, the F-18 still costs only about half as much as the state-of-the-art F-14. And, no doubt, as the Navy claims, much of the increase in cost has been due to inflation. The Navy also is fond of pointing out that the F-18 is generally superior to the two veteran planes it is to replace.

But that isn't the best comparison if taxpayers want to measure both the return on their tax dollars and the modernization of the country's defenses, critics charge.

Chief among those critics is U.S. Rep. Joseph P. Addabbo (D-N.Y.). A House subcommittee he chairs determined that the Navy would do better to ignore the F-18 and instead buy just F-14 fighters and Grumman A-6 bombers. That would be cheaper than procuring all three, as the Navy intends to do, the panel claims. Rep. Addabbo is hardly a neutral critic, however, since he represents an area affected by the Long Island-based Grumman's fortunes.

But Navy test pilots don't like the new jet either, confidentially damning it as too clumsy and slow to be an "operationally suitable" fighter. And Navy tests indicate the plane so far hasn't shown the range of one of the aircraft it is to replace.

The Navy may soon decide whether to go ahead with full production of the F-18. With $6 billion already spent on development, and with strong political backers in both the administration and Congress, it's not likely the project will be stopped on the runway.

That's a shame. As difficult as it is to toss away $6 billion, it's even harder to part with several times that amount on something that is neither fish nor fowl — unless one considers how fast it "gobbles" taxpayers' money.

The Courier-Journal
Louisville, Ky., December 15, 1982

TAXPAYERS who worry that President Reagan is giving the armed services everything they want, regardless of cost or efficiency, are only partly right. In fact, this administration is determined to give military brass *more* than they want.

That's obvious in Mr. Reagan's insistence that the nation spend $30 billion or so to build and deploy 100 MX missiles in "dense pack" silos — even though a majority of the Joint Chiefs of Staff finds the dense pack plan incomprehensible.

The same sort of impulse buying has prompted the Pentagon's top weapons-review panel to approve plans for purchasing more than 1,300 FA-18 naval fighter-bombers, at a cost of $40 billion. The FA-18 has been severely criticized by those who should know best: Navy test pilots. The pilots complain that the plane is "not operationally suitable" for one of its main missions, as a carrier-based light bomber. Specifically, the FA-18 lacks sufficient combat range when loaded down with bombs and rockets. It also is too heavy to be safely stopped by existing carrier-deck arresting gear.

President Reagan defended the FA-18 at a press conference last month, assuring a questioner that he had "access to information close to the source." But his source must have neglected to tell him that the FA-18's range as a bomber is about 160 miles less than that of the A-7, the plane it would replace. Yet the A-7 costs only about half as much as an FA-18 and is preferred as an attack bomber by pilots who have flown both.

So an administration determined to squeeze every loose nickel it can find from social programs seems content to pour tens of billions of dollars into a Navy plane that is only second best (to the F-14) as a fighter and is unsuitable as a bomber. Presumably, potential adversaries will be cowed into submission not by the FA-18's combat capabilities but by its price tag.

Newsday
Long Island, N.Y., December 15, 1982

The United States can certainly afford a strong defense, but with economists predicting a $185-million federal deficit, it can't afford a wasteful one. If it spends money on weapons it doesn't need, there won't be enough for the ones that are vital to the nation's security. Congressional leaders have an obligation to remember that, even when their own parochial interests are at stake.

Consider the Navy's $1-billion-plus order for 63 new FA-18 fighter-bombers this fall. Within a month of the order, the Navy's own test pilots filed a scathing report recommending that the plane not be approved for sea duty.

The FA-18 was conceived as a light, low-priced replacement for earlier fighters. But it was so heavily modified during development that, in the pilots' estimation, it no longer performed significantly better than existing planes. As a fighter, it doesn't match the speed, range or armament of Grumman's F-14, which the Navy also uses. As an attack plane, it has such limited range that it may not be able to reach targets from ships a safe distance offshore.

So how did the Navy react to its pilots' evaluation? It reaffirmed its intention to buy more of the planes — up to 1,300 of them. Rep. Joseph Addabbo (D-Ozone Park) insists that the Navy could save $1 billion simply by buying more of its present fighter and attack planes instead of the FA-18.

Now the Defense Department must decide what to do. Although the Navy says the new plane can be modified to meet its needs, enough doubts have been raised to justify putting the whole program on hold until the people who have to fly the plane are satisfied with its performance.

For various reasons, however, that may not happen. There's a natural tendency in Washington to try to justify the initial investment in a weapons program by pushing it to completion, whether it works well or not. And quite a few military and bureaucratic careers may be threatened when a program is canceled.

Beyond that, the FA-18 has strong political support because it will funnel money and jobs into many congressional districts. And one of its strongest backers has been House Speaker Tip O'Neill, whose Massachusetts district includes many of the people who will build the plane's General Electric engines.

O'Neill is the dominant figure in the House of Representatives and the most powerful Democrat in Washington. No federal agency wants to alienate anyone with that much clout, even if O'Neill is making no special effort to exercise it. But as the Defense Department tries to decide how to handle its FA-18 problem, it should remember that it's supposed to be buying a weapon, not an employment program or congressional influence. It would be unforgivable if Navy combat pilots ended up flying planes that risked lives because of the bureaucratic momentum and political muscle behind the FA-18.

THE SACRAMENTO BEE
Sacramento, Calif., December 2, 1982

The controversial F-18 Hornet is an example of a good idea gone sour. The Navy conceived its development 10 years ago as a low-cost plane with a double punch — combining fighter-plane capabilities with those of an attack bomber. Through its development stages, however, the plane has had so many add-ons and modifications that even Navy test pilots complain it's inferior either as a fighter or as a tactical bomber.

The question now before the White House and Congress is whether to go on with this $40 billion project, trying to fix the Hornet's problems and then begin full-scale production, or simply to cancel it as a bad deal. On the basis of the F-18's performance tests, and the extreme technological difficulties of modifying basic components this far along, the latter course may prove the wiser one.

The decision on the Hornet is distorted by a variety of political considerations. Navy brass whose careers have been linked to its success and who have influential friends on Capitol Hill want to see it approved. The corporate giants involved, McDonnell Douglas Corp. of St. Louis and Northrop Corp. of Los Angeles, are competing for defense dollars with Grumman Aerospace Corp., manufacturer of the A-6 attack plane which the F-18 would supplant. General Electric Co., maker of the F-18 engines, is located in the Massachusetts congressional district of House Speaker Thomas P. "Tip" O'Neil. Altogether, contractors and subcontractors in 37 states would receive work orders if the Hornet receives the go-ahead. The congressmen in those states will not easily surrender the federal dollars and the thousands of jobs the F-18 would mean. They are ever alert to such economic considerations when it comes to spending on weapons.

That's a powerful array of political clout weighing against the opinion of low-ranking Navy test pilots, the ones who, it would seem, are best able to judge the F-18's value. Earlier this month, they forwarded to Navy Secretary John F. Lehman their assessment of how the F-18 had performed under simulated combat conditions. Although the report was classified, it had hardly reached the Pentagon before its damaging conclusions leaked to the news media. The test pilots criticized the Hornet's power and maneuverability, its combat range, the effectiveness of its radar, and other characteristics.

Notwithstanding those criticisms, a Navy council of top brass has recommended going ahead with F-18 production; a Defense Department panel will take up the question early this month. Lehman has yet to make his recommendation, but it must come soon so that committees in Congress can take up the proposed multibillion-dollar authorization. Some Navy officials believe design changes can be made to meet the Hornet's shortcomings, but an impressive body of experts familiar with the project say those would run the cost — already more than triple the original estimates — to prohibitive levels. What's certain is that as it is designed now, there's no point in building it.

The San Diego Union
San Diego, Calif.,
January 28, 1983

It's a most serious matter that three respected members of the House Appropriations Committee have charged the Navy with manipulating public funds to conceal large cost overruns in the $40 billion FA-18 jet fighter program.

At the request of committee members, Secretary of Defense Caspar Weinberger has properly initiated an audit to determine if money appropriated for the plane's combat equipment was used illegally to pay for increased airframe costs.

If the audit substantiates the charges, there should be certain punishment for responsible civilian officials and military officers.

The accusations have credibility, coming from Appropriations Committee Chairman Jamie Whitten, D-Miss., Rep. Joseph Addabbo, D-N.Y., chairman of the defense appropriations subcommittee, and Rep. Jack Edwards of Alabama, the senior subcommittee Republican.

Committee members are upset and not just because of any overrun coverup. Not obtaining committee permission to switch public funds from one program to another is flouting the authority of Congress.

Moreover, any cost overruns should be a matter for settlement between the Navy and the contractor, McDonnell Douglas. Then, the Navy could make a reasonable argument to Congress for necessary additional funds.

But building planes without fighting equipment only means the Navy would try to whipsaw Congress in the future by saying more money would be required to put the plane in combat condition.

An illegal coverup of cost overruns would be disgrace enough. Unfortunately, the charges come when President Reagan's plans for bolstering the nation's defenses are under increasing attack.

Secretary of Defense Weinberger should move quickly to put the Navy's house in order. An FA-18 scandal must not discredit the overall need for strengthening the national defense spending.

Arkansas Gazette.
Little Rock, Ark., January 28, 1983

During his political incarnations as secretary of Health, Education and Welfare and as director of the Office of Management and Budget, Caspar Weinberger was known in some circles as Cap the Knife. His proclivity for trimming the budgets of social programs was recognized and duly noted.

In his present assignment as secretary of Defense, Mr. Weinberger is in the process of earning fame as Caspar the Friendly Juggler. His credentials for claiming the title are based on his skill in making apparent concessions to the need for fiscal responsibility and in moving appropriated funds around from one project to another in ways Congress never intended.

As just about everyone knows, President Reagan is experiencing a bit of trouble with his budget. Having come to office on the promise that he would submit a balanced budget in 1983 — later retargeted for 1984 — Mr. Reagan faces the prospect of a deficit that may set a new record in each of his years in office.

The 1982 shortfall was about $111 billion, which was a high mark by a comfortable margin. The figure is likely to approach $200 billion this year then move up from that benchmark.

Since the Defense Department budget absorbs a high-and-rising percentage of the total outlays, there are those who claim it probably contains a measure of waste. People who are familiar with military spending know about the occupational tendencies of generals and admirals to spend the money in the name of defense without considering the bookkeeping. Procurement officers are not seriously disturbed by over-runs.

If Mr. Weinberger were still in his old incarnation as Cap the Knife, he would attack the problem gleefully. With the judicious application of his old skills, he could slice away a few hundred million here or a billion there without damaging the defense capability of the country. With a little luck, he might find a moth-balled battleship that some tradition-minded admiral had discovered and targeted for restoration with the sole justification that it would impress the natives and, in the process, provide luxurious quarters for the commanding officer. Mr. Weinberger could save a billion or so by chopping off the project.

The Secretary has provided little help in the way of trimming defense spending. He recently agreed to reduce outlays in the coming fiscal year but he explained that part of the saving would come from expected lower prices for fuel. Confusion among the Organization of Petroleum Exporting Countries, rather than the application of the knife, should be credited with these savings — if they come.

Mr. Weinberger insisted that if other budget reductions are granted, he will expect to recapture them in later years.

Jugglers (or is it magicians?) sometimes claim the hand is quicker than the eye. Some members of Congress have sharp eyes and were not fooled at all when Mr. Weinberger juggled appropriations for the Navy's new F-18 plane.

The F-18, a McDonnell-Douglas creation, experienced a bit of trouble in the early stages of production because cost over-runs threatened to get out of hand. The plane also came up short of expectations in its advance flight tests. Twice last year, the Pentagon considered canceling the F-18 because of problems related to price and performance.

Last summer, Navy Secretary John Lehman announced, with considerable fanfare, that the price problem was under control and the Defense Department could go ahead and buy a flock of the planes. The shortcomings in performance could be corrected.

Now it comes out that Caspar the Friendly Juggler had solved the price problem with a neat little trick that had been used quite effectively in the Pentagon back when he was saving money for HEW. He held the cost of the plane to $22.5 million each by purchasing a stripped-down version. Pods containing infrared and laser target-locating systems were left off with the assumption the gear could be purchased later and paid for out of future budgets. Funds appropriated for maintenance and service-related equipment were juggled over to another column and used to pay for the planes. Requests for other equipment were padded so that the "savings" could be diverted to the main purchase — that of stripped-down planes that could be equipped later.

Representative Jamie Whitten (Dem., Miss). chairman of the House Appropriations Committee, Representative Joseph Addabbo (Dem., N.Y.), chairman of the Defense Appropriations subcommittee, and Representative Jack Edwards (Rep., Ala.), the ranking Republican on the subcommittee, have challenged Mr. Weinberger on his juggling act. Apparently they believe the control of cost over-runs has been "done with mirrors."

We hear a great deal about the "declining readiness rate" of the Defense Department and about the need to step up spending to overcome the problem. Improvement is not likely to come from purchasing planes stripped of their sophisticated equipment and serviced in shops that lack specialized testing gear.

Come to think about it, that was the approach used for purchasing military equipment in the early and middle part of the 1970 decade. There are those who say the practice contributed to the decline in the readiness rate and opened the window of vulnerability that we hear about today.

We are not likely to correct the old problem with the practices that caused it in the first place.

The Seattle Times

Seattle, Wash., January 27, 1983

THE Pentagon, buoyed by the Reagan administration's virtually unlimited defense budgets, has been riding high. So high, apparently, that the Navy feels it can play games with Congress.

Three key congressmen who have a large say over defense funding wrote a properly sharp letter to Defense Secretary Caspar Weinberger, accusing the Navy of violating the will of Congress — perhaps even breaking the law — in quietly juggling funds to cover the rising costs of the new F-18 fighter.

The F-18 has been under heavy fire for price and performance problems. Now that congressional investigators have uncovered the Navy's version of a shell game, reconsideration should be given to canceling the troubled and super-costly program.

ST. LOUIS POST-DISPATCH

St. Louis, Mo., January 26, 1983

The McDonnell Douglas F/A-18 fighter-bomber is again in trouble with Congress and is faced with the threat of a cutoff of production funds. The controversy this time involves the Navy and the way in which it has been handling the plane's funding.

The F/A-18 program, since its inception, has been plagued with skyrocketing cost overruns and more than a fair share of technical problems. At $40 billion, this Navy and Marine aircraft has now become the single most expensive Pentagon procurement program, far more costly than even the MX missile or the B-1B bomber. What the House Appropriations Committee rightly fears is that the Navy — in an attempt to hide new cost increases and to protect the program — is shifting excess development and procurement funds from one program account to another. The committee is also concerned that the Navy may be padding certain budgets and postponing the purchase of support equipment without telling Congress. The exact amount is unclear, but it could involve between $300 million and $800 million.

There is most certainly an element of pure politics involved in these latest charges — one of the primary F/A-18 critics is Rep. Joseph Addabbo, a longtime proponent of the rival Grumman F-14 fighter and A-6 attack aircraft. However, these latest charges are far too serious to be dismissed out of hand.

If the Navy is robbing Peter to pay Paul to hide F/A-18 cost overruns, then the Congress and citizens have a right to know. The Navy and McDonnell Douglas proclaim the F/A-18 to be one of the most advanced fighter-bombers in the world today. That would count for little if the cost of these aircraft becomes so high that they cannot be purchased in reasonably effective numbers or the program's runaway cost forces the cancellation of other vital projects.

St. Louis, Mo., March 22, 1983

Is the Navy trying to pull a fast one? That is the question that is raised by the Pentagon decisions to proceed with full-scale production of the light bomber version of the F/A-18 McDonnell Douglas fighter-bomber while postponing — for at least a year — a final determination of how many of the new planes to buy. The move is certain to provoke congressional questions as to its legality.

By law, the Pentagon must tell Congress when the cost of a new weapon project rises above 15 percent of the program's current cost estimate. But if Congress doesn't know how many of the aircraft are in the total production run, it cannot determine the cost of the plane. The official plan calls for 1,366 Navy and Marine F/A-18s at a cost of $40 billion. The per-aircraft cost of the F/A-18s now in production is supposed to be $22.5 million, but, if the total run is less than 1,366,

the per-unit cost will much higher. And the Navy is doing more than just hinting that it may not buy the full order.

Last year, the Pentagon decided to deploy all F-14 fighter squadrons on all but the Navy's two smallest and oldest aircraft carriers. It also decided to procure some 366 AV-8B Harrier fighter-bombers for the Marines. Those two decisions alone could result in a cut of approximately 400 F/A-8 aircraft from the current program. In addition, there remains legitimate concern about the plane's combat capabilities as a bomber.

Congress and the American people have a right to know if the U.S. is getting its defense dollar's worth out the the F/A-18. But that can't be done unless the Pentagon lives up to the letter of the law and reports its true procurement plans.

St. Louis, Mo., June 22, 1983

Is the Navy "cooking the books" on the F/A-18 fighter-bomber program?

The answer would appear to be Yes. Separate reports by the General Accounting Office, the House Appropriations defense subcommittee and the Pentagon's own inspector general have uncovered serious irregularities in the Navy's management of the F/A-18. In short, the reports charge that, in order to hide major cost increases, the Navy made unauthorized transfers of funds from engine and weaponry accounts to other parts of the program. Rather than having a per unit price of $22.5 million, the F/A-18 will cost about $28 million per plane.

This creative bookkeeping means that Congress, in order to pay for the Navy's first 253 F/A-18s, will have to come up with another $1.2 billion. This is on top of the already authorized $5.2 billion, and it is no small matter. Even at the current official

price of $40 billion for 1,366 F/A-18s, this program is the single most expensive Pentagon arms project.

• The Navy hotly denies the charges of juggling the books, and the plane's defenders maintain that most of the cost increases are due to inflation.

Still, there are questions. The charges of Navy mismanagement would be one thing if they were the program's first, but the fact remains that the F/A-18 — for all its advanced capabilities — has been plagued with serious technical and cost problems. The most recent one involves the short combat range of the bomber version.

As rich as the U.S. may be, it cannot afford open-ended cost increases in any arms program. Before the situation gets any worse, Congress has a duty to get to the bottom of this controversy and, at the same time, see if the F/A-18 is worth the money.

Chicago Tribune

Chicago, Ill., March 24, 1983

In the neatest trick of the week, the Pentagon has ordered full production of the controversial F-18 Hornet fighter-bomber while deferring for at least a year the decision on how many are actually to be built.

By law, Congress is to be notified whenever unit cost of a weapon exceeds the original estimate by 15 percent or more, but with no idea of how many are to be built, the Congress has no figure for the unit cost. Estimates have ranged from $9.9 million to $30 million, and there are indications the program has already had cost overruns of $500 million.

Worse, the Defense Department has yet to decide what role the F-18 is to play. It was designed as a double threat to replace two highly effective Navy aircraft—the F-4 fighter and the A-7 light bomber. It has performed well as a short range, if highly expensive, fighter, but Navy test pilots have repeatedly been unable to achieve the required 550-mile bomber range when it is loaded down with bomber instrumentation and armament.

Often it has fallen 100 miles or more short of range, a flaw that would require carriers using it to move dangerously close to enemy coasts. With its heavy weight, it taxes the restraining gear necessary for safe carrier landings.

One of the more distressing aspects of today's high-tech, blank-check military is that missions are increasingly being designed for weapons systems, instead of vice versa. The Army's expensive new DIVAD anti-aircraft gun proved useless at its intended mission of shooting down maneuvering airplanes, so it was reassigned the mission of shooting at hovering helicopters, a task that can be performed well with cheaper anti-aircraft weapons.

The same seems to be happening with the F-18 Hornet.

In case the Pentagon and the White House haven't noticed, the public and the Congress are no longer content with "war is not cost effective" as an answer to budget questions. It seems not too much to ask for the Defense Department to know what mission a weapon is to perform, whether it can perform it and how many will be needed to perform it before anyone starts writing out the check.

Part IV: The Defense Budget & The Economy

Ultimately, the size of the defense budget depends not only upon national security considerations but upon the health of the national economy. While it might be argued that every weapon proposed by the Defense Department is necessary to adequately defend the United States and its allies, this line of reasoning becomes unconvincing in the face of an enormous and growing federal deficit that threatens to strangle the economy. During World War II and for several decades afterward, it was possible to spend open-handedly for defense without endangering major industries or the spending power of consumers; such government spending actually stimulated the other sectors of a then-robust economy. Now, however, for reasons too complex to explore here, there are difficult choices to be made. More federal spending means less money for consumption and for industry investment; a ballooning federal deficit means increased unemployment. This is the "guns vs. butter" predicament. And, as many editorial writers point out, legislators must also consider the cumulative effect of so much government spending on industries which are also important to national security, among them oil and steel.

It is, of course, very difficult politically for legislators to reduce significantly the largest portion of federal spending, for the so-called "entitlement" programs. The Reagan Administration's attempt to shore up both defense and industry has inevitably cut into this area of federal spending, resulting in furious congressional debates that pit social programs against defense. In the end, Congress is forced to make "guns vs. guns" decisions, and here the legislators are dependent upon the expertise of defense officials and analysts. Many of the editorial debates over the funding of particular defense programs in the following pages reflect the conflicting testimony offered by different experts during congressional hearings. Frequently, because of the overwhelming economic and political pressure to cut back on defense spending and their own lack of technical or classified defense knowledge, legislators settle on a budget that embraces every Administration request but allocates less than requested per program.

Carter's Budget Calls for 12% Defense Spending Increase

President Carter presented Congress Jan. 28, 1980 with what he called a "prudent and responsible" $615.8 billion budget for fiscal 1981. The budget, built upon an unusual forecast that a mild recession would occur in the first half of 1980, called for a sizable 12% increase in defense spending. The $142.7 billion in defense outlays for 1981 represented 23.2% of federal spending. (Budget authority was set at $158.2 billion.) The country must bolster its strength in a "sometimes hostile world," Carter cautioned. Spending on research was the only other sector of the budget to be favored with an increase above the inflation rate. (After allowing for inflation, the proposed defense spending increase would be about 3.3%.)

The Defense Department's budget contained major programs to increase American ability to protect Middle Eastern oil fields and to respond to growing Soviet naval power. Under the new spending plans, the military would get nearly $100 billion more over the next five years than the Carter Administration had projected in 1979. Defense spending was to grow at an average annual rate of 4.6% in "real" or inflation-adjusted terms. One of the major elements in the budget was the beginning of a $9 billion, five-year program to develop a quick-strike, or Rapid Deployment Force, for use in trouble spots around the world. It also called for $6.12 billion for 17 new ships and the modernization of two more.

About 49% of the fiscal 1981 defense budget would go for pay and pensions of the armed forces, which was a change from recent years when the Pentagon's personnel costs had eaten up more than half its spending. Increases in military hardware programs were cited as the difference. The Pentagon planned to increase the ranks of active-duty personnel by 14,000 to 2,059,000, and reserve and national guard ranks by 36,000 to 868,000 in fiscal 1981. Congress had also been asked to tie military pay increases for certain specialties to wages in the private sector and to increase military pay by 7.4% in fiscal 1981, while keeping pay increases for other federal workers at 6.2%.

St. Petersburg Times

St. Petersburg, Fla., January 25, 1980

As Soviet aggression threatens America's access to vital Middle East oil supplies, the question is not whether this nation should be strong but how it will be strong.

One of President Carter's answers is a show of military strength through increased defense spending. Citing a massive Soviet arms buildup, Carter has proposed that the United States increase its defense budget an average of 4.5 percent above inflation in each of the next five years.

With some doubt cast on America's military superiority, it was necessary to send to our friends and foes overseas the message of strength implicit in Carter's proposal.

NONETHELESS, there are potential domestic problems arising from increased defense spending that must not be ignored.

National Urban League President Vernon Jordan's recent admonition that greater defense spending to counter crises like Afghanistan not overshadow spending on social needs should not be forgotten in the months ahead when the 1981 budget is hammered out.

The only way to meet both domestic and foreign policy needs, without increasing the already devastating tax burden, is to eliminate waste from all government spending. If this is not accomplished, America will once again be forced to wrestle with the philosophical issue of more guns or butter.

When Carter campaigned for the presidency, he promised to cut $5-billion to $7-billion from the defense budget by eliminating *waste*. That goal is as worthy now as it was then.

National security cannot be purchased merely by spending more money. The effectiveness of military spending depends as much on how resources are allocated in the defense budget as on the size of the budget.

It is President Carter's responsibility to assure taxpayers that they will get their money's worth from increased military spending.

WASTE HAS reached a most alarming level in the armed forces. In the name of defense, the brass hats have built planes that won't fly, torpedoes that miss their targets, aquatic trucks that sink, a space communications system that remains mute and a "supertank" that breaks down when dirt is sucked into its turbine engines. In addition to such flops, large-scale cost overruns on good equipment are rampant in military spending.

In President Eisenhower's notable "farewell address," the former general warned of the unwarranted influence of the military-industrial complex. "The potential for the disastrous rise of misplaced power exists and will persist," he cautioned.

Today, 19 years later, we must still heed Eisenhower's warning.

The Boston Globe

Boston, Mass., January 22, 1980

One of the first orders of business for the Congress reconvening today is final action on the Defense Department budget. Given Iran, Afghanistan and the submergence of the SALT 2 treaty, there is reason to fear Congress will spend money for programs that add neither to our security at home nor to our ability to respond effectively to incidents abroad. Every effort must be made to restrain that impulse.

The preliminary signs are not encouraging. Just before the recess, the Senate voted overwhelmingly in favor of a $2.1 billion aircraft carrier that President Carter has been trying to kill for more than two years. Election-year politics will make all such proposals even more attractive than they were before the Soviet invasion of Afghanistan.

The MX missile system is a vivid example of a project that has been changed by events. The system, which involves mobile missiles that the Soviet Union would have difficulty in tracking, has been justified by its sponsors on the grounds that, in the presence of a strategic arms limitation treaty, it would ultimately permit the use of fewer missiles.

Now SALT has been put into limbo by the Iranian and Afghan crises, perhaps unwisely and unnecessarily. In its absence, one of the most convincing arguments for MX is lost. Nevertheless, Congress, which has already voted $670 million for preliminary development of the $30 billion system, is expected easily to defeat an attempt to kill it in the next few days. It would make far more sense to postpone the MX development until the SALT treaty issue is resolved.

The Near East crisis will have other ramifications regarding the loss of highly trained technical personnel to the private sector. It costs about $1 million to train a naval pilot, for example. One response is a bill that would add $700 million to the President's proposed 7 percent military pay increase, concentrating the funds in those areas of greatest personnel attrition. Such increases can only reverberate through military pay schedules in future years.

Additional military projects beckon those who may feel that the time is ripe for new programs or the revival of older programs. The B1 strategic bomber, laid to rest two years ago by the Carter Administration, is sure to have fresh sponsors. The Senate Armed Services Committee had added a net of more than $300 million to the Administration's $43.6 billion weapons and research budget, adding such items five naval vessels, development of smaller aircraft carriers and aircraft for them, artillery rockets, and expanded production of the Army's newest battle tank, the M-60.

Congress might do well to postpone its decisions in those matters until the crisis atmosphere has subsided. If it acts in haste on such matters now, the danger is that we will have decades during which to repent at leisure as we pay the bills for premature judgments.

THE STATES-ITEM
New Orleans, La., January 29, 1980

President Carter's proposed 5 percent increase in defense spending, discounted for inflation, figures to play havoc with domestic economic goals and cause the American people to sacrifice, ready or not.

Given the new defense mood in the country and in Congress, there is a good possibility Mr. Carter will get more from Congress than the $142 billion defense spending increase he seeks. That means, says Sen. Majority Leader Robert C. Byrd of West Virginia, that "it may not be possible" for Congress to keep the fiscal 1981 federal deficit to the $15 billion level the president had been shooting for.

Many leading economists expect the increase in military spending to further fuel inflation and possibly eliminate the slight recession which had been forecast for this year.

The prospect, then, is for no tax cut for consumers in the foreseeable future; no reduction in inflation, which stood at 13 percent in the Consumer Price Index at the end of the year; an increase in inflation psychology, a further slowdown in private saving, which already is at a record below 4 percent; a firmer grip on the money supply by the Federal Reserve Board to counter inflation and, consequently, no material decline in interest and mortgage rates.

Such is the price the nation can expect to pay for the president's response to the new Soviet military threat. It is unrealistic for Mr. Carter or anyone else to suggest that it can be otherwise.

Yet there is no question that the increase in military spending is needed in the interest of national security.

St. Louis Globe-Democrat
St. Louis, Mo., January 31, 1980

The success of a con artist is dependent upon his ability to appear absolutely sincere and betray no guilt, no matter how big the lie he tells.

President Carter has mastered this technique as perhaps no president before him. Thus he was able to claim that his $615.8 billion budget for fiscal 1981 is "prudent and responsible" and "continues the strategy of restraint that I proposed, and the Congress accepted, for the 1980 budget."

Prudent? How could the fourth consecutive deficit budget be prudent when Jimmy Carter promised he would balance the federal budget when he became president?

Restraint? How could the budget show restraint when it has been increased 25 percent in just two years?

Even Carter's inference that his proposed increase in defense spending is sufficient to meet the Russians' huge military buildup is phony.

His plan to spend $142.7 billion for defense in 1981 is cited as a "real increase" of 3 percent after inflation. This is far short of the 5 percent minimum that most military authorities say will be needed to begin matching the tremendous Soviet expenditures.

In 1979 the Russians spent $165 billion on defense, which is more than 25 percent more than the U.S. spent. It can be seen that a piddling 3 percent increase is not going to begin closing the gap in defense spending to any great degree.

In terms of the gross national product, the 1981 defense expenditure equals only 5.2 percent, just barely above the 5.1 percent being spent in fiscal 1980. But it is less than half the 11 percent to 12 percent of GNP that

the Soviets have been spending on defense.

The welfarists, who have become accustomed to expect a greater redistribution of taxpayers' money every year, are crying crocodile tears and claiming they aren't getting their usual much larger handouts in the 1981 Carter budget.

The fact is that income transfer payments to individuals are continuing to grow at a fantastic rate. In 1981 they will comprise 43 cents of every budget dollar. Another 15 cents of every dollar will go for federal grants to states and local governments, a large proportion of which also will be distributed to individuals. But defense spending will take only 24 cents of each tax dollar.

President Carter isn't even leveling with the American people when he claims the deficit for his 1981 budget is $15.8 billion. This figure doesn't include "off-budget" spending which will be $18 billion, making the true deficit $33.8 billion.

This $33 billion deficit will cause more inflation at a time when inflation has reached 13.3 percent, the highest rate in 33 years. When the nation already is $847 billion in debt, the last thing it needs is more debt. The crushing load this imposes is seen in Carter's request for $79.4 billion just to pay interest on this massive national debt.

If Americans were not complacent and conditioned to accept the wasting and misuse of their money by federal officials, they would recognize that President Carter is easily the biggest spender ever to come down the pike. He's also one of the most deceitful when he poses as a penny-pincher while showering taxpayers' money with abandon on his favorite charities.

The Birmingham News
Birmingham, Ala., January 29, 1980

This budget for 1981 is prudent and responsible. It continues the strategy of restraint that I proposed, and the Congress accepted, for the 1980 budget. At the same time, it proposes selected, essential increases in areas of high priority and great national concern. In this way, it seeks a balance between our needs for budgetary restraint and our needs for specific expenditures.—President Jimmy Carter in his budget message to Congress

★ ★ ★

THE PREAMBLE TO Mr. Carter's budget for Fiscal Year 1981 is redolent of hypocrisy. One wonders how he could make such a claim with a straight face. How can any responsible person with pretensions of honesty and integrity claim that a $615.7 billion federal budget is prudent, responsible and restrained?

Does the administration perceive the public to be so ignorant, stupid and powerless as to believe such statement or to be unable to take corrective measures to halt the growth of government and its ravenous appetite for more and more money that the budget symbolizes?

And what of Mr. Carter's campaign promises of four years ago? This $615.7 billion budget denies almost every promise he made to the American people when he was running for office and it represents almost total capitulation to Democratic leftists who will not permit any increases in the defense budget unless there are complementary increases in welfare spending.

For instance, only 42 percent of the $615.7 billion will go for expenditures mandated by the Constitution and 9 percent of that will go for debt service which yields nothing tangible for the public. Welfare, in its many anonymous forms, will eat up 58 percent of the $615.7 billion, with 15 percent going to state and local governments in the form of grants.

Clearly, the White House has rejected the warning in California's Proposition 13 and from the Treasury Department that Americans are showing signs of no longer supporting the federal taxing system and the uses to which taxes are put.

In its historical perspective, the budget is even more frightening. For instance, when Mr. Carter took the oath of office barely three years ago, the federal budget was $365.6 billion. The $615.7 billion Mr. Carter wants to spend next year represents an increase of more than $250 billion in a four-year period or an increase of more than 68 percent. Restrained? Prudent? Responsible?

The money the Carter administration will pay out just in debt service in FY 1981 is more than the average total federal budget for the years between 1941-45 when the U.S. was locked in total war. The average yearly expenditures for those years were a modest $66 billion. Debt service alone next year will be about $73.8 billion and the national debt will climb to $939.4 billion with every man, woman and child in the country obligated for $4,229 of that debt. Prudent? Restrained? Responsible?

The last year the federal government had a truly balanced budget — 1960 under President Dwight Eisenhower (The balanced budget in 1969 was done with mirrors and the Social Security Trust Fund) — the budget was only slightly more — $76.5 billion — than next year's $73.8 billion for debt service.

Mr. Carter also failed to explain in his message how a 9 percent increase — adjusted for inflation — in federal spending with a $15.7 billion deficit will affect inflation. When the man from Plains, Ga., took the oath of office, the inflation rate was 4.8 percent. Figures just released by the federal government for 1979 put the inflation rate at 13.3 percent. The $615.7 billion in federal spending is almost certain to sustain that figure with another heavy drain on Americans' pocketbooks.

And while Mr. Carter, the great defender of human rights and freedom, would be the last to reconize it, Americans' own tax dollars are being used by the federal government to diminish Americans' freedoms. With each new bureau and agency — two new Cabinet departments for Mr. Carter — and the additional money necessary to fuel them, personal freedom is increasingly threatened.

A $615.7 billion budget: Prudent, restrained and responsible? Hardly. Not even in the Land of Oz.

DESERET NEWS

Salt Lake City, Utah,
January 30, 1980

The ink was hardly dry on President Carter's new budget before it started getting bipartisan criticism that he wasn't spending enough for defense.

The criticism is certainly understandable in view of the way Russia no longer bothers to conceal its aggressive designs on its neighbors. These and other threats might one day dry up foreign sources of oil on which the U.S. heavily depends.

But where were these critics during the past 10 to 15 years that the Soviets have been consistently and decisively outspending the U.S. on military preparedness?

Where were these critics when Congress repeatedly looked upon the defense budget as the first place to cut and acted as if social services were the only programs that deserved more money?

And specifically where do these critics propose to economize now in order to find more money for defense than President Carter is proposing?

After double-digit inflation is taken into account, Mr. Carter's proposed 1981 budget represents an increase of just 3.3% for defense. If we're going to catch up with Russia, we'll have to exert a greater effort than that. Currently, the Soviets are spending 50% more for military purposes than is the U.S.

The trouble is that in recent years the U.S. has spent itself into a box that limits our fiscal maneuverability. A 3.3% increase in defense spending translates into an additional $15.3 billion, for a total defense budget of $142.7 billion. That $142.7 billion amounts to 23.3% of the entire federal budget. Another 75% supposedly can't be controlled because federal dollars for various federal "entitlement" programs are legally obligated even before the money is spent.

Even if all other funds not already committed were devoted to defense, the critics could add only 1.7% more to President Carter's military spending plans — unless they sharply increased the federal deficit.

But a strong military posture isn't the only thing that keeps the nation safe. So does a strong economy. Yet more red ink in the budget would mean more of what is generally conceded to be the worst ailment that already besets our economy — namely, inflation.

It's hard, then, to see how the U.S. can correct overnight a defense problem that has been a decade or more in the making.

None of this is any secret to the Soviets. Even if they never attack the U.S. directly, the Russians know they can afford to act more aggressively, as the invasion of Afghanistan is demonstrating. And the more aggressive the Russians become, the greater becomes the risk of a major Soviet miscalculation.

The world is going to be a much more dangerous place until the U.S. puts its fiscal house in better order.

Again the federal budget is in the red. President Carter's 1981 budget says spend $616 billion, collect $600 billion in revenues and end up $16 billion short.

A $16 billion deficit would be the lowest in seven years. That is less than half of fiscal 1980's estimated $40 billion deficit. But squeezing the deficit down to $16 billion will mean tight self-discipline — and no tax cut.

Arms spending is going to make the job harder. The president has the public's approval to raise his 1981 defense money to $158 billion. That is a 5% real increase, above inflation.

To afford such arms costs will require rigid control over most other programs. With inflation roaring upward from a 13.2% annual rate, being ordered to hold spending at the same level means an actual decrease.

But obviously there will have to be belt tightening all over the federal government. We expect to hear some howling wherever this starts pinching — whether in help to the handicapped or to medical education or to farmers hurt by the embargo.

Carter's decision not to cut taxes is 100% correct. Tax cuts now would be inflationary. Inflation was at a 13.2% rate in the year just closed. But in its last month it increased 1.2%, a 14.4% rate if continued for a year. That is explosive.

Tax cuts would reduce revenues. That would make it all the harder to scrape up the money needed to pay that $616 billion in planned federal expenses. Unless hard times hit, a tax cut is out.

Most Americans will have to help foot that bill out of earnings that taxes and soaring prices have caused to dwindle.

Cost-of-living increases in pay automatically bump many wage earners upward into higher tax brackets. Though they are still at their old social level, and getting no more in real dollars, they have to pay higher income taxes.

In the retail markets they have to pay the ever-higher prices at the gasoline pump, the supermarket checkout line, the utility company

---

THE PLAIN DEALER

Cleveland, Ohio, January 29, 1980

window or at their neighborhood bar.

Carter's windfall profits tax on oil companies will be enacted. It will bring in more federal revenue. That revenue is supposed to be spent mainly to lead to developing new energy sources. But the money for it all will come out of consumers' pockets, and the consumers' profit from that investment is in the remote future.

Carter's plan to fight inflation, if he had any plan, has been a failure so far. He now hopes to beat back inflation with this not-at-all lavish budget.

It contains no big spending bulge except in armament and defense. It has only one small youth-jobs experiment in its social spending areas. Charles L. Schultze, economic adviser to the president, calls the budget "very restrained, very severe."

Restraint might slow inflation to Carter's projected level of 10.4% in this fiscal year and less than 9% in fiscal 1981. Achieving that may be all the victory Carter or the nation can expect.

The Washington Post

Washington, D.C., January 29, 1980

THE CARTER ADMINISTRATION wants you to know that its budget for 1981, published yesterday, is tight as a drum. It's rigorous, responsible and severely anti-inflationary, according to a chorus of official voices. Maybe so—but you shouldn't let your attention be diverted from the current budget, which seems to have become strangely fatter since last fall.

The budget for 1981, which doesn't go into effect until next October, is at present a secondary matter. It will be largely formed by questions that have not yet been answered. One question is whether, and how much, President Carter will decide to increase defense spending. The present version is based on policy as it stood last summer, with the 3 percent annual rise to which the United States has been committed for the past two years. If there is to be a reaction to events in Afghanistan and the Persian Gulf, it will have to be added to the budget that appeared yesterday. The other question is, of course, whether the recession forecast continuously since last spring will actually appear, and when. These open questions make writing the budget more uncertain than usual—and the labor of reading it less enlightening than ever.

Instead, it is useful to look at the three-year pattern that is emerging from last year to next. That pattern is not reassuring. The Carter administration is letting the current budget go slack; it is an election year. Restraint is postponed until next year.

The budget for fiscal 1979, which ended last September, turned out to be significantly more restrictive than the White House expected, mainly because inflation pushed up tax receipts. But, oddly, the consequences were the opposite of those you'd normally expect. Unemployment ran lower than forecast, and inflation notoriously went nearly twice as high. It was a warning that the administration was still underestimating the force of inflation and overestimating the danger of unemployment.

A year ago, when it brought out the 1980 budget, the administration emphasized that it had kept the deficit under $30 billion. Congress, with great travail, managed to do the same. Its second budget resolution, passed last November, held the deficit to $29.8 billion. But now the administration reports that it's going to be about $10 billion larger than that. There is the money for the embargoed grain, and for more mortgage assistance, and for transportation, and for a little of this and a little of that.

When the federal government steps up defense spending, the wave of inflation begins as soon as the contractors begin tooling up. That happened in 1965, and the seeds of the present inflation were planted then—when Lyndon Johnson refused to seek the increase in taxes necessary to offset it.

Perhaps it is unrealistic to suggest a tax increase in an election year. Certainly Mr. Carter thinks so. The administration would prefer that you concentrate on all the rigor and restraint that, at least according to present plans, will come after the election in the next budget. But it's the current budget that counts—and that one is moving toward a higher deficit and higher inflation.

Newsday

Garden City, N.Y., January 31, 1980

The $616 billion budget President Carter sent to Congress contains a lot more money for defense without painful cuts in social spending, and almost no new social programs.

That makes the 1981 budget far more inflationary than the administration would like you to believe. And because it doesn't seem likely to stand the test of its many economic and political assumptions, the budget tells us more about Carter's priorities than about taxes and spending.

The priorities—defense over health and economic security; energy production over conservation—need far more searching examination than the current crisis atmosphere has allowed. In Carter's view, badly needed health and welfare reforms must wait. So must balancing the budget itself.

The projected deficit, based on relatively optimistic assumptions of less inflation, more revenues and a mild recession, is $16 billion. That sounds pretty impressive until you realize the figure is predicated on no tax cuts and ratification of the Strategic Arms Limitation Treaty. Without SALT II, there's no telling how high defense spending might take us and inflation.

The total 0.2 per cent spending increase projected by the budget, after inflation, is more than accounted for by a 3 to 3.5 per cent increase in defense spending alone. And that's on top of what now appears to be a 4 per cent real increase in defense spending in the current fiscal year, which ends Oct. 1. Those increases are clearly inflationary.

But it's the other implications of such heavy emphasis on defense that should prompt Americans and their elected representatives into deep reflection on how best to insure the nation's security. Afghanistan and Iran notwithstanding, rejoining the arms race may not be it.

Oregon Journal

Portland, Ore., January 29, 1980

President Carter has conceded that he must miss his target of a balanced budget by 1981.

The budget he has sent to Congress proposes $15.8 billion in red ink. Nonetheless, staggering though the figure may be, it represents considerable movement toward a balanced budget, for it is the lowest deficit in seven years and is considerably under the deficits above $50 billion that were common a few years ago.

Apart from lowering the deficit and heading toward a balanced budget, there is little satisfaction to be found in the president's budget.

It assumes that the nation will be in a recession for the first half of the fiscal year, which begins in October. It expects 7.5 percent of the work force to be unemployed. Yet, recession and unemployment notwithstanding, it predicts inflation will be slowed only slightly, still running at more than 10 percent.

On top of all that, the gluttonous defense budget is about the only one that gets an increase over inflation.

Defense sops up nearly one-fourth of all federal revenue and there seems to be no limit. It is a fair question to wonder whether the American people are getting their money's worth out of the Pentagon, a question that Congress ought to explore. But given the mood sparked by the Iranians and the Soviets, the climate may not be right to call the Pentagon to account.

Some additional funds are intended for employment for the young and housing for the poor.

But most of the "people programs," along with energy, education, health and the like, will continue only at present levels.

Given the conditions of the times, the budget may be the best one could hope for, but it contains little satisfaction.

THE MILWAUKEE JOURNAL

Milwaukee, Wisc., January 30, 1980

President Carter's $616 billion budget is pitched to an election year. It naturally attempts to be all things to all people — and fails. However, measured against sometimes conflicting national needs, the budget seems fairly sensible.

The budget is not as austere as the White House suggests. Yes, the 1981 deficit is held to an estimated $16 billion, far less than this year's projected $40 billion. But the president has not balanced the budget as he originally pledged. Moreover, federal spending as a percentage of national output continues to be much higher than Carter promised for this budget period — 22.3% vs. 21%.

Prodded by the need to get tougher with the Russians and to bolster his own image as a leader, Carter also has beefed up defense spending, but not as high as the 5.5% he lately promised to defense hawks. Yes, the 5.5% figure is there. Carter wants to *authorize* that level of increase in defense funding. But his *actual* spending plans call for only a 3.3% increase.

However, that bit of razzle-dazzle on defense spending seems for the good. The capacity of the defense-aerospace industry is very tight. It is doubtful that the industry could absorb large influxes of new orders without significantly aggravating inflation within the defense sector. Even now, defense spending is generally considered highly inflationary because it pumps money into the economy without producing products that can be consumed by the public.

Overall, however, Carter's budget does a fairly good job of juggling various needs — to fight inflation (still the nation's top economic priority); to avoid costly, deep recession; to provide for a stronger defense; to meet critical domestic requirements. It is a tricky balancing act and success will largely depend on Congress.

Carter's slim budget deficit, for example, depends upon Congress passing his federal pay reform and hospital cost containment proposals, something that lawmakers have been deplorably loath to do.

Congress also could easily pull out the inflation stops by giving Carter more money than he wants. That may sound strange, given all the legislative talk of cutting government spending and balancing budgets. But a fiscal splurge is a real possibility because of the congressional mood to give the Pentagon everything it wants.

A larger federal deficit resulting from greater-than-planned defense spending could send inflation soaring. As it is, the White House estimates that inflation will remain in double digits this year. Overly big defense hikes could insure the entrenchment of inflation in a double-digit rut.

HERALD·JOURNAL

Syracuse, N.Y., January 29, 1980

Every year toward the end of January, we examine a new federal budget.

But the document is so huge, physically and financially, we do little more than walk around the monster, kick it here and there, and look for new gadgets and gimmicks added to "sell" what we know will cost us hard-earned cash.

This year, President Carter put before Congress a new re-election tool.

It's big: $615.8 billion.

Last year, he called for $531.6 billion in federal spending.

He tries to convince us that with this projected $615.8 billion in spending, we're on our way toward eliminating the federal deficit and, at the same time, spending more for national defense.

Last year, he projected $33 billion in the new debt; the debt really went to $39.8 billion; this year, he predicts $15.9 billion.

That's progress toward fighting our enemy "within," inflation.

Inflation is taking more out of incomes now than at any other time in the last 30 years.

It is an enemy.

About defense:

Last year, the president asked Congress to authorize $139.3 billion for the Pentagon. This year's request is up by $19.4 billion with $5.4 billion of the new spending added after the Soviet invasion of Afghanistan.

The $5.4 billion will pay for new missile development and strengthening U.S. forces in NATO.

Said Carter:

"The long decline in real spending for defense that began in 1969 has been reversed.

"I plan increases in my defense budgets through 1985."

Obviously he expects to win this fall.

On the inflation front, Carter abandoned his 1976 campaign pledges to balance federal spending with income and is proposing, now, to narrow the deficit in fiscal 1981 which begins next October and, note this, to bring the budget into surplus after the election.

He is narrowing the deficit from the current $39.8 billion to $15.8 billion by a series of budget maneuvers that surface every four years: Selling federal assets from the strategic stockpile, speeding up certain tax collections (a la Rockefeller), forcing states and local governments to make good welfare and hospital care frauds, imposing a lid on federal pay.

There's no doubt, in our mind, that defense objectives will be achieved, given time.

But we're worrying about the absence of a determined attack on inflation other than uncertain deficit manipulation.

Presidential budget estimates of debt don't hold, not after Congress has worked over appropriations.

Today, inflation eats up all incomes — Social Security, weekly paychecks, interest on investments, welfare aid.

Consider paying $2 a gallon for gasoline.

Shocking, isn't it, to think about telling filling station attendants to "fill 'er up" and paying him $40 or $50 for a tank of gasoline.

Remember? Once, the prospect of $1-a-gallon didn't seem frightening.

Carter Opposes Defense Increase in Budget Resolution

On May 22, 1980, House-Senate conferees ended two weeks of budget discussions by approving a package calling for an $18 billion increase in defense spending for fiscal 1981, or $3.2 billion more than President Carter had proposed. At the White House May 27, Carter told community leaders that the $153.7 billion allocation for the military in the budget resolution cut into funds for programs for the jobless and the cities, "... those very things that prevent a recession from getting out of hand." His decision to oppose the budget resolution brought strong criticism from some members of Congress. House Majority Leader Jim Wright (D, Texas) noted that only a day before his unfavorable remarks about the resolution, the President had told crewmen on the aircraft carrier *Nimitz* that he would support a military pay increase bill. Although Carter maintained that his proposed military budget of $150.5 billion was "adequate," and had been "approved by the Joint Chiefs of Staff, the Secretary of Defense, and others," the four service chiefs and chairman of the Joint Chiefs told a different story before Congress May 29. All five officers contended that greater military expenditures were needed to counter the Soviet threat. Liberal Democrats and many conservative Republicans, however, joined to vote down the compromise budget resolution in the House May 29 on the grounds that it called for too much defense spending.

The Evening Gazette

Worcester, Mass., May 23, 1980

The United States will spend about $126 billion for national defense in the current fiscal year. President Jimmy Carter is asking for about $159 billion in defense authorization for the coming fiscal year, beginning July 1. Of that, perhaps $140 billion or so will actually be spent before July 1, 1981. There is always a lot in the pipeline.

But the president's proposals seem too little to some in Congress. The House Armed Services Committee is recommending an extra $6 billion for military hardware alone, and the Senate Budget Committee wants to increase the average total defense budget to nearly $200 billion a year over the next five years.

The more the military experts and congressmen study what the Soviet Union has been doing, the more urgent is the demand for beefing up our armed forces. We may not yet be No. 2, but things are heading that way if nothing is done.

We are a long way from 1976 and the presidential campaign in which Jimmy Carter promised to cut back our "swollen" military establishment. Carter himself is urging higher defense spending to help offset the immense Soviet buildup.

The Committee on The Present Danger, an independent group concerned with the rising Soviet threat, says that we need to spend even more on arms. Its new position paper calls for an increase of $26 billion in defense spending next year, and a total increase of about $260 billion (1981 dollars) over the six-year period ending in 1985.

The CPD, which studies military equations very carefully, says that the United States must "recognize the consequences for the United States of the Soviet push for military superiority" and must "come forward with programs capable of arresting and containing the Soviet drive."

The CPD says that "an ominous and political and military threat" looms over the world and it will last until at least 1989. During that period, we will be vulnerable to a so-called Soviet "second strike."

The CPD wants the country to add, during the next five years, five active Army divisions, nine tactical air wings (six Air Force, three Navy-Marine), 10 additional tactical airlift squadrons, a doubled strategic airlift capability, and enough ships to create a 650-ship Navy by 1990. And it wants defense manpower increased from the current 2,045,000 to 2,347,000 by 1985.

Unlike the Congress, which is wary about mentioning the draft, the CPD says that a "democratic and equitable Selective Service System should be instituted as changing circumstances require."

As we see it, there is no question that the United States needs to increase its military strength, despite the call for government economy.

As to just what items we need in our arsenal — the B-1 bomber, the cruise missile, the MX system, the neutron bomb — those decisions are beyond the capabilities of lay persons. But we and most Americans have a gut feeling that the United States cannot afford to become clearly inferior to the Soviet Union in the realm of military power. As is so clearly shown by Afghanistan, Angola, Ethiopia, Yemen, Czechoslovakia, Hungary, and Vietnam, the Soviets want military might so they can extend their power and influence, either diplomatically or directly.

If they are tempted someday by our perceived weakness to move in where we feel we have to take a stand, the danger of World War III will be immeasurably intensified. A few billion additional dollars spent now and for the next few years might well be enough to stabilize the security of the world.

THE SUN

Baltimore, Md., June 2, 1980

Ideally, the federal budget should be balanced in two ways. Revenues should equal outlays, and military spending should be in equilibrium with the costs of meeting domestic needs. Most politicians swear obeisance to this ideal, and then proceed to flout it. Until runaway inflation finally created a public uproar, the government would regularly flee its responsibilities by running up huge deficits. It was a cruel and mindless approach that loaded the burdens of inflation on the poor and the elderly.

This year, things were supposed to change. President Carter, who had been elected promising a balanced budget, finally made a gesture toward fulfilling this pledge. He scrapped his January budget and came up with a ledger balanced by hook, if not crook. Ah, the applause from those pretending the president had finally done what they had always demanded. Yes, by golly, the budget would be balanced—despite a new consensus to beef up the military.

Now, watch what happened to make a shambles of the budget process. First, a hawkish Senate Budget Committee added $5.2 billion to Mr. Carter's defense budget while slashing domestic spending. Then the House Budget Committee approved a bill with more money for butter and less for guns. Finally, a compromise emerged that gave the Senate hawks about two-thirds of what they wanted. But it did not last for long.

The president, who has endured the taunts of Senator Edward Kennedy for his lack of compassion and social justice, could not resist the temptation a week before the big "Super Tuesday" primaries to intrude clumsily into the congressional budget process. He demanded that the compromise budget be defeated because it was weighted too heavily toward the military.

Democratic legislators, encouraged by their president, lost no time plunging their knife into the budget. One would think this marked a show of concern for the urban poor and the jobless. But one would be wrong. Before House Speaker O'Neill could gavel adjournment, the chamber adopted a resolution supporting the lavish defense spending figure Mr. Carter has assailed.

And what of the Republicans' role in this charade? Why, they were doing their bit to make this a tawdry spectacle. A close study of GOP rhetoric reveals a diminishing commitment to the once sanctified balanced budget. Republicans, as a group, seem ready to accept deficits to pump up military spending. Yet they are not anxious to approve higher taxes to prevent this deficit from soaring out of sight. Instead, the GOP is junking its austere principles and rallying around the most enticing theory since the free lunch: slash taxes spectacularly and sit back while the revenues from a stimulated economy roll in (supposedly). Thus Republicans had no trouble joining the assault on the budget.

Now comes picking-up-the-pieces time. We hope the Budget Committee conferees can fashion a face-saver to salvage the important process now under assault—drafting budgets in a rational and honest way. Alas, they can expect precious little help from the cynical hypocrites who litter the Washington political scene.

CHARLESTON EVENING POST
Charleston, S.C., June 2, 1980

"One day he goes on the Nimitz and says 'Whoopie! You're heroes and I'll raise your pay.' Then two days later he tells a civic group that the budget is goldplated and we must cut defense. That's the height of hypocrisy.... He doesn't want a balanced budget. He wants a campaign budget." — Sen. Ernest F. Hollings

We share completely the anger and frustration expressed by the new chairman of the Senate Budget Committee at President Carter's political duplicity in pressuring liberal House Democrats to reject a conference committee report on the 1981 budget. The budget compromise hammered out with great difficulty by Sen. Hollings represents but a modest step toward redressing the serious imbalance between defense spending and election year social spending in the budget advocated by the administration. How Mr. Carter can maintain that the $6.8 billion additional Hollings wants for defense is not needed is simply incomprehensible.

Let us cite just one small example with which Charleston's Navy community should be familiar: Some ships fresh from overhaul are being denied traditional refresher training before departure on extended overseas deployment. There is no money to pay for fuel; there are not enough ships in our one-and-a-half-ocean Navy to maintain the three-ocean commitments assigned by the president. Poorly trained and poorly manned ships are disasters waiting to happen. Similar situations undoubtedly exist in all the services.

President Carter's commitment to an adequate defense budget was nakedly displayed earlier in the year when, in order to meet his pledge of a 3 percent growth in real spending next year, he ordered *cuts* in spending this year.

Sen. Hollings has launched one of the strongest attacks by a Democrat on a Democrat president in memory. The attack is well deserved, and we commend him for it.

The Des Moines Register
Des Moines, Iowa, June 4, 1980

How much of a difference is there between President Carter and Congress on military spending?

Carter urged Congress last week to defeat the 1981 budget proposed by the House-Senate conference committee because it contained too much money for the military and too little for jobs programs, aid to the cities and other social programs.

Senator Ernest F. Hollings (Dem., S.C.), chairman of the Senate Budget Committee, charged that Carter was a "hypocrite" guilty of "outrageous, deplorable conduct" for contending that the proposed budget earmarked too much money for the military.

The proposed congressional budget called for $153.7 billion in military outlays in fiscal 1981. Carter had urged in the revised budget he submitted to Congress in March that $150.5 billion be spent on the military in 1981. That would appear to be $3.2 billion less than the House-Senate conference committee proposed.

But Hollings and other congressional leaders cited a recent Congressional Budget Office "unofficial estimate" that Carter's March budget actually would cost $153.1 billion.

They noted that, on Memorial Day, Carter promised the sailors on the U.S. aircraft carrier Nimitz that he would support increased pay and benefits for U.S. military personnel. The CBO estimates that this bill, which is pending in Congress, would add another $600 million to Carter's budget. Hollings said that this would bring the cost of Carter's budget up to $153.7 billion — exactly what the House-Senate conference committee had proposed.

A White House budget official said last week that the administration was sticking by its March estimate that Carter's military budget would cost $150.5 billion.

Who's right?

Expenditures are determined not only by what Congress has budgeted but by the rate of inflation, the speed with which the Pentagon moves on authorized military construction programs and by international developments. Only time will tell whether the Carter administration or the CBO has the most accurate guess.

There is no question, however, that important differences exist between Carter and Congress on military spending.

The military outlay budget is the one that gets all of the press attention because this is the figure assigned to the military in the effort to balance the federal budget. But the military *authorization* budget is a much better guide to the long-term direction of U.S. military policy. The authorization budget includes spending for the coming year, plus military projects that may take several years to complete.

The Carter administration has suggested an authorization budget of $164.5 billion for fiscal 1981; the House-Senate conference committee called for $171.3 billion.

As part of his five-year military plan, Carter has suggested that $186.9 billion be authorized for the military in fiscal 1982, $209.3 billion for fiscal '83, $228.3 billion for fiscal '84 and $253.2 billion for fiscal '85.

The House-Senate conference committee did not lay out a five-year military program. But the Senate Budget Committee called for authorizations of $204.6 billion in fiscal 1982; $234 billion in fiscal '83; $264.6 billion in fiscal '84; and $293.1 billion in fiscal '85.

Over the next five years then, Carter wants $1,042 billion authorized for the military, while the Senate Budget Committee wants $1,167 billion. This is a difference of $125 billion.

This $125 billion could be better spent fighting soil erosion, increasing foreign aid, rebuilding America's cities. The Carter administration needs to fight to convince Congress to adopt its more reasonable authorization figures.

After all, the administration has asked Congress to authorize over $1 trillion for the military over the next five years. This should be sufficient.

Richmond Times-Dispatch
Richmond, Va., June 1, 1980

President Carter, who would like to remain in the driver's seat as America careens toward its rendezvous with 1984, already is speaking fluent Orwellian. In the controversy over the federal budget in general and military spending in particular, the kernel of Mr. Carter's argument is: Strength is weakness, less is more.

The House's desire to invest $6 billion more than the president recommends for such important defense equipment as two new submarines, a refurbished aircraft carrier, 24 F-18 fighters and a complement of new strategic weapons launchers could, according to Mr. Carter, "adversely affect today's military readiness by forcing offsetting reductions in the operations and personnel accounts." Carterism's perverse logic is expressed, too, by Defense Secretary Harold Brown, who told the Senate Armed Services Committee that increased defense spending would tip the budget into imbalance, putting "undue stress on our scarce economic resources and, ironically, jeopardiz[ing] the added military capability we all seek."

The United States simply isn't resourceful enough, Carter logic leads one to conclude, to equip and man the armed forces according to the minimal standards the Joint Chiefs of Staff say are needed to meet the Soviet threat. Then why doesn't the president be done with expense and procrastination and simply hoist the white flag? Probably because he knows that, in truth, no one is "forcing" him to cut the military operations budget to balance off increases in the procurement budget. No one is "forcing" him to insist, against the urgings of the Joint Chiefs for military spending at 6 to 7 percent of Gross National Product, that the defense budget be held at 5 percent of GNP.

During recent weeks Congress has voted on numerous proposals to boost the defense budget while trimming some domestic programs that no one correctly could consider vital. Each was voted down after intense lobbying by the White House. Mr. Carter's personal lobbying encouraged the House to reject the House-Senate compromise budget because, as he put it, the budget provided too much for defense and not enough for jobs, the needs of the cities and other "human needs." The president's argument is wildly perverse. He opposes a House provision of $907 million to build two nuclear submarines at Newport News. The thousands of jobs that project would provide seem not to count in Mr. Carter's ledger of "human needs."

Because of ideological commitment, or perception of a political coalition to be held together, or both, Mr. Carter is trading away our national security for a pottage of welfare state programs. This he has been doing ever since he took office, but now he is showing his intentions unashamedly, in an effort, it is said, to co-opt the left-wing support that threatens to go to to John Anderson. Andersonism without Anderson, weakness pursued aggressively: these are the pathetic preposterosities served up by Mr. Carter. One only can hope that, in providing for the national defense, Congress will offer something better, and that the voters will send Mr. Carter a one-way ticket back to Plains.

Sentinel Star
Orlando, Fla., June 9, 1980

THE HOTTEST fight in Washington these days is over how much money the president and the Congress are willing to spend on national defense.

Neither Mr. Carter nor the Congress seems able to decide the crucial matter of how much money is needed or where the money, once appropriated, should go.

However, one thing is certain.

If the United States is to maintain a credible defense posture, the military must be given a larger slice of the national budget than it has been getting. American defense spending has declined dramatically over the last two decades while the Soviet Union's has been progressing at geometric rates.

In 1952, American military expenditures accounted for 49 percent of the national budget. Last year it was less than 24 percent. From 1960 to 1980, federal non-defense expenditures rose from 9.5 percent of the gross national product to 17.2 percent of the GNP. A recent federal study shows that more than half of that increase in the non-defense share of the GNP was paid for by a reduction in the defense share from 9.1 percent of the GNP in 1960 to 5.2 percent in 1980.

The issue is further complicated by Mr. Carter's constant waffling and egregious porkbarreling by some of Capitol Hill's most influential defense spending champions. Mr. Carter has changed his signals on defense allocations no less than four times in the last three months, a fact that is driving congressional budget-makers up the marbled walls.

Some of those same budget-makers, ever vigilant to defend their home turf above all else, are force-feeding reluctant military leaders a diet of obsolescent aircraft, ships and other physical assets which the generals simply don't want. But the planes and boats in question just happen to be produced on the home turf of some very influential senators and congressmen.

Defense planners have repeatedly stated that acquisition of materiel, while a pressing concern, is not the biggest defense need. Retention of skilled technicians and career cadre is.

Keeping highly trained personnel can be accomplished best by two successive steps: institution of the draft and overhauling pay scales to dramatically increase incentives for those trained in crucial skills to remain in the service.

One reason why the draft is necessary is that it would assure the availability of a reliable manpower pool and free "incentive" money for the needed skill groups.

The military could help its budget pleas by further elimination of some of the excess that remains despite the vows that all is bare bones already.

A recent congressional study shows that millions of dollars in military expenditures could be more wisely used if redirected from present areas. Such as:

● Non-essential but politically sensitive bases could be closed with potential savings of $400 million a year.

● $50 million a year is lost through assigning personnel to off-base housing while on-base housing remains vacant.

● $20 million a year could be saved by greater use of the regular mail system in lieu of costly teletype transmissions.

● It costs $3 billion a year to constantly transfer personnel. Longer tours could save $600 million annually and raise morale as well.

The greatest savings of all — up to $6 billion — could be realized by reforming the military's 20-year-and-out pensioning system that now allows, in fact encourages, retirement as early as the age of 38. The increasing load the present pension system imposes on the Pentagon budget underscores the need for creation of incentives to serve a full 30-year term.

If the prime military retirement age were raised to 50, it would yield annual savings of $2.3 billion.

The solutions to the crucial problem of where we get the money to defend ourselves are available and run the gamut from short-term to long-term relief. But all would take measures of courage such as putting the greater good above lucrative contracts for local constituencies, reforming what amounts to wasteful spending traditions and not playing political football with the national defense.

The Hartford Courant
Hartford, Conn.,
May 23, 1980
With whom is America at war?

What military threat, what impending conflict of major proportions, what quantifiable weakness justifies a $20 billion increase in defense spending in the next federal budget?

The tragic Soviet invasion of Afghanistan, and the nightmare that is Iran, have become predictable fuel in an election year for an explosion of frightening and emotional rhetoric from persons who know better, and their words have come alive in a budget document that declared war not on America's enemies, but on America's poor.

The $613.3 billion federal budget agreed to by House and Senate negotiators is a saddening message to America that in times of war hysteria, social compassion will give way to a new round of inflationary military purchasing.

The balanced budget that now goes to the full House and Senate for approval, is balanced in the ledger books, but not balanced in terms of what America needs in 1981. When the impact of the deepening recession increases its toll on the poor, either the balanced budget will crumble under the weight of welfare needs, or America will be a nation well prepared for war, but sadly deficient in the art of peace.

St. Louis Globe-Democrat
St. Louis, Mo., June 2, 1980

The public got its first view of how sharply the Joint Chiefs of Staff differ with President Carter on national defense as they testified before the House Armed Services investigation submcommittee.

President Carter is fighting the fiscal 1981 defense budget of $153.7 billion because it is $3.2 billion more than he asked. Rep. Samuel S. Stratton, chairman of the House Armed Services investigation subcommittee, suspecting that the president once more had ignored the advice of his Joint Chiefs on the budget, asked the White House to send the Joint Chiefs of Staff to testify.

When the administration balked, Stratton threatened to subpoena the Joint Chiefs. Only then were they allowed to testify, and Stratton was able to bring out into the open what had been reported behind the scenes for a long time. The Joint Chiefs took full opportunity of this rare "unmuzzling."

Every one of the Joint Chiefs or his representative strongly criticized President Carter's irresponsible budget with some of the most scorching indictments of a chief executive heard in many years.

The unanimous opposition underscores the deceitfulness of President Carter. Just prior to addressing 7,000 weary sailors on the aircraft carrier Nimitz, ordered home so Carter could use it as a Memorial Day backdrop, he said he will support a $1 billion military pay increase. Thus Carter gave the impression he is giving full support to the Navy when, in fact, he has cut ship-building programs to ribbons and

consistently has refused to provide salary schedules necessary to reduce the shortage of 20,000 petty officers.

Here is how the Joint Chiefs responded when asked if President Carter's budget was adequate:

"Right now we have a hollow Army," said Gen. E.C. Meyer, Army chief of staff.

"I don't believe the current budget responds to the Army's needs for the 1980s," added Meyer. **"There's a tremendous shortfall in the ability to modernize quickly."**

Commandant Robert Barrow of the Marine Corps minced no words when asked if Carter's defense budget was adequate. He replied:

"In a word, no,"

General Lew Allen Jr., Air Force chief of staff, said, "increased defense spending is needed to meet the increased danger."

Admiral James D. Watkins, deputy to Adm. Thomas B. Hayward, chief of naval operations, said Carter's fiscal 1981 budget "fell short of Navy requirements."

Gen. David C. Jones, chairman of the Joint Chiefs of Staff, said at first he thought Carter's defense proposals were "not unreasonable." But, he added: "That was before (the Soviet invasion of) Afghanistan and I would have a different view now."

Americans can thank Rep. Stratton for exposing how the Joint Chiefs have been ignored and muzzled, imperiling Americans who thought all along the president was listening to their expert counsel on the nation's security.

The Courier-Journal

Louisville, Ky., June 3, 1980

THIS YEAR'S edition of the annual guns-vs-butter battle on Capitol Hill has been especially intense — and confusing. Some of the congressional confusion merely reflects the public's mixed feelings about national security, balancing the budget and curbing domestic spending. But much of it can be laid at the White House doorstep of Jimmy Carter.

Mr. Carter has been all over the political map on the issue of military spending. Back in January, right after the Soviet invasion of Afghanistan, he proposed a $572 billion fiscal 1981 budget that included $146 billion for defense. But he warned at the time that the defense figure probably would rise. And sure enough, two months later he was pushing a revised '81 budget with $150 billion for the Pentagon.

Meanwhile, Congress has been working up its own figures. The House produced a budget with over-all spending almost exactly the same as Mr. Carter's revised budget, but with slightly less for defense.

The more hawkish Senate proposed giving the Pentagon about $5 billion more than the Carter budget allowed.

A Senate-House conference committee produced a compromise that, at least on defense, came closer to the Senate version. At that point, Mr. Carter came apart at the political seams. In the role of President-as-fiscal-conservative, he warned that the conference committee budget was wasteful and would actually harm national security by giving the Pentagon more than it could wisely spend.

But it was the President-as-superpatriot who greeted the carrier *Nimitz*, back from nine months at sea, and told the crew it was time the U.S. started paying its men and women in uniform a living wage. What made his carrier pep-talk especially surprising was the fact that he had threatened, only a few months earlier, to veto a bill that would boost military pay.

Mr. Carter's ambivalence quickly infect-

ed Congress. When the conference committee's budget came before the House last week, it was voted down by an overwhelming margin. Liberal Democrats, including Speaker O'Neill, couldn't stomach the combination of heavy spending on defense and what they regarded as stinginess on social programs. House Republicans joined the attack — but from the right — arguing that the compromise budget was too big over-all and relied too much on inflation-spurred tax increases.

The Executive Branch's contributions to the debate were mixed. On the one hand, the White House lobbied to defeat the conference committee's handiwork on pretty much the same grounds that prompted House liberals to oppose it. On the other hand, the Joint Chiefs of Staff trooped to Capitol Hill and in a rare display of independence argued against their Commander in Chief. In their view, the conference committee's budget did *not* propose too much for the Pentagon. In fact, they said, the military needs a heck of a lot *more*.

Was President wooing liberals?

The upshot was that, though the House rejected the compromise budget, it also resolved not to cut that budget's share for the military. The whole confusing business left most of the Democratic leadership in both houses fuming at Mr. Carter. Even Speaker O'Neill, who was on the same side as the White House, said he wished the President hadn't butted in.

So do we. It's not that the President doesn't have a right and an obligation to speak out forcefully on what he considers irresponsible spending, for defense or anything else. But effective leadership requires some consistency on the issues. Mr. Carter's comments on defense in recent weeks have given the impression either of total disarray at the White House or of political opportunism. His opposition to higher defense spending, for instance, looks very much like an attempt to erode liberal support for Senator Kennedy.

This impression undermines even the valid arguments Mr. Carter may have against specific military expenditures. He made sense the other day, for instance, when he warned against questionable items in a weapons procurement bill for the current fiscal year, including revival of the B-1 bomber and a plan to refurbish a rusty World War II battleship.

But these sensible objections are lost in the confusion over Mr. Carter's position in the broader guns-vs-butter battle. Does he believe, as he indicated after the Soviet move into Afghanistan, that the U.S. must be prepared to intervene militarily to protect the oilfields of the Persian Gulf? If he does, there's no question but that the Pentagon budget must grow substantially. Or he believe the U.S. can get by with small, incremental increases in defense spending, and that the top priority should be a balanced budget?

It's hard to tell. And that says loads about a man who not only is a candidate for president, but has already been in the White House three and a half years.

THE INDIANAPOLIS NEWS

Indianapolis, Ind., June 4, 1980

As an example of effective American leadership, last week's budget fiasco was high farce taken from the pages of Jonathan Swift.

President Carter and House Speaker Tip O'Neill demonstrated to the nation that in times requiring political giants, they are Lilliputians of limited vision.

The budget fiasco unfolded as a series of extraordinary events occurred in ordinary fashion that left the Democratic leadership marching in one direction, with the congressional troops taking off in the other. That last week's events focused attention upon this nation's commitment to a strong defense, it was healthy. In every other respect it was not.

Perhaps President Carter set the tone when he submitted a fiscal 1981 budget proposal to Congress and then withdrew it in favor of another. He pledged support for higher military pay to sailors on the *Nimitz*, and then proceeded to break tradition by lobbying hard against the increased military spending contained in the congressional compromise budget resolution.

The resolution before the House last week contained $153.7 billion for defense spending: That was $2 billion less than was voted by the Senate, $5.8 billion more than was approved by the House and $3.2 billion more than the President recommended. The House listened to President Carter. It voted down the compromise last week, returning it to conference committee.

Then the Joint Chiefs of Staff, in a rare move of public dissent with the President, testified that military spending should be increased even more than Congress was considering. The House also listened to the Joint Chiefs. It instructed its negotiators to keep the high military spending amount. Hence, the budget farce continues.

And while the breakdown in the process partially is attributable to a lack of leadership, it is not a balance-the-budget issue. The President's visions of a balanced budget rest on revenues derived from an import oil fee and tax withholdings on savings accounts that are unlikely to pass Congress. Actually balancing the budget will require realization across the nation, as well as in the Congress, that we cannot afford to make pets of everyone's projects.

Nor can the debate be considered a classic guns-versus-butter argument. The Joint Chiefs of Staff testified in favor of military spending amounting to 6 or 7 percent of the gross national product; the rise is currently projected for roughly 5 percent. A GNP giving 90 percent priority to butter is not giving precedence to guns.

If anything, the breakdown demonstrates the President is out of step with the people. The latest Sindlinger poll for the Heritage Foundation shows two-thirds to three-fourths of the public believe Congress should spend as much money as necessary to meet U.S. defense needs. President Carter, responding to the Soviet invasion of Afghanistan, requested a real growth in military outlays of 3.1 percent; the downed compromise budget included a 5.2 percent real increase.

The budget should include amounts sufficient to help get military personnel out of the food stamp lines. It should stem the trend that finds us outmanned by the Soviet Union in Army and Marine divisions, number of tanks, number of ships and ICBMs.

A strong leader would not only lobby for such a budget, but would take the hard stands necessary to control social spending programs that play leapfrog with inflation. A strong leader is required — precisely what Mr. Carter has so ably demonstrated he is not.

The Cleveland Press

Cleveland, Ohio, June 3, 1980

In a classic example of having one's cake and eating it, too, the U.S. House of Representatives overwhelmingly has rejected a proposed 1981 national budget of $613.3 billion.

The compromise resolution had been painfully worked out by a House-Senate conference committee and promised the country its first budget surplus (about $500 million) in 12 years.

But liberals, mostly Democrats, opposed it because it devoted too much money to defense and too little to social programs. Conservatives, mostly Republicans, disliked it because the surplus was to be achieved not by slashing government spending but by sharply increasing the tax burden.

The House then turned around and instructed its conferees, who must now go back to the Senate, to insist on the compromise defense spending total of $153.7 billion.

Although this was $2 billion less than the Senate wanted, it was $5.8 billion more than the House approved last March and $3.2 billion more than President Carter recommended. It represented a 13 percent (before inflation) increase over fiscal 1980 defense spending.

"They're going in both directions at the same time," complained House Budget Committee Chairman Robert Giaimo, D-Conn.

Majority Leader Jim Wright of Texas also said of the schizoid behavior of the House that "I'd like to have more money for military defense. I'd also like to have more money for social programs I believe in. I'd like to have a bigger surplus, and I'd like to have money for a tax cut."

So would Jimmy Carter. One day he promises sailors aboard the aircraft carrier Nimitz a raise in pay. The next he tells community leaders the compromise budget is too heavily weighted on the side of defense.

Obviously, the nation can't have all the defense and all the social programs everybody wants and have both a surplus and a tax cut. Something has to give, and in the absence of decisive leadership by the administration, Congress will have to choose what it will be.

The expectation is that there will be some token increases in social programs in a new compromise budget, but that the $153.7-billion defense total will remain pretty much intact.

Realization of the deteriorating state of the nation's armed forces and the burgeoning power of the Soviet Union is beginning to sink in. The very fact that the House tried to pay homage to the ghost of the Great Society and to Mars at the same time shows that it has at least begun gumming the bullet of higher defense spending.

The Dallas Morning News

Dallas, Texas, June 3, 1980

AMID THE furor over President Carter's battle against major defense spending increases, the part played in the debate by the Joint Chiefs of Staff gets overlooked. That is too bad, for what the service chiefs did, in their testimony before a House subcommittee last week, was remarkable.

What they did was to dissent from the commander in chief's defense budget, saying the military must have more money to do its job.

All five said so, though politely, respectfully, as befits serving officers loyal to their leader. In fact, the politeness of the Joint Chiefs has rankled many staunch friends of the military during Carter's administration. The chiefs, who came out for the Panama Canal treaty and — though with much hard swallowing and lip-biting — for SALT II, have been widely branded as apologists for Carter, saluting fervently whenever he proposes something.

No salutes were thrown to the President's defense spending plans as the chiefs testified the day of the House's vote on the overall budget. For instance, Adm. James D. Watkins, vice chief of Naval Operations, said more money was needed for the United States to deploy a 3-ocean fleet. Army Gen. Edward C. Meyer said the Carter budget "does not meet the Army's needs of the '80s."

What are the specifics here? The defense authorization bill, passed by the House on May 21, provides a strong indication. The House wants to build 72 F18 and 30 F14 fighters, Carter only 48 and 24, respectively. The Carter budget contains no money for the A6E all-weather bomber; the House voted to build 12. The House bill contains $333 million for the Marine Corps' top priority AV8B Harrier jump jet; Carter ignored the plane.

So does the House think $600 million necessary to start work on a strategic weapons aircraft, much like the B1 bomber that Carter scrapped. The House bill budgets much more money for ship-building than does the President.

It is things of this nature that the Joint Chiefs are talking about. And all honor to them for so talking. The muzzles they supposedly donned when Carter became president have been doffed, at least for the moment. To say what the chiefs said the other day took a higher-than-battlefield species of courage. The commander in chief will not take kindly to what he doubtless deems "insubordination," but the nation should reflect that the chiefs have done a public service.

RAPID CITY JOURNAL —

Rapid City, S.D., June 4, 1980

The debate over the 1981 federal budget is again centered around the guns-vs.-butter issue.

A compromise budget resolution hammered out by House and Senate conferees which proposed $153.7 billion for defense was rejected by the full House on May 29 and sent back to another conference.

President Carter and the Democratic leadership in the House opposed the budget compromise because in order to keep the budget in balance and still provide more for defense, money for other programs had to be trimmed.

Although Democrats and Republicans voted against the budget compromise, a second vote that same day instructed House conferees to maintain the defense spending figure.

Although that instruction is not binding, its sentiment coincides with the findings of a nationwide public attitude study by the Sindlinger polling organization. Taken before the budget compromise was rejected, the study indicated the public favors higher defense spending within the context of a balanced budget.

When offered a variety of alternatives, 56.7 percent of the nearly 1,400 respondents said Congress should find ways to increase defense spending by reducing non-defense spending within a balanced budget. A fraction over 21 percent felt Congress should increase defense spending even if it means higher taxes or a budget deficit. Nine percent felt Congress should give up its efforts to balance the budget because when it's balanced, defense spending forces non-defense spending to be cut. Only 6.5 percent supported the fourth alternative — that Congress should not increase defense spending if it will unbalance the budget.

An increase in defense spending would not place undue stress on the nation's economic resources. Military outlays as a percentage of gross national product remain well below the historical levels that have prevailed in peacetime since World War II. Budget deficits are not due to the Pentagon but to the huge increases in transfer payments to individuals over the last decade.

The added tensions in the Persian Gulf area, the continued Soviet arms buildup, the need to boost morale in the all-volunteer armed forces and the obvious public sentiment for increased defense spending should signal Congress to stay close to the defense spending figure worked out in the initial attempts at compromise.

Los Angeles Times
Los Angeles, Calif., June 4, 1980

Most members of Congress know by now that the probable meaning of the last few weeks of bad economic news will be a $50 billion budget deficit a year from now.

They won't admit that publicly until they have to —when the final vote on next year's budget is taken a month before the election this fall.

Part of their reluctance is political. Nobody wants to spend a long summer defending another huge and possibly inflationary budget deficit.

Part is sheer helplessness. With every 1% increase in the unemployment rate, the federal government loses $20 billion in taxes and spends $5 billion more to help the unemployed pay their bills. The recession, then, will cause the bulk of the deficit.

But, basically, Congress will put off acknowledging the deficit because it knows, or at least senses, that promises of balanced budgets and of unlimited amounts of aid for anything that ails anybody are hopelessly out of touch with the real world.

Profound changes are coming in tax policy, in the way America does business abroad, in the mission of its armed forces and in the relationships between government and industry. And this budget is where the changes must start.

But Congress is like a search party that hears voices but cannot tell where they are coming from or exactly what they are saying. It needs a base camp and some time to sort out the conflicting voices. This budget, balanced or not, is its base, and this summer is all the time that it can spare to choose its directions.

That is why it seems both dangerous and pointless for President Carter and the hard-line liberals and conservatives in Congress to be arguing over how to balance a budget that in fact will not be balanced.

A Senate-House conference committee has agreed on a budget of $613.3 billion for the next fiscal year. Of that, $153.7 billion is for defense—more than the House wanted and less than the Senate wanted.

Carter objects because, he says, it contains too much for defense and not enough for social programs. This ignores the clearest voices that the search party can hear—the ones coming from the Middle East and Afghanistan, which say that, with the Soviet Union in a position to interfere with the source of half of America's imported oil, defense budgets no longer can be squeezed to make room for social programs.

In the past, Congress resolved arguments between social programs and defense programs by giving both sides everything they asked for. Not this time.

This time, Congress must hold the tightest line possible on the first budget vote to have any margin at all for a tax cut—and the tax cut, not balance, is what the budget debate should be all about.

America's automobile industry is in serious trouble. Its steel industry cannot compete with more efficient producers abroad. Its plastics industry prospers in large part because the oil that it uses as raw material is priced below world levels.

The country cannot pay cash for everything that it imports; it runs up a bigger tab every year with foreign producers. Its economy has stumbled for the second time in five years; by the time that it recovers its balance, at least 9% of the workers in the United States will be out of jobs.

That is a description of a country that must spend carefully, giving its highest priority to tax cuts that can begin to deal with the very problems that make another deficit inevitable: low productivity, inflation, a failure to compete in fields in which the United States once dominated, such as steel and automobiles.

Carter intervened at a crucial time. Even if his view were to prevail, it would produce a relatively small, largely political, shift of funds from defense to social programs.

In the end, it could serve no purpose other than distracting Congress from more important goals and from its search for ways to deal with coming changes. It may be smart politics, but it is not wise government.

THE BLADE
Toledo, Ohio, June 3, 1980

WHATEVER the outcome of the haggling in Washington over a fiscal 1981 federal budget, there is no doubt that political considerations have taken precedence over hard-headed economics, both on Capitol Hill and in the White House.

Some congressmen seem genuinely interested in arriving at a balanced budget that will stand up. Others, while paying lip service to the idea, continue to fall into predictable spending patterns, depending on whether they are more oriented to domestic programs or to a stronger defense budget. Most of them know full well that balancing a budget on paper is an exercise in semantics and that later appropriations can change the picture completely.

Congressional hypocrisy was bad enough. But then President Carter, who has blown hot and cold on both domestic and defense spending — depending largely on the political climate or his audience at the time — made things even worse. The President had adopted what appeared to be a forthright position for increased defense outlays in the wake of the Iranian and Afghanistan crises. But then, faced with domestic criticism in his re-election campaign, he came out strongly against a Senate-approved federal budget which included a defense bill of $153.7 billion, marginally higher than Mr. Carter's latest request.

That reversal followed a presidential pledge made when Mr. Carter greeted crewmen of the aircraft carrier Nimitz returning from the Middle East that he would support a military pay increase which would add $700 million to the 1981 defense budget. The turnabout also followed public statements by the Joint Chiefs of Staff that defense spending needs to be increased in view of the nation's global responsibilities.

The President's flip-flop brought an unprecedented blast from Sen. Ernest Hollings, South Carolina Democrat and chairman of the Senate Budget Committee, that Mr. Carter was guilty of "outrageous, deplorable conduct" and "the height of hypocrisy." And the senator was backed by other heavyweights of the President's own party, such as majority leaders Robert Byrd in the Senate and Jim Wright in the House.

The President does not have a lock on playing politics with federal budgets. But what Mr. Carter does, particularly in the area of national defense, has a direct bearing on how the nation's actions and statements are accepted abroad. The latest squabbling along the Potomac, due in large measure to Mr. Carter's abrupt changes in course, do not promise to enhance American credibility in that respect.

THE SACRAMENTO BEE
Sacramento, Calif., June 7, 1980

In recent weeks, the federal budget process has deteriorated into a guns-or-butter debate: arms vs. social programs. Such arguments, however, have served only to create false dilemmas that lead to gross and misleading simplifications. The issue is not which course the nation must choose, but rather in recognizing and accommodating two vitally important national concerns: a strong defense posture and a sound domestic program. They are not mutually exclusive.

Within that framework, the House and President Carter acted properly in rejecting a compromise $613.3 billion 1981 budget proposal, which contained the largest peacetime military increase in the nation's history at the expense of social programs for those most likely to suffer the ravages of inflation and of a deepening recession. The House-Senate compromise proposal called for $153.7 billion in defense spending, $3.2 billion more than the president requested. To achieve that, the congressional panel gouged deeply into domestic programs, including transitional aid to cities, jobs, mass transit, and income security, an aggregate $4.8 billion below administration requests under the compromise.

The result is a dangerously shortsighted budget that promises to prolong a business and housing slump, and exacerbate a rising unemployment rate. Because of reduced tax revenues and increased expenditures in unemployment and food stamps that a recession brings, the $500 million surplus projected in the budget would be wiped out. A balanced budget the White House and Congress had struggled to achieve would be balanced on paper only.

Consequently, it was best that the House discard the so-called compromise document that was neither fair nor economically wise. A balanced budget need not be achieved in the way that the House-Senate compromise, so-called, tried to do it. The budget conference committee, which now reshapes the budget, must obviously take into account the need for a strong military, but it cannot do so without compassion for those who stand to suffer most during the very tough times ahead. In a $613 billion budget, there is room for both.

Higher Defense Spending Approved in Compromise 1981 Budget

Congress approved preliminary spending limits for 1981 June 12, after many weeks of debating a balanced budget for the upcoming fiscal year, which would begin in October. The tentative budget resolution called for a total of $613.6 billion in expenditures, leaving a $200 million surplus. The Senate vote on the budget resolution was a lopsided 61–26, while the close House vote, 205 to 195, was largely split along party lines. The budget provided the same amount in defense outlays for 1981 as had the compromise budget rejected by the House in May ($153.7 billion), but cut $800 million from the Defense Department's future-year spending authority. That change was enough to win the support of many House Democrats who had objected to the earlier budget. The compromise was opposed, however, by all but 10 Republican House members. The Republicans contended that the budget was not really balanced and did not provide enough military spending or a tax cut.

(Congress Dec. 5 passed the final fiscal 1981 appropriations bill for the Defense Department. The $160.1 billion compromise reflected congressional concern about military manpower shortages and the combat readiness of forces in the field. Both houses of Congress had added money to the President's defense spending recommendations, ending with a bill that was $5.6 billion more than President Carter had requested for the defense budget. It was signed into law Dec. 16.)

THE SAGINAW NEWS

Saginaw, Mich., July 10, 1980

What some like to call the "Pentagon war machine" has been exposed as a clunker with worn parts, creaky wheels and rusty springs. It still grinds along, but lack of maintenance has severely limited its range and power.

Back into the shop it went, a tow job prompted by serious doubt whether U.S. capability would match the fine rhetoric about defending our interests in Europe, the Middle East or anywhere else.

Last week the U.S. Senate, not usually known for its willingness to work on this type of vehicle, started the repair job with unusual dispatch and dedication.

The work won't come cheap. The $51.9 billion weapons procurement bill approved by the Senate 84-3 is the largest in U.S. history, and almost $6 billion more than President Carter had recommended. But the Senate, over the past year, could see as well as the American people that our armed forces were stretched to the limit and beyond, by such relatively small-scale assignments as patrolling the Persian Gulf area and sending a rescue team into Iran.

Noteworthy parts of the Senate package are $8.4 billion for shipbuilding to shore up a fleet outnumbered three to one by the Soviets and half the size it was on Dec. 7, 1941; $91 million for research on a new strategic bomber to replace the B-52s so old some are piloted by children of the original pilots; and $16.5 billion for aircraft, including helicopters which presumably would function in the desert.

But one of the most needed features was an 11.7 percent pay raise for military personnel.

Partly because of the recession, the armed services, excepting reserve units, are managing to recruit up to strength.

Keeping the recruits, especially after they've been trained in vital skills, is another matter. Veteran service personnel, noting great differences between their military income and what civilians earn doing the same work, act accordingly. They get out.

Pay in the lower ranks verges on the scandalous. Starting earnings are less than the federal minimum wage. Former Defense Secretary Melvin Laird estimates at least 100,000, and as many as 250,000, military families may be eligible for welfare. Nearly a fifth of the Air Force qualifies for food stamps.

America is asking its armed forces to be ready to take on an increasingly dangerous burden. The least we should do is give them the equipment they need and pay them a living wage.

We strongly believe that in a nuclear world, the best way to resolve dangerous situations is to talk them out. But when words fail us, we had better be sure our armed forces will not. And the price of failure would far exceed our investment in those who serve.

Post-Tribune

Gary, Ind., June 18, 1980

One of the better bets seems to be that that budget Congress balanced last week ain't.

"Ain't" in balance, we mean, or, more precisely, "ain't" likely to stay that way.

With their own campaigns as well as a presidential election coming up, members of Congress suddenly felt they had to make a show of creating that balanced budget so long pledged and seemingly so much in tune with the tax revolt syndrome. So, with some last minute finger crossing, both houses agreed to a tentative $613.6 billion 1981 fiscal year budget which would provide a narrow $200 million surplus.

Well, Hooray, **except** —

— The $153.7 defense budget is $3.2 billion over President Carter's desires yet is about to include a 25,000-man cut in Army strength which the president opposes, so something expensive has to give.

— Congressional estimates are for a 7.5 percent jobless rate, yet it's already reached 7.8 with other economists in agreement it will go higher, and a percentage point increase in joblessness costs $20 to $25 billion a year in federal revenue.

— Not only joblessness, but other economic pinches indicate increasing pressure for higher social program spending than is now provided — and could also bring election-year pressure for a tax cut.

— The first congressional action of note after the tentative budget OK was House committee action to restore threatened Saturday mail delivery at a cost of $500 million — not such a major figure in a $600 billion plus discussion, but every half billion counts.

Well, one could add more "excepts," no doubt, but even with these one can understand how House Speaker Thomas P. "Tip" O'Neill, who pushed so hard for budget balancing, already is saying he "can't conceive" how it can stay that way.

THE LOUISVILLE TIMES
Louisville, Ky., July 8, 1980

Concern over Afghanistan and Iran gets the blame this time, but the results are the same as always — a frenzy of expensive saber-rattling on Capitol Hill at budget time.

This year, however, the lawmakers elected to guard the nation's purse have outdone themselves in ripping it open. Last Wednesday, with only three dissenting votes, the Senate approved a $51.3 billion defense authorization bill, $5.9 billion more than the President asked. At that, the Senate version was cheaper than the $53.1 billion measure the House passed a month earlier.

Between the two versions, it is hard to imagine any pork-barrel Pentagon project that possibly could have been left out, unless it was raising the *Monitor* and refitting it with a nuclear engine. The measure goes now to a conference committee to work out the differences. Sharp scissors would be the best tool for the job.

Here are examples of likely places to start cutting:

✔ Nuclear attack subs. The President asked funds for one, the Senate gave him two and the House insisted he take three. Three would cost $907 million.

✔ F18 fighters. The House authorized 72 and the Senate, 60. The administration says it needs no more than 48.

As extravagant and unneeded as all this hardware is, at least it would be usable if the manpower were available to use it. Some of the worst boondoggles in the bill don't fall in that category.

The best-known, of course, is the MX missile, which is supposed to be a defense against Soviet intercontinental ballistic missiles. The MX program would disperse 200 Minuteman missiles over 4,600 launching tracks.

In the absence of a new arms limitation treaty, however, the Russians might just be spurred to build enough ICBMs to destroy all 4,600 tracks — if they don't first come up with some other method of defanging the MX in the many years before it can be in place. In the meantime, we — not the Russians — will environmentally scar large sections of our western states, at a cost of up to $40 billion.

But the MX isn't the only weapon likely to be obsolete before it is complete. Congress brought that old zombie, the strategic bomber, back to life. The Carter administration put the B-1 program to rest in 1977 after deciding it wasn't needed.

But now the House has authorized $600 million for development of a bomber based on the B-1 design. The Senate voted $91 million, giving the Pentagon the choice of whether to buy a variant of the B-1, an entirely new "advanced technology" aircraft or a stretched version of the FB-111. The Pentagon's assertion that the B-52 is fine was ignored.

Congress was even deafer when it came to arguments against bringing the 37-year-old battleship *New Jersey* and carrier *Oriskany* out of mothballs at a cost of nearly $600 million. Defense Secretary Harold Brown asked that it not be done, and Sen. John H. Chafee, a former secretary of the Navy, called it "a Rube Goldberg scheme." Even Adm. Thomas Hayward, chief of naval operations, has said he doesn't want the ships in service until the President and Congress "first solve the problem of inadequate, non-compensated personnel .... "

It will require about 5,000 personnel to man the two ships at a time when the Navy is desperately short-handed. The Senate defense bill also includes an 11.5 per cent across-the-board pay hike for active-duty military. But it remains to be seen if that can attract the people necessary to operate and care for all the high-priced hardware that most of the money would be spent on.

And remember: 1981 was to be the year of the balanced budget.

Los Angeles Times
Los Angeles, Calif., July 3, 1980

Higher defense spending by the United States is an unfortunate necessity; the world is dangerous, and the armed forces are no more immune to inflation than anyone else. But several of the extra items being tacked onto the military budget by Congress are neither necessary nor even helpful.

The $51.9 billion military-authorization bill passed by the Senate on Wednesday is $5 billion higher than President Carter's request. The Senate bill must now be reconciled with a House-passed measure that is even more expensive.

There is genuine concern on Capitol Hill that the Carter Administration is not moving rapidly enough to overcome deficiencies that have been allowed to develop in this country's military capabilities.

Unfortunately, though, this seems to be a case where congressional back-seat driving is going too far.

The most glaring case in point is the insistence of both the House and the Senate on spending more than $300 million to reactivate the New Jersey, a retired battleship of World War II vintage.

Backers of the battleship move contend that, because new warships take so long to build, refitting the New Jersey with missiles would be a quick and cost-effective means of building up naval power to meet the growing Soviet challenge at sea. The truth is, however, that the Navy would be hard put to man the battleship properly if it had it in service.

There is a strong case for a manned strategic bomber to replace the aging B-52s, which are older than most of the men flying them, in the 1990s and beyond. The question is whether the best option is to resurrect the B-1 project, canceled by Carter in 1977; to convert the FB-111 fighter-bomber, or to develop a new bomber entirely.

The Senate, by voting to require the Pentagon to make up its mind by next February and to have the new strategic bomber flying by 1987, is trying to move faster than the Air Force itself believes is necessary.

The approval of an extra nuclear attack submarine, at a cost of $413 million, owes more to the lobbying ability of Adm. Hyman Rickover than to military need.

Since the House was even more extravagant in some respects—approving two additional attack submarines instead of one, for example—it will be difficult at this point to bring the military-authorization bill down to earth in the House-Senate conference committee.

Fortunately, legislative authorization is meaningless until backed up by appropriations actually providing the money. There is still time, therefore, for a common-sense balancing of need and resources to prevail.

The Virginian-Pilot
Norfolk, Va., July 6, 1980

In Europe, the United States is commonly perceived as a fading military and economic power.

The United States Senate has just fired three volleys of repudiation of that perception.

Volley 1: It approved $1.6 billion to develop a shuttle system to keep 200 MX missiles moving among 4,600 launching points.

Volley 2: It approved the development of a new strategic bomber, to be in operation by 1987.

Volley 3: It authorized an 11.7 percent pay raise, effective October 1, for the 2 million men and women in the armed services.

The volleys were fired as President Carter struck another blow for national preparedness: He ordered all young men born in 1960 and 1961 to register for the draft.

The measures are important for substantive as well as symbolic reasons.

The MX missile will provide insurance against a Soviet first-strike capability. Senator John Glenn, D-Ohio, proposed a study to determine whether the missiles could be mounted on trucks to roam the nation's Interstates. Senator John Tower, R-Texas, gave the appropriate response: "The MX has already been studied to death."

The new strategic bomber would help the United States recoup some of the ground lost when President Carter canceled the B-1 program in 1977. It would replace the venerable B-52, which is wearing out and growing obsolete. The House has approved a bill to resurrect the B-1. The Senate measure is more flexible. It would explore the options of building the B-1, a stretch-FB111, or a new advanced-technology aircraft.

The pay raise should help the armed forces recruit and retain the personnel for a high-technology defense. And the draft registration sould cut the military's reaction time in event of a crisis.

The substance of these measures is important. But the symbolism shouldn't be underrated.

America's military strength has declined as Soviet strength has grown. Our European allies are no longer confident of our military superiority. President Carter's erratic foreign policy has committed us to defend areas they're not sure we can defend. The European perception is of an America growing weaker and less reliable.

Such a perception could disastrously undermine the common effort needed if the Western allies are to checkmate Soviet expansionism. It could even tempt the Europeans to abandon faith in America and seek a separate and tragic accommodation with the Soviet bloc.

It is vital, therefore, that the Europeans be reassured that the United States is both willing and able to maintain unquestioned military parity with the Soviets.

The signals emanating from Capitol Hill this week have been the right ones. They mark a long-overdue turning point in American military preparedness, and in American military prestige.

THE ARIZONA REPUBLIC
Phoenix, Ariz., July 6, 1980

WHILE the Soviet Union preached detente and arms limitations, Russian arms factories in fact were working overtime producing airplanes, ships, tanks, and missiles.

This buildup has had one central purpose — to become the world's dominant military power, and thereby be in a position to either use force or the threat of force to expand its influence without hindrance from the United States.

The Kremlin has demonstrated, in Afghanistan, that it has the capacity and willingness for aggression, and will use its men and weapons to prop up faltering Marxist regimes by crossing another nation's borders.

Russian weaponry also is poised along NATO's flanks in Europe, where NATO grounds forces would be overrun in a matter of hours by Soviet and Warsaw Pact units.

As the Soviet Union's military capabilities increased dramatically, America's military establishment shrunk, and the quality of its fighting capacity deteriorated.

Angered by the invasion of Afghanistan, stunned by public demands for strength in defense, and humiliated by the sorry state of the military, Congress passed the largest arms-buying bill in its history last week.

Conferees must now reconcile the difference between the Senate's $51.9 billion appropriation, and the House's $54 billion.

Although some of the appropriation will go for modernizing America's missile weaponry and intercontinental delivery systems ($1.5 billion for the MX missile, and $91 million for reviving research of a new long-ranbe bomber like the scrapped B-1), most of the funds are committed to rebuilding conventional forces for tactical warfare.

At least $42 billion will go for new ships, for 569 new tanks, for 525 new airplanes and helicopters, and for development of a new long-range transport for deployment of materiel and men.

The emphasis on tactical equipment, instead of on missiles, confirms the concern that the United States and its allies face a period of regional conflicts that cannot be fought with intercontinental missiles, but with ground forces, tactical air power and naval units.

The Persian Gulf is an example. So, too, is South Korea, where President Carter has reversed his policy to withdraw American ground forces because of continued North Korean threats to unify the two countries by force.

Congress' generous appropriation for a military buildup cannot but help deliver a message to the Kremlin, and reassure American allies who have become nervous about our willingness and ability to meet the Soviets on equal terms.

But the quantative gap between Russian and American forces is now so great that it will be years before the United States can claim even parity with the Soviets.

The State
Columbia, S.C., June 17, 1980

THE ARDUOUS congressional budget process is over for the time being, the House and Senate having finally agreed to a compromise hammered out by their budget committees.

An impasse developed on the guns-versus-butter issue. One recalls that during the Vietnam war, the Johnson administration tried to give the nation both guns (defense spending) and butter (social programs), and large deficits were the result.

This year a liberal coalition in the House, backed by President Carter, rejected the first joint budget resolution on the grounds that it provided too much for defense and too little for social programs, the kind that appeal to the various Democratic constituencies.

That budget projected a surplus at the end of fiscal 1981 of $500 million, the first since Congress began preparing guidelines to curb unplanned and restrained spending.

When the President helped defeat that version on the House floor, S.C. Democrat E. F. "Fritz" Hollings, new chairman of the Senate Budget Committee, charged that Mr. Carter "doesn't want a balanced budget; he wants a campaign budget."

There's some truth there, but it is also true that many congressmen also wanted a budget with goodies that will enhance their chances of re-election.

It is also probably true that Senator Hollings and others who fought hard to keep the higher defense figures have hopes of tapping the public's desire for a beefed-up military posture in the light of recent international developments. Polls show this mood exists, and there is little doubt a sharp increase in military spending is needed to bolster America's strength in weapons and to help recruit and retain military personnel by increasing pay.

Throughout this jockeying over guns and butter, Congress managed to keep its eye on the goal of a balanced budget. The final compromise achieved a paper balance by cutting the expected surplus from $500 million to $200 million, which is peanuts. The enlarged defense figure for 1981 was retained, but authority for future spending in that area was trimmed by a modest amount.

Almost no one believes that the country will wind up next year with a surplus. One reason is that balance was achieved partly by putting in the budget resolution instructions to other congressional committees to raise $4.2 billion in new taxes and to cut already approved programs by $6.4 billion. This is unprecedented, and one wonders if the appropriations and tax-writing committees will comply.

The main reason that the budget is likely to fall out of balance is the recession, which will reduce tax revenues and increase the need for spending for such things as unemployment benefits. This reality will have to be dealt with in the final budget resolution, due Aug. 28.

The recession brought the goal of a balanced budget under fire from, of all sources, the U.S. Chamber of Commerce, which prefers $25 billion in individual and business tax cuts to stimulate the economy.

We are pleased, however, that Congress clung to the goals of higher defense spending and a balanced budget at this time. Both have symbolic as well as real value. If more red ink ahead is unavoidable, it's better to start the year with a paper balance than with a built-in deficit. The budget also signals Congress' intention to curb runaway spending.

The defense outlays will not only provide good-paying and much-needed jobs here at home, but it will tell our allies and enemies around the world that America intends to hang tough.

Congress Receives Defense Requests from Reagan

The Reagan Administration presented to Congress March 4, 1981 a defense budget that would substantially increase expenditures and future commitment to a military buildup. In fiscal 1981, the defense budget plan called for a $6.8 billion increase in the supplemental appropriation requested by President Carter in January. In fiscal 1982, budget authority would increase $25.8 billion over the Carter request, to $222.2 billion. From 1983 through 1986, Reagan's plan would increase the Pentagon budget by about 7% annually in real, or inflation-adjusted terms. (The Carter budget had projected real increases of 5% for each of those years.)

Of the $25.8 billion Reagan added to Carter's fiscal 1982 request, $4.2 was earmarked for new ships, as a first step toward expanding the Navy's fleet by a third in the coming years. The Reagan budget also called for the development of a new long-range bomber, construction of a nuclear aircraft carrier, and reactivation of two battleships and a conventionally powered aircraft carrier. Military pay would be increased again, in addition to an 11.7% pay boost already effected in fiscal 1981.

The biggest Air Force program, the MX missile, was more or less put on hold pending review of the Pentagon plan to base it in 4,600 shelters along 8,500 miles of routing in Utah and Nevada. Reagan requested $2.95 billion for the MX, compared with $2.93 billion budgeted by Carter.

ST. LOUIS POST-DISPATCH
St. Louis, Mo., March 6, 1981

As a candidate for president, Ronald Reagan suggested "the possibility of an arms race" as a means of putting pressure on the Soviet Union. Now, less than two months in office, Mr. Reagan has decided to see what an all-out escalation in military spending will do. The president has asked Congress to increase the Pentagon budget by more than $38 billion dollars between now and the end of fiscal 1982. By fiscal 1986, under Mr. Reagan's plans, the Pentagon budget would reach $386 billion, more than double the current one of $171 billion.

Those increases are breathtaking, even by the standards of the healthy second and third helpings the Defense Department usually gets out of the nation's treasury. The Carter administration, for example, was scarcely considering a cutback in military spending, having committed itself to after-inflation increases on the order of 5 percent a year. For fiscal 1982, the Reagan administration is asking for raise of nearly 15 percent in total obligational authority. When you consider that to compensate for these prodigious increases, the administration is proposing to cut nearly $45 billion out of more than 80 federal programs — food stamps, school milk, education for the handicapped, black lung benefits and so forth — this year, the magnitude of what the president is proposing to do becomes starkly clear.

At a time when the nation is neither at war nor is threatened with war, before Congress chooses guns over butter it has a deep responsibility to demand from the administration compelling evidence that the nation's security requires such an imbalanced deployment of its resources. No responsible citizen can have any interest in weakening America's defenses; and no reasonable person would argue that there are not places where the military could use not merely wiser spending but more spending as well. But it should take considerably more than Defense Secretary Weinberger's mere assertion that the U.S. cannot "afford to temporize any longer in the face of the Soviet threat" or the pipsqueak example of El Salvador to persuade Congress to provide the kind of money the administration is asking for.

The fact is that simply spending more money will not make the nation stronger or more secure. The Soviet Union is powerful enough to remain a potent military rival no matter how much money is spent. The great danger, as we see it, is that the administration and Congress will delude themselves into thinking that cranking up the arms race will prove a substitute for shrewd diplomacy or sound and principled policies. In fact, wasting money in scraping the rust off aging World War II battleships or building a manned strategic bomber in the age of the missile will not make the Soviet "threat" any more remote.

There are some places, to be sure, where the administration is on the right track: more money for military pay to stem the hemorrhage of trained personnel; more money for maintenance and operations, so that troops and machinery stay ready to go; more money for certain conventional weapons, so that commitments to Europe and the Middle East remain credible. But selected increases, prudently managed, are a far cry from the blank check the administration is proposing.

Make no mistake about it: Mr. Reagan is attempting to pull off a revolution in the country's priorities. Common sense, fiscal responsibility, concern for other national values — all of these cry out for a careful appraisal of what he wants. Congress must not fail to provide it.

DAYTON DAILY NEWS
Dayton, Ohio, March 17, 1981

That U.S. defense readiness must be brought up to par with that of the USSR is a given. The Carter administration concurred. So did the last Congress in passing a $171 billion 1981 defense budget.

Thus whether President Reagan has a mandate to close conventional and deterrent gaps in U.S. security is not at issue in appraising his Big Bang military budget — more than double current funding through 1986, starting with a $32.6 billion increase between now and next year.

Neither at issue are increases in military pay and manpower; one-third of our striking power, much of it unnecessarily complicated, is neutralized by lack of personnel and maintenance.

The questions that want debating are, what are the objectives of this most massive and costly naval-air-ground buildup in peacetime history? Does its design meet, or exceed, our needs for protection of strategic interest zones — Western Europe, Mediterranean, Middle East, Persian Gulf, Pacific, the Americas?

As to the first question, Congress is expected to work a genetic miracle. It is asked to hatch a $1.5 trillion military egg unfertilized by any carefully formulated public policy, whether to govern its use or restraint, counter its inflationary effect, cushion its social and economic impact, coordinate it with our allies' policies and capabilities, or employ it as leverage in arms control negotiations.

Before his confirmation, Defense Secretary Caspar Weinberger said it would take him months to gauge the relative merits of all the weapons and projects on the Pentagon wish list. Has he since decided to buy everything offered and figure out later what to do with it?

Instead of providing some rationale for his plans, Mr. Weinberger offered the Senate Armed Services Committee a lame generalization: The defense budget is "the second half of the administration's program to revitalize America."

And an implication: Public investment in building a more humane society has to be slashed to accommodate unprecedented military expansion.

And an assumption no cautious NATO ally would buy without first seeing it tested in a resumption of U.S.-Soviet arms talks: "It is neither reasonable nor prudent to view the Soviet military buildup as defensive in nature."

Admittedly, military preparedness has to be planned ahead, its hardware bought in installments. The Reagan administration is asking Congress and the public to buy a global military policy the same way: Make a commitment now to an enormous drain on national resources, including investment capital, strategic minerals, fuel, and find out later why we're doing it.

the Charleston Gazette

Charleston, W. Va., March 17, 1981

CONGRESS has before it the defense budget increases wanted by the administration. We suggest that instead of rushing to pick up the tab Congress give the proposals a long, hard look before moving.

We agree that the nation needs to maintain adequate defense systems. But we are not impressed by the tiresome comparisons showing the Soviet Union to be far more powerful than the United States — who among us is willing to trade our defense establishment for theirs? Still we can appreciate the need, for instance, to protect Middle East oil resources if worse comes to worse.

To Congress we recommend the counsel of Edmund Muskie, given shortly before he left his job as secretary of state:

"We must be prepared to defend our vital interests if they are endangered ... but we must also recognize that our security over the longer term is best assured if, working with others, we are effective in addressing the conditions that breed instability and conflict."

Adding to the earth's burden of military hardware may be the least effective way of achieving stability and peace. As military stockpiles build, there is a temptation to use them. History has shown this to be the case.

THE CHRISTIAN SCIENCE MONITOR

Boston, Mass., March 9, 1981

Defense is a difficult, complex subject. But when the President of the United States asks Congress to authorize an astronomical $222 billion for the fiscal 1982 military budget — at a time of financial squeeze on all other areas of government spending — the American people ought to take more than a casual interest. In five editorials, which will appear this week, we shall examine some of the issues involved and, we hope, stir discussion.

Let it be said at the outset that the nation's defense is not an area in which to take risks. The armed forces clearly must be adequate to meet security needs, and we doubt any American would begrudge the funds — and sacrifice — required to maintain defense at a demonstratively safe level. That the unceasing Soviet military buildup poses new challenges to the West is a matter of general agreement. The question is exactly what should be done about that challenge.

Our major concern is that the subject receive honest analysis and debate within the government. It would be unfortunate if an exaggerated "Russian menace" became the excuse for bloating the US budget with unnecessary arms programs. The military services always want more weapons and the temptation to push for them under an assertively prodefense administration must be strong. The defense industry — that military-industrial complex which President Eisenhower warned about — is avidly awaiting huge contracts. Defense Secretary Caspar Weinberger, even before he has had time to study the complicated problems involved, has called for a $33 billion jump in military appropriations over the Carter budgets for 1981 and 1982. Are these requests based on meticulously thought out plans — or are they designed in large part to set a national tone of toughness vis-à-vis the Soviet Union? And perhaps for domestic political purposes?

Authorizing money before it is determined what the money is to be for is putting the cart before the horse. The United States needs a sound, long-range military- policy. And, as former chairman of the Joint Chiefs Maxwell Taylor notes, the first requirement of such a policy is to know what US foreign-policy and security goals are and, to determine these, what dangers can be expected in the decade or two ahead. Then, says General Taylor, the Pentagon can work out the missions which must be performed and the weapons systems best suited to performing them. "By making task adequacy the standard for force strength," he writes, "our military policy will meet the legitimate requirements of national security without need to resort to a mindless arms race with the Soviets."

Has this precision homework been done?

There is not much evidence yet that it has. Instead, much is heard about generalized Soviet arms "superiority" and about the Russians "outspending" the US in defense. Such unqualified statements are misleading. It is hard to conceive that the United States, with more than 9,000 strategic H-bombs, is in a position of overall inferiority to the Russians, with their 6,000 some H-bombs. There are areas in which the Russians have an important advantage (most notably in conventional weapons) and areas in which the US has the clear edge (accuracy of warheads). Overall, most military experts, whatever their disputes over detail, appear to agree that the two superpowers *at present* are in rough equilibrium with each other. This is not to deny areas of US vulnerability — a dated bomber force, a stretched-thin Navy, poor combat readiness, for instance — which must be addressed. But calm determination of actual need will serve the national interest better than broad overstatement.

In this connection, comparing US outlays with those of the USSR is an unreliable business. Most CIA estimates of Soviet spending are based on what it would cost the US to duplicate the Soviet military effort. Yet such a comparison is often fallacious. The Russians, for instance, pay their military far less than does the US and have a more manpower-intensive army. So, as the Center for Defense Information in Washington points out, whenever the US boosts military pay by $1, the Soviet dollar cost increases by almost $2 — making the Soviet Union appear far more threatening than it is.

Furthermore, even if CIA estimates are taken as a guide, the picture is not complete without comparing NATO and Warsaw Pact spending, and here NATO is the undisputed leader. Figures put out by the London-based International Institute for Strategic Studies show the Atlantic alliance considerably outspending the Eastern bloc. NATO also has more men under arms.

However, the basic point is not how much is spent, but how efficiently and effectively it is spent — whether the arms and personnel at hand are sufficient to their mission. Here attention must be given not only to the state of current weapons systems and manpower but to Western defense strategy itself — to organization and doctrine as well as equipment.

One innovative concept heard these days comes from a group of defense analysts who say that, with new strategies, the US could have a much stronger defense — and without big increases in spending. These specialists, led by retired Air Force colonel John Boyd, argue that the US armed forces are weighed down by a cumbersome, expensive strategy based on overwhelming an enemy by superior numbers of soldiers and weapons. They favor instead "maneuver warfare," a strategy based on defeating an enemy by agile attacks at its weak points with smaller, more cohesive divisions and with smaller, cheaper, and less sophisticated planes, tanks, and ships. Ironically, this is the strategy of the Soviet Union, which maintains large numbers of lean divisions for swiftly overpowering the adversary in intense but short campaigns.

This is not to accept the Boyd group's call for institutional reform at face value. It may not be valid and we are in no position to judge its merit. But it does raise intelligent questions, and it is therefore hoped that Mr. Weinberger and his aides are looking at this and other analyses as they consult with NATO allies and work out a long-term military policy. Challenging conventional thinking could open up fresh ideas and approaches.

One other major item concerns us: moving forward as quickly as possible on SALT. We appreciate that Mr. Reagan needs time to review the whole platter of arms control issues before starting talks with Moscow. But, meanwhile, it is disquieting to hear voices calling for scrapping of the 1972 ABM treaty and other changes. The years ahead are likely to be marked by a higher level of US-Soviet military competition and tension, which would make nuclear arms control even more crucial if the superpowers are to preserve a balance and contain the risks of nuclear war. Both sides are developing new systems, such as counter-silo capabilities. Both are scurrying to keep up with new vulnerabilities. This spiral, driven by military institutions on both sides, needs to be broken.

Economics alone should bring both sides to the negotiation table. It is hard to imagine the Reagan administration will not be eager to pursue arms control — and to scale down its budget projections — when it realizes the impact on the US economy of rising defense costs. Few believe the President will be able to balance the budget and cut taxes without also curbing arms outlays.

Other issues could be touched upon, including the massive defense-budget waste which the outgoing US comptroller general says runs into billions of dollars annually. Subsequent editorials will deal with the MX, bombers, naval strategy, and the draft. But the main point we would make today is that US security cannot be bought by throwing dollars at the very real problem of Soviet military growth. Americans want to be assured that the White House and Congress are applying standards of cost-effectiveness, efficiency, and legitimate purpose as they seek to put the nation's defenses in proper order.

Richmond Times-Dispatch
Richmond, Va., March 8, 1981

When he submitted a new defense budget to Congress last week, President Reagan flashed an important message to Moscow. No longer, the president warned, will the assumption that the Soviet Union genuinely favors peace constitute a factor in the United States' defense equation. The Reagan administration will assume instead that Russia remains committed to belligerent expansionism and that, therefore, the United States should prepare militarily for a possible collision with that communist nation.

Throughout most of its four years, the Carter administration labored under the delusion that by exercising restraint in military matters it could encourage the Soviet Union to do likewise. It allowed American armed forces, and especially the Navy, to deteriorate alarmingly. But instead of reciprocating by moderating its own actions, Russia expanded and strengthened its armed forces and became steadily bolder in the use of power to spread its influence. Its invasion of Afghanistan and its fomentation of civil strife in Latin America are examples of its adventurism.

Even in its weakened military condition, the United States would not be a pushover for the Soviet Union. But as the Persian Gulf crisis — sparked by turmoil in Iran and by Russia's aggression in Afghanistan — vividly illustrated, the United States is inadequately prepared to respond with conventional military forces to Soviet threats to American interests in distant areas. The United States had no rapid deployment force that it might have sent to the area, and it had to raid a Pacific task force to find ships to form an American naval presence in the Gulf area.

Mr. Reagan's defense spending proposals are designed to overcome the deficiencies that developed under the Carter administration. An especially commendable feature of his plan is expansion of the Navy from 450 ships to 600 over a five-year period. Initial appropriations would include funds for a cruiser and a submarine and to start work on a *Nimitz*-class nuclear aircraft carrier. The plan also provides for development of a new manned bomber capable of penetrating Soviet defenses and for the purchase of additional F-15 and F-16 fighters. There would be money, too, for another pay increase for military personnel, who have been miserably conpensated for the past few years.

It is imperative that Congress react positively to the Reagan proposals. Of course it has an obligation to examine the recommendations carefully and to check especially for signs of waste, which exists in the Pentagon as surely as it exists in other agencies of the government. But Congress' objective should be the same as Mr. Reagan's: to develop a military program that would enable the United States to rebuff any threat to its security at any point on the globe.

The Dallas Morning News
Dallas, Texas, March 7, 1981

IF YOU have doubts about the Reagan administration's commitment to national defense, prepare to shed them now. The White House weighed in a few days ago with a request for $32.6 billion in additional military spending in 1981 and 1982.

The figures translate, as Defense Secretary Weinberger explained, into 4 percent more this year for the military and 13 percent more in the next fiscal year, compared with increases proposed by the Carter administration.

"This is a lot of money," said old John Stennis, the Mississippi Democrat, who until this year chaired the Armed Services Committee, "but I believe you'll get your money."

We believe so, too. And how exhilarating is the belief. Just a few years back, Weinberger and his boss, President Reagan, would have been laughed out of Washington for proposing to give "the Pentagon" so much money. That the Defense Department's headquarters was in the old days of the '60s and '70s more an epithet than a building — a word to be spat out between clinched teeth — speaks volumes about our present military predicament.

Yes, the old days — days when in many circles it was fashionable to despise soldiers as a class. In these misbegotten days there was a vogue phrase: Reorder the priorities; which, freely translated, meant, let's cut the Pentagon's swollen budget and spend the money on conquering poverty, improving education and so on. The defense budget, which once consumed about half of federal spending, shrank by fiscal 1980 to less than a fourth. Indeed, in 1980, Congress sliced $900 million from the Carter administration's budget for military operations and maintenance.

This would have mattered less had not the Soviets been busily beefing up their own military — so busily indeed that no military expert thinks us any longer superior to the Soviets. We are — at best — roughly equal for the moment; for the near future, we will not even be equal, thanks to the parsimony of the past.

President Ford's long-range program to strengthen the military was systematically dismantled — the MX missile, scheduled for 1983 deployment, put off until 1986; the B1 bomber canceled; the Trident SSBN and cruise missile programs stretched out. With reason Weinberger submits that "we have not, as we thought, saved money by reducing military spending in the last decade. We have merely postponed spending, and now we must resume it in a time when high inflation gives a false impression of just how much we are really devoting to our defense needs."

What is the old saying? Penny-wise, pound-foolish? Surely that describes this country to a T. And now that we know what is wrong with us, let us give Secretary Weinberger his money, every cent of it.

The Des Moines Register
Des Moines, Iowa, March 9, 1981

It is not just the size of the increases in President Reagan's military budget, although these are stunning. What is more striking is the fundamental shift in foreign policy and military strategy that it implies.

Reagan wants Congress to authorize an additional $33 billion in military spending over the next 18 months on top of the already-large increases proposed by former President Carter. Between fiscal 1983 and 1986, Reagan wants to boost military spending by 7 percent a year, after adjustment for inflation — $1.5 trillion over the next five years.

The Reagan budget is aimed at giving the United States a military force that could be much more aggressive around the globe. Defense Secretary Caspar Weinberger told Congress that the nation must have a "credible" military presence in the Middle East and Persian Gulf to protect the oilfields.

The budget calls, too, for a substantial buildup of the Navy, particularly its ability to take on the Soviet navy in or near Soviet home waters.

Perhaps most significant, the Reagan budget proposes an accelerated buildup of strategic nuclear forces, a buildup that Reagan believes would induce the Russians to engage in more realistic arms-control talks.

The Reagan budget assumes that the buildup of Soviet military power is the predominant security concern of the United States. We don't belittle it, but the country is faced with other, potentially more dangerous threats to its security. During the 1970s, the OPEC cartel did more harm to the United States than the Soviet Union did. Reagan proposes to offset the dangerous U.S. dependency on Mideast oil with a military presence in the Persian Gulf region. Yet he calls for cutbacks in federal energy programs aimed at boosting energy production and conservation.

Turmoil in Third World nations such as El Salvador will continue to trouble the United States. A strong military is one way to respond to such turmoil. But Third World turmoil is often caused by desperate economic conditions. President Carter sought to meet this threat head-on by sending more economic aid to the Third World, but Reagan wants to cut back aid.

Without doubt, the gravest single threat to the national security is the nuclear-arms race. Yet Reagan wants to build up the already-large stockpile of nuclear arms in the hope that this will make Russia more willing to bargain on nuclear-arms reduction. It would be less costly and less dangerous to seek meaningful nuclear-arms control now.

We believe that Reagan's military strategy and foreign policy are unbalanced. He puts too much emphasis on the military, too little emphasis on diplomatic, economic and technological remedies.

The Soviet Union has made heavy sacrifices to build up its military, but the Soviets lack the economic power and the technological genius of the United States, and they certainly lack the American tradition of civil and political rights.

This country is stronger than Russia in all of these areas and ought to capitalize on its real strengths in designing foreign policy and military strategy.

Newsday

Long Island, N.Y., March 10, 1981

Anyone who thinks arms control is no longer important simply hasn't absorbed the implications of the military spending plans the Reagan administration outlined for Congress last week.

Those plans call for a $6.8-billion boost in defense spending authority for the current fiscal year. For fiscal 1982, which begins Oct. 1, Reagan's people want $222.2 billion—$25.8 billion more than the Carter administration proposed. The Reagan five-year plan projects a cumulative total of $1.3 *trillion* in military spending. Meanwhile, as domestic expenditures level off, the defense portion of the federal budget would increase from 24 per cent to 32 per cent.

The administration's rationale for enormous increases in defense spending when everything else in the budget is being cut was summarized last week by Defense Secretary Caspar Weinberger: "Simply put, we are being forced into a continuing and, apparently, long-term military and political competition with the Soviets, and we are not maintaining a competitive position."

Just where the military competition stands today is a matter of sharp debate; the Central Intelligence Agency is often accused of overestimating Soviet defense outlays. But no one denies that the Soviet Union has improved its relative position over the past decade.

Whether the Russians are doing as well in the political competition is another question, although Poland and Afghanistan suggest that they're not. And one of the puzzles Congress must consider is whether funding every procurement program the Pentagon comes up with is the best way to achieve U.S. political goals abroad.

Still, it's clear that a policy of unilateral restraint has few followers in Washington these days. It might be different if

Jimmy Carter's decisions not to produce the B-1 bomber or deploy the neutron bomb had brought a response in kind from Moscow, but they didn't. What they brought was a continuing Soviet buildup in Europe, including multi-warhead nuclear missiles, and Soviet policies that could threaten the West's access to Mideast oil.

As a result, the Carter administration pushed NATO to accept new U.S. missiles in Europe and announced a "Rapid Deployment Force" whose main mission would be to head off a Soviet blitz in the Persian Gulf. Now Reagan wants to resuscitate the manned bomber and the nuclear aircraft carrier. He wants to take a carrier and two battleships out of mothballs. Instead of reducing the fleet, he wants to increase it by a third, from 456 ships to 600. He wants, above all, to let the Russians know that they cannot win the military competition by default.

It's by no means clear that reviving

discarded weapons is the way to do this, but some of the administration's other proposals show greater promise. Speeding up defense procurement should save money in the long run, for instance. Raising pay scales ought to reduce some of the military's manpower problems.

If the Kremlin is convinced that Reagan means business, there's always a chance it will slacken its own military buildup. Leonid Brezhnev is now talking about a freeze on nuclear weapons in Europe—a frivolous proposal if its only purpose is to keep the West from catching up. But military spending, which is inflationary enough in this country, is an even heavier burden on the weaker Soviet economy.

That's why, no matter how much Washington sees fit to spend on defense, it must never close the door to arms-control negotiations as long as there's a live possibility that they might produce greater security at lower cost.

The Cleveland Press
Cleveland, Ohio, March 6, 1981

President Reagan has asked for a surge in military spending, and in a capital that has turned pro-defense there is no question that Congress will go along. The question is whether the Pentagon can use its windfall wisely.

When Defense Secretary Caspar Weinberger outlined the new defense budget to the Senate Armed Services Committee, no one argued with his stated goal: to regain military superiority over the Soviet Union.

In fact the committee was so supportive that one doubts the spending plans will get the scrutiny they deserve.

Weinberger proposed to more than double the Pentagon budget in five years, from $171 billion in 1981 to $368 billion in 1986.

The spending wave would give each of the services just about everything it wants.

No prudent, patriotic person would deny that Moscow has engaged in a massive military buildup in recent years, while the United States has shortchanged its defenses. But this does not mean that some of the bigger items on the Pentagon shopping list should not have to justify themselves.

For example, the Navy wants to reactivate two World War II battleships and use them as cruise missile launchers. As far back as the 1920s Gen. Billy Mitchell proved that battleships were vulnerable to air attack. Are we now to believe that the two battlewagons, in this era of guided missiles, could survive off the Soviet Union's coast to fire their weapons?

Or take the Air Force's prime desire, a fleet of new manned bombers. Since existing bombers could stand off from Russia's ferocious air defense system and launch cruise missiles, why build a penetrating bomber that would cost so much more in dollars and lives?

In the past conservatives blasted liberals for wanting "to throw money" at social problems. Liberals now can do their psyches (and the country) some good by talking about conservatives throwing money at defense problems and making them prove the need for each new weapon.

THE BILLINGS GAZETTE
Billings, Mont., March 2, 1981

President Reagan's war on incompetence, inefficiency and waste shouldn't stop at the front door of the Pentagon.

We laud his efforts to clean up government, to give welfare only to those who need it and to sweep away picky-picky regulations.

What is hard to understand is the apparent key to the treasury he wants to give the military. The Reagan administration plans to spend more billions on the military than it will be able to save if it can implement all of its cost-cutting measures on the rest of the government.

But why exempt the military from the waste eradicators and boondoggle busters?

There are just as many dreamers, schemers and turf protectors in the military as there were to be found in the New Deal, New Frontier, Great Society, War on Poverty and all those other slogan-boosted programs which the president so disdains.

Most everyone who has served in the armed forces of the U.S. knows of the wasteful and inefficient manner in which they are operated. The president himself should realize that from his own questionable role in World War II.

His trust in the military as budget watchers is scary. These are the people who have been buying weapons that don't fire in field conditions, planes that carry out their missions only on the drawing boards and an array of costly — and often malfunctioning — missiles.

These are the same people who spend millions developing military posts with all the amenities of country club life only to abandon them when some other fantasy comes along.

We realize the nation has to be defended, even to the point of being able to carry that defense to foreign shores. That doesn't mean the defense apparatus needs to be top-heavy with brass who seem to spend most of their time scheming to get more money out of Congress for such far-fetched things as the MX system.

The military may well need a bigger budget to accomplish its purpose. Before getting it, the armed forces should clean up its act. It should be forced to prove that what is now being spent is going for defense not featherbedding and fantasy.

Minneapolis Tribune
Minneapolis, Minn., March 8, 1981

President Reagan's defense program attempts too much, too fast, at too great a risk to the U.S. economy. Increases over defense budgets offered by the Carter administration may be necessary; certainly higher military outlays would be consistent with Reagan's campaign statements. But the kind and quantity of additions now proposed deserve the strong challenge they will surely get from Congress.

Western Europe is a leading candidate for stronger defense. According to a study by the Congressional Budget Office, NATO ground forces would be inadequate against the 120 Warsaw Pact divisions that the Soviet Union would probably use if it attacked Western Europe. The study argues that neither battlefield nuclear weapons nor NATO troop reinforcements would correct the imbalance.

Since imbalance increases the possibility of such an attack, some of Reagan's proposals seem prudent: a strengthened army and marine corps, larger stocks of ammunition and spare parts. The Carter budget included nothing for the A10 — a heavily armored, low-altitude attack plane that is basically a tank-killer. The 60 A10s in the Reagan budget could be $600 million well spent.

Another Congressional Budget Office report offers an example of substantial increases that would improve strategic and conventional forces. The total in the fiscal year beginning next October would be $213 billion, $9 billion less than the Reagan proposal. It includes more ground divisions, ships and vehicles, and various options for improving nuclear forces (for example, a speed-up in production of the the Trident II submarine-based missile).

In contrast, the administration wants to plunge into an extraordinarily wide range of new or rapidly expanded programs. For example, its proposed concentration on big, costly naval ships raises basic questions of strategy, economy and usefulness. So does its request for a new fleet of long-range bombers and for $4 billion to buy tanker airplanes for air-to-air refueling.

In one sense, it is true that current U.S. defense expenditures represent a comparatively small proportion of national wealth. A study by the Carnegie Endowment points out that in the Korean and Vietnam Wars, defense outlays as a proportion of gross national product rose faster and higher than they would in the Reagan defense budget. But the Carnegie report also points out important differences: First, the economy then was growing faster than it is now. Second, federal payments to individuals now account for half the federal budget, compared to less than a quarter in 1960.

Reagan's economic program envisions faster economic growth through deregulated, reinvigorated private enterprise; but any growth increases are likely to be gradual. A rapid defense increase could be financed by higher taxes; but Reagan's plan is to cut them. It could be financed by cuts in other programs; but while some reductions can and should be made, inordinate increases in defense spending could cause inordinate cuts in basic human services. A rapid, sustained defense increase also could be achieved by larger federal deficits; but the resulting inflation would drive defense costs still higher, and Reagan hopes eventually to balance the budget.

The problem is not whether to improve national defense. Some improvements, such as more competitive military pay, are essential. The problem is trying to push large, across-the board increases through Congress with inadequate consideration for the military and economic wisdom of doing so. Those are among the considerations Congress must supply.

DESERET NEWS
Salt Lake City, Utah, March 17, 1981

One of the few areas to escape President Reagan's budget-cutting ax in his recent recommendations was defense. The president is seeking $4.8 billion in increased defense spending to create "a margin of safety . . . by rebuilding the nation's defense capabilities."

Increased defense spending, coupled with slashes in social programs under the Reagan plan, would boost the defense share of the budget from 24 percent in 1981 to 27 percent next year, and 37 percent by 1986.

Reagan's proposed increase is on top of the $196.5 billion fiscal 1982 defense budget called for in the Carter budget recommendations. The Carter budget called for 5 percent real growth in defense spending in fiscal years 1983 through 1986.

Also included in the earlier Carter budget recommendation was 14.1 percent real growth in research, development, test and evaluation for fiscal 1982 over FY 1981. That itself represents a hefty increase in defense outlays after years of neglect.

But there should be at least two caveats in the drive to beef up U.S. defenses:

— Dollars should not be wasted on useless or misguided weapons systems that add little to total U.S. defense capabilities.

— The burden of providing increasingly-expensive and complicated planes, ships, tanks, and other weapons of war is so onerous that the Reagan administration should immediately seek new talks with Russia on limiting Warsaw Pact and NATO forces.

Since the prospect of ratifying SALT II has practically vanished, it becomes increasingly important to start negotiations on a new pact to limit nuclear arsenals — one of the most expensive weapons systems ever designed. Getting the Russians back to the bargaining table is going to take some diplomatic effort. But the effort must be made, and in good faith.

Before those defense dollars are committed, some tough questions must be answered:

—How much should the U.S. spend on improving conventional forces and how much on expanding the nuclear arsenal? That question has considerable implications for the MX program.

— How much should be allocated to improve combat readiness of equipment already in the field, instead of buying new hardware?

— Which conventional combat arms will give the greatest security for the least dollars? Is it more important, for example, to purchase 20 more F-15 fighter planes or one more nuclear attack submarine?

— And finally, how can the Russian threat be countered the best without having to match plane-for-plane, ship-for-ship, tank-for-tank? Battle tactics and new weaponry development shift so rapidly that yesterday's equipment may be obsolete in tomorrow's war.

Merely increasing the defense budget is not the answer to all-around better capabilities. Any radical production surge is bound to be limited by bottlenecks in producing certain key components — like large titanium forgings used in aircraft.

Paring waste and fraud out of the military budget is even more important when dollars are diverted from other worthwhile programs to provide a better defense. And most important of all must be the continued search to provide a lasting basis for peace and an effective reduction of armaments.

THE SACRAMENTO BEE
Sacramento, Calif., March 15, 1981

There can be no doubt that the American military is in need of funds to improve combat-readiness and upgrade certain weapons systems. But neither the Carter administration's last defense budget nor the Reagan administration's enlargement of it is the way to achieve those ends. As a quid pro quo for Senate approval of the SALT II agreement, the former president agreed to future purchases of more new weapons and equipment than his own Pentagon thought it could deploy. Reagan has essentially taken over this indiscriminate wish list and asked for all of it now — nearly a 30 percent spending increase over the next year and a half.

Never mind that the Pentagon itself is still debating such fundamental questions as how fast a buildup is practical, whether money is better spent on more weapons or on more sophisticated weapons, and whether the new Rapid Deployment Force should be set up as a trip-wire or a holding operation. Never mind that Carter's array of future programs never did have much relation to actual strategic or tactical needs. Why should that affect spending decisions?

The only fault Caspar Weinberger, the new defense secretary, could find in the undifferentiated list he inherited was that Carter had "failed to provide full funding for the many programs (he) conceded were necessary but felt unable to afford." The only modifications Weinberger proposed were the addition of 150 ships and a new fleet of long-range bombers. Of the meager $3.2 billion Reagan's people claim to have streamlined off Carter's military spending plans, $2.7 billion involved no program changes at all: It was merely a statistical adjustment created by changing the estimate of future inflation.

This does not mean that Weinberger has come up with any particular justification for buying more hardware, for use in more simultaneous crises, than the military has the plans or soldiers to deal with. If the Reagan defense budget is based on any global strategy, it is only the strategy of being everywhere at once. "We must not pursue a defense strategy that (merely) anticipates a point-to-point response to (Soviet) actions," Weinberger announced, "but rather one which permits us to take full advantage of Soviet vulnerabilities." This, at the same time that we are to be building a "credible presence" in Southwest Asia and the Middle East, maintaining our standby capability in Europe and improving our intercontinental nuclear arms.

Even if the United States had investment dollars, personnel and raw materials to spare, this seems to be a breadth of military preparedness that there is no good reason to strive for. But given the domestic realities of severe inflation, military personnel shortages, and a troubled industrial base which is already the victim of unprecedented worldwide competition for investment dollars and raw materials, this refusal to make choices is particularly dangerous. A spending program so massive that it threatens the domestic economy undermines what, in fact, is our strongest military asset.

It is incumbent upon the Congress to bring a modicum of common sense to bear on this spending frenzy. Appropriations for even the most inarguable of purposes — military pay raises, for instance, and the large sums needed for maintenance, supplies and spare parts for existing military equipment — must still be scrutinized for cost-effectiveness and practicality. Such dubious undertakings as Reagan's proposal to enlarge the naval fleet by one-third, when many of our existing ships are now idle for lack of middle-level officers to run them, require even closer examination.

Apparently the Reagan team did not think about such things, but before Congress agrees to refurbish World War II battleships, it had better find out where they can possibly be used now, given their admitted vulnerability. Before it agrees to order the next generation of electronic gadgetry, it had better find out whether, as one recent Pentagon study suggested, increasing the military's technological sophistication actually reduces its combat readiness.

More important, Congress had better determine which military objectives we can afford — and which we even want — to pursue. Only then can it decide which new defense expenditures are realistic or necessary. Like kids in a toy shop, Reagan's military planners have demonstrated precious little discrimination. Congress does not have the same luxury.

House, Senate Pass 1982 Defense Authorization Bill

There was little effective objection to President Reagan's defense budget in Congress following his March proposals, although the military was nearly alone among major government programs in escaping budget cuts. The Senate May 14 passed a record defense bill authorizing $136.5 billion for defense programs by a 92 to 1 vote; the House passed a $136.1 billion bill July 16 on a 354 to 63 vote. The similar bills included authorization for weapons procurement, military research, and operations and maintenance in fiscal 1982.

Floor debates in the Senate and House preceding passage of the bills concerned such issues as the MX missile system's cost and basing problems, the need for measures to cut waste in the Pentagon budget and the enforcement of draft registration. The Senate, faced with the prospect of a filibuster by Sen. Mark O. Hatfield (R, Ore.), deleted from its bill a provision requiring the Health and Human Services Department to make available to the Selective Service System the names and addresses of those men required to register for the draft. The provision was passed by the House. Major cost-reduction amendments were defeated in both houses, but both the House and Senate passed amendments that would enable Congress to block whatever basing plan the President chose for the MX missile.

THE MILWAUKEE JOURNAL
Milwaukee, Wisc., May 10, 1981

There is an alien aboard President Reagan's whizzing economic spacecraft — and it could devour the progress Reagan hopes to achieve through aggressive tax cutting and budget slashing.

The alien is defense spending, which Reagan proposes to increase over the next five years at a rate three times as great as the military buildup for Vietnam. So far, the magnitude of that boost has been largely ignored in the debate over Reagan's budget and tax packages.

Yet, so vast an increase — from $180.7 billion in 1981 to $374.3 billion in 1986 — is bound to cause problems for Reagan's economic recovery scheme. Adding to the concern is the real possibility that the huge sum projected by Reagan could actually be conservative.

Reagan is basing his defense spending estimates on very optimistic assumptions about the decline of inflation over the next five years. If Reagan is wrong about achieving a 4.9% inflation rate in 1986 — and his figure is at least 1.5% below other estimates for that year — then defense spending could balloon much more than he anticipates. For instance, at the 7% inflation rate estimated by the Congressional Budget Office, defense spending in 1986 would total $426.5 billion — a cool $52 billion above Reagan's projection!

The administration argues that it can safely feed large sums of money to defense because the Reagan economic program surely will curb inflation and restore economic health to the economy. The budget cuts eventually are supposed to produce a balanced federal budget, which will signal the nation that inflation is on the wane. Meanwhile, tax reductions supposedly will induce people to save and invest in a more productive, competitive economy, which in turn will produce more tax revenue for government.

The Reagan "supply-side" economic formula is risky at best. However, the bulge in defense spending makes the plan even shakier. If the president is wrong and holds to his Pentagon spending proposals, they not only could wipe out any hope of balancing the budget, but also could cause mushrooming federal deficits that would exacerbate inflation. Instead of a 4.9% inflation rate, the country could see double digits again.

Further, the kind of military spending that Reagan is proposing almost surely would heighten inflationary pressures within the defense sector of the economy. Defense and aerospace industries already face a squeeze on technical talent and production capabilities. Massive outlays for defense also would affect America's competitive position in other industries. If the big money goes to defense, so will the best talent, draining innovation from the other industries that must compete worldwide if the US is to prosper.

As Wisconsin's Rep. Les Aspin put it: "The whole point of the supply-side philosophy is to generate more investment in the civilian sector so we can become more competitive. The defense budget just does the opposite."

It is time for Congress to scrutinize the beast that Reagan proposes to let loose. It is time to vigorously debate the defense spending issue.

Rocky Mountain News
Denver, Colo., May 6, 1981

GIVEN the mood of the country and of Congress, there's little doubt the Reagan administration will get most of what it wants in increased defense spending — at least initially.

The president has proposed boosting defense outlays by about 25 percent in fiscal 1982, up to $222 billion, and spending a total of $1.5 trillion in the five fiscal years ending in 1986.

Most Americans would agree, we believe, that if that's what it will take to bring the nation's military strength up to the point it should be, then that's what will have to be spent. But the key word is "if."

It is interesting that so-called "hard-liners" in Congress are as concerned, perhaps even more concerned, about the "if" as liberals are. This includes even Sen. John Stennis, D-Miss., former chairman and now ranking minority member of the Senate Armed Services Committee and perennial advocate of increased defense spending.

Stennis says he told Defense Secretary Caspar Weinberger "that you're going to get you money this year. The years you've got to worry about are the following years, because if it's not handled well, there'll be a backlash."

Another member of the commitee, Sen. Carl Levin, D-Mich., also warns of a public revolt against defense spending unless Congress demonstrates that it is cutting the fat out of the Pentagon's budget and using the money for muscle.

The people see an effort being made to eliminate waste and fat in domestic programs, he says, "but they don't see the same effort being made in the defense budget."

We have the uneasy perception that the Reagan administration is much too willing to shovel gobs of money onto the Pentagon in the faith that it will all be spent wisely and well. This is the same approach to social problems that has so discredited the liberals.

Thus it is highly encouraging that some of the Pentagon's best friends in Congress are demanding that the military prove its need for its responsible use of all those forthcoming billions.

Rockford Register Star
Rockford, Ill., May 19, 1981

Most Americans agree that there is a need to modernize and expand U.S. defense capability in some areas. Updating of tactical forces to meet small-scale emergency situations, for example, has almost universal support.

But there is less than general agreement on the need to give the Pentagon everything it wants — an MX missile system, a B-1 bomber, a large standing army, a fleet of World War II battleships which were terribly vulnerable 38 years ago, for examples. Rep. Les Aspin, D-Wis., is among those who doubt the need to give the generals and admirals everything on their wish lists.

Aspin suggests that many of the most expensive Pentagon requests would be of no real value — a fact many generals and admirals admit — and that their cost would be too high.

He questions the need for proposals to increase military spending from $162 billion this year to $343 billion by 1986 and wonders if some of those dollars couldn't accomplish more to assure the security of this country if they went instead into strengthening the U.S. economy.

To support his case, Aspin uses the projected $226 billion military budget for 1983 and points out that if the money were used instead for peaceful purposes it could:

—Convert power plants from oil to coal at a saving of 350,000 barrels of oil a day.

—Modernize the U.S. steel industry so it could once again compete on the world market.

—Rebuild much of the nation's deteriorated highway and rail network.

—Retool the nation's auto industry so it could produce small, fuel-efficient cars at a cost competitive on the world market.

Aspin thus reminds Americans of something most have forgotten: In the 20th Century, our national security always has been founded on a strong economy and the world's greatest industrial production capacity.

If that economy and that world leadership in production capacity are lost, no number of Pentagon tanks, airplanes, battleships or bullets will stop a major enemy war machine.

Houston Chronicle
Houston, Texas, May 18, 1981

The U.S. Senate voted overwhelmingly last week for a record $136.5 billion military spending bill, but tacked on some qualifications in the process. The size of the appropriation and the nature of the amendments are significant.

The funds are only part of the administration's defense budget request for fiscal 1982, which totals $222 billion. That amount of spending is required to begin the process of restoring this nation's defense capability, which was allowed to slip dangerously under the previous administration. The size of the Senate vote, 93-1, indicates that the necessity for a stronger defense posture has been recognized.

Another point made by the senators is that Congress is going to expect more bang for the buck. The Senate amended the appropriation bill to call for public reports on cost overruns of more than 15 percent on research and development contracts and 10 percent on procurement contracts. It also restricted the granting of contracts of more than $500,000 without competitive bidding. And it voted an amendment designed to bar dealings with firms which have a history of poor performance.

Defense Department officials will say that such restrictions are not needed, that their contracts are open books and that their decisions are made on the basis of what is best for the country. Granting that all of this is true, there are enough problems in defense procurement to rate a second look and full disclosure. Recent congressional hearings, for instance, revealed U.S. submarine production difficulties, with work on one giant Trident submarine running almost three years behind schedule.

The affirmative Senate vote is but the first of many that will be needed over many years in both houses of Congress to insure that our defenses are adequate. A one-year burst of spending won't do the job. An increase in funds voted by Congress now will not put badly needed equipment in the hands of supply sergeants for months. Major items, such as ships and bombers, will not be operational for years. A sustained effort to match the unprecedented military buildup of the Soviet Union is essential.

THE ATLANTA CONSTITUTION
Atlanta, Ga., May 14, 1981

The people of the United States — a substantial majority of them in any case — are currently in a mood to accept and support big increases in military spending. What more certain sign of this could one want than the 92-1 Senate vote last Thursday approving a record military budget of $136.5 billion for the fiscal year beginning Oct. 1?

The one negative vote was cast by Sen. Mark Hatfield, R-Ore., who said the huge boost in military spending — approximately $30 billion more than President Carter had requested before leaving office in January — made "meaningless" the severe budget cuts proposed in non-military government spending. But the overriding support for the increased military spending was made abundantly clear in that such frequent and strong critics of military spending as Sens. Ted Kennedy, Howard M. Metzenbaum, Paul F. Tsongas and Paul S. Sarbanes, all liberal Democrats, voted for the military budget.

Let's be very careful, however, and not let this great surge for military spending be wasted. In the flush of such a tremendous Senate victory (with strong support also expected this week from the House), the Reagan administration and the Pentagon could "blow" their opportunity to strengthen America's military forces in the way they need to be.

Let's be certain that we don't have any more terrible examples of military boondoggles and new-weapons cost overruns of many billions of dollars — the kind we have had far too many of in past years, the kind that soured so many Americans on military spending, especially when the need for government spending on social needs, health needs, employment needs and other "human needs" were so great. Even now, there are charges that current programs building nuclear submarines are costing far more than projected.

So, Georgia Sen. Sam Nunn was dead-center on target with this concern when he offered an amendment, adopted without dissent, to the military budget that would give Congress a greater role in overseeing military programs that exceed their budgeted costs. The provision would require "a report to Congress on these programs that experience substantial cost overruns and mandates an accompanying defense plan for correction." If the reports are not submitted, further spending on the weapon system would be prohibited.

The increased military budget is needed. It's clear that military weakness on our part invites aggression and "pushing" and "adventurism" by the Russians. That has been clearly demonstrated to Americans in the past year or so — Afghanistan, for example, and there's plenty of Soviet activities and influence in Africa, the Caribbean and Central America. But let's spend our military dollars with very tight fists and let's be very tough with military agencies and military contractors who aren't similarly tight-fisted — or the public support for such spending will once again disappear, and without that support the spending would soon decline. And America would continue to grow weaker.

The Salt Lake Tribune

Salt Lake City, Utah, May 16, 1981

It is distressing to see a program one favors in principle being railroaded through a pliable Congress and expanded beyond reason as a result.

The reference is to the $136.5 billion military authorization bill which sailed through the Senate Thursday with but one dissenting vote.

A certain amount of military muscle building seems justified by present world tensions. And, things being what they are, even modest overreaction to a perceived national security threat can be accommodated. But there is good reason to believe, and we suspect many Americans feel it in their bones, that the all-out, no-holds-barred military,

spending of the gung-ho Reagan administration is at best a sure-fire formula for mammoth waste and probably worse than that.

Since President Reagan won election partly because he promised to restore this country's once unchallenged military supremacy, he can hardly be faulted for losing no time in getting to work at that all but impossible task. But we are unconvinced the country can afford the Reagan arms buildup at this inflation-buffeted time. And even if money was no object, the Reagan "buy everything the generals want" attitude is not in the best interest of defense or anything else. Even so, it is not primarily with Mr. Reagan that we take umbrage.

It is the roll over and play dead

Congress that must bear most of the blame if the worst fears of defense spending critics come true. In the Senate vote Friday, even longstanding military spending moderates such as Sen. Edward M. Kennedy, D-Mass., Sen. Howard M. Metzenbaum, D-Ohio; Sen. Paul S. Sarbanes, D-Md., and others voted in favor. And the vote was preceded by only two days of so-so debate in which few serious challenges were raised.

No doubt these senators and others felt resistance was useless in view of the president's obvious support. But hard questions should have been asked and answers given. The urgent need for all those billions of dollars in military spending is far from clear to the people at large. And enough defense experts have pronounced Reagan defense spending plans excessive to require detailed explanation to the contrary. But the Senate didn't inquire and there is not much hope the House will do any better.

As noted, we believe a strengthening of this country's military capacity is called for in light of new international challenges. We find it difficult to accept, however, the Reagan premise that President Carter's relatively modest military spending increases were so far off the mark as to require the added billions called for by his successor. After all, Mr. Carter, who approved the multi-billion dollar MX development and laid elaborate plans for a rapid deployment force, was not exactly a military spending Scrooge.

The Des Moines Register

Des Moines, Iowa, May 21, 1981

The Senate last week took a major step toward launching the largest peacetime military buildup in American history when it rubber-stamped a $136.5 billion military shopping list.

The bill is the largest chunk of the $226 billion that President Reagan wants Congress to spend on the military in the coming year. It includes $73 billion for developing and buying new weapons and $63 billion for operating and maintaining the armed forces.

It authorizes projects — such as the MX nuclear missile, development of a long-range bomber to replace the B-52 and a major expansion of the Navy — that will have a direct bearing on the U.S. role in the world for years to come.

The Senate Armed Services Committee said it expects the administration to boost military spending as needed to keep pace with inflation. The Congressional Budget Office calculates that inflation could add $6.4 billion to the military budget next year alone. By some estimates, the administration's five-year figures may be $150 billion below actual costs.

Congress, therefore, may be forced to make even deeper cuts in social spending in order to offset the inflationary increases in military spending.

The Senate, however, was in no mood to consider such serious questions. It approved the $136.5 billion military shopping list by a

vote of 92-1, the kind of margin usually reserved for Mother's Day resolutions. Senator Mark Hatfield (Rep., Ore.) cast the lone negative vote. The tenor of the Senate "debate" was illustrated by the rejection of two amendments offered by Senator Carl Levin (Dem., Mich.).

The first would have required direct approval by Congress of the administration's plans for basing the MX missile, a highly controversial question, before the program could get under way. The bill reported by the Armed Services Committee lets the administration go ahead with a basing plan without prior approval, although Congress will be allowed to vote it down. Although the Levin amendment was no more than common sense, the Senate voted 59-39 to kill it, with both of Iowa's senators voting with the majority.

The second Levin amendment would have cut $200 million in obvious fat, as recommended by the General Accounting Office and supported by the National Taxpayers Union. The Senate rejected this saving by 66-29. Apparently, in the Senate's present uncritical mood, what the Pentagon wants, the Pentagon gets.

The Senate could have supported an increase in military spending without abandoning its duty to critically examine the budget. A tough-minded evaluation could have led to a stronger and more effective military.

TULSA WORLD

Tulsa, Okla., May 18, 1981

LAST DECEMBER, the Defense Department made its quarterly review of prices it expects to pay for weapons and found that the total increase was $46.2 billion.

Give or take a billion dollars or so, that just happens to be the amount of money President Reagan hopes to cut from the new budget he inherited from President Carter.

In other words, the latest round of price increases for weapons alone will neatly offset the entire saving Reagan plans to achieve in non-military programs next year.

What this tells us is that any serious move to turn the Federal spending picture around must sooner or later touch the Pentagon.

This does not mean that weapons purchases need be drastically cut. Indeed, many management experts believe the military services could actually buy more weapons for the same money they are now spending if they could improve their purchasing methods.

In other words, the need is not to cut back on defense, but to cut back on waste. Partly due to the

Army's awkward contracting system, the cost of the XM-1 tank has gone up so dramatically the Army has been forced to reduce its order by 20 machines and is negotiating to cut the contract by an additional 45.

Since defense is second only to income security programs in total Government expenditures, any effort to save money elsewhere without staunching the fiscal hemmorhage at the Pentagon is bound to be disappointing. Yet neither the Administration nor Congress seems greatly alarmed. The Senate Thursday passed the first big part of a $222.2 billion defense spending program with very little debate and no demands for serious reforms.

This is not a liberal-conservative issue. One of the most persuasive voices for improving military purchasing and manpower programs is the Heritage Foundation, a conservative think tank which has great clout in the Reagan Administration. Perhaps the Foundation's proposals for modernizing military organization and business management practices will soon get some attention.

Minneapolis Star and Tribune
Minneapolis, Minn., June 21, 1981

An overdue debate has begun about the negative effects of a massive defense build-up. Most discussion so far has focused on finances. Rapidly expanding military budgets may cause uncontrollable economic damage. The damage would show up in unbalanced budgets, high-cost federal borrowing and postponed tax cuts. It would also entail an unproductive skewing of economic choices. Skilled workers making missiles and submarines cannot build new housing or drill for oil. Scientists and engineers designing neutron bombs cannot design office machines and cars. Nor can what the Pentagon must buy raise the level of civilian goods and services or keep the nation competitive in world trade.

The stronger the emphasis on rearmament, in short, the weaker will be progress against inflation or toward a revived economy. Thus, for economic reasons alone, militarizing America on the scale Reagan proposes — Pentagon budgets growing almost 10 percent annually, after inflation, through 1986 — is a dubious enterprise. But such massive spending raises questions that go beyond economics. Even if the country could readily afford the military growth, citizens would have to ask whether that sort of investment supports or contradicts American ideals. To us it looks like a deep contradiction. And the contradiction is all the more striking for being at odds with cherished elements in President Reagan's own political philosophy.

Reagan, for example, is tireless in his conviction that government should curb its intrusions in the private sector. But beefing up the government's world military power maximizes such intrusions, rather than making them less. Production and markets must be shaped to military ends that business and consumers would not choose by themselves. Indeed, nowhere is the line more blurred between private enterprise and government control than in industries that depend on congressional spending and Pentagon contracts. Their number will increase as the war machine grows. But the strength and resilience of the private sector will shrink.

Reagan also believes strongly that government should be scaled close to the people, its powers dispersed and subject to local scrutiny. That ideal does not fit comfortably with an emphasis on global military might. A gargantuan government defense establishment — whether protecting the Persian Gulf or proposing MX missiles for Utah and Nevada — embodies power in a uniquely distant way. It is centralized, secretive, inaccessible and unelected. However necessary in a military machine, these are not the features, and do not promote the habits, of democratic self-governance.

Just there is the dilemma. To defend U.S. democracy by asserting armed power around the world detracts from the strength of democracy at home. The objections Reagan raises to the welfare state — that it saps enterprise, breeds dependence, weakens local government — can be doubly directed at the warfare state. Yet the Reagan administration wants warfare budgets that make even the most extravagant welfare spending look cheap by comparison.

In the absence of a demonstrated national-security emergency, such budgets should not be uncritically granted. Militarizing America is not the way to make America strong.

ST. LOUIS POST-DISPATCH
St. Louis, Mo., July 24, 1981

The House passage of the 1982 Defense Authorization Bill clearly shows that President Reagan's rearmament drive is moving at full-speed. The bill authorizes more than $136 billion for new weapons and operations. When military pay and construction costs are added, the total 1982 Pentagon budget will be above $220 billion. Even this incredible sum may not be enough.

The Pentagon has issued a new report on procurement which has raised the cost estimates for 37 of the top 47 weapons systems by $4.3 billion over last year's report. This massive increase is above inflation rates and has not yet been added to the administration's $1.46 trillion five-year defense budget plans. According to a *Washington Post* report, procurement cost increases and other unanticipated bills could add as much as $10 billion to the Pentagon's 1982 budget alone.

Even while these cost growths are eating away the administration's budget plans, Defense Secretary Caspar Weinberger is planning even greater military spending. In order to support the Reagan administration's plans for fighting a possible long-term, conventional war with the Soviet Union, Mr. Weinberger wants to establish a prepared industrial base that would allow U.S. defense industries, in the event of a crisis, to absorb upwards of half of the U.S. GNP — or about *$1.5 trillion* — in a single year.

What Secretary Weinberger is suggesting would require spending tens — if not hundreds — of billions of additional dollars for stockpiling strategic materials, modernizing weapons plants and maintaining full-scale production lines, all in the name of a questionable military strategy.

The Reagan administration's runaway rearmament plans may or may not threaten the Soviet Union, but they are certainly threatening the U.S. treasury.

THE TENNESSEAN
Nashville, Tenn., June 14, 1981

A ray of fiscal sanity may be emerging within the Reagan administration on plans for a massive military buildup from 1982 through 1986 — a plan that would cost $1.488 trillion dollars.

According to White House sources, efforts are being undertaken within the top levels of the administration to slice as much as $10 billion in 1983 and another $10 billion in 1984 from the military spending plan.

President Reagan is committed to increased weapons development. But he has also pledged to balance the budget by 1984. As many economists have noted, it will be difficult, if not impossible, to eliminate budget deficits without trimming the defense plan.

Defense Secretary Caspar Weinberger almost surely will resist attempts to reduce the Pentagon budget. But budget director David Stockman is expected to take the lead in pushing for savings. There will be some fireworks.

There have been serious questions all along whether a defense department buildup of the size first contemplated by the administration is possible within a relatively short time. The first problem is that of skyrocketing costs. The second is of production facilities.

Quarterly reports issued by the defense department on cost changes showed at the end of last year a $47.6 billion increase in the price of 47 weapons systems. The Air Force has just informed the administration that a modified version of the B1 bomber will cost more than $200 million per airplane, twice the cost of the B1 when it was cancelled by President Carter.

In the one year period from March 1980 to March 1981, the cost of the ground launched cruise missile increased 54% and the F18 jet fighter had a 21% hike. So, the unit costs of the various weapons systems are increasing at rates far beyond that of inflation.

Even if it were possible to spend the money on a veritable wish list of missiles, airplanes and ships, the question is whether production facilities around the nation can be expanded to produce the quantities that are wanted.

Literally billions will have to be invested in plant additions, retooling and training. Over a relatively short period of time that would be an enormously expensive undertaking.

There is the ultimate question whether, if the money were available, the defense department and the defense industry could absorb large amounts of new money in a practical way. The defense department, as profligate as it is, often cannot spend the money it has on hand. At the close of the last fisal year, it had more than $90 billion in unspent balances — money appropriated, but not actually spent.

Mr. Reagan cannot have his defense cake and a balanced budget at the same time unless the American economy is turned around and begins performing in ways that the most optimistic of economists do not foresee.

The hard choices, then, for the administration will be that of lowering its defense budget sights and making the necessary cuts in spending. And these may by necessity be more than $10 billion a year for two years. That, in turn, will require some hard priorities in terms of need for weapons systems.

But before it spends some $600 for each and every person in the United States, the administration is going to have to decide what it needs worst and what it can do without in terms of national defense.

THE CHRISTIAN SCIENCE MONITOR

Boston, Mass., July 13, 1981

Few quarrel with President Reagan's determined efforts to balance the federal budget. Few quarrel with the President's desire to strengthen the nation's military posture. But it is hard to see how these objectives can be reconciled until the administration tackles defense spending with the same eye to cost-saving as it has applied to social programs. It does not appear to have done so thus far — but realities may soon jolt it in this direction.

From the Pentagon comes news that the military budget for fiscal 1983 will probably run $2 billion to $10 billion more than estimated. Deputy Defense Secretary Frank Carlucci told the Washington Post that to accommodate expected cost increases in the next few years will require raising the military budget by 9 percent after inflation instead of 7 percent as planned. Even a 7 percent real growth, it seems, would not be enough to obtain everything the President wants — a new bomber, higher military pay, more ships. Needless to add, raising the military budget even beyond its present high levels imperils the goal of balancing the budget, a point Mr. Carlucci made.

Voices that have been warning the Reagan administration about underestimating defense costs have proven to be right. In recent committee hearings Sen. Mark Hatfield disclosed that the Pentagon had raised the cost estimates for 37 of its 47 major weapons systems by more than $4 billion in a single budget year. To name but a few items: the Army's Patriot missile increased by $285 million, the Navy's F-18 fighter by $607 million, and the Air Force's F-16 by $172 million.

"We are spending more and more dollars to buy less and less," said Senator Hatfield.

The answer obviously lies in more efficient defense spending — choosing carefully what weapons are to be purchased (the most sophisticated, for instance, are not necessarily the best in war conditions), improving procurement practices, riding herd on defense industries to stay within cost estimates. Even many conservative economists believe the administration needs to slow down its military planning and take stock before plunging the nation into an unrestrained arms buildup. They note that, although there is slack in the economy at the moment, it will be running closer to capacity in the years ahead and that competition for manpower, supplies, and manufacturing capacity could push up costs and prices — undermining the effort to revitalize American industry.

This is no argument for short-changing defense. Certainly the American people are prepared to pay whatever cost is required to maintain an adequate military force. But they are skeptical of simply letting the competing services run rampant with their shopping lists and they strongly support arms negotiations with the Soviet Union as a means not only of safeguarding world peace but of keeping costs within reason.

Interestingly, this was the view, too, of a former US president whose life historians are closely scrutinizing these days — Dwight Eisenhower. Not unlike President Reagan, Ike insisted on holding down budget deficits, but he accomplished this in part by preventing runaway defense spending. He warned of the "military-industrial complex" and of the impact on the economy of an arms race with the Russians. "Someday," he wrote, "there is going to be a man sitting in my present chair who has not been raised in the military services and who will have little understanding of where slashes in their estimates can be made with little or no damage. If that should happen while we still have the state of tension that now exists in the world, I shudder to think of what could happen in this country."

Presidential parallels can only be drawn so far, perhaps. But given the era of both peace and prosperity which the United States enjoyed during the Eisenhower years, it might serve President Reagan well to study these words from a predecessor of good Republican credentials. If Mr. Reagan wants a dynamic, vigorous economy he, like Ike, will have to make sure the US does not put intolerable strains on its economy by producing too many arms.

THE ATLANTA CONSTITUTION

Atlanta, Ga., July 20, 1981

It's official, the United States is about to embark upon the costliest military spending in its history. During 1982, America will spend somewhere in the neighborhood of $136 billion to increase her military might in just about very area of defense imaginable. OK, it's good to be militarily prepared, but the Reagan administration should not be given carte blanche privileges by Congress.

For years, the Department of Defense by far has been the most wasteful government agency. Reagan should voluntarily step forward and apply the same stated standards for defense spending as he has used in cutting the federal budget for other departments.

One measure to do this was defeated by the House before approving the record defense budget measure, which is similar to one already passed by the Senate. The amendment offered by Rep. Pat Schroeder, D-Colo., would have forced the president to scrutinize the defense budget and eliminate $8 billion in waste and fraud. Reagan would have been ordered to send Congress a list of savings by Jan. 15 outlining the areas of savings in the budget. Mrs. Schroeder made some good points that are worth repeating.

"The president's war on waste, fraud, abuse and mismanagement has, up until now, been limited almost entirely to domestic social programs," she said. "That war cannot be won unless we allow our army of auditors to cross the Potomac and establish a beachhead at the Pentagon." Mrs. Schroeder is certainly on target.

The administration is setting itself up for stiff opposition by groups who will continue to oppose Reagan's cutbacks in social programs and redirection of those funds to defense spending. It will be difficult to sincerely convince opponents that he is doing the "right" thing when, in effect, his supporting the total defense budget is actually condoning waste, fraud and mismanagement. Opponents will see the move in that light.

In an effort to do nothing about what's wrong with the budget, the House did approve a weak substitute amendment that will require the president to make recommendations for savings, but without any target amount. That's like saying do what you can, but don't worry about it.

The budget for all defense spending for 1982 is expected to be around $220 billion That's an hefty sum to spend on defense when it will actually do little to stimulate a stale economy or provide additional jobs. Such a budget makes little sense to the average American. But consider that the production of combat planes for the Navy and Marine Corps will cost $34.1 million apiece; $1.9 billion for continued work on a new manned bomber; and more than $600 million to reactivate various battleships and carriers. With those astronomical figures, it does not take long to use up a few hundred billion dollars.

Unless the administration addresses the big three in the defense budget — waste, fraud and mismanagement — it will be a budget for the skeptics to attack with good reasons.

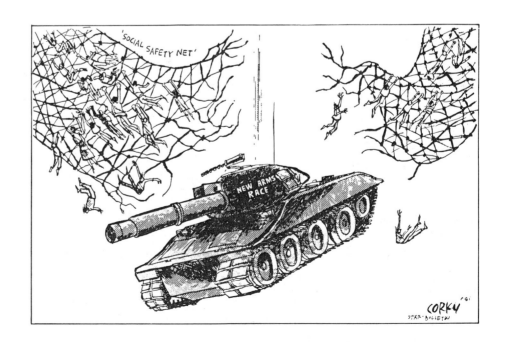

Cuts in Military Spending Announced to Offset Budget Deficit

The Reagan Administration, concerned by persistent warnings that the federal budget deficit for fiscal 1982 would far exceed forecasts, cast about during the summer of 1981 for ways to cut government spending. (A larger deficit meant more government borrowing, which meant higher interest rates, which would erode business confidence in the President's economic recovery program.) Murray Weidenbaum, chairman of the President's Council of Economic Advisers, asserted Aug. 30 that "no part of the budget should be sacrosanct" in considering further budget cuts. President Reagan Sept. 12 called for a reduction in projected military outlays of $13 billion over the next three years. Under Reagan's plan the defense budget for the 1982 fiscal year, which began Oct. 1, 1981, would be decreased by $2 billion; the remaining $11 billion in cuts would come in 1983 and 1984. This decrease represented only 2% of the $652 billion in planned military spending for the three years. The announced cuts were far less than White House budget Director David Stockman and other top White House advisers, in a fierce Administration battle, had represented as necessary to achieve Reagan's goal of a balanced budget by 1984; the outcome represented a victory for Defense Secretary Caspar Weinberger.

Los Angeles Times
Los Angeles, Calif., August 30, 1981

Economists, politicians and a lot of plain folk have been puzzled all along as to how President Reagan could possibly meet all three of his fundamental budget goals: Cut taxes, increase military spending by 7% a year after adjustment for inflation, and still balance the budget by 1984.

It turns out that there is no rabbit in the hat. Important as the refurbishing of American military power is, the money simply will not be available to move as rapidly as the Administration had hoped.

For days, Budget Director David A. Stockman has been making the case that budget deficits for fiscal 1982 and beyond now threaten to be much larger than anticipated. As a result, he says, additional spending cuts must be made if there is to be any realistic prospect of the lower interest rates that are essential to the success of Reagan's economic program.

The President apparently is ready to concede that, considering the large reductions that have already been made in domestic spending programs, the defense budget can no longer remain immune. White House spokesmen have taken to describing the 7% figure for increased defense spending as a "target" rather than as a hard-and-fast commitment.

Last week's visit to the ranch by Stockman and Defense Secretary Caspar W. Weinberger was part of an effort to determine just how much fudging is required.

There is little disagreement among defense analysts that a U.S. military buildup is indeed necessary. The Soviet Union has been outspending the United States for the past decade, with disturbing effects on the military balance of power.

Russia's strategic nuclear forces are numerically superior to ours, and are rapidly closing the gap in such qualitative measures as missile warhead accuracy. Years of tight budgets and questionable Pentagon management have left U.S. conventional forces outnumbered and outgunned in a number of important respects.

The Navy is spread far too thin. The Army, because of its long orientation toward the defense of Europe, is ill-equipped for desert warfare. The Air Force lacks sufficient airlift capability for quick movement of substantial forces. All the services have inadequate inventories of ammunition and spare parts, and all suffer from shortages of the trained manpower needed to operate and maintain highly complex equipment.

President Carter, in response to the invasion of Afghanistan and the growing threat to the oil-rich Persian Gulf region, began a program of rearmament. But Ronald Reagan entered the White House with a greater sense of urgency—a sense of urgency that is widely shared in Congress and the country.

The military budgets for fiscal 1981 and 1982 have basically been enlarged versions of those inherited from Carter. But Weinberger's five-year plan is more ambitious. If carried out in full, defense spending authorization would rise from $176 billion this year and $222 billion next year to $373 billion in fiscal 1986.

This would include a $200-billion package of steps to improve the nation's strategic nuclear deterrent. It would also include a one-third increase in the size of the Navy and substantial improvements in the nation's airlift and sealift capabilities.

Purely in terms of the burden on the taxpayer, the full Reagan defense program would not be unacceptably heavy. It would constitute 7% of the gross national product and a quarter of the federal budget—well under the figures that prevailed through the 1950s and 1960s.

Unfortunately, things are not that simple.

Thanks to the defense management mistakes of past Administrations, the defense industry might not be able to digest the new orders without delayed deliveries and inflated prices.

Even more to the point, the looming budget deficits constitute a genuine threat to the national security in themselves; if high interest rates are prolonged, the accompanying recession will shrink tax revenues and make even larger cuts in the defense budget necessary.

The military budget is so complex that knowing where to cut is a challenging, even overpowering, task. But certain general observations are in order:

—To the degree that the choice must be made, it is more important to beef up this country's conventional, non-nuclear forces than to carry out the full program of improving the nuclear deterrent.

—Within the conventional forces, it is more important to rebuild depleted inventories of ammunition and equipment, to sharpen maintenance capabilities and to hang onto trained manpower than it is to buy this or that weapons system.

—Weinberger should listen a little harder to the minority voices within each service that argue against "goldplating" weapons with unnecessarily complex and fragile technology.

The first priority should be lean, tough combat forces that are ready to roll in fact as well as on paper.

The Pittsburgh Press
Pittsburgh, Pa., September 9, 1981

It didn't take the military long to join the game being played by some of the mayors and governors around the country.

The game is known as "crying wolf," and the scenario is starkly familiar:

Taxes rise to the point where citizens rebel and demand budget cuts.

"All right," the citizens are told, "if you won't provide the money, we'll have to lay off policemen and firemen and cut back on aid to the mentally retarded. And maybe even eliminate high-school football."

The idea, of course, is to pick out what's most popular or most essential — not what's merely desirable — and mourn its imminent demise. For by crying wolf in this manner the officials often buffalo the people into ponying up the additional money the taxpayers would rather save.

★ ★ ★

Thus, the Pentagon now is warning that if President Reagan cuts a total of $30 billion from the fiscal 1983 and 1984 defense budgets, our military power will disappear and we'll all have to learn to speak Russian.

The plain truth is that Mr. Reagan has to find ways to get waste out of the defense budget, which is slated to rise to an enormous $226 billion next year.

Many other programs — from food stamps and school lunches to welfare — are being put through the wringer. If the Pentagon turns out to be sacrosanct it will turn into bad public policy and guarantee that Mr. Reagan won't achieve his goal of balancing the budget in 1984.

★ ★ ★

From Defense Secretary Caspar Weinberger on down, the military is saying that budget cuts would mean bringing back an Army division from Europe and deactivating it, mothballing aircraft carriers and grounding the B-52 bomber.

In effect, the Pentagon is saying: Touch our budget and we'll jettison the muscle and keep the fat, and you'll be sorry.

Mr. Reagan should call the Pentagon's bluff, and at the same time salvage his economic program.

As a starter, he could save $100 billion by cancelling the MX missile, especially since nobody knows where to base it.

He could close military bases that are kept open only to waste money and keep congressmen happy.

And he could retire redundant generals and admirals (probably as many as one out of every three) without damaging America's military muscle. Indeed, there would then be room to walk in the Pentagon corridors, and fewer brass hats to dream up horror stories about budget cuts.

The Washington Post
Times Herald

Washington, D.C., August 6, 1981

SEN. PETE DOMENICI, chairman of the Senate's Budget Committee, delivered a gentle but unambiguous caution the other day to the Pentagon. There's going to be a large increase in real defense spending, he said. But it probably won't be as large as the figures currently projected for the years ahead in the budget documents.

If the budget is to move toward balance, further rounds of severe cuts in spending will be required. In that process, Mr. Domenici observed, very little if anything is going to be sacred, and the military budget is going to get the same scrutiny as all the rest. Some procurement schedules, and the introduction of new defense systems, may have to be spread out over longer periods than the Defense Department currently expects.

The defense estimates in President Reagan's budget, particularly for the years after 1982, were not calculated from specific program requirements. They were calculated, in great haste, by a very new administration, as signals to indicate a degree of urgency and a general intention. Many people agree that defense spending had fallen to a point by the middle 1970s that required an accelerated rate of rebuilding. But there are also limits to the speed at which money can be spent efficiently.

Government spending responds to the unpredictable movements of the national economy, and budgeting is necessarily a constant process of revision. Political debate gives an artificial and misleading air of precision to a budget, as partisans insist on their own forecasts and write specific numbers into law. Mr. Domenici was making the valuable point—especially valuable, in this year of extraordinary budget debate —that all of these estimates and projections have to be used with the knowledge that reality can rapidly seize and bend them. A budget sets policy, but it can't promise to control the future. With massive strains already becoming apparent in the next several years' budgeting, it seems pretty clear that not all of the defense figures can be fitted in.

What will constitute success for the Reagan budgets? As the inevitable question goes, is the strategy going to work? The economic indicators would not have to follow the projections precisely, to persuade people that the administration's budget program is having a healthy effect. The Reagan plan promises very high economic growth rates beginning next year. Suppose that the growth rate is only half that high, but that unemployment declines and both inflation and interest fall sharply lower. Wouldn't most people accept that as success? The test for defense will be similar. Except perhaps for defense contractors, few will greatly care whether military spending touches a certain published figure on the last day of fiscal year 1984. The real question will be whether the administration can show that it has built a defense capability stronger and more reliable than today's.

Washington, D.C., September 3, 1981

AMERICAN PRESIDENTS detest changing their minds in public. But, awkward though the exercise might be, it's preferable to sticking with a bad position. The financial markets are now assisting Mr. Reagan in his decision to review defense spending. They find Mr. Reagan's forecasts of the budget deficits to be unrealistic as long as the administration holds to its past projections of defense spending and Social Security.

The administration apparently intends to launch a Social Security bill soon after Congress reconvenes next week. Now the White House says that defense outlays are going to have to be scaled down as well. The figures are not precise, but they establish a general order of magnitude.

The changes announced this week won't make much difference in spending during 1982. The defense budget runs with tremendous momentum, and substantial changes can be imposed only over a period of several years. The Reagan defense budget for 1982 is larger by only a small margin—about 2 percent—than the figure that President Carter proposed last winter just before leaving office. For the immediate future, Mr. Reagan's willingness to cut back on defense is important chiefly as a conciliatory gesture toward those senators, Republican as well as Democratic, who are uneasy about last spring's extraordinarily high estimates. The cooperation of those senators is going to be essential to the administration this fall in getting other kinds of spending cuts—in Social Security, among other things—that have earlier effects.

For the fiscal year 1984, the White House is evidently now proposing a level of defense spending that is almost exactly the same as that in the Carter budget last January. The original Reagan program in March called for an annual increase in defense spending, throughout his term, of about 8 percent a year in real terms—that is, after inflation. He is now evidently proposing to bring that rate of increase down to about 6 percent, the track that the Carter administration was on.

No doubt some of the Democrats will charge him with copyright infringement, while some of the military—and, especially, military contractors—will cry betrayal. But there's a sense of reality to the revised Reagan numbers that the earlier ones lacked. In view of the Carter budget, they can also claim to be based on a broad bipartisan consensus—not necessarily a bad thing in national defense.

The White House is inclined to blame this revision on poor performance by the American economy. That is one accusation the economy does not have to bear. The original Reagan budget was based on economic forecasts that were far too optimistic, and everybody knew it. If anything, the behavior of the economy is currently more satisfactory than most people expected six months ago. Who, for example, thought then that unemployment would fall this summer? The arithmetic showed from the beginning that there was not room for both Mr. Reagan's tax cut and Mr. Reagan's defense increase. The tax cut has been enacted, and defense spending inevitably must be fitted to it.

American defense policy has repeatedly got into trouble by putting too much emphasis on budget totals, and not nearly enough on how that money will be spent. The Reagan defense figures of last March were worked up in great haste, with no clear sense of program requirements, to indicate a certain direction and intention. The new numbers reflect not only economic necessity but also a clearer judgment of what's actually needed and how fast it can actually be achieved. Military strength depends on not only the number of dollars available but also the wisdom with which they are spent. The dollars will be adequate. Wisdom is always the scarcer commodity.

THE BLADE
*Toledo, Ohio,
September 1, 1981*

PRESIDENT Reagan has demonstrated that he can and will stand fast when it comes to backing his proposals for change in government. But in considering the scaling down of his proposed defense outlays for the next few years, he has shown that he also is willing to trim sail somewhat when that appears to be the thing to do.

There still will be considerable growth in defense spending, but the way his fiscal 1982 budget is shaping up and in view of current economic factors, he is wise to consider some cuts in proposed increases. The problem is that a tentative defense budget of $225 billion for fiscal 1982 might help send the deficit for that year higher than the $45 billion that has been anticipated. And Mr. Reagan is still hoping to come close to balancing the federal budget by 1984.

With the drastic cuts already being made in various social and other domestic programs and with income-tax reductions already authorized for the next three years, there clearly will have to be some limit to the increases in defense spending that can be funded. So the President and his staff are going over their options with an eye to bringing outlays to something less than the 7 per cent increase, after inflation, that was being contemplated.

As the elements of the Administration's so-called supply-side economics are rapidly being put in place, Defense Secretary Weinberger made the pertinent point that a strong economic base is necessary to serve as a stable foundation for a strong defense establishment — and part of that base is a federal budget in closer balance. Or, as the Economist put in in its most recent issue, the termites of economic failure can destroy the foundations of political power. And political power, of course, is essential to any credible national defense.

Also, limiting increases in the defense budget by judicious trimming is likely to make the President's cuts in domestic programs more palatable. In that way Americans could end up with more butter — in the form of a stronger economy — along with more guns.

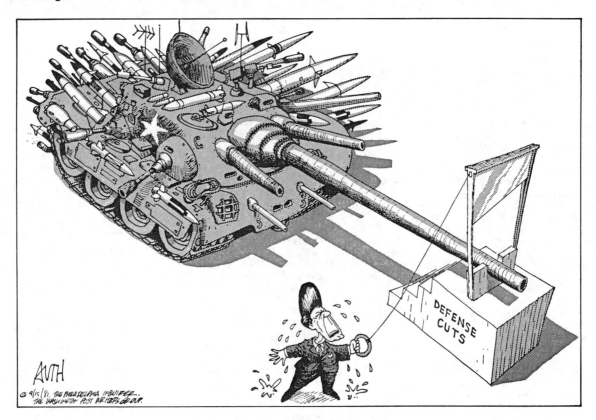

The Charlotte Observer
Charlotte, N.C., September 4, 1981

The Reagan administration apparently has decided it will have to moderate its defense spending goals to have any hope of reaching its economic goals. Even as we applaud that decision, we should remember that Mr. Reagan is a magician of sorts, an illusionist who draws our vision to what he wants us to see, creates the perspective in which he wants us to see it, while the sleight of hand goes on outside our view.

That isn't necessarily a criticism. The technique is one of the secrets of his extraordinary effectiveness so far. The president doesn't use it to deceive, but simply to put the best light on what he is doing and disarm those who oppose him. But a certain wariness may be in order.

Mr. Reagan came into office vowing to cut the fiscal 1982 budget by almost $50 billion, then claimed victory when a congressional budget resolution projected cuts of about $35 billion. Those who worried about budget cuts breathed a sigh of relief, having salvaged almost $15 billion.

Similarly, he called for a 30% tax cut spread over the next three years and ended up with something less than that, claiming victory while letting those who feared the impact of deep tax cuts take comfort in having minimized the damage.

Now, having let critics of the defense budget agonize for months over the prospect of giving the Pentagon $1.6 trillion over the next five years, Mr. Reagan, according to aides, is ready to accept cuts of $20 billion to $40 billion in that figure. So the headlines can announce that Mr. Reagan has made a "major concession," and the critics can praise his decision. Suddenly the levels of defense spending that remain after the cuts, amounts that otherwise would appear outrageously large, seem moderate.

And it still isn't clear, of course, exactly what the figures mean. While some aides talk about defense budget cuts as high as $40 billion, others say the administration is sticking to its goal of a annual increase of 7% above inflation. Another says his understanding is that 7% is a "cap," not a commitment. And different aides seem to have different notions about what defense budget figures the 7% would apply to.

While we welcome the news that Mr. Reagan is cutting the defense budget, we ought to remember that when a magician saws a woman in half, she always emerges in one piece.

TULSA WORLD
Tulsa, Okla., September 2, 1981

SHOULD the huge projected increase in defense spending be trimmed to allow President Reagan to attain a balanced budget in 1984?

The indications are the President is about to decide it should, with good reason.

It is true the U. S. needs to bolster its defense spending to make up for years of allowing the military to decline at a time when Soviet Russia has intensified its military buildup.

But the practicalities of the state of the U. S. military contracting industry indicate that no amount of money will quickly bring back the productive capacity that has been allowed to deteriorate over several years.

The evidence is that even if the President decides to reduce the amount of his defense increases by as much as $40 million annually, as suggested, the military-industrial establishment will still be hard-pressed to spend the rest of the money targeted on defense in an orderly, productive way.

Politically, it is clear that if the Administration expects to be able to cut spending on other Government services any more than it has, it must yield on the military spending issue.

Economically, as well as politically, Reagan must deliver on promises to lower inflation and interest rates to spur the kind of economic expansion needed to finally whip those problems.

Already, a big reversal in military spending has been made. The 1981 fiscal year contains a big increase for the military and if substantive cuts are made in 1982, the military budget will still contain a 19 percent increase after inflation is considered.

A change in the direction in military preparedness is badly needed. But that has been achieved and it will serve no real value in sticking with a level of spending that outstrips the ability of the defense establishment to carry it out with efficiency.

The Dallas Morning News
Dallas, Texas, September 4, 1981

THE new catch phrase in Washington is, let's cut defense spending. Or, more properly, let's cut back the huge increase that President Reagan has budgeted for the Pentagon.

The administration notes the stock and bond markets' acute indigestion, which is due to widely advertised fears of larger-than-predicted deficits. Accordingly plans are afoot to scale back military spending.

Given Reagan's commitment to the "rearming of America" one can surmise the cuts will be no greater than necessary.

At that, many defense-spending critics are unlikely to be appeased. Such as MIT's Lester Thurow argue that the more we spend on the military, the less that consumers will have left over to consume. Inevitably the cry goes up from liberals that, so fat is its budget, the Pentagon won't even miss what's taken away.

Siren voices like these must be resisted. Why do Thurow et al suppose we are increasing the military budget — for the fun of it? In fact, America faces two critical situations — one economic, one military. Neither can be neglected.

The root cause of both predicaments is the same: Congress' decision, during the late '60s and most of the '70s, to slight military spending, using the money to fuel a colossal expansion of social programs. At the same time defense programs were being deferred or canceled for lack of money, the government was stoking the inflationary fires by printing money to pay for yet more lavish social programs.

The day of reckoning arrived in 1979-80, when double-digit interest and inflation rates hammered the economy, just as the Soviet Union started to pass us in overall strategic nuclear strength.

Enter Ronald Reagan, striving to fight on two fronts at the same time. And a ticklish job it is. To the President's critics there seems an inherent contradiction in cutting taxes and beefing up military spending. The contradiction is resolved when we reflect that disaster is likelier to overtake us if we don't than if we do tackle both problems at once.

A healthy economy is of the essence, but what good is such an economy if it cannot be adequately defended by the military? Can a 7 percent prime rate fend off Soviet missiles?

America's military needs are many: A replacement for the B52 bomber, development of the Stealth bomber, the MX missile system, however we decide to base it. Besides this, conventional-war stocks are low, military personnel are underpaid, the Navy is in sore need of ships.

Cut if we must the military's budget, but better yet would be to wait for the President's tax and budget cuts to begin rejuvenating the economy. The need for a prosperous — and a safe — America is what we seem to recall the last election's being about.

St. Louis Globe-Democrat
St. Louis, Mo., August 19, 1981

It isn't surprising that budget director director David A. Stockman is reported planning to recommend cuts in defense spending of $20 billion to $40 billion in an effort to help balance the budget by 1984.

The Office of Management of Budget, which Stockman heads, consistently has recommended cuts in defense in the last two decades. Unfortunately, its recommendations too often have been accepted in the past, with the result that defense spending in the last 12 years actually fell by about 35 percent when adjusted for inflation.

But there is a big difference today. President Ronald Reagan is in the White House and he is backed by a much more defense-minded Congress than has been the case in a long time. Reagan has made it clear he wants to spend as much on defense as is required to meet the increasing Soviet military challenge.

Therefore, unless Stockman can demonstrate how cuts can be made without jeopardizing the goals set out for strengthening the nation's conventional and strategic military power, his chances of getting his way are slim.

Stockman in this case appears to be taking the short-range view of defense, failing to consider the fact that it may take five to 10 years of much higher defense spending to make up for all the years that previous administrations were actually cutting back defense.

Much of this increased spending is needed just to meet a whole host of serious shortages of weapons, equipment and ammunition in all of the armed services, including those stationed in Europe. The "bare bones" budgets of more than a decade simply didn't provide enough money to develop many necessary new weapons systems such as the M-1 battlefield tank, new ships, new planes and new strategic weapons systems.

Therefore, to look at the first two Reagan defense budgets as though they can be considered apart from the military needs of the armed forces would be a serious mistake. It would be surprising if Reagan acceded to Stockman's requests.

The Chattanooga Times
Chattanooga, Tenn., September 7, 1981

On the campaign trail last year, candidate Reagan repeatedly pledged to reduce federal spending — except for defense expenditures, which he said should be increased to offset the Soviet threat — and to balance the federal budget. Opponents warned that a collision between those goals was inevitable. The collision occurred last week during a sort of White House "summit" conference on the outlook for future federal budgets.

Central to the Reagan economic recovery plan is a balanced federal budget, which the White House has promised by 1984. But Budget Director David Stockman told the president, in effect, to forget that goal — unless the White House can come up with an additional $75 billion in spending cuts in the next two years. Thus a rhetorical conflict has developed between Mr. Stockman and Defense Secretary Caspar Weinberger, with the latter saying there would be no steep cuts in defense spending and the former asserting he had told Mr. Weinberger the defense budget had to be squeezed. One report this week was that Mr. Reagan is expected to reduce planned defense spending by upwards of $30 billion to avoid jeopardizing his pledge of a balanced budget.

But even that cut leaves $45 billion still be trimmed from the federal budget by fiscal 1984. Moreover, the $150 billion, three-year tax cut is virtually certain to cause higher deficits. Mr. Reagan's aides, for example, have warned that this year's deficit will be considerably higher than the $42.5 billion the administration has projected; perhaps as much as $60 billion.

President Reagan, then, faces some tough decisions. He can ask Congress to slash even deeper into domestic programs for the fiscal 1983 budget he will present in January, reducing expenditures by $30 billion. And he will need to trim another $45 billion in the fiscal 1984 budget. But to do both without requiring the Pentagon to absorb substantial losses will jeopardize the fragile coalition Mr. Reagan has put together in the House.

The key to the dispute is Mr. Reagan's original goal of increasing military appropriations 7 percent a year for five years. At the California meetings with Mr. Reagan, aides changed that concept somewhat: the 7 percent was actually a "cap," not an absolute pledge of minimum increases. More important, Pentagon officials now contend that even if Congress authorizes a 7 percent yearly increase, that does not mean all the money has to be spent in a single year.

One truly ironic aspect of this debate is that the administration's shifts concede, in effect, that the defense budget inherited from President Carter is actually bigger than originally thought. That's quite a switch for those who just a few months ago was describing it as a danger to the nation's security.

To his credit, Mr. Reagan has sincerely tried to keep his campaign promises. But evidence is growing that the goals of drastic defense spending increases and a balanced budget are mutually exclusive. It would be regrettable, but not a national tragedy, if the administration abandoned the goal of a balanced budget — if achieving it dictated even more drastic cuts in domestic spending, such as the politically sensitive Social Security program. Similarly, if he is determined to reduce federal spending, it must be made clear early on that defense is not sacrosanct.

We'd rather see Mr. Reagan sacrifice a couple of campaign slogans rather than the nation's social fabric.

Oregon Journal

Portland, Ore., September 5, 1981

Congress returns to Capitol Hill on Wednesday, and more budget-cutting is anticipated. This time the administration seems ready to concede that it will have to cut defense spending or the federal budget deficit will be out of sight by 1984 and interest rates will be somewhere in the stratosphere.

Defense spending previously has been sacrosanct. President Reagan pledged he would increase defense spending, and he meant it. After inflation, defense spending is supposed to rise a real 7 percent a year.

The last round of budget cutting was so harsh that state governments, welfare and food stamp recipients and benefactors of other social programs don't know yet how much bleeding will be required. When those budget cuts finally are felt, millions of Americans will ache. The crying from the pain hasn't been heard yet.

Something has to give and the logical place to slash is in the military budget. Military personnel have won justifiable pay raises under the Reagan administration. The obvious is to eliminate, maybe defer, major weapons systems.

The MX missile system is a likely candidate. The Reagan administration has been split about how to deploy the new missile, whether to put it in the ground in Utah and Nevada, place it in airplanes or hide it on or under the oceans. Withholding a decision on the MX or delaying another major defense expenditure will cause less suffering than cutting deeper into social programs or Social Security.

ALBUQUERQUE JOURNAL

Albuquerque, N.M., September 5, 1981

Ronald Reagan came to power with solid backing for the improbable triangle of a huge defense buildup, supply-side oriented tax cuts and a balanced budget. Or, starting with a big deficit, he was going to spend more, take in less, and balance the budget.

But the economy, as measured by Wall Street, is not following the script. As interest rates soar and the Dow Jones average plummets, the subject of military cuts has entered the arena for the first time since Reagan took office. And high time, too. The cuts are there; if Reagan is truly committed to a balanced budget, and his aides say he is, he must find them.

Reagan promised that the tax cut approved this summer by Congress would stimulate the economy sufficiently in inflation-free growth to finance his projected $1.6 trillion defense buildup — largest in U.S. history — and still get the budget balanced by the target date of 1984. Now the administration acknowledges much greater budget cuts must be found if that is to happen.

Along with the tax cut, Congress also followed Reagan's lead by authorizing about $35 billion in cuts in social programs, which directly affect millions of lower and middle-income Americans. The Reagan team has now suggested more budget cuts for social programs, this time along with a suggestion that military cuts be found too.

David Stockman, current budget director, has reportedly suggested certain reforms that would cut up to $20 billion annually from defense outlays. That is not much when one considers Reagan plans to spend an average of over $300 billion a year.

The Pentagon is a huge institution. It is foolish to assume there is no waste and over-indulgence in a department that large. Moreover, few allege the U.S. military is weak, only that it could use some strengthening to counter the Soviet military buildup.

As the Reagan team considers overall cuts, its long-range military strengthening strategy will be a top priority. It may find that costly new weapons programs can wait while current readiness (manpower, logistics supply lines, etc.) is given adequate attention. Quantity of weaponry is meaningless without quality people and a quality apparatus to back it up.

With big social cuts already approved, the Defense Department is starting to look like a sacred cow when it comes to budget cuts. Even if Defense loses, say, $30 billion yearly, another $45 billion in social cuts will need to be found.

Reagan is right: those additional social cuts won't be politically palatable unless he can trim the Defense Department, too. And from all appearances, he can.

The Birmingham News

Birmingham, Ala., September 11, 1981

As the administration prepares to weather darkening economic clouds, the apparent decision awaiting President Reagan is not whether to cut back on his proposed increase in defense spending, but by how much — and where.

Following a lengthy session Wednesday with Defense Secretary Caspar Weinberger and budget director David Stockman, the president said he would give himself a week to come to a decision on the problem. Mr. Reagan's stated goal remains to balance the federal budget by 1984 while maintaining a 7 percent real growth in defense spending. The present defense spending plan would allow several billions of dollars in cuts before dipping into that 7 percent level, but to what degree and in what specific areas the cuts come will say a very great deal about the real defense goals of the administration and the sense of reality which it has in reaching them.

Clearly, certain priorities exist. Military pay, especially in the career grades, must be raised in order to retain highly trained personnel. The reserves and supply of such basic materiel as ammunition and spare parts must be improved. Efforts must be continued to refit the Air Force with the new generation of fighter aircraft. Research and development of new weapons systems must be not only continued but accelerated.

These would appear to be among the absolutely essential ingredients of any defense spending plan. Beyond them and certain other spending areas, the going gets very tough — and expensive. The estimated cost of the proposed MX missile system, for example, hovers around the figure of $100 billion, and although this would be spread out over the course of several years, its impact on the level of spending cannot be described as other than dramatic. Other defense options, such as development of the B-1 bomber, manufacture and deployment of the neutron bomb and achieving a true, three-ocean Navy, also carry staggering price tags.

Deciding which among these is absolutely essential to the national defense interests of the United States is an unenviable job. Each has its strong adherents, and their arguments, taken in isolation, are certainly persuasive.

It is the president's job, however, to balance such arguments against the breadth of the defense spectrum. And, further, to balance the entirety of the defense budget against its affect on the larger budget of the federal government and the whole of the American economy.

In that context, it is clear that the level of increase in defense spending must be held down if the president is to have any hope of balancing the total budget and thereby achieving the economic goals which are crucial to the health of the nation. For, if the economy is allowed to weaken further, the underpinning, not only of the defense establishment, but of the whole federal government and the nation, must weaken as well. Without the foundation of a healthy, growing economy, military might alone, even if it could be achieved under such conditions, would not be enough to sustain the nation.

Against that backdrop, the president is due the full support of the American people as he goes about the business of balancing the essential elements of the national equation of needs and interests. It is doubtful that all parties will agree fully with the decision he will reach next week, but all should recognize that even the most arguably excellent of specific ideas must be placed in the greater context of the general national good.

The Morning News
Wilmington, Del., September 3, 1981

The classic cartoon of the man who stubbornly ignores all warnings and paints himself into the corner of the room farthest from the door may still be funny despite its age. It isn't funny when the president of the United States and the secretary of defense place themselves in a similar predicament.

President Reagan and Caspar Weinberger have adamantly insisted since January that the nation's security demands and that its pocketbook can support massive increases in defense spending — to a total outlay of $1.5 trillion over the next five years. Forget the anticipated $48-billion cuts in social programs and the president's promised tax reductions, defense spending would be increased by 7 percent a year without jeopardizing Mr. Reagan's promise to balance the federal budget by 1984.

Now the president and Mr. Weinberger find themselves in that corner, and their glistening promises, like wet paint, lie between them and the only way out. President Reagan and his advisers insisted for weeks that the projected $42.5-billion federal budget deficit for fiscal 1982 was still accurate. Now they have been forced by economic realities to concede that they are going to have to cut $10 billion to $15 billion more to hold the deficit at that level.

And they may have to reduce projected increases in spending for 1983-84 by as much as $30 billion.

Political realities have forced them finally to look to ballooning defense spending for a major part of those reductions. While Mr. Weinberger remained firm in behalf of the Pentagon, other presidential advisers had begun to concede the possibility of a little economy in defense spending.

At last, the Reagan administration's tenet that you don't solve national problems by throwing more money at them will apparently apply to the Pentagon as well as to the rest of the government.

Where could economies be made? Take for instance the Navy's F-18 fighter. The Pentagon planned to build 1,377 of the aircraft, at a total cost originally estimated at $16 billion. The estimated cost of the planes is now $38 billion, more than double the original.

The infantry fighting vehicle so coveted by the Army was planned at a cost of $900,000 each. Make that double, now $1.8 million each and probably certain to rise.

There are many such examples in a $226-billion budget, created by the long-range programs through which military improvements are obtained as well as the certainties of cost overruns and continued inflation. Such galloping increases in the costs of defense programs demand the same vigilance against waste and fraud that the president insists upon in other government programs.

Sen. Mark Hatfield, the Oregon Republican who is chairman of the Senate Appropriations Committee, warned several weeks ago: "If this cavalier disregard of fiscal restraint continues in the area of military expenditures, the federal deficit will be driven to unprecedented heights and will make meaningless the sacrifices the American people have made in cutting domestic programs."

A growing number of Americans have begun to echo that sentiment. It is reassuring to learn that even the president, reluctant as he may have been, has been forced by the facts of life to recognize that there are economic limits even to what the nation can afford to spend on defense, if there is to be anything left to defend.

The Idaho STATESMAN
Boise, Idaho, September 4, 1981

The Reagan administration at last is coming around to reality on its goals for defense spending and the federal budget. The Associated Press reported this week that the administration plans to chop $20 billion to $30 billion from its defense-spending plan. Also, presidential counselor Edwin Meese III said last week that the administration can't afford to finance all of its proposed defense programs and still balance the federal budget. Because of Meese's position, his comments usually are taken as a sign of Reagan's thinking.

We've said all along that Reagan could not possibly balance the budget if he spent his projected $1.6 trillion on the military in the next five years. To keep the budget in balance with that much defense spending, Reagan's economic program would have to instantly increase national productivity by 3 percent — an increase unprecedented in American history. Furthermore, Reaganomics also would have to shrink inflation to 5.1 percent.

It's all right to be optimistic and to hope that such miracles will occur. It's foolish to bank on them and commit ourselves to new, long-term military expenditures that will mean bigger, uglier deficits if the miracles don't appear.

Strengthening the military is an important goal, but part of that strengthening process is reform and elimination of waste. There's ample evidence that waste within the military is easy to find.

Earlier this year, for example, Sens. Howard Metzenbaum, D-Ohio, and Barry Goldwater, R-Ariz., wrote a letter to Secretary of Defense Caspar W. Weinberger suggesting that the defense budget could be cut easily without sacrificing military capability. They cited a government study that said "modest improvements" in efficiency could save $16 billion a year.

Likewise, both the General Accounting Office and the House Appropriations Committee have reported that as much as 10 percent of the Pentagon's budget is wasted.

The obvious conclusion to be drawn from such statistics is that the Defense Department is a classically fat bureaucracy in dire need of the budget knife.

It's unclear now whether a cut of $30 billion from the defense plan would be sufficient to bring the federal budget into balance by the administration's target date of 1984. But if Reagan and crew pare their defense-spending plan they will go a long way toward alleviating questions that have been raised about their ability to control federal spending.

THE LINCOLN STAR
Lincoln, Neb., September 15, 1981

President Reagan's weekend decision to cut down the Pentagon's ration of gravy by a comparatively few driblets over the next three years will have two negative effects.

First, it will not silence critics of his economic recovery program who rightly point out that not everyone, as had been promised, will "sacrifice" in bringing down inflation, unemployment and interest rates. He cannot argue any longer that his program is "fair."

The military is reported "jubilant" at Reagan's decision to cut only $13 billion in actual appropriations over the next three years (and a total of $22 billion in long-term obligated spending) from projected military spending increases. Have you ever heard of anyone who is sacrificing being "jubilant?" Budget Director David Stockman

wanted $30 billion cut from defense spending over the next three years. According to the Defense Department, the final figure means that the military will not have to sacrifice a single new weapons system nor affect any troop reductions. It will simply stretch out planned-for phased increases in troop strength and armaments.

Second, Reagan's kind treatment of the military places his program in even greater jeopardy in dollar terms, fairness aside. Much greater cuts will have to be taken from domestic programs, including pension and entitlement programs — and the first cuts haven't been felt yet. It won't sell politically.

The only other alternative is to restore some of the tax cuts.

Something's gotta give.

SAN JOSE NEWS
San Jose, Calif., September 15, 1981

SOME compromise.

The Reagan administration is making much of the "agreement" between Budget Director David Stockman and Defense Secretary Caspar Weinberger to trim increased military spending by $13 billion over three years. But it's about as much of a compromise as the Charge of the Light Brigade was a draw between the British cavalry and the Russians at Balaklava.

The issue was never whether to *cut* defense dollars; even with the $13 billion reduction, they're going to grow, at least by the 7 percent annual increase promised by Reagan on the campaign trail. The military buildup will be stretched out over a longer period than the administration originally planned; even so, the Pentagon's budget will rise like a Minuteman missile — to nearly $182 billion in the fiscal year starting Oct. 1, to $215 billion the next year, and to $242 billion the year after that.

Despite Stockman's stated desire to trim the defense increase by $27 billion for 1983 and '84, and despite earlier noises from the White House staff that trims of up to $30 billion would be considered, the decision came down to a matter of bureaucratic infighting. If Reagan has any hope of holding the budget deficit to anywhere near a mere $42.5 billion next year, the necessary hatchet jobs will carve deeper into social programs, not into the Pentagon's purse. In other words, Weinberger won, and won big.

When U.S. sailors on a $2 billion carrier like the Nimitz qualify for food stamps and earn the same money as a McDonald's cashier, there's an obvious need to increase military pay. Strengthening our conventional forces — and our ability to move them quickly — also are high-priority needs that should be met now. But exotic new strategic weapons systems are another, more debatable question.

Nevertheless, the Washington Post Sunday quoted Pentagon sources as saying the $13 billion nibble at their budget won't force cancellation of the MX, the B-1 or any other massive new hardware procurement.

There's a real question as to whether the armed services can efficiently absorb so much money as quickly as Weinberger and Reagan are determined to give it to them. But this administration seems hellbent on throwing money at the target of military superiority over the Soviet Union, as though dollars could buy a quick fix for national security. In fact, there is no quick fix. The Russians aren't the sole threat to global peace; weapons certainly aren't the sole means of securing it. A lot of what's involved is Third World turmoil, and that involves socioeconomic, nationalistic and political problems, as well as military ones.

But all that seems lost on the White House. The result is a defense spending surge too rapid even for the Republican-dominated Senate. The proposed $13 billion trim is so puny as to "make it very difficult to get where we have to go" in fighting inflation, Senate Budget Committee Chairman Pete Domenici said Sunday. "A majority of my committee and a majority of the Congress are looking for larger cuts than that."

So, obviously, is Wall Street. Reagan carefully timed the news of the $13 billion slowdown for weekend release, so the news would be out in time for the opening of Monday's trading. The reaction on the New York Stock Exchange: More blahs on Monday.

Domenici and the stock market gurus are right on this one. If Reagan really wants to shore up the economy, he's going to have to speed up military spending a little more slowly. The president claims he put a safety net under the truly needy. But he's put a pedestal under the Pentagon.

ST. LOUIS POST-DISPATCH
St. Louis, Mo., September 17, 1981

Last weekend, President Reagan announced that the Pentagon's share of budget balancing reductions would be limited to $13 billion over the next three years. The Office of Management and Budget had requested a cut of up to $30 billion between now and 1984. But after strong objections from Secretary of Defense Caspar Weinberger, the president rejected the OMB suggestion as being too radical. Mr. Reagan defended the limited reductions on the basis that the military has been the "poor relative" when it comes to federal funding.

In reality, Mr. Reagan did not cut anything — he only reduced the rate of planned Pentagon budget increases. The military will still get 98 percent of what it wanted. Pentagon officials freely admitted that Mr. Reagan's trims would not harm any of the major military procurement programs; at most, it might lengthen the production runs of some weapons. The cuts most likely will be made in operations and maintenance.

Even taking the $13-billion trim into account, Mr. Reagan's military spending will still be over $25 billion more than the already sizable increases that were planned by the Carter administration for the 1982 through 1984 defense budgets. Moreover, the Pentagon's 2 percent reduction looks tiny compared to the 25 percent or greater cutbacks inflicted earlier this year on some social programs.

To their credit, Republican leaders in the Congress were quick to send up storm warnings. Sen. Peter Domenici, chairman of the Senate Budget Committee, warned that greater military cuts are called for. "I feel that the overall cuts in defense should be more in the neighborhood of $30 billion," Sen. Domenici said. In addition, House Minority Leader Robert Michel argued that, "Defense simply could not be sacrosanct."

Many Wall Street analysts were also unhappy about the small size of the president's military cuts. Investors fear that the combination of decreasing federal tax revenue and skyrocketing military spending will lead to additional federal borrowing from the private sector. If that happens, not only would interest rates remain high, but it could set off a new round of inflation.

What is most surprising is how ill-timed the announcement was. The president made his Pentagon as "poor relative" remark just a couple of days after the administration announced that it was cutting milk rations for 27 million school children from lower income families and was considering counting ketchup as a "vegetable" in the school lunch program. These changes were necessary because of the full one-third cut in school lunch program funding made earlier this year.

President Reagan's refusal to allow the Pentagon to shoulder its fair share of the budget balancing burden is certain to cause a bitter fight on Capitol Hill. The president should follow the solid advice of his conservative allies in Congress and increase the Pentagon's share of the budget cutbacks. It is the only fair and just thing to do.

The Times-Picayune
The States-Item
New Orleans, La., September 15, 1981

Faced with the necessity, both economic and political, of trimming the defense budget he has pledged to increase, President Reagan has swung a careful ax gently. His announced $20 billion cut over the next three years translates into some $13 billion of actual expenses, and does not significantly damage the overall trend toward bigger defense expenditures.

The economic argument for trimming back the defense budget is that by some estimates the 1984 federal budget will be in deficit by $70-75 billion rather than in balance, as Mr. Reagan had projected. The political argument is that since budget cutting has been concentrated on what is called "social" spending — programs that have large constituencies and vocal champions — some balancing cuts in the defense budget's "guns" to match the shrinkage in the "butter" budget are necessary to defend the administration against charges of domestic heartlessness and foreign belligerence.

Three-year economic projections made during the unsettled times of a turning point are hazardous, and many projections conceal in themselves a degree of tendentiousness in the projectors. The Democrats, as the outs, will foresee much worse futures than the Republicans, and all projections are conditioned by their assumptions and methods.

But the term "butter" does not now mean what it did when President Lyndon Johnson, preparing to plunge into the Vietnamese war, decided we could have both guns and butter. Butter then meant vast federal spending on the social programs gathered under the rubric of the Great Society. Now butter is best thought of as the domestic economy as a whole, and Mr. Reagan rightly argues that we might have to curb our appetites for the moment in order to get more from a better organized and more efficient economy later.

The present-day equivalent of a war that forces choices is the clear need to improve, expand and revitalize our defense forces. The announced cuts are relatively modest — they will require, for example, not building as many new Navy ships or buying as many F-15 fighters as planned, not stockpiling as much ammunition as planned, and stretching out increasing our military manpower.

But because of a decades-long Soviet build-up in military capability across the board while we marked time or poured all our energies into the Vietnamese war, we are in the position of having to play catch-up in the most elementary military requirements. We must take care that whatever cuts are made in the defense budget do not damage the basic need to have — and to be seen to have — the force necessary to deter armed confrontations.

SYRACUSE
HERALD·JOURNAL
Syracuse, N.Y., September 15, 1981

President Reagan retired to Camp David and, before emerging, sent word he had bitten the bullet and will trim defense spending by $13 billion over the next three fiscal years.

The $13 billion is in the form of "first instance" appropriations. When follow-through appropriations are cut, eliminated dollars will add up to $21 billion.

Upon listening to Wall Street economists, the $13 billion should have come in around the $30 billion mark; otherwise, they fear he's indulging in cosmetic surgery.

Worse, we think, is the administration's failure to embrace a defense strategy that sets clear, build-up priorities. Instead, Secretary of Defense Weinberger lets us and the financial markets and the country's economic pundits believe "there's literally nothing that we did not need."

We're told the Pentagon must have everything, from soup to nuts, and if that creates inflation, too bad.

With this approach, how can the president, and especially his No. 1 budgeter, David Stockman, and his chief defense manager, Weinberger, tell where to cut what?

No wonder we're uneasy, not only about the economy, but about this country's arms buildup.

For evidence, examine the Bernstein reports published on the Op-Ed pages.

The Star-Ledger
Newark, N.J., September 15, 1981

President Reagan has returned to the fiscal drafting board in another effort to pare the new federal budget to reasonable proportions, drawing even more leaner lines to reduce spending ceilings for 1982.

Without another round of cuts — as much as $18 billion — the deficit could rise to $62 billion, substantially more than the Administration has anticipated. The Reagan White House now talks in a wistful perspective about achieving its objective of a balanced budget by fiscal 1984, the end of the President's term.

In spite of the need for deep new spending cuts, Mr. Reagan is reluctant to move with the same vigor in reducing military outlays that he did with the civilian sector.

Mr. Reagan has rejected recommendations by his chief budget aide, David Stockman, to reduce defense spending by at least $25 billion and as much as $40 billion over the next three fiscal years.

Instead, the President has sided with Defense Secretary Caspar Weinberger by limiting Pentagon budget curtailments to a modest $2 billion in 1982, and by an overall $13 billion over a three-year span.

That will mean the Administration will have to knock off at least another $14 billion in non-military expenditures to keep the estimated fiscal 1982 deficit at $42 billion, the White House fiscal goal.

* * *

These civilian spending curtailments will be harder to come by, not only in budgetary terms but also resistance from Congress in the wake of the relatively small military cutbacks. The defense budget is the only government area with which the Administration has been liberal, with increases of up to seven per cent in each of the next five years, weighted for inflation, a total outlay of $1.5 trillion.

On the sheer size of the Pentagon budget alone there should be sufficient flexibility for at least $10 billion in reduced defense commitments. Regrettably, the President has decided otherwise, characterizing the military establishment as a "poor relative" in comparison with "overgrown and extravagant" domestic programs.

Under the proposed Reagan budget policies, it is not beyond the realm of fiscal possibility that these roles will be radically altered — the social programs will be severely trimmed while defense spending will be permitted to expand in an open-handed manner.

This does not mean that our military capability does not require a significant upgrading. But there is room for a budgetary accommodation by the defense sector to temporarily defer some commitments as a means of holding down an unacceptable rise in a projected 1982 deficit.

THE TENNESSEAN
Nashville, Tenn., September 15, 1981

IN defending his plan to make no more than minor reductions in the Pentagon budget, President Reagan called the Defense Department a "poor relative," which is like calling King Midas a pauper.

Last week, the White House announced that Mr. Reagan plans to trim the Pentagon budget by no more than $13 billion over the next three years. That is not a cut but more like a nick. Before Labor Day, Mr. Reagan's budget advisers were pressing for cuts of between $20 billion and $40 billion in the defense budget to avoid the possibility of the deficit going sky-high.

But in the struggle between budget director Mr. David Stockman and Defense Secretary Caspar Weinberger, the latter seems to have won. In a memorandum to Messrs. Stockman and Weinberger, Mr. Reagan said that in fiscal 1982 defense spending would be $181 billion; in fiscal 1983 it would be $214.9 billion and for fiscal 1983, it would be $242.6 billion.

"When you stop to think," Mr. Reagan said, "we've been cutting a budget that has been overgrown...and extravagant over the years, while in the same years Defense has been a poor relative and we have not been keeping pace with a needed military buildup."

Since 1976, the Defense Department has had increases averaging about 3% a year. That may not sound like much of a percentage, but it is not peanuts when applied to total budget authority. That was $125 billion in 1979 and has been increasing.

Even with cuts of $20 to $30 billion, Mr. Reagan's defense spending plans would be substantially more than the $1.28 trillion, five-year program put into effect by the Carter administration. The President could make the cuts and still maintain he his meeting his promised goal of boosting defense spending by 7% a year.

Mr. Reagan's pledge to get out the budget knife again may be addressed as much to Wall Street as anywhere else, since it has never believed that he could cut taxes and raise defense spending without some massive deficits.

If the President is going to cut military spending only slightly, then he is going to be forced to find places to trim at least $14 billion in non-defense spending next year and some $63 billion in the following years.

It is going to be increasingly difficult to find places for such cuts in the non-military sector without some serious dangers to the economy and the social fabric of the country. Huge military expenditures tend to be a drain on the civilian sector, in terms of capital, expertise and plants

Furthermore, simply throwing dollars at the defense establishment doesn't necessarily guarantee more and better defense. The various armed services are already busy with their wish lists of various weapons systems of questionable value. The MX missile system, for example, promises to be an expensive and massive boondoggle without any proven increase in terms of national security.

The Congress is going to be reluctant to make further and heavier cuts in non-defense spending and it should be. There are good and sufficient arguments for adding more muscle to defense, especially the conventional forces of the military.

But there would be sufficient money to do that even if Mr. Stockman's original goal of cutting $20 billion to $30 billion in 1983 and 1984. If Mr. Reagan is unwilling to squeeze the Pentagon more than a little, then it will be up to the Congress to make some necessary cuts.

Record 1982 Military Spending Bill Passed

Both chambers of Congress Dec. 15, 1981 approved a record military appropriations bill of $199.8 billion, only slightly under President's Reagan's requested $200 billion. The bill, passed by a 334 to 84 vote in the House and by a vote of 93 to 4 in the Senate, essentially approved the strategic weapons plan outlined by Reagan in October. It was a compromise, reached by House and Senate conferees, between a House bill of $197.44 billion and a Senate bill of $208.67 billion. The final figure was agreed upon after two features of the Senate version, the $4.8 billion for increased military pay and $1.6 billion to cover anticipated inflation and cost overruns, were eliminated from the bill. The final version included a Senate amendment that restricted spending on hardened silos for the MX missile, allocating most of the earmarked research funds to alternative basing schemes.

Detroit Free Press

Detroit, Mich., December 6, 1981

ONE OF David Stockman's early frustrations on the job, as recounted in the now famous Atlantic Monthly article, was his inability to get across the intractable logic of numbers to his colleagues in the Reagan administration and Congress. Cuts in social services wouldn't be enough to restore the budget's stability, he said, if you increase defense spending and cut taxes.

Budget Director Stockman at first expected that Defense Secretary Caspar Weinberger and Congress would come to realize this and serve as his allies. "There's a kind of swamp" of $10 billion to $20 billion to $30 billion "worth of waste that can be ferreted out" of the defense budget, he said. The problem with the Pentagon, he said, was "blatant inefficiency, poor deployment of manpower, contracting idiocy." Mr. Weinberger, he predicted, would get at the problem, because "he's not a tool of the military-industrial complex . . . he hasn't been steeped in its excuses and rationalizations and ideology for 20 years."

The last few weeks have proven Mr. Stockman's prediction terribly wrong. Both the U.S. House and Senate have approved record military appropriations inflated by the expensively ineffective B1 bomber and MX missile system. In both houses, attempts were made to excise the B1 and the MX from the budget or to divert the funds to more urgent defense needs. The one successful attempt was the Senate's overwhelming vote to transfer most of the next year's MX funding to research on alternatives to the president's plan to base the missiles in fixed, hardened silos. Otherwise, our lawmakers went along with the White House wish list for reasons that had more to do with the "excuses and rationalizations and ideology" of the past 20 years than with military wisdom.

Even some congressmen who voted for the B1 and MX acknowledged that politics counted for as much as defense considerations. Rep. Elliott H. Levitas, D-Georgia, said the MX plan was "naive, childish and foolish" but to vote against the president would be "unconscionable." House Majority Leader Jim Wright of Texas said many congressmen feared they would be branded "weak on defense" in next year's elections if they voted against the B1.

The same sentiments pervaded the Senate, which was under great pressure from the White House to regard the B1 and MX votes as a litmus test for what the president called "American resolve in the face of an ever-growing Soviet challenge." Sen. Carl Levin, D-Mich., wisely saw through the rhetoric. He co-sponsored an amendment, also supported by Michigan's other senator, Donald Riegle, to cancel the B1 and use most of the money instead for needs such as fuel, ammunition and improvements in the Rapid Deployment Force, which is now little more than a new title for existing units.

"Readiness items are shortchanged," Sen. Levin said. "Conventional items are shortchanged." He is absolutely right. And his colleagues who voted for two of the least useful weapons systems in recent history are wrong.

The current incarnation of the MX leaves it as vulnerable to Soviet attack as the Minuteman it is supposed to supplant. The B1 perpetuates the inadequacies of the B52 it is designed to replace. The only difference they make to our welfare is cost.

In an era committed to the end of funny money, this means real dollars taken away from real, not symbolic, military needs. However impressed our representatives think their consititutents will be with the high-priced signal they are sending to the Russians, the signal the Russians are receiving is quite different. It is difficult to work up much fear of a nation that lacks the transport capability or the reserves to sustain more than a few weeks of conventional fighting anywhere, a nation that lacks the money for training and spare parts and that can't even find the "resolve" to conscript its citizens.

But there are no Russians voting in next year's election. So we continue to get empty, politically cheap gestures so costly in tax dollars that the essentials of our citizens' security — conventional defense, health and public safety programs, and a productive economy — fall by the wayside.

The Kansas City Times

Kansas City, Mo., December 9, 1981

The $208 billion arms bill approved by the Senate has a long way to go. Such issues as the B-1 bomber and the MX missile and its basing still are far from decided.

But unless the world suddenly declares peace and beats everything into plowshares overnight, the money figure probably will be in the neighborhood of ultimate expenditures. It looks enormous and it is. But it really is not out of line as a share of the gross national product. In the past we have spent proportionately more on the military.

What makes it seem a greater burden than ever is the fact that so much is being cut out of various domestic areas in the Reagan program to beat inflation and lower the rate of the deficit. And studied from that angle it really is a greater burden. In the end, it may not be politically feasible.

Like most of our dilemmas, this one took a while to become apparent, and it will take a while to resolve. The combined Vietnam War-civilian production economy of the 1960s and '70s was the beginning of rapidly compounding inflationary woes. Then, in the mid-1970s, in terms of comparative dollars, the Carter administration did cut the military back from Nixon-Ford projections when the Soviets were building steadily. There was something of a return to the starve-or-splurge military budgets of the past. Many damaging omissions occurred, not least among them a deterioration in real pay for service people that only now has been redressed.

Afghanistan and other awarenesses struck Mr. Carter near the end of his term. On Jan. 15, 1981, he proposed much greater defense obligational authority and outlays. By then, however, Mr. Reagan had been campaigning on a theme of "not enough" and "too little, too late."

So now the ante has been upped to include the B-1, the MX missile in some unknown form, a Rapid Deployment Force that ideally would use the new C-17 transport aircraft and exotic roll-on, roll-off ships, and a new generation of weapons systems for the Army and Navy.

From the military point of view, every bit of it probably can be justified. It is difficult ever to have enough when the responsibility is national security.

But that is where civilian government enters the picture. In this country it does have the supreme authority. As always, it must weigh priorities. It cannot always do the instantly popular thing or follow the formula for sure-fire, momentary applause.

The United States needs now what it has needed since 1945: A program of steady, reasonably long-range military planning and expenditures that will not operate on a boom-or-bust cycle that has us spending first not enough and then, in a panic, too much.

This is the time to spend more. But not beyond the willingness of the people to pay for it in hard times when businesses are going broke, the unemployment lines lengthen, and domestic programs are dying. In the end, Congress will have to find a compromise that will both protect and conserve.

THE LINCOLN STAR
Lincoln, Neb., December 4, 1981

The last time we checked, the U.S. Senate had not got its beserk military spending spree under control.

Its version of the defense appropriations bill is several billions higher than the House's measure, and the Republican majority in the Senate has succeeded in channeling excessive amounts of money into strategic weapons while defeating amendments aimed at beefing up manpower and conventional warfare needs. One military analyst published a study this week asserting that there is no longer a conventional arms race because the Soviet Union is so far ahead. Democrats, including Nebraska's Jim Exon, who has taken a leading role, have fought for more funds for manpower and basic readiness. But those efforts have been defeated, and more funds have been voted for the kind of weapons systems with which the U.S. already enjoys massive overkill capability,

The Congress seems intent, too, on spending vast sums of money on obsolete or politically hamstrung weapons systems. The B-1 bomber, for example, a multibillion-dollar turkey that ought to be junked with funds sunk into the next generation bomber, and the MX missile system, which will waste billions as a sitting duck for Soviet missiles because of its vulnerable basing mode — a slap-dash arrangement arrived at by the president and some western buddies in the Senate, none of whom knows much about nuclear warfare. Regrettably, Exon has joined in support of these wasteful systems.

The current mood in Washington still seems to be to grab the last can of dogfood away from elderly pensioners but to spare no expense when it comes to enriching defense contractors and trying to sate the ravenous appetite of Pentagon brass.

But will the United States have a more adequate, realistic defense for the last part of the century because of the current spending spree? Probably not. The cruel cuts in domestic spending are made in order to insure, as Sen. Fritz Hollings, D-S.C., says, that the United States is "over-prepared for nuclear war and unprepared for conventional war."

What's happening in Washington should please no one except the aging leadership in the Kremlin and the American defense contractors, who must be laughing all the way to the bank.

BUFFALO EVENING NEWS
Buffalo, N.Y., December 12, 1981

Congressional support for rebuilding U.S. defenses is commendable, but that does not mean that Congress should automatically approve every military proposal that is presented to it. The Senate last week followed the example of the House in approving a $208.6 defense appropriation bill, including funds for the B-1 bomber and the MX missile.

The defense appropriation represents a sizable increase in spending and demonstrates a proper U.S. determination to strengthen our lagging military might, especially in view of the ominous Soviet arms buildup of recent years.

The measure was not, however, above criticism. Critics of the B-1 presented strong arguments that the plane was unnecessary in view of the plans to develop the new radar-evading "Stealth" bomber by 1990. The B-1 could be obsolete some three years after it was put into service.

Designed to replace the aging B-52 bomber as one leg of the "triad" of nuclear deterrents, the B-1 is supposed to be able to penetrate Soviet defenses better than the B-52, but there is no guarantee that it would be able to do so. However, with the advent of cruise missiles, the airborne deterrent seems secure, and there is no urgent need to build the B-1.

Nevertheless, the expenditure of $2.4 billion was approved to start work on the B-1. The dominant feeling in the Senate was that failure to vote the funds would be undercutting the president at a time when he was entering important arms-reduction negotiations with the Soviet Union. President Reagan, indeed, reinforced this feeling, declaring that any vote against his key proposals would send "a dangerous and misleading signal of weakening American resolve in the face of an ever-growing Soviet challenge."

The president also plans to spend some $5 billion in reinforcing missile silos for the new MX missile, and the current appropriation bill sought $354 million to begin this work. While the need to develop the MX missile is clear, the stationary MX cannot be considered an invulnerable leg of the triad at a time when the Soviet ICBMs are becoming ever more accurate. Thus the Senate wisely voted to study options to the hardened silos.

Passage of the overall $208.6 defense package was in general a welcome step toward rearming America, even though the senators turned back several attempts to make judicious cuts here and there. Mr. Reagan is proposing increases in defense spending totaling $99 billion over three years, and it is hard to believe that there is not some fat in that spending schedule that could be trimmed in these difficult times.

The Senate measure must now be reconciled in conference with the $197.4 billion defense bill approved by the House last month. No one can be happy about such huge military outlays, but there is no substitute for a strong defense in deterring potential adversaries and keeping the peace.

The Times-Picayune
The States-Item
New Orleans, La., December 10, 1981

The Senate has passed a record military spending bill — $208.7 billion — that will now have to be dovetailed with the House's $197.4 billion bill. Most of the argument and attention centered on appropriations for the B-1 bomber and the MX missile, but those controversies should not obscure the fact that major investments are needed in our military forces, primarily in the less dramatic area of conventional arms.

There should be little argument that down on the ground — where the tanks, personnel and equipment carriers, rifles, tactical rocket launchers and such operate — we need more. If some view domestic warnings as self-serving, they might heed the the authoritative British Jane's new military manual on armor and artillery.

The U.S.-Soviet race in conventional arms, Jane's says, is really no race at all because the Soviets are so far ahead and "members of the North Atlantic Treaty Organizaton suffer inflation and budget problems." The Soviet Union, which has its own economic problems, can displace them because its command economy serves the government and is not responsive to public opinion or voter pressure. It can hide military spending in phony budgets for non-military departments, so that what it spends is far more than its announced defense budget. And it has a minimum-wage conscript army, while half our defense budget is devoted to military salaries.

Jane's puts the Western problem succinctly "Unless the United States and other members of NATO can slow down the rapidly increasing costs of weapons systems of all types, the outlook for the West is bleak." Many factors bear on such costs, but a continuing charge against weapons procurers is that they go for the breakdown-prone super-complex instead of the dependably simple, which increases research and development costs and the time it takes to get into actual production.

The Soviets may just be getting into production with their T-80 supertank — the U.S. equivalent is the M-1, of which we now have 100, equipped with old guns — but they have in Europe 3,000 older taks that Jane's says are better than current NATO armor.

Nuclear weapons were welcomed, in a way, for making war unthinkable but it was nuclear war they made unthinkable — and that not entirely. But in an ironic twist, they also made conventional war the only kind available. The world has seen perhaps a dozen such wars since World War II without tripping the nuclear wire. But deterrence works also in conventional warfare, and to make it work — and to be able to fight if fighting is forced upon us — our strength must be both real and visible.

Minneapolis Star and Tribune

Minneapolis, Minn., December 9, 1981

President Reagan worries a lot lest Congress send the Soviets a signal of faltering resolve about a massive buildup of American weapons hardware. Such a signal would go out loud and clear, Reagan told the Senate last week, if spending were trimmed for big-ticket items like the B1 bomber or MX missile. So the Senate fell in line and sent the signal the president wanted. It handily beat back some budget-conscious amendments and approved a $209-billion Pentagon appropriation for this fiscal year. That's even more than Reagan requested, and $11 billion more than the House passed last month.

Perhaps the Soviet Union will be duly impressed. But signals for the Kremlin can be heard on Main Street, too, and may carry a different message from what the signal-senders hope. Few people doubt that rocket diplomacy by the Soviet Union requires a strong response by the United States. Many do doubt, however, that the weapons extravagance relied on by Reagan is a proper centerpiece for American foreign policy. And it's obvious to many more, even in the administration, that military spending at the level approved last week confounds all strategies for achieving non-inflationary economic growth at home.

So the signal from the Senate is bad news for America, however it may be heard by the listeners in Moscow. The signal tells us that the truly weak resolve in Washington today is the resolve to be hard-headed about control of government spending. Uncritical support of the military requests means continued acquiescence in overgrown central government, ballooning federal deficits, interest-rate pressure, renewed tax increases, entrenched inflation and a sluggish private sector. That is not the way to make America strong.

The TENNESSEAN

Nashville, Tenn., December 9, 1981

SENATE passage of the largest appropriations bill in history for defense gave President Reagan nearly everything he wanted, but there were some gathering clouds on the horizon about the 1983 Pentagon budget.

After five days of debate on the defense spending measure, Senate passage left very little that the President could complain about. One item that may have been disappointing was disapproval of his interim plan to place MX missiles in existing Minuteman and Titan silos. The senators approved 90 to 4 an amendment designed to keep the Pentagon from spending research funds on the silo approach.

The interim scheme to deploy three dozen or more MX missiles in older silos has not pleased very many, because that basing plan would leave the MX just as vulnerable to a Soviet attack as the present missile system is said to be.

There is some sentiment in the Senate for a mobile basing plan, but there is no agreement on just what it should be — a problem that Mr. Reagan faced before coming up with an interim solution, that of superhardening existing silos with additional concrete armor.

Efforts to delete funding for the B-1 bomber failed, and that is unfortunate. The B-1 is too expensive to begin with, and it may be obsolete almost as soon as it becomes operational.

The Senate would have served defense purposes better if it had deleted the $2.4 billion for the B-1 and redistributed the major part of that for conventional weapons and improvement of the combat readiness of forces in the field with such needed items as ammunition, spare parts and training.

During the debate, Sen. Ernest Hollings, D-S.C., said, "We've got thousands of bombers coming out of our ears. We aren't short of bombers, but we are short of ammunition...and that's a disgrace."

What the defense effort is getting instead is a bomber of uncertain worth and a missile system that may not be deployable, simply because of the expense and technical problems in almost any basing mode. There certainly have been any number of basing options suggested, and all are constrained by the enormous outlays needed to do the basing.

But the symbolic battles in the Senate over defense spending did raise some hints that the road may be rockier for President Reagan when he submits his 1983 budget for the Pentagon. Some influential Republicans were complaining about the Pentagon's relative immunity from the kind of austerity imposed on most domestic programs.

Sen. Robert Dole, R-Kan., warned that he will "insist" that defense programs "accept some share of the cuts" in the 1983 budget. Such a warning from the Finance Committee chairman was lent some weight by an amendment to make cuts in procurement and research titles by 2%, and one to eliminate a 3% cushion added to the B-1 and MX programs. Both lost, but the latter failed by a single vote.

So, there is restiveness in the GOP-controlled Senate over the fact that domestic programs are all feeling the budget-ax while the Pentagon only suffers the slightest of nicks. The next Pentagon budget is unlikely to fare so well, and it should not.

RAPID CITY JOURNAL

Rapid City, S.D., December 4, 1981

In approving funds for the B-1 bomber and the MX missile, the U.S. Senate signalled that it's willing to bolster the nation's deterrent capability with available technology rather than continuing a search for an invincible weapon.

For a time it appeared that Congress would deny funds for the MX until the administration came up with an invincible basing mode. There was also considerable sentiment for bypassing the B-1 and spending the money for the Stealth bomber because it looked to some legislators, as drawing board systems often do, like the invincible weapon.

The crucial task facing any bomber pitted against the Soviet Union is the penetration of increasingly formidable air defenses — radars, missiles and interceptor aircraft.

Some of the reluctance to fund the B-1 was based on a CIA analyst's report that there would be practically no difference in the ability of B-52s and B-1s to pierce Soviet defenses.

Defense Secretary Caspar Weinberger doesn't agree. He claims the aging B-52s will be unable to penetrate the Russian shield beyond the end of 1985.

The Pentagon maintained the CIA was talking about the wrong B-1. The new aircarft, the B-1B carries more

advanced defenses than the original which will enable it to reach Soviet targets more easily. The radar cross section of the B1-B will be one tenth that of the original B-1 and one-hundreth that of the B-52. Weinberger says the B-1B will be able to penetrate Soviet air defenses well into the 1990s.

The strategic weapons proposals advanced by the Reagan administration recognize there is no invincible weapon, no once-and-for-all answer. It therefore proposes to do what it can.

It makes sense to continue with planning and design of the MX. The decision may be made some day to protect them with an anti-missile system. And if they are built, they might as well be deployed in silos instead of storing them in warehouses.

It also makes sense to build the B-1, the airplane we have rather than one we don't have.

The danger in rejecting weapons like the MX and B-1 because they are not the ultimate or because they are not invincible is that the nation could be left with none at all.

Military commanders throughout history have discovered that even if their weapons aren't invincible, it's better to have some of them than none.

TULSA WORLD
Tulsa, Okla., December 7, 1981

THE U.S. Senate Friday passed a record $209 billion defense spending bill — $8 billion more than the president requested and $11 billion more than the House approved.

Only four years ago, total defense outlays were $105 billion. In that short time, defense spending has nearly doubled. It now takes up more than one-fourth of all federal spending.

The military spending bill now goes to House-Senate conference committees, where the final proposal is expected to reflect the President's initial request.

The Senate vote points up an unhappy but obvious fact about the nation's economic problems: as long as defense spending remains sacrosanct, chances of balancing the budget are near zero.

When the administration first took office, there were indications that the budget could have been balanced without any substantive cuts in existing programs. Eliminating fraud and waste would have taken care of things if defense spending had been held in line and tax revenues had not been cut.

Soon thereafter, Budget Director David Stockman convinced the administration that, in fact, some $40 billion in real cuts would have to be made. Those cuts were made, though defense was left untouched.

Now it is clear, in light of the Kemp-Roth tax cut bill, that more cuts are needed. Only two big targets are available: defense and entitlement programs.

Some cuts have already been made in entitlements, and further adjustments need to be made. But the possibility of more such cuts is slim unless defense spending also faces the ax. Politically, the Reagan honeymoon is over. Congressmen will vote on proposed cuts more with an eye to the 1982 election than to the mandate of the 1980 Reagan sweep. Don't expect them to cut such politically sensitive programs as Social Security without seeing some economies in defense spending.

The Dispatch
Columbus, Ohio, December 26, 1981

CONGRESS LAST week approved a $199.7 billion defense spending package which will strengthen the nation's deterrent forces and will help it respond effectively to crises around the world.

The bill represents a $28 billion hike in the Pentagon budget over last year and contains the major elements President Reagan had called for earlier this year.

The B-1 bomber is there, a project needed to replace the aging B-52 fleet and keep the U.S. air power strong through the next 15 years. The B-1 effort will have great impact in central Ohio where several thousand jobs will be created over the next five years as Rockwell International gears up for the aircraft's production.

The MX missile is there, too. The controversial weapon will be produced and stored temporarily in existing silos while a permanent basing system is decided upon. Earlier plans called for a huge race-track system in Utah and Nevada.

The rapid deployment force is also included in the spending package, as is money to fund construction of bases needed to train and house the force.

In passing the bill, members of Congress expressed confidence that the programs included in the package will enhance the nation's security, but some noted that future funding for on-going projects — such as the B-1 and MX — will be difficult. "We face funding crises in 1983, '84 and '85 that will be substantial," said Sen. Ted Stevens, R-Alaska, floor manager for the bill in the Senate.

The funding problem will be left to future deliberations. The important thing now is that the defense buildup is in place and the action needed to keep the nation strong and secure has been taken.

The Des Moines Register
Des Moines, Iowa, December 18, 1981

Congress cast a vote for bigger budget deficits and inefficient use of the public's money when it gave final approval to almost $200 billion in military spending. Iowans should be proud that five of their six representatives in the House voted against this bloated bill (see following editorial).

The United States needs a military establishment strong and effective enough to defend its national interests. To just throw money at the Pentagon indiscriminately, as this bill does, is not the most effective way to reach that goal.

The bill provides $199.7 billion during this fiscal year, some $28 billion more than last year. Total military spending is almost certain to be several billion higher than the $199.7 billion figure, because the House-Senate conference committee — eager to give the appearance of cutting the Senate's $208.7 billion proposal — struck out money needed for military-pay raises already approved.

Those raises will cost about $4.8 billion. Where will that money come from? Chairman Joseph Abbaddo (Dem., N.Y.) of the House defense-appropriations subcommittee, admitted, "... We will undoubtedly have a large supplemental [military] request ... next month."

This enormous military budget could have been cut substantially if Congress had been willing to take a more critical look at some of the weapons requested by the Reagan administration, especially nuclear weapons.

The B-1 bomber is of doubtful utility. The fleet of B-52s, though aging and losing their ability to penetrate Soviet air defenses, can serve as cruise-missile launchers well into the 1990s. By that time, the Stealth bomber, which could get past Soviet defenses, should be ready.

Cutting out exotic weapons such as the B-1 and the MX missile and restraining spending on frills like military bands ($100 million) would not have weakened U.S. military capabilities. Some of the money saved might have been devoted to worthwhile domestic programs that have been cut too deeply by Congress. The rest could have reduced the ballooning federal deficit.

The result would have been a healthier economy and a stronger United States. It is tragic that Congress passed up this opportunity to strengthen the nation.

Military Outlays in Fiscal 83 Budget Set Peacetime Record

The Reagan Administration Feb. 6, 1982 unveiled a $757.6 billion federal budget for fiscal 1983 that projected a substantial and politically risky deficit of $91.5 billion. The only block of the budget to enjoy substantial growth was the military, while most domestic spending was slated to be frozen or cut in real terms (after inflation was accounted for). The fiscal 1983 defense request of $215.9 billion represented 28.5% of the federal budget; an additional $42 billion was sought in obligational authority. (Obligational authority referred to all funds Congress would be asked to appropriate in 1983, even those that would not actually be spent in 1983, and included funds appropriated but not spent during the previous year.) The gap between authorized funds and planned spending was the largest in U.S. peacetime history, signifying a large-scale commitment to future military spending. Part of a five-year plan to increase U.S. forces and modernize weapons, the budget placed an overwhelming emphasis on seapower and airlift capability, shifting away from the traditional focus on land battles in Europe. The biggest jumps in spending would be in weapons procurement and research, which were to be increased by 37% and 22%, respectively.

Chicago Tribune

Chicago, Ill., February 12, 1982

Much has been made of the political and economic problems caused by the large defense spending increases in President Reagan's new budget. But another equally serious risk is that by overplaying the military buildup hand the administration will weaken the fragile consensus that Mr. Reagan and his supporters put together in favor of strengthening U.S. defenses.

It is beginning to look as if Mr. Reagan put his defense proposal on the table in expectation that a bipartisan effort will be made in Congress to trim it down. In one way, this is quite shrewd. It gives members of Congress a chance to assert themselves in an election year. But there are also dangers in this approach.

First, the arguments against increased defense spending may spread much farther than Mr. Reagan expects. They may, in fact, create a public climate reminiscent of the mood of the 1970s when any defense spending was unpopular.

Second, by asking for more than he can get and then being turned down in Congress, Mr. Reagan will be sending the wrong signal to the Soviet Union. The administration has wanted to demonstrate to the Soviets and the world that the United States has the will to do what it must in order to protect its vital security interests. It is a tricky business to create and nurture this kind of consensus, and an even trickier one to make it credible to allies and adversaries. Provoking a fight with Congress over defense spending—especially a losing fight—is hardly the way to make the point.

Defenders of the Reagan defense budget point out that actual spending in fiscal 1983 will not be predominantly for hardware. The big capital proposals the administration has revived—the B-1 bomber, the MX missile, the accelerated shipbuilding program—will not start costing big money until after 1983, they say. First year spending will go for personnel costs, operations, maintenance and the like.

It is in some ways a peculiar argument to make on behalf of the defense budget. For one thing, it suggests that the worst is yet to come, which will hardly be reassuring to investors worried about future as well as present deficits. For another, it literally invites cuts in areas where cuts ought not be made. The most dangerous legacy of the period in which defense spending was unpopular is the decline in military readiness rather than in the lack of big, new weapons systems.

President Reagan was absolutely right to campaign and govern upon the proposition that national defense deserved a higher priority than it had been getting in the past. He was right to emphasize budget cuts in areas outside the Pentagon. But the art of governing is at least in part an art of proper degrees. And by tilting his latest budget too far in the direction of defense, he has endangered the very consensus he has worked so well and so hard to create.

The Wichita Eagle-Beacon

Wichita, Kans., February 9, 1982

Compared to the $756.6 billion — more than three-quarters-of-a-trillion-dollars — spending total that President Reagan has proposed for fiscal 1983, a $215.9 billion outlay for military programs may not seem dramatically impressive. But that total represents a $33.1 billion increase in the Pentagon's budget at a time domestic programs are being cut back, sharply, and it will contribute to a second projected budget deficit of more than $90 billion.

The first federal budget whose preparation Mr. Reagan has been able to control totally calls for a red-ink total of $91.5 billion; a record $98.6 billion deficit is anticipated at the end of fiscal 1982. The budget-balancing goal Mr. Reagan optimistically set for himself less than two years ago has been missed by a very large distance.

Yet, Mr. Reagan proposes a defense build-up program that calls for the spending of $1.6 trillion over the next five years. The question

that haunts many minds is whether the nation can afford such an ambitious armament buying program at a time when the national debt already exceeds $1 trillion and is expected to be increased by interest payments alone by some $182 billion over the next four years.

Many of Mr. Reagan's admirers find the budget disappointing. Sen. Bob Dole, R-Kan., chairman of the Senate Finance Committee, is quoted in the Wall Street Journal as saying the projected deficits are too large and that there "isn't a clear enough signal that we really mean business" in the fight against inflation. The Journal itself editorially suggests "Mr. Reagan and his team may lack the courage of their convictions."

Another way of putting it is that defense has to yield its share as deeper and deeper cuts in federal programs reduce the alternatives that are available.

DESERET NEWS

Salt Lake City, Utah, February 8, 1982

When President Reagan sent Congress today a long list of programs to be cut as a means of saving $26 billion on the next federal budget, a major item was missing.

Notably absent from the list of proposed cutbacks was the Defense Department, even though the military accounts for a major part of all federal spending.

Up to a point, this omission is understandable. Since the mid-1960's, the military budget has been declining as a percentage of the gross national product after inflation is taken into account. Moreover, America simply must become stronger in the face of an unrelenting Soviet military buildup.

But there's still room for wondering if this situation justifies the 18% increase in the defense budget that President Reagan is proposing for fiscal 1983. With such an increase, 29 cents of every federal dollar would go to the Pentagon and other defense-related agencies.

As part of his budget message, President Reagan proposed some new management initiatives that are basically a renewed attempt to curb waste in federal spending. Yet the Pentagon never seems to be singled out by the administration as a prime target for such savings even though it should be.

Plenty of Pentagon-watchers insist the U.S. is spending too much on ultra-deluxe, super-sophisticated weapons that don't always work out under battlefield conditions. Still other observers are concerned that too much emphasis and money are being devoted to strategic weapons — including such dubious ones as the MX missile — at the expense of America's conventional forces.

Even more important than military hardware, in the estimation of other experts, is the need to reverse the trend toward centralization and bureaucratization of the armed forces that has stifled initiative and impeded the services' ability to react and innovate.

Moreover, no matter how much America strengthens itself militarily, there will still be a major chink in the nation's armor if it remains weak economically. In this connection, one recent study notes that of 13 major industrialized nations, those that spent a smaller than average share of their economic output on defense experienced faster growth, greater investment, and higher productivity during the past two decades.

This is not to suggest that the military be short-changed. Rather, it is to urge that U.S. defense programs be scrutinized much more closely to determine their need, cost, and effectiveness.

The News and Courier
Charleston, S.C., February 12, 1982

A measure of the bankruptcy of new ideas on the part of President Reagan's critics is that they are gradually zeroing in on cutbacks in national defense as a means of reducing a large and troublesome deficit. It is traditional when "benefits" that Congress passes out are threatened, to look toward defense as a reservoir from which money can be diverted.

In that respect, the president's plans for huge spending on military forces may serve the country well apart from what they do to rebuild strength depleted by previous administrations. Attracted by what looks like more money than is strictly necessary, Congress may well take some swipes at defense in order to make up losses elsewhere. If it does, that is in keeping with history. Defense has always served as "surge tanks" for government spending in general. And, as long as the swipes don't get too close to the bone, they may prove useful in diverting attention from other important parts of the president's program. The president may, in fact, have planned things that way.

Congress can and often does turn to cutting defense in an effort to balance a budget. Many times it has no choice, thanks to its own mistakes. Defense is about the only area of government spending that is not locked in concrete for one reason or another. It can be tailored to meet the needs of the situation. Spending in all departments of government should resemble defense spending in that it should never be cast in concrete. One of the chief attractions of President Reagan's program to take power from Washington and give it back to the states is the opportunity it offers to shatter rigid patterns of spending which result in government's always having to spend more because it never gets a chance to spend less.

The Houston Post
Houston, Texas, February 28, 1982

Public and congressional concern over the size of the deficit in President Reagan's red-ink budget is focusing attention on his $216 billion defense-spending request for fiscal 1983. The president insists that his proposed military budget is drawn so tightly it cannot be cut much without endangering national security. But with a deficit nudging $100 billion, it is inconceivable that defense outlays will be immune from scrutiny with a view to reducing them.

One of the most comprehensive analyses of ways to save Pentagon funds was prepared by Sen. David F. Durenberger. The Minnesota Republican outlined $26 billion in cuts he claims could be made over the next five years without jeopardizing the nation's safety. The administration plans to spend $1.4 trillion on arms in that period.

Durenberger's proposals, however, would snip only $3 billion from fiscal '83 defense spending. The bipartisan Congressional Budget Office, by contrast, has a list of cuts it says would reduce the Pentagon budget by $14 billion in the coming fiscal year and by a total of $64 billion by 1987. Even the Heritage Foundation, a conservative think tank that favors strong national defense, says as much as $10 billion could be saved by curbing waste and inefficiency in the Defense Department.

The administration also has been faulted for failing to develop its own defense strategy. Instead, say its critics, it has simply added billions to the Carter administration's defense spending proposals without giving sufficient consideration to alternative means of strengthening our defenses. Among the cost-cutting measures suggested by advocates of a leaner defense budget are: Eliminate the B-1 bomber, slow the Navy's shipbuilding program and switch some aircraft carriers and submarines from nuclear to conventional models, and hold a proposed military pay raise to the governmentwide 5 percent rate rather than increasing it to 8 percent as recommended by the administration.

To declare the $216 billion arms budget sacrosanct is both unrealistic and politically indefensible. Cuts can and will be made. What and how much remains to be seen, but before the defense-budget surgeons begin to operate, they should have a clear understanding of our security needs and commitments to the rest of the free world. Besides defending our own shores, we must be prepared to conduct military operations in Europe and the Pacific and protect the Persian Gulf oil pipeline. It would be a grave mistake to damage the military muscle we need to meet these responsibilities.

It should further be noted that we were spending a larger percentage of our gross national product on defense during most of the 1950s and 1960s than we would be at the end of the administration's proposed military buildup in 1987. But, of course, we weren't running $100 billion deficits in the '50s and '60s. The trick now is to strike a set of budgetary priorities that will give us the arms we need to defend ourselves and our allies at a cost that won't make a basket case of the economy.

The Dispatch
Columbus, Ohio, February 19, 1982

IT SEEMS LIKELY that Congress will trim President Reagan's proposed defense spending for the 1983 fiscal year. Cuts and economies can be made without jeopardizing the president's plans to strengthen this nation's security forces.

When Reagan sent Congress his proposed 1983 budget, it included an estimated deficit of $91.5 billion. It called for total defense outlays of $215.9 billion in 1983. Many lawmakers, Republican and Democratic alike, are alarmed by the size of the deficit and the effect it could have on the nation's economic recovery efforts. The lawmakers, many of whom face re-election this November, are looking for ways to reduce the size of the deficits.

Reagan is standing firm in his opposition to revamping tax cuts he pushed through Congress last year. They are essential to his goal of revitalizing the economy. While some further budget cuts are probable in social programs, it is very likely that the lawmakers will cut Pentagon programs, too. If they move carefully, money can be saved and the defense buildup continued.

For instance, the General Accounting Office (GAO) reported this week that undetermined millions of dollars are being wasted by improper accounting procedures involving foreign arms sales. These deals should include provisions for foreign governments to pay for the administrative overhead incurred by the Pentagon in processing these deals. A 3 percent fee has traditionally been charged, but the GAO believes that doesn't come close to covering actual costs.

Also this week, Donald Kendall, chairman of the U.S. Chamber of Commerce and a strong Reagan supporter, estimated that between $10 billion and $15 billion could be saved by eliminating waste and mismanagement in the Pentagon. He joins a growing list of respected individuals and groups who believe huge sums could be saved if proper procedures were followed. The list includes U.S. Sen. Mark Hatfield, R-Ore., chairman of the Senate Appropriations Committee, the National Conservative Foundation and the House Appropriations Committee, in addition to the General Accounting Office.

And Congress and the White House should re-examine the decision to spend $100 billion developing and deploying the MX missile system.

In addition, the administration should take a second look at its decision to spend some $377 million primarily for the development of chemical weapons. President Nixon halted chemical weapon production nearly 13 years ago and renounced any use of germ warfare weapons. The administration's decision to resume production at accelerated levels reverses national policy that extends back even beyond Nixon's prohibition.

A strong defense relies on the economy's ability to finance military activities. The Pentagon — even for its own sake — should be included in the fight to restore the health of the economy.

Boston Sunday Globe

Boston, Mass., February 14, 1982

The fight over President Reagan's profligate Pentagon spending plan promises to be more than a watershed in the Reagan presidency. With any luck it will force a historic, overdue debate that goes past budgetary issues to underlying questions about military doctrines, definitions of national interest and the nature of threats. It will produce a new generation of national security policies that for the first time are related to the 21st-century world rather than to the world of World War II.

Such a debate will take a while to develop, perhaps as much as two or three years, but when it does, it will go beyond the more-is-better, less-is-better arguments of the recent past. A whole set of Administration assumptions on confrontational diplomacy, arms control and nuclear "war-fighting" doctrines will be examined in public. Some of those assumptions may survive, but others, like germs, will wither in the sunlight.

Administration thinkers are going to find this process acutely uncomfortable, but it is going to be healthy for the country. That's the good news about Reagan's defense budget: It can serve as an unintended catalyst for change.

The dismay on Capitol Hill was nearly universal last week when the monster budget was rolled out. Reagan is proposing a 20 percent increase in new spending authority, from $214 to $258 billion, while making brutal cuts in domestic spending and running up deficits of around $100 billion. The combination of daredevil economics, disregard of social needs and political insensitivity shivered the timbers of fiscal conservatives and provided Democrats with an instant rallying point.

Defense Secretary Weinberger came into the job with no background in defense, but he is experienced in the basic bureaucratic art of defending a budget. For a year he has been weaving a seamless web of arguments to deflect the expected attacks. His main points have been the "relentless" Soviet military buildup, the developing Soviet "global reach and grasp," the theoretical "window of vulnerability" to Soviet missile attack and the "neglect" of American defense needs, attributed mainly to Jimmy Carter. This is stitched together with the assertion that "no one can deny this alarming trend" and that patriots will make the sacrifices required "if we wish to keep our freedom."

Those arguments, booming away, have been like the old battleship Missouri softening up a beach with its 16-inch guns. When invasion day arrived last week (time to publish the first full budget under the Reagan presidency), the Defense Department unveiled additional tactics for securing the budgetary beachhead.

With Weinberger's "rearm America" ordnance still whistling in overhead, Deputy Secretary of Defense Frank Carlucci delivered two new lines: First, the budget should be sacrosanct because all kinds of cutting, cost savings and managerial magic have already been achieved. Second, 93 percent of the budget is locked in due to past commitments, and only 7 percent is "really" new – which means that even if you look for places to cut, you can't find any. Furthermore, you can't save by cutting new programs, because they don't cost much the first year anyway. So goes Pentagon Catch-22.

That may be malarky, but it's the kind of malarky that over the years has often silenced citizens and cowed congressmen, who on complicated issues give leaders the benefit of the doubt. How, then, to respond?

There is certainly a potential military threat, primarily from the Soviet Union. In some respects the United States needs to back its foreign policy with a stronger defense. After Vietnam, the Pentagon was under-funded for a few years in certain categories, especially having to do with "readiness": stocks of spare parts, ammunition and budgets for maintenance and training. The Soviet military establishment now is about equal to our own in many respects. Military spending is bound to be painful because many categories, from fuel to high-tech weaponry, are subject to higher than usual rates of inflation.

Having acknowledged that, it is still true that the Pentagon budget is riddled with waste, including some spending patterns that are genuinely dangerous because they support military programs and doctrines that will reduce our national safety rather than enhance it.

One example is the latest generation of land-based intercontinental missiles, the MX, which is beginning to look as if it will provide the worst of both worlds: It will be lethal, because if produced in numbers, it will be powerful and accurate enough to threaten the Soviet land-based deterrent. That will put the Soviets on a hair-trigger. Furthermore, it provides the "war-fighting" school around Reagan and Weinberger with a suitably precise tool for "limited" strikes, which they are now busily imagining.

The other side of the MX is that, in fixed bases on land, it will be nonsurvivable. That will increase pressure to build an antiballistic missile system, which would kill the SALT 1 treaty, which stopped ABM development, and would lead to wildly expensive (and probably ineffective) new technologies, such as laser stations in space.

The 600-ship Navy built around carrier groups might seem innocuous, but it too is dangerous. Not only is it enormously expensive, but it is based on a naval doctrine that was sound from the Spanish American War to World War II, but is ludicrous today. The idea is that if a regional war breaks out, say in Europe or the Mideast, the Navy will zip around and sting the Russian bear on his neck, shoulder blades and backside, sweeping the Soviet fleet from the high seas and bombing its home bases. That splendid and anachronistic strategy (virtually guaranteeing nuclear strikes against US fleets) is the underpinning of Reagan's 600-ship Navy.

The defense budget is like one of the unfortunate Christmas fruitcakes, where the cake part – which is no doubt nourishing – is laced with glistening chunks of unidentified substances, fruits and nuts that are quite unappetizing and possibly wholly indigestible. Programs such as the B-1 bomber, the large aircraft carrier, the 600-ship Navy, the production of binary chemical munitions, the fixed base MX missile, the antiballistic missile, the M-1 tank, the AH-64 attack helicopter, and dozens of others each present different problems and deserve critical attention. That will take time.

Perhaps the best immediate response to the indiscriminate Weinberger budget is to meet it with an equally simplistic remedy: Increases in "real" spending after inflation should be slashed at least in half, from 10 percent to 4 or 5 percent. The Pentagon should be ordered to live within that cap and to use that money first on readiness accounts, rather than on new hardware. That's a crude approach, but no more crude than the Weinberger wish-list in which all the services were encouraged to ask for anything they could think of.

The point, after all, is to block helter-skelter waste and to freeze development of dangerous, swashbuckling military doctrines until there has been serious public discussion about whether they make sense. The occasion for such a debate is Reagan's unintended gift.

Tulsa World

Tulsa, Okla.,
February 15, 1982

PRESIDENT Reagan is well advised to stand firm on his commitment to increase U. S. defense readiness. On that, he is joined by Republicans and Democrats alike.

But the problem is timing.

It is unlikely, maybe even impossible, for the nation's defense industry to move quickly and efficiently on the programs planned. The danger is a hasty effort to place billions in new defense contracts, only to see the contractors bog down in getting the actual goods into production.

Whether the entire Reagan defense budget is approved or not, we are not going to see an immediate improvement in U. S. defense readiness.

After years of winding down defense spending, the ability of U. S. defense contractors to produce equipment and armaments is low.

The obvious question that Reagan and Congress should be considering is how to leave the total defense commitment at increased levels while recognizing that actual expenditures should be slowed considerably. This would give both the defense department the contractors time to build up the production capacity more slowly and more efficiently.

Slowing the actual spending would obviously help cut the budget deficits for the next few fiscal years, which would help to give the rest of the Reagan program a chance to work.

Perhaps the most important aspect of the military buildup is the commitment. But having made that, there is no sense in rushing pell mell to spend the money in such a way as to guarantee waste and inefficiency.

The Washington Post
Times Herald
Washington, D.C., February 9, 1982

THE SEASON IS starting in which the annual ritual debate over defense expenditures takes place. The documents produced so far by the Reagan administration—the proposed federal budget itself and the defense secretary's report to Congress —and the immediate reaction to these documents by the critics, suggest that, in certain respects, only the numbers and the names of the players have changed. The broad lines of argument remain the same.

To the charge that the country cannot afford these gigantic expenditures, that they are both helping to ruin the economy and absorbing funds direly needed for social services, come the equally familiar replies. These are that defense expenditures as a percentage of GNP are relatively modest, that much is needed in the way of modernization and improved readiness for American forces, that social spending (if you include the big insurance programs) is still the far larger share of budget costs, that no duty of government takes priority over the duty to protect the populace from external threat and so on. All of it true—on both sides of the argument: we can't afford it, but if it is necessary, of course, we can.

From here the argument will veer off to what is meant by necessary and from there to various strategies and weapons systems and whether they are any good or not, and sooner or later there will be some congressional cuts—and after that, maybe in a few months, everyone will agree that the "wrong" cuts were made. Much sighing all around. A high-ranking officer in the Pentagon will allege that he had to counsel against going into some place or other because we have let our military resources run down so, and a complaining congressman will swear that the latest fighter-bomber plane won't fly and costs twice as much as it was supposed to. Then everyone will get ready for the debate the following year.

Don't be misled by our weariness with this debate into thinking that when it starts up we don't plan to be there, sinking into the dreadful details with everyone else concerning costs and weapons characteristics and the rest. But for now, before all that gets going, something else strikes us as far more urgent to consider. Before you can reach the question of "how much is enough," you really have to have some rudimentary idea of what it is supposed to be enough for. The Defense Department's careful descriptions of the kinds of engagements (and deterrent effects) various weapons systems and force levels are intended for and its verbal tour of the trouble spots of the world do not satisfy this need. And here, it seems to us, you come right up to the huge, troubling question concerning this country's defenses and its defense expenditures: it often seems as though the elaborate military enterprise itself is a work of fantasy, that it is absorbed in anxieties and contingencies and scenarios that have little connection with the actual world in which we live.

To some extent this is a result of interservice politics and bargaining—plans are made and weapons procured that do more for the various services' self-images than for their ability to defend. But there is more. Look at the places that, from a national security point of view, have troubled our government most in recent years—Afghanistan, Iran, Poland, El Salvador—and consider that in each, somehow the circumstances have been deemed "complicated" in ways that made irrelevant the kind of forces that we have at our disposal. This is not a suggestion that this country should have "gone into" any of those countries in a military way, only a comment on the split-screen quality of our costly national defense establishment. There is our military enterprise and then there is what we do around the world.

The fact is that however much improvement may be needed in this country's military forces, the show of strength that is relevant and required now has to do with political will on the nonmilitary diplomatic and economic front. It's all very well to talk tough about weapons and forces and their great potential. But a country that is not willing to sustain a grain embargo or other nonmilitary pressures that are controversial and inconvenient at home, really isn't going to impress anyone with lots of added hardware. You can agree or disagree with the substance of Secretary Caspar Weinberger's blast, in his report to Congress, against current trading arrangements with the Soviet Union. Maybe it wasn't even his to have brought up in such a report. But, right or wrong, there is a certain relevance to it: the real questions concerning this country's strength in its conflicts around the world are only partly questions of force levels and organization. They are, in much larger part just now, questions of national purpose and credibility on a variety of nonviolent fronts.

THE COMMERCIAL APPEAL
Memphis, Tenn., February 21, 1982

WHAT MESSAGE is President Reagan sending to Congress when he says his administration has ruled out reductions in defense spending and delays in tax cuts in spite of the prospect of a record budget deficit?

What options is he leaving Congress, when he invites "specific suggestions" for limiting the deficit? Some new sources of tax revenue could be tapped. Congress could — and should — close the loophole that allows wealthy companies to buy and cash in the unusable investment tax credits of weak businesses.

But the President seems to be pointing mostly at social programs. He seems to be saying, in effect, "I've cut about as much as I think I can get away with. But I'll be glad to consider more cuts if you're willing to recommend some and take the heat from the voters for it."

That's the way, it appears, that Reagan would like to set up the confrontation over his proposed budget. Congress, however, doesn't have follow the President's lead. And, indeed, it seems to be moving in another direction.

The big budget battle may very well be over defense.

REPUBLICANS AS WELL as Democrats are joining a rising chorus of complaints about the amount of defense spending that the administration has proposed and about how that spending would drive the deficit up.

Here's a sampling:

• House Republican leader Robert Michel of Illinois: "Some of my House members felt pole-axed when they were first presented with a $90-million deficit by Reagan . . . I've never seen a defense budget that couldn't be cut."

• Rep. Newt Gingrich (R-Ga.): "If you're cutting widows and orphans, you have to be at least critical of every penny you're spending on generals and admirals. We're clearly not going to get Reagan's defense budget . . . (It's) clearly a fantasy."

• Ted Stevens of Alaska, the Senate's No. 2 Republican: "We're going to cut defense some way."

• Sen. Paul Laxalt (R-Nev.), one of the President's closest friends in Congress: "I can't believe there can't be substantial savings effected out of that (defense) budget without threatening weaponry or our basic defense."

• Senate Majority Leader Howard Baker of Tennessee also has said that defense can, should and will be cut.

Aside from the deficit, there are other reasons for challenging the proposed spending levels and their purposes. Military analysts have questioned whether the administration has gone off in all directions in a dash to get ahead of the Soviet Union without tailoring spending programs to clearly defined military strategy and practical military needs.

SOME SUPPORTERS of heavy defense spending agree, for instance, that the B52 bomber should be replaced, but they argue that the proposed B1 isn't an effective alternative because it probably won't be able to penetrate Soviet detection systems by the time it becomes operational.

Why should we build two nuclear-powered aircraft carriers, others argue, when precision-guided weapons from ships, aircraft and shore would make the carriers sitting ducks?

What good will it do to spend $19 billion on 7,000 M1 tanks, the critics ask, when the tank's transmission is so delicate that it can't dig itself into a hull-down position on a battlefield? The Army's answer is high-speed bulldozers to accompany each tank company — at a cost of $1 million each.

And, after all the new weapons, planes and ships are built, where will the armed forces get the personnel to man and use them? Gen. Edward C. Meyer, the Army chief of staff, told Congress recently that the President's global military strategy involved "tremendous risks" because the armed forces were too small to carry it out. So far, there's no indication that the President is considering a peace-time draft.

Reagan said Thursday that to "back away on national defense" would send the wrong signal to friend and foe alike. What signal is he sending now, especially to friends?

ACCORDING TO CHANCELLOR Helmut Schmidt of West Germany, Western Europe is in danger of political and economic destablization as a result of a world economic crisis that projected U.S. deficits could make much worse.

"Europe is in greater danger than the Americans have understood so far," Schmidt said last week. "The fabric of the economy and the society is endangered by the deepest recession since the middle '30s.

In addition, the projected U.S. deficits have been called a threat to the world's economic health by the finance ministers of France, Britain and Belgium because of the effects those deficits would have on world interest rates.

While back at home, the Congressional Budget Office has said that Reagan's five-year defense budget could be reduced by $64.4 billion by abandoning the questionable B1 bomber in favor of development of the more sophisticated Stealth aircraft and making a number of other cuts.

Congress isn't listening only to the President's offer of a poor choice or none. It may listen to him even less as the budget debate continues. At least, we can hope so.

Post-Tribune

Gary, Ind., February 15, 1982

It requires no exceptional insight to see that President Reagan's proposals for defense spending are unrealistic. He wants everything.

The rigidity of his stand and the enormity of the defense budget almost assure bitter arguments and in the end, some sizable cuts.

He has made a mistake. The military spending cuts won't necessarily be the most intelligent cuts. Because there are no real priorities in the military proposals, members of Congress are likely to just whack where they can.

Big spending and strength obviously are not synonomous. Why is that so difficult to see? Looking ahead five years or so, the bill for defense could be more than $1.5 trillion. What is the president preparing the country for — a "limited" nuclear war? "Regular" wars? Peace?

The lasting strength of America is not in glamorous tools of war, in nuclear supercarriers. It is in a healthy economy and a creative populace. The economy, though down, is by no means out. But it is being .battered. The proposed military spending buildup will batter it more. The price is high.

If the president cannot set realistic priorities in the total budget, he should at least set some in the military proposals. Even some military experts say that shifting spending from the most costly planes and ships would cut total costs and still allow for a build-up in necessary equipment.

Members of Congress will set some military priorities if the administration does not, and their cuts could be damaging. A united effort between Congress and the Pentagon is the only sensible, safe answer. But first, the president and the Pentagon people have to listen.

There is, besides the priority problem in the Pentagon's spending, a geographical bias, as the accompanying chart shows. The sunny South does nicely, and so does the West. But the Midwest and Northeast are something else. Those discrepancies may explain why some southern and western politicians are less critical of the plan to pour out the military dollars.

It will be a victory for nobody if the administration, in demanding so much, reaps a bitter harvest for us all by being unrealistic.

The San Diego Union

San Diego, Calif., February 14, 1982

Congress, transfixed by a projected $91 billion deficit, is looking for ways to cut federal spending without incurring the wrath of voters in November. Increasingly, this is translating into a consensus that the $215 billion fiscal 1983 defense budget must be cut, and that Pentagon spending hikes planned for 1984 and 1985 must also be reduced substantially.

Before this sentiment snowballs into an unstoppable avalanche, Congress and the American people ought to stop and think long enough to put defense needs into proper perspective.

For all the wild headlines about Mr. Reagan's $1.6 *trillion,* five-year defense buildup, the President is really proposing to spend only $200 billion more than President Carter had allocated for the 1981-86 period. We say "only" because adding $200 billion to the defense bill over a five-year period works out to $40 billion per year, or roughly 5 percent of the federal budget in any year between now and the mid 1980s.

Still, $40 billion a year is hardly loose change. Wisely spent, it ought to help the U.S. military recover at least some of the ground lost during the decade of the 1970s when Soviet military spending exceeded that of the United States by some $240 billion overall and $355 billion for actual weapons purchases.

Assuming the Reagan defense budgets through fiscal 1986 remain substantially intact, the United States will then be spending 7 percent of its gross national product on defense. That will compare to 15 percent or more for the Soviet Union, providing the Russians continue to ratchet up their military spending by 4 or 5 percent each year as they have been doing relentlessly since the mid-1960s.

With luck, the fiscal 1986 U.S. defense budget may approach the magnitude of the Kremlin's military budget, although even this achievement would be misleadingly reassuring because the Soviets spend a much higher percentage of their defense budget to buy armaments.

In defense terms, the legacy of the 1970s is one of U.S. military deficiency across the board. The Air Force still lacks a modern strategic bomber. The Navy is at least 150 ships short of the minimum needed to fulfill existing foreign and defense policy commitments. Modernization of weapons for U.S. ground forces is a decade overdue, and far behind comparable Soviet programs that are churning out arms at three times the rate the Reagan buildup would reach in 1986.

The strategic nuclear picture is the most ominous of all. Far from closing the now-famous "window of vulnerability," current Reagan programs are actually postponing the day when the threat of a Soviet first strike is effectively neutralized. Adopting a survivable basing mode for the MX missile would help to cancel the vulnerability of the U.S. nuclear deterrent, but would also cost more than the administration has now allocated for the MX program.

All this is not to say that the Pentagon's budget is inviolable, or that it could not be pared without cutting into desperately needed muscle. But sharply reducing the Navy's shipbuilding program, or canceling the B-1 bomber, or scrapping the MX would only compound the nation's already acute strategic problems.

Moreover, as Budget Director David Stockman noted last Sunday, most of the funds for these and other new weapons programs do not show up in the Pentagon's budget until the mid or late 1980s. Arbitrarily lopping off $10 billion or so from the '82 defense budget would almost certainly require sharp reductions in service pay and benefits, plus funds for such readiness items as spare parts, fuel, munitions stocks, and training.

These were precisely the kinds of cuts made during the 1970s that put enlisted personnel on food stamps and grounded half the planes in even the best Air Force squadrons.

What is needed instead are redoubled efforts by Secretary of Defense Caspar Weinberger to ferret out and eliminate the costly waste and duplication that continue to infect the Pentagon bureaucracy. This waste is now doubly intolerable because it inflates the overall budget deficit while subtracting funds available for actual improvements in the nation's security.

The procurement reforms initiated by Secretary Weinberger, and especially the multi-year purchasing he has recommended, would help to insure that every dime spent buys added security. But much more must be done to simplify weapons development programs and to expand competitive bidding in lieu of the negotiated contracts favored by too many in the Pentagon.

The pressure from Capitol Hill should help Mr. Reagan and Mr. Weinberger to understand that waste, duplication, and defense industry profiteering must be attacked ruthlessly.

The alternative is to stand by while Congress, now showing signs of panic over the looming deficits, carves billions out of the defense budget with too little regard for the effect on the nation's defenses a few years hence.

Wisconsin ⚜ State Journal
Madison, Wisc., February 19, 1982

President Reagan and the Pentagon can argue as much as it wants about efficient military spending, two questions remain:

Q. Are all these weapons, all these ships, all this equipment, all these nuclear and conventional bombs really needed?

Congress has shown by past actions that it believes the military must be strengthened, but the Reagan budget is overkill. It provides for everything from the on-again, off-again B-1 bomber program that would be obsolete before it would be used to the grossly expensive and unproven MX system.

The Reagan budget can be cut plenty, while still improving military preparedness.

Q. If other programs must be reduced, why should the military be spared — especially in light of its record of waste, fraud and inefficiency?

Answer: It shouldn't be spared.

It won't be easy to cut back defense spending, but what is easy these days?

Part of the difficulty is because many members of Congress who are screaming against defense spending are the same ones who have refused to close most of the 634 bases the Defense Department recommended by closed to save $443 million year. Close the other guy's bases, they say, but don't close mine.

These are the same members of Congress who approved the $41-billion worth of military projects in past years that must still be paid for.

The moment of truth will come when members of Congress have to vote on military cuts that affect their constituents. Look for members from non-military states, like Wisconsin, to do much of the proposing. They don't have to take heat from potential voters who depend on military installations for a living.

If all else fails, why not cut the defense budget across the board and let the Big Brass at the Pentagon sort out what programs they really want and trim or discard the others.

Above all, President Reagan must not jeopardize his good start in taking the American people away from the high-tax, high-spending practices of the past by insisting on his swollen defense budget.

In the middle of his term, President Jimmy Carter reacted to international criticism of "weakness" in America's foreign posture — much related to defense capability.

It led Carter to abandon his campaign pledge to reduce defense spending by $7 billion yearly "without damaging our military capability."

Instead, Carter proposed sharply increasing military budgets. In 1979 and 1980, he wanted annual *real* increases (above infla-

tion) of 3 percent in military spending; in 1981 that rose to an 8 percent real increase, with a 5 percent real increase from fiscal 1982 on.

In his farewell budget for fiscal 1982, Carter proposed a 14.7 percent increase in the defense budget from the fiscal 1981 budget to $184.4 billion. Incoming President Reagan, who had campaigned for increased military spending, wanted more and got it raised to $188.8 billion by a willing Congress.

In fact, Congress frequently spent more than the Carter administration had proposed on military arms, in particular.

Big 1982 budget

In the face of recession and an estimated $91.5-billion deficit, Reagan has continued with his accelerated defense spending, only this time Congress isn't going along.

Congressional resistance is coming from Democrats and Republicans alike.

In fiscal 1982, the Reagan administration is expected to spend $182.8 billion on the military; this is $6 billion less than was budgeted.

In fiscal 1983, Reagan is asking for military outlays of $215.9 billion or $28.1 billion (14.3 percent) more than was budgeted in fiscal 1982.

Defense spending gets even more massive in terms of obligational authority, which is the amount of money that can be contracted to spend, even if not spent

within the fiscal year.

In fiscal 1983, Reagan is asking $258 billion in obligational authority, which represents an increase of $31.7 billion or 14 percent over the $226.3 billion in the fiscal 1982 budget.

What defense dollars buy

Under the new budget, every category of military spending increases but the emphasis is on weapons purchases (up 37 percent), research (22 percent).

The big gainers under the increased obligational authority will be new ships for the Navy (up more than 100 percent) and for nuclear weapons (up 43 percent).

The Reagan administration argues effectively that $13.5 billion of the increase in obligational spending is included to hold down spending in later years.

Item: The Reagan administration is using higher, and more realistic, inflation estimates for weapons to avoid cost overruns that have been customary up to now.

Item: It is providing multiyear contracts to bring down long-term costs of ships, weapons etc.

Also, the Reagan administration can point out that $41 billion in military outlays will be paid in fiscal 1983 for arms, ammunition, equipment and the like that Congress had approved in earlier years.

Pentagon Officials Warn Budgetmakers of Soviet Threat

As President Reagan's five-year, $1.6 billion defense plan came under congressional scrutiny in March and April of 1982, the dilemma facing budgetmakers became clear; while many legislators felt that the substantial U.S. military buildup called for in the budget was necessary, most felt also that a decrease in the defense budget was essential to reduce projected federal deficits. The Administration, however, remained adamant in its refusal to recommend reductions. Testifying before the Senate Budget Committee March 3, Weinberger declared: "We did not submit a budget that we believe has any unnecessary requests in it."

Pentagon officials appeared before Senate and House committees and subcommittees to tell their members, sometimes in closed sessions, that even the proposed budget figures were not large enough to meet the current Soviet military threat. One secret, two-hour presentation, dubbed the "threat briefing," reportedly included detailed photographs of Soviet equipment taken by U.S. spy satellites. Senior planners for the armed services told the Senate Armed Services committee that the extent of U.S. commitments abroad was threatening their ability to meet potential threats, and that if the proposed size of the forces was cut, the number of commitments would also have to be decreased.

The Des Moines Register

Des Moines, Iowa, March 12, 1982

One might suppose that President Reagan's plans for spending $1.6 trillion on the military over the next five years would satisfy the Pentagon. Not so. The Defense Department recently told Congress that not even this fantastic sum would pay for the ambitious military strategy laid out by the Reagan administration.

The Washington Post reports that this was the unanimous advice provided by the senior planners for the nation's four military services in testimony before a Senate Armed Services subcommittee in late February.

The chief planner for the Army testified that, to carry out Reagan's strategy, the Army would need more divisions than the president's budget provides. The Navy's chief planner likewise said that more seagoing battle groups would be needed. And the Air Force warned of a need "considerably greater than the 40" tactical fighter wings now budgeted.

● One might argue that their testimony proves a need to sacrifice even more non-military programs and pay more taxes to provide more than Reagan's $1.6 trillion.

● A more reasonable view, expressed at the hearing by Senator Sam Nunn (Dem., Ga.), is that "we had better go back to the drawing boards on strategy." For the military strategy espoused by the Reagan administration is filled with wild-eyed ideas that not only would be terribly expensive but would be of questionable benefit to the national security.

Nunn is concerned with the Reagan administration's interest in what it calls "horizontal escalation." Under this plan, if the Soviet Union attacked American interests somewhere in the world, this country might strike back by attacking a Soviet weak point, such as Poland. Nunn, one of the leading military experts in the Senate, believes that a much larger armed force would be needed to carry out this strategy.

The Reagan military budget calls for "modernization of all components of U.S. strategic forces to ensure their ability to survive an attack and retaliate." Yet the United States already has enough nuclear weapons to annihilate the Soviet Union.

Such grandiose plans fail to recognize that there are limits to what this country ought to spend on its military forces during peacetime. The strategy places too great an emphasis on military solutions to world problems, and too little emphasis on diplomacy, economic aid and a human-rights policy — all of which probably are more effective tools in an era of unwinnable war.

If Congress hopes to bring the dangerous deficit down to a safe level, it will have to cut, rather than increase, Reagan's military budget. And the administration ought to work out a strategy more in line with what is affordable — and what is needed.

SYRACUSE
HERALD·JOURNAL
Syracuse, N.Y., March 29, 1982

When Ronald Reagan was between elections, he helped organize the Committee on the Present Danger. Once, he sat on its board of directors.

Today, more than 40 current and one-time members of the committee work in his administration. They've helped the president, his Security Council and Defense Secretary Caspar Weinberger shape the administration's higher-than-ever military budgets.

The committee, however, isn't happy.

Its members look at the $1.6 trillion the administration intends to spend on defense during the next five years and flatly declares:

"Not enough."

The "present danger," they maintain, will threaten the U.S. until the administration beefs up its trillion-dollar plan by another $100 billion.

The country's businessmen see a more imminent danger, that of continued run-away inflation.

The National Association of Manufacturers, the U.S. Chamber of Commerce and, more recently, the Business Roundtable composed of heads of 200 major companies advise slowing down military spending. The coming deficit of $91.5 million threatens recovery, they contend. They fear another shot of inflation.

The roundtable suggests rebuilding defenses on a slower schedule and delaying 1973's projected 10 percent income tax cut.

We can't agree with their tax-cut recommendation, but we do agree with their armament-buying slowdown contention.

Stepping up defense spending from $187.5 billion for this year to $221 billion for next year risks a new surge of inflation.

The extra dollars can be squeezed out of the Pentagon.

Do so. Bring down the projected deficit. But strengthen buying power with tax cuts. They're our pump primer.

Otherwise, we risk an economic "present" danger.

The Dallas Morning News

Dallas, Texas, March 22, 1982

Jimmy Carter greatly weakened our defense capability vis-a-vis the Soviets. But even Carter was starting to wake up toward the end of his administration. His secretary of Defense, Harold Brown, knew that the arms race always proceeded thusly: We race fast, they race fast; we slow down, they race fast.

The most unpleasant reality President Reagan has had to face up to, then, is the need to rearm. By the end of the Carter era the Soviets were outproducing us in virtually all categories of weaponry, so the newly elected Reagan was stuck with trying to start us on the road to economic recovery while at the same time beefing up our defenses. His critics now thrust to undercut both programs by suggesting that the tax cuts be rolled back and the defense budget be cut. Social-welfare spending, of course, is sacrosanct in the critics' view.

The facts are these: Social-welfare spending, as a percentage of the federal budget, has doubled in 20 years; defense spending has been cut in half — at the very time the Soviets were proceeding with the biggest buildup in the history of the world.

It is highly appropriate, then, that the respected Committee on the Present Danger, which the President used to belong to, should point out that Reagan's proposed defense allocations are, if anything, too low, and at best "minimally" adequate. Committee chairman Charls Walker advocates spending $1.5 trillion more than the President has proposed to spend over the next five years. The committee thus adds yet more evidence, already mountainous, that the Pentagon ought not be chief focus for budget cutters.

Rocky Mountain News
A Scripps-Howard Newspaper   Reg. U.S. Pat. Off.   Colorado's First Newspaper—Founded in 1859

Denver, Colo., March 17, 1982

EVEN if President Reagan got the entire $1.6 trillion he wants the nation to spend on defense over the next five years, it wouldn't be enough, says the Pentagon.

At a recent Senate Armed Services subcommittee hearing, the senior planners of the four military services agreed that they will need more Army and Marine divisions, more Navy ships and Air Force wings than the five-year plan provides to be able to carry out all the missions the plan sets forth.

In declassifying the testimony, the Defense Department has more or less made official the leak that so upset the administration a couple months ago.

This was to the effect that Pentagon specialists had calculated that it would take possibly another $750 million on top of the $1.6 trillion to fulfill all the administration's military objectives.

If the stupefying sum of $1.6 trillion isn't going to do the defense job, then maybe the job needs to be redefined.

The defense budget is already a tempting target for people in Congress worried about the huge federal deficits projected for the next few years. There is no way they will go along with even larger defense proposals.

We don't know which is the greater danger — spending too little on defense or spending too much. Unfortunately, we are not convinced the Pentagon can wisely spend $1.6 trillion, let alone $2 trillion-plus.

THE WALL STREET JOURNAL
New York, N.Y., March 25, 1982

President Reagan's huge defense budget is getting plenty of attention in the current political struggle over budget cuts, and we can see no reason at all why it should be overlooked. Our fear is not that someone might cut the defense budget but that the cuts will be made in ways that have in the past insured that we would receive the least, rather than the most, bang for a buck. The politics of putting defense spending on a rational basis are themselves formidable, but that is where the focus on defense spending should be directed.

Disinvestment was the watchword of the military budget in the 1970s. The Nixon and Ford administrations hoped to use the mislabeled "peace dividend" after the Vietnam war to offset the rising costs of social service programs. Just before leaving office, President Ford chucked that position and proposed an ambitious plan to upgrade our arsenal and our readiness. Jimmy Carter quickly scotched those proposals, and for almost his entire term, he left the military to languish as entitlements spending raced out of control.

During the decade of the '70s, military preparedness grossly deteriorated. Because of a dearth of spare parts, repair chiefs cannibalized aircraft and vehicles in order to keep at least some planes flying and some tanks rolling. Skilled troops left in droves due to poor pay and benefits. Even ammunition was in short supply. Strategic programs, such as the new nuclear bomber, were scrapped, or as with the Trident submarine and cruise missile, stretched out. In the meantime, the Soviet Union was embarked on the most massive military buildup in world history, and now is superior to the U.S. in almost every category of strategic and conventional force.

Those calling for major defense cuts—the figures run as high as $30 billion for fiscal 1983—would have us repeat the mistakes of the past decade. Readiness would remain impaired; procurement contracts would be so stretched out as to cost more over the long run; the troops' morale might again ebb.

As opposed to popular impression, most of the defense budget will be spent on manpower and conventional readiness. Strategic forces will consume less than 10% of the Total Obligational Authority in next year's budget. Spending on general purpose forces will amount to $106.5 billion out of total budget authority of $258 billion. The next largest expenditure item is training, medical and other general personnel activities, which will total $44.2 billion. That compares with $23.1 billion that will be spent on strategic weapons such as the MX missile, Trident submarine and the B1 bomber.

There are few quick ways of making large savings in the defense budget without sacrificing readiness. For instance, the Office of Management and Budget calculates that if every defense procurement program costing $500 million or more were killed, it would save $49 billion in obligational authority— but only $6.5 billion in outlays next year. Of the $216 billion that actually will be spent next year on defense, more than a quarter comes from money provided in the fiscal 1982 budget and earlier years on long-term procurements.

This situation, of course, leads to the temptations to which previous administrations and Congresses succumbed—reducing readiness by cutting funds for maintenance, munitions and manpower, or stretching out longterm procurement contracts even though that just increases the costs of these programs in future years. It's these practices that have gotten us into the defense jam we're in today.

There are ways of trimming military spending. Cutting unnecessary expenditures to maintain obsolete bases, killing pet programs of some services and consolidation of procurement programs among the branches of the military make economic sense but always face political obstacles. The most efficient way is the one most often avoided in the past—to fund long-term procurement projects fully in order to optimize the Pentagon's bargaining leverage with contractors. To a large degree, the administration's proposals aim to do that.

However, this policy trades large apparent costs now for large savings in the future, whereas the instinct in Congress is to do exactly the opposite. It has been that instinct that has ballooned our present costs. The best defense for the Reagan defense budget is not that it is sacrosanct but that it attempts to remedy some of those past sins. By all means the defense budget should be looked at carefully. But controlling defense costs is a long-term effort. Attempts to trim a single year's budget can lead, indeed most typically have led, to shortsighted cuts that over time only make an adequate defense more costly.

The Seattle Times
Seattle, Wash., March 8, 1982

THE BATTLE over President Reagan's massive military budget threatens to eclipse all other congressional issues in fury and scope. And if the relevant committees do their jobs properly, their concerns will involve much more than the cost-effectiveness of the individual components of the president's program.

Broadly speaking, those larger concerns could be placed in three categories:

● **Strategy.** By the looks of things, the Pentagon has no comprehensive, strategic defense plan other than to "defend the world." The idea appears to be to spend billions of dollars toward developing a capability to wage any kind of war just about anywhere.

Obviously, the Russians must be kept guessing. No one suggests that plans for meeting specific contingencies be spelled out in public hearings.

Yet, to set priorities on spending for specific arms programs, Congress must be given some concept of national strategic priorities. The U.S. was thought to have learned in the Vietnam War that it could not be policeman to the world. There is ample reason today to doubt that the lesson was learned.

● **Organization.** The valedictories of two departing four-star generals have freshly alerted the nation in recent days to the fact that the military-command structure needs an overhaul.

Gen. David C. Jones, who will retire in June as chairman of the Joint Chiefs of Staff, says the Joint Chiefs system impedes effective decision-making because every member of that body except the chairman wears two hats. The leaders of the individual services, who also are on the Pentagon's "board of directors," naturally devote much of their efforts to defending turf. Their parochial service interests often conflict with the broader view. The inevitable results are unsatisfactory compromises.

Jones favors legislation that would, among other things, assign the statutory role of chief military adviser to the chairman of the Joint Chiefs, rather than to the Joint Chiefs as a body.

Gen. Volney F. Warner, who formerly headed the Readiness Command, which includes all nine Army divisions and 40 Air Force tactical air wings in the continental U.S., retired early after he was unable to persuade Defense Secretary Weinberger and the Joint Chiefs to realign the command structure.

In a letter to the president, Warner charged that "the Joint Chiefs . . . have subverted the unified command system in creating ad hoc headquarters to meet each new military crisis," and that "this proliferation of headquarters without any attendant increase in forces — not one soldier, sailor, airman or marine — is ineffective and creates a facade of readiness that simply does not exist."

● **Economy.** In his letter Warner said, "The president urgently needs a National Security Council that balances the execution of civil and military programs and the threats to national security posed by the economy as well as by the Soviets."

It may be unusual for a general to recognize — but Congress surely should — that unrestrained military spending can wreck the economy, which is truly the nation's first line of defense. Ultimately, only a sound economy can support an adequate military force.

The Oregonian

Portland, Ore., March 15, 1982

In its debate of the Pentagon budget, Congress should demand to know whether the $1.6 trillion cost of the administration's five-year defense plan is understated by half and whether even the lower figure buys too much hardware for the armed forces to swallow in so short a time.

Recent Senate Armed Services Committee hearings strongly suggest that the price tag of the ambitious defense plan may be understated by as much as $750 billion over the five-year period. Testimony shows that even if the $2.35 trillion is hurled at the so-called "horizontal escalation" defense strategy, U.S. forces probably would be unable to accomplish their combat goals.

The thrust of some of the testimony is that even with gigantic expenditures on rearming, the nation will be no closer to closing the gap with the Soviet Union five years from now than it is at present. Fred C. Ikle, undersecretary of defense for policy, testified that the armed forces would not have the "reasonable assurance" of being able to carry out the strategy now charted by the Pentagon's civilian bosses. Top Pentagon planners envision the United States as being able to fight several conflicts around the world simultaneously or to defend against a Soviet assault in one area while attacking the Soviet Union from another.

There is another aspect that should not be overlooked in this eerie and ominous budgetary fire dance. What good will it do the country to spend untold billions on an "iffy" defense strategy if it exhausts the country's economic base in the process?

Sentinel Star

Orlando, Fla., April 2, 1982

WITH as little fanfare as possible, the Reagan administration has released a report showing that the costs of 44 major weapons systems in the Reagan military spending program have increased 33 percent since the last report to Congress was issued Dec. 31. The figures are startling.

The report shows that buying the 44 biggest weapons will cost an estimated $454.8 billion instead of the December estimate of $340.3 billion. That's a $114.5 billion increase. Even more amazing is that the costs of both the B-1 bomber and two nuclear aircraft carriers were not included in the report.

Defense spokesmen explained that the huge increases were based on two factors: One was $97 billion in additional orders, and the other was a $16 billion increase attributed to a more realistic estimate of inflation.

Administration spokesmen denied that the figures were either unexpected by them or that they would require changes in the Reagan budget goals of spending $258 billion on military items in fiscal 1983 and a total of $1.6 trillion on the military through fiscal year 1987.

But if those figures didn't come as a surprise to the president, they will surely come as a surprise to Congress, Wall Street and the American public. Even giving the president the benefit of the doubt that the increase has already been considered in his ambitious budget, the psychological impact of the report will be major.

The fiscal 1983 budget proposal is now before Congress and the report released so quietly by the Pentagon is bound to fire up an already heated budget debate. Slipping that news past Congress is akin to slipping a bull elephant into the PTA bake sale.

Lincoln Journal

Lincoln, Neb., March 22, 1982

Last Friday's Pentagon announcement — that the cost of paying for 44 new major weapons system wanted by President Reagan will cost the country a staggering $114.5 billion more than previously estimated — was underpublicized.

The Reagan administration has caught on to the shrewd technique of waiting until Friday afternoon to disclose disagreeable information. That's when the Washington press corps often is short-staffed and the rest of the media is caught in the crush of preparing for weekend publications or telecasts. In such a situation, some spot stories may escape the kind of attention they deserve.

Nevertheless, the nation will not overlook an 85 percent cost increase of the Reagan military expansion program. For it cannot be overlooked.

Or tolerated.

There can be no quarrel that the United States must improve its defense capability in several areas, essentially relating to air and sea lanes supremacy, readiness, equipment and other non-nuclear military aspects.

But there certainly can be a quarrel with the notion that to keep peace among the fiercely competitive service arms and their civilian-industrial allies, the country simply has to purchase the top items in the weapons-system shopping list of each.

The United States should tailor its military forces smartly to meet what are deemed to be the military's integrated mission. Period. We should not be spooked by what the Soviet Union and any other potential adversary may be doing, like building a trillion tanks or missiles.

One senses the radically escalating and potentially bankrupting military costs result from a White House inability to rebut the worst-case-scenario generals and admirals and their civilian supplier allies, from those who think there can be such a thing as a limited nuclear war, from those who think a nuclear war is "winnable."

Dwight Eisenhower, where are you when we really need you?

LYNDON JOHNSON WAS HERE

REAGAN CONTINUES ARMS BUILDUP WITHOUT TAX INCREASES. —NEWS ITEM

Arkansas Gazette.
Little Rock, Ark., March 29, 1982

The Reagan administration has said that it plans to spend $1.6 trillion on the military through fiscal 1987. This is a whopping sum indeed, but already there is evidence that the total will amount to much more.

In any event, the Pentagon is required to submit quarterly estimates to Congress, and the one that came in last week shows that 44 of the largest weapons projects are expected to cost $114.5 billion more to build than was estimated just three months ago. At 33 per cent, this is the biggest quarterly increase estimate ever made, but it does not include many other defense expenditures. It does not include, for example, changes made since the December 31 report on weapons costs of the B1 bomber and two nuclear-powered aircraft carriers. This estimate alone is expected to reach $37 billion.

The United States must have adequate defense, but there has to be a point at which it weakens inself by spending beyond all reason. That point may be near.

DESERET NEWS
Salt Lake City, Utah, March 23, 1982

"Speak softly and carry a big stick," is the old motto for America's defense. But what if the stick gets so heavy that Uncle Sam can't lift it?

Even the most hawkish defense advocates are likely to be staggered by updated cost estimates for the 44 biggest U.S. weapons projects planned between now and the mid-1990s.

A report quietly released by the Pentagon a few days ago showed that those weapons are expected to cost $454.8 billion — $114 billion more than an estimate made only three months earlier.

And even that is understated because the figures don't include the B-1 bomber and two giant nuclear aircraft carriers costing at least another $37 billion.

Also not included in the report are secret projects such as "stealth" aircraft invisible to radar, plus hundreds of less expensive weapons systems, and the cost of operating and maintaining all these armaments.

Given the penchant for cost over-runs in procuring military weapons, the estimates may translate into even higher figures by the time the weapons are delivered.

A limited breakdown of the weapons cost was made available. It showed that the figure for Tomahawk cruise missiles quadrupled to $12.6 billion since the last quarterly report; F-14 fighter planes tripled to $35.8 billion and F-15 fighters more than doubled to $40.6 billion.

Most of the increase in these and other systems listed by the Pentagon is due to larger quantities being ordered and new features being added to the weapons. The military seems to be on a spending binge.

The nation's defenses need to be bolstered, but the improvements ought to be made carefully, with an eye on what we can reasonably afford and what is most urgently needed. And at the same time, savings should be made in other areas of the military budget. Our military needs to be hard and lean, not soft and bloated.

If the administration, the Pentagon and Congress get carried away with military spending, the bristling armaments may end up defending a bankrupt and economically demoralized nation.

The Washington Post
Washington, D.C., March 16, 1982

SECRETARY WEINBERGER was arguing before the National Press Club the other day that cutting defense spending would mean lost jobs.

Defense jobs—because they generally involve highly skilled workers and large amounts of scarce raw materials—are among the most expensive jobs in the economy. The Defense Department estimates that the added $33 billion in defense outlays requested in the administration's budget would increase employment in defense-related industries by about 347,000 jobs. Each directly created job would thus cost almost $100,000.

The secretary's estimate of 350,000 jobs lost for each $10 billion cut from defense spending, however, takes account of the indirect effects of defense spending as it ripples out through the economy. This brings the average cost for each job down to about $30,000.

What's the matter with this estimate? Simply that it assumes that, if the money were not spent on defense, it would be buried in a hole or stashed away under someone's mattress. This, of course, wouldn't happen. The money would either be spent on other government functions, used to reduce the deficit or returned to taxpayers as a tax cut. Any one of these uses would produce more jobs than would defense spending.

For example, either a tax cut or spending on public works—such as highways and urban renewal—would produce about 50 percent more jobs than the same amount of money spent on defense. Low-wage public service employment would create about three times as many jobs when all direct and indirect effects are taken into account.

There are reasons for increasing defense spending, but job creation isn't one of them.

Herald American
SYRACUSE

Syracuse, N.Y., March 7, 1982

On his way west, President Reagan burned the airwaves with comment about congressional budget-cutting ideas.

"Many of these are not genuine budget alternatives at all but political documents designed for saving legislators' political hides rather than saving the economy."

After cooling down, he telephoned Senate majority leader Howard Baker in an effort to separate the sheep from the goats:

"I wasn't talking about us," he said.

Despite his recognition of GOP alternatives, Reagan is digging in.

He's sticking by his tax-cut guns.

He should.

That's the route to an economic pickup. We won't feel the impact of the July, 10 percent personal income tax cut until three or four months later. But federal pump priming would take longer.

Reagan is equally stubborn in his resistance to shrinking the 18 percent defense spending increase.

The president should think again.

The reason is apparent.

Secretary of Defense Caspar Weinberger's 1982-83 defense catalogue is a replate of President Carter's, hastily enlarged to reflect the Reagan imprint for 1981-82.

Weinberger and Reagan refuse to look again at the big-ticket items — aircraft carriers, planes, tanks — and, upon weighing their minuses and pluses, tell Congress:

"We can cancel this, but must build that."

As examples, the Wall Street Journal cited the following asked-for appropriations:

● $1 billion for 48 new Army AH-64 attack helicopters with the Army so upset by ever-higher costs its procurement people refused to sign the contract;

● $363 million for the Navy's P3 patrol plane although the Navy at one time decided to cancel additional purchases because its P3 inventory will last five years;

● $4.8 billion for the B1 bomber plus billions more for duplicate weapons; namely, $500 million to upgrade B52s due for replacement by B1s, $864 million for cruise missiles designed to supplant B1s, unknown millions for bombers based on F15 and F16 fighters;

● $2 billion to buy 776 of the new M1 battle tanks (7,000 is the ultimate goal) with $230 million for light, rapid deployment force tanks and with unknown millions set for development of a new generation of tanks.

Results of this "let's buy everything, old and new approach" are seen as:

● Undermining arguments for a rational military buildup;

● Creating a counter force in Congress to cut maintenance, supplies, pay, thereby crippling the services' capabilities, especially their recruiting capacities;

● Confusing means and aims; namely, the purchase of heavy weapons designed for Europe while current demand is for lighter equipment, easily deployed worldwide.

The Army Times, no carping Pentagon critic, examined the new budget and concluded:

"The Pentagon seems to be saying, 'We want it all.' By submitting such a budget request, the administration risks destroying the delicate consensus on national defense."

The consensus, as the president has discovered, is being destroyed in the Congress.

If he touches down on his return to Washington from his California ranch, he'll discover consensus is being destroyed in the country.

Decisions that discriminate don't come easily, particularly in the White House. They must be made or the House and Senate will choose and discard.

Congress Passes '83 Authorization, Cuts Chemical Arms Funding

Congress Aug. 17–18, 1982 approved a $178 billion compromise defense authorization bill for fiscal 1983. Only $5.4 billion less than President Reagan had originally requested, the bill amounted to a 36% increase over the fiscal 1982 defense authorization. The $178 billion total worked out by conferees, actually higher than the amount originally approved by either the House or the Senate alone, included funding for nearly every weapons system the President had sought.

The compromise bill restored funds to build the controversial MX missile that the Senate had eliminated from its version of the bill, although it authorized funding for only five of the nine missiles the Administration had requested. It also withheld $874 million for basing the missile until plans for a satisfactory basing system were submitted. The conferees struck out a provision included in the House version that would have required the Pentagon to comply with the unratified second Strategic Arms Limitation agreement with the Soviet Union. In the only major setback for the Administration, the bill eliminated $54 million that Reagan had requested for production of new binary nerve gas shells.

ST. LOUIS POST-DISPATCH
St. Louis, Mo., August 24, 1982

President Reagan's 1983 Defense Authorization Bill has rolled through Congress with only minor cuts. Halfhearted attempts to trim wasteful and militarily questionable programs were beaten back.

The final version of the bill that came out the House-Senate conference committee, and that was approved by both chambers, authorizes a total of $178 billion for 1983 defense spending — just $5.6 billion less than the president's original request and nearly $47 billion *higher* than the comparable 1982 budget. The bill provides $86.5 billion for arms procurement, $23 billion for research and development, $68.3 billion for operations and maintenance and $152 million for civil defense. When the funding for military construction and military manpower are added, the total 1983 Pentagon spending authorization will be close to Mr. Reagan's original request of $258 billion.

Even the most controversial weapons were approved. The 1983 orders for two nuclear-powered aircraft carriers, seven B-1B bombers and 776 M-1 tanks were approved as requested. In the cases of the AV-8B, F-18 and F-16 fighter-bomber programs, Congress increased the purchase requests by 41 planes.

The only programs where the administration suffered any major problems were the MX missile, chemical weapons and civil defense. In the case of the MX, Congress approved ''only'' $989 million for production of five missiles rather than the $1.4 billion for nine missiles that was originally requested. The joint conference committee was worried about the final basing plans for the MX. Besides reducing the buy, the committee placed on hold $874 million in additional MX funds until after Mr. Reagan reports to Congress on a final basing scheme in December.

The only outright defeat for the president was the deletion of $54 million for the start of production of a new type of nerve gas. That was done because it was such a small amount and because it was such an emotional issue. Congress also cut $100 million from the administration's 1983 civil defense budget. However, the $152.3 million which was approved still represents real growth (i.e. over-and-above inflation) of 10 percent over this year's budget.

What must be kept in mind, however, is that this is very much of a preliminary victory for Mr. Reagan. It is rather easy for any president to get the hawkish armed forces committees of both houses to approve the Pentagon's wish list in the authorization bill. However, the House and Senate Appropriations committees are the hands that hold the purse strings and if they don't appropriate funds for these programs, the weapons won't be built.

Both appropriations committees — and particularly the one in the Democrat-controlled House — fortunately take a far more critical view of the Pentagon's spendthrift programs. This is where the real budget fight is planned, and major cuts are expected. Action on the Pentagon's appropriation bill is still months away, but a sense of the mood can be seen in the fact that earlier this month the House Appropriations Committee sliced more than $1 billion out of the administration's $8 billion military construction budget request. Whether Mr. Reagan likes it or not, the decisive battle for the defense budget is yet to come.

Houston Chronicle
Houston, Texas, August 30, 1982

While Congress debated long and loud over a tax bill, the largest military weapons bill in U.S. history was approved with relatively little discussion. The conclusion can be drawn that President Reagan has succeeded in convincing Congress, and the public, that this nation must rebuild its defenses.

Having a strong defense seems such a basic requirement that it is easy to forget that this nation in recent years carelessly allowed its military strength to deteriorate. There were those in Washington who slashed away at military budgets, crying fraud and waste. Plans for a new bomber were rejected. The U.S. Navy was shrunk. Army divisions were cut. New missiles were delayed. Those who pointed with alarm finally were proven correct by events in Iran, Afghanistan and Poland.

This new military authorization bill includes $86.5 billion for more planes, ships, tanks and other weapons plus $23 billion for research and development and $68 billion for operations and maintenance. The Air Force will begin buying 50 transport planes and the U.S. Navy gets $17.9 billion for 24 vessels, including two nuclear-powered aircraft carriers. The total spending is $178 billion, compared with $130 billion authorized for 1982.

While funds for the new MX missile are included, allocations for ammunition, tanks and the crucial supplies required to sustain a conventional military engagement actually decrease the chances of nuclear warfare. Previous administrations worked on the theory that a conflict would escalate to a nuclear exchange in weeks. A five-year program of which this new spending bill is a part will increase the ability of U.S. forces to engage in sustained conventional warfare, reducing the necessity to resort to nuclear weaponry.

For those who believe that strength is the best deterrent to war, passage of this measure is good news. It is the start of a rebuilding process that will take many years. President Reagan has succeeded in reversing a trend that would have made this nation a second-rate power.

The Chattanooga Times
Chattanooga, Tenn., August 6, 1982

To its great credit, the House has rejected the Pentagon's request, backed by the Reagan administration, for $54 million to begin production of a new type of chemical weapon. The amount involved is infinitesimal in light of the $177 billion defense authorization bill, but the principle is more important. And if the House can persuade Senate members of the conference committee to agree, then the United States will be able to maintain its 13-year moratorium on the production of chemical weapons.

The Reagan administration says the binary chemical weapons — in which two harmless substances are combined after firing to produce a lethal nerve gas — are needed to deter the use of chemical warfare by the Soviets. But that argument is hypocritical in light of the administration's condemnation of the Soviets' documented use of chemical and biological weapons in Afghanistan and Southeast Asia. Actually, it would be more sensible, not to mention cheaper, to equip our armed forces with the proper protection against chemical warfare.

Chemical weapons, like nuclear ones, make warfare especially immoral for the simple reason that they are indiscriminate. The gas from such weapons is carried by the wind, attacking all in its path, so they cannot be controlled once used. Obviously they cannot be restricted solely to military targets. And just as obviously they cannot be classified as defensive weapons; if used in this country, they would kill American as well as enemy forces.

The United States and the Soviet Union have been negotiating since 1976 on a proposal to prohibit the production and use of chemical weapons. When it rejected funding for binary weapons, the House urged the administration to place special emphasis on those talks. We hope the White House is listening. Negotiations are obviously a better way of trying to ensure that neither civilian population — American or Russian — is exposed to chemical warfare.

Wisconsin ▲ State Journal
Madison, Wisc., August 9, 1982

President Reagan has made a strong case for increased defense spending in the 1983-85 budgets, and Congress has bought it.

The defense-authorization bill passed by the Democrat-controlled House reduced by only 1 percent Reagan's request for military spending in fiscal 1983, placing the figure at $175.3 billion.

With that slap on the wrist, the House approved most major defense spending proposed by the administration, ensuring final approval by Congress.

A few days later, Reagan said in a news conference that he felt bound by *overall* budget ceilings agreed to by Congress for fiscal 1984, but added that he doesn't consider himself bound by the specific cap on military spending. He said he believes he should have flexibility on individual programs. He specifically mentioned defense.

The reference was brief. The president did not elaborate then or later.

Was Reagan saying he might restore the 1-percent cut?

Perhaps, but the New York Times has quoted unidentified Pentagon spokesman to the effect that the administration could call for an 11-percent increase in defense spending in fiscal 1984. That 11-percent figure has become almost biblical in origin and authenticity as critics have jabbed Reagan for high defense spending.

The president deserves it, whether or not he intends to increase defense spending by 1 percent or 11 percent. He not only unlocked the doors for criticism with his off-handed reference to not feeling bound by the budget ceiling for defense spending, but he failed to consult with congressional leaders — Republican and Democrat — on his plans.

Reagan has enough economic problems without needlessly antagonizing Congress and stirring up critics.

Rocky Mountain News
Denver, Colo., August 10, 1982

IT'S hard to understand why the White House is making such a big thing of not being bound on fiscal 1984 and 1985 defense spending by the budget compromise worked out with Congress in June.

The compromise called for spending $30 billion less over the next three years than President Reagan had proposed several months ago. But Reagan said last week that he doesn't feel bound by the $23 billion in cuts that had been agreed on for the final two years.

That's bad news for two reasons. First, it damages Reagan's credibility. Some of his most faithful lieutenants on Capitol Hill — Republican Leader Howard Baker, for one — were shocked that the White House would take the compromise so lightly.

Second, it's just plain bad timing. Congress is not finished with the fiscal 1983 budget, and the hornet's nest stirred by Reagan could jeopardize progress on that.

The White House went along with the defense cuts in order to get Congress to make further reductions in domestic programs. Members of Congress might well say now that if Reagan doesn't feel bound by the defense cuts, they won't feel bound to make the agreed upon cuts in social spending.

As if to pour salt in the wounds, someone at the Defense Department leaked a story the other day that the department has nearly completed work on a proposed fiscal 1984 military budget several billion dollars above the compromise projection for that year.

It may be true, as the White House says, that a congressional budget resolution is not legally binding for more than one year. But a bargain is a bargain.

Barring some national emergency requiring military spending beyond the compromise figures, the president ought to keep his end of the deal. As fat as the Pentagon budget is — by fiscal 1985 it will be approaching $300 billion — there shouldn't be any great strain in forgoing $23 billion.

St. Louis Globe-Democrat
St. Louis, Mo., August 20, 1982

President Reagan, despite sniping by perennial foes of increased military spending, got most of what he wanted in the $178 billion defense authorization bill approved overwhelmingly by the Senate and House.

The $178 billion is $5.6 billion less than President Reagan requested for fiscal 1983 but it is a sizable boost over the $130 billion authorized for 1982. Perennial foes of increased defense spending tried to knock out such programs as the new MX intercontinental missile, the B-1 bomber, and other strategic weapons systems but in the end were defeated by heavy margins in both houses.

The compromise bill did, however, eliminate money for chemical weapons that Reagan had wanted to start producing after a 13-year moratorium by this country in order to offset the massive chemical warfare program of the Soviet Union.

The measure authorizes $86.5 billion for purchase of more planes, ships, tanks, missiles and other weapons, plus $23 billion for research and development, $68.3 billion for operations and maintenance, and $152 million for civil defense.

This represents the first sizable down payment in the Reagan program for upgrading and modernizing our conventional and strategic forces to make up for more than a decade of defense cutbacks which have allowed the Soviet Union to surpass this country in a number of crucial areas of defense.

In approving the Reagan defense proposals by such wide margins, 78 to 21 in the Senate and 251 to 148 in the House, members of Congress gave the White House the strongest support on national defense that any administration has had in more than 20 years.

It does appear that after decades of undercutting national defense, the majority in Congress now is working with President Reagan in his program for rebuilding America's strength. This bodes well for peace because the growing military strength of this country should make the risk of war unacceptable to any possible aggressor.

THE SUPERPOWERS WILL SPEND ONE MILLION DOLLARS PER MINUTE ON ARMS THIS YEAR.
— NEWS ITEM

AUTH

THE MILWAUKEE JOURNAL
Milwaukee, Wisc., August 4, 1982

Even if Ronald Reagan were able to walk tolerably well on water, his administration still would face as complicated an agenda as any recent president has. Why, then, does he needlessly create fresh sorrows, as in the fuss over future defense spending? It is a mystery.

Is also a severe annoyance, especially to Republican leaders on Capitol Hill. They feel, with reason, that the president has left them naked unto their enemies by his recent dipsy-doodle on defense.

For no obviously logical reason, the White House wafted out the word that the president did not consider himself bound by defense spending ceilings for the 1984 and 1985 budget years. Military spending is, of course, an explosive issue as the federal deficit takes on the dimensions of something from outer space.

Elaborating on the simmering issues at his press conference last week, Reagan said that, yes, he felt bound by the *overall* budget ceilings agreed to by Congress and accepted by the White House. But he wants "flexibility with regard to individual programs" — that is, defense.

The quick lads at the Pentagon, who don't need much encouragement anyway, now are cooking up a 1984 budget proposal that reportedly calls for a startlingly high outlay of about $247 billion. That would be an 11% increase in real growth over the 1983 military budget; with inflation tacked on, the jump would be 17%.

What obviously follows is that to stay within the overall budget ceilings, Reagan will be asking Congress for a far more drastic slice in domestic spending than Congress had anticipated — or will be eager to accommodate.

The president's assertion that he is not bound by the spending ceilings for specific catergories of the budget may be technically correct. But it was politically dumb and not a little devious for Reagan to permit Congress to think it had an agreement upon which to consider the next two budgets — and then suddenly to saw off the limb.

Sen. Howard Baker and Rep. Robert Michel, the respective GOP leaders, say they will try to change the presidential mind. Reagan should listen intently to them. If he sends up 1984 and 1985 defense proposals substantially higher than the ceilings, there is likely to be a very short parade following his leadership.

Reagan is going to have to learn to say no to Defense Secretary Weinberger one of these days. Soon.

THE TENNESSEAN
Nashville, Tenn., August 19, 1982

WHEN the Reagan administration presented its largest-ever peacetime military spending plan in February, there was a chorus of congressional voices calling for less military spending in the coming fiscal year. It was no more than wasted breath.

The Senate has now approved a compromise $178 billion military weapons bill, and the Pentagon simply rolled over its critics like a tank. Sen. James Exon, R-Neb., said the bill was a blank check for the defense department to "purchase virtually anything that pops. We are throwing gobs of taxpayer money for almost anything for sale or on the drawing boards," he said.

The weapons systems that were the best choices for cuts simply sailed through with hardly a nick from congressional cutting knives. These include the MX missile, the B-1B bomber, nuclear aircraft carriers, refurbished battleships, the M-1 tank and a plethora of other "big ticket" items.

The bill authorizes $86.5 billion for procurement of more planes, ships, tanks, missiles and other weapons, plus $23 billion for research and development, $68.3 billion for operations and maintenance, and $200 million for civil defense.

Both the House and Senate had previously cut money for deployment of the MX missile, pending a decision by the administration on where and how the missile would be placed. But the conference committee voted to restore the funds.

Authorizing production before a deployment plan is worked out is putting the cart before the horse. And the MX is a very doubtful cart in any case. Sen. John Tower, R-Texas, added fuel to the controversy over the missile this week by declaring that the MX will need an anti-ballistic missile system to protect it, no matter what basing system is chosen.

The cost of that would be another awesome amount of spending, making the MX the most expensive boondoggle in the world.

What is chilling about the MX and some other systems is the likelihood of higher and higher cost overruns. These have been fairly commonplace in the defense department. As far back as 1972, the General Accounting Office reported that weapons prices were averaging 40% above cost estimates. What they are now is anybody's guess.

But as a harbinger of the future, overruns of even 50% on weapons systems could make the defense budget go much higher than anticipated and make the present budget deficit projections look like small potatoes.

Defense Secretary Caspar Weinberger has maintained that military spending should be measured "against the threat" and not against social or economic costs. But that is an upside-down view of things. With an economy in shambles no amount of weapons systems would provide invulnerability.

Nobody argues that the nation shouldn't have a sound and adequate defense. But surely that can be provided without simply throwing taxpayer money at the Pentagon to buy any and all of the exotic weapons system that it thinks it would like to have. That is neither sound fiscal policy nor rational defense planning.

The Charlotte Observer

Charlotte, N.C., August 30, 1982

Murray Weidenbaum, the Reagan administration's chief economist until last Wednesday, had something important to say before leaving his White House post. In an interview held for release until after his departure, he said the administration's defense spending plans are overwhelming the other elements of its economic policy. Thus, despite non-defense budget cuts, the federal government faces awesome deficits over the next few years.

Weidenbaum

The fact that Mr. Weidenbaum stated the obvious shouldn't diminish the impact of his remarks. He speaks as someone who favors a strong defense, and his objection to the president's proposed defense budgets is based on economic considerations, not a philosophical disagreement over spending priorities.

Unrealistic, Unnecessary

Many different people criticize the Reagan defense strategy for many different reasons. But the most immediate concern — and perhaps the only one with any chance of influencing Ronald Reagan — is the one expressed by Mr. Weidenbaum: that it is unrealistic, unnecessary and economically suicidal to try to increase the defense budget from $182 billion to $356 billion over the next five years.

"... these crash efforts rarely increase national security," he said. "They strain resources, create bottlenecks."

Mr. Reagan's response to such concerns in the past has focused on two elements, both irrelevant.

First, he has said the United States must increase its military might to avoid becoming vulnerable to intimidation or coercion by the Soviet Union. No one has to take issue with that goal in order to suggest that Mr. Reagan is putting an unnecessarily high price tag on it.

And he considers the deficit projections too high, because he believes a strong economic recovery will generate higher revenues than those projections anticipate. But that suggests that a wasteful, extravagant program is fine as long as there's enough money to pay for it — a point of view Mr. Reagan and other conservative Republicans have often attributed, with disdain, to liberal Democrats.

The president seems to ignore the ultimate impact of staggering deficits and a ruined economy on the nation's ability to maintain the kind of manpower and produce the kind of firepower it may need. Attempting an unrealistic defense buildup could force the United States someday to make in midstream the kinds of hard choices that ought to be made now; and if that happens, billions of dollars will have been wasted.

More For The Money

Mr. Reagan also seems to ignore the possibility — indeed, the probability — that a tough attack on waste and cost overruns and an intelligent approach to setting defense priorities would produce a functionally stronger defense for less money than he now proposes to spend.

Defense Secretary Caspar Weinberger apparently is no help in this regard. His approach to shopping for new weapons systems and the other defense needs seems to be to buy out the store and never quibble about the price. But that is *our* money Mr. Weinberger and Mr. Reagan propose to spend, and we have a right to demand more conservative and intelligent stewardship.

Ronald Reagan has demonstrated — most recently on the tax bill —that while he is something of an ideologue he has no desire to go down on sinking ships. Mr. Weidenbaum was not alone among White House advisors in believing the administration needs to restrain its defense-spending plans. Maybe his parting counsel will encourage others on the staff and among Republicans in Congress to push that point with more vigor and urgency.

Voices Of Common Sense

If that happens, perhaps Mr. Reagan again will heed the voices of experience and common sense.

At a time when the nation's economic health still hangs in the balance, such a decision could mean the difference between success and failure for his presidency — not only in economic matters, but also in assuring the nation an adequate, credible defense.

RAPID CITY JOURNAL—

Rapid City, S.D., September 2, 1982

Critics of defense spending and defense planning notwithstanding, the need for maintaining U.S. defenses and for planning to win even a nuclear war are essential.

Congress recognized that when it cleared a $178 billion military spending bill which will enable this country to continue to play catch-up with the Soviet Union.

The authorization bill, for the year beginning Oct. 1, represents an increase of 36 percent. The compromise legislation passed the House by a 251 to 148 margin and the Senate 77 to 21.

Lawmakers gave President Reagan most of what he requested in arms spending. Funds for five MX missiles, a fleet of 50 C-5 transport planes and three Boeing 747 freight carriers are included in the bill as well as authorization for a number of other major weapons systems which were backed by the administration.

Although maintenance and repair funds are provided in the bill, they will fall far short of covering the substantial backlog of work needed at military installations such as improvements to dormitories and other structures at Ellsworth Air Force Base.

The authorization bill contains $152.3 million for civil defense which indicates that Congress and the administration are not going to knuckle under to threats of nuclear or conventional warfare from a possible aggressor.

The concept that any nation could win a protracted or extended nuclear war is difficult to accept. However, that doesn't relieve the administration and defense officials of the responsibility to plan for one while, at the same time, pursuing all avenues to prevent a nuclear exchange.

The best hope for avoiding nuclear war is for the Soviet Union and the United States to negotiate a reduction in their nuclear stockpiles. It is in the best interest of this country to conduct those negotiations from a position of strength. Therefore, while those negotiations are carried on, the United States must continue to maintain and upgrade its capability to wage war and to be prepared with contingency plans to protect its citizens in the event the worst happens.

The military spending bill approved by Congress represents a substantial commitment of the nation's resources for military needs. But in view of the Soviet Union's continued military buildup, the expenditure hardly can be avoided.

Weinberger Announces 3% Cut in 1984 Defense Spending Plans

Defense Secretary Caspar Weinberger told reporters Jan. 11, 1983 that, "in response to economic problems," he had recommended a reduction in defense spending proposed for 1984. The recommendation before President Reagan called for a reduction of $11.3 billion from the proposed appropriation of $284.7 billion. Appropriations, or the budget authorized by Congress, are not all spent in the year they are voted by Congress. Thus, the full $11.3 billion would not be saved in fiscal 1984. In terms of outlays, or the actual amount that the Pentagon would spend during the year, Weinberger estimated that the reduction would lead to $8 billion in savings.

About half of the cutback was attributable to lower inflation rates and fuel prices, the secretary said, and the rest would come from diminished military and civilian pay raises scheduled for 1984, reduced training programs and deferred military construction. While the U.S. would still be able to meet its military security responsibilities, Weinberger said, "no one should believe that these reductions will not adversely affect some of our military capabilities," such as readiness and training.

The decision about where to cut the defense budget had been reached without consultation with the Joint Chiefs of Staff, according to Gen. Charles Gabriel, the Air Force's chief of staff. If they had been asked, Gabriel said during a meeting with reporters Jan. 13, the Joint Chiefs would have recommended a cut in arms programs rather than in pay.

THE MILWAUKEE JOURNAL
Milwaukee, Wisc., Januaary 13, 1983

When President Reagan minimizes the significance of his $8 billion cut in planned defense spending for 1984, his assessment — sad to say — is quite accurate.

The administration's revised spending proposal still calls for a $31 billion increase over the outlays planned for fiscal year 1983. That comes to 10%, in inflation-adjusted dollars. And the administration's commitment to excessive military outlays in future years remains unaltered.

About half of the $8 billion "cut" represents no scaling back at all in real terms; it is merely an adjustment of numbers to reflect lower-than-expected inflation and reduced fuel costs. The remaining $4 billion of the reduction would be achieved by holding down expenditures for military construction, salaries and training.

Until those latter cuts are spelled out, the justification for them will be hard to assess. They might be in areas that should not be trimmed. In any event, they obviously are very small in relation to the country's fiscal needs.

In order to make significant savings, without impairing basic defense, the administration needs to eliminate some of the questionable strategic weapon systems that represent a huge cost burden in coming years. Leading candidates are the B-1 bomber, the MX missile, a Nimitz-class aircraft carrier and the M-1 tank. Regrettably, the administration's latest proposal contains no concessions on those items.

The best that can be said about the proposal is that it may possibly mean the president and Defense Secretary Weinberger finally see a need to budge. Still, as Sen. Slade Gorton (R-Wash.) noted, it is "only a first step."

Detroit Free Press
Detroit, Mich., January 17, 1983

DEFENSE SECRETARY Caspar Weinberger's proposal for an $8 billion cut in next year's military spending is, as Sen. Carl Levin said, "not enough and in the wrong places." The second half of that opinion is shared by the Joint Chiefs of Staff, who dislike any reductions in their funding but especially dislike Mr. Weinberger's plan to focus those reductions on troop pay and training.

And with good reason. Under Gen. Edward Meyer, its chief of staff, the Army in particular has made admirable efforts toward rebuilding the quality and morale of its personnel. After the disastrous early years of the All-Volunteer Force, when intelligence and educational levels of recruits plummeted, the Army tightened its screening procedures and reinstituted many of the educational benefits of the former GI Bill to attract more college-bound high school graduates.

Much of the Army's recent recruiting success must be attributed to the recession and high unemployment. But not all of it. Getting enough bodies was never the problem. Getting well-qualified personnel and retaining them at the senior-enlisted and field-grade-officer levels were.

The Army's renewed emphasis on the human factor is one of the healthiest developments in the military in recent years. But however critical that factor might be on the battlefield, it has failed to excite defense contractors with weapons to sell, congressmen who think their resolve against the Russians is measured by the weapons systems they vote for, or, apparently, Mr. Weinberger.

Half of Mr. Weinberger's proposed cut can be dismissed as artificial, since it is the result of savings from lower inflation and fuel costs that would have occurred anyway. The other half would come from a pay ceiling, reduced training and deferred military construction. A pay freeze can be justified on the basis of economy and equity if it applies to all federal employes. Training cutbacks cannot.

Instead of scuttling the basics of military readiness, Mr. Weinberger should try cutting such expensive and useless projects as the B1 bomber and the MX missile. According to a recent study by the conservative Heritage Foundation, defense budgets since the mid-1970s have consistently underestimated the full cost of procuring weapons systems. This has built enormous inflationary pressures into the budget, resulting in fewer weapons and inadequate maintenance. The spending increases initiated by the Reagan administration have been largely absorbed by existing programs, without increasing American fighting ability.

Even without the threat of budget cuts, Mr. Weinberger should have undertaken long ago a serious review of military priorities, eliminating exotic weapons to save the indispensable ones — and to make sure that we have enough of those indispensable weapons and the people to operate them.

The Seattle Times
Seattle, Wash., January 13, 1983

DEFENSE Secretary Weinberger's heretofore unshakable belief in the inviolability of his budget was dented this week when he agreed to recommend an $11.3 billion reduction in defense-budget authority for the next fiscal year.

Weinberger said nearly half of his proposed reduction is traceable to lower fuel costs "and the effect of reduced inflation."

The concession to the facts on inflation constituted belated recognition of a point made by this state's Slade Gorton last month during the Senate's climactic battle over the fiscal-1983 defense budget.

Gorton proposed a $5.6 billion reduction — amounting to a 3.3 percent cut, but exempting operations and maintenance.

He pointed out with unquestionable logic that inflation now is lower than had been forecast when the fiscal-1983 budget was drafted, so the Pentagon should need less money to buy the same amount of equipment.

And he predicted that

Sen. Slade Gorton

Congress will reject the continued large defense-spending increases that will be needed to follow through on the large weapons-procurement increases in fiscal 1983.

If steps are not taken now to restrain future spending, Gorton warned, "we shall find that the steps we will be taking in two or three years will require much greater cuts in readiness and in weapons systems themselves."

But the Senate failed to fall in line with Gorton's argument, voting 52-45 to table his budget-reduction amendment. However, Gorton sees the closeness of the vote as "a strong indication that next year's military budget will bear the same intense evaluation as the rest of the federal budget."

Now that even Weinberger has seen the logic of Gorton's inflation-factor point, there is every reason to think that Congress at last will apply the kind of tough scrutiny the Washington senator rightly calls for.

The Idaho STATESMAN

Boise, Idaho, January 24, 1983

The need for Defense cuts over and above those proposed by the Reagan administration is fast becoming obvious to almost everybody except President Reagan and Defense Secretary Caspar Weinberger.

In the past, the administration has dismissed critics of the Defense budget as better-Red-than-deaders who would leave the country vulnerable to Communist aggression. That's a little hard to say about Republican Senate Majority Leader Howard Baker, who wants to cut the fiscal 1984 military budget $15 billion, as compared with the $8 billion recommended by Reagan.

Five former U.S. Treasury secretaries, including Republicans William Simon and John Connolly, who could hardly be called liberals, go further than Baker. Simon and Connolly, along with Democrats Michael Blumenthal, Henry Fowler and Douglas Dillon, think that for the sake of the country's economic welfare, the fiscal 1984 defense budget should be cut $25 billion.

A coalition of three leading business groups, the National Association of Manufacturers, the American Business Conference and the National Federation of Independent Businesses, has made a similar proposal, saying the Pentagon budget could be trimmed $18 billion to $23 billion.

Both groups suggested cuts in weapons systems, an area ignored by Reagan's budget cutters. The Reagan-Weinberger savings would come from lower inflation, lower-than-expected fuel costs, reducing training and delaying military pay raises and military construction.

That won't do the job. If the administration is going to make inroads into future deficits, which threaten to rise above $300 billion, it must also eliminate unnecessary and marginal weapons systems. Over the years of development and assembly, such weapons projects build expenditures into future budgets that are almost impossible to eliminate. If they are not killed while still on the drawing board, the only way to cut future military spending will be to reduce manpower and maintenance and operation, places the military cannot afford to trim.

Among potential candidates for the budget knife are two nuclear aircraft carriers that will be sitting ducks for enemy aircraft and missiles; reactivation of the battleships USS Missouri and USS Wisconsin, also highly vulnerable targets; an anti-tank gun that won't penetrate the armor on the front of one of the Soviet's main battle tanks; and a computer-operated anti-aircraft weapon that military officials agree does not work but is still under development.

The evidence indicates we are building weapons systems we wouldn't need, even if we could afford them. Buying them now — when the president's advisers can shoot for nothing better than holding the deficit to an astronomical $200 billion — may be catastrophic.

The question the country must ask is why pay for a record defense buildup that weakens our economic base, the true source of America's strength.

The Birmingham News

Birmingham, Ala., January 23, 1983

In the face of the nation's mountainous budget deficit, now estimated in the neighborhood of $200 billion, the need to reduce government spending has become more than obvious. Even if other action is taken to increase revenue — that is, raise taxes — there seems to be a consensus that outgo must in some way be reduced if there is to be any semblance of a balance.

And increasingly, the defense budget is becoming a favorite theme of those looking for places to cut. The very size of the defense charge bill — recently set by Congress at $231 billion for fiscal 1983 — makes it an easy target, and President Reagan's repeated vows of defense inviolability in the face of cuts in social service areas, in truth, has done little to reduce the attractiveness of the target.

It should be noted, however, that in addition to the spending reduction recently endorsed by Mr. Reagan and Defense Secretary Caspar Weinberger (based on lower oil prices and a smaller military pay increases), Congress already has reduced the defense budget from administration-requested levels.

The fiscal '83 spending of $231 billion represents a considerable increase, to be sure, over the $205 billion budget for fiscal 1982, but still falls considerably short of the $250 billion requested by the administration. In fact, as pointed out by a recent study by *Congressional Quarterly*, the 7 percent cut in the administration's original request was the deepest in a defense request since the early 1970s. In addition to the oil-related and salary cuts, the reduction came in a variety of areas, with much of the big money cuts tracing to procurement of new weapons systems. The celebrated Congressional rejection of administration plans to begin buying MX missiles saved $998 million, for instance, while another $493 million was pocketed by Congress' decision to slow procurement for Pershing II missiles — the intermediate weapon designed to strike Russian targets from bases in Western Europe which had suffered from both political attacks and poor performance in early trials.

Overall, however, the thrust of defense spending remains intact. And just what is that thrust — what part of the budget is going for what purposes?

The total $231 billion breaks down roughly this way: $45 billion for active duty personnel; $16 billion for retired personnel; $67 billion for operations and maintenance; $80 billion for procurement; $23 billion for research and development.

In other words, in a very loose sense, if you pictured the Defense Department getting your dollar bill, a quarter of it would be spent on personnel, another on operations — the here-and-now of defense — with the rest going for procurement and research and development. Nearly half of the budget — $103 billion of the total $231 billion — is to be spent on the future, whether that means purchase of operational fighter planes or in research which might not produce actual results for years to come.

At the same time, it is the very large total of this spending which presents the most tempting area for budget-cutting — especially the massive amount listed under procurement, a heading without a somehow more respectable tone of "research and development."

But what, exactly, will these 80 billions of dollars buy? These are the major purchase areas:

• For strategic warfare: In addition to $2.5 billion for continued MX development, spending includes $4.6 billion for the first seven production-line versions of the B-1 bomber and its continued development, $532 million for modernization of existing B-52 bombers, $548 million for cruise missile procurement, $1.5 billion for a new Trident submarine and $634 million for 66 Trident missiles.

• For ground combat: $1.36 billion for 855 new M-1 tanks, $783 million for 600 new M-2 armored personnel carries, $695 million for 48 Apache anti-tank helicopters, $356 million for 20 A-10 antitank planes, $779 million for 376 Patriot long-range missiles, $214 million for 2,256 Stinger portable short-range missiles and $134 million for 12,000 TOW anti-tank missiles.

• For airlift and sealift: $800 million for 50 more C-5 transport planes, $144 million for buying used, wide-body civilian aircraft, $915 million for procurement of KC-10 cargo and refueling aircraft and $379 million for an LSD-41 cargo ship.

• Naval warfare: $6.6 billion for two nuclear aircraft carriers, $300 million for modernization of the battleship U.S.S. Iowa, $2.9 billion for three cruisers, $1 billion for two nuclear hunter submarines, $646 million for two escort frigates.

• Tactical aircraft: $1.24 billion for 39 F-15s, $1.71 billion for 120 F-16s, $235 million for eight A-6E bombers, $875 million for 24 F-14 fighters, $2.1 billion for 84 F-18 fighters and $702 million for 21 Harrier vertical-takeoff bombers.

Those items, of course, are only the high points of procurement. Other billions will go for a variety of like purposes, ranging from additional missile purchases to buying bullets for officers' handguns. As staggering as some of the individual bills may be — $3.3 billion for a single aircraft carrier, for instance — it is the cumulative total, representing more than 10 percent of the total federal budget of $765.17 billion, which most overwhelms.

Yet, those who would cut are faced with the classic problem of defining how much is enough in defense spending. Given the varying assessments of Soviet military might, who would deny the Army the anti-tank weapons which might save American lives? Who would say no to an aircraft carrier which might stabilize a crisis situation by its mere presence, and thus avert war? Who will cut back on the fighter planes which will determine air superiority?

The overall problem represents a national vexation which probably is beyond solving by rational consensus. It is important, however, for the average citizen to understand, at a minimum, the dimensions of defense procurement and what it will provide for the national defense before undertaking to compare the dollars being spent in other areas of budgeted spending.

ST. LOUIS POST-DISPATCH
St. Louis, Mo., January 6, 1983

In an attempt to pre-empt the critics of runaway military spending, Defense Secretary Caspar Weinberger held a hard hitting press conference recently to defend the administration's program. "To falter now would be to undo our present gains and endanger our future safety," he warned.

It was a classic Weinberger performance — raising the specter of the Soviet menace while stonewalling all questions on the real military necessity of certain prized Pentagon weapon programs. It is a tactic that he has employed successfully for the past two years; but the approach is starting to wear more than a little thin.

Secretary Weinberger and his top aides have yet to come to grips with a very fundamental problem: even without triple-digit deficits, there is just not enough money to go around to pay for all of the Pentagon's programs planned for the 1980s and into the early 1990s. The Navy wants to build up the fleet to 600 ships. The Army and Marines both have major new procurement programs. Besides its numerous tactical aircraft programs, the Air Force is lobbying hard for its new strategic arms — the MX missile and the B-1B and Stealth bomber projects. In addition, there is the ever increasing expense of manpower, training, operations and maintenance.

Secretary Weinberger will publicly justify any and all of these programs on the vague logic that they are necessary for opposing Soviet aggression somewhere in the world. Yet, as many in Congress correctly perceive, the Reagan administration does not have a clear-cut, rational military strategy. That is the issue that must be addressed by the new Congress — and satisfactorily answered by the administration — before this nation can proceed on its defense program.

THE INDIANAPOLIS NEWS
Indianapolis, Ind., January 22, 1983

The Reagan administration is headed in the right direction in reducing the next Defense Department budget by $11.3 billion.

Defense Secretary Caspar Weinberger announced the $11.3 billion reduction in budget authority for the 1983-84 fiscal year, claiming that much of the reduction is due to the Reagan administration's fight against inflation. Fuel costs will be lower than anticipated, according to Weinberger, and some spending on training and construction will be deferred.

The reductions, he added, will not affect the buildup of major weapons that the administration claims is essential for national security.

Obviously Weinberger lost an arm-wrestling contest within the administration. Some Reagan advisers think defense spending needs to be trimmed to reduce massive Federal budget deficits.

Other informed critics outside the administration have questioned the extent of the military buildup. Retired Adm. Hyman Rickover has warned of waste and overkill. Former Defense Secretary Melvin Laird also thinks the Navy buildup is excessive. "The Navy is going wild by making all these commitments on ships," he has said. "It hasn't been proved to me that you need a Navy that large. I don't think we can afford it."

Business groups have offered similar criticism, raising concerns about the growing Federal deficit. The National Association of Manufacturers, the American Business Conference and the National Federation of Independent Business recently formed a coalition to call for defense spending reductions by $18 billion to $23 billion, as well as other cuts in the domestic section of the budget.

Until this recent announcement, Weinberger was adamant about defense spending levels. Any cuts, he contended, would endanger security. Now he has wisely backed off from that dogmatic and unreasonable stance.

No doubt there are more cuts to be made, and not just due to changing estimates based on inflation predictions. These are minor reductions he is proposing, and there's bound to be more fat to be trimmed.

Herald — News
Fall River, Mass., January 13, 1983

The Secretary of Defense, Caspar Weinberger, has announced that he has recommended an $11.3 billion decrease in the spending authority of the Defense Department.

The announcement ends speculation that the President, even in the face of skyrocketing government deficits, would refuse to agree to budget cuts in the appropriations for the Pentagon.

Evidently the speculation, as is so often the case, was ill-founded.

Perhaps the reports of a tug of war between the Defense Secretary and Budget Director David Stockman were equally ill-founded.

Even so, the announcement by Weinberger will be interpreted as a victory for the Budget Director.

In any case it sets the stage for other reductions in budgetary proposals by the President.

Weinberger, in announcing his recommendations for a truly substantial decrease in the defense budget, said it had been made possible by the administration's success in curbing the inflation.

He went on to point out that Pentagon long-range planning naturally enough took into account the factor of inflation in estimating its expenses and the costs of new weapons.

With inflation merely a pale shadow of its former self, it is possible for the Pentagon to reduce its estimates of future outlays.

This, according to Weinberger, was the principal reason for the cutback he is recommending in the Defense Department's budget.

Perhaps so, but it seems more likely that it is a response to the clamor from Congress for a cut in military spending and Stockman's insistence that cuts in social programs the administration is expected to recommend would stand no chance of acceptance unless the Defense Department's appropriation was also cut.

Whatever the background of Weinberger's decision, there is no question but that the President will accept his recommendations, or that they will be well received on Capitol Hill.

Indeed it disposes of the charge that the President and his cabinet are inflexible in their thinking.

On the contrary, the administration, now in the final stages of preparing the new budget, is evidently making a real effort to reduce the appropriations it seeks and therefore the government's deficit.

The announcement by the Secretary of Defense effectively undercuts many of the false assumptions of the administration's opponents in and out of Congress.

It also implies that the President is determined to present a budget at the end of the month which will command serious consideration.

In spite of all the face-saving explanations for Weinberger's decision, the fact seems to be that cutbacks in defense spending were imperative if the administration expected its new budget to have a chance of acceptance.

With that in mind, the President apparently chose to be realistic about Pentagon spending in order to give the budget a better chance.

This capacity to adjust to political realities is one of the reasons why Ronald Reagan is President as well as one of the reasons why his opponents are unwise to underestimate his skill.

The announcement by Secretary Weinberger really means that President Reagan has not lost any of his ability to move with the times or to take his opponents off-guard.

These enviable capacities have stood him and the country in good stead before, and they evidently will again.

THE INDIANAPOLIS STAR

Indianapolis, Ind., January 16, 1983

Cuts of $11.3 billion in proposed fiscal 1984 defense spending — which were recommended by Defense Secretary Weinberger and approved by President Reagan — prove that the defense budget is not holy writ engraved in granite.

The nation might save multi-billions more, and at the same time strengthen U.S. security through appointment of a Cabinet-level defense cost control boss to oversee the President's five-year, $1.6 trillion defense buildup — to chop out fat, root out corruption, hear out whistle-blowers, curb extravagance, restrain inter-service rivalry and halt flagrant cost overruns, duplication and other waste costing hundreds of billions of dollars.

The man for the job should not be a dove or partisan of unlimited social spending but a patriot with the grit of an Eisenhower or Patton and a killer-instinct toward fraud and mismanagement.

Cost-cutting is not the principal duty of Secretary Weinberger, even though his recommended cuts show he is able to do it just as he was when, as HEW secretary, he was nicknamed "Cap the Knife." Now his mission is to provide the nation with what, in his studied opinion, based upon the analyses of civilian and military experts, is the best possible defense.

This task would generally run counter to that "super-watchdog" concentrating on negative aspects of the massive defense program.

The cost boss would need an investigative staff with subpoena powers. His targets would include cost overruns, fraud, kickbacks, bribery, failure to meet contract specifications, needless duplication of weapons, ammunition, equipment and servicing, decisions to manufacture combat-unworthy weapons and equipment, and contracting procedures needing improvement.

He would report directly to the President, who as commander-in-chief of the armed forces would be able to issue executive orders for action when necessary or could request reports to the appropriate committees of Congress.

His would be a complex and thankless task made no simpler by the realization that it was false economizing — the failure to provide an adequate anti-missile defense system — that made a costly British warship prey to a relatively cheap Exocet missile during the Falkland Islands war.

His task might be improved by getting the views of combat troops and others familiar with weapons and equipment in use, instead of 'through the channels" hype Soldiers' gripes often are justified and if acted upon could produce better equipment, servicing and combat procedures.

Probably few combat soldiers would disagree with the Heritage Foundation's charge that money is wasted on fancy weapons that "are prone to break down" when simpler, cheaper alternatives are available.

It helps put the picture of U.S. military capability into perspective to realize that the greatest military effort in history which led to the greatest victory — victory in World War II — was accomplished not by a "military establishment" but by a thrown-together civilian army led by a largely mongrel officer corps and a clutter of maverick geniuses, working not out of marble halls but old ramshackle buildings all around the world.

They produced the momentum that smashed the Nazi and Japanese war machines. After the war the Pentagon, which was completed on this date in 1943, bureaucratized war planning and fell into the stagnation that the Heritage critics charge is the chief affliction of U.S. defense today.

As for President Reagan's five-year defense spending proposal for 1983-87, it breaks down to an expenditure of $876 million a day — or $608,500 a minute.

Spending like that calls for gimlet-eyed watching by a guardian as patriotic as Stephen Decatur and as tough as Old Ironsides.

The Des Moines Register
Des Moines, Iowa,
January 18, 1983

The Reagan administration's agreement to cut $8 billion from its military asking is a breakthrough. But it is far from what thoughtful critics mean when they call for reductions.

In the presentation, the extent and the selection of the cuts, the administration showed clearly that it has failed to grasp what is worrisome.

Defense Secretary Caspar Weinberger presented the $8 billion reduction with the assurance that about half is accounted for by lower inflation rates. This is a dandy plug for a development for which President Reagan feels insufficiently congratulated. It reflects a lack of recognition that military spending, like all government spending, is subject to waste — waste such as the $4.5 billion the Air Force secretary estimates is lost in keeping members of Congress happy with less-than-efficient purchases and siting of military bases; waste such as the 24-cent rivet that costs the Pentagon a dollar, or the $12,000-a-month Navy contract that turned out to cost $350,000.

Cutting only $8 billion out of a $281 billion budget (less than 3 percent) is a token, despite White House denials, and as such it is dangerous: It can be hauled out to fend off requests for real action.

Compare the proposed $8 billion cut with the $34 billion that Reagan wants to spend to build 100 B-1 bombers while work goes ahead on the more advanced Stealth bomber; or with the $25 billion he wanted to spend on the ill-planned dense-pack scheme for the MX missile; or with the $100 billion he has advocated spending on shipbuilding over the next five years.

Most distressing, the $8 billion cut offers no hope that the administration is beginning to see that such schemes are not only a huge strain on the budget but are far from synonomous with national security.

Besides inflation, Weinberger said, his cuts are accounted for by lowered personnel, operating and training costs. These are not the best areas to cut. We would feel far more secure with well-paid, well-trained armed forces, adequately housed and provided with reliable equipment, than with the new weapons — grandiose as they are horrible.

Perhaps reality seeps only slowly into minds as hardened with ideology as those now running America's military establishment. Perhaps this $8 billion, no matter how inadequate, speaks of a dawning awareness. We hope so.

Democratic Budget Plan Passed by House Scales Back Defense Spending

The House dealt President Reagan a major legislative defeat in March, 1983 by adopting, 229 to 196, a fiscal 1984 budget resolution drafted by the Democrats. Four Republicans from the Northeast joined 225 Democrats in voting for the plan, which cut Reagan's proposed increase in military spending for fiscal 1984 by $9.9 billion and restored funds to many domestic programs the Administration wanted to shrink. The House plan reduced Reagan's increase in defense spending for 1984 from 10% to approximately 4%, according to the Democrats' estimate, and maintained major entitlement programs, such as welfare and food stamps, at existing levels. More of a political than an economic statement, the Democrats' budget plan would have to be reconciled with the one adopted by the Senate, then sent to congressional committees for more detailed allocations within the general goals. Commenting on the Democrats' first budget victory in three years, House Speaker Tip O'Neill (D, Mass.) said: "The people believe that Reagan policies are unfair and have gone too far. This evening, the House voted to restore fairness and balance to our national policies." Less than a week earlier, the President had delivered a strong attack against the House Democratic budget plan. "Nothing could bring greater joy to the Kremlin than to see the United States abandon its defense rebuilding program after barely one year," Reagan warned.

THE TENNESSEAN
Nashville, Tenn., March 29, 1983

THE whopping vote last week in the House on a Democratic budget plan is both an indication of a changed political balance and a rejection of President Reagan's soak-the-poor and pet-the-Pentagon policies.

Although there were some defections among Democratic conservatives, the "boll weevil" coalition had no muscle of the kind that gave Mr. Reagan budget victories in 1981 and 1982.

The budget resolution approved in the House would sharply slow administration defense spending, holding increases to 4% after adjustment for inflation. That is not likely to hold in the reconciliation and appropriations process, but it appears now that the President will not come close to the 10% after-inflation increase for the military that he wants.

With whopping deficits forecast ahead, it is essential that defense spending be cut, especially in those areas of "gold-plated' and dubious weapons systems.

At the same time, the Democratic budget resolution would put the brakes on Mr. Reagan's efforts to slash more or dismantle scores of domestic programs. Many have been cut already to the bare bones. Although there will be additional funding for many of the programs that would be slashed under the Reagan budget, including such things as child care, low-income fuel assistance and Aid to Families with Dependent Children, again the final figures may not add as much as the resolution now projects.

But considering the size of earlier cuts and the long duration of the current recession, obviously there are needs that should be addressed with a little more common humanity than the Reagan administration's budget does.

Mr. Reagan has criticized the House vote and sought to convince the public that it was a "dangerous" step brought on by the "liberal wing" of the Democratic party. But the 225 Democrats who voted for it represent a cross-section of philosophical attitudes. The consensus seemed to be that Mr. Reagan's budget is out of kilter in terms of priorities and unrealistic in terms of defense spending.

The Republican-controlled Senate will take up the administration budget after the Easter recess. And, among its membership — both Democrats and Republicans — exist some of the same feelings about priorities. So it is extremely doubtful that Mr. Reagan will get his asked-for loaf on defense, although he is busy turning up the heat and asking voters to do their bit in gaining approval of his budget.

What is possible is a compromise budget that gives less to defense than asked and more to social welfare spending than sought. Since the Congress has been able to compromise on such things as the Social Security reform package and the jobs aid and recession relief measures, it is clearly possible for the lawmakers to shape a budget that reflects both the economic and political realities that exist in Washington and in the country.

Mr. Reagan may try to convince the public otherwise, but there can be no harm in debating the nation's priorities in terms of its spending. And that is what the Senate will be expected to do.

The Kansas City Times
Kansas City, Mo., March 25, 1983

This is getting to be a dated comment, we know, but it's still valid: Democrats in the House, who are carrying the torch for the party while Ronald Reagan is president, still have not come up with a distinct program of their own for economic recovery. They want less for defense, more for jobs creation bills and more for social welfare programs. That's pretty simple and predictable, isn't it? They'd change the mix, risk increasing the deficit to spend more on federal jobs programs, and not show anywhere how that would improve the overall budget picture, the out-year deficits and so on. They would spend $863.6 billion in the 1984 fiscal year, compared to Mr. Reagan's plan to spend $848.5 billion. Their deficit would be $174.5 billion, compared to the president's $188.8 billion. They would raise $30 billion in new taxes and cut the defense increase from 10 percent to 4 percent.

Maybe the House Democrats don't need a program that fits the times. Maybe all they need is to take the Reagan program — and ignore it. Or show that the president, after two years of recession with less than bright chances for recovery, is a weakened man. Heck, maybe the Democrats do have the right idea. It just doesn't seem quite kosher, though, if what they mean to do is shame the president and turn back to their comfortable old ways of deficit spending to put the drive back into recovery in the private sector. The deficit is becoming ever larger, inflation is down to a livable rate for once and there are encouraging signs that a genuine start-up is under way.

Is this showdown necessary, except in the political sense? Do the Democrats offer a better plan for economic revival and for buttressing the national security apparatus than the Reagan White House has? Why, the Reagan budget didn't even get a vote before the House Budget Committee, which is under Democratic control. A Democratic budget blueprint was approved Wednesday on a vote of 229-196. Four GOP members voted with the Democrats.

What should be obvious to Democrats and Republicans alike is that any rejection of the Reagan budget for 1984 ought to be followed by preparations for dealing with the future. For instance, the Democratic budget resolution would restore cuts made in Medicaid for low-income families, food stamps, child nutrition, Aid to Families with Dependent Children, etc. It would not necessarily reform those programs and the services they provide. Pertinent questions of eligibility and management raised by the Reagan cuts two years ago are not answered by the Democrats. Have they found ways to make those programs less costly and more efficient while still meeting the needs of the "truly needy?"

This is what's wrong with the House Democrats' approach. They showed up Mr. Reagan all right. They have not advanced the conduct of public policy by turning back to the same formulas that got them where they are today — without control of one-half of the Congress and with a Republican in the White House. That's the temptation always before this bunch of Democrats — to go back, not forward. Such a mistake, for a mere tactical victory.

The Chattanooga Times

Chattanooga, Tenn., March 28, 1983

By a vote of 229 to 196, the House has adopted the Democrats' version of a fiscal 1984 federal budget, a document House Republicans have sourly observed could be more accurately called the "Revenge on Ronald Reagan Act of 1983." The Republicans' problem, however, is that they have forgotten a familiar political axiom: You can't beat something with nothing.

Before critics go off the deep end in savaging the Democrats' temerity in actually offering an alternative to the budget President Reagan presented in January, consider this: The GOP did not offer a budget of its own. To put it more bluntly, no one in the party was willing to introduce the president's budget as an alternative to the Democrats'. House Majority Leader Jim Wright of Texas accurately observed, "We have a choice of this budget or no budget at all."

The Republicans complained that their amendments had been ignored. And Mr. Reagan charged that the Democratic budget, because it contained less for defense than what he wanted, would bring joy to the hearts of those in the Kremlin. The wisdom of such a charge is questionable, for in effect it amounts to accusing the Democrats of knuckling under to the Soviet Union; members of his own party must have been embarrassed at the president's inflamed outburst, especially when many GOP congressmen consider the White House's defense request excessive.

With the House vote on the first budget resolution, the fight will now shift to the Senate. At the president's request, drafting of a budget was suspended last week just before the Senate Budget Committee, which Re-

publicans dominate, was expected to hand the president a defeat by voting for a smaller increase in defense spending than the 10 percent he contends is necessary.

The House budget includes a 4 percent increase in defense spending after inflation is factored in. But it reflects a logical question that asks whether every weapons system the administration has requested is actually essential to the national security. Anyone who read *Time* magazine's recent cover story on massive waste in defense spending, not to mention the flawed procurement system, would have to conclude it is not.

The Democrats' budget proposes $863.6 billion of spending, revenues of $689.1 billion and a $174.5 billion deficit in 1984. The president's proposed budget contained $848.5 billion of spending, $659.7 billion in revenue and a deficit of $188.8 billion. Neither, obviously, is satisfactory, especially in terms of the planned deficits. Similarly, neither is in final form; one reason the president's budget hasn't been introduced is that even members of his own party had assured him that, in its present form, the document would be defeated.

The Democratic budget will be useful in helping to define the budget debate that will resume after the Easter recess. But President Reagan will have to restrain himself, forgoing the antagonistic rhetoric directed against the "liberal wing" of the Democratic party. He should know by now that progress in fashioning a reasonable budget for 1984 will require bipartisan cooperation, not partisan, confrontationist rhetoric.

The Philadelphia Inquirer

Philadelphia, Pa., March 29, 1983

To hear President Reagan talk, you might think that comrade Yuri Andropov and his Politburo colleagues were turning handsprings of joy over the budget approved by the Democratic-controlled House Wednesday.

In a brief appearance a few days before he went on television with his appeal to "restore our military strength," Mr. Reagan called the House budget a "dagger aimed straight at the heart of America's rebuilding program." He declared that "nothing could bring greater joy to the Kremlin than seeing the United States abandon its defense rebuilding program after barely one year." He went on to declare:

"I'm not going to sit still for a proposal that makes a huge increase in taxes, guts our defense program, repeals many of the overdue welfare reforms that we have enacted and adds an incredible $181 billion in domestic spending to what we have proposed."

Now Mr. Reagan is, of course, entitled to make his case, but this kind of hyperbole does not exactly enhance the quality of what passes for the political dialogue. Is it not possible to make a case without the innuendo that those who disagree are dupes, willing or otherwise, of the Kremlin? The approach is of a piece with Mr. Reagan's approach toward those who favor a bilateral and verifiable nuclear freeze, and it demeans those who make it.

Beyond that, it is simply not a fact that only Democrats — and, according to Mr. Reagan, members of the "liberal wing" of the Democratic Party — are unhappy about the size and shape of the administration's budget, especially

its military budget. It was only by dint of a personal plea from the President that the Republican-controlled Senate Budget Committee, headed by Sen. Pete V. Domenici of New Mexico, staved off a humiliating defeat for Mr. Reagan by agreeing — reluctantly — to put off for three weeks consideration of its own budget with sizable cuts in the administration's requests for military spending.

It was not "liberal" Democrats but conservative Republicans who, objecting to the President's refusal to make concessions on defense, declared, "I think the President is wrong" (Sen. Charles E. Grassley of Iowa), and "Every time the President has intervened in the budget process he has been wrong" (Sen. Slade Gorton of Washington).

The President's rhetoric departs from reality in other ways. The "huge increase in taxes" contemplated in the House committee budget amounts to $30 billion — nearly $70 billion less than last year's increases that Republicans as much as Democrats thrust upon Mr. Reagan and that Mr. Reagan himself, once he accepted them, fought for. It is also almost exactly the amount of revenue that would be lost from the third round of tax cuts scheduled to go into effect July 1. Postponing tax cuts is not the same as a "huge increase in taxes," whatever else may be said about the idea.

The administration is proposing to increase Pentagon outlays by 10.3 percent, after allowing for inflation. The Senate Budget Committee has been considering an increase of about half that. The House calculates its increase

at about 4 percent — $9.9 billion for the next fiscal year and projected military spending through fiscal 1988 of $1.6 trillion as against the administration's projected $1.8 trillion. That hardly sounds like a plan that "guts our defense program."

As for that "incredible $181 billion" allegedly added to domestic spending, it might seem incredible that the President neglected to note that the House version would cut the fiscal 1984 deficit anticipated by the administration from $188.75 billion to $174.45 billion.

Quite a number of members of Congress, in both chambers and in both parties, think that the strength of this democratic society has something to do with child nutrition and care for the elderly, with education, with mass transit, with thriving cities, with getting the American people back to work. Most of them favor a steady military buildup, but they are troubled, and rightly, by the prospect of an enormous military buildup that creates astronomical deficits for this generation and astronomical bills to be paid by future generations.

The defense debate, Mr. Reagan declared in his televised speech, "is not about spending arithmetic," and he is right. It is also not about what the Kremlin wants but what the Congress wants, and what the American people want and need. The larger debate is about priorities, about fiscal responsibility. It's about fairness. Mr. Reagan warns against making defense "the scapegoat of the federal budget." Neither should it be made a sacred cow.

THE ARIZONA REPUBLIC
Phoenix, Ariz., March 25, 1983

THE Democratic majority in the House has thrown down the gauntlet to President Reagan.

By completely rewriting his fiscal 1984 budget, the Democrats have set the stage for a knock-down-drag-out fight.

For personal, philosophic and political reasons, neither they nor the president are willing to compromise on the issue.

The conflict, therefore, is certain to last well into the fiscal year, forcing the government to operate during the first months of the year on continuing resolutions.

That's a terrible way to run a government. It makes change difficult and longterm planning impossible.

And it creates uncertainties that can adversely affect the economy.

What the Democrats did specifically was to cut Reagan's defense buildup by more than half, raise $30 billion in new taxes, and restore $33 billion of his proposed cuts in social and welfare programs.

With only a handful of exceptions, the Democrats have long felt uncomfortable with the Defense Department's appetite for more and more expensive weapons.

In addition, most of them feel it's possible to reach arms limitation agreements with the Soviet Union without so great a defense buildup as Reagan wants.

They have always opposed Reagan's tax-cutting program, saying it favors the rich.

And they believe that cuts in social and welfare programs already have gone too far.

The party's traditional constituency are those who benefit most from social and welfare programs — union workers, the unemployed, the destitute, minority groups and women — so the Democrats naturally have political as well as philosophic reasons for believing as they do.

In contrast, Reagan's tax program and reducing the size of the federal government are the very heart of "Reaganomics."

Reagan cannot abandon them without becoming merely a caretaker president.

Reagan, moreover, considers the Democrats naive about the Russians.

He believes the Soviets will never seriously discuss arms limitation unless the United States achieves clear strategic superiority.

House Speaker Thomas P. O'Neill has a personal stake in the battle. He wants to restore the prestige he lost during the first two years of the Reagan administration when Reagan rode roughshod over him in the House.

Reagan has a personal stake, too. He cannot run for re-election as a failure. And, should he decide not to run, he does not want history to remember him as a failure.

The clash inevitably will have a tremendous impact on the 1984 presidential campaign. In fact, the difference in philosophies could become the central issue of the campaign.

The Dispatch
Columbus, Ohio, March 27, 1983

THE BUDGET plan passed last week by the Democrats in the U.S. House of Representatives represents an outrageous attempt to return to the discredited free-spending ways of another age. If allowed to become law, it would scuttle the economic recovery charted by President Reagan and his congressional allies.

Enactment of the Democratic budget would mean the institution of additional taxes which would drain billions of additional dollars from consumers and the private business sector. But this new tax revenue would not be used to close the deficit gap the Democrats have been screaming about. No, this new money would be used to fund an expansion of governmental spending programs that would negate the progress that has been made during the past two years to bring federal growth under control.

Anyone who is fed up with big government, ever-rising taxes, recessions, high unemployment and inflation had better let his or her voice be heard in Washington so that this Democratic package is not voted into law.

The Democratic budget plan calls for spending in fiscal 1984 of $863.6 billion — $15.1 billion more than the amount proposed by Reagan. The Democrats want to collect $689.1 billion in revenues — $29.4 billion more than Reagan wants to collect. But even with this increased revenue, the Democrats expect a $174.5 billion deficit — a figure only $14.3 billion less than what Reagan proposes.

These numbers do not tell the whole story, however. The Democratic package represents a shift in priorities that would drain funds needed for national defense and use them to increase social programs that were cut during the last two years. To continue to fund these spending programs beyond fiscal 1984, the Democrats would have to raise $40 billion in new taxes in fiscal 1985 and $50 billion in fiscal 1986.

The Democrats want to limit defense increases to a level estimated by the Congressional Budget Office to just 2.3 percent above current expenditures after inflation is taken into account. (The Democrats say their plan includes a 4 percent hike but part of that increase is for pay raises which the CBO attributes to inflation.) Reagan, by contrast, wants to increase defense spending by 10 percent above the inflation rate.

While Reagan's increases may be unattainable and specific programs may have to be reduced or eliminated, the 2.3 percent rate proposed by the Democrats is simply inadequate if this nation is to meet the challenge posed by the massive Soviet military buildup.

But the Democrats contend that the money Reagan would spend on national security could be better used by increasing the food stamp program, child nutrition efforts, child care, Aid to Families with Dependent Children and other social programs designed to aid the needy.

While these are worthwhile programs necessary to help those in need, spending for them cannot be allowed to get out of hand. Making large numbers of people dependent on these government programs robs them of the incentive to pursue productive lives and deprives them of the opportunity for personal growth.

And the high levels of taxation needed to fund the programs would prevent the private sector from creating the employment opportunities needed to foster individual and financial freedom. The combination of high taxes for social programs at the expense of national security would make this nation vulnerable to apathy from within and threats from without.

The nation must demand more than the spending and taxing free-for-all proposed by House Democrats. Their plan certainly is not free, and it would be injurious to all.

THE PLAIN DEALER

Cleveland, Ohio, March 25, 1983

At last there appear to be guarantees of a process returning to Washington that has been missing in recent years. The success of Democrats in passing their own budget plan in the House signals the return to Capitol Hill debates of two healthy and vital participants in the budgetary procedure — the House and the Senate.

In successfully passing their budget plan, Democrats have gained an important face-saving victory after two years of humiliating defeats. It was the first tax and spending plan passed by either house that President Reagan has opposed.

The budget calls for a $30 billion increase in new taxes, the restoration of $33 billion in spending for social programs, and an increase in defense spending of only 4%, as opposed to the 10% increase desired by the administration. It also projects a slightly smaller deficit than the budget proposed by the administration.

There are the more liberal elements of the party who would have preferred less than the 4% growth in defense spending, and more conservative members who would liked to have seen a smaller increase in new taxes. But one reason for the Democratic success was their ability to put together a budget that did not go to extremes; it remained enough of a compromise to hold the troops together, yet offered enough to all segments to gain the support it needed for passage.

The victory has important political meaning as well. It provides Democrats with a crucial bargaining chip in future negotiations, which will begin once the Senate takes up the issue after the Easter recess.

How will the president approach these negotiations? Will he place as much priority on the proposals for a $30 billion tax increase and a $33 billion increase in social program spending as on the defense issue? Probably not. But it is most apparent that he is not going to get all he wants.

Just recently he asked a Senate budget committee to delay a vote on defense spending when it became evident the committee would recommend an increase much less than the 10% the president had requested. But now Senate Republicans, at least, have a little more negotiating leeway with House Democrats, who have capped defense spending at 4%.

President Reagan knows there is virtually no way that he will succeed in getting a budget with a 10% increase in defense spending. The very best he can hope for is 7% or 8% from the Senate, leading to a 5% or 6% increase after a House-Senate compromise. The president's nationally televised speech shortly after the Democratic victory was delivered with that in mind.

In talking about weapons systems for the future, as the president did in his speech, he hopes to gain enough support and leverage to get the weapons systems he desires for the present. But he will have to negotiate for them nevertheless, as well as for practically everything else he wants in the budget. So, too, will the Democrats. And that's the kind of vital and healthy democratic process that has been missing for too long.

Newsday

Long Island, N.Y., March 27, 1983

In President Reagan's view, if the 1984 federal spending targets approved by the House of Representatives last week were passed into law, they would bring "joy to the Kremlin." What's more, he said he regarded them as "a dagger aimed straight at the heart of America's rebuilding program."

Those comments were a typically hyperbolic revelation of Reagan's political pique at being handed the first important budgetary defeat thus far in his presidency.

What the House approved was in fact an entirely sensible Democratic alternative to the administration's proposed budget for the fiscal year that begins Oct. 1. The $836.6 billion House package includes a smaller increase in 1984 defense expenditures than Reagan wants. And instead of the $1.8 trillion he requested for military spending over the next five years, the House approved $1.6 trillion. That's surely enough to continue the enormous military buildup the Reagan administration has begun.

The House budget would also restore some of the deep cuts made during the past two years in domestic social programs. And it envisions $30 billion more in tax revenues and a deficit that would be $15 billion lower than the administration's projection.

On the whole, it's a fair and realistic approach to federal spending as the country begins to recover from the recession.

Reagan has expressed fear that the House proposal would jeopardize the income tax cut scheduled to go into effect on July 1. The Democrats are indeed likely to seek to cancel, defer or cap that tax reduction. But since many economists consider the enormous budget deficits projected by the administration to be the principal threat to sustained economic recovery, the July tax cut may well be something the country can't afford.

The spending targets adopted by the House are only a framework to be fleshed out later. But they constitute a solid basis on which to work with the Senate and the White House to craft a responsible federal budget.

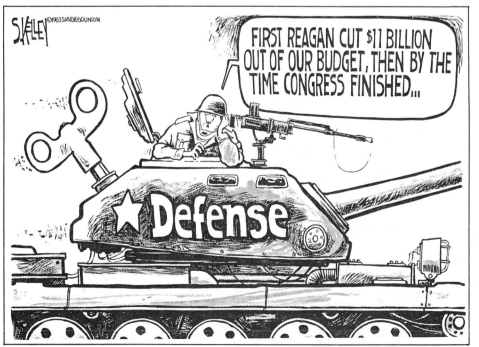

FIRST REAGAN CUT $11 BILLION OUT OF OUR BUDGET, THEN BY THE TIME CONGRESS FINISHED....

Defense

Senate Panel Halves Defense Increase Sought by Reagan

A second major defeat for the Administration on budgetary issues occurred in April, 1983 when the Senate Budget Committee rejected the President's proposed 10% boost in defense spending. Instead, the committee approved, on a 17 to 4 vote, a 5% increase for fiscal 1984. Committee Chairman Pete Domenici (R, N.M.) said he found the Administration's assertion that the country could not be adequately defended without a 10% increase "incredulous." A 5% increase was "what we can afford" and represented a "serious effort at reducing the deficit," Domenici said. Many of the senators expressed annoyance at Reagan's refusal to compromise. Sen. James Exon (D, Neb.), an unquestionably pro-defense member of the committee, accused the President of "framing the debate in terms of politics." The committee's plan called for $3.3 billion less in outlays during fiscal 1984 than Reagan had requested.

Post-Tribune
Gary, Ind., April 10, 1983

If President Reagan listens, he can hear the Senate Budget Committee's call to reason on military spending. It's an insistent call, coming from a committee controlled by his own party. The committee voted for a 5 percent increase in the military budget, half what the president has demanded.

The call to reason is not a call for military weakness, but for common sense: Military strength and economic strength go together. The 5 percent increase "is more nearly what the country can afford," a committe member said.

The president showed signs several days ago that he sees the need to re-assess his position on arms generally. He said, "All of us are going to have to take a fresh look at our previous positions. I pledge my participation in such a fresh look and my determination to assist in forging a renewed bipartisan consensus."

That unusual presidential eloquence may mean that he will accept, with some grace, the message even his fellow Republicans are writing in Congress.

Now he should talk candidly about the defense budget, piece by piece. The pieces that don't fit a defense policy Americans can accept should be put on hold. America's military ambitions, even if supported unanimously, must be limited by the country's resources and ability to pay.

The Times-Picayune
The States-Item
New Orleans, La., April 12, 1983

By insisting on a 10 percent increase in the defense budget, President Reagan has provoked a revolt among Senate Republican ranks that is threatening to spill over into other policy issues of importance to the administration and the country.

Bearing out the advance warnings of Senate Republican leaders, the Senate Budget Committee, with the support of eight Republicans, voted 17 to 4 to reduce Mr. Reagan's proposed defense budget for next year to 5 percent after inflation. Facing the prospect of defeat in the full Senate, Mr. Reagan wisely has decided to seek a compromise and could end up with an increase of about 7 percent.

Growing opposition even among Republicans to the president's defense proposal reflects the concern not only in Congress but in the nation over the huge federal deficits and the threat they pose to economic recovery. Fear of the deficits is widely viewed as the main reason interest rates have not fallen more in response to declining inflation. Real interest rates — those posted after inflation is figured in — remain high by historical standards.

Opposition is stiff among Democrats and increasing among Republicans to severe addi-tional cuts in social programs, particularly with unemployment hanging high. That leaves defense as about the only place left where substantial cuts can be made to reduce the deficits.

Further reflecting concern over the deficits and the growing unwillingness of some Republicans to back the president's programs without question was the call by five Republican senators to repeal this year's 10 percent income tax cut, the final stage of the three-year tax cut voted during Mr. Reagan's first year in office. Tax indexing, which would reduce tax rates to adjust to inflation beginning in 1985, also faces growing opposition.

Should they form a coalition with Senate Democrats, the five liberal GOP senators — Lowell Weicker of Connecticut, Charles McC. Mathias Jr. of Maryland, John Chafee of Rhode Island, Robert Stafford of Vermont and Mark Hatfield of Oregon — could upset the 54-46 Republican majority in the Senate that Mr. Reagan has relied upon to enact his programs.

Characteristically, Mr. Reagan appears to be ready to compromise, at least on the defense budget, only after he has encountered insurmountable opposition to his original position.

The Detroit News
Detroit, Mich., April 10, 1983

Voodoo economics has come home to roost in the Republican-controlled Senate Budget Committee. Faced with a deficit that has not receded in the face of President Reagan's wand-waving, the committee had little choice but to halve his requested 10 percent increase in the military budget for the next fiscal year.

After the rebuff — characterized by chairman Pete V. Domenici (R., N.M.) as "a reprimand to the people who advise" the President — the White House sent out a note asking for reconsideration.

It was the Senate, though, that had given Mr. Reagan time to reconsider, backing off a scheduled March 17 vote that was headed against the President. The Senate pleaded for cutbacks; it waited.

But instead of confronting fiscal reality, the President launched a public relations campaign to shore up his original position, compounding bad judgment with bad form. "We were misled," huffed Sen. Howard Metzenbaum (D., Ohio).

Sadly, the misleading goes far beyond horse-trading on a committee vote. Without acknowleging the inflationary implications of widening a deficit during economic hard times, Mr. Reagan is scurrying around warning of Soviet military superiority — a stance that not even the Joint Chiefs of Staff swallow.

The truth of the matter is that the frantic catch-up ball Mr. Reagan would have the United States play in the arms race has more potential for destabilizing the economy and ultimately the national security than any immediate Soviet threat.

Keep in mind, the committee is not exactly proposing slashing the military budget: It would be allowed to grow to $267 billion for 1984 (Mr. Reagan wanted $280.5 billion). It is simply telling the President that you can't rob Peter to pay Paul when Peter has been down on his luck.

The Wichita
Eagle-Beacon
Wichita, Kans., April 11, 1983

By cutting President Reagan's proposed defense spending hike in half, the Senate Budget Committee succeeded in sending a stern message to the White House. While the passage of a 5 percent increase — rather than 10 percent — is as not substanital as some Pentagon critics had hoped for, it clearly signals some type of compromise will be necessary.

The growing public discontent with administration calls for additional cuts in domestic programs — while refusing to accept significant reductions in the Pentagon budget — has forced the Republican-controlled budget committee to take a stand that constitutes the second major defeat on defense appropriations the president has encountered this year.

While it seems certain the president will receive less than he has proposed, the issue now is how much less and to what degree administration cooperation is forthcoming to reach an acceptable compromise. It was the lack of compromise during the three-week delay in the Senate Budget Committee vote that angered many senators and resulted in the 17-4 vote to cut military buildup funding.

There also are serious questions about how the Penatgon currently handles more than $200 billion in federal tax dollars. Reports from the General Accounting Office cite frequent cost overruns, and other examples of waste and mismanagement. Resolution of those types of problems are essential to restoring public and congressional confidence. President Reagan now should begin the necessary compromise process, rather than allow the stalemate between himself and Congress to erode needed public support further.

Newsday
Long Island, N.Y., April 11, 1983

A month or so ago, President Reagan pleaded with the Republican leaders of the Senate Budget Committee to delay a vote on defense spending until after Congress' Easter recess. He wanted time to marshal his political forces and he hoped the senators would hear from the folks back home that they favor sharply increased defense spending.

The President's delaying tactic didn't work. Whatever message the senators got during the Easter break, they no sooner returned to Washington than the Budget Committee rejected Reagan's defense spending plan by a vote of 19-2 and passed a resolution cutting in half the increase that he and Defense Secretary Caspar Weinberger proposed.

The administration contends that annual increases of 10 per cent — beyond the estimated 4 per cent needed to keep up with inflation — are absolutely essential for the nation's survival. The Senate Budget Committee instead adopted as its target a 5 per cent real spending increase. The full House had previously approved a budget resolution calling for increases in defense spending of about 4 per cent after inflation.

It's still too early to tell where Congress will aim its defense spending and whether any programs will be targeted for actual cutbacks. But the sense of the Congress is clear: The nation neither needs nor can afford the huge military buildup Reagan envisions.

Reagan remained committed to that buildup despite repeated warnings by congressional leaders in his own party that his defense budget would not pass. Their pleas with Reagan and Weinberger to search for savings in the military budget were met with an almost insulting response: Instead of real reductions, the administration offered paltry savings resulting from lower inflation, reduced fuel costs and a less costly basing mode for the MX missile.

Last Friday on this page we reviewed some major issues that must be addressed before America embarks on a vast military buildup. Regrettably, the administration apparently refuses to confront those issues or to make its priorities known to Congress. That's no way to devise a national defense strategy that's fiscally and militarily sound.

THE ATLANTA CONSTITUTION
Atlanta, Ga., April 11, 1983

Nothing could be more clear: Congress is not — repeat, not — going to approve the 10-percent increase in defense spending that President Reagan has requested and that he is holding out for. If the president does not soon admit this, and begin working with Congress, he risks leaving the development of the nation's defense to the congressional committee structure, which congressional leaders themselves recognize as a poor mechanism for such decisions.

The Democrat-controlled House voted last month to hold defense spending to an increase of 4 percent over inflation. Now the Republican-controlled Senate Budget Committee has approved a 5-percent increase, with eight Republicans, including Chairman Pete Domenici (R-N.M.), joining nine Democrats to halve the president's proposal. The committee earlier voted to reject the president's proposal by a devastating 17-2 margin.

And the vote by the Senate committee, unlike the House vote, came after the president made his "Star Wars" pitch on television for his full defense budget. This time, the famous Reagan communications magic did not work. The president was unable to pull an Easter rabbit out of the hat. Members of both parties returned to Washington from their recess with grass-roots instructions to keep the outlandish size of the Reagan budget deficits in mind when funding defense.

The president's argument with Congress so far is only over gross figures, but in time, as actual appropriations decisions have to be made, that will narrow down to specifics.

What portion of the defense budget should go to upgrading conventional forces? What part to strategic weapons? Should the B-1 bomber be mothballed in favor of awaiting the developing Stealth technology? Can MX missile deployment, once a basing mode is settled on, be stretched out?

Ronald Reagan

All of these questions, and more, have to be figured into an overall concept if the result is to be a reasonably balanced, effective defense.

Clearly, such complex work should not be left solely to the legislative process, with its susceptibility to pork-barrel politicking and its potential for manipulation by defense contractors. Even when Congress is taking its responsibilities soberly — and in this matter, it is — it is an imprecise instrument for making such fine and interlocking decisions. It needs the administration's good-faith participation.

If Reagan's intransigence to date has been a negotiating technique, in the manner of W.C. Fields playing his cards close to his vest, well and good. But both houses of Congress, and the leaders of both parties, have now staked out their positions, too. It is time for the president to become part of the solution. We are not, after all, taking about a mere game here. The quality of the nation's basic military defense is at stake. Reagan was elected to lead, not to stand pat.

The Pittsburgh Press
Pittsburgh, Pa.,
April 10, 1983

The U.S. Senate Budget Committee's vote to give President Reagan only half of the increase in defense spending that he wants is his worst budgetary defeat since taking office. And one for which he himself is largely responsible.

The committee, which recommends overall spending limits to the Senate, is dominated by Republicans. Yet the president lost, 17 to 4, as eight GOP members opposed his demand for a 10 percent boost, over and above inflation, in military outlays.

Mr. Reagan simply got hit by a backlash.

Few members of either house are convinced that the Pentagon budget should grow by 10 percent in real terms when many other programs are being cut or constrained.

There also is a suspicion, well-founded, that the Defense Department is trying to take advantage of Mr. Reagan's pledge to "rearm America" by insisting on every expensive weapon on its wish list.

Earlier, the Democratic-controlled House voted to hold the inflation-adjusted hike in military spending to 4 percent for the next fiscal year, which starts Oct. 1.

When the two houses finish their haggling in conference, the increase will probably be 5 percent.

★ ★ ★

Between now and then, you should brace yourself for a lot of doomsday talk by Mr. Reagan, Defense Secretary Caspar Weinberger and the military brass about how the Russians are coming and we can't defend ourselves with a mere pittance.

But when all the smoke has lifted, it will be seen that the budget committee has trimmed outlays for next year by only $3.3 billion, leaving a tidy sum of $241.4 billion.

Moreover, the committee has voted for a steady, long-term, 5-percent-after-inflation defense buildup.

Our NATO allies, who are closer to the Soviet Union and more directly threatened, are boosting their military spending by no more than 2 percent. So the committee's budget is hardly parsimonious.

Indeed, a Defense Department which is incapable of looking after our national security with $241 billion a year — that's spending at the rate of *$27½ million an hour* — must be inadequately led and badly managed.

The Washington Post
Times Herald
Washington, D.C., April 10, 1983

AN ACUTE political interest attaches to the 17-4 vote in the Senate Budget Committee, which is controlled by President Reagan's own party, to cut in half the 10 percent rate of increase in real military spending that he had requested and strenuously lobbied for. The counterpart committee in the Democratic-controlled House had already voted for no more than a 4 percent rate of increase. It appears Mr. Reagan is headed for a major defeat.

Respectful of his mandate, Congress gave the president almost everything extra he wanted for defense in his first two years, notwithstanding the impact on current budgets and future deficits. This year, however, Congress decided it was safe and reasonable and necessary to demand a more solid strategic rationale. It made a parallel new demand for assurance that the Pentagon would spend the money wisely. On both counts, strategy and management, Mr. Reagan has come up short.

The current picture, however, cannot be attributed entirely to administration failings. Congress has worked hard in the last few years, and it has generated and been hospitable to a considerable body of expertise. A serious and wide-ranging defense debate has taken place. The upshot is that the legislators have improved their capacity for a responsible defense role. It is not anti-defense "liberals" who are in the saddle, notwithstanding presidential attempts to brush off skeptics in those terms. In both parties and both houses, conservatives dominate the defense opposition.

It is wise to listen to Sen. Sam Nunn's warning that legislators tend both to debate weapons systems rather than strategy and to end up protecting the programs dearest to their constituents and cutting the wrong things. Similarly, it is wise to be wary of a meat-ax approach based simply on cutting the budget by a given percentage.

Congress is, nonetheless, increasingly receptive to strategic approaches to defense: to approaches that measure the requirements of national security as well as the resources available to meet them. We publish in Topic A today one such approach, in which William Kaufmann, a high-level consultant to nearly every defense secretary from Robert McNamara to Harold Brown, suggests ways to buy more usable defense than would the Reagan budget, for less money.

Even without further increases in defense spending, the nation's arsenal would be expanding greatly as a consequence of various expansion votes of the last few years. The procurement budget has risen from $35 billion to $80 billion just since 1980. The budget committee's plan for 5 percent annual real growth means the nation would commit almost $1.7 trillion to defense over the next five years. The current focus on the rate of increase should not distract attention from the central fact that an immense buildup is already going on.

The Chattanooga Times

Chattanooga, Tenn., April 9, 1983

President Reagan and Congress, especially the Senate, remain at swords' points over the 1984 defense budget, with Mr. Reagan still adamantly clinging to his proposal for a 10 percent increase in defense spending in real dollars. It appears increasingly likely he'll have to settle for less: On Thursday, the Senate Budget Committee voted 17-4 (eight Republicans were in the majority) for a 5 percent increase. Mr. Reagan hopes the committee will reconsider later. But the administration may have become a victim of itself. Its argument for a 10 percent increase hasn't been helped by Defense Secretary Weinberger's penchant for playing games with the defense numbers.

Mr. Weinberger has argued for months that the administration's increased emphasis on sound managerial practices would soon start to reduce the rapidly escalating costs of new weapons systems. It appeared the administration had met its goal when the Pentagon recently published its quarterly Selected Acquisition Report, a study of weapons program costs. According to the SAR, the total price of 40 major weapons dropped by nearly $18.5 billion, about 4 percent over the figure three months ago.

But things are not always what they seem. It soon became evident that the "savings" resulted not from promised hard-headed management but from semantic gimmickry and what might be called "creative accounting."

Consider the Trident nuclear missile program, for example. The SAR said that the cost for that program had declined by $11.3 billion in one quarter. But that was because the Pentagon classified the last seven submarines (out of 15 in the program) as Trident IIs, thus apparently creating a new type of Trident. But it really didn't. The Navy's Trident II submarine is the same as the Trident I; the only difference is that the former carries the Trident II missile. More to the point, the Trident program actually *increased* over the past quarter by $2.7 billion, about 9 percent.

Take another case, the Pentagon claimed in the SAR that the cost of its air-launched cruise missile program declined by $4.2 billion because the production total was cut. But that saving will be overcome by the cost of the new stealth model of the same missile. How much is problematical; the cost is secret. Then there was Mr. Weinberger's boast a few months ago of an $8 billion reduction in the defense budget — a reduction due mostly to lower estimates of inflation.

Members of Congress aren't stupid, and neither are the American people. When the Pentagon tries to fudge the defense budget with such semantic double-talk, it should not be surprised at the cynically skeptical response.

EVENING EXPRESS

Portland, Maine, April 7, 1983

President Reagan's stubborn insistence on a 10 percent increase in the national military budget flies in the face of political reality.

The president, having made the best case he can for the increase and finding little support for his position either in Congress or among the public at large, has nothing to gain and much to lose by digging in his heels at this point.

The Democrat-controlled House of Representatives has already passed a resolution with much smaller military increases than the president proposed for 1984. Leaders of the Republican-controlled Senate have warned Reagan that his spending goal can't even make it through that body's budget committee.

By refusing to back away from his demands, Reagan has left fellow Republicans in Congress little choice but to abandon him on this issue. By courting defeat even at the hands of his own political party, Reagan sacrifices still more of a president's most precious commodity: the ability to lead through consensus.

True, we demand that our political leaders stand firm on principle. But there is such a thing as principled compromise. Effective leadership depends upon an ability to deal with reality without selling out.

By the same token, Congress has a responsibility, when it disagrees with presidential policies, to offer reasonable alternatives. Compromise is a two-way street.

But by hanging tough on his proposal for a 10 percent military budget increase when there is no chance left of winning it, Reagan merely gives up any opportunity to control the details of the compromise that inevitably must come.

True leadership demands a more flexible approach.

Rockford Register Star

Rockford, Ill., April 12, 1983

President Reagan's stubborn, uncompromising stance on the 1984 military budget suffered a well-deserved and overwhelming rebuff last week by a Senate committee controlled by his own Republican Party.

The Senate Budget Committee's vote of 17-4 in favor of a smaller increase in Reagan's plans for military spending next year seems to have established a firm ceiling on the Pentagon budget hike, since a House committee already has voted for an even smaller military spending increase.

It now appears likely that House-Senate conferences will grant a military spending increase of no more than five percent (after inflation). The president has demanded a 10 percent increase.

It should be noted that the Senate committee funding level will not leave the Pentagon destitute. It would increase military spending to a whopping $241.4 billion during 1984.

The Senate committee vote reflected, among other things, Republican displeasure with Reagan's refusal to budge even a bit on his military spending plans. The committee had postponed its vote for weeks to give the president time to offer some sort of compromise, but none was forthcoming.

Repeatedly, Senate Republicans had warned Reagan his plan wouldn't pass without modification, but the president stood fast. All his intransigence got him, however, was the worst budget defeat of his administration.

Cutting in half Reagan's military spending proposal is but a single step in the critical process of chipping away at the ruinous federal budget deficits that have been projected. Additional steps in the area of domestic spending will be required if the Congress is to bring the budget under any semblance of control.

It strikes us as ironic, though heartening, that Congress has had to seize the reins in this budget-paring process from a so-called fiscal conservative in the White House who won't, when it comes to military spending, practice the kind of budgetary restraint that he has made a career of preaching.

Impact of Defense Spending on Unemployment, Economy Debated

It is often assumed that peacetime defense spending is good for the nation as a whole, stimulating the economy by providing jobs and funnelling capital into defense-related industries. This is the view often expressed by Administration officials and cited in congressional debates over defense budgets. Studies conducted in 1981 and 1982, however, threw doubt upon the basic premise that defense dollars significantly reduced unemployment or stimulated economic development. Firstly, it was pointed out, the creation of jobs in the defense sector does little to alleviate overall unemployment because the jobs provided require highly skilled workers. Secondly, according to some analyses, if the same amount of money were spent in the civilian sector as were spent on the military, the number of jobs created as a result would be greater by a third to a half. Viewed only as an economic stimulant, then, defense spending may be one of the least efficient methods. In addition, opponents of the military buildup argued that the increased spending for defense starved other sectors of the economy and drove up inflation. Opponents of this view point out that historically, involvement in wars has almost always been good for the U.S. economy.

The Hartford Courant
Hartford, Conn., November 1, 1981

The reported drop last week in the index of leading economic indicators should add more fuel to the White House debate on how best to lower the federal budget deficit.

As the recessionary trend persists, the projected deficit grows worse. It now appears that the budget will be about $100 billion in the red by 1984.

High deficits contribute to both high interest and inflation rates.

Such deficits cannot be overcome with the president's latest package of spending cuts, primarily in the non-defense area, and "revenue enhancements." This week, the president is expected to recommend further non-military cuts.

Sooner or later — and preferably sooner — the administration will have to face the inherent contradiction in insisting on the need for federal tax- and budget-cutting and the simultaneous need for massive increases in defense spending.

The five-year plan unveiled in March by the administration would more than double the annual Pentagon budget to $368 billion by 1986. Total military outlays over the next five years would be nearly $1.5 trillion, half again as large as the entire national debt.

One of the principal factors in setting off the inflationary trend in this country in recent years was the enormous expenditure for the Vietnam War. In terms of its procurement increase, the Reagan buildup may exceed the buildup for the war.

These expenditures are relatively nonproductive. Military outlays concentrate enormous amounts of capital in a narrow area, starving the rest of the economy of investment funds it needs to compete in tightening worldwide markets.

The result will be worse inflation, higher interest rates and a further slowdown in the economy's real growth.

Further, the defense increase siphons into military areas the skilled labor already in short supply for some industries, such as electronics and machinery. The nation's civilian industries would become even less competitive on the world market as American resources shift to weapon production.

There is, it is true, a strong case to be made for modernizing the U.S. armed forces, but the size of the proposed military expenditures merely distorts the economy while providing no more real security.

The United States already has more strategic nuclear weapons than the Soviets, yet there are plans to build about 17,000 new nuclear weapons during this decade.

The president just last month proposed spending $180 billion over the next six years for the deployment of 100 MX missiles and for 100 B-1 bombers, which even the administration admits would provide the nation with a temporary advantage at best.

Further slashes can be made in ambitious plans to construct more warships for the Navy, which is already far superior to the Soviet navy.

The administration cannot continue to treat military spending like a favorite, fat child — at least not if it wants to leave itself a chance of reaching its goals of a balanced federal budget, a manageable inflation rate and revitalized economy.

Military spending is not isolated from the rest of the economy. When it is excessive and wasteful, the entire economy is debilitated. Until the administration recognizes it as part of the problem, it will fail to find an adequate solution.

ST. LOUIS POST-DISPATCH
St. Louis, Mo., October 3, 1981

As the nation prepares to confront record increases in military spending for the remaining years of the Reagan administration, the question may fairly be asked as to whether those outlays will be good for the economy as a whole. As weapons systems move from the drawing board to testing and development to production, will they benefit the lot of the American people?

The answer, in a word, is No. Indeed, far from improving the nation's economic situation, the massive increases in military spending will harm it. Instead of adding jobs to the economy, the Reagan defense budgets are likely to subtract them. And just as Pentagon outlays contribute to the unemployment problem, so will they exacerbate the already high level of inflation, for defense spending produces neither goods nor services that the public can buy with its increased spendable income.

An idea of just how heavy a burden the Pentagon budget imposes on the economy can be got from the newly released third edition of a study by Employment Research Associates of Lansing, Mich. Entitled "The Empty Pork Barrel," the study shows that in 1977 and 1978, the military budget averaged $101 billion and the nation suffered a net loss of 1.015 million jobs — a ratio of 10,000 jobs for each $1 billion spent on defense. If those ratios remained constant for fiscal year 1982, in which the Reagan administration proposes to spend $188.8 billion on the military, some 1.8 million jobs would disappear. In the two years studied, ERA found, 29 states, including Missouri, lost employment because of the negative impact of Pentagon outlays. New York, where 288,200 jobs disappeared, suffered the biggest decline. Missouri showed a net employment loss of 4,500 positions. ERA blames the correlation between lost jobs and defense spending on the effect of taxes.

When people pay high taxes, the researchers found, their buying power is reduced. "This means that they build fewer houses, buy fewer cars, take fewer vacations and vote lower taxes for their state and local governments," the study notes. Lower state and local taxes mean reduced services, which, in turn, result in a loss of public-sector jobs.

The effect of the Reagan tax cuts on the job-loss/defense spending correlation remains to be seen, of course. But the fact remains that as long as the government is forced to finance record defense costs, money for other sectors of the economy will remain tight.

In this connection, the ERA, drawing on Bureau of Labor Statistics figures, points out that every $1 billion spent in the civilian-industrial sector produces 27,000 jobs but a comparable amount spent on the military results in only two-thirds that many jobs. Military expenditures go typically for the production of technologically complex items, which means that more money is spent on equipment and specialists than on hiring basic workers. As a result, the billions that the government will pour into the defense sector is a particularly poor investment for rejuvenating the national economy.

Conventional wisdom still holds that defense contracts are good for the economy; and in narrow circumstances that is true enough. But whatever the looming defense expenditures will provide in the way of armaments, the fact remains that they will detract from America's economic strength — and hence its overall security.

THE ANN ARBOR NEWS

Ann Arbor, Mich., October 7, 1981

IT'S always good to have safe assumptions challenged. Held to the harsh light of closer analysis, conclusions safely jumped to have a way of falling apart.

For example, one would think that heavy defense spending would create more jobs, especially in an industrial state such as Michigan. Wrong, says Employment Research Associates of Lansing.

"Contrary to long held and popular belief," the firm said in a study released recently, "military spending is not good for the economy. It does not create employment — it generates unemployment."

The reason for the relationship between defense spending and jobs is that if people are paying high taxes, a substantial portion of which goes to defense, their buying power is decreased, according to ERA.

"This means (people) build fewer houses, buy fewer cars, take fewer vacations and vote lower taxes for their state and local governments," which in turn reduce services, often by eliminating jobs.

ERA'S STUDY found that for every $1 billion spent on defense, the nation lost 10,000 jobs. Among the states showing the highest net job losses during 1977 and 1978 was Michigan. Only New York and Illinois lost more.

That was under President Carter. The Reagan administration's commitment to greater defense spending will, apparently, cut purchasing power still more and keep unemployment high.

A billion dollars spent on Pentagon projects produced 18,000 jobs. The same amount spent in the civilian-industrial sector would have created 27,000 jobs, says the report of the period 1977-78.

"Raising the military budget at a time when unemployment is growing and inflation is high directly undermines the stated goals of the (Reagan) administration," the report goes on.

WILL THIS STUDY by Employment Research Associates give pause to local and statewide efforts to attract more defense dollars to Michigan? Not likely.

Whether it will even challenge some comfortable assumptions is open to question.

It sounds like one more variation of the guns vs. butter argument. President Johnson thought the country could have both. Instead, it got a fierce inflation his successors tried gamely to control.

Now we have Reaganomics and supply-side thinkers who say we can open the defense spigot, cut social spending, bring down inflation and balance the budget.

The ERA study, if on target, speaks in a language (job losses) politicians understand. That's worth remembering as election year 1982 slides into view and the first crack voters have at judging Reagan's performance.

THE INDIANAPOLIS STAR

Indianapolis, Ind., November 17, 1981

Higher military spending means fewer civilian jobs, according to a Michigan researcher. Bigger defense budgets also drive industry out of the Frost Belt, spur inflation, rob non-military industries of capital and redistribute income on a scale far exceeding that of welfare, Marion B. Anderson, director of Employment Research Associates of Lansing, concludes in "The Empty Pork Barrel: Unemployment and the Pentagon Budget."

She argues that reduced military spending would lessen these evils while stimulating employment and prosperity.

This may be a good idealistic theory but the record of history shows that it has seldom worked out that way. For example, in 1940 military spending amounted to a mere 1.5 percent of the Gross National Product. But the unemployment rate was 14.6 percent.

Five years later, in 1945, military spending was 38.3 percent of the GNP and the unemployment rate was 1.9 percent. Also in that year a dollar, based on 1957 100 cents=$1 purchasing power, bought $1.47 worth of goods. Of course that was at the height of the U.S. World War II effort.

So consider a peace year, 1955. In that year the defense budget amounted to 58.2 percent of total federal outlays and 10.5 percent of the GNP. Far from being a year of high inflation, rising unemployment and severe economic distress, 1955 was a year of enviable prosperity.

The unemployment rate was a low 4.4 percent. The dollar — 1957 base — was worth $1.07. Reasonably-priced houses and cars were being built in record numbers and average-income Americans were buying them. Productivity was high, the economy was growing and incomes of all classes of working people were rising.

In the years that followed, except during the major phase of the Vietnam War effort in the late 1960s, the level of defense spending fell. In 1975 it dropped to 26.7 percent of total federal outlays and 6 percent of GNP. But there was no spurt of growth and prosperity, or crop of new jobs, or drop in inflation. In that year the unemployment rate reached 8.5 percent. The purchasing power of the dollar dropped to 54 cents.

After reaching a low of 24.3 percent of total federal outlays and 5.5 percent of GNP in 1977, defense spending is increasing. Why was there no business boom when defense spending reached its lowest level?

Defense is not the villain that proponents of lavish social welfare spending often make it out to be. The fact is, high taxation and social welfare spending combined are the heavy-growth factors that dominate the federal budget.

The military cannot fairly be said to be starving social welfare. Total spending on social welfare now amounts to more than 20 percent of GNP, well over $400 billion a year. In the 1982 federal budget Defense is allotted $184 billion and the Department of Health and Human Services $250 billion — the largest but still only one of many multibillion-dollar areas of federal social welfare spending.

Certainly defense spending should not be used as a tool of economic policy. Yet in an economy as large as that of the United States, there is little cause to believe that proposed increases in defense will cripple the civilian economy. Indeed the record would suggest that the opposite is true.

The TENNESSEAN

Nashville, Tenn., March 12, 1982

SECRETARY of Defense Caspar Weinberger, arguing before a Senate committee against a $40-billion cut in his record budget, has taken a new tack. He says slashing military programs would not only amount to "unilateral disarmament," but would cost the U.S. 350,000 jobs.

Until now, the administration hasn't mentioned the jobs issue, perhaps because criticism of the Pentagon budget has focused mainly on whether costly hardware like the MX missile and the B-1 bomber is needed.

The Senate Budget Committee, however, is increasingly skeptical, not only about these weapon systems, but about the Pentagon's entire authorization bill for 1983. The committee would like to see it shaved by 6% and wants to know where cuts can be made that will do the least harm to defense.

Mr. Weinberger doesn't want to make *any* cuts, so he resorted to an emotional appeal about all the jobs that $40 billion will create. The threat of Reaganomics has been to slash jobs, which has sent unemployment soaring. Concern for jobs comes very late indeed.

And it didn't persuade. What the committee is worried about is the prospect of $100-billion or more deficits — not to mention the trillion-dollar national debt. Both lead to heavy federal borrowing, which exerts upward pressure on interest rates. The resulting higher cost of money makes private-sector investment in new plant and equipment, and thus new jobs, increasingly difficult.

Putting $40 billion into new defense weapons may well create some factory and white collar jobs, but not nearly as many as a healthy economy could provide. Mr. Weinberger needs to find a better argument for his defense budget.

Nashville, Tenn., October 26, 1982

A new study analyzing the impact of military spending on the U.S. economy has concluded that, for every $1 billion the Pentagon spends on military purchases, it costs the nation 18,000 jobs compared to how consumers would have spent the money.

The analysis, by Employment Research Associates of Lansing, Mich., of the impact of defense spending on 156 industries, concluded that the military budget for 1981 of $154 billion caused a net loss of 1,520,000 jobs to the industrial and commercial base, even though military spending generated 1,764,000 jobs in defense-related industry.

That illustrates a dilemma about defense spending. If the Pentagon wants to build a tank, that is what it gets. It is unproductive in terms of the economy, except for salaries of workers who build it. It uses resources that could be more advantageous elsewhere. But the military needs tanks and planes and missiles for the security of the country, so the economics of a tank vs. a locomotive, for example, is an exercise in value judgment.

The real problem of defense spending is that there is an enormous amount of unnecessary spending by the Pentagon, there are wasteful defense systems, and there are cases of just plain waste.

Defense studies that began under former President Jimmy Carter and continued under President Ronald Reagan recommend significant reform of the procurement process, one being multi-year purchasing strategies that would be cheaper.

The General Accounting Office has frequently cited unnecessary expenditures in the federal government, almost half of these being in the Defense Department. The GAO suggestions could save some $16 billion. The problem is putting them into effect.

Still another problem is getting more standardization of parts and weapons among the armed services. One small example of that is the helicopter. The Air Force A-10 attack helicopter is effective against tanks and pretty good at ground support. But the Army wants the AH-64 aircraft for ground support. The program would cost $3 billion to $4 billion, almost twice as much. Both services could use the A-10, but the Air Force doesn't want the Army to use its aircraft.

The Reagan administration is so insistent on a military buildup and growing defense budgets that it has decided to strenthen the military by funding some of the same programs that were rejected by the Nixon, Ford and Carter administrations.

These include the B-1 bomber, which will be superseded by the Stealth bomber not long after it is operational, the M-1 tank, and the Division Air Defense Gun, called DIVAD, at $10 million a copy, and which has not lived up to expectations.

There is no argument about keeping this country militarily strong, although the cost will be high in terms of future deficits and their impact on the economy. The issue is whether the Pentagon should continue to waste money through inefficiency and through "gold-plated" weapons systems of doubtful efficiency and efficacy on the battlefield. One way or another, the nation is going to have to get a handle on defense spending.

Lincoln Journal

Lincoln, Neb., February 28, 1983

There's a school of history which holds that for all its innovative efforts, Franklin D. Roosevelt's New Deal did not pull the United States out of the Great Depression. What did was World War II. From that line grows a notion that we may be able to correct some of what now ails us economically by increased military spending.

Beware of such a seductive analysis. At the very least, it is arguable; certainly, if millions of men are not also channeled from civilian life into the armed forces, as they were in the early 1940s.

Defense Secretary Caspar Weinberger's stated position is that 35,000 new jobs are created for every $1 billion spent by the Pentagon. Directly opposing that contention is the analysis of a specialized economic consulting firm. It's conclusion is that for every $1 billion "tranferred from purchases by the taxpayer to purchases by the Pentagon," commerce and industry suffer a net loss of 18,000 jobs.

Employment Research Associates of Lansing, Mich., applied the Bureau of Labor Statistics' 156-sector "Input-Output" computer model of the American economy. It compared all jobs likely to be generated by increasing military spending to what jobs hypothetically might be created if the same sum were filtered through the private individual and business spending stream.

The conclusion: President Reagan's $238.6 billion defense budget for the coming fiscal year will cut employment 720,000, net.

In some ways, the analysis tracks with warnings given in Lincoln by liberal economist Lester Thurow during a November 1980 visit. Because late 20th century military spending is so geared toward high technology, it is inevitably capital intensive versus labor intensive. Moreover, it will soak up engineers and scientists needed for private sector rejuvenation, Thurow said.

In this connection, a report from the Commerce Department is worth reflection. It notes that while 20 of the nation's 250 largest industries today are dependent upon military contracts for the biggest share of their business, the number will grow to 29 industries by 1987 under the accelerated military spending charted by President Reagan. There will be additional industrial impacts and dislocations of product distribution channels.

More than half of all the output of makers of television, radios and aircraft engines will go to the military, as will 28 percent of all optical and engineering instruments. A Newhouse News Service survey projects small-arms manufacturers will have to trim their output for civilian hunters and sportsmen to 60 percent as against the present 75 percent.

While the American industrial plant currently has excess capacity, this redirection of certain product lines may not be too noticeable. But factor in recovery, and the picture changes.

Which is to conclude that there's government spending and there's government spending, and the two are not necessarily the same.

THE MILWAUKEE JOURNAL
Milwaukee, Wisc., June 15, 1983

Defenders of President Reagan's trillion-dollar military buildup frequently cite the need to counter the threat to national security posed by the Soviet Union. Only rarely is it recognized the US military buildup is itself threatening this country's national security. That threat is perhaps not as visible as the Soviet military machine, but it is authentic.

Like the nuclear triad of air-, sea- and land-based missiles, the US national security rests on more than one leg. It requires not only a strong military arsenal, but other kinds of national strengths — economic, political, social, even moral. Reagan is trying to strengthen the military leg of the national security, but his preoccupation with that effort is allowing the other legs to weaken. Consider some worrisome signs:

— In Denver the other day, the US Conference of Mayors complained about the large and growing problems that fester in the nation's cities.

— Many critics say that the nation's schools have been shortchanged. They ask a pertinent question: How long can this country remain free and strong in the computer era if its citizens lack basic educational skills?

— America's business leaders complain they won't be able to rebuild factories and become competitive in world markets because massive government spending is making investment money too expensive.

— Some economists worry that, as the military-industrial complex grows in size, power, and affluence, it will attract a disproportionate share of top talent — talent that won't be available to conduct vital non-military research needed to solve pressing social and economic problems.

— Some public health officials are concerned that diversion of resources away from nutrition programs can impair the brain development of many infants, leaving a terrible legacy for the future.

Of course, the military establishment produces a product, just as a factory does. That product is absolutely indispensable: military strength. Moreover, Pentagon officials have estimated that every $1 billion in military spending creates as many as 60,000 jobs.

But Employment Research Association, an economic consulting firm, argues that many more jobs are produced by non-military government spending. And even those who argue for stupendous spending on the military have raised questions about what the administration wants to buy and how the program is being financed.

A study done for the conservative Heritage Foundation has raised serious doubts about the Army's new M-1 tank and the Air Force's Maverick missile. Other independent studies have shown how billions could be safely trimmed from the military modernization program and warned of the danger of cutting funds devoted to maintaining weapons that already exist.

To be sure, the US cannot afford to ignore the Soviet military buildup, and Afghanistan is there to show that the Soviets are willing to use what they have. At the same time, it would be equally wrong to base this country's military program only on what the Soviets do.

The important thing is to have a balanced strategy that produces the combination of strengths that will be needed to meet the combination of dangers that this complex age presents.

ALBUQUERQUE JOURNAL
Albuquerque, N.M., June 11, 1983

Heavy military expenditures cannot be justified on any basis other than strategic necessity. That's the inescapable conclusion of the Council on Economic Priorities, a New York-based independent, non-profit organization.

The group concluded that increased military spending means fewer jobs for Americans, not more, as the Reagan administration maintains. In a study comparing 17 industrialized nations, the council found that military spending is one of the least effective ways to create employment.

Defense Secretary Caspar Weinberger has argued that each $1 billion cut from the defense budget would cost 35,000 jobs. Weinberger's claims that military spending has side benefits in employment, economic growth and technological advances are not supported by the statistics.

The study found that about 28,000 direct and indirect jobs are created for every (constant 1981) billion dollars spent on military procurement. In contrast, the same billion would create 32,000 jobs if spent for public transit, 57,000 jobs if spent for personal consumption or 71,000 jobs if spent for education.

The jobs military spending creates are in the groups with the lowest unemployment rate — white collar jobs in science and engineering.

The national unemployment rate is 10.1 percent and economists predict that it will drop less than half a percent the remainder of the year. During the past five years there has been a 4.4 percent increase in jobs — approximately 2,000 jobs a day — while the population has grown at a 5.4 percent rate.

If part of those billions of defense dollars were freed for the private sector of the economy, the unemployment rate would drop faster and more new jobs would be created.

The Defense Department seems to be using an old fashioned smoke screen to try to convince Congress and the public that what's good for the Defense Department is good for the employment rate. Weinberger and company should stick to national security arguments rather than playing with the nation's employment statistics.

The Birmingham News
Birmingham, Ala., October 26, 1982

Few would doubt that the Pentagon's $154 billion budget can be trimmed by several billion, with obvious economies, and with waste and abuse eliminated. The cuts should be made. And the conclusions of a firm called Employment Research Associates defense spending has caused a net loss of 1,520,000 may be well grounded.

But they seem self-serving and skew logic when such conclusions are isolated from the impact of government spending in other areas. For instance, how many jobs have been lost because of spending for environmental purposes; how many by the monumental welfare programs and how many by funding the Departments of Energy and Education and regulatory agencies?

Defense is one of the very essential tasks and responsibilities of government, mandated by the Constitution. So one is inclined to ask: How many jobs would have been created if the federal government stuck to only the responsibilities mandated by that document and left many other tasks to those more capable of succeeding at them?

Index